Refo500 Academic Studies

Edited by
Herman J. Selderhuis

In co-operation with
Christopher B. Brown (Boston), Günter Frank (Bretten),
Barbara Mahlmann-Bauer (Bern), Tarald Rasmussen (Oslo),
Violet Soen (Leuven), Zsombor Tóth (Budapest),
Günther Wassilowsky (Berlin), Siegrid Westphal (Osnabrück).

Volume 92

Kees Teszelszky

The Holy Crown and the Hungarian Estates

Constructing Early Modern Identity
in the Kingdom of Hungary

Translated by Bernard Adams

Vandenhoeck & Ruprecht

Bibliographic information published by the Deutsche Nationalbibliothek:
The Deutsche Nationalbibliothek lists this publication in the Deutsche Nationalbibliografie;
detailed bibliographic data available online: https://dnb.de.

© 2023 by Vandenhoeck & Ruprecht, Robert-Bosch-Breite 10, 37079 Göttingen, Germany,
an imprint of the Brill-Group (Koninklijke Brill NV, Leiden, The Netherlands;
Brill USA Inc., Boston MA, USA; Brill Asia Pte Ltd, Singapore; Brill Deutschland GmbH,
Paderborn, Germany; Brill Österreich GmbH, Vienna, Austria)
Koninklijke Brill NV incorporates the imprints Brill, Brill Nijhoff, Brill Hotei, Brill Schöningh,
Brill Fink, Brill mentis, Vandenhoeck & Ruprecht, Böhlau, V&R unipress
and Wageningen Academic.

All rights reserved. No part of this work may be reproduced or utilized in any form or by any means,
electronic or mechanical, including photocopying, recording, or any information storage and
retrieval system, without prior written permission from the publisher.

Cover design: SchwabScantechnik, Göttingen
Proofreading: Patricia Edgar, Köln
Partly translated and edited by: Bernard Adams, Zánka
Typesetting: le-tex publishing services, Leipzig
Printed and bound: Hubert & Co. BuchPartner, Göttingen
Printed in the EU

Vandenhoeck & Ruprecht Verlage | www.vandenhoeck-ruprecht-verlage.com

ISSN 2198–3089
ISBN 978-3-525-57344-0

For Marika, Matyi, Peti and Ágica
In memory of Ágnes R. Várkonyi and László Péter

Nationalism arises from the lack of knowledge about one's own culture.*

---

* "Nationalisme ontstaat bij de gratie van het ontbreken van kennis over de eigen cultuur." in Kees Teszelszky, *De sacra corona regni Hungariae: De kroon van Hongarije en de ontwikkeling van vroegmoderne nationale identiteit (1572–1665)* [De sacra corona regni Hungarias. The crown of Hungary and the development of Early Modern national identity (1572–1665). PhD thesis (Groningen: University of Groningen, 2006) (thesis page).

Content

Abbreviations 11

Preface 13

Introduction: concepts and context 17

I. A changing symbol of authority: the meaning and tradition
   of the Holy Crown up to 1526 33
   The visible and invisible crown 33
   The concept of the crown in Hungary 38
   The origin of the cultus of the Holy Crown 40
   The cultus of the Holy Crown around the reign of
   King Mátyás Corvinus 45

II. The Holy Crown and the Hungarian Estates:
    the transformation of the Estates from a cultural to a
    political community 51
    The concept of *natio* in Medieval Hungary 51
    The concept of *natio* and the Holy Crown in the work
    of István Werbőczy (1517) 54
    The concept of *natio* and the cultus of the Holy Crown after
    the Battle of Mohács (1526) 59
    The formation of a Hungarian nation of Estates after the Battle
    of Mohács (1526) 62

III. Emperor Rudolf II, Habsburg rule in Hungary and the Holy Crown 67
     The Emperor Rudolf II's political background 67
     The Illésházy case and the crown 71
     The work of Elias Berger a Grünenberg 77
     The dispute on the decline of Hungary (1602–1603) 83
     The speech of Demeter Naprágyi (1603) 85

IV. The Bocskai Rebellion (1604–1606) 89
    The cause of the rebellion 89
    Bocskai's court in Hungary 92
    The body of the crown and the free towns of Hungary 97

        The song on Bocskai and the crown 105
        The justification of the Bocskai Rebellion in *Querelae* 112

V.   The Ottoman crown of Bocskai 125
        The request for a new crown 125
        The presentation of and handing over of the Ottoman crown (1605) 127
        The myth of the refusal of the Ottoman crown 132
        Bocatius' Hungaroteutomachia 138

VI. The return of the Holy Crown to Hungary 167
        The end of the Bocskai rebellion and the testament of Bocskai (1606) 167
        Archduke Matthias Habsburg in Hungary 173
        Elias Berger as historian of the Habsburg family 178
        The theory of Illésházy and Berger concerning the crown 190
        The transferring of the Crown from Rudolf to Matthias (1608) 193
        István Illésházy's speech of 1608 and the work of Berger (1608) 198
        The coronation of Matthias as King of Hungary (1608) and its
        description by János Jeszenszky 213

VII. Péter Révay's History of the Holy Crown (1613) 225
        Questions and problems 225
        Péter Révay's life and oeuvre 230
        The interpretation of the book on the Holy Crown 234
        Destiny, Christendom and the Holy Crown 263
        The description of the outlook of the crown 278
        The reign of King Mátyás II 285
        Révay's book and the shaping of national identity 287

VIII. The effect of Révay's book on the crown 295
        The Sylvester Bull 295
        The debate on the apostolic nature of the crown 299
        Annales ecclesiastici regni Hungariae (1644) 312
        The aftermath of Révay's work and national identity 318

Conclusion 325

Epilogue 329

Images 331

List of images 349

Bibliography 351
    Primary sources 351
    Research literature 363

Index 393

Abbreviations

EK	ELTE Könyvtára, Budapest, Hungary (University Library of ELTE)
ELTE	Eötvös Loránd Tudományegyetem (Eötvös Loránd University)
MOE	Magyar Országgyűlési Emlékek - Monumenta comitialia Regni Hungariae
MOL	Magyar Országos Levéltár, Budapest, Hungary (Hungarian National Archive)
MTAK	Magyar Tudományos Akadémia Könyvtára, Budapest, Hungary. (Library of the Hungarian Academy of Science)
ÖStA Wien, HHStA	Österreichisches Staatsarchiv Wien, Haus-, Hof- und Staatsarchiv, Vienna, Austria
OSZK	Országos Széchényi Könyvtár, Budapest, Hungary (Hungarian National Library)
SNA	Slovenský národný archív, Slovakian National Archive, Bratislava, Slovakia

Note on personal and geographical names.

The names of kings of Hungary and important persons in this book are written in the Hungarian form. Geographical names from locations in the Early Modern Kingdom of Hungary are also written in the Hungarian spelling.

Preface

The crown of the kingdom, Crown of St István and Holy Crown of Hungary, these names alone indicate how old and important a symbol this crown jewel has been in Hungarian public thinking. The royal diadem was highly respected from the second half of the thirteenth century. It was believed that it was the headgear of the first Hungarian king, St István (reigned between 1000/1001–1038). Subsequently, at the beginning of the fourteenth century, the view developed that only those rulers who were crowned with the Holy Crown could be considered legitimate Hungarian kings. Since the fifteenth century, specifically since 1440, the Hungarian Estates considered it their own possession and therefore called it *corona regni* or Crown of the Kingdom. The crown became a symbol of state power and noble rights (and the noble constitution) in the codification of the customary law of the Hungarian kingdom compiled by István Werbőczy (ca. 1460–1541).

The importance and symbolic role of the crown increased further in the seventeenth century. During the Bocskai rebellion against Habsburg rule in Hungary between 1604 and 1606, the rebels would have liked to see the crown jewel as a symbol of legitimizing power on the head of their prince and leader, István Bocskai. They demanded that the Holy Crown, which had been in Prague for some time, be returned to Hungary. Following the Vienna Peace Treaty of 1608 between the rebellious Estates and the Habsburgs, this wish was granted. In the same year, Emperor Rudolf, who opposed the peace treaty, was forced to retreat before his brother Archduke Matthias and the Hungarian, Moravian and Austrian Estates allied with him: among other things, he abdicated the Hungarian royal throne and placed the Holy Crown at his brother's disposal. For contemporaries, the return of the Holy Crown to Hungary and the coronation of Matthias as king symbolised the reconciliation between the orders and the Habsburg court, and the enactment of religious and confessional rights. Thus, the perception was created that the crown staying "at home" in the kingdom would guarantee the country's freedoms.

Some members of the Protestant intellectual elite were the first to formulate this idea, including among others Péter Révay, the guardian of the crown, who wrote a crown history in 1613, and made the above idea (that the prosperity of the country depends on the location where the crown is kept and the degree of the crown's esteem) one of the key ideas of his work.

But the other reason for the rise in the value of the coronation jewel is now linked to the Catholic side of the Hungarian Estates. The imperial court and the Hungarian clergy used the alleged apostolic title of St István against the Holy See in order to widen their own room for maneuver in the matter of the appointment of Hungarian bishops, a power which the Holy See wanted to secure for itself (especially in the case of the bishopric of Bosnia which was of missional importance). For the Habsburgs and the Hungarian episcopate, the main basis of argument was a legend about St István, the so-called Hartvik legend, written at the turn of the eleventh and twelfth centuries. According to this, the Pope sent a crown to Vajk, the Grand Prince of the Hungarians (the later St István), calling him "the true apostle of Christ" and entrusting him with the government of the churches in Hungary. Thus, the crown jewel also became important in the narrative of the Hartvik legend as "material evidence" of the apostolic authority granted by the Pope.

Later, the Holy Crown would become an important element in the propaganda of the Virgin Mary, Patroness of Hungary, one of the main motifs of the counter-reformation efforts in Hungary. The Medieval Hartvik legend is again the source for this, since it includes the claim, among other things, that the holy king St István, who founded the state, offered himself and his country to Mary. The scene of the dedication of the country became a popular and frequent theme in Catholic art of the period, in the iconography of which the Holy Crown embodied the offered Hungary.

In his book, Kees Teszelszky has explored this long process of the interpretation and use of the Holy Crown as a symbol, which has changed over time and according to political actors and interest groups. At the same time, an important part of his book is an examination of how the crown as an abstract concept is related to the formation of Hungarian national identity in Hungary in the Early Modern period. He also discusses the role of the crown in the representation of the state and the Hungarian Estates.

The focus of his book is to examine how the Holy Crown is used as a symbol of power and politics in the early seventeenth century. The author's great merit lies in the fact that he accurately traces the process and stages of this growth in importance, and clarifies the driving forces behind it. The author's detailed analysis of Péter Révay's *Commentarius* (1613), the seminal work of Hungarian crown research mentioned above, is also a very valuable part of the book. Teszelszky rightly points out the narratives and the main message of this small volume. This main message is *concordia*, the importance of agreement between the Hungarian Estates and the Habsburg king, between one denomination and another. According to Révay, as Teszelszky points out, the pledge of this concord is respect for the crown and the constitution of the Estates it has embodied, as well as for the peace treaty of 1608. Teszelszky has also thoroughly explored the reception and impact of Révay's work, which was fundamental to the development of views on the Holy Crown.

Kees Teszelszky's book thus contributes a great deal to the history of the Hungarian Holy Crown as a political symbol and to the exploration of the changing views associated with it. In addition, his work always takes into account the international, European context of these views, as well as the political literature of the various periods (e. g. Bodin, Lipsius, etc. in the sixteenth and seventeenth centuries), and indicates their influence on political thought in Hungary. His work thus also provides valuable contributions to the history of European ideas. I would therefore recommend this work to all interested readers.

Written in Székesfehérvár, the former coronation city of the Hungarian kingdom, on 28 April 2022.

Gergely Tóth, PhD.

Associate Research Fellow, Eötvös Loránd Research Network, Research Centre for the Humanities, Institute of History (Hungary).

Introduction: concepts and context

> We have, each of us, a life-story, an inner narrative, whose continuity, whose sense, is our lives. It might be said that each of us constructs and lives a 'narrative', and that this narrative is us, our identities. If we wish to know about a man, we ask 'what is his story – his real, inmost story?' – for each of us is a biography, a story. Each of us is a singular narrative, which is constructed, continually, unconsciously, by, through and in us – through our perceptions, our feelings, our thoughts, our actions; and, not least, our discourse, our spoken narrations. Biologically, physiologically, we are not so different from each other; historically, as narratives – we are each of us unique. To be ourselves we must have ourselves – possess, if need be re-possess, our life-stories. We must 'recollect' ourselves; recollect the inner drama, the narrative, of ourselves. A man needs such a narrative, a continuous inner narrative, to maintain his identity, his self.[1]

Identity and the formation of identity are important parts of human personality. According to Oliver Sachs, the development of identity in the human mind is a continuous reworking of past memories and experiences, which gain new meaning according to the actual context. This book is about one of the most important elements of the political narratives in the history of Hungary in past and present: the Holy Crown of Hungary and the way in which it has been used to construct and alter a form of identity.

This book analyses the construction of an Early Modern national identity on the territory of the Kingdom of Hungary by providing a case study of the so-called Magyar Szent Korona or Holy Crown of Hungary. This object, also known as the crown of St István, is one of the most widely used symbols of modern Hungarian nationalism in our times, but has been in use for ages in the political culture of Hungary.

My research concentrates on the relation between the change in the meaning of the Holy Crown and the construction of an Early Modern national identity between 1572 and 1665. Using a constructivist method of research (following the work of Quentin Skinner[2]), an attempt is made to answer the question of how the Hungarian political community and its relation to the Holy Crown was depicted, in what way the function of the crown legitimised this depiction, how the image,

---

1 Oliver Sachs, *The Man Who Mistook His Wife for a Hat and other Clinical Tales* (New York: Summit Books, 1985) 110.
2 Quentin Skinner, *Visions of Politics: Volume I: Regarding Method* (Cambridge: Cambridge University Press, 2002).

function and meaning of the crown changed, and how this change can be explained. My primary sources will be texts and images in which a certain political message is disseminated through the use of a certain concept or image of the crown and the nation.

My discussion of the views of the crown and of national identity supposes, of course, that the concept of a national identity is a meaningful one in the context of Early Modern Hungary. Questions of when and how a nation, national consciousness, or a sense of national identity took shape have been topics of lively debate among historians, sociologists and political scientists in recent decades. The debate has been between primordialists, who assume that national identity is as old as mankind, and modernists, who cannot imagine the existence of nations and national consciousness before the nineteenth century.[3] The ethno-symbolists, as represented by Anthony Smith, differ from this perspective, as they stress the sense of national identity as an ideology constructed by the use of symbols and images of the nation, in which these symbols played an important role.

In my research I am not so much interested in the question whether a Hungarian nation as such did exist. Instead, I will focus on how Early Modern politics on the territory of the Kingdom of Hungary was legitimised by the use of a concept of the nation and a certain meaning of the crown and its holiness, as expressed in texts, images and rituals.

The starting point of my approach is the notion of Ferenc Eckhart (1941) and László Péter (1966 and 2003): that the *Szentkorona-tan* or Doctrine (or Theory) of the Holy Crown is a modern invention, which makes it impossible to explain the meaning of the crown in Hungarian political culture in the Early Modern period. Still, the formulation of this doctrine has had a tremendous influence on the way in which the history of the crown and the nation has been written and the notion of the Holy Crown in modern-day politics in Hungary. We therefore need briefly to explain this doctrine, its origins and its reception.

---

3 Karl Deutsch, Eric Hobsbawm, Ernest Gellner, and Charles Tilly can be considered as the most influental modernists. Karl W. Deutsch, *Nationalism and Social Communication* (Cambridge, Mass: M.I.T. Press, 1966); Charles Tilly, "Reflections on the History of European State-Making" in Charles Tilly and Gabriel Ardant, eds., *The Formation of National States in Western Europe* (Princeton, N.J.: Princeton University Press: 1975) 3–83; Eric Hobsbawm, *Nations and Nationalism since 1780: Programme, Myth, Reality*, 2nd ed. (Cambridge, Cambridge University Press, 1992); Ernest Gellner, *Nations and Nationalism* (Ithaca: Cornell University Press, 1983). On the debate on Early Modern collective identities in the context of Central European see: Balázs Trencsényi and Márton Zászkaliczky, "Towards an intellectual history of patriotism in East Central Europe in the Early Modern period," in Balázs Trencsényi and Márton Zászkaliczky, eds., *Whose Love of Which Country?: Composite States, National Histories and Patriotic Discourses in Early Modern East Central Europe* (Leiden-Boston: Brill, 2010) 1–74.

The Doctrine of the Holy Crown was invented when modern nationalism was gaining ground on Hungarian soil. The concepts of the nation and the Holy Crown were used as arguments in providing legitimacy of political power in Hungary from the end of the eighteenth century. Historians and jurists started to research the roots of their nation and the Medieval history of the Crown in order to support the claims to sovereignty on behalf of the Estates against the power of the Habsburg dynasty. These political strivings resulted in a political ideology in which a notion of the crown and an idea of the nation were combined: the famous so-called *Szentkoronatan* or Doctrine of the Holy Crown.[4] There was also a fundamental change in the way that historians in Hungary regarded the political history of their country in Medieval times.

The creators of this doctrine in the nineteenth century, Imre Hajnik and Győző Concha, based their ideas on the famous and influential codification of Hungary's customary laws by the Hungarian jurist István Werbőczy (ca. 1460–1541).[5] Werbőczy finished his manuscript of *Tripartitum opus juris consuetudinarii inclyti Regni Hungariae* in 1514. It was published for the first time in 1517 and many times since then, but was never ratified by the king.[6]

In the opinion of Hajnik and Concha, a single phrase in this work ("*membra sacrae coronae*" or members of the Holy Crown) summarised an age-old organic state concept of Hungary.[7] On the basis of this concept king, church and nobility divided power among themselves in the mystical body of the Holy Crown. These

---

4 László Péter, "The Holy Crown of Hungary, Visible and Invisible," The Slavonic and East European Review, 81(2003) 32; László Péter, *Hungary's Long Nineteenth Century: Constitutional and Democratic Traditions in a European Perspective*, Miklós Lojkó, ed. (Central and Eastern Europe: Regional Perspectives in Global Context) (Leiden- Boston: Brill, 2012) 15–113.

5 Imre Hajnik, *Egyetemes európai jogtörténet a középkor kezdetétől a franczia forradalomig* [General European history of law from the medieval beginning till the French Revolution] (Budapest: Eggenberger, 1875); Győző Concha, "Közjog és magyar közjog. Viszontválasz a Nagy Ernő jogtanár úr Közjogáról írt bírálatomra adott válaszra [Public law and Hungarian public law. Respond to Ernő Nagy law teacher's answer to my criticism of his Public Law]," *Magyar Igazságügy*, vol. 35/2 (1891) 46–62. See also: József Kardos, *A szentkorona-tan története: 1919–1944* [The history of the holy crown doctrine: 1919–1944] (Budapest: Akadémiai Kiadó, 1985) 27–28; Barna Mezey, "Utószó [Afterword]," in Ferenc Eckhart, *Magyar alkotmány- és jogtörténet* [Hungarian constitutional and legal history], Barna Mezey, ed. (Budapest: Osiris, 2000) 423–424; Péter, "The Holy Crown of Hungary," 481–485.

6 Stephanus de Werboecz [Werbőczy], *Tripartitum opus iuris consuetudinarij inclyti regni Hungarie* (Viennae Austriae: Joannes Singrenius, 1517). Hereafter: *Tripartitum*. Modern edition and English translation: Péter Banyó, János M. Bak and Martyn Rady, eds., *The Customary Law of the Renowned Kingdom of Hungary: A Work in Three Parts Rendered by Stephen Werböczy (The "Tripartitum")* (The Laws of Hungary Series I: 1000–1526: Vol. 5.) (Charles Schlacks Jr Publisher and Central European University: Idyllwild and Budapest, 2005). See also: Martyn Rady, *Customary Law in Hungary: Courts, Texts, and the Tripartitum* (Oxford: Oxford University Press, 2015).

7 *Tripartitum*, Partis I. Tit 4. § 1. 58.

three words – *membra sacrae coronae* – served as historic legitimation of the modern sovereignty of the Hungarian nation. László Péter wrote about this way of thought:

> It is, then, a remarkable feat of nineteenth-century scholarship that it was on Werbőczy's authority that this metaphor, used in a single instance and in a very different context, could become the main evidence for evolution towards the concept of a unified system of public law and political authority."[8]

The codification of the Doctrine of the Holy Crown as a primordial state doctrine was mainly the work of Ákos Timon (1850–1925), who was a professor of constitutional law and the history of law in Budapest and a disciple of Hajnik.[9] His main work, in which he elaborated this doctrine, was published in 1902, six years after the celebration of the millennium of the occupation of the territory of Hungary.[10] According to Timon, the ideas about the nation and the crown to be found in Werbőczy even predated this work. He stated that the Doctrine of the Holy Crown was a unique and ancient Hungarian construct, and as such the fruit of the constitutional spirit and political character of the Hungarian nation.

Despite the efforts of nineteenth century academics, the Doctrine of the Holy Crown became state doctrine only after the dissolution of the Habsburg Empire in 1919. The only time that the notorious Doctrine played a dominant role in Hungarian political and academic life was during the Twenties. This was a direct result of the Treaty of Trianon (1920), under which Hungary lost two-thirds of its territory and a large part of its ethnic Magyar population. The crown became the symbol of the claims to the lost territories of the Kingdom of Hungary.[11] The kingdom had lost its king, but its crown and its symbolic meaning remained at the very heart of Hungarian politics.

In 1931 Ferenc Eckhart (1885–1957) published an article that caused a great commotion; in it he struck a devastating blow at the historical theory represented by Timon and similar nationalists.[12] The attack came from an unexpected direction, because the author of the publication was likewise a lecturer in the history of State

---

8 Péter, "The Holy Crown of Hungary," 452.
9 On Timon: Kardos, *A szentkorona-tan*, 29–31; Mezey, "Útoszó," 423–424; Péter, "The Holy Crown of Hungary," 485.
10 Ákos Timon, *Magyar alkotmány- és jogtörténet különös tekintettel a nyugati államok jogfejlődésére* [The Hungarian constitutional and legal history in light of the legal development in western countries] (Budapest: Grill Károly Könyvkiadóvállalata, 1902).
11 Kardos, *A szentkorona-tan*, 38–247.
12 Ferenc Eckhart, "Jog és alkotmánytörténet [History of law and constitution]," in Bálint Hóman, ed., *A magyar történetírás új útjai* [The new roads of Hungarian historiography] (Budapest: Magyar Szemle Társaság, 1931, ²1932) 269–320.

and Law at Budapest University.¹³ The storm and opposition that broke out in Hungarian political and academic circles all but cost the author his post.¹⁴ What caused the argument was that the conservative legal expert had removed a very important ideological pillar in the demands for political rights of the Hungarian nation living in the Carpathian basin, and of their territorial claims. He demonstrated that the image which the lawyers and politicians had formed of nation, State and crown was risible in the light of foreign research. Despite the consternation in political circles, not a single academic made a serious attempt to refute Eckhart's views.

Ten years later Eckhart reworked his original article on the concept of the crown into a monograph which appeared in 1941, during the war.¹⁵ In this he stated that the concept of the crown had undergone continual change in the course of Hungarian history. Over the years more and more ideas had become attached to it without any constant and unvarying concept of the Holy Crown coming into being, as his opponents had postulated. Eckhart also demonstrated that the Hungarian conception of the crown was by no means a unique phenomenon, but that similar formulations existed everywhere in Europe, and that these too had gone through the same stages of development. Furthermore, he showed that Timon's argument for the antiquity of the Doctrine was built on the quicksands of nationalism. His final conclusion was that the Doctrine of the Holy Crown had to be regarded as a modern development.

In its time Eckhart's essay met with such criticism because it subjected to critical examination the two pillars of the Doctrine of the Holy Crown – the conception of the crown itself and the organic notion of the State. Furthermore, his essay was not based on the axiomatic principle of the nation. He had examined the original textual context of hundreds of Medieval sources in which the term *corona* appeared and analysed the variation of the semantic content of the concept on the basis of textual comparison.

Eckhart's purpose was to write an essay which would reveal the way in which thought in Hungary on the subject of the crown had varied, and to compare this with similar notions throughout Europe. In the light of semantic change Eckhart attacked Timon's reasoning, according to which the corporate organisation of the

---

13 For Eckhart's biography see: György Bónis, "Ferenc Eckhart," *Zeitschrift der Savigny-Stiftung für Rechtsgeschichte: Germanistische Abteilung* 75/1 (1958) 596–600; Mezey, "Utószó," 407–439, Péter, "The Holy Crown of Hungary," 495–500; Zoltán József Tóth, *Szemelvények a Szent Korona-tan 20. századi történetéből. Az Eckhart-viták története* [Excerpts from the twentieth century history of the Doctrine of the Holy Crown] (PhD thesis, Miskolc University, 2005) 4–19.
14 László Péter, "The Holy Crown of Hungary," 496–499.
15 Ferenc Eckhart, *A szentkorona-eszme története* [The history of the Doctrine of the Holy Crown] (Budapest: Magyar Tudományos Akadémia, 1941, Máriabesnyő–Gödöllő: Attraktor, ²2003). Page numbers are those of the modern edition.

State had come into being in Hungary in the course of the development of the feudal social system and the growing significance of the crown.[16] In his opinion the Hungarian nobility had no legal say in matters of succession to the throne and legislation, and did not share power with the king. According to Eckhart the only connection between the development of the concepts of State and Crown was that the crown was the symbol of royal power within the boundaries of the Kingdom, while from the fourteenth century onwards it was used in Europe as a synonym for the Hungarian State. Treaties were made with other Medieval States in the name of the Crown of Hungary, and in making treaties the king acted as a representative of the Crown. In Eckhart's view, this special meaning of *corona* does not refer to the corporate state structure but was simply a function of kingship in international relationships.[17]

In introducing the development of the balance of political power in Medieval Hungary, Eckhart explains his opinion that in the Middle Ages the structure of the corporate State did not exist.[18] He does not examine balances of power from the point of view of the Hungarian State or the nation-state, but concentrates on the analysis of the relationships between the King of Hungary and the nobility on the basis of the meaning of the terms *respublica* and *regnum*. In the thirteenth century the term *respublica* emerged as a concept designating the body of the Estates, and it was only much later, in a law of 1386, that it was used in the sense of "country" (*regnum*). Until that time the term *regnum* was used primarily for kingship, the rights of the ruler as a whole. The second meaning of *regnum* referred to the circle of advisers surrounding the king, but the third meaning referred to that area of territory within the boundaries of which the rights of the ruler were valid. In the said law, and in following centuries, the word *regnum* was used in the sense of *respublica*.

The election of the king by the *regnum*, or rather the Estates as a body, first occurred in 1387. In Eckhart's view, this election was the first step on the road to the formation of the dualist State, in which there existed the required equilibrium between the king and the Estates with regard to the balance of power.[19] He states that in the same period royal power and the concept of *corona* became separated. In sources connected with the 1387 election of the king he encountered both *corona regia* (royal crown) and *corona regni* (crown of the country). As he sees it, after that date the *regnum* played a constantly growing role in political life, which led to the alteration in the significance of the crown. He believes that it was a result of

---

16 *Ibid.*, 35–41.
17 *Ibid.*, 41.
18 *Ibid.*, 42–56.
19 *Ibid.*, 44.

the enhanced political role of the *regnum* that the crown became a symbol of the Medieval Kingdom of Hungary in the eyes of the inhabitants of the country.[20]

In his view, these changes led to the distinction that was made in the fifteenth century between the crown as a symbol of the State and the crown as a symbol of royal power. He supports this by referencing events surrounding the election of the king in 1440 and a charter issued in connection with it.[21] Because of the view that he expressed on the Medieval State, this is the most debatable part of Eckhart's essay.

Eckhart interprets the contents of the said charter of 1440 as the formulation by the Estates of the mystery of the crown. He posits, however, that it may not be inferred from this that the king shared power with the *regnum*.[22] In fact, 1440 saw the first free election of the king by the Hungarian Estates, as on this occasion, unlike in 1387, the election was conducted not on the usual basis of descent. Furthermore, the transfer of power took place not through the collaboration of the high clergy and the aristocracy, but by means of an election held by the assembled Estates. This change, states Eckhart, did not mean that the Estates had become members of the crown, but was an expression of the fact that their political presence and influence were growing, which was also revealed by the ever more frequent use of the term "crown of the kingdom" (*corona regni*).[23]

As a consequence of the change in meaning, the term *corona* acquired a territorial significance.[24] In the fifteenth century *corona* denoted the Kingdom of Hungary, within the frontiers of which the ruler was clothed with complete power. From the fact that *corona* was conceptually linked to the idea of territorial integrity it followed that every individual piece of land taken from the Kingdom reduced the property of the crown. Loss of territory was regarded as injury to the Holy Crown. As the king regained lost territory it became once more the property of the crown. This action was deemed the recovery of the property of the crown. The property of the crown included not only territory but also towns. Certain territories and towns constituted the immediate property of the crown and were therefore inalienable, that is, the king was not able to make gifts of them or to mortgage them. In 1514 a law was enacted specifying which territories and towns enjoyed such status; which previously had been decided by the ruler. According to Eckhart, the Hungarian crown thus became synonymous with State interest and State property.[25]

---

20 *Ibid.*, 57–59.
21 *Ibid.*, 58–62, for the text of the charter see *ibid.*, 205.
22 *Ibid.*, 58–59.
23 *Ibid.*, 59–60.
24 *Ibid.*, 64–65.
25 *Ibid.*, 66–68.

On the basis of his research, Eckhart posits that the concept of the crown as a symbol of State integrity was brought into line with organic constitutional theory only in the sixteenth century.[26] He states that the organic view was known in Hungary as early as the thirteenth century, but that no political significance was attached to it. In that period the king, the great ecclesiastical and lay landowners, together with the common nobility, constituted the body of the *regnum*. The idea that every individual that took part in the Diet was a member of the *regnum* dates from the fourteenth century. A century later the royal council regarded itself as the body of the *regnum*, while its members were the magnates. At the same time, the entire nobility began to be referred to as members of the *regnum*. Eckhart states that this organic metaphor does not indicate the power of the members of the body politic but alludes to a Medieval State guided by consensus. In the course of his examination of the development of the Hungarian concept of the crown and that of the organic concept of the State, Eckhart comes to the conclusion that both concepts had a European ecclesiastical background and were not mutually linked in Hungary until the sixteenth century at the earliest.

According to Eckhart's research, the Hungarian concept of the crown and European organic constitutional theory first come together in Werbőczy's book of law of 1514. Werbőczy uses the concept of the crown in three different ways.[27] The first of these occurs most frequently and designates royal power in the traditional sense. The second meaning too, that relating to territory, had long been familiar in Hungary. Werbőczy uses the word *corona* in a sense other than the traditional only once, namely on the solitary occasion when he calls the nobility "members of the Holy Crown" (*membra sacrae coronae*). Eckhart, however, emphasises that Werbőczy states nowhere that the entire Hungarian nobility were members of the crown or had political power.

Eckhart makes a claim which astounded his contemporaries, namely that in the *Tripartitum* the concept of the crown had nothing to do with the Doctrine of the Holy Crown.[28] In the book, Werbőczy makes not a single use of the organic metaphor in writing about the crown, with the exception of the passage mentioned; he does not examine the question in detail and does not return to the concept in the remaining chapters of the book. According to Eckhart, the function of the particular section of text that touches on the crown was only to support the author's statement to the effect that all members of the nobility were equal and enjoyed the same privileges. In his opinion, In his opinion, Werbőczy wished to support his own earlier argument about the equality of the nobility by referring to his organic

---

26 *Ibid.*, 97–116.
27 *Ibid.*, 125.
28 *Ibid.*

metaphor. Werbőczy wished to support his own earlier argument about the equality of the nobility. He further states that it is not at all clear from Werbőczy's work that the nobility had a share with the king in executive power in keeping with the organic view. These observations of Eckhart's are in direct contradiction to the dominant ideology of his time, the 1930s.

Eckhart supports his statement by examining the way in which the new conception of the crown that had been formed was received in the period following the publication of the *Tripartitum*.[29] In his opinion the Medieval significance of the crown was still valid in the Early Modern period too; the crown was simultaneously the symbol of royal power and the power of the State, and subjects owed it fealty. The only meaning of *corona* that acquired constantly greater significance in the Early Modern period was the interpretation of the concept that linked it to territory. The change of meaning ensued because after 1526, with the Turkish invasion and the dual election of kings, three powers were ruling the country. Eckhart also states that in this period the crown was elevated to a symbol of the integrity of the country.

Eckhart did not find a single source in which the notion of *corona* was approached on the basis of the organic notion of the State.[30] The concept of "members of the crown" was used nowhere except in legal proceedings where – as in Werbőczy's law book – it arose as a metaphor in the defence of the rights of the nobility.[31] Other than usage connected with court cases, no source was found in which the nobility demanded political rights as members of the crown. In Eckhart's opinion, therefore, the Doctrine of the Holy Crown is a modern invention. His final conclusion is that Werbőczy's passage referring to "members of the crown" had served as a source of modern ideology aimed at guaranteeing the political rights of the nobility only since the eighteenth century.[32]

According to Péter, Eckhart's conception of the Hungarian State in the Medieval period is problematic.[33] In his later writings Eckhart lays emphasis on the special structural characteristics of Hungarian political institutions, the way in which the powers of king and *regnum* complemented one another. In his opinion both king and *regnum* enjoyed power bases founded on independent institutional systems and mutually complemented one another on a number of points, but did not constitute a unity. The sole link between the power of the ruler and the rights of his subjects was the covenant entered into at the coronation of the new ruler. The over-arching system of law, however, which has been a distinguishing feature of the State since

---

29 *Ibid.*
30 *Ibid.*, 164–153.
31 *Ibid.*, 151.
32 *Ibid.*, 175.
33 László Péter, The Holy Crown of Hungary, Visible and Invisible, *The Slavonic and East European Review*, 81(2003) 498–499.

the eighteenth century, did not yet exist. Péter states that in his monograph of 1941, Eckhart had changed his previous opinion and held that a kind of state-notion had existed in Medieval Hungary too.[34] In his book on the history of Hungarian law five years later, Eckhart maintained unaltered his position on the Medieval Hungarian State.[35]

In Péter's opinion this is why the small amount of academic criticism of Eckhart's monograph was aimed at the statement that the crown was a symbol of the Medieval State and the embodiment of the Medieval notion of the State. In his 1941 review of Eckhart's book, József Deér argues that in the Middle Ages *corona* could not have been a synonym for State.[36] He observes that in Medieval texts the term *corona* occurs in the sense of kingship rather than State. Deér also emphasises the importance of the role of the crown from the perspective of justifying the power of the king, and points out that Eckhart devotes insufficient attention to this function. In his view, the growing significance of the crown was linked not so much to the development of the Hungarian notion of the state as to the king's intention to legitimise his own power. He considers that from this it follows that the Hungarian crown, as object and concept alike, had a double significance for the king. He interprets Werbőczy's conception of the crown as an attack on this idea by means of which his book undermined the power of the king and justified the theory about the nobility.

Neither Deér nor Péter, however, offers an explanation of what caused the strange change in Eckhart's thinking about the existence of the Medieval state and, at the same time with the benefit of hindsight, we can agree with them both in their criticism of their compatriot.[37] The reason for the conceptual change that may be observed in Eckhart's work is to be found in the ideological background of his time, and in the formulation of general opinion on state and nation. The expert on Hungarian law took strong objection to the views of his contemporaries on the roots of Hungarian political power, and never publicly withdrew that criticism. He did, however, alter his opinion concerning the origin of the state. It may be supposed that he did this on the one hand to take the wind out of his opponents'

---

34 *Ibid.*, 499; Eckhart, *A szentkorona-eszme*, 44, 46–47, 49–51, 63.

35 Ferenc Eckhart, *Magyar alkotmány- és jogtörténet* [Hungarian constitutional and legal history], (Budapest: Vörösváry Soksz., 1946, Máriabesnyő–Gödöllő: Attraktor, ²2000) 98–103.

36 József Deér, "Eckhart Ferenc: A szentkorona-eszme története," [The History of the Doctrine of the Holy Crown] *Századok*, 76 (1941) 201–207. In the opinion of László Péter, this is the only serious criticism of Eckhart's work.

37 See R. van Caenegem, "Law and Society," in James H. Burns, ed., *The Cambridge History of Medieval Political Thought c. 350–c.1450* (Cambridge: Cambridge University Press, 1988) 174–183; J.P. Canning, "Introduction: Politics, Institutions and Ideas," in *ibid.*, 360–361; and: *id.*, "Law, Sovereignty and Corporation Theory, 1300–1450," in *ibid.*, 463.

sails from an ideological point of view, and to make them accept his other ideas. On the other hand, however, the change of his opinion can also be linked to the then current perception of the Hungarian State. Like the majority of his compatriots, Eckhart did not accept the terms of the Peace Treaty of Trianon (1920), due to which the Hungarian kingdom lost two-thirds of its territory. The academic theses concerning the existence of the Medieval Hungarian State that he propounded in 1931 could have been used as arguments against the territorial demands of the country, as on the basis of these the conclusion could be reached that there had been no continuity between Medieval Hungary and twentieth-century Hungary.[38] With regards to Eckhart's political views, it is probable that in his work that appeared in 1941 he reassessed his views on the continuity of Hungarian statehood and adjusted them to his personal political ideas.

Another point of criticism of Eckhart's work is the striking paradox which escaped Péter's attention. As will be discussed in detail later, this contradiction is connected to the way in which Eckhart introduced his academic conclusions. On the one hand, Péter states that Eckhart was the first to refute the Doctrine of the Holy Crown, and that indeed chimes with everything that we can read in his essay. It is an undisputable fact, on the other hand, that in Hungary Eckhart is regarded as the leading researcher of that doctrine. He is quoted in countless modern studies as the best overall expert on its development. In other words, Eckhart is seen not as the man who refuted Werbőczy's Doctrine of the Holy Crown, but as he who described it and also popularised it. It is forgotten that the main thrust of Eckhart's essay is that there is no historical basis for the Doctrine of the Holy Crown. His 1941 article on the crown is utilised to uphold precisely what the work essentially refutes, in other words the fact that the doctrine appears for the first time in Werbőczy's work.

So, what is the reason for readers' failure to understand what Eckhart has to say? The explanation for the contradictory reception of his essay is that he himself inadvertently caused the misunderstanding due to which the content of his book was, and still is, misinterpreted. Because of the attack on his 1938 work he clothed the substance of his 1941 essay in the ideological guise of a Holy Crown doctrine in the hope that this time it would meet with a more favourable reception; he did not, however, reckon on his thoughts being interpreted in two ways.

When one reads Eckhart's work one sometimes wonders whether he doubted his own conclusions. In speaking of the sixteenth and seventeenth centuries, he states that the concept of the crown seemed to have been "a retrogressive development", because "the Holy Crown began once again to signify royal power rather than the character of the State".[39] A few pages further on he refers again to the meaning of

---

38 Eckhart, 'Jog és alkotmánytörténet,' 269–320.
39 Eckhart, *A szentkorona-eszme*, 130.

Werbőczy's passage, and asks, concerning the Doctrine: "Did not the doctrine itself have any influence on Werbőczy's concept?"[40] After that he analyses a seventeenth-century reference to "members of the crown" and announces: "I have found the first trace of this teaching of the *Tripartitum* in the intellectual world of the Bocskay insurgency..."[41] He ends the chapter with the following conclusion: "The young plant of the Doctrine of the Holy Crown, tended by the hand of Werbőczy, now began to bear fruit, be it ever so little."[42] By virtue of this, the essay takes a surprising turn: Eckhart thinks that he has found the key to the Doctrine of the Holy Crown and at the same time it is clear that he cannot break with the predominant ideological current of his time.

After Deér's review of 1941 appeared it was more than twenty years before Eckhart's deductions were re-evaluated. The British-Hungarian legal historian László Péter wrote his dissertation on the significance of the Holy Crown in 1966; in it he examined the topic further and at the same time was critical of Eckhart's work.[43] In 2003, however, he published the results of further research in an article, after the revival of the cultus of the Holy Crown in 2000.[44] This article may be regarded as the most significant publication on the subject of the crown since the publication of Eckhart's book. Péter states that it is a mistake to attempt to account for the development or history of the Doctrine of the Holy Crown, because this quickly leads to the false conclusion that the concept of the crown is a synonym for the Hungarian State. This view he shares with Deér's criticism of Eckhart. Then he repeats Eckhart's conclusion with regard to Werbőczy. He too is of the opinion that the term "members of the crown" is a metaphor that Werbőczy called on to support his thesis that "one and the same liberty" applies to the nobility.[45]

In addition, Péter states that Werbőczy did not apply the term "members of the crown" to all the nobility but only to those that had received grants of land from the king, that is, some thirty percent of the entire nobility. In this connection he reaches the following conclusion:

> The context in which Werbőczy used the organic metaphor was clearly *fidelitas*, service and land donation rather than the political rights of the *communitas*.[46]

---

40 *Ibid.*, 150.
41 *Ibid.*
42 *Ibid.*, 151.
43 László Péter, *The Antecedents of the Nineteenth-century Hungarian State Concept: A Historical Analysis. The Background of the Creation of the Doctrine of the Holy Crown.* (PhD thesis, Oxford, 1966).
44 Péter, "The Holy Crown of Hungary"
45 *Ibid.*, 451.
46 Péter, *The Antecedents of the Nineteenth Century*, 14.

Péter finds no constitutional reference in Werbőczy's work to anything that would legitimise the sovereignty of the nation. In his view Werbőczy fused together two concepts: that of the crown of the *regnum*, in the sense of the nobility's right to elect the king, and the conflicting dogma that all the nobles that had received grants of land were equal, as they were under an obligation to no one but the lawfully crowned king. Péter ends his account with the following conclusion:

> In sum, the evidence is simply not there in Werbőczy that his organic crown metaphor even prefigured the idea of political authority, let alone a system of public law, residing in the Holy Crown as a corporation which comprised the king as head and the noble *ország* as its members.[47]

He therefore reaches the conclusion that the Early Modern political meaning of the term *corona* is connected exclusively with the king, but that the Doctrine of the Holy Crown is devoid of any historical foundation.[48] Taking into consideration the ambiguous nature of Eckhart's work and its reception, we may regard Péter as the first and only writer to unambiguously and publicly call into question the historical basis of the Doctrine of the Holy Crown.

To this day the conclusions of Eckhart and Péter have not been refuted, and indeed no one has so much as tried. We must, however, make a critical observation regarding both essays. In their works the writers do not tackle the questions formulated in the introductions, and in fact do not present an over-arching picture of the changes in significance of the crown. The actual purpose of the research of each is the refutation of the modern Doctrine of the Holy Crown. It is evident that in their essays they struggle feverishly to achieve that, but they only touch lightly on the Early Modern development of the significance of the crown. They are satisfied with finding no source between 1517 and 1790 that alludes to the crown's organic idea of the State, and they say not a word about the survival of Werbőczy's alleged Doctrine of the Holy Crown.

Neither Eckhart nor Péter carried out extensive research on the presence of the crown in Early Modern Hungary. For them, it was enough to prove that this doctrine did not exist before the modern period by carefully studying Medieval legal sources, charters and the contents of Werbőczy's codification. They did not pay attention to the rich crown tradition in the political literature and art of Hungary and its relation to the development of national identity in the period after 1514.

---

47 *Ibid.*, 452.
48 *Ibid.* Bak says the same in one of the last notes in his dissertation of 1973. See: János M. Bak, *Königtum und Stände in Ungarn im 14–16. Jahrhundert* (Wiesbaden: Steiner, 1973,)123, note 34.

For them, only the connection between the concept of the crown and the rise of modern nationalism was relevant.

My study fills this gap in the research of Ferenc Eckhart and László Péter. I will focus on the development of the narrative of the Holy Crown and the construction of an idea of the nation on the territory of the Early Modern kingdom of Hungary. Following Benedict Anderson, I will define a nation not as an objective or subjective collective, but as a mental, cultural and linguistic construct.[49] My analysis will focus on the functionality of the idea of the nation for the legitimation of political goals, in the first place those of the Estates of the Kingdom of Hungary. The notion of the Hungarian nation will therefore first and foremost refer to the nation of Estates. We shall consider the formation of national identity in such a way as to show the nature of the connection between the variants of the image that has been formed of the erstwhile concept of the nation and the coronation tradition. We shall also examine the role of the crown in legitimating the political message that existed in the imagination of the nation of Estates. We shall set the final development and collective depiction of the Kingdom of Hungary in the political and social framework between 1526 and 1664. The latter year is the date of publication of the latest item of literature on the crown that will be discussed: the book Mausoleum by Ferenc Nádasdy. We shall also shed light on one formulation of the political concept of community, which legitimized the demands of the nation of Estates on the basis of the significance of the crown, and in this way show the nation of Estates to have been independent in a peculiar political context.

We shall approach the formation of Early Modern national identity through the following questions: How were the nation of Estates of the Kingdom of Hungary and its relationship to the Hungarian crown depicted? What was the legitimising function of the Hungarian crown? In what ways did this image and function vary? How may these variations be explained?

According to our study, as a result of the crisis over the legitimation of the reign of King Rudolf in Hungary (1572–1608), in the period 1600–1608 the crown acquired a role of importance to the Estates. In this way its image too was changed. The process eventually led, in the period 1608–1613, to the formulation of a political concept of the crown which met the demands of the nation of Estates. This is the period in which the crown figures both emphatically and more frequently than in earlier times, and it appears in works on the State as an almost independent person. This is supported by the comparatively great number of works on the crown that appeared.

---

49 Benedict Anderson, *Imagined Communities* (London – New York: Verso, 2006) (revised edition) 5–7.

The first chapter of this study introduces the origin and history of the Hungarian crown jewels, the Medieval Hungarian monarchy, and the development of the tradition of the Holy Crown in the Middle Ages. The importance of the crown to the Hungarian kings' claim to power increased in the course of the Middle Ages. This was mainly because of violent succession to the throne. The crown did not have a constant meaning, and an intentional development of the tradition of the crown reached its peak during the reign of Mátyás Corvinus. Additionally, the alleged significance of the crown, which was introduced in the work of István Werbőczy at the beginning of the Early Modern period and summarised in the nineteenth-century Doctrine of the Holy Crown, is examined critically using the ideas of Timon Ákos, Ferenc Eckhart, and László Péter.

The second chapter explains the methods of research employed, and gives an analysis of the development of national identity and the meaning of the crown in the Kingdom of Hungary in the period around 1526. Applying the notions of *natio*, *regnum*, and crown, an explanation is given of how in Hungary the transformation from a cultural to a political community took place. The influence on this transformation of the tripartition of the Kingdom after the battle of Mohács in 1526 is also discussed. During this period, the crown began to symbolize the unity of the as yet divided political community and of the kingdom.

The third chapter discusses the changed legitimising function of the crown in the period between 1572 and 1603 during the rule of King Rudolf. Because of the political weakness of King Rudolf, the crown was used increasingly in political literature to strengthen the demands of the Hungarian political community. We can observe the beginning of a development in the course of which not only the abstract legal expression *corona* but the closely defined interpretation of the crown and the Hungarian Estates too, serve as justification of the political ideas of the Hungarian Estates which conflict with Habsburg royal power.

The fourth chapter describes the changes in the meaning of the crown and the image of the Hungarian Estates during the Bocskai Rebellion (1604–1606). It was the first uprising in Hungary against Habsburg power. In order that the political goals of the Bocskai Rebellion might have been made acceptable, new political ideas and concepts had to be formulated, and as a result the image of the Hungarian Estates changed, as did the legitimating significance of the crown.

During the insurrection the function of the Holy Crown changed from a symbol of the legitimacy of royal power to one of the political claims of the Hungarian Estates. This development is shown mainly in the creation of the fiction of the refusal of the Turkish crown which was written down by János Bocatius and in the hitherto unknown work of Bocatius, *Hungaroteutomachia*. I will argue in the fifth chapter that the use of the Holy Crown in the representation of the Hungarian Estates can be traced back to the work of the intellectual circle around Bocskai in 1605, in which Bocatius played a decisive role.

Elaborating on the important legitimising function of the crown in political culture, the sixth chapter further explains a number of texts and events which demonstrate this new importance of the Hungarian crown after 1606. This development is set against the content of Bocskai's political testament, the creation of the court of Archduke Matthias in Hungary in 1607–1608, the transfer of the Hungarian crown from Rudolf to his brother Archduke Matthias, and the latter's coronation in Hungary in 1608 as King Mátyás II. The ideas of Mátyás II, István Illésházy, Elias Berger, Péter Révay and János Jeszenszky are used to show how the political compromise between the new Habsburg king and the Hungarian Estates was legitimised by images of the crown, Hungarian *communitas*, and the Kingdom of Hungary.

The seventh chapter focuses on Révay's political thinking on the crown and national identity. It elaborates on the origin of his book on the crown and the political community, the intellectual context of his thinking and the reception of his ideas about the crown. The central thesis of this chapter is that the way in which Révay constructed national identity can be traced back to the method used by Jean Bodin to analyse history. Furthermore, Révay creates the notion of the sovereignty of the Hungarian political community using a fiction of the sacral influence of the Holy Crown on the history of Hungary. These constructs of Révay's concerning the crown (and not those of Werbőczy or the Doctrine of the Holy Crown) determined Hungarian national identity in the Early Modern period, as is shown by the reception and popularity of his work concerning the crown until the rise of modern nationalism at the end of the eighteenth century. I will also try to explain this description by Révay of the holiness of the Crown.

The eighth and last chapter treats part of the reception of the work of Révay using the story of the so-called Bull of Sylvester: an eleventh-century fiction made up in the seventeenth century. By explaining the role of the crown in the seventeenth-century negotiations between the Habsburg kings of Hungary and the popes about the right to appoint bishops, it appears that because of Hungary's changed political situation the ideas of the Lutheran Révay acquired a new meaning with a strong Catholic and Habsburg bias. This meaning has lasted until our time and is still present in today's politics and culture in Hungary.

I. A changing symbol of authority: the meaning and tradition of the Holy Crown up to 1526

The visible and invisible crown

"Let every soul be subject unto the higher powers. For there is no power but of God: the powers that be are ordained of God." (Rom 13:1) The words of the apostle Paul were used from the Late Antiquity to add a divine legitimation to earthly rule. This concept was made tangible by a crown jewel and made visible by the symbolism of the coronation ritual. A crown became the symbol of the divine legitimation of the rule of the king. The divine authority was transferred to the person of the ruler through the crowning with a crown during the coronation. The crown, the king and the coronation ritual became rewarding subjects to express one's political and religious thoughts about power and authority in literature and art.[1]

In Medieval Europe the Latin word *corona* was ascribed two meanings in political texts, which Ernst Kantorowicz has described in detail.[2] On the one hand it designated the visible object (*corona visibilis*), and on the other the conceptual content associated with it (*corona invisibilis*). As an object, the crown was a golden ornament for the head, circular or wreath-like in shape, which was used at the coronation of princes.[3] In the conceptual sense the crown was an expression of the fullness of royal power, acquired by the king through the grace of God at the time of coronation, which embraced all the royal rights, obligations and privileges necessary for the governing of the country (*regnum*) (see image 2).

The Latin word *corona* had significance among the political elements of the Medieval Kingdom of Hungary similar to that in the rest of Europe. On the one hand it was used to denote the circular head-dress, on the other hand it meant the power of the king. From the birth of the Kingdom of Hungary in the eleventh

---

1 See: Joachim Ott, *Krone und Krönung: die Verheißung und Verleihung von Kronen in der Kunst von der Spätantike bis um 1200 und die geistige Auslegung der Krone* (Mainz am Rhein: Philipp von Zabern, 1998).

2 Ernst Kantorowicz, *The King's Two Bodies: A Study in Medieval Political Theology* (Princeton: Princeton University Press, 1957) 336–337.

3 For the medieval crowning of Hungarian kings see: Vilmos Fraknói, *A magyar királyválasztások története* [The history of the elections of Hungarian kings] (Budapest: Athenaeum, 1921, reprint: Máriabesnyő–Gödöllő: Attraktor Kft, 2005) 5–123; Emma Bartoniek, *A magyar királykoronázások története* [The history of Hungarian coronations of kings] (Budapest: Magyar Történelmi Társulat, 1938) 8–67; Erik Fügedi, *Kings, Bishops, Nobles and Burghers in Medieval Hungary*, ed. János M. Bak. (London: Variorum, 1986) 1–185.

century both meanings were current, and both may frequently be found in the Latin hagiographies of saints, in charters and other documents.[4] The earliest known occurrence of *corona* with a Hungarian possessive suffix, in the form *coronaja* (his crown) dates from 1350. Later, during the course of the fifteenth century, this develops into the Hungarian *korona*.[5]

In what follows we shall accordingly use the word *crown* in three senses. In the material sense, following Kantorowicz, it will mean the head-dress of Medieval origin which served through the centuries as the coronation jewel of the kings of Hungary (see image 1).[6] It has a long and eventful history, as can be seen by its worn outlook.[7] It has been stolen, buried and was even in exile in the USA after WWII. In modern usage it is most frequently referred to as the *Hungarian Holy Crown*, the *Holy Crown of Hungary*, the *Hungarian crown* or *St István's crown*, written with or without initial capitals according to political, religious or academic views. Used in the abstract sense, the concept of the crown embraces all political connotations relevant to the royal power with which the ruler of the Kingdom of Hungary was clothed in coronation.

The concepts of the tradition of the Hungarian Holy Crown and its *cultus*, and the legitimate significance of the crown, arising from the already quoted work of László Péter, denote a whole series of shifting political and religious views regarding the crown. The *cultus* of the crown finds expression in the use of the adjective holy, the belief that it was associated with King St István, and the reverence accorded the diadem as a sacral object. In Kantorowicz's perception the meanings of *corona visibilis* and *corona invisibilis* are interwoven in Hungarian tradition; the reality of the material crown physically supports the notions, deriving from them its power and mystical nature.[8] The original function of the *cultus* of the crown was the legitimation of kingly power (the crown as an abstract concept).

According to János M. Bak's definition, the coronation jewel is an object used on the occasion of the coronation. By coronation we understand a set series of symbolic and ritual acts, which in the Middle Ages and under the *ancien régime*

---

4 Iván Boronkai and Ibolya Bellus, eds., *Lexicon Latinitatis medii aevi Hungariae*, vol. III, (Budapest: Argumentum Kiadó - Akadémiai Kiadó, 1991) 1991, 407–408.

5 Loránd Benkő et al, eds., *A magyar nyelv történeti-etimológiai szótára* [The Hungarian language historic-etymologic dictionary], vol. II (Budapest: Akadémiai Kiadó, 1970) 579–580.

6 Cf. Sándor Radnóti, "The Glass Cabinet. An Essay about the Place of the Hungarian Crown," *Acta Historiae Artium* 43 (2002) 83–111.

7 For an excellent English language overview of the history of the holy crown, see: János M. Bak and Géza Pálffy, Crown and Coronation in Hungary 1000–1916 A. D. (Research Centre for the Humanities, Institute of History and the Hungarian National Museum, 2020).

8 Kantorowicz, *The King's Two Bodies*, 339–340.

rendered the king's power legitimate and made it visible to the public.⁹ Bak lists the symbols of the transfer of power under three headings. To the first belong those which played a part in the ceremony of coronation or initiation. To the second may be ascribed those representative, real, imaginary, or only depicted symbols which the ruler bore on his body, held in his hands, or displayed. The third category includes such symbolic objects as were connected to deceased rulers.¹⁰

In Hungary the first group consists of the crown, the orb, the coronation sword, the sceptre and the coronation cloak.¹¹ To the second group belong those crowns which, strictly speaking, should not be reckoned coronation insignia, but played a certain role in Hungarian political history.¹² The third group consisted of funeral crowns, grave crowns and votive crowns all used in Hungary or by Hungarian rulers and which sometimes look similar to the Holy Crown.¹³

Although under Bak's definition a wide variety of objects may be listed among the coronation insignia of Hungary, only one of the crowns bears the name of *Magyar Szent Korona* (Holy Crown of Hungary). Because of the political and religious significance of the symbol of majesty the question of the origin of this crown has to this day not been satisfactorily answered.¹⁴ To the best of my knowledge no foreign expert has recently studied the tangible crown from close by. Despite its importance in the history of art hardly anything has appeared about it in any foreign language.¹⁵

---

9 János M. Bak, Introduction: Coronation Studies – Past, Present and Future, in János M. Bak, ed., *Coronations: Medieval and Early Modern Monarchic Ritual* (Berkeley: University of California Press, 1990) 1, 10.
10 János M. Bak, "Magyar királyi jelvények a középkorban [The Hungarian crown jewels in the Medieval period]," *A Hadtörténeti Múzeum Értesítője* 4 (2002) 17–21.
11 Éva Kovács and Zsuzsa Lovag, *A magyar koronajelvények* [The Hungarian crown jewels] (Budapest: Corvina Kiadó, 1980); Róbert József Szvitek and Endre Tóth, eds., *A koronázási jelvények okmányai* [The charters of the crown jewels] (Budapest: Magyar Nemzeti Múzeum, 2003) 33–265. It should, however, be noted that the objects used at coronations varied.
12 These were the so-called Bocskai crown, the Rudolf crown and the Brassó crown of which we will read later.
13 One of the finest Hungarian votive crowns is that dating from 1635 which may be seen on the St István reliquary in the Cathedral of Zagreb. György Tarczai, *Az Árpád-ház szentjei* [The saints of the House of Árpád] (Budapest: Szt. István Társulat, 1930) 57.
14 For an account of the problem see Kálmán Benda and Erik Fügedi, *A magyar korona regénye* [The novel of the Hungarian crown] (Budapest: Zrínyi Nyomda, 1979) 17.
15 There is ample literature on the subject but scientifically based studies have been very few. The most important of these are: Alexius Horányi, *De Sacra Corona Hungariae, ac de Regibus eadem redimitis Commentarius*, (Pest: Typis Trannerianis, 1790); Sámuel Décsy, *A magyar szent koronának és az ahoz tartozó tárgyaknak historiája* [The history of the Hungarian holy crown and the objects which belong to it] (Vienna: Alberti Ignátz, 1792); István Veszprémi, *Magyar országi öt különös elmélkedések, I: A Magyar Szent Koronáról* [Five special reflections, I: on the Hungarian Holy Crown] (Pozsony: Simon Péter Weber, 1795); Arnold Ipolyi, *A magyar szent korona és a koronázási jelvények története és műleírása* [The history and description of the Hungarian Holy Crown and the crown jewels]

It is almost certain that in its present form the Holy Crown does not date from the time of István I (997–1038). Its lower section, the *corona Graeca*, is probably a Byzantine woman's crown such as may be seen in portraits of Byzantine rulers. The age of the crown has been assessed from these illustrations, and on this basis, it was made or modified in or about the second half of the eleventh century.[16] It came to Hungary in about 1075 as a gift from the emperor of Byzantium. The transference of the emperor's likeness on a crown proclaimed his suzerainty both within the Byzantium Empire and within the realm of foreign diplomacy with the Kingdom of Hungary.[17]

Less is known about the origin of the upper section, the *corona Latina*, but it is unlikely that it was ever a crown in its own right. The enamels on it pre-date the second half of the eleventh century, but when the cross-bands were made is unclear.[18] The majority of experts agree that the two sections were joined in the reign of Béla III (1173–1196), but a number dispute this.[19] On the basis of

---

(Budapest: Magyar Tudományos Akadémia, 1886); Patrick Kelleher, *The Holy Crown of Hungary* (Rome: American Academy in Rome, 1951); Albert Boeckler, Die "Stephanskrone", in Percy Ernst Schramm, ed., *Herrschaftszeichen und Staatssymbolik: Beitrage zu ihrer Geschichte vom dritten bis zum sechzehnten Jahrhundert* (Stuttgart: Hiersemann, 1956); Magda von Bárány-Oberschall, *Die Sankt Stephanskrone und die Insignien des Königreiches Ungarn* (Wien–München: Verlag Herold, 1961); *id.*, "Localization of the Enamels of the Upper Hemisphere of the Holy Crown of Hungary," *Art Bulletin* 31/2 (June 1949) 121; Josef Deér, *Die heilige Krone Ungarns* (Wien: Herman Bohlaus, 1966); Éva Kovács and Zsuzsa Lovag, *A magyar koronajelvények* [The Hungarian crown jewels] (Budapest: Corvina, 1980); Ferenc Fülep, Éva Kovács, Zsuzsa Lovag, eds., *Regni Hungariae I: Studien zur Machtsymbolik des mittelalterlichen Ungarn* (Budapest: Népmuvelési Propaganda Iroda, 1983); Iván Bertényi, *A magyar szent korona* [The Hungarian Holy Crown] (Budapest: Kossuth Kiadó, 1996); Endre Tóth and Károly Szelényi, *A magyar szent korona. Királyok és koronázások* [The Hungarian Holy Crown. Kings and coronations] (Budapest: Kossuth Kiadó, 2000); David Buckton, "The Holy Crown in the history of enamelling," *Acta Historiae Artium* 43 (2002) 14–22; Géza Pálffy, "A Szent Korona balesete 1638-ban [The accident of the Holy Crown in 1638]," in József Jankovics, ed., *"Nem sűlyed az emberiség!"… Album amicorum Szörényi László LX. Születésnapjára* [Mankind is not lost! Album amicorum for the sixtieth birthday of László Szörényi] (Budapest: MTA Irodalomtudományi Intézet, 2007) 1431-1444; Cecily J. Hilsdale, "The Social Life of the Byzantine Gift: The Royal Crown of Hungary Re-Invented," *Art History* 31 (2008) 602–631; Bak and Pálffy, Crown and Coronation in Hungary 1000–1916 A. D. (Research Centre for the Humanities, Institute of History and the Hungarian National Museum, 2020).

16 Deér, *Die heilige Krone*; Tóth and Szelényi, *A magyar szent korona*.
17 Hilsdale, "The Social Life of the Byzantine Gift," 602–631; Cecily J. Hilsdale, *Byzantine Art and Diplomacy in an Age of Decline* (Cambridge: Cambridge University Press, 2014) 11.
18 Endre Tóth, "A Szent Korona apostollemezeinek keltezéséhez [On the origin of the Holy Crown's plates with the apostles]," *Communicationes Archaeologicae Hungaricae* (1996) 181–209.
19 Tóth and Szelényi, *A magyar szent korona*, 30–31. According to Deér the present crown was made for István V (1270–1272) in 1270, when Queen Anna fled to Prague with the former crown after the death of King Béla IV. Deér, *Die heilige Krone*, 206–209.

our information on its origin and age, the crown that we know today cannot be unreservedly identified as one of those referred to in sources of the eleventh and twelfth centuries.

A similar problem arises when we investigate the connection between the crown and its historical depictions.[20] Endre Tóth classifies the forms in which the Hungarian crown is historically depicted into three groups.[21] The first he calls the semantic crown group. This contains the depictions of the crown made on a European pattern, occurring in artistic creations and medals from the eleventh to the fourteenth centuries. The second category contains depictions of the crown made in the fifteenth and sixteenth centuries made after the coronation of Mátyás I. in 1464, by which time certain features of the present-day Hungarian crown may be perceived (for instance image 2). The third group consists of detailed and more or less accurate illustrations which were printed between 1608 and 1790 and circulated widely (see image 10-17). Examples of European-style depictions may be seen, for example, on the heads of kings in the fourteenth century *Illustrated chronicle* (Hungarian: *Képes Krónika*). The best-known example in the second group is a coloured ink drawing in the Fugger chronicle from Munich, made between 1547 and 1555, and which is considered the earliest accurate depiction of the crown (see image 4).[22] The depictions in the third, and at the same time latest, group date from the time of Mátyás II (1608-1618), of which we will read in the fifth and sixth chapter (image 6-11).

According to János M. Bak it is certain that the Hungarian crown familiar today was used as a royal crown and the coronation jewel of the Hungarian kings from the early fourteenth century, yet the first accurate depiction of it dates only from the mid-sixteenth century.[23] He believes that earlier depictions of the crown cannot offer information on its exterior. Therefore, in his view, we cannot make any deductions with regard to the earlier appearance of the Hungarian crown from depictions made before the sixteenth century. In the case of depictions that may be listed in categories 2 and 3, however, the connection between the real crown and its illustration is beyond doubt; these may therefore be regarded as important sources for the study of the appearance of the crown and the shifts in its significance.

---

20 Kees Teszelszky, "A magyar korona megjelenése a kora újkori képzőművészetben [The depiction of the Hungarian crown in Early Modern art]," *Művészettörténeti Értesítő* 60/1 (2011) 1-10.
21 Szvitek and Tóth, *A koronázási jelvények okmányai*, 9-21.
22 Bayerische Staatsbibliothek, Cgm 895, fol. 308v. On this image and other depictions, see: Enikő Buzási and Géza Pálffy, *Augsburg - Wien - München - Innsbruck. Die frühesten Darstellungen der Stephanskrone und die Entstehung der Exemplare des Ehrenspiegels des Hauses Österreich. Gelehrten- und Künstlerbeziehungen in Mitteleuropa in der zweiten Hälfte des 16. Jahrhunderts* (Budapest: Magyar Tudományos Akadémia Történettudományi Intézet, 2015).
23 János M. Bak, "Magyar királyi jelvények a középkorban [The Hungarian crown jewels in the medieval period]," *A Hadtörténeti Múzeum Értesítője* 4 (2001) 20-21.

The concept of the crown in Hungary

In order to understand the later development of the concept of the Crown we must study the origins of royal power in Hungary. The institutions of *king* and *kingdom* came into being as the result of political, religious and cultural changes which transformed the loose Hungarian tribal association of the tenth century into a Christian kingdom on Western European lines. The transformation which the Hungarian people underwent in the tenth century strongly resembles – in Pál Engel's opinion – that which was played out during that time in the milieu of other pagan nations in Europe.[24] The transmutation of pagan tribal confederacies into Christian kingdoms generally took place as follows: a member of one of the leading families would assume power, force the tribe to accept Christianity, create a Christian ecclesiastical organisation, and re-organise the power structure in accordance with the monarchic principles of Christian Western Europe. After that, in justification of his own power and the legitimacy of the assumption of that power, he himself would adopt the title of king *(rex)*, or cause a relative to do so. The new king would then be crowned with the symbol of Christian rulers, the crown. The end result of the transformation would be a Christian kingdom and the country would irreversibly become part of Christian Europe. In the political transition former observances would be adapted, new ones introduced, symbols and terms brought into use that were in keeping with Christian political ideas, and new institutions could be created.

The formation of the Christian kingdom and St István's governance are among the most visited topics in Hungarian history.[25] Numerous historians have used the image that has been formed of the first king in order to project on the past the socio-political problems of the present.[26] To this day it is common practice to link the birth of the kingdom to other similarly sensitive topics such as the connection between the Holy Roman Empire and the Kingdom of Hungary, the

---

24 Pál Engel, *The Realm of St. Stephen. A History of Medieval Hungary 895–1526*, Tamás Pálosfalvi, tr. (London–New York: I. B. Tauris, 2001) 18–25.

25 On Szent István, see Bálint Hóman, *Szent István* (Budapest: Egyetemi Nyomda, 1938); Thomas von Bogyay, *Stephanus rex* (Wien–München: Herold, 1976); György Györffy, *István király és műve* [St István and his work] (Budapest: Gondolat, 1977); Péter Erdő and József Török, eds., *Doctor et apostol: Szent István tanulmányok* [Doctor et apostol: studies on St István] (Budapest, Márton Áron Kiadó, 1994); Iván Bertény, *Szent István és öröksége: Magyarország története az államalapítástól a rendiség kialakulásáig, 1000–1440* [St István and his heritage: the history of Hungary from the beginning of the state till the formation of the estates, 1000–1440] (Budapest: Kulturtrade, 1997). See also the extensive bibliography in: Engel, *The Realm of St. Stephen*, 402–405.

26 Sándor Őze and Norbert Spannenberger, "Zur Reinterpretation der mittelalterlichen Staatsgründung in der ungarischen Geschichtsschreibung des 19. und 20. Jahrhunderts," *Jahrbuch für Geschichte und Kultur Südosteuropa* 2 (2000) 62; Péter, "The Holy Crown of Hungary," 426–431.

role and situation of the Catholic Church in Hungary, the place of the country in Central Europe, the relationship of Hungary to neighbouring countries and the connection between Hungarian and European culture.[27]

The most significant ceremony that served as justification of the power carved out in Central Europe by the Árpád dynasty was the coronation of Prince István as a Christian king, which took place in Esztergom either on Christmas Day 1000 or 1 January 1001.[28] Like the crown of St István, his coronation too is a topic that is frequently discussed.[29] From the debates of the past two hundred years we may state that such St István legends as the *legenda maior* (1077) and *legenda minor* (twelfth century) are not to be regarded as reliable sources on the coronation.[30] Even the references to King István's power in various official documents provide no definite answer to the question of how the ceremony was conducted.[31] According to the chronicle of Thietmar von Merseburg (c.1015) all that is certain is that some kind of coronation jewel played a part in the course of the coronation ceremony.[32] By the ceremony of coronation the House of Árpád gained the ultimate divine approval of its assumption of power.[33] The show of force that accompanied the assumption of power and the enforcement of baptism in an effort to consolidate the acceptance of Christianity took place in Hungary as elsewhere in Europe.

---

27 Gyula Szekfű, "Szent István a magyar történet századaiban [St István in the centuries of Hungarian history]," in Jusztinián Serédi, ed., *Emlékkönyv Szent István király halálának kilencszázadik évfordulóján* [Book to commemorate the 900th anniversary of the death of King St István], vol. III, (Budapest: Magyar Tudományos Akadémia, 1938, revised ed. 1988) 1–80; Katalin Sinkó, "Árpád versus Saint István. Competing Heroes and Competing Interests in the Figurative Representation of Hungarian History," in Tamás Hofer, ed., *Hungarians between "East" and "West": three Essays on Myths and Symbols* (Budapest: Néprajzi Múzeum, 1994) 9–26; Őze and Spannenberger, "Zur Reinterpretation," 61–77; Péter, "The Holy Crown of Hungary," 426–431.
28 János Karácsonyi, *Szent István király oklevelei és a Szilveszter-bulla* [The charters of King Sz. István and the Bull of Sylvester] (Budapest: Magyar Tudományos Akadémia, 1891) 160–164.
29 Péter, "The Holy Crown of Hungary," 427–429.
30 See László Péter's thoughts on the subject and Zoltán Tóth, *A Hartvik-legenda kritikájához (a Szt. Korona eredetkérdése)* [On the critics of the Hartvic-legend (the question of the origin of the Holy Crown] (Budapest: Ranschberg, 1942); Jozsef Deér, "A magyar királyság megalakulása [The formation of the Hungarian kingship]," in *A Magyar Történettudományi Intézet Évkönyve* [The yearbook of the Hungarian Institute for the Study of History] (Budapest: Magyar Történettudományi Intézet, 1942, reprint Budapest: Attraktor, 2010) 1–88.
31 József Gerics, "Szent István királlyá avatásának körülményeiről [About the circumstances of the coronation of St István]," *Művészettörténeti Értesítő*, 33 (1984) 97–101.
32 Robert Holtzmann, ed., *Die Chronik des Bischofs Thietmar von Merseburg und ihre Korveier Überarbeitung: Thietmari Merseburgensis Episcopi Chronicon* (Berlin: Weidmann, 1955) 198.
33 Jenő Szűcs, "König Stephans "Institutionen" – König Stephans Staat," in Jenő Szűcs, *Nation und Geschichte. Studien,* trans. Johanna Kerekes (Köln–Wien: Böhlau, 1981) 258.

The origin of the cultus of the Holy Crown

In László Péter's opinion, the tradition concerning the genesis, origin and significance of the crown of St István arose in a manner different from that of the crown-tradition in other European countries. In the course of the Middle Ages the crown and the ceremony of coronation as means of confirming the power of rulers decreased in significance everywhere except in Hungary.[34] Royal power was rather legitimised by the ruling dynasty's divine right to the throne.[35] Péter is of the opinion that a different development can be observed in Hungary, departing from the European trend in three ways.[36] Firstly, the Crown acquired political significance much later in the Kingdom of Hungary than in other countries of the Christian world. Secondly, the tradition persisted all through the Middle Ages. Thirdly, the tradition of the crown flourished not only in the Middle Ages but lives on even since the Medieval Kingdom of Hungary came to an end in 1526.

The origin and substance of the cultus of the crown actually resided in the belief that in coronation, together with the original crown of the first ruler, the power and holiness of St István I descended upon the new ruler. The kings that followed István I and their subjects all traced their ownership, liberty and other rights and obligations back to the *auctoritas* of the founder of the kingdom, and thereby instigated the formation of the cultus of the holy rulers of the House of Árpád.[37] The reason for the power struggles that broke out constantly in Hungary in the Árpád period was the view that every member of the royal family was suitable to rule and at the same time had a right to the throne as they were all blood relatives. After István I died in 1038, closeness to the ruler by descent in the blood-line was a weightier justification in the power struggles of posterity than whether or not they were crowned with St István's crown. As blood relationship to the Árpáds was considered more important than István's coronation jewel, the tradition of the crown is rooted in the cultus of the Árpád dynasty. The beginning of the dynastic cultus was marked by the sanctification of two members of the House of Árpád in

---

34 Radnóti, "The Glass Cabinet," 83–111; Péter, "The Holy Crown of Hungary," 432. On the meaning of a crown in Europe, see: Jean Dunbabin, "Government," in James H. Burns, ed., *The Cambridge History of Medieval Political Thought c. 350–c. 450* (Cambridge: Cambridge University Press, 1988) 498–501.

35 See among others Janet L. Nelson, *Politics and Ritual in Early Medieval Europe* (London: Hambledon Press, 1986); Sergio Bertelli, "*Rex et sacerdos:* The Holiness of the King in European Civilization," in Allan Ellenius, ed., *Iconography, Propaganda, and Legitimation* (Oxford: Clarendon press, 1998) 123–145.

36 Péter, "The Holy Crown of Hungary," 432.

37 Ibidem, 431–432.

1083, when King István and his son Imre, who died young and was never crowned king, were elevated to the ranks of the saints.

Gábor Klaniczay believes that through this canonisation the power of the rulers of Hungary also acquired a further sacral legitimacy over and above that of the ceremony of coronation.[38] László I (1077–1095) was guided by weighty political considerations when he initiated the canonisations. After he and his brother, the later Géza I, had dethroned the rightful king, Salamon (1063–1074), László ruled for seven years without being crowned. He owed his throne to the constant struggles for it between the Christian and pagan relatives of István I and the discord that affected the country's well-being. After the canonisation Salamon fled from Hungary. The cultus of the sanctified members of the dynasty reinforced László I in power, and in 1197, long after his death, he too was elevated to sainthood.

In Klaniczay's opinion, by his policy of canonisation László I followed the example of the Western-European ruling houses, but was also drawn to it by a personal element.[39] István I became the first king to be canonised in Europe because he had followed a policy of Christianity. He had earned his sainthood not through martyrdom but by his efforts as a Christian ruler to convert his people to Christianity. It is therefore no wonder that the symbol of the power of the ruler, the crown, played a key part in the life of the sainted king.

The text regarded as the beginning and culmination of the cultus of the crown of St István, is known as the Hartvik legend.[40] Its author was probably Arduin, bishop of Győr in the time of Könyves Kálmán (Kálmán the Learned, 1995–1116).[41] He worked up into a *Life of St István* the legends (*legenda maior* and *legenda minor*) that had arisen about the first king, incorporating into the text *topoi* from *Lives* of European saints together with occasional allusions to topical politics and ecclesiastical matters.[42]

---

38 Gábor Klaniczay, *Holy Rulers and Blessed Princesses. Dynastic Cults in Medieval Central Europe*, Éva Pálmai, tr. (Cambridge: Cambridge University Press, 2002) 123–134.
39 *Ibid.*, 122–134.
40 Emma Bartoniek, ed., "Legendae Sancti Stephani regis maior et minor atque legenda ab Hartvico conscripta," in Emericus Szentpétery, ed., *Scriptores Rerum Hungaricarum tempore ducum regumque stirpis Arpadianae gestarum* Vol. II (Budapestini: Typ. Reg. Univ. Litter. Hung., 1938) 363–448. On the legends see Carlisle A. Macartney, *The Medieval Hungarian Historians. A Critical and Analytical Guide* (Cambridge: Cambridge University Press, 1953) 165, and Klaniczay, *Holy Rulers*, 305–308.
41 Gyula Pauler, "Ki volt Hartvich püspök? [Who was Bishop Hartvich]," *Századok*, 16 (1883) 803–804.
42 For the construction and content of the text see Klaniczay, *Holy Rulers*, 124, 128, 135–147, 305–308; Macartney, *The Medieval Hungarian Historians*, 165–170; Carlisle A. Macartney, "The Hungarian texts relating to the Life of St István," in Carlisle A. Macartney, *Studies on Early Hungarian and Pontic History*, László Péter and Lóránt Czigány, eds. (Aldershot: Variorum, 1999) 351–374.

Hartvik's most interesting addition is the earliest account of the miracle involving the pope and the crown.[43] According to Hartvik's narrative, Pope Sylvester II (999–1003) presented István with a crown and an apostolic cross because of a vision that he had seen in a dream. In this an angel appeared to him and commanded him to send the crown originally intended for King Mieszko of Poland to István instead.[44] The Pope obediently asked Bishop Asztrik, István I's envoy, to hand the crown and apostolic cross to the Hungarian ruler as symbols of royal power.[45] Klaniczay considers that the details that Hartvik wove into the story must be seen as: "… a liturgical-sacral dimension, a form of the ruler's divine legitimation that went back to the Imperial Holy Roman traditions of the Ottonians and Carolingians."[46] Hartvik also recorded the ceremony of the coronation and István's publicly spoken last words. According to his evidence King Istvan, on his death-bed, presented the crown – symbolising his kingdom – to the Virgin Mary, and thus Mary became the patron saint of the country.[47] In Klaniczay's view, this must be seen as a liturgical act properly belonging to István's coronation.[48]

László Péter believes that the description of the miracle of the royal crown marks the start of the cultus of the crown of St István.[49] We still may not, however, assert unequivocally that Bishop Hartvik intended to establish a cultus of the crown. His aim in writing the *Legend* was to support his king in his struggle for power, and the way to do that was, as he saw it, by emphasising the sainthood of King Kálmán's ancestor. The role of the crown in this tale is marginal, but it serves the writer's political purposes, as the main theme is the justification of the sainthood and holy nature of King István I. The story of the miracle of the crown and the Pope's gift serves as an argument confirming István's sainthood, by means of which Hartvik wishes to increase the respect in which his king is held.

From the point of view of the cultus of the crown of St István, the significance of the Hartvik legend lies in the continuation of the attributes with which the crown is peculiarly clothed. The importance of the role of the crown in the Hartvik legend was later regarded as genuine, and – as we shall see – a number of selected details acquired independent existence in art and literature.

Despite the existence of the cultus of St István, nothing is known about the peculiar significance of the crown in the eleventh century. The earliest document in which the term *sacra corona* occurs dates from 1250, that is, more than two hundred

---

43 *Legendae Sancti Stephani regis maior et minor*, 401–440.
44 *Ibid.*, 412–414.
45 *Ibid.*, 414.
46 Klaniczay, *Holy Rulers*, 135.
47 *Legendae Sancti Stephani regis maior et minor*, 385–387.
48 Klaniczay, *Holy Rulers*, 136.
49 Péter, "The Holy Crown of Hungary," 426.

years after István I's death.⁵⁰ Again the contrast with the development that had occurred in the rest of Europe is striking, as by that time the term had fallen into disuse outside Hungary.⁵¹ According to Hungarian historians the nomenclature Holy Crown refers to the link between the crown and its religious significance, and to the fact that for that reason supernatural powers were attributed to the crown in the Middle Ages.⁵² The Slovak legal historian Josef Karpat refuted this idea when he revealed the frequency of occurrence of the term and its context. According to his statement, the term *sacra corona* occurs only seven times in official documents between 1256 and 1291, and furthermore, as in the rest of Europe, in connection with the king as a sacral leader.⁵³ In his view, the term has nothing to do with any sacral object.

Karpat's theory is, however, contradicted by the fact that in Hungary the crown was regarded as a very important object from the second half of the twelfth century on. This is the time – the years not long after the emergence of the St István legend – when the first references to guarding the royal crown appear.⁵⁴ At that time the crown was guarded by the *custos* of the Basilica of Székesfehérvár, the church where the Árpád kings were crowned and St István was buried. Székesfehérvár was therefore the centre of the St István cultus, where the king annually convoked the nobility to celebrate the memory of the holy king.⁵⁵ It seems obvious, therefore, to deduce that as early as then some connection existed between the crown and St King István.

The political situation that pertained at the end of the thirteenth century, when the last Árpád kings were on the throne, encouraged the development of the cultus of the crown. It was an increasingly difficult task for the more remotely descended to demonstrate their blood relationship to St István, and so they looked for other links to the first ruler of the House of Árpád to justify their claims to power. This may explain why the coronation jewel was associated with St István in 1290. After ascending the throne under dubious circumstances, András III (1290–1301), distant descendant of the first king and at the same time last scion of the Árpád dynasty,

---

50 Letters patent of the church of St Adalbert, Esztergom, 1256, in Josef Karpat, "Corona Regni Hungariae im Zeitalter der Arpaden," in Manfred Hellmann ed., *Corona Regni. Studien über die Krone als Symbol des Staates im späteren Mittelalter* (Darmstadt: Wissenschaftliche Buchgesellschaft, 1961) 298–299.
51 Benda and Fügedi, *A magyar korona regénye*, 25.
52 Eckhart, *A szentkorona-eszme*, 26, Benda and Fügedi, *A magyar korona regénye*, 25; Péter, "The Holy Crown of Hungary," 433.
53 Karpat, "Corona Regni," 298–299. Karpat refers only to charters and had not examined any other types of documents.
54 Bertényi, *A magyar szent korona*, 78. Nevertheless, in 1163 the crown was stolen for the first time. This theft was followed by a series of others.
55 *Ibid.*

proclaimed that he wore "the crown of St István".[56] This phrase marks the beginning of the tradition of the crown of St István.

After the House of Árpád became extinct in 1301 the crown acquired an important role in the legitimation of royal power. The special symbol of majesty was given a legitimising function in the ceremony of coronation as the crown of St István had to be used for the crowning of the ruler.[57] The crown was of constantly increasing significance in enabling the rulers of Hungary to enhance their standing among their subjects, as usually they could only cling to power at the price of lengthy disputes over the succession. The papal legate Gentilis di Montefiori commented as early as 1309 that "… so great is the respect that gilded the Hungarians' Holy Crown that it almost seemed as if it were in the crown that royal power resided."[58]

The reason for the change that followed in the early fourteenth century was the struggle for the throne in which Károly Róbert (1308–1342), the first king of Hungary from the House of Anjou, emerged supreme. It was only after three coronations that the French prince could call himself rightful ruler of Hungary, as only the final coronation was performed "with the Holy Crown" (*cum corona sancta*).[59] This is the period described by the Illustrated Chronicle (*Chronicum Pictum, Képes krónika*), composed by Márk Kálti (Marcus de Kalt) at the request of Lajos the Great (1342–1382).[60]

The Chronicle describes the sacral nature of the crown in the following way, and miniatures illustrate it.[61] First, the chronicler refers to the miracle of the crown of St István and points out that the first king received it as a gift from God.[62] A few pages later he tells of the life of King St István. In Klaniczay's view, Kálti attaches a new motif to the biography of the sainted king, linking him to the crown.[63] He describes how László I and his brother Géza I took up arms against King Salamon, rightfully crowned but unworthy of the throne. In the passage describing the decisive battle with Salamon in 1070 László sees a vision of an angel placing a golden crown (*corona aurea*) on Géza's head. László took this to mean that they were going to win

---

56 Benda and Fügedi, *A magyar korona regénye*, 29.
57 Péter Váczy, "Az angyal hozta korona [The crown brought by the angel]," *Életünk*, 19 (1982) 456–460.
58 "[…] cui multum reverentiae atque auctoritatis ex dicti regni incolarum opinione defertur, quasi in eo sit ius regium constitutum." Quoted by Emma Bartoniek. Emma Bartoniek, "Corona és regnum," *Századok*, 68 (1934) 321.
59 Stanisław Sroka, "Methods of Constructing Angevin Rule in Hungary in the Light of Most Recent Research," *Quaestiones Medii Aevi Novae*, 1 (1996) 77–90; Bak, *Königtum und Stände*, 13–22.
60 Marcus de Kalt, *Chronicon Pictum. Képes Krónika* [Illustrated chronicle], László Mezey, ed., and László Geréb, tr., vol. I–II, (Budapest: Magyar Helikon, 1964).
61 Péter, "The Holy Crown of Hungary," 434.
62 "*Porro beatus Stephanus, postquam regie celsitudinis coronam diuinitus est adeptus* […]". *Chronicon Pictum*, vol. II, 98. Kálti nowhere mentions the ceremonial surrounding St István's death. *Ibid.*, 102.
63 Klaniczay 157.

the battle, and that by the will of God his brother was to gain the crown and the kingdom.[64] A few pages more, and Kálti describes a miraculous event called *The discovery of the Holy Crown (De invencione sacre corone)*, which befell the crown in the middle of the fourteenth century.[65] It occurred during the contest for the throne between Károly Róbert of Anjou, the Czech Vencel and the Bavarian Otto that Otto had hidden the crown and other coronation regalia in a small wooden box and was secretly carrying them with him, when in the dark the box fell from the carriage onto the roadway. It lay in the dust on the busy road for some time, and was found by those transporting it only next evening. By this tale the chronicler meant to reveal a divine warning: the crown was not to be on Otto's head for long. The fact, however, that the crown was recovered by those transporting it, and thus did not fall into inappropriate hands, he took as a sign that "… Pannonia was not to be deprived of its angel-given crown".[66]

The starting-point of Kálti's thinking is the granting of the crown in the time of St István, from which it is clear that the crown had received from God a supernatural significance. Kálti later quotes another story connected to the crown, in which he imparts an unmistakeable message in the words of King László: he that wins the crown will triumph, for God is with him. In the end a miracle of the crown would take place in his own time, which he explained by a parallel with St László's vision: crown and kingdom would come to his benefactor Károly Róbert in an assumption of power sanctioned by God. The comparison conveyed an up-to-date political message.[67] This piece of fiction is the earliest known example of the texts in which the ordinance of God, the sacral significance of the crown and the rightfulness of royal governance are yoked together.

The cultus of the Holy Crown around the reign of King Mátyás Corvinus

In the period preceding the reign of Mátyás Corvinus (1458–1490) the cultus of the crown underwent further development. On this occasion too the cause was a

---

64 "*Tunc beatus Ladizlaus subiunxit: 'Dum staremus hic in consilio, ecce angelus Domini descendit de celo portans coronam auream in manu sua et impressit capiti tuo, unde certus sum, quod nobis victoria donabitur et Salomon exul fugiet debellatus extra regnum. Regnum vero et corona tibi tradetur a Domino.*" *Chronicon Pictum*, vol. II, 132–133, miniature ibid., vol. I, 83.

65 *Ibid.*, II, 171–172.

66 "*Quid est, quod a nullo inventa, sed ab ipsis, qui portabant, nisi quod ne Pannonia data sibi corona ab angelo privaretur.*" *Ibid*. II, 172; miniature *ibid.*, I, 135.

67 On the László cultus, see, Klaniczay, *Holy Rulers*, 167, and the older studies in László Mezey, ed., *Athleta Patriae: tanulmányok Szent László történetéhez* [*Athleta Patriae*: Studies on the history of Saint László] (Budapest: Szent István Társulat, 1980).

struggle for the succession, to which the death of Albert Habsburg (1437–1439) gave rise. The immediate cause of the trouble was the theft of the crown in 1439 by a lady of the court of King Albert's widow, Erzsébet of Luxemburg. In 1440 the queen had her three-month old son crowned king, under the style of László V, with the crown thus obtained: he ruled from 1440 until 1457.[68] After that the Hungarian crown was pawned to Holy Roman Emperor Friederich III for 2,500 forints.[69]

The event is of significance as a deliberate if futile attempt at undermining the sacral status of the crown.[70] In the year of the coronation of László V the Hungarian Estates elected an anti-king in the person of Ulászló I. As the Hungarian crown was missing from the coronation regalia Ulászló was crowned with St István's reliquary. On the occasion the Estates proclaimed in a document that the coronation of the king had taken place by the will of the "… inhabitants of the country…" *(regnicolae)*, and for that very reason their consent determined "…the validity and force of a crown…" *(efficacia et virtus corone)* used for the coronation.[71] In other words: coronation performed with the new crown jewel clothed the ruler with the same power as if he had been crowned with the crown of St István. At the same time the Estates declared that if the *sacra corona* was not available the symbolism, mystery and force of the old crown would be transferred to the new coronation jewel.[72] This plan, however, did not succeed, because Ulászló I died before the crown returned to Hungary, and after his death his grants of estates *(donatio)* were not recognised.[73] After this incident it became a factor of vital importance for pretenders to the throne that they should possess the Hungarian crown for the validation of their claims to power.

---

68 The handmaid account of the theft is recorded in a fifteenth-century German manuscript: ÖNB, cod. 2920. English edition: H. M. Bijvoet Williamson, ed., and tr., *The Memoirs of Helene Kottanner* (Woodbridge, Suffolk: Boydell & Brewer, 1998). On the theft: Benda and Fügedi, *A magyar korona regénye*, 50–80; Emma Bartoniek, *A magyar királykoronázások története* [The history of the Hungarian coronations] (Budapest: A Magyar Történelmi Társulat 1939, reprint Budapest: Akadémiai Kiadó, 1989) 64–65; Fraknói, *A magyar királyválasztások*, 55–58.

69 The earliest known description of the crown also derives from this giving in pawn. Károly Mollay, "Jegyzetek [Notes]," in *A korona elrablása*, 86–87.

70 Bálint Hóman – Gyula Szekfű, *Magyar történet* [Hungarian history], Vol. II, (Budapest: Egyetemi Nyomda, ³1936) 419; Bartoniek, Corona és regnum, *Századok*, 86 (1934) 325; Bartoniek, *A magyar királykoronázások*, 386; Eckhart, *A szentkorona-eszme*, 58–63; Eckhart, *Magyar alkotmány- és jogtörténet*, 80–82; Deér, *Die heilige Krone Ungarns*, 191–192, Péter, "The Holy Crown of Hungary," 435.

71 Martinus Georgius Kovachich, *Vestigia comitiorum apud Hungaros* (Budae: typis Regiae Universitatis, 1790) 235–240.

72 "… et si eadem recuperari non potuerit, omnis deesset efficacia ac quodlibet signaculum, mysterium et robur eiusdem in hanc modernam coronam intelligantur et harum serie de omnium nostrorum … ". Ibid.

73 Péter, "The Holy Crown of Hungary," 435.

Despite the significant changes that took place in the fifteenth century, historians have to this day scarcely interested themselves in examining the meaning of the crown in the sources that have come down to us from the period 1440–1450. In those years, to name but two, reference is made to the crown in a sermon of 1453 by János Vitéz (1408–1472), Archbishop of Esztergom[74], in letters of Eneas Silvius Piccolomini, the later Pope Pius II[75] and in a poem of Janus/János Pannonius (1432–1472), the celebrated humanist.[76] We will examine the latter source because of its special subject.

Pannonius' poem was composed in 1463, a year before the crown returned to Hungary. In the epigram the poet links the destiny *(fatum)* of the Emperor with the Habsburg emperor's evident reluctance to return "…our crown…".[77] In the first few lines of the poem Pannonius sketches the grim fates of a number of kings, then announces that Friederich should not hide behind his imperial rank because by so doing he tempts fate. Apart from Kálti's *Képes krónika*, this poem is the earliest known text about the crown in which the author adduces historical examples in linking together the Hungarian crown and the fate of the ruler.

During the reign of Mátyás Hunyadi the significance of the crown underwent further change. When Mátyás appeared on the Hungarian political scene in 1458 there were several reasons why he had very great need of the Hungarian crown to support and justify his rightful claim to power. Mátyás was elected king by the will of the common nobility despite the wishes of the aristocracy.[78] He had no royal blood in his veins as he was of common nobility extraction, and his lowly birth

---

74 Iohannes Vitéz de Zreda, "Oracio in legacione ultima ad dominum Fredericum imperatorem pro rependis corona et hereditate domini regis Ladislai," in Iván Boronkai, ed., *Opera quae supersunt / Iohannes Vitéz de Zredna* (Budapest: Akadémiai Kiadó, 1980) 238–242.
75 Eneas Silvius an den Erzbischof von Gran, Dionys Szécsy; Wien, [Anfang Oktober] 1445. Tritt mit Entschiedenheit dafür ein, daß Ladislaus als König von Ungarn anerkannt werde", in Rudolf Wolkan, ed., *Der Briefwechsel des Eneas Silvius Piccolomini. I. Abteilung: Briefe aus der Laienzeit. I. Band: Privatbriefe. (1431–1445)* (Fontes Rerum Austriacarum) (Wien: Hölder, 1909) 548–558, "Eneas Silvius an Leonhard Laiming, Bischof von Passau; Wien, 28. Oktober 1445. Ausführliche Darlegung der Thronfolgefrage in Ungarn.", in *ibid.*, 563, 569–570, 575; "XCV. K. Friedrich an Papst Eugen IV.; [Wien, Anfang Februar 1445]. Bittet ihn um seine Unterstützung in Ungarn, damit Ladislaus zum Könige gewählt werde,", in Rudolf Wolkan, ed., *Der Briefwechsel des Eneas Silvius Piccolomini. I. Abteilung: Briefe aus der Laienzeit (1431–1445). II. Band: Amtliche Briefe* (Fontes Rerum Austriacarum) (Wien: Hölder, 1909) 158, "XCVI. K. Friedrich an das Kardinalskollegium; [Wien, Anfang Februar 1445.] Bitte, dahin wirken zu wollen, daß das erbetene Schreiben des Papstes möglich rasch an der Reichstag nach Pest gelange," in *ibid.*, 159.
76 On Pannonius, see Marianna D. Birnbaum, *Janus Pannonius - Poet and Politician* (Zagreb: Jugoslavenska akademija znanosti i umjetnosti, 1981).
77 Janus Pannonius, "De corona regni ad Fridericum Caesarem," in Sándor V. Kovács, ed., *Jani Pannonii opera omnia* (Budapest: Tankönyvkiadó, 1987) 202.
78 Fraknói, *A magyar királyválasztások*, 73–85.

impeded his efforts.[79] At the time the Hungarian crown was in the possession of Friederich III Habsburg, the Holy Roman Emperor. He was prepared to relinquish it only if Mátyás complied with certain political conditions and paid 80,000 forints to redeem it.[80] The most important of the conditions was that concerning the succession. This required that should Mátyás die without leaving a male heir a Habsburg would succeed him on the throne. Friederich adopted Mátyás as his son, however, so that his lowly origin might no more be used as an argument against his royalty. After lengthy discussions Mátyás agreed to comply with the conditions. In 1464 the Holy Crown was welcomed back on Hungarian soil on the occasion of its glorious return to Hungary at Sopron.[81] The letter written by a Transylvanian Saxon delegate informs us of the jubilation of those present.[82]

That return of the crown to Hungary and the tradition of the Holy Crown played an important part in the justification of Mátyás' power is made clear by the work of his Italian humanist and Mátyás' court historian Antonio Bonfini (1427/1434–1502), *Rerum Hungaricarum decades* (1496/7). In those years the tradition of the crown gained new life. In his work Bonfini gives an account of two new elements with which Mátyás enriched the tradition. These are the "public role" of the crown and the enquiry into the external appearance of the coronation jewel.

The first new element was that the crown played its public role as a physically existing object by being displayed to the people on its return to Hungary. Before Mátyás' reign, it had been seen in public only on the occasion of a coronation. Bonfini writes: "... And so the crown, which had been in the emperor's possession for twenty-four years, was borne into Sopron, beribboned, with unrivalled pomp and festive rejoicing, as if it had descended from Heaven."[83] It was proclaimed throughout the country that "... the Holy Crown which has been regained will be exposed in Sopron for three days to the view and scrutiny of all that are moved by love and respect for it".[84]

This new role can also be recognised in Bonfini's account how the Holy Crown came to Hungary almost 500 years earlier. The court historian tells us with what great pomp and circumstance prince István, together with the assembled priests and bishops, received the crown in Esztergom, and how Asztrik handed the symbol

---

79 Volker Honemann, "The Marriage of Matthias Corvinus to Beatrice of Aragon (1476) in Urban and Court Historiography," in Martin Gosman, Alisdair MacDonald and Arjo Vanderjagt, eds., *Princes and Princely Culture, 1450–1650*, (Leiden – Boston: Brill, 2005) 213.
80 Antonio Bonfini, *Rerum Ungaricarum decades* (Basiliae: Robertus Winterus, 1543) decadis III, liber X, 534.
81 *Ibid*.; Benda and Fügedi, *A magyar korona regénye*, 80–90.
82 *Ibid.*
83 Bonfini, *Rerum Ungaricarum decades*, decadis III, liber X, 534.
84 *Ibid.*

of majesty to the king.⁸⁵ His account of events, however, differs from that of Hartvik, but is much more alike to how Mátyás received the crown in Sopron.

In addition to describing the role played by the crown on its reception in Sopron and the event that occurred in 1000, the sources also inform us that in 1476 King Mátyás appeared before the people on the occasion of his marriage to his second wife, Beatrice of Aragon in 1476, wearing the Hungarian crown.⁸⁶ The author, being present, was even able to describe the appearance of the crown, which is one of the earliest descriptions known: "… eine köstliche crone, reich von golde, dorein vorsaczt sein XXV grosse diamant, balas und rubin, ein schoner zaphir gros, nymant meynet einen köstlicheren gesehen hette."⁸⁷ The public role of the crown was, in any case, not an exclusively Hungarian peculiarity, as in 1412 Ulászló Jagelló of Poland had entered Krakow amidst similar ceremonial with the Polish coronation regalia that had been retrieved after being kept in Hungary since 1382.⁸⁸

The other new element in the tradition of the crown is the explicit interest in the external marks on it. This is primarily directed at the question of whether in fact it was the original crown that the Habsburg ruler had given back, or whether he had merely been content with a show of satisfying the Hungarians' demands. Bonfini's account tells how the Hungarian delegation examined the jewel closely before it was handed over to see that it was identical with the Holy Crown.⁸⁹ The authenticity of the symbol of majesty was established on the basis of "… a certain identifying mark …", says Bonfini (which would have been a cracked sapphire). The writer also at hints interest in the external features of the crown in his remark that on the entry to Hungary at Sopron "… the people might examine the crown…". After its return the first more or less faithful depictions of the crown began, the best known of which appeared in János Thuróczy's printed chronicle of 1488 (see image 2) and the map of Wolfgang Lazius (see image 5).⁹⁰

It seems contradictory that Mátyás Corvinus, whom we regard as a Renaissance ruler with a humanist view of the world, should revive a Medieval cultus. In fact, however, he was forced to fall back on an ancient tradition in order to realise his ambitions, because in a society that relied on a Medieval tradition that was the

---

85 *Ibid.*, decadis II, liber X, 175.
86 "[…] Doruff is gestigen Mathias mit der hiligen cron des konigreichs zi Hungernn vffgesazt, seine regalia anhabende […]", G. Roth, ed., *Peter Eschenloer, Geschichte der Stadt Breslau* (Münster: Waxmann, 2003) 995.
87 *Ibid.*
88 A. Gieysztor, "Gesture in the Coronation Ceremonies of Medieval Poland," in János M. Bak, ed., *Coronation, Medieval and Early Modern Monarchic Ritual* (Berkeley: University of California Press, 1990) 163.
89 Bonfini, *Rerum Ungaricarum decades*, decadis III, liber X, 533.
90 Joannes de Thurocz, *Chronica Hungarorum* (Augsburg: Erhard Ratdolt, 1488).

only way for him to legitimise his power. Bak opines that Mátyás Hunyadi had one foot in the Renaissance culture of Medieval Italy, and the other in the Medieval traditions of the Kingdom of Hungary.[91] Mátyás had at his disposal the virtues of both Renaissance rulers (philosopher-kings) and of the anointed Medieval kings who preserved the traditions of St István. The blending of the Medieval cultus of the crown and the culture of the Renaissance court explains why the tradition of the crown flourished especially in the reign of the Renaissance king. How great the significance of the crown was under Mátyás is shown by the remark made, according to Bonfini, by the Palatine Mihály Guti Országh in 1495: "Him that you see crowned with the Holy Crown, worship him, regard him as a sacred king, even if he is an ox."[92]

From the significance of the crown outlined above we may draw the conclusion that the tradition of the crown altered continuously in Hungary from the establishment of the kingdom on. The tradition, as conceptualised by Bonfini in his work at the end of the Middle Ages, was the fruit of centuries of development of political culture in Hungary. In the rest of Europe dynastic descent played a more important role in succession than did the coronation regalia. In Hungary, contrary to this, the role of dynastic considerations diminished because of a series of violent changes of ruler. Variation in the tradition of the crown was the consequence of the struggle to find a new means of justifying the lawfulness of the ruler's power, as kings could no longer base their esteem on such traditional footing as descent from sainted ancestors. As the result of this development the Medieval tradition of the Holy Crown reached its zenith during the blossoming of the Hungarian Renaissance under King Mátyás Corvinus.

---

91 Janos M. Bak, "The Kingship of Matthias Corvinus: a Renaissance state?," in Tibor Klaniczay and József Jankovics, eds., *Matthias Corvinus and Humanism in Central Europe* (Budapest: Balassi, 1994) 45–46.

92 "*Quencunque sacra corona coronatum videris, etiam si bos fuerit, adorato, & pro Sacrosancto rege ducito,& observato.*" Antonio Bonfini, *Rerum Ungaricarum decades quatuor cum dimidia*, Iohannes Sambucus ed., (Francofurti: Andreas Wechelus, 1581) decadis IV, liber III, 564.

II. The Holy Crown and the Hungarian Estates: the transformation of the Estates from a cultural to a political community

The concept of *natio* in Medieval Hungary

The development of the meaning of the Holy Crown during the Medieval period is closely related not only to the change in royal power, but also to the root of the development of an early national identity. The birth of national identity in Hungary was a result of the changing of the meaning of the concept of natio, as Jenő Szűcs explained in his ground-breaking study of the chronicle *Gesta Hungarorum* (1282–1285).[1] According to Szűcs, the seeds of national identity were sown in the Hungarian Kingdom when the cultural community of Hungarian noblemen was transformed into a political community.

Szűcs presented this transformation through a study of the development of the meaning of the word *natio in Medieval* Hungarian sources. This concept was used to project an image of a cultural community with common interests, which were legitimised by shared cultural values and characteristics. According to Szűcs, the membership of a certain nation (*natio*) became even more important for a thirteenth century Hungarian nobleman than his noble descent.[2]

When authors of chronicles of the eleventh and twelfth centuries wrote of the origin of the Hungarian people as a *populus* they scarcely referred to the pagan past. He also states that the historical sources only show the Hungarians through the deeds of the House of Árpád. Chronicles, legends, charters and decrees speak rather of "the king's people", "the people of the realm" – *gens regis* or *populus regni*. What made the inhabitants of the Kingdom of Hungary into the Hungarian people was that they were subjects of the Hungarian king.

In the thirteenth century the word *Hungarus*, derived from *Hungaria*, designated a person born and living on the territory of the Kingdom of Hungary.[3] In the 1200s, in Szűcs's opinion, the meaning people (*populus*) previously attached to *gens* changed, thanks to Master P (the chronicler known as *Anonymus*). In his work *Gesta Hungarorum* (Deeds of the Hungarians) he devoted attention primarily to

---

1 Jenő Szűcs, "Theoretical Elements in Master Simon of Kéza's Gesta Hungarorum (1282–1285)," in László Veszprémy and Frank Schaer, eds. and tr., *Simonis de Kéza Gesta Hungarorum* (Budapest and New York: Central European University Press, 1999) xli.
2 *Ibid.*, liii, xli, lxxxv–ic.
3 *Ibid.*, lxx.

the nobility of Hungary – *nobilissima gens Hungariae*.⁴ He no longer treated the nobility simply in terms of the links binding them to the ruler. He wrote of the acts of the nobility (*gesta nobilium*) in the time before the conquest by the Hungarians of the Carpathian Basin and of the people's pagan past. After the appearance of the *Gesta* the history of the pagans also received more attention in the political thinking of the Kingdom. From the early thirteenth century on there came a series of writers who made use of pre-Christian motifs in order to legitimise certain political aims of king and nobility alike.⁵

The next stage in the change of meaning of *natio* can be observed in the work of Simon Kézai (Simon de Kéza).⁶ A notary at the court of László IV, between 1282 and 1285 he wrote a chronicle likewise titled *Gesta Hungarorum*. In his book he treats of the origin of the Hungarian people, the connections between the Huns and the Hungarians and the political concept of *natio*. In Szűcs's view Kézai made use of his knowledge of Roman and canon law in writing his book, and at the same time one can sense in it the influence of the French and German epic tradition.⁷ The knowledge and experience that he had gained in studying and travelling in Europe are reflected in the work.⁸

Kézai's most significant innovation is his use of the term *natio* in a positive way, in connection with the people's pagan past.⁹ In earlier Hungarian and European chronicles, legends and legal documents the term *natio* was used for the negative depiction of alien, barbarian, possibly pagan peoples. The term *gens* was reserved for a writer's own people. According to Szűcs, Kézai was the first Hungarian writer to apply the term *natio* to his own people in a good, positive sense, by which he came into line with European practice.¹⁰

Kézai also tried to prove that the Hungarians stemmed from the pagan Huns.¹¹ He supported this by a linguistic argument. According to him, the Huns quite certainly spoke Hungarian, as the Hungarians' legendary tribal chieftain Hunor was, as the name showed, a Hun. After Kézai, the idea of a blood relationship between Huns and Hungarians left an indelible mark in Hungarian political thought, and also

---

4 *Ibid.*, lx. For an English translation of this work of anonymous, *Gesta Hungarorum* see Martyn Rady, "The Gesta Hungarorum of Anonymus, the Anonymous Notary of King Béla: A Translation," *The Slavonic and East European Review*, 87/4 (2009) 681–727.
5 Szűcs, "Theoretical Elements," lxii–lxv.
6 *Ibid.*, xli–xlii.
7 *Ibid.*, xlviii, lxxvii–lxxxiv.
8 *Ibid.*, ic–civ.
9 *Ibid.*, lxv.
10 *Ibid.*, lxvi–lxvii.
11 *Ibid.*, lxxvi.

became an important topic from the cultural point of view.[12] According to Szűcs, the sudden emergence of the Huns in Hungarian chronicles had a political source.[13] From Kézai's work it appeared that the desire of the Hungarian nobility was to know that their new-found status, liberty and wealth were safe against the power of the king. This power was legitimised by the political and religious meaning of the symbol of royalty, the Hungarian crown. Kézai endeavoured to support the demands of the nobility by emphasising that the rights of the nobility were of greater antiquity than the power of the king.[14] According to him, the liberty and wealth of the nobility pre-dated Christianity and the kingship. His argument was that since these rights were more ancient than the royal power, the claims that the nobility made vis-à-vis the king were to be regarded as legitimate. In Szűcs's view, the most significant argument with which Kézai tried to support the political ambitions of the Hungarians was that they were descended from the Huns.[15] On the basis of this relationship the members of the Hungarian *natio*, including the king, were the rightful possessors of the territory of the Kingdom of Hungary because Attila's people had legitimately occupied it at an earlier historical time.[16] In Kézai's view that occupation was at least as rightful as the establishment of the kingship, because God had bestowed on the Huns their own role in the history of Christianity.[17] From that it followed that the king was equal with the other members of the *natio* not in respect of descent alone, but that the claims of the nobility were more ancient than those of the ruler. Furthermore, these demands (like the coronation of the king) also served as Christian justification for the Huns' divine mission.

In addition to the significance of the crown, another form of justification of power emerged as a thirteenth century consequence of the development of the concept of *natio*.[18] The political significance of the relationship to the Huns legitimised not only the rights of the nobility but also the power of the king in the Kingdom of Hungary. As the power of the nobility grew in the final decades of the century, so the ruler's political situation changed, and with the extinction of the House of Árpád the country was plunged into a crisis over the succession. At this time the political content of the belief in Hunnish origin tended to undermine the role of the crown,

---

12 Tamás Hofer, "Construction of the 'folk cultural heritage' in Hungary and rival versions of national identity," in *idem*, ed., *Hungarians between "East" and "West": three Essays on Myths and Symbols* (Budapest: Néprajzi Múzeum, 1994) 34–35; Gyula Németh, "Hunok és Magyarok [Huns and Hungarians]," in Gyula Németh, ed., *Attila és Hunjai* [Attila and his Huns] (Budapest: Akadémiai Kiadó, 1940) 265–271.
13 Szűcs, "Theoretical Elements," lxix–lxxi.
14 *Ibid.*, lxxi.
15 *Ibid.*, lxxii–lxxiii.
16 *Ibid.*, lxvii–lxix.
17 *Ibid.*, xlv–xlvii, liii–liv, lxi, lxxii.
18 *Ibid.*, lxxxiv.

as it had functioned as the primary justification of royal power. According to Szűcs, it may be seen in a German source as early as 1290 that the Hungarian nobility called on the relationship to the Huns to prove title to their estates in Hungary.[19] After the thirteenth century the concepts of *natio* and relationship with the Huns were further developed in every Hungarian chronicle and historical narrative about the Estates of Hungary.

The concept of *natio* and the Holy Crown in the work of István Werbőczy (1517)

The crown gained a place in the early sixteenth century representation of the Hungarian Estates because the concept of *natio* and the tradition of the Holy Crown were yoked together. The political background to this was that in the first quarter of the century the Kingdom suffered a domestic crisis.[20] After the death of Mátyás Corvinus in 1490 a struggle for the succession broke out between Maximilian Habsburg, two members of the Polish Jagiello dynasty (Ulászló II and Jan I Olbracht), and János Corvinus, Mátyás' illegitimate son. On 14 July 1490 Ulászló II was elected king. From the moment that he ascended the throne there was no doubt but that his position was insecure. On entering Hungarian territory, he was made to accept the main conditions of election (*capitulationes electorales*), under which the new king was almost completely dependent on the will of the magnates.[21] Furthermore, in the first year of his reign he was still in a state of war with his opponents. As a consequence of his weak position he lost the regions of Bohemia and Austria that had been conquered by Mátyás, his personal income fell, and the magnates and aristocracy came into the ascendancy as they were well aware of how to add to their rights and privileges. His personal power was seriously weakened as during the dispute over the throne he was forced to mortgage a number of royal castles and towns – indeed, to make gifts of some – so that the income of the treasury was greatly reduced.[22]

---

19 *Ibid.*, lxxi.
20 Engel, *The Realm of St. Stephen*, 345–347.
21 Emma Bartoniek, "A koronázási eskü fejlődése 1526-ig [The development of the coronation oath till 1526]," *Századok*, 5(1917) 37.
22 Pál Engel, Gyula Kristó and András Kubinyi, *Magyarország története 1301–1526* [History of Hungary 1301–1526] (Budapest: Osiris, 1998) 342–345.

The weakness of the king's rule led to radical societal and political changes.[23] Very important decisions, affecting the whole country, were taken in the Diet. The country was led by an aristocratic oligarchy, which opened the way to social injustice, the robbing of the servile class, the impoverishment of the peasantry and the common nobility, and arrested the development of the provincial towns.[24] The greatest political change in 1514 was that in consequence of their victory over the insurgents the nobility acquired even greater power. An attempt was made to exploit this domestic political situation by the common nobility and their principal spokesman Werbőczy; it was at this Diet that he presented the codification of Hungarian law, containing his programme.[25] In the *Tripartitum* Werbőczy confirmed the position of the nobility vis-à-vis the king and the aristocracy in terms of power. The Estates approved Werbőczy's work and accepted the codification, but after intervention by the aristocracy the king never ratified it.[26] It was printed for the first time in 1517 in Vienna.[27]

---

23 Marianna D. Birnbaum, *Humanists in a Shattered World. Croatian and Hungarian Latinity in the Sixteenth Century* (Columbus: Slavica Publishers, 1986) 13–20; Engel, Kristó and Kubinyi, *Magyarország története*, 342–345, Bak, *Königtum und Stände*, 62; Péter László, "Ius resistendi in Hungary," in Péter László and Martyn Rady, eds., *Resistance, Rebellion and Revolution in Hungary and Central Europe: Commemorating 1956* (London: University College London School of Slavonic & Eastern European Studies, 2008) 45.

24 Engel, Kristó and Kubinyi, *Magyarország története*, 349, 363.

25 Vilmos Fraknói, *Werbőczi István életrajza* [Biography of István Werbőczi] (Budapest: Magyar Történelmi Társaság, 1899); Gábor Hamza, ed., *Tanulmányok Werbőczy Istvánról – Studien über István Werbőczy* (Budapest: Professzorok Háza, 2001); Martyn Rady, *Customary Law in Hungary: Courts, Texts, and the Tripartitum* (Oxford: Oxford University Press, 2015); Martyn Rady, "Stephen Werbőczy and his Tripartitum," in János M. Bak, Péter Banyó and Martyn Rady, eds. and trans., *The Laws of the Medieval Kingdom of Hungary*, Volume 5, The Customary Law of the Renowned Kingdom of Hungary: A Work in Three Parts Rendered by Stephen Werbőczy (The 'Tripartitum'). The Laws of Hungary (Series I: Volume 5). (Idyllwild, CA and Budapest: Charles Schlacks Jr and Department of Medieval Studies, Central European University, 2005) xxvii–xliv.

26 Bálint Hóman and Gyula Szekfű, *Magyar történet* [Hungarian history], Vol. II, (Budapest: Királyi Magyar Egyetemi Nyomda, 1936) 588. Although the king supported Werbőczy's work by granting it a charter he did not disseminate it, so that no decree was issued and it did not acquire the force of law. Engel, Kristó and Kubinyi, *Magyarország története*, 365.

27 István Werbőczy, *Tripartitum opus iuris consuetudinarij inclyti regni Hungarie…* (Viennae Austriae: Joannes Singrenius, 1517). I have quoted from this edition: István Verbőczy[!], *Werbőczy István Hármaskönyve, Sándor Kolosvári and Kelemen Óvári, eds., and trans.* (Budapest: Magyar Tudományos Akadémia, 1894). A modern edition and English translation: János M. Bak, Péter Banyó and Martyn Rady, eds. and trans., *The Laws of the Medieval Kingdom of Hungary, Volume 5, The Customary Law of the Renowned Kingdom of Hungary: A Work in Three Parts Rendered by Stephen Werbőczy* (The 'Tripartitum'). The Laws of Hungary (Series I: Volume 5) (Idyllwild, CA and Budapest: Charles Schlacks Jr and Department of Medieval Studies, Central European University, 2005).

Werbőczy's most significant thesis was that the "...equality before the law of the members of the nobility..." formed the basis of the system of law of the Kingdom of Hungary. This thesis, however, stood much more for a political programme than for the legal and political reality perceptible in the country at the time.[28] The political map of Hungary was characterised by a fluctuating tug-o'-war for power between the common nobility and the powerful aristocratic oligarchy. The reason for this was the advantageous position that the aristocracy held through inheritance, as these families could claim big holdings of land and were able, generation after generation, to fill the most important national offices. They held more potent implements of power than did the common nobility. The latter were only lesser landowners, or had no land at all, and could only exceptionally rise to higher positions of power. Furthermore, because of their powerful position the aristocrats played a decisive part in the National Assembly when elections of king took place, and also had the capacity to influence important decisions of the king or National Assembly so as to serve their own interests.

Werbőczy's political programme aimed to change the balance of power in the country. In the *Tripartitum* he gathered together such measures as were to be taken for the limitation of the power of the aristocracy and the weakening of their position, and would at the same time enhance the influence exerted by the common nobility on the decisions taken by the king. His first objective was that all nobles should be able to participate in national politics.[29] The second was that the entire nobility should be able to take part in the election of the king.[30] The third purpose, however, was to cause the recognition of the power of the nobility vis-à-vis the king.[31] After that he developed the programme into a political theory based on the doctrine of the equality of the nobility and supported by the concept of "one and the same liberty" (*una eademque libertas*).[32] This programme had been conceived as early as 1351, during the reign of Lajos the Great (1342–1382), but had not been realised.[33]

Werbőczy therefore sought and found an argument to support his idea. This was the concept that he formed of the crown. His political thinking was based on his adaptation of the symbolic meaning of the crown, the already existent concept of the crown and the Medieval crown tradition. In his opinion royal power was based on the legal postulation that the entire territory of the country – which was the property of the crown – was the concern of the king. Werbőczy elaborated his

---

28 Engel, Kristó and Kubinyi, *Magyarország története*, 365; Martyn Rady, *Nobility, Land and Service in Medieval Hungary* (London: Palgrave Macmilan, 2000) 3; Péter, "The Holy Crown of Hungary," 449.
29 *Tripartitum*, II, 3. *Qui possint condere leges, et statuta?* (Who may lay down laws and statutes?)
30 *Tripartitum*, I, 3.
31 *Tripartitum*, I, 2.
32 *Ibid.*
33 Hóman and Gyula Szekfű, *Magyar történet*, II, 589.

notion of the equality of the nobility on the basis of this premise, behind which was the belief that the country in its entirety was the property of the crown. He stated that only persons who received grants of land from the king could rise to the nobility.[34] It was thanks to this grant that the nobleman enjoyed rights, privileges and liberty.

It followed from this that all the rights of the nobility were of identical origin because the king granted them through the crown. Thus, every member of the nobility was endowed with the same liberty. Werbőczy therefore made no distinction between prelate, high clergy, baron, big landowner and simple nobleman: in his view every nobleman possessed one and the same liberty.[35]

The political notion of the liberty and equality of the nobility may thus be taken as strengthening royal power to the detriment of the influence of the nobility. Werbőczy's intention, however, was not that but the strengthening of the common nobility. He therefore distinguished in his theory between the noble as a person and the nobility as an institution, which he saw as paralleling the Medieval distinction (referred to above) between *rex* and *corona*.

His final conclusion rendered his purposes unambiguous. Because the nobility had existed already in pagan times, even before the first king of Hungary was crowned, he regarded the institution of the Estates as more ancient than the kingship. He supported his statement with the legends of origin which, through the premise that he elaborated, acquired new political significance.

What inspired Werbőczy in this was Kézai's concept of *natio* (mentioned above), with which he had become familiar through the 1488 work of János Thuróczy.[36] Werbőczy too was of the opinion that Huns and Hungarians shared a common origin. This belief was based on the origin-legend that spoke of the mythical ancestors of the Hungarians, Hunor and Magor.[37] He was convinced that the Hungarians, like their ancestors, "… had migrated from Scythia into Pannonia."[38] Werbőczy also stated, as did Kézai, that the distinction between noble and non-noble originated from the willingness of the nobles to take up arms and fight for the Estates. In the pagan world, any that were not prepared to do battle became servile.[39]

The author continued his reasoning with an account of the myth of the origin of royal power in Hungary. He believed that the Hungarian people had adopted the Christian faith through the joint operation of the Holy Spirit and "our sainted

---

34 *Tripartitum*, I, 3, §6.
35 *Tripartitum*, I, 2, §1.
36 Elemér Mályusz, "Az Eckhart-vita," *Századok*, 64(1931) 416; Eckhart, *A szentkorona-eszme*, 201–203; Thuróczy, *Chronica Hungarorum*.
37 *Tripartitum*, I, 3, §1 and §5.
38 *Tripartitum*, I, 3, §1.
39 *Tripartitum*, I, 3, §1–§5.

king".⁴⁰ They then of their own accord (*sponte*) elected István king and crowned him. As Werbőczy writes,

> The Hungarian commonwealth, by its free will, set the right to ennoble and to grant land, which enriched the noble and consequently distinguished them from the ignoble, together with complete power, rule and ownership, under the jurisdiction of the Holy Crown and consequently clothed therewith our prince and king.⁴¹

According to Werbőczy's assumption, from that moment on the nobility had the exclusive right to elect the king, and the king alone could elevate to noble rank.

This should not be taken as a claim for the nobility to have sovereignty vis-à-vis the king, but as an attempt to justify certain rights peculiar to them alone.⁴² The power of the king, in Werbőczy's view, corresponded to the Medieval concept of the crown. He defined it as that power by which one could distinguish between noble and ignoble on the basis of grants of land from the crown. The king received this power on ascending the throne, and that agreed with the gist of the tradition of the crown.

The essence of Werbőczy's theory is the view of voluntariness (*sponte*) with which he proposed to support certain political rights of the nobility.⁴³ One of these was the right freely to elect the king. Since the Hungarians had chosen their first king by a free election, freely to elect the king remained their right. A second right, linked to the first, was the right of the nobility to participate in the making of laws. Pointing to his own time, Werbőczy states that the Hungarians had since ancient times had the right to take part in the making of the country's laws, and that he explains by the fact that the nobility itself had brought power to the sphere of influence of the Holy Crown.⁴⁴ Intervention by the nobility was, however, limited to expressing a view as to whether a law infringed their liberties.⁴⁵ Werbőczy was therefore not asserting that the nobility shared power with the king through the crown.

By showing the legitimising role that the crown played for the nation (*natio*), Werbőczy revived Kézai's ideas. Kézai had been writing for an Árpád king who needed no such device to justify his claim to power because his blood relationship

---

40 *Tripartitum*, I, 3, §6.
41 *Tripartitum*, I, 3, §6; II, 3, §1–§2.
42 Szűcs remarked in his essay on Kézai: "In contemporary European theories the populus is never 'sovereign' in the modern sense, it merely provides, in the wake of the ruler's assumption of its original power, a kind of limited 'historical' source for the present." Szűcs, "Theoretical Elements," cxiv–cxv.
43 *Tripartitum*, II, 3, §2.
44 "*Prout et temporibus nostris fieri consuevit.*" *Tripartitum*, II, 3, §2.
45 *Tripartitum*, II, 3, §3.

with the sainted king confirmed that his power was lawful. By working the significance of the crown into the idea of natio, he actually altered its legitimising role. Its meaning, if only to a limited extent, did support the political demands of the nobility. Until the appearance of the *Tripartitum* in 1517 the tradition of the crown had supported the power of the king.

On the basis of this tradition, the king had been able to assert that István had created the Hungarian nobility and, through the crown, had empowered his legitimate posterity to elevate to the nobility. Werbőczy refuted this tradition, as through the notion of *natio* he was essentially saying that even before the kingship existed the Hungarian nobility had been a body that enjoyed certain liberties. In his view the power of the first sainted king had sprung from the will of a pagan nation, since the Estates themselves had subordinated the power of the ruler to the jurisdiction of the Holy Crown. In other words: by his theory, Werbőczy legitimised election of the king by the nobility, and that was symbolised by the crown too.

The few that grew up in the early sixteenth century of the change in the legitimising role of the crown had a great influence on the formation of the identity of the Hungarian nation. By reviving the Hun-Hungarian legend Kézai had shown a cultural body to be a political body with certain rights vis-à-vis the king. This Werbőczy complemented with his theory about the tradition of the Crown. In this way some aspects of Kézai's premise acquired new political significance and supported the rights of the nobility freely to elect the king and to participate in law-making. The influence of the Hungarian lawyer could be detected even before the National Assembly of 1524, when the common nobility wished to elect their own leaders "…in the style of the great Attila".[46] Werbőczy's new ideas, therefore, marked the end of the first period of the development of the national identity of Hungary.

The concept of *natio* and the cultus of the Holy Crown after the Battle of Mohács (1526)

In addition to Werbőczy's compilation of law, the Battle of Mohács in 1526 had the greatest effect on the development of the idea of nationhood. The clash of the armies of the Ottoman Empire and the Kingdom of Hungary meant the end of the Medieval kingdom. After 1526 the principal characteristic of the Estates was lack of political cohesion.[47] Within the Estates conflict arose over how to resolve the

---

46 Engel, Kristó and Kubinyi, *Magyarország története*, 383.
47 Ágnes R. Várkonyi, "Vienna, Buda, Constantinople," *The New Hungarian Quarterly*, XXV(1984) 3; Ferenc Szakály, "The early Ottoman Period, including Royal Hungary, 1526–1606," in Peter F. Sugar, Péter Hanák and Tibor Frank, eds., *A History of Hungary* (Bloomington: Indiana University Press,

political crisis. The majority of the Estates chose as king one of the most influential landowners, János Szapolyai, and he was eventually crowned on 11 November 1526. On 17 December of that year a minority decided to choose Ferdinand Habsburg (1527–1563), who was likewise crowned on 3 November the following year.[48] In the struggle between the pretenders, Szapolyai was worsted. Süleyman took advantage of the internal strife in Hungary and offered Szapolyai the status of vassal. The political discord led to territorial division and the country was split into three; the west came under Habsburg domination, the east and Transylvania became a Turkish protectorate and the central area was absorbed into the Ottoman Empire.

A second phase of the change in the significance of the crown began after the disaster of Mohács. Ágnes R. Várkonyi has argued in a number of essays that after the collapse of the kingdom the Hungarian crown became the symbol of the unity hoped for by the country and the Estates.[49] The crown acquired a new legitimising role in that it was not merely a symbol of the political goal of the divided Estates, their endeavours towards the reunification of the country, but also represented them vis-à-vis the king. Both in Hungary and abroad the man who had been crowned with the Hungarian crown and was at the same time actually in possession of the symbol of majesty was seen as the rightful king.

According to Várkonyi, in the course of time the crown became the symbol of the political unity of the country. In 1526 and 1527 both Ferdinánd and János Szapolyai were crowned with the Hungarian crown. In 1529, after the siege of Buda, the sultan succeeded in appropriating the crown and other regalia; later that year he presented them to János Szapolyai in a splendid ceremony, and offered him not only Buda but the entire Kingdom of Hungary.[50] In Várkonyi's opinion,

---

1990) 85; Géza Pálffy, "The Impact of the Ottoman Rule on Hungary," *Hungarian Studies Review*, XXVIII(2001) 109–111.

48 For "the twin coronation" see Benda and Fügedi, *A magyar korona regénye*, 109–117.

49 Ágnes R. Várkonyi, *Három évszázad Magyarország történetében 1526–1790. Vol. I. A megosztottság évszázada; 1526-1606* [Three centuries in the history of Hungary, 1526-1790. Volume I: the century of division] (Budapest: Korona, 1999) 81; Ágnes R. Várkonyi, "'...Jó Budavár magas tornyán...' A magyar államiság szimbólumairól Mohács után [...'On the high tower of good castle Buda...' On the symbols of the Hungarian statehood after Mohács]," in *Hagyomány és történelem* [Tradition and history](Eger, 2000) 77–100; Ágnes R. Várkonyi, "A korona és a Budai vár [The crown and the castle of Buda]," in *Tanulmányok Budapest múltjából* [Studies on the past of Budapest] 29(2001) 37–47; Ágnes R. Várkonyi, "A magyar államiság Mohács után [On the Hungarian statehood after Mohács]," in Jenő Gergely and Lajos Izsák, eds., *A magyar államiság ezer éve, kultúra és tudomány a magyar államiság ezer évében* [Thousand year of Hungarian statehood, culture and science in the thousand years of Hungarian statehood] (Budapest: ELTE Eötvös Kiadó, 2001) 121–139; Ágnes R. Várkonyi, "Az egység jelképei a megosztottság másfél évszázadában [The symbols of unity in hundred fifty years of division]," *A Hadtörténeti Múzeum értesítője - Acta Musei Militaris in Hungaria* [The bulletin of the Military Museum], 4(2002) 59–69.

50 Benda and Fügedi, *A magyar korona regénye*, 118–120.

the sultan intended this gesture as an adaptation of the Christian tradition of coronation by which to establish the balance of power in this part of Europe to serve his own interests. He made use of coronation, as previously, as a symbol of the legitimation of power. Likewise, he had a crown made for himself too, in Venice.[51] In the correspondence that he carried on with Christian rulers the sultan boastfully styled himself "distributor of crowns among the rulers of the world".[52]

To the sultan the use of this symbol was merely a means of gaining himself a place in the European power structure. In 1530 Ferdinánd sent an ambassador to Süleyman with the request that he recognise him as King of Hungary.[53] The sultan refused, but in the Treaty of Nagyvárad (1538) he agreed with János Szapolyai and Charles V that János would surrender the crown to Ferdinánd but that Charles would end all support for warfare against the Turks.[54] The agreement meant the nominal reunification of Hungary. In order to prevent this actually happening, in 1541 Süleyman invested the castle of Buda, thus driving a wedge between the western and eastern parts of the country.[55]

The surrender of the crown in 1551 was an expression of the symbolic reunification of Hungary. On 21 July 1551 János Szapolyai's widow Izabella handed it over to Ferdinánd Habsburg's ambassador in the church of St Michael in Torda, and made a speech to those present.[56] This included the prophetic words: "Henceforth you will never crown with this crown a king of your own nation and blood anymore."[57] The political unity of the country was declared in the Treaty of Speyer in 1570. János Zsigmond, heir to János Szapolyai, relinquished the title of king and was then elected prince of Transylvania, thus creating the Principality of Transylvania (*Principatus Transylvaniae*) within the kingdom. The Principality officially belonged to the Kingdom of Hungary and recognised the supremacy of the Habsburg rulers, but in practice was a vassal of the Ottoman Empire.[58]

The surrender of the crown is, for various reasons, almost forgotten, but it remains a very significant symbolic milestone in the history of the crown and Hungary. It is

---

51 Gülru Necipoğlu, "Süleyman the Magnificent and the representation of power in the context of Ottoman-Habsburg-papal rivalry," *Art bulletin*, 71(1989) 401–427; Otto Kurz, "A gold helmet made in Venice for Sultan Sulayman the magnificent," *Gazette des Beaux Arts*, 74(1969) 249–258.
52 Geoffrey Parker, "The political World of Charles V," in Hugo Soly and Willem Pieter Blockmans, eds., *Charles V 1500–1558 and his Time* (Antwerpen: Mercatorfonds, 1999) 155.
53 *Ibid.*, 161.
54 R. Várkonyi, "'...Jó Budavár magas tornyán..'" 80–81.
55 László Makkai, "The Crown and the Diets of Hungary and Transylvania in the Sixteenth Century," in R. J. W. Evans and T. V. Thomas, eds., *Crown, Church and Estates* (London: Palgrave Macmillan, a division of Macmillan Publishers Limited, 1991) 81.
56 Miklós Istvánffy, *Historiae de rebus Ungaricis* (Coloniae Agrippinae: Hieratus, 1622) 298.
57 *Ibid.*
58 R. Várkonyi, "'...Jó Budavár magas tornyán..'," 82.

to be regarded as the antithesis of the occasion in 1464 when Ferdinánd Habsburg surrendered the crown to Mátyás Corvinus. The ceremony of surrender that took place in Mátyás' time may be seen as the confirmation of the new king's Central-European kingdom and of his position in respect of power vis-à-vis the Habsburg emperor. The content of the 1551 ceremony was precisely the opposite of that, as it emphasised the assumption of power in Hungary by the House of Habsburg. It is furthermore apparent from Queen Izabella's words that the Hungarians were quite clear that the surrender meant de facto an end to the free election of the king, the single constitutional right of the Hungarian nobility. The Hungarian national kingship was being relinquished for a higher purpose, nothing less than the political unity of Hungary, which was eventually realised with the recovery of the Turkish-occupied territories. The crown came into the foreground more and more as the symbol of the desire for the Kingdom of Hungary to be reunited. It was given its first important symbolic role when the political situation desired by the country – reunification – was portrayed by the Hungarian crown in the coronation of Ferdinánd's successor Maximilian (1563–1572).[59]

The formation of a Hungarian nation of Estates after the Battle of Mohács (1526)

Politically, the Kingdom of Hungary consisted of a number of provinces, to wit Hungary, Croatia, and Slavonia, together with Transylvania. In all cases a separate Diet was maintained, since we may speak of political communities with their own independent administrations.[60] Despite this, in the national assemblies the provinces formed one *regnum* or rather country. The cohesion of the *regnum* was strengthened by the person of the king.

In László Péter's opinion, in Hungary during the period under discussion the balance of power between the king and the Estates is best described by the expression "structural dualism".[61] The principal distinguishing feature of this system

---

59 Thomas DaCosta Kaufmann, *Variations on the imperial theme in the age of Maximilian II and Rudolf II* (New York: Garland Publishers, 1978) 5–15, 26–27, and the description: *Commentariolus de coronatione Maximiliani II.*, OSZK Ms. Lat. 2275, fol. 162–173. Hungarian edition and translation: János Liszty, "II. Miksa beiktatásának rövid leírása [Brief description of the inauguration of Maximilian II.]," in *A korona kilenc évszázada* [Nine centuries of the crown], Tamás Katona ed. (Budapest: Helikon, 1979) 176–191.
60 Péter, "The Holy Crown of Hungary," 447.
61 *Ibid.*; László Péter, "Die Verfassungsentwicklung in Ungarn," in Adam Wandruszka, Peter Urbanitsch, and Alois Brusatti, eds., *Die Habsburgermonarchie, 1848–1918. Verfassung und Parlamentarismus*, Bd. 7 (Wien: Verlag der Österreichischen Akademie der Wissenschaften, 2000) 239–261.

was that regnum and rex lived side by side as jurisdictions and powers, mutually complementing one another.⁶² In an ideal case, king and regnum solved political differences by discussion in the National Assembly. The Hungarian regnum consisted of persons summoned to the National Assembly, who formed the Estates (Hungarian *rendek*, Latin *status et ordines*).⁶³ The high clergy and aristocracy took part in national assemblies personally, and the common nobility of the counties, together with the free royal towns, through their representatives.⁶⁴

According to Géza Pálffy, after 1526 there was a significant change in the way the *regnum* worked.⁶⁵ Three separate courts, those in Vienna, Hungary and Transylvania, took over its role and task, the natural consequence of which was that the self-determination, independence and importance of the Hungarian royal court ceased to be. In his essay on the changes that took place in the Hungarian court Pálffy states that with the transformation the gap between the court and the regnum widened significantly.⁶⁶ The most important political decisions were taken in the Habsburg court in Vienna (and for a short while in Prague). The king did not even live in Hungary, for which reason the Estates had the opportunity of personal contact with him only at National Assemblies. Other than on such occasions the regnum tried to exert influence on his policies through emissaries, which led to the steady erosion of the political influence of the Estates in Hungary.⁶⁷

---

62 "Kronen und Land, (…) waren auch zwei im wesentlichen getrennte Recht- und Machtsphären, die einander ergäntzen und in Wiederspruch und Anpassung nebeneinander funktionierten." *Ibid.*, 249, also Rady, *Nobility, Land and Service*, 158–161; Kálmán Benda, "Az országgyűlések az újkori magyar fejlődésben [The Diets in the Early Modern Hungarian development]," in Kálmán Benda and Katalin Péter, eds., *Az országgyűlések a kora újkori magyar történelemben* [The Diets in the Early Modern Hungarian history] (Budapest: MTA Történettudományi Intézet: Országos Pedagógiai Intézet, 1987) 4–5.
63 See *Tripartitum*, I, 2, §1.
64 Erik Fügedi, *The Elefánthy: the Hungarian nobleman and his kindred*, ed. Damir Karbic, with a foreword by János M. Bak (Budapest: Central European University Press: 1998) 63–68; Rady, *Nobility, Land and Service*, 169–173.
65 Géza Pálffy, "Der ungarische Adel und der Kaiserhof in der frühen Neuzeit (eine Skizze)," in Václav Bůžek and Pavel Král, eds., *Šlechta v habsburské monarchii a císařský dvůr (1526–1740)* [Nobility in the Habsburg Monarchy and the Imperial Court (1526–1740)] (České Budějovice: Historický ústav Jihočeské univerzity, 2003) 133–152; Géza Pálffy, "A magyar nemesség I. Ferdinánd bécsi udvarában [The Hungarian nobility in the Viennese court of Ferdinand I.]," *Történelmi Szemle*, 45/1–2(2003) 45–59; Géza Pálffy, *The Kingdom of Hungary and the Habsburg Monarchy in the Sixteenth Century*, Thomas J. and Helen D. DeKornfeld, tr., (Boulder, Colorado: Social Science Monographs–Wayne, New Jersey: Center for Hungarian Studies and Publications, Inc. – New York: Distributed by Columbia University Press, 2009. (East European Monographs, DCCXXXV.; CHSP Hungarian Studies Series, 18.)
66 Pálffy, "Der ungarische Adel," 135–140.
67 Pálffy points out that the proportion of Hungarian nobles at the Habsburg court was minimal (3–4%), whereas previously in Buda it had reached 30–40%. Pálffy, "A magyar nemesség," 59.

In Pálffy's view, the other great change was that the Hungarian aristocrats became integrated into the structure of the Habsburg court.[68] This process began in 1527, and similar changes took place in the Czech court during the same period.[69] Members of the Hungarian aristocracy were given court titles and official positions, and were involved in Habsburg imperial decision-taking, so that they became ever more closely bound to the Habsburg ruler and their links with the Estates became weaker and weaker.[70] The consequences presented the common nobility with new opportunities to influence the ruler. Lacking their own court, the Diets acquired a more important role for the Estates in the formulation and achievement of the political demands of the *regnum*. At the same time the political influence of the Hungarian aristocratic courts grew, as did that of the princely court of Transylvania. This explains why after 1526 the Hungarian Estates tried to influence the court by another strategy.

The most important forum for the political influence of the Estates was the Diet held in Hungary. According to Kálmán Benda, material for debate in the Diet was furnished by motions proposed by the king to which the Estates replied in writing (specific grievances might be submitted), to which the king would respond and a further response from the Estates would follow.[71] The process continued until agreement was reached. The preparation of responses and counter-responses required a great deal of time, discussions were protracted, and almost all compromise agreements between the Estates and the ruler could only be reached with difficulty in roundabout fashion.

The Hungarian humanist János Bocatius speaks of these problems when in 1611 he writes, concerning the Hungarian Diet enactments of 1604:

> If anyone is unaware of how these enactments came into being I will tell you. At some diet or other in Pozsony the delegates present make proposals, of these one or another is approved, and those approved are submitted to the king for confirmation and ratification. This is done as follows: After the royal preamble the clauses are appended in order like the pages of a book; on each individual page are the royal and imperial great seal and signature, and the pages are then sent back to the magnates and the representatives of the counties and free towns. Among the enactments from the National Assembly there

---

68 Pálffy, A magyar nemesség,"; Pálffy, "Der ungarische Adel," 140–145.
69 Volker Press, "The Imperial Court of the Habsburgs," in Ronald G. Asch, and Adolf M. Birke, eds., *Princes, Patronage and the Nobility. The Court at the Beginning of the Modern Age, c.1450–1650* (London: German Historical Institute, 1991) 302–303.
70 Benda, "Az országgyűlések," 4; Géza Pálffy, "A bécsi udvar és a magyar rendek a 16. században [The Viennese court and the Hungarian estates in the sixteenth century]," *Történelmi Szemle* 3–4(1999) 331–369.
71 Benda, "Az országgyűlések," 5.

remained some in German too, but these were by then obsolete because they had been amended by deletion or insertion, without the knowledge or agreement of the National Assembly and always to the detriment of the liberties of the country. As had happened in the past so it was in 1604 too, when foreign enactments were interpolated.[72]

In modern-day literature in Hungary about the formation of national identity much emphasis is laid on the role in Hungarian political thinking of Werbőczy's coinage *natio Hungarica*.[73] The reception in Hungary of the legal idea expressed in the *Tripartitum*, and widely familiar, was very positive. For that very reason scholars have assumed that Werbőczy's work and the view that he developed of the origin of the Hungarian people influenced the formation of the national identity. Katalin Péter, however, believes that Werbőczy's concept of the nation had hardly any effect on Hungarian political thinking.[74] The ethnicity of individual members of the *regnum* was therefore much less important to the nation of Hungarian Estates that modern historians have suggested.

We may use as an excellent example the case of naturalised persons who, as foreigners, were ceremoniously made members of the Estates and who, after taking the oath of loyalty, enjoyed the same rights as their peers. At the Diet of 1608 Charles Liechtenstein and another Austrian aristocrat were "…received among the Hungarians…" (*recipiuntur in Hungaros*).[75] They were granted membership of the Hungarian Estates on account of their loyalty (*fidelitas*) and willingness to help (*servitus*), and after taking the oath of loyalty became, as the saying was, "good citizens of the fatherland". It should be noted that Bocatius, himself of Sorb extraction though a Hungarian nobleman, also complained in 1611: "…foreign names have been smuggled onto the roll of Hungarian magnates."[76] It may be seen from the ceremony that to members of the *regnum* the idea of the Hungarian Estates was bound up with the concept of the politically active man, faithful to the fatherland. The ethnic character of the Estates (and with it Werbőczy's premise)

---

72 János Bocatius, *Öt év börtönben [1606–1610]* [Five years in prison], Ferenc Csonka, ed. and trans. (Budapest: Európa Könyvkiadó, 1985) 29.
73 Jenő Szűcs, *Nation und Geschichte. Studien*, Johanna Kerekes, tr. (Köln–Wien: Böhlau, 1981) 100.
74 Katalin Péter, *Papok és nemesek: Magyar művelődéstörténeti tanulmányok a reformációval kezdődő másfél évszázadból* [Priests and nobles: studies on cultural history from hundred fifty years after the beginning of the Reformation] (Budapest: Ráday Gyűjtemény, 1995) 213.
75 "Matthiae II. decr. a. 1608 post cor. (I) 2, art. 27. Articulus 27. D. Carolus princeps a Liechtenstein, una cum fratre Maximiliano: in Hungaros recipiuntur," in Kálmán Csiky, Sándor Kolozsváry, Gyula Nagy, Kelemen Óváry, Lőrinc Tóth and Márkus Dezső, eds., *Corpus juris hungarici: magyar törvénytár, 1000–1895. Vol. 3. 1608–1657, évi törvényezikkek* [Corpus juris hungarici: Hungarian law collection, 1000–1895. Vol. 3. Law articles from the years 1608–1657] (Budapest: Franklin-Társulat, 1896) 38–40.
76 "*Sperantes ipsos; juxta praestitum ab iis juramentum, bonos cives patriae futuros.*" Ibid., §2, 40.

was only emphasised when the rights of the Estates had to be justified vis-à-vis the king, or to counter some threat from abroad.

III. Emperor Rudolf II, Habsburg rule in Hungary and the Holy Crown

The Emperor Rudolf II's political background

The turning point in the history of the meaning of the crown and the nation in Hungary took place during the rule of Emperor Rudolf II as King Rudolf I of Hungary between 1572 and 1608. The balance of power between the king and the Estates after 1526 described in the last chapter was disturbed by the political ambitions of the king. These led to the clash between king and the Hungarian Estates, which started with the famous conflict between Rudolf and István Illésházy in 1600 and eventually led to the Bocskai Rebellion in 1604.

In the last quarter of the twentieth century the reign of Emperor Rudolf II became the focal point of scholarly interest.[1] In 1973 there appeared from the pen of Robert Evans what was considered a ground-breaking study of Rudolf's political ideals and the intellectual background to his thinking. Evans stated that Rudolf's time as emperor was marked by significant political, religious and cultural changes in which his personality and Weltanschauung played a decisive role.[2] In his view, a ruler was endowed with absolute power in order that he might preserve the harmony of the universe.[3]

Rudolf strove for the spiritual and political unity of Christendom, to bring an end to religious strife, to keep peace in the Habsburg Empire and to defend Europe against the threat from the Ottomans. His reign came at the time of the so-called Long War (1591–1606), the first serious attempt at retaking occupied territory. In this effort he was supported by an international humanist élite, partly belonging to the court, who were in contact with one another. This intellectual circle included Catholics and Protestants alike, but despite their differences over faith scholars, writers, artists, politicians and churchmen formed a group that shared the Habsburg

---

1 Robert J.W. Evans, *Rudolf II and his World. A Study in Intellectual History 1576–1612* (Oxford: Thames and Hudson, 1973, 1997) 11; Frances A. Yates, *Astrea: The Imperial Theme in the Sixteenth Century* (London and Boston: Routledge, 1975) 12–28; Thomas DaCosta Kaufmann, *Variations on the Imperial Theme in the Age of Maximilian II and Rudolf II* (New York: Garland Publishing, 1978); Hugh Trevor-Roper, *Princes and Artists. Patronage and Ideology at Four Habsburg Courts 1517–1633* (London: Thames and Hudson, 1976) 85–127; Anton Gindely, *Rudolf II. und seine Zeit*, vol. I–II (Prague: Tempsky, 1863–1865).
2 Evans, *Rudolf II*, 2–3.
3 *Ibid.*

ruler's opinions. The members of this group gave expression to these thoughts in their works, which appeared, for example, at the investitures of new rulers.

The coronation was an important event which an emperor could use to make known his political ambitions. The art historian Thomas DaCosta Kaufmann defined the coronation of Habsburg emperors as "…the visual expression of the power of the House of Habsburg…".[4] The function of such an event was to authenticate the rightfulness of the emperor's power by celebrating the imperial cult.[5] The inspiration for this was the ceremonial with which, it was supposed, the person of the emperor had been glorified in the ancient Roman Empire.[6] The onlookers had to be convinced of the emperor's virtue and the correctness of his intentions, which were displayed by means of symbolism (the coronation regalia and insignia of the House of Habsburg), depictions employed (former emperors as Hungarian kings and Roman emperors) and performances (staged battle-scenes in which the emperor was shown as victor).

Another function of the coronation was the strengthening and legitimating of the existing social order.[7] On the occasion of Rudolf's coronation in Pozsony in 1572 the Hungarian Estates (the aristocracy and high clergy together with the representatives of the common nobility and the royal towns) stated publicly by their presence and participation that they acknowledged their subject status. Furthermore, the various Estates had prescribed roles at the coronation which both reflected and confirmed their situations in society.[8] At the focal point of the celebrations was the person of the king, which was consonant with the significance of the ruler's social position.

As early as the sixteenth century the Habsburg rulers had an authoritarian conception of the exercise of Hungarian royal power.[9] They were scarcely tolerant of the Estates' commenting on the policies of state and refrained from appointing a palatine. This Habsburg view of power was at odds with the views that the Hungarian Estates had formed of their rights. The first clash came in 1572, shortly after the coronation, when Rudolf (and Maximilian) and the Hungarian Estates differed

---

4 DaCosta Kaufmann, *Variations*, 6–7.
5 *Ibid.*, 12–13.
6 Yates, *Astrea*, 1–28; Ladislav Daniel, "The Myth of the Prince between Rome and Prague around 1600," in Lubomír Konečný, Beket Bukovinska, and Ivan Muchka, eds., *Rudolf II, Prague and the World: papers from the International Conference, Prague, 2–4 September, 1997* (Prague: Artefactum, 1968) 50.
7 DaCosta Kaufmann, *Variations*, 12–13.
8 "Descriptio coronationis in regem Hungariae Posonii," in Márton György Kovachich, *Solennia inauguralia serenissimorum...* (Pestini: Typis Matthiae Trattner, 1796) 23–28, and the description in the ms by the hand of Rudolf's court historian: [Elias Berger], *Descriptio Coronationis Serenissimi Principis ac Domini; Dni Rudolphi Archiducis Austria. etc.: in Regem Hungariae inaugurati, Posonij die Vigesima quinta Septembris Anno Dni 1572 d: 26. Sept: ...*, ÖNB, codex 8674, fol. 13r.–31v.
9 Evans, *Rudolf II*, 78–79.

over the matter of the election of the king. Rudolf defended his own claim to power by alluding in depictions and literature to future victories over the Ottomans which could only be achieved thanks to his monarchy.[10]

Since the cultus of the crown had become connected to the rights of the Estates through the election of the king of Hungary, no change in significance is to be seen in literary sources at this period.[11] *Corona* meant royal power in the Kingdom of Hungary.[12] Copies of the coronation regalia of Hungary, Bohemia and the Holy Roman Empire were produced for the lying-in state of Maximilian II in 1577 and were depicted on the cover of the description of his funeral ceremony.[13] In the same description of this ceremony by Johannes Benessovinus, the term *sacra corona* occurs, and there is an allusion to its "heavenly origin".[14] The fact that the Hungarian crown – together with the other crowns of the Habsburg Empire – was placed in Rudolf's Prague art collection as a mere work of art demonstrates his political ambitions to perfection.[15]

A good example of the side-lining (even if unintentional) of the use of the tradition of the crown is the text, circulated in a handbill in 1572, written by the court historian János Zsámboky (Sambucus, 1531–1584) titled "Concerning

---

10 Nicolette Mout, *Bohemen en de Nederlanden in de zestiende eeuw* [Bohemia and The Netherlands in the sixteenth century] (PhD dissertation, Leiden: Universitaire Pers, 1975) 77; Frances A. Yates, *The Occult Philosophy in the Elizabethan Age* (London: Routledge, 1979) 87–89, Karl Vocelka, *Die politische Propaganda Kaiser Rudolfs II. (1576-1612)* (Wien: Verlag der Österreichischen Akademie der Wissenschaften, 1981) 13–331; Géza Galavics, *Kössünk kardot az pogány ellen. Török háborúk és képzőművészet* [Let us gird on the sword against the heathen. Turkish wars and art] (Budapest: Képzőművészeti Kiadó, 1986) 27–32.
11 See e. g. the epitaph of Maximilian II, father of Rudolf, written by Hungarian court historian of the Habsburg family Sambucus in which the Hungarian crown is not mentioned. Iohannes Sambucus, "In moerore funeris Maximiliani II. Laudatiuncula," in Antonio Bonfini, *Rerum Ungaricarum decades* (Hanovia: Typis Wechelianis, apud Claudium Marnium, & haeredes Ioannis Aubrii, 1606) 816–826.
12 Thomas DaCosta Kaufmann, "Remarks on the Collections of Rudolf II: the *Kunstkammer* as a Form of *Representatio*," *Art Journal*, 38–1 (1978) 22–28.
13 Johannes Benessovinus, *Brevis et succincta descriptio pompae funebris, in honorem sacratissimi ac gloriosissimi monarchae, divi Maximiliani II ... conscripta* (Pragae: Melantrichus, 1577) (cover).
14 '*Eodem ordine ferebant Hungariae proceres, ensem, sceptru omum & sacram coronam, quam anno 1022. ad preces D. Stephani Regis coelo delapsam putant.*' Benessovinus, *Brevis et succincta descriptio pompae funebris*, B2v. See also: József Podhraczky, "Mikor és miért vitette Rudolf király Prágába a' magyar koronát [When and why did King Rudolf bring the Hungarian crown to Prague]," *Tudománytár Értekezések* XI (1842) 374.
15 For the use of the crown by the Habsburg dynasty in the sixteenth century see: Géza Pálffy, "Magyar címerek, zászlók és felségjelvények a Habsburgok dinasztikus–hatalmi reprezentációjában a 16. században [Hungarian family crests, flags and crown jewels in the dynastic–power representation of the Habsburgs in the sixteenth century]," *Történelmi Szemle* 3–4 (2001) 241–277.

Rudolf's crown".[16] The author does not even once refer to the Holy Crown or crown of Hungary, but instead uses the neutral terms *diadema* and *corona*. He also calls the Hungarians *genus Ungaricum* or *natio*, and, in view of the Ottoman menace, emphasises the importance of social harmony (*concordia*) through the power of the House of Austria (*Domus Austriae*). We must not forget that Sambucus had a quite special position as court historian of the Habsburg dynasty and, according to Gábor Almási, could write his works in relative autonomy.[17] He did not have, and perhaps did not want, to legitimate the political claims of the Hungarian Estates.

According to Katalin Péter, it is a striking fact that the coronation regalia had not been kept in Hungary since 1551, and the handbill does not turn its attention to this. We know of no source that refers to the absence from Hungary of the crown.[18] From this it may be deduced that at this time the tradition of the crown was unimportant to the Hungarian Estates even for the purpose of legitimating their rights. Other than in the ceremony of coronation the king made no use of the tradition of the crown for the legitimation of his power.

According to Várkonyi, the personal coronation jewel that Rudolf had made in 1602 hints at the reduced significance of the Hungarian tradition of the crown in the legitimation of royal power.[19] The plan for the new crown reflected Rudolf's conceptions, and the notion that the unity of the Habsburg Empire found expression in the person of the emperor.[20] On the crown, three fields depict the Hungarian, Czech and imperial coronations, while a fourth presents in allegorical form Rudolf's victories against the Ottomans. The first relief shows the ceremonial sword strokes which Rudolf made after the Hungarian coronation as a sign of his promise to defend the country.[21] In a second relief Rudolf is glorified as the conqueror of the Ottomans and defender of the Habsburg Empire. These depictions allude to the

---

16 Ioannis Sambucus, *De corona serenissimi Rodolphi regis Ungariae, &c. Archiducis Austriae, &c. 25. Septemb. 1572. ad status Regni, & alios Ioan. Samb. oratiuncula* (Viennae Austriae: typis Blasii Eberi 1572).

17 Gábor Almási, *The Uses of Humanism: Johannes Sambucus (1531–1584), Andreas Dudith (1533–1589) and the Republic of Letters in East Central Europe* (Leiden – Boston: Brill, 2005) 172–178.

18 Katalin Péter, "A haza és a nemzet az ország három részre hullott állapota idején [The Fatherland and Nation in the time the country was divided in three parts]," in Katalin Péter, *Papok és nemesek. Magyar művelődéstörténeti tanulmányok a reformációval kezdődő másfél évszázadból* [Priests and nobles: studies on cultural history from hundred fifty years after the beginning of the Reformation] (Budapest: Ráday Gyűjtemény, 1995) 226–227.

19 Várkonyi, "A magyar államiság," 83.

20 Hermann Fillitz, *Die österreichische Kaiserkrone und die Insignien des Kaisertums Österreich* (Vienna – München: Herold, 1959) 16; Galavics, *Kössunk kard*, 42; Beket Bukovinská, "Zu den Goldschmiedearbeiten der Prager Hofwerkstätte zur Zeit Rudolfs II," *Leids Kunsthistorisch Jaarboek*, 1 (Delft: Primavera Press, 1982) 71–82.

21 Vocelka, *Die politische Propaganda*, 127, 307–310.

promises made by Rudolf at the coronation and their imminent fulfilment. The new crown was both a symbol of the power of the Habsburg ruler and at the same time a sign of his political ambitions.

During Rudolf's reign it became obvious that his policies were unsuccessful. Stalemate developed in the wars with the Ottomans, his capacity to govern left something to be desired, and tension between subjects and ruler sprang up within the Habsburg Empire. As king he infringed the rights of the Estates more and more frequently, among them that of freedom of exercise of religion. It further undermined the power of the king that in consequence of the continuous warfare on the eastern frontier and the European financial crisis the Habsburg imperial treasury was empty.[22] Rudolf attempted to remedy the economic situation by mortgaging the crown lands and by renting for cash certain privileges without considering the interests of the creditors, the banking houses of Prague. This policy constantly led him into confrontation with his subjects.

The Illésházy case and the crown

With regard to the legitimation of royal power in Hungary, the most significant and far-reaching conflict was that between the king and the aristocrat István Illésházy (1540–1609) over an estate which had been mortgaged to the latter. Illésházy was the wealthiest Hungarian landowner and the most influential politician and political thinker of his time.[23]

Illésházy's life is an excellent example of the new social mobility of the age in Hungary and Central Europe. He was a man that made the fullest use of his talent, position and connections to extend his power and wealth to the utmost, and at the same time to adapt sensibly to the changed political and economic circumstances. Illésházy's marriage to Kata Pálffy, widow of the very wealthy János Krusich of Lepoglava in 1581, made him one of the richest aristocrats in Lower Hungary. His

---

22 Gindely, *Rudolf und seine Zeit*, vol. II, 36.
23 Although Illésházy was one of the most significant political figures of his time in Central Europe no recent biography of him is known. The first known account of his life was the eulogy delivered at his funeral: [Elias Berger], *Oratio funebris in exequiis illustrissimi comitis, palatini Stephani de Ilieshaza comitis Trenchinien: et Liptovien:* ([Kassa: S.N.], 1609). Another brief biography, containing little original material, is that by József Podhraczky, "Illésházy István nádor élete [The life of Palatine István Illésházy]," *Új magyar múzeum* [New Hungarian Museum], I (Pest, 1856) 299–321, 370–390. More recent biographies, abridged in form, are: Péter Ötvös, ed., *Pálffy Kata leveleskönyve: iratok Illésházy István bujdosásának történetéhez 1602–1606* [Correspondence book of Kata Pálffy: documents on the exile of István Illésházy] (Szeged: Scriptum, 1991); Ferenc Szakály and István Hiller, "Illésházy István (1540–1609)," in Árpád Rácz, ed., *Nagy képes millenniumi arcképcsarnok* [Great illustrated Millennium portrait hall] (Budapest: Rubicon–Aquila–Könyvek, 1999) 82–83.

wife's relatives included some of the leading aristocratic families in the Empire. In the year that he was elected palatine Illésházy was *főispán* (lord-lieutenant, *comes*) of the counties of Trencsén and Liptó, and *alispán* (*vicecomes*) and chief officer of the royal court in Pozsony.[24] He owed his wealth to the estates – among them the affluent market towns of Szentgyörgy and Bazin – which he held in mortgage from the king.[25] Emissaries from these properties regularly complained to the king of the excessive sums that they were made to pay to the mortgagee.[26]

The townspeople attempted to escape Illésházy's domination by requesting the king to elevate them to the status of royal towns, by which the towns would have become the inalienable property of the crown and the king would never again have been able to mortgage them.[27] Not only economic advantage but also political rights came with the status. Each of the free royal towns might send a representative to the National Assembly, and the towns enjoyed the right to vote in the election of the king.[28] The two towns eventually agreed with Rudolf that he would redeem the mortgage before it fell due, and in exchange the towns would replace the premium of the mortgage which Illésházy had been paying into the treasury. Lázár Henkel, one of the richest financiers, supported the towns with loans.[29]

According to Ágnes R. Várkonyi, this was not the only occasion when the interests of Illésházy and Henkel had clashed. Henkel had acquired the copper mine at Besztercebánya in northern Hungary, the cheapest route for delivery from which lay through Illésházy's land, and the use of his serfs could have simplified the operation. The landowner took every opportunity to frustrate this. Henkel, however, was far too powerful a businessman to shrink from Illésházy. He controlled almost the

---

24 Éva S. Lauter, "A Palatinus Regni Hungariae a 17. századi Magyarországon [The Palatinus Regni Hungariae in seventeenth century Hungary]," in Ildikó Horn, ed., *Perlekedő Évszázadok. Tanulmányok Für Lajos történész 60. Születésnapjára* [Moving Centuries. Studies offered to Lajos Für for his sixtieth birthday] (Budapest: Eötvös Loránd Tudományegyetem Budapest Bölcsészettudományi Kar Középkori és Kora–újkori Magyar Történeti Tanszék, 1993) 216–217.
25 László Makkai, "A Habsburgok és a Magyar rendiség a Bocskai–felkelés előestéjén [The Habsburgs and the Hungarian estates at the dawn of the rebellion of Bocskai]," *Történelmi Szemle*, 13 (1974) 162–163.
26 Árpád Károlyi, *Illésházy István hütlenségi pöre* [The infidelity case against István Illésházy] (Budapest: Magyar Tudományos Akadémia, 1883) 15–16.
27 The request for elevation to privileged status was not unprecedented, because Rudolf's father Maximilian had similarly granted that favour to the town of Modor. *Ibid.*
28 István H. Németh, "A szabad királyi városi rang a kora újkorban [The free royal town rank in the Early Modern period]," *Urbs. Magyar Várostörténeti Évkönyv*, I (2006) 109–122.
29 Ágnes R. Várkonyi, "A nemzet, a haza fogalma a török harcok és a Habsburg–ellenes küzdelmek idején (1526–1711) [The notion of nation and fatherland in the time of the Turkish wars and the struggles against the Habsburgs]," in Ágnes R. Várkonyi, ed., *Magyarország keresztútjain. Tanulmányok a XVII. századról* [Hungary's crossroads. Studies of the seventeenth century] (Budapest: Gondolat, 1978) 339.

whole business of supplying grain to the army, and when the treasury, although owing him almost a million, applied to him for a further loan Henkel was not prepared to advance more credit except on his own terms. Várkonyi believes that this was the final link in the chain of the series of exchanges as the result of which the dispute between the Austrian and Hungarian businessmen became a dispute between the Hungarian aristocrat and the Habsburg emperor.[30]

On 5 September 1598, therefore, despite Illésházy's objections Rudolf bestowed on Szentgyörgy and Bazin the rank of royal free town.[31] Illésházy challenged the king's right to decide in the matter. and appealed against the decision. As he saw it, the king had infringed the law of the land by elevating the towns and had abused his powers to the detriment of subjects. The king regarded such open criticism of his exercise of power as lèse-majesté and prosecuted Illésházy. In this way what was essentially a disagreement of an economic nature changed into one of national policy concerning royal power and its legitimation.

The political background of the century-long Hungarian opposition to the power of the Habsburg ruler – and thus the clash between Rudolf and Illésházy – has always attracted much attention in studies of Hungarian history. Already in 1843 Pál Jászay described the event as an ideological difference of opinion between the Hungarian Estates and the autocracy of the king.[32] In his view, the question at the centre of the suit brought against Illésházy was whether the king had the right to bestow on individual towns the sort of privileges enjoyed by the common nobility.

In 1883 Árpád Károly refuted Jászay's views of the political nature of the case by an examination of the economic background of affairs between the wealthy magnate and the cash-strapped emperor. In his essay he showed that both parties to the dispute were placing weighty material interests at risk in the action. Illésházy advanced the political argument only out of self-interest.[33]

Neither historian, however, came to a fully correct conclusion because both interpreted the complex political background incorrectly. The case appeared to turn on the mortgaged property of the crown, but this matter of real estate had deeper political roots. The cause of the disagreement was a difference in the views held by the king and the Estates concerning the exercise of royal power in Hungary. This political tension surfaced at the time of the case and in the period that followed. As this tension between king and Estates had been in existence since the coronation in

---

30 *Ibid.*, 340.
31 Matthias Bél, *Notitia Hungariae novae historico geographica*, vol. II (Viennae Austriae: Paulus Straubius, 1736) 115–116.
32 Pál Jászay, *A' sz. kir. városok szavazatjoga országgyűléseken* [The right to vote of the free royal towns during the Diets] (Pest: Heckenast, 1843).
33 Károlyi, *Illésházy*, 61, 66.

1572 it made sense for Illésházy, as a good politician, to make use of such arguments borrowed from the political events of the day as best served his personal interests.[34]

The debate over King Rudolf's authority began with a letter of complaint from Illésházy to the *Camera Hungarica* (Hungarian Treasury) dated 8 November 1600.[35] In this he questions the legality of the king's decision by describing the limits of the extent of royal power on the basis of the defined meaning of *corona regni Hungariae*. In this argument the term corona has two interpretations. The more important is *ius coronae regni Hungariae* (the rights of the crown of the Kingdom of Hungary), by which Illésházy understands the whole of the law of the land. The second meaning of the term is the crown lands themselves, by which he means the inalienable property of *corona regni Hungariae*.

The explanatory statement begins with Illésházy's views concerning *ius coronae regni Hungariae*. He states that by virtue of his royal power the ruler has at all times the right to redeem his pledge.[36] He does not, however, have the right to bestow privileges on the towns, as that runs contrary to the law of the land. He justifies this statement as follows: the towns had been mortgaged in the time of Rudolf's father Maximilian with a rider to the effect that they might not be gifted or sold to anyone other than the mortgagee. This rider conferred a privilege on Illésházy as mortgagee. At his coronation Rudolf had promised to respect privileges bestowed on his subjects by his predecessors. In Illésházy's opinion, furthermore, the king had sworn to adhere to *ius coronae Hungariae*, that is, to uphold the rights of the crown of the Kingdom of Hungary and to keep its laws. These laws, however, defended the privileges of its subjects.

If the king elevated Szentgyörgy and Bazin to the status of royal free towns, he breached Illésházy's privilege, and with it *ius coronae Hungariae*, the rights and laws of the crown of the Kingdom of Hungary. Illésházy pointed out that by such acts royal power could lose its legitimacy. If the king broke the law, respect for him

---

[34] This circumstance is also evident from Illésházy's apologia after the case and his struggle for rehabilitation. See *inter alia* the correspondence on the affair that he conducted for years in his "minute book" which contains copies and documents, among his papers in the Hungarian National Library. In this (sadly, undated) correspondence he repeats again and again the same arguments used in his first letter to the Treasury. Stephanus Illésházy, *De Rebus Hungaricis Prothocolon*, OSZK Fol. Lat. 2336, fol. 16–18. See also the edited letters of Illésházy in: Ötvös, *Pálffy*, especially: 102–105. Károlyi used sources from HHStA when writing his book about Illésházy, which were send by Illésházy to the court in Prague or to the *Camera* in Vienna or Pozsony. The original documents about the Illésházy case from the Illésházy family archive can be found in: MOL P 1341. Raktári szám 2. fasc. 10–12 and MOL E 200 *Acta diversarum* 24. tétel. (Illésházy).

[35] Published in Károlyi, *Illésházy*, 170–172. The concept of the petition can be found in: MOL P 1341. Lad. 1 fasc. 10–12. fol. 1.

[36] Károlyi, *Illésházy*, 170.

would be forfeit. Thereby, in his view, the State itself could lose its foundation. In brief: the breaching of Illésházy's privilege could mean the end of royal power and the Kingdom of Hungary.

In the second section of his plaint, Illésházy sets out his views on the property of the crown. He begins with the statement that the two towns are the inalienable property *coronae regni Hungariae*. The king's decision to elevate them to the status of free royal towns was an infringement of the law, since in so doing he took way the property of the crown.[37] This he explained by the fact that the pledge had not reverted to the crown but had been donated to the citizens of the towns.[38]

Then Illésházy turns to the question of how this action by the king offended against *ius coronae regni Hungariae*, and why this gift was contrary to law. According to the law, because of the legal position in Hungary it was not permissible to make an ennobling donation of land to a provincial town, a royal free town or any other kind of community. A place of habitation, in contrast to a natural person such as a nobleman, was in law perpetual. If the king granted an estate to a nobleman, it reverted to the crown after the beneficiary's death. Property that had once been granted to a community could never revert to the crown but must remain in perpetuity in the possession of the community, as the community never died. From this it followed that the two towns which had, by elevation of status, been donated to their own communities, had been in perpetuity taken from the crown and would never return to its ownership. Such a donation was therefore contrary to law, because infringement of the rights of the crown and of the property of the crown were equal. Illésházy ends with the words: "He proposed to complain to the authorities of this infringement of the law and to oppose the king's decision in order on the one hand to obtain justice for himself and on the other to defend the law of the land."[39]

At this point, however, it must be observed that – as Várkonyi comments – Illésházy naturally saw no objection at all to infringing the law of the land if it was to his advantage.[40]

Illésházy's document on the manner of the exercise of royal power and on its limits and legitimacy set in motion a debate. According to Károlyi, it brought two important questions onto the agenda.[41] The first was whether the king had the right to elevate provincial towns to royal free status. The second was whether Illésházy or any other subject had the right to oppose the power of the king or to restrain the king in the exercise of that power. The essence of the problem was whether or

---

37 *Ibid.*, 171.
38 *Ibid.*
39 *Ibid.*, 172.
40 Várkonyi, "A nemzet," 338–339.
41 Károlyi, *Illésházy*, 40.

not royal power had any limits. In his document Illésházy made it clear that by his policies the king was not only attacking the rights of an individual person, but also undermining the legitimacy of his own royal power. This debate was carried on by an exchange of correspondence with the king and the resulting suit for lèse-majesté which lasted until 1603, but Illésházy continued to protest until he was pardoned and received compensation under Mátyás II (1608–1619) in 1608. He passed away in 1609.

The difference of opinion between Illésházy and the king is evident in the vocabulary used in their correspondence. In order to make his arguments effective, Illésházy speaks on several occasions of the "rights of the crown of the Kingdom of Hungary" (*ius coronae regni Hungariae*). In Rudolf's replies, this term does not occur, as he adduces exclusively his own majesty (*maiestas*) as the source of his correctness. Illésházy took the view that the king's legitimacy was based on the promises which he had made to respect the law of the land and on the terms of which the Estates had elected him. These promises were specified in the coronation oath and confirmed in the act of crowning with the crown of Hungary. In Rudolf's eyes the source of his power – despite the law of the land or the promises which he himself had earlier made – was the sovereignty of his person.

The Habsburg court took Illésházy's words as an attack on the omnipotence of the king, and therefore accused him of lèse-majesté with the intention of taking possession of his estates. On 16 January 1601, the king sent an answering letter in which he declared that Illésházy's views constituted an intolerable restriction on royal command, authority and power.[42] According to Rudolf he might, on the basis of his royal rights, authority and power *(per jurem, autoritatem potestatemque nostram regiam)*, elevate individual towns to royal free status just as he could ennoble commoners. At the same time the Vienna court too was preparing to support the royal claim to power, as is shown by a passage in a letter from the *Hofkammer* (Court Treasury) to Archduke Matthias, dated 5 February 1601. In this it states that Illésházy's attack on the emperor "…offended against royal power, rights and majesty…" and for this reason, something had to be done "…for the defence of royal prerogatives, rights and authority."[43]

That the king's power was really under attack is made clear by the following move by the Hungarian Estates: in the same year as Illésházy wrote his document the

---

42 *Ibid.*, 172–174.
43 "(…) noch gröber gemacht, indem er sich nit allain gantz scharfer und hitziger Anzüg gegegen Ihrer Majestät gebracht sondern auch der königliche Macht, Jus und Autorität angreift und dieselbe seines Gefallens zu constringiern und tu engen vermaint: so werden demnach Ihr fürstl. Durch. hierüber Ihrer Majestät Notturft und was diesorts zu Rettung dero königlicher Regalien, Rechten und Reputation vonnöten, ohne der Hofkammer Massgebung zu bedenken wissen." Quoted in Károlyi, *Illésházy*, 39, note 1.

delegates to the National Assembly refused to admit those from the town of Modor, as the Estates did not recognise it as a free royal town.[44] According to Károlyi, this exclusion was suggested by Illésházy.[45] By this refusal the Estates made it public that they did not recognise the king's right to elevate individual towns to royal free status, and by this political act opposed his wishes themselves. Thus began opposition to the power of the king in the Kingdom of Hungary, which cumulated in the Bocskai Rebellion in 1604.

The work of Elias Berger a Grünenberg

During the time that the debate over the legitimacy of royal power was taking place (1600-1603) the significance of the crown underwent a change, as did the associated image of the Hungarian Estates. In the background to this change was growing dissatisfaction with the king's policies, and there were constantly growing political and religious tensions in Hungary.

The first text in which this change of significance may be noted was written in 1600 by the Viennese court historian Elias (Illés) Berger a Grünenberg (Bergerus Pannonius, Perger, Bergher, Bergher Bergerus a Grinberg/Grimberg, 1562-1645).[46]

---

44 Makkai, "A Habsburgok," 169.
45 Károlyi, *Illésházy*, 43.
46 For Berger see József Podhraczky, "Berger Illés magyar történetíró [Elias Berger Hungarian historiographer]," *Tudománytár Értekezések* XII (1843) 351-366 (on the question of whether Berger was a Hungarian and a Catholic) and Vilmos Fraknói, "Berger Illés magyar királyi historiographus [Elias Berger Hungarian royal historiographer]," *Századok* 6 (1873) 373-390, quote: 374 (Fraknói describes Berger's work as worthless.) Other writers such as Evans and Vocelka, repeat this opinion of Fraknói's uncritically without carrying out further research. There is no appreciation of Franknói's work in their essays. Evans, *Rudolf* II, 128, Vocelka, *Die politische Propaganda*, 79. Béla Holl, *Ferenczffy Lőrinc. Egy könyvkiadó a XVII. században* [Lőrinc Ferenczffy. A book publisher in the seventeenth century] (Budapest: Magyar Helikon, 1980) 149-170. Interest in Berger has increased again more than twenty years ago. See: Péter Kulcsár. "Berger Illés történeti művei [The historical works of Elias Berger]," *Magyar Könyvszemle* 110 (1994) 245-259 and László Szörényi, "Berger Illés eposza a Szent Keresztről és a magyar történelem [The epic of Elias Berger on the Holy Cross and the Hungarian history]," in Marianne Rozsondai, ed., *Jubileumi csokor Csapodi Csaba tiszteletére* [Jubilee bouquet in honor of Csaba Csapoi] (Budapest: Argumentum, 2002) 298; László Szörényi, *Hunok és jezsuiták: fejezetek a magyarországi latin hősepika történetéből* [Huns and Jesuits: chapters from the history of Hungarian Latin heroic epic writings] (Budapest: AmfipressZ, 1993) 15-24; Eva Frimmová, "Humanista Eliáš Berger v službách Habsburgovcov [Humanist Elias Berger in the service of the Habsburgs]," in Miloš Kovačka - Eva Augustínová - Maroš Mačuha, eds., *Zemianstvo na Slovensku v novoveku. Časť 2. Duchovná a hmotná kultúra* [Developments in Slovakia in the Early Modern period. Part 2. Spiritual and material culture] (Martin: Slovenská narodná knižnica, 2009) 100-115; Kees Teszelszky, "Elias Berger Historia Ungarica című művének keletkezése és háttere (1603/4-1645) [The origin and background of the work Historia Ungarica by Elias Berger (1603/4-1645)]," in

Berger was born in Breznóbánya, Zólyom county, in the northern part of the Hungarian Kingdom.[47] His father, Péter Berger, was a Lutheran minister, and frequently had to move house (Zsolna and Biccse) because of his Calvinist sympathies and iconoclastic activities.[48] He studied in Heidelberg from 1593, and became a teacher in the Lutheran schools in Trencsén and later Pozsony. His relatives in Bohemia were also teachers, and in fact one was a professor at the Charles University in Prague.[49]

In about 1600, Elias chose himself another career. He became a court poet and historian in the service of the Habsburg dynasty and the Catholic and Lutheran aristocrats of Hungary and Moravia. He successfully published his first works in Latin verse and entered the circles in Prague near the Habsburg court. In 1603 he was appointed *Poeta Laureatus* with support of Archduke Matthias, but against the will of the Hungarian *Camera*. As a crown on his new career, he was ennobled in Prague on 25 April of the same year together with his six brothers Johannes, Daniel, Peter, Jeremias, Stephan and George.[50] He received this honour on the basis of his literary work as *poeta laureatus*: "... *in describendis carmine heroico divorum* ...".

In his capacity as court historian and poet it was his principal task to legitimate the political interests of those that employed him by writing of historical events in precisely the required manner. It is therefore not correct to attribute to him any given religious or political convictions, as his writings reflect first and foremost the current political intentions of his employer. For this reason, his oeuvre is peculiarly suitable for the analysis of the shifts that took place in Hungarian political thinking and the formation of national identity.

Gergely Tóth, ed., *Clio Inter Arma. Tanulmányok a 16–18. századi magyarországi történetírásról [Clio inter arma. Studies on history writing in Hungary between the sixteenth and the eighteenth century]* (Budapest: MTA Történettudományi Intézet, 2014) 149–168.

47 Fraknói, "Berger Illés," 375. I am not sure about the year of his birth. Fraknói derived it from a letter by Berger written in 1644 close to his death in which he stated to be 82 years old. His last letter written by him dates from 25 January 1645, so he must have died in that year. MOL, E 204 "Perger" Elias 1645.01.25, f. 1–2.

48 On Peter Berger see ms: OSZK, Fol. Lat. 3415, fol. 54v.

49 Antonín Truhlář and Karel Hrdina, eds., *Enchiridion renatae poesis Latinae in Bohemia et Moravia cultae*, vol I. (Praha: Academia, 1973) 194–195; Péter Kulcsár, ed., *Inventarium de operibus litterariis ad res Hungaricas pertinentibus ab initiis usque ad annum 1700 – A magyar történeti irodalom lelőhelyjegyzéke a kezdetektől 1700-ig [Inventory of all historic literature on Hungary from the beginnings till 1700]* (Budapest: Balassi Kiadó, 2003).

50 On the basis of Elias Berger's merits, he and his relatives received their nobility and armorial bearings on 25 April 1603. MOL, R64, 25 April 1603. George Berger was a Lutheran priest like his father and also wrote at least one verse, Jeremias Berger was a teacher and a poet and became later a professor at the Charles University in Prague.

In 1600 Berger composed an epic about the meaning of the double cross that is seen in the arms of the Kingdom of Hungary, and which is the symbol of the Árpád-dynasty of the first Hungarian kings.[51] The work about the cross and the country consists of twelve stanzas, more than 161 pages. He dedicated the work to János Kuthassy, the then archbishop of Esztergom and Primate of Hungary. Until his death in 1601 Kuthassy was an important patron of the arts and a well-known preacher, and between 1592 and 1593 the most important man in Hungary as the representative of the king, as there was no viceroy.[52]

By virtue of its content Berger's first work is usually mentioned as evidence that the author had converted to Catholicism, which in turn is seen as his first attempt at gaining admission to the better circles of society. The political weight of the subject, content and publication of written material are all the greater in the case of the advancement of an intellectual in need of assistance: he had to support the political ambitions of the Hungarian Estates vis-à-vis the king, as we shall later see. As Berger was only a poor teacher when he began the poem it may be supposed that János Kuthassy commissioned him to rewrite it and also paid for its publication. At the same time, it is probable that the work was drafted on the basis of Kuthassy's Catholic ideas.[53] We do not really know on what occasion the work was written. The content of the publication was probably connected to the dissatisfaction of the Estates with the Habsburg ruler's policy in Hungary and the struggle against the Ottomans.

The reason why Berger received this task is very likely connected to a tangible object in the possession of Archbishop Kuthassy related to the True Cross of Christ. Kuthassy owned the now-called *Esztergom Staurotheke*: a Medieval Byzantine reliquary made to display a fragment of the True Cross.[54] The Archbishop donated

---

51 Elias Berger, *Rapsodiae de cruce insigniis regni Hungarici et sanctissimis, et de gestis pro Cruce Christi inclutorum Hungariae Regum Faelicissimis: secundum fidem historicam pro Immortali Gloria Hungariae, pro nomine Christi tot seculis Pugnantis* (Olomutii: Typis Georgij Handelij, 1600).
52 Truhlář and Hrdina, *Enchiridion renatae*, vol. III, 115–116.
53 For the connection with patrons of dedications in the Early Modern period see Brian Richardson, *Printing, Writing and Readers in Renaissance Italy* (Cambridge and New York: Cambridge University Press, 1999) 49–76; Natalie Zemon Davies, *The Gift in Sixteenth-Century France* (Oxford: Oxford University Press, 2000) 36–37; Arnoud Visser, *Johannes Sambucus and the Learned Image* (Leiden and Boston: Brill, 2005) 111–120.
54 Paul Hetherington, "Studying the Byzantine Staurothèque at Esztergom," in Christoph Entwistle, ed., Through a Glass Brightly: Studies in Byzantine and Medieval Art and Archaeology Presented to David Buckton (Oxford: Oxbow books, 2003) 82–9 4; György Ruzsa, "Quand la staurothèque byzantine d'Esztergom est-elle arrivée en Hongrie?," in Anna Tüskés, ed., *Omnis creatura significans: Essays in Honour of Mária Prokopp* (Budapest: CentrArt, 2009) 47–48; Philippa Couch, *Esztergom Staurotheke* (undergraduate thesis, London, Courtauld Institute of Art, University of London, 2010; Iván Szántó, "The cross-cultural heritage of a Byzantine reliquary," in Dragana Cicović Sarajlić, Vera

this reliquary to the Cathedral of Esztergom after his death in 1601, where it is still present in the Archiepiscopal Treasury of Esztergom. According to the text of the will of Kuthassy, this sacral object reached Hungary already in 1190 in the time of the Árpád dynasty, which would have enhanced its symbolic value.[55] The reliquary had been made in the form of a double cross: the same cross as which is present in the coat of arms of the Árpád dynasty and the Kingdom of Hungary and which is displayed after the title page in the work of Berger.

The aim of the work was to persuade the Habsburg ruler to defend the Kingdom of Hungary against the Ottomans. In support of this message the writer indicated the Habsburg dynasty's God-given mission to defend Christianity against the heathen.[56] In this Berger follows the argument of the Hungarian Estates, repeated in his own time, that the defence of the entire Christian world would be guaranteed if the Kingdom of Hungary were successfully defended against the Ottomans. In Berger's view, it follows from that, that the king of Hungary had received from God the mission to defend Hungary, and with it Europe.

Berger uses the image of the True Cross to put his political message over to the emperor. He interprets the cross as a symbol of Christ's struggle against the pagan threat.[57] He draws a parallel between Christ's struggle and the war waged by the king of Hungary by linking together the meaning of the cross and the double cross in the Hungarian arms. He develops this analogy in his epic by creating the concept of the sign of the Cross. In so doing he explains in allegorical manner how the cross of Christ, fashioned from the wood of Paradise, could have come onto the Hungarian crown and the arms of the Hungarian State. The meaning of this image is that it is the sacred mission of the Hungarians and their kings to take up the struggle against the heathen for the defence of Christianity.

The epic begins with an account of heraldic symbols from antiquity and Berger's own time. After comparing a variety of symbols, the poet comes to the conclusion that no people have armorial bearings as majestic as the Hungarians' as the "true cross of Christ" is depicted on them. According to him, the double cross is a token that the Hungarians are "soldiers of Christ", which means that they are to be regarded as the defenders of the Christian faith. Berger gave colour to this device by observing

---

Obradović and Petar Đuza, eds., *Traditional and Modern in Art and Education* (Kosovska Mitrovica: University of Prishtina, 2018) 23–31.

55 Jeffrey C. Anderson, "The Esztergom Staurotheke," in Helen C. Evans and William D. Wixom, eds., *The Glory of Byzantium: Art and Culture of the Middle Byzantine Era, A.D. 843–1261* (Exhibition catalogue) (New York: The Metropolitan Museum of Art, 1997) 81.

56 Szörényi, "Berger Illés," 298.

57 The double cross also played a part in Werbőczy's book of laws, when he writes: '*Unde ab illius tempore, gens Hungarica, duplicatam crucem pro armis, ac insignibus habere pariter, et gestare consuevit.*' *Tripartitum*, Part. I. Tit. 11. § 3, 70–72.

the histories of Christianity and of Hungary from the point of view of the working of the Cross in history. The Hungarians received the token of the cross from the pope, since it was he that sent a double cross to the first king, István. By virtue of this gift the significance of Christ's first True Cross was transferred to this symbol of the Hungarian people, and the Hungarians may thereby be regarded as crusaders (*crucigeres*). The Hungarian kings had defended these armorial bearings by their glorious wars against the heathen and in the struggle with the people beneath the "sign of the half-moon" – the Ottomans. Berger further declares that the struggle between the Hungarian cross and the half-moon was a contemporary revelation of the eternal struggle carried on by Jesus against Satan. Christ fights against evil through the appearance in this world of the token of the cross.

Next, Berger returns to his own time, when, based on the device of the cross, he states that thanks to their role as kings of Hungary, the Habsburg emperors have become bearers of the true cross. This invention of the author has to be examined in the light of the way in which Rudolf had justified the rightfulness of his claims to power. He regarded the successes won in the course of the struggle against the Ottomans as the most important source of the legitimacy of the emperor's endeavours to acquire omnipotence in the empire. According to Berger, Rudolf owed his position as omnipotent ruler not to his imperial crown but to the fact that he was king of Hungary.

The writer therefore legitimates the political ambitions of the Hungarians by attributing the existence and history of the nation to the revelation of the will of God. He shows that the life of the Estates is of immediate significance from the point of view of the justification of the power of the king. In doing so, he goes so far as to elaborate in the epic on various elements of Hungarian history which support the demands of the Hungarian Estates concerning rights, but which are at odds with the image of the Habsburg dynasty as omnipotent rulers. In this way he refers to Attila, first ruler of the Hungarians, whom various Medieval writers and Werbőczy regard as the prime mover of the political independence of the Hungarian Estates. He also mentions the Golden Bull of András II, on the basis of which the Estates have the right to oppose the king. At the same time, he glorifies the national king Mátyás Corvinus, who was not particularly popular with the Habsburg dynasty because of his capture of Vienna in 1485. Berger's poem must therefore be seen as an epic of symbols of the Hungarian Estates and the Hungarian nation, rather than a work glorifying the person of the Habsburg ruler. This comes as no surprise if we keep in mind that Kuthassy had commissioned its writing.

By creating this work, Berger set in motion a literary change which acquired great importance in the formation of national self-identity in Hungary in the Early Modern period. The literary historian László Szörényi states that the epic meant a turning-point in Latin literature in Hungary because it can be seen as the first national epic of the Hungarians.[58] This national character is also evident from the impact of the work, as despite its Catholic subject Protestants too took a positive view of it.[59] Accordingly the wealthy Protestant bourgeois patron of the arts András Asztalos mentions it in a letter of 1610 to Albert Szenczi Molnár.[60] In this, the dual interpretation of Berger's work is pointed out and the political and religious content sharply separated. But how did Asztalos know of the content of the work? Berger himself presented him with a copy with a long dedication in verse in which Asztalos is named as the "patron of the Muses" (*patronus musarum*).[61] From this it is evident that Berger intended his work as a national epic for people of all religions in the Kingdom of Hungary.

With this new sort of portrayal of the Hungarians, and by interpreting a national symbol in a politically tinged text, Berger initiated a cultural change which was maintained much later, in works of a political origin in the early seventeenth century. It was his basic thought that since the Magyar race had sacred obligations to Europe the continued existence of the Kingdom of Hungary was indispensable for the maintenance of the power of the Habsburg dynasty – a thought which would be used both at the time of the Bocskai rebellion (1604–1606) and during the reign of Mátyás II (1608–1618). The more that pressure jeopardising the continued existence of Hungary and the Estates continued to grow, the more this message was voiced in ever more forceful expressions, ever more powerful images, and more and more enthralling ceremonial.

It is important to remark that Berger did not write a single word about the crown of Hungary in his work about the cross. He only started to use the symbolic meaning of the crown in his epic about the importance of archdukes as the pillars of the House of Habsburg published in 1602. In this work, one verse can be found about the holiness of the crown.[62]

---

58 Szörényi, "Berger Illés," 298; Szörényi, *Hunok*, 15–24.
59 The wealthy bourgeois and patron of the arts András Asztalos refers to Berger's work in a letter of 20 February 1610 from Nagyszombat to the Protestant humanist and theologian Albert Szenczi Molnár. See Judit P. Vásárhelyi, ed., *Szenczi Molnár Albert válogatott művei* [Selected works of Albert Szenczi Molnár] (Budapest: Magvető, 1976) 603–604.
60 *Ibid.*
61 Berger, *Rapsodiae*, Pannonhalmi Könyvtár [Library of Pannonhalma], RMK III. 948 (cover).
62 Elias Berger, *Domus augustissimae Austriae. Columnae sidera Caesares monarchae archiduces* (Viennae Austriae: Ex Officina Typographica Francisci Kolbij, 1602) L3r. (poem with title: *sacra tutela corona*). On this work, see: Zaynab Daloul, "Berger Illés és a Domus Augustissimae Austriae columnae sidera c. eposza," in Enikő Békés and Imre Tegyey, eds., *Convivium Pajorin Klára 70. Születésnapjára* [Convivium for the seventieth birthday of Klára Pajorin] (Debrecen and Budapest: Institutum Doctrinae Litterarum Academiae Scientiarum Hungariae, 2012) (Classica, Mediaevalia, Neolatina, Vol. 6) 63–73.

The dispute on the decline of Hungary (1602-1603)

At the time when Berger was beginning to publish, the Reform, Lutheran and Catholic writers in Hungary were debating the reason for Hungary's decline and the success of the Ottoman invaders.[63] The debate was essentially centred on the question of which branch of faith had caused the decadent state of the country and against which should the struggle be taken up.[64] The Catholic view was that God was punishing the Hungarians by means of the Ottomans because the Lutherans had neglected the true faith. The Protestants were of the opinion that the sins of the Catholics had roused God to anger, and the Ottoman hordes were His implements. In their view the only possibility for the Hungarians to be set free from their sins (and the Ottomans) lay in a return to the purer forms of the faith. This question had not only religious aspects but also political ones. The debate was about the future of the country, the political and religious freedom of Hungary and the extent of royal power.

The Protestant minister István Magyari (?-1605) made a highly significant contribution to the debate in 1602.[65] Court chaplain to Ferenc Nádasdy, he had fought with distinction against the Ottomans, and his ideas were either those of his employer or were inspired by him.[66] The Jesuit Péter Pázmány (1570-1637) began to publish a year later, and his first pamphlet was in response to Magyari's book.[67]

---

63 On this debate see Hóman and Szekfű, *Magyar történet*, vol. III., 283-284; István Bitskey, *Hitviták tüzében* [In the fire of the religious debates] (Budapest: Gondolat, 1978) 178-192; István Bitskey, "A vitézség eszményének változatai a XVI-XVII. század fordulójának magyar irodalmában [The variants of the ideal of gallantry in the seventieth and eightieth century Hungarian literature]," in *Hagyomány és korszerűség a XVI-XVII. században* ed. Tivadar Pétercsák (Eger, 1997) 208-209.

64 This question was raised in Hungary as early as 1538 in the chronicle published by the Protestant minister András Farkas. See Katalin Péter, *A magyar nyelvű politikai publicisztika kezdetei* [The start of journalism in the Hungarian language] (Budapest: Akadémiai Kiadó, 1973) 6-7; László Makkai, "Mindszenti Gábor emlékirata [The memoir of Gábor Mindszenti]," in László Makkai, ed., *Mindszenti Gábor diáriuma öreg János király haláláról* [The memoir of Gábor Mindszenti on the death of old King János] (Budapest: Európa Kiadó, 1977) 36-37.

65 Tibor Klaniczay, ed., *A magyar irodalom története* [The history of Hungarian literature], vol. II (Budapest: Kossuth Könyvkiadó, 1964) 60-62.

66 László Makkai, "Magyari és műve [Magyari and his work]," in István Magyari, *Az országokban való sok romlásoknak okairól* [On the causes of the many disasters in Hungary], ed. Tamás Katona (Budapest: Magyar Helikon, 1979) 187-206.

67 Péter Pázmány, *Felelet az Magiari Istvan sarvari praedicatornak az orzag romlasa okairul irt könivere* [Answer to what István Magyari write about the causes of the many disasters in Hungary] (Nagyszombatba: typ. capituli Strigoniensis, 1603). Ten years later he repeated his arguments in: Péter Pázmány, *Isteni igazságra vezérlő kalauz* [Guide to Divine Truth] (Posonban: [S.N.], 1613). Pázmány was the toughest disseminator of the Catholic faith, a leader of the counter-Reformation and the most influential 'ecclesiastical politician' of his time in Hungary. It was due to his efforts that the

In their writings both deal with the question of why Hungary and the Hungarian nation had fallen into ruin after the flourishing period of the reign of Mátyás Corvinus, and each of them places the blame on the other's denomination. In support of their arguments, they adduce analogies and parables from the Bible, Classical literature and Hungarian history. Thus, works similar to Berger's were produced in which religious symbols acquired a new, political significance while political themes were given a religious filling.

Pázmány was the first Catholic writer to make use of the meaning of the crown as an argument to support his personal political beliefs. Like Magyari, he analyses Hungarian history in his exposition. He illustrates the indissoluble link between the Catholic religion, the Hungarian nation and the Kingdom of Hungary with images and themes borrowed from the already mentioned work of Antonio Bonfini. He states that the pope presented St István with the crown after a miraculous event, and thus *orzagunknac Coronaia* (the crown of our country), came about.[68] The tradition of the crown therefore justified the important role of the Catholic religion in Hungary.

The Catholic writer also employed another theme connected to the crown. He mentions that St István dedicated his country to Virgin Mary, who thus became the patron saint of Hungary (*"Magiar orzag Patronus" – patrona Hungariae*).[69] According to Éva Knapp and Gábor Tüskés, this is the first occasion on which use is made of the topos *patrona Hungariae* in Hungarian religious polemic literature.[70] Thus Pázmány's work marks the beginning of the use in polemic of the tradition of the crown, Mary as the patron saint of Hungary, and the connection between the two themes and the Estates.

---

majority of the aristocracy of Hungary – including the Nádasdy family – returned to Catholicism. Klaniczay, *A magyar irodalom*, vol. II, 120–137; Emil Hargittay and Ágnes Varga, "A hitvitáktól a gyakorlati politikáig (Pázmány Péter politikai pályájának alakulása) [From the religious discussions to the practical politics (the development of Péter Pázmány's political career)]," in Béla Varjas, ed., *Irodalom és ideológia a 16–17. században* [Literature and ideology in the sixteenth and seventeenth century] (Budapest: Akadémiai Kiadó, 1987) 316. Magyari replied to Pázmány in a eulogy that he wrote on Ferenc Nádasdy. See: Gábor Kecskeméti, *Prédikáció, retorika, irodalomtörténet* [Sermon, rhetorics, history of literature] (Budapest: Universitas, 1998) 146–148.

68 Pázmány, *Felelet*, 421.

69 Pázmány relies on Bonfini for this. See: Antonio Bonfini, *Rerum Ungaricarum decades* (Basiliae: Robertus Winterus, 1543) decadis II, liber I, 185.

70 Éva Knapp and Gábor Tüskés, "Magyarország – Mária országa [Hungary—the country of Mary]," *Irodalomtörténeti közlemények*, 5–6(2000) 585. The first wood-cut depicting Mary as *patrona Hungariae* was also printed during this period. It may be seen from Wolfgang Lazius' map of 1556 that the title originated earlier (see also illustration 6 for the crown image on the map).

In the same year as Pázmány's work appeared Berger published his epic *Idyllia de virtute bellica*, to which he prefixed a twenty-two page dedication to Magyari's patron Ferenc Nádasdy (1555-1604).[71] As the Nádasdy family plays a leading role in this extended epic and the author praises effusively the deeds and qualities of various members of that clan it is highly likely that Ferenc Nádasdy commissioned the work to mark some special occasion. In the introductory dedication the poet uses biblical and Classical references and examples from Hungarian history to describe the ideal Hungarian aristocrat, who sacrifices himself for the governing power and the defence of the realm.[72] After that he sings in six idylls of the Hungarians' war against the Ottomans as a heavenly battle between good and evil.

The content of the work can be compared to that about the cross *Rapsodiae*: the Hungarian race has received from God the high calling of defending Christianity against the heathen. It is noticeable that on this occasion Berger makes no use of a cross-myth, but – with the Hungarian aristocrat in the principal role – displays the Hungarian aristocratic Estate as God's weapon in the war against the heathen. He portrays the Nádasdys as knights of Christ or Christian heroes, defending Christian Europe against the pagans. In this way he gives a new twist to the current Catholic-Protestant debate by stating that Christian Europe depends on the Hungarian aristocratic Estate – in the present instance a Lutheran family – if it is to be saved. By this message he legitimates the position adopted by the Nádasdys, as a powerful Lutheran aristocratic family in Hungary, against the Catholic Habsburg emperor. Berger's epic is thus a novel step, rising above sectarianism towards the formation of national self-awareness.

Why did Nádasdy support the publication of such an epic, when a year before he had assisted in the publication of Magyari's anti-Catholic pamphlet? The answer is to be found in the fact that the publication of the works served different political purposes. Magyari's was intended to bolster the position of the Protestants in Hungarian internal politics, that is, it had domestic political significance. Berger's, on the other hand, aimed at strengthening the European position of the Lutheran aristocrat within the Habsburg Empire.

The speech of Demeter Naprágyi (1603)

In 1603, when Pázmány's and Berger's works appeared, the Crown did in practice serve as justification for the Estates' political ambitions against royal power. The

---

71 Elias Bergerus, *Idyllia de virtvte bellica, fortitvdine, is est de militiae christianae origine, progressu u u dignitate utilitate. Additis panegyribus in exemplo dvcis et herois antiqvis et veris comparati avthore Elia Bergero poeta lavreato caeseo.* (Pragae: Typis Chumanianis, 1603).
72 *Ibid.*, 2*–22*.

idea emerged in an important speech on behalf of the *Status et Ordines* (Hungarian Estates),[73] given by Demeter Naprágyi, bishop of Transylvania, in the presence of the emperor after five emissaries – one of them Péter Révay, author of a subsequent work on the crown – had presented the king with a memorandum on 15 April 1603. According to István Szamosközy, court historian to Prince István Bocskai, Illésházy was one of its authors.[74]

The memorandum complained to the king about Hungary's current woes, most grievous of which was that the Estates were given no say in the affairs of the country.[75] They resented the king's autocratic exercise of power and the fact that they had little influence on the government of the country, on executive power and the administration of justice.[76] They declared that the king no longer involved the Hungarian Royal Council in decision-taking, as had been the case previously and as still was the custom in other parts of the Habsburg Empire. It was their view that lawlessness prevailed in Hungary, because many lawsuits were concluded by royal command. In the speech that he made on the occasion of the presentation of the memorandum, Naprágyi first said that the Hungarian crown, as an object, was of importance in legitimating royal power. He called on Rudolf as king of Hungary to remember the ancient customs of the country and to involve the Hungarians in the taking of his decisions. He supported his argument by reminding the king of his coronation with the Holy Crown, the most important element of the legitimation of his power as king of Hungary:

> Who would there be that should not honour Your Majesty as sons honour the father who shows them great devotion? For since in 1572, when, to the common cries of the assembled Estates as they wished Your Majesty good fortune, the angelic crown of St István was placed on your august head, they have experienced nothing other than Your Majesty's virtues, particular solicitude and unfailing conscientiousness in the performance of Your

---

73 Petrus de Rewa [Péter Révay], *De monarchia et sacra corona regni Hungariae centuriae septem...* (Francofurti: Thomae Mattiae Götzii, 1659) 108.
74 Erzsébet Abaffy and Sándor Kozocsa, eds., *Magyar nyelvű kortársi feljegyzések Erdély múltjából. Szamosközy István történetíró kézirata* [Contemporary historic notes in the Hungarian language from the Transylvanian past. István Számosközy's historical manuscript] (Budapest: Magyar Nyelvtudományi Társaság, 1991) 158.
75 MOE, XI, 157–159.
76 "Supplicatio Regni Ungariae," in Gábor Kazinczy, ed., *Gr. Illésházy István Nádor följegyzései 1592-1603. és Hidvégi Mikó Ferencz históriája 1594-1613. Bíró Sámuel folytatásával* [Notes by Count Palatine István Illésházy 1592–1603 and the history of Mikó Ferencz Hidvégi 1594–1613. With the sequel of Sámuel Bíró] (Pest: F. Eggenberger, 1863) 120–129.

duties, that divine providence stands beside You, and that Your Majesty has evinced such sympathy towards Your Hungarian subjects as toward no other people in Your empire.[77]

According to Naprágyi, the power of the king was not limitless since it depended on the assent of his subjects. The bishop opined that the Hungarians obeyed their king because it had been with their consent that he had been crowned "…with the angelic crown of St István…". In his view, royal power was dependent on whether or not the king kept the promises which he had made at his coronation. In Naprágyi's thinking, the crown was the symbol of the legitimacy implemented in the coronation through the acclamation. When the king broke his promises and abused his power, he then at once forfeited his power in the eyes of his Hungarian subjects. Naprágyi's speech was regarded by his contemporaries as a significant piece of work, and for that reason it is to be found in many and varied contemporary political and historical anthologies of the day.[78]

On the basis of sources from the period 1600–1603, the following development in the significance of the crown and of national self-awareness of the Hungarian Estates may be observed. Illésházy used the expression *corona regni Hungariae* in a strictly legal sense, as a reference to the laws of the land that limited the power of the king. In their politically slanted writings Pázmány and Naprágyi speak of the material crown of St István and clothe it with supernatural significance. For Berger, the crown denotes the divine mission of the Hungarian race, which justifies the rightfulness of their political demands from the king. These meanings of the crown display the start of a development in the course of which not only the abstract legal expression *corona* but the closely defined interpretation of the crown and the Hungarian Estates too serve as justification of the political ideas of the Estates which conflict with royal power.

---

77 "… *Quid est cur non debeant Maiestatem Vestram eo, quo filii parentem pientissimum* (!), *amore prosequi? quando ab eo solo tempore, quo anno 1572 omnium Ordinum ejus Regni fausta acclamatione, corona S. Stephani Regis angelica augusto Maiestatis Vestrae capiti imposita fuit, nihil in ea praeter virtutes heroicas, singularem curam, diligentiam in rebus agendis assiduam, providentiam plane caelestem, et in gentem Hungaricam praeter alias, quas imperio suo subjectas habet, propensionem animadverterint.*" "Habita coram caesare in audientia 15. Aprilis per Hungariae Legatos, Reverendissimos et Magnificos Dominos Demetrium Nápragy Episcopum Transylvaniae, Joannem Joo, et Petrum Révay, Anno Dni 1603," in *ibid.*, 114–120.
78 *Ibid.* (Written by Illésházy), ÖNB, Cod. 8464, fol. 183r. (Written by Berger), MOL I 7, Vol. 34, fol. 61r.

IV. The Bocskai Rebellion (1604–1606)

The cause of the rebellion

The outcome of the lasting political tension between the Habsburg king and the Estates in Hungary after 1600 was a rebellion that broke out in 1604. This turmoil was the first significant uprising against Habsburg authority in the kingdom. Its military and political course led to a change in ideas and notions in Hungary about the king, the Estates and the crown, which was expressed by a change in symbols and rituals relating to Habsburg rule, the kingdom and the crown.

The preceding period was mainly characterised by the extinction of respect for the Habsburg king because of decisions taken to the detriment of the Estates. As is plain from his reaction to the petition and speech of 9 May 1603, the king repudiated the open criticism of his rule and Naprágyi's admonitions as to the legitimacy of his power.[1] As for the lack of involvement in the affairs of the country, Rudolf writes that as the Hungarian Lords of the Council were a long way off he was obliged to take decisions without them, and the question of royal power was not open for discussion. The awkward situation that had prompted the Estates' petition therefore remained unaltered. The court ultimately overruled the resolutions of the National Assembly. The king hastened the end of the Illésházy case, caused Miklós Istvánffy, president of the judicial college, to falsify the verdict, and gave orders for the arrest of Illésházy.[2] He summoned Illésházy to Prague to give a personal account of his injuries to his emperor.[3] Illésházy thereupon fled into Poland, having – probably – been warned of Rudolf's true intentions by Archduke Matthias.[4] After that Illésházy's estates were expropriated and further lawsuits instituted against other aristocrats.

The immediate cause of the rebellion was the dissatisfaction in Hungary (tax reforms, unpaid salaries of the mercenaries, religious affairs, expropriation of lands) incited by the king's misuse of power.[5] The conflict was triggered by the threat to

---

1 MOE, X, 327–329.
2 Károlyi, *Illésházy*, 87–90.
3 Published in: Sándor Szilágyi, "Három uralkodoi levélke [Three tiny letters of rulers]," *Történelmi tár* 2 (1879) 389.
4 Károlyi, *Illésházy*, 117.
5 Zoltán Angyal, *Rudolfs II. ungarische Regierung; Ursachen, Verlauf und Ergebnis des Aufstandes Bocskai* (Budapest: Athenaeum, 1916); Géza Lencz, *Der Aufstand Bocskays und der Wiener Friede* (Debreczen: Hegedüs und Sándor, 1917); Kálmán Benda, *Bocskai István* [István Bocskai] (Budapest: Művelt Nép, 1955); László Nagy, *A Bocskai-szabadságharc katonai története* [The military history of the Bocskai

István Bocskai (1557–1606) of having his lands too expropriated; he was a Transylvanian aristocrat at Rudolf's court and a councillor of the prince of Transylvania. Bocskai sought the support of the Hajdús and with their aid resisted the king's forces. Following this he united Rudolf's dissatisfied subjects from a wide range of ethnic, religious and social backgrounds in a rebellion against the king. Surprise attacks took a large part of the Kingdom of Hungary from the king's troops, which constituted the success of the first rebellion of the Hungarian Estates against Habsburg power.

The Bocskai rebellion brought about a profound change in Central Europe, as it was the first test of armed strength between the Estates and the possessor of royal power in the Habsburg realm.[6] The conflict began in 1604 and brought the Habsburg Empire and the Estates to a crisis; it seemed only to be settled with the establishment of the *Confederatio Bohemica* in 1619.[7] The most important feature of this crisis was that the leading figures in the Estates' rebellion sought potential supporters and allies both at home and abroad.[8] Alliances and other links went beyond the lines of religion, legal differences and national boundaries. In order that the grounds for these bonds might be made acceptable new political ideas and concepts had to be formulated, and as a result the image of the Hungarian Estates changed, as did the legitimating significance of the crown.

From the outset Bocskai gathered about him a court to lead the rebellion against Rudolf. The political aim of the opposition was to reach agreement with the Habsburg emperor that would also be favourable to the Hungarian Estates.[9] Accordingly, the court was organised so as to enable this purpose to be attained as effectively as

---

rebellion] (Budapest: Akadémiai Kiadó, 1961); László Makkai, "A Bocskai-felkelés [The Bocskai rebellion]," in Zsigmond Pál Pach and Ágnes R. Várkonyi, eds., *Magyarország története 1526–1686* [History of Hungary 1526–1686], vol. I (Budapest: Akadémiai Kiadó, 1987) 709–775; Gábor Barta, "Az Erdélyi Fejedelemség első korszaka [The first period of the Transylvanian principality] (1526–1606)," in Béla Köpeczi, ed., *Erdély története* [History of Transylvania], vol. I (Budapest: Akadémiai Kiadó, 1987) 532–537; Sándor Papp, Török szövetség - Habsburg kiegyezés. A Bocskai-felkelés történetéhez [Turkish Confederation - Habsburg Compromise. On the history of the Bocskai uprising] (Budapest: Károli Gáspár Református Egyetem - L'Harmattan, 2014) 41–99.

6 Gottfried Schramm, "Armed Conflicts in East–Central Europe 1604–1620," in Evans and Thomas, *Crown, Church and Estates*, 176–195; Péter László, "*Ius Resistendi* in Hungary," in László Péter and Martyn Rady, eds., *Resistance, Rebellion and Revolution in Hungary and Central Europe: Commemorating 1956* (London: Hungarian Cultural Centre, UCL, 2008) 65; Rady, "Bocskai," 63.

7 Joachim Bahlcke, "Modernization and state-building in an east-central European Estates' system: the example of the Confoederatio Bohemica of 1619," *Parliaments, Estates and Representation*, 17/1(2010) 61–73. DOI: 10.1080/02606755.1997.9627014.

8 Joachim Bahlcke, *Regionalismus und Staatsintegration im Wiederstreit* (München: Oldenbourg, 1994) 310–311.

9 László Nagy, *"Megint fölszánt magyar világ van..." Társadalom és hadsereg a XVII. század első felének Habsburg-ellenes küzdelmeiben* ["It is again an uplifted Hungarian world ..." Society and army in the

possible in a short time. For this reason, the whole household was temporary in nature and had no fixed abode.¹⁰ The most important tasks included the direction of military operations, arranging negotiations with the Habsburg court, building up international relationships, finding financial support, controlling domestic government, convening Diets and obtaining support at home and abroad for Bocskai's policies.

From the point of view of the aspirations behind the political goals of the rebellion it was a fundamental task to undermine Rudolf's authority in Europe. Bocskai's policy was aimed at offering armed support to the nobility against a rightful king from a mighty ruling house, who enjoyed great respect in Europe and had such powerful allies as Spain and the pope.¹¹ This was, furthermore, the first rebellion in Central Europe against the power of the Habsburgs, and was without historical precedent.¹²

Because of its peculiar nature the rebellion cannot be viewed as a local political event being played out in isolation from the rest of Europe.¹³ It could only achieve its desired success if Bocskai was able to know for certain that he had the support of powerful foreign allies. A good third of the activity of his household was therefore directed at convincing Hungary and Europe of the rightfulness of the rebels' cause and of Bocskai's role as leader. The political message of Bocskai and his followers can be traced in correspondence, speeches, proclamations, minutes of Diets, pamphlets,

---

first half of the seventeenth century in the struggle against the Habsburgs] (Budapest: Zrínyi, 1985) 235.
10 István Bitskey, "Bethlen Gábor és a két Rákoczi György irodalompolitikája [The literature politics of Gábor Bethlen and the two György Rákoczi's]," *Magyar Könyvszemle* 102 (1980) 3. On the mobility of the court, see: László Nagy, *Kard és szerelem: török kori históriák* [Sword and love: stories from the Turkish period] (Budapest: Gondolat, 1985) 76–79; Kálmán Benda, "Bocskai István székhely nélküli fejedelmi udvara [The mobile princely court of István Bocskai]," in *Magyar reneszánsz udvari kultúra* [The Hungarian Renaissance court culture], ed. Ágnes R. Várkonyi (Budapest, 1987) 158–165.
11 Wilfried Schulze, "Estates and the Problem of Resistance in Theory and Practice in the Sixteenth and Seventeenth Centuries," in Evans and Thomas, *Crown, Church and Estates*, 171.
12 Bahlcke, *Regionalismus*, 310.
13 Ágnes R. Várkonyi, "A Bocskai-szabadságharc nemzetközi háttere (Európai jelenlét és a magyar történelmi távlat) [The international background of the Bocskai freedom war (European presence and the Hungarian historical perspective)]," in Klára Papp and Annamária Tóth-Jeney, eds.,*"Frigy és békesség legyen..." A Bécsi és a Zsitvatoroki béke* ["Let there be joy and peace..." The Peace of Vienna and Zsitvatorok] (Debrecen: Debreceni Egyetemi Történelmi Intézet, 2006) 21; Kees Teszelszky, "Üzenet az utazótáskában. Diplomáciai kapcsolatok Németalföld és Magyarország között a Bocskai-felkelés alatt [Message in a trunk. Diplomatic relations between The Netherland and Hungary during the Bocskai Uprising]," in Nóra G. Etényi and Ildikó Horn, eds., *Portré és imázs. Politikai propaganda és reprezentáció a kora újkorban* [Portrait and image. Political propaganda in the Early Modern period] (Budapest: L'Harmattan, 2008) 127–147.

soldiers' songs, pictures and ceremonies.[14] The writings and pictures met with a favourable reception in parts of Europe, and evoked a counter-blast from the Habsburg court.[15]

Bocskai's court in Hungary

The propaganda campaign against the king was conducted by a group of court politicians (*familiares Aulae Botschkai*, as Bocatius calls them) in 1605.[16] The members of the group were all humanists and occupied places at the top of the cultural élite in Hungary, though their positions with regard to religious, ethnic and social factors were varied. Some of them, like Bocskai, belonged to the Habsburg court. Within the group the most respected strategist and theoretician was the Catholic aristocrat Mihály Káthay (?-1607), who filled the office of chancellor to Bocskai. The humanist János Rimay (1569/1573-1631) played an important political and intellectual part.[17] Bocatius functioned as emissary and court historian, and also wrote on political subjects, as did János Szappanos Debreceni and István Szamosközi.[18] The Calvinist minister Péter Alvinczi also belonged to Bocskai's court. In addition, there were a number of secretaries in Bocskai's service such as the humanist Simon

---

14 Katalin Péter, *A magyar nyelvű politikai publicisztika kezdetei* [The beginnings of the Hungarian language political criticism] (Budapest: Akadémiai Kiadó, 1973) 5-7; Nóra G. Etényi, "A Bocskai-szabadságharc európai propagandája [The European propaganda of the Bocskai rebellion]," *Confessio* 3(2006) 24-34.

15 For Bocskai's connections with the Dutch envoy Brederode see: Teszelszky, "Üzenet," 127-147; Kees Teszelszky, *True Religion: a lost portrait by Albert Szenci Molnár (1606) or Dutch-Flemish-Hungarian intellectual relations in the early-modern period* (Budapest: ELTE BTK Középkori és Kora Újkori Magyar Történeti Tanszéke and the Transylvania Emlékeiért Tudományos Egyesület, 2014) 81-183.

16 "Confessiones I [Ultimo mense Augusto 1606]" in Ioannes Bocatius [János Bocatius], *Opera Quae Extant Omnia: Prosaica*, ed. Franciscus Csonka (Bibliotheca Scriptorum Medii Recentisque Aevorum, n.s. 12) (Budapest: Akadémiai Kiadó, 1992) 161. We learn this from Bocatius, who divulged all sort of things about members of the Bocskai court and their activity, both in the course of his interrogations while a prisoner in 1606 and in his memoirs. See also: *Ibid.*, 236.

17 Rimay wrote a chronicle of the rebellion, now unfortunately lost. See: Géza Szentmártoni Szabó, "Balassi Bálint halála [The death of Bálint Balassi]," in János Rimay, *Balassi epicedium*, ed. Pál Ács (Budapest: Balassi Kiadó, 1994) 82.

18 Klaniczay, *A magyar irodalom története*, vol. I, 430-431; István Sinkovics, "Szamosközy István [István Szamosközy]," in István Szamosközy, *Erdélyi története [1598-1599, 1603]* [The history of Transylvania], trans. István Borzsák, ed. István Sinkovics (Budapest: Magyar Helikon, ²1977) 20-23. Unfortunately, Szamosközy did not complete his history, and the most important years of the rebellion are missing from the ms. The importance that Bocskai attached to this work is evident from the fact that in his will he left Szamosközy 2,000 forints for its publication, while he gave Szappanos Debreceni only 200 in gratitude for his. [István Bocskai], Testamentaria dispositio... MOL P 287 Forgách család. Series 1. 34. cs. Fasc. T. 34, fol. 30-31.

Péchy. Illésházy only joined Bocskai in the spring of 1605 and soon became his most important adviser.

It would be wrong to think that because of a strict division of responsibilities at court every political work and the ideas deriving from it can be attributed to a definite author.[19] Bocskai's court has to be regarded as an intellectual workshop in which thoughts that circulated by word of mouth were given expression by various people in a variety of works and styles. It is clear from the correspondence of members of the court and from the registers of Bocatius' interrogation and his confession after imprisonment that these intellectual products came about more or less as joint works.

Numerous examples of the way in which the court functioned can be found in Bocatius' writings. For example, he writes concerning certain letters titled *Litterae sigillatae ad Electores Imperii* that Illésházy and his secretary had drafted them, and that the final version had been written by Rimay. Bocatius had then carried these letters to the German princes in December 1605.[20] On Bocskai's instructions Bocatius reworked one of Rimay's writings so that it could be used in verse form on a monument.[21] In one of his letters to Bocskai himself, Illésházy advises him on how to write his (political) testament, which the prince later dictated to his secretary Simon Péchy in the presence of Alvinczi and his adviser Pál Örvéndy.[22] From these and other examples it may be deduced that works on the significance of the crown too were produced in a similar interactive manner.

With regard to the connection between the change in the significance of the crown and the functioning of the court it is important to consider the theory by which Bocskai's policy was legitimated.[23] The substance of the question is whether

---

19 See *inter alia* the debate on the *Querelae* in: László Nagy, "Ki volt a szerzője a szabadságért fegyvert fogott magyar rendek Európához intézett kiáltványának? [Who was the author of the declaration to Europe by the Hungarian estates who took up arms for freedom?]," in Béla Varjas, ed., *Irodalom és ideológia a 16–17. században* [Literature and ideology in the sixteenth and seventeenth century] (Budapest: Akadémiai Kiadó, 1987) 175–187.
20 ÖStA Wien, HHStA, Ungarische Akten, Fasc. 433.
21 "Responsoria" and "Confessiones," in Bocatius, *Opera Quae Extant Omnia: Prosaica*, 224, 227, 236–237. The ms of the verse can be found under ÖStA Wien, HHStA Ungarische Akten, Fasc. 149 C, fol. 49r. It should be noted that on release from prison Bocatius offered Rudolf that he would prepare a pamphlet against Bocskai. *Ibid.*, 237.
22 Illésházy's letter to Bocskai, 23 August 1606, Szepesvár, published in József Jankovics, ed., *Literátor-politikusok levelei Jenei Ferenc gyűjtéséből (1566–1623)* [Letters of writers and politicians from the collection of Ferenc Jenei (1566–1623)] (Budapest – Szeged: JATE, 1981) 38–40.
23 Ferenc Eckhart, "Bocskai és hiveinek közjogi felfogása [The concept of public law of Bocskai and his adherents]," in *Emlékkönyv Károlyi Árpád születése nyolcvanadik fordulójának ünnepére* [Book of remembrance to celebrate the eightieth anniversary of the birth of Árpád Károlyi], ed. Sándor Domanovszky (Budapest: Sárkány Nyomda, 1933) 133–141; Eckhart, *A Szentkorona-eszme*, 146–151; Eckhart, *Magyar alkotmány- és jogtörténet*, 35; Kálmán Benda, "Habsburg-politika és rendi ellenállás

Bocskai and his followers took Werbőczy's work as grounds for the justification of the rebellion against the rightful emperor, or whether they made use of Calvin's ideas. According to Eckhart the former was the case, while Benda is convinced that the latter was equally possible. Benda had to tackle the problem that although the Catholic Káthay was the most significant theoretician of the rebellion there were also Lutherans and Calvinists in the court, and Bocskai called himself a Calvinist. Benda solved the problem by stating that Bocskai took his political theory from Werbőczy, and his Calvinist ideas reinforced this, as a result of which the rebellion found support in all social circles.[24]

It may be asked whether the rebellion, in which Bocskai appears in the role of a ruler sent from God and standing for the true Calvinist faith, may be viewed as a war of religion against the Catholic king. In a number of works the leader of the rebellion is portrayed as precisely that. This image, however, is insufficiently refined, as it is not in keeping with the previously outlined political aims of the rebellion. For the attainment of their goals Bocskai's court politicians had to win over a very wide public both at home and abroad. An excessively Calvinist message would have offered the emperor's theoreticians far too easy a target and would have aroused unease abroad.[25] Furthermore, dissatisfaction with the Habsburg emperor's policies was widespread among Protestant and Catholic subjects alike.

[The Habsburg politics and Estate resistance]," *Történelmi Szemle* 13/3 (1970) 420–426; Kálmán Benda, "A kálvini tanok hatása a magyar rendi ellenállás ideológiájára [The influence of Calvinist ideas on the resistance ideology of the Hungarian Estates]," *Helikon* 17 (1971) 322–329; Kálmán Benda, "Le droit de résistance de la bulle d'or hongroise et le Calvinisme," in Béla Köpeczi and Éva H. Balázs, eds., *Noblesse française, noblesse hongroise: XVIe-XIXe siècles* (Budapest: Akadémiai Kiadó, Paris: Éditions du CNRS, 1981) 155–161. Gyula Gábor has researched the connection between Bocskai's title and the legitimation of his power, see: Gyula Gábor, *A kormányzói méltóság a magyar alkotmányjogban* [The governor's dignity in Hungarian constitutional law] (Budapest: Athenaeum, 1931) 151–159; Benedek Varga, "Szempontok a Bocskai-felkelés ideológiájának európai kontextusához [View points on the European context of the ideology of the Bocskai Rebellion]," *Studia Caroliensa* 1 (2006) 29–41; Martyn Rady, "Bocskai, Rebellion and Resistance in Early Modern Hungary," in László Péter and Martyn Rady, eds., *Resistance, Rebellion and Revolution in Hungary and Central Europe: Commemorating 1956* (London: UCL SSEES, 2008) 57–66; Kees Teszelszky and Márton Zászkaliczky, "A Bocskai-felkelés és az európai információhálózatok: Hírek, diplomácia és politikai propaganda, (1604–1606) [The revolt of Stephan Bocskai and the European information networks: News, diplomacy and political propaganda, 1604–1606]," *Aetas - Történettudományi folyóirat* 27/4 (2012) 149–121; Márton Zászkaliczky, "The language of liberty in Early Modern Hungarian political debate," in Quentin Skinner and Martin van Gelderen, eds., *Freedom and the Construction of Europe*, vol. I (Cambridge, Cambridge University Press, 2013) 274 – 295.

24 Benda, "Habsburg-politika," 425.

25 A pamphlet written in name of Bocskai, published in 1606 and 1608, in which he defended himself against the charge of heresy and served in the defence of Protestantism in Hungary. [István Bocskai], *Apologia et protestatio...* (Bartphae: Jacobus Klös, 1606, ²1608). See also Kálmán Révész, "Bocskai István apológiája [The apology of István Bocskai]," *Protestáns Szemle* 18 (1906) 285–309; Judit P.

In any case, the Calvinist school of thought was too limited in Hungary to serve as a basis for a nationwide community of interest.

It is therefore more likely that in their writings and correspondence the members of Bocskai's household formulated political messages aimed at the specific audience associated with each particular event, and for that purpose made use of such arguments, topics and ideas as had the most convincing effect at the moment in question. It was not so much the source of the thoughts or the persons of their authors that was decisive as to whether they were used or not, but rather the persuasive force of the ideas that helped them attain their political goals. This accounts for the observation that those who served up these ideas were of differing religious and political backgrounds, and yet expressed views which seemed contrary to their own personal religious convictions. In Bocskai's court intellectual workshop, therefore, there must have been an exceptional wealth of topics and ideas concerning the form that the rebellion took.

In the political thinking of the court prime of place was occupied by showing the inhabitants of Hungary as true Christians whose continued existence and independence were menaced by the heretical Austrian tyrant Rudolf. The Hungarian struggle for freedom against the emperor was conducted in the spirit of this contrast, and appeared in numerous different forms in plans linked to the subject. The thinkers of Rudolf's court showed the sympathisers as a part of the Hungarian Estates (*natio* or *gens*) opposed to Rudolf's Austrian people. The Kingdom of Hungary – the fatherland (*patria*) – was depicted as a country which the Ottoman and Habsburg Empires threatened to swallow up.

The concept that interpreted the Hungarian Estates as a *natio* underwent a significant change at the end of the sixteenth century. The beginning of the process is seen in the verse of Bálint Balassi (1554–1594). Balassi influenced Illésházy,[26] Rimay and those in their intellectual entourage, including Káthay, Révay and the brothers Mihály and Imre Forgách. This circle formed a complete cultus around the person of Balassi, who was killed at the siege of Esztergom in 1594.[27] His character and death were what inspired the numerous poems by Rimay and Káthay which Rimay gathered into a memorial volume.[28] In these poems an idealised portrait is painted of Balassi: he is shown as a tragic Christian knight and wordsmith who

---

Vásárhelyi, *Eszmei áramlatok és politika Szenci Molnár Albert életművében* [Lines of thought and politics in the life work of Albert Szenci Molnár] (Budapest: Akadémiai Kiadó, 1985) 17–20.

26 For the connection between Balassi and Illésházy see: Sándor Eckhardt, "Balassi Bálint utóélete [The reception of Bálint Balassi]," *Irodalomtörténeti közlemények* 72/4(1955) 421–427.
27 Klaniczay, *A magyar irodalom története*, vol. I, 448–481 and *idem*, vol. II, 18–21.
28 János Rimay, *Balassi epicedium*, ed. Pál Ács (Budapest: Balassi Kiadó, 1994).

sacrificed himself for Christendom on the field of battle.²⁹ According to Tibor Klaniczay, the Balassi-cultus bolstered the self-confidence of Hungarian nobles like Rimay, and at the same time may be regarded as a source of inspiration for the political thinking about Hungarian society that took place at the time of the rebellion.³⁰

In addition to the changes that ensued in the thinking about the Hungarian Estates, it may also be observed that Hungarian came to be used more and more often instead of Latin. Numerous tracts on the condition of Hungary and other works on national topics were written in the national language. At the end of the sixteenth century – and especially at the time of the rebellion – use of the term *magyar nemzet* (Hungarian nation) became more and more frequent in political literature and correspondence.³¹ Other political terms, on the other hand – such as *regnum* and *corona* – were not translated into Hungarian.

As a consequence of these changes, poetry on national subjects came into being.³² This genre grew up in the intellectual environment that formed around Bocskai. Rimay wrote one of the first such poems, which marked the start of a new poetic tradition in Hungary, full of grief for the loss of *haza* (fatherland) and *nemzet* (nation).³³ These poems in the Hungarian language were an important medium for the spread of the new political ideas.

During the rebellion the concepts *nemzet* or *natio*, used in the sense of the Hungarian Estates, served as a starting-point for political thought. The function of this imagery was to justify the rightfulness of rebellion against the emperor. Bocskai and his followers formed their ideas on the account of the concept of *natio* to be found in Werbőczy's book of laws. In their view the rightfulness of the rebellion of the *natio* gained justification because the emperor had pursued lawless policies

---

29 Tibor Klaniczay, *Reneszánsz és Barokk (tanulmányok a régi magyar irodalomról)* [Renaissance and Baroque (Studies on the ancient Hungarian literature)] (Budapest, Szépirodalmi Könyvkiadó, 1961) 293; Klaniczay, *A magyar irodalom története*, vol. I, 459–461; István Bitskey, "A vitézség eszményének változatai a XVI-XVII. század fordulójának a magyar irodalmában [The changes of the idea on heroness on the border between the sixteenth and seventeenth century]," in Tivadar Pétercsak, ed., *Hagyomány és korszerűség a XVI-XVII. században* [Tradition and actuality in the sixteenth and seventeenth century] (Eger: Eger Heves Megyei Múzeumi Szervezet, 1997) 203–212.

30 Tibor Klaniczay, *Stílus, nemzet és civilizáció* [Style, nation and civilisation], Gábor Klaniczay and Péter Kőszeghy, eds., (Budapest: Balassi Kiadó, 2001) 44–45; Bitskey, "A vitézség," 212.

31 Klaniczay, *A magyar irodalom*, vol. II, 21–23; Sándor Eckhart, ed., *Rimay János összes művei* [All the works of János Rimay] (Budapest, 1955) 200.

32 Klaniczay, *A magyar irodalom*, vol. II, 96.

33 János Rimay, "Kiben kesereg a Magyar nemzetnek romlássán, s fogyássán [In which he laments the decay and decrease of the Hungarian nation]," in Eckhart, *Rimay János összes művei*, 83–84.

to the detriment of his subjects.³⁴ In a number of letters Bocskai accounts for the outbreak of the rebellion as the consequence of Rudolf's rule, which was proving fatal to the Hungarian *nemzet* and *haza*.³⁵ The prince and his followers interpreted the content of Werbőczy's *natio*-concept more broadly by counting other groups in Hungarian public life as belonging to the Estates. In this way the greatest possible political support for opposition to the emperor could be mobilised. The change of the image of the Hungarians and the formation of the concept of the Estates were the result of this development.

The body of the crown and the free towns of Hungary

The change in meaning of the concept of the Estates began in the spring of 1604 with a Catholic reform in Hungary; this is regarded as the cause of the outbreak of the Bocskai rebellion – or rather, such it was declared by the rebels and their followers.³⁶ At the same time as anti-Protestant regulations were brought in, a debate was taking place over whether the citizens of the royal free towns had the right to freedom of religion. In the theoretical political background of the conflict was the question of what political and religious rights accompanied the status of royal free town in the possession of the crown.³⁷ In time, the debate became centred on whether the citizens of the royal free towns enjoyed the same freedom in the practice of religion as did the Hungarian Estates, or whether the king might compel them to convert back to Catholicism. The towns found the answer by referring to their status as property of the crown to validate their political and religious demands.³⁸

---

34 Bocatius gave a summary of this in: "Olympias Carceraria," in Bocatius, *Opera Quae Extant Omnia: Prosaica*, 125.

35 Bocskai's letter to Illésházy from Kassa, 16 June 1605. Partly published in: Pál Jászay, "A' magyar nyelv' történetének vázlata [Sketch of the history of the Hungarian language]," in *A' magyar tudós társaság' évkönyvei* [The year books of the Hungarian academic society], vol. VI (Buda: a Magyar királyi egyetem, 1845) 279–280. On the same day Bocskai wrote to Miklós Istvánffy and the Thurzó brothers for a similar purpose. See: Eckhart, *Rimay,* 199–200; Andrea Molnár, *Fürst Stefan Bocskai als Staatsmann und Persönlichkeit im Spiegel seiner Briefe 1598–1606* (München: Trofenik, 1983) 129–130.

36 See: *Warhafftige Newe Zeitung/ Wie und was massen sich des Sigissmundi Bathori Mutterbruder Steffan Botschkai genandt/ gegen unserm Christlichen Keyser/ sampt den Deutschen Kriegsvolck/ Trewlos und Meineydig verhalten/ dem Türcken gehuldet unnd sich ihm untergeben* (Prag: Nickel Strau, 1605). See also: István H. Németh, *Várospolitika és gazdaságpolitika a 16–17. századi Magyarországon* [City politics and economical politics in sixteenth and seventeenth century Hungary] vol. I. (Budapest: Gondolat, 2004) 109–112.

37 Eckhart, *A szentkorona-eszme*, 139.

38 Németh, *Várospolitika*, vol. I., 496–498.

Eckhart was of the opinion that one of the first uses of the theory of the crown derived from Werbőczy's book of law could be detected in the arguments adduced in the debate.[39] He bases this statement on those passages in which the royal free towns – with reference to their status as property of the crown – are referred to as parts of the body of the country (*membra regni*) or simply of the Holy Crown (*membra sacrae coronae*).[40] According to him, in these places we are confronted with an interpretation of Werbőczy's organic common-law concept (the Doctrine of the Holy Crown) that applies to the royal free towns.[41] Eckhart explains the meaning of terms quoted as follows: since the authors regard the royal free towns as limbs of the body of the crown while the nobility possess their rights on the same basis, the citizens of the towns enjoy the same rights as do the nobility. From this it follows that the royal free towns, as nobility, enjoy religious freedom as do the nobility.[42]

By this interpretation of Eckhart's the above seventeenth century references are fundamental to the development of the legitimating significance of the Hungarian crown. János Bak and László Péter regard the Doctrine of the Holy Crown as a nineteenth century invented artificial tradition. In contrast, according to Eckhart there was a process of development – leading from the sixteenth century book of laws to the political idea of the nineteenth century – one point of which was the interpretation in 1604 of the royal free towns as part of the body of the crown. If Eckhart is right, we may certainly speak of the use of the Doctrine of the Holy Crown as early as the start of the seventeenth century, but in that case this doctrine is no invented artificial tradition and there may be a question here of a living tradition.

Neither Péter nor Bak refer in their work to the debate in the Early Modern period on the political significance of the crown, and furthermore both of them fail to consider Eckhart's analysis; we cannot therefore expect an answer to this question from them. In addition, they have never examined Eckhart's idea critically but have put it forward again and again as a historical extension of the Doctrine of the Holy Crown or evidence of the use of the theory in the seventeenth century.[43] This is why in the following section we shall consider the passages referring to the crown in such a way as to link them to their time in political terms.

---

39 *Ibid.*, 150; Eckhart, "Bocskai és hiveinek," 141.
40 Eckhart, *A szentkorona*-eszme, 140–141, 150–151.
41 *Ibid.*, 151.
42 *Ibid.*
43 Benda, "Habsburg-politika," 418; Gábor Nagy, ed., *Magyar história 1526–1608: forrásgyűjtemény* [Hungarian history 1526–1608. Collection of sources] (Debrecen: Tóth Könyvkereskedés és Kiadó, 1998) 409, note 855; Bahlcke, *Regionalismus*, 311; Thomas Winkelbauer, ed., *Österreichische Geschichte, Ständefreiheit und Fürstenmacht: Länder und Untertanen des Hauses Habsburg*, vol. I (Wien: Ueberreuter, 2003) 146–147.

In the debate over whether the citizens of the royal free towns might enjoy the same right of freedom of exercise of religion as the nobility, three arguments were used that were framed in metaphors of legal and political content. The first argument in favour of the citizens was that the towns were not dependent on the king since they were property of the crown, which the towns depicted metaphorically as part of the body of the country or part of the body of the crown. The second argument against the citizens free practice of religion said that there was no place in the country for Protestants. This was advanced by the use of the organic metaphor of the country. The third argument – also against the citizens – was derived from the idea that the towns were property of the kin', so that it was within the king's rights and power to decide which religion the citizens should follow. The interaction of the arguments and images led to some regrettable formulations, and it was on the basis of these that Eckhart developed his concept of the continuity of the Doctrine of the Holy Crown.

The first argument was applied in a petition of the Protestant Estates to Archduke Matthias as governor of Hungary.[44] The petition, with which the debate over the free exercise of religion by the royal free towns began, was presented in April 1604 on the occasion of the Diet in Pozsony. On the grounds that the towns were the "property of the Hungarian crown" (*peculium Regni Coronae*), the Estates requested that free exercise of religion be maintained in the royal free towns too.[45] Since the towns were the property of the Hungarian crown, the petitioners considered that they constituted one body together with the other Estates of the Kingdom of Hungary: "… *nobisque incorporatae sunt*…".[46] And as the other Hungarian Estates enjoyed freedom of religion, the citizens, because of the status of their towns, constituted part of the country (*regnum*) and therefore possessed the same freedom as the nobility. In this document the term *membrum* does not occur.

In the response to the proposal of the Protestant Estates, addressed on 6 April 1604 to the Archduke Matthias, the Catholic members of the Hungarian royal council applied the second argument.[47] By making use in the document of the organic metaphor of the country, the authors describe Hungary as a Catholic country on the basis of the shared conviction of the king and the Estates. The function of this metaphor was to give the impression that the Catholic faith was naturally and inseparably linked to the history of Hungary and to the structure and

---

44 "Ordinum et statuum Regni Hungariae pars," in MOE, vol. X, 510–512.
45 *Ibid.*, 511.
46 *Ibid.*
47 "A magyar királyi tanács katholikus tagjainak véleménye a protestáns rendek vallás-sérelmi föliratai, illetőleg folyamodásai ügyében [The opinions of the catholic members of the Hungarian Royal Council on the Protestant Estates' religious contempts and appeals]," in MOE, vol. X, 519.

character of the Hungarian Estates. Contrary to what the Protestant Estates had stated, the Protestants were not members of this class – said the council.

In the document the second argument was formulated as follows. The council declared that Hungary was a community consisting of a head and limbs, where the king was the head and the subjects the "limbs" (*membra*).[48] They quoted Werbőczy's book of laws and called the king apostolic (*Apostolus*). For this style he had his forebears, the saintly kings, to thank – said the authors.[49] The limbs are formed by the "high clergy, barons and magnates" (*Praelati Barones et Magnates*), who were all scions of notable Catholic families.

The political aim of this organic image of a Catholic country was to persuade the Habsburg power to deprive the Protestants of their rights because, as faithless and "erroneous heretics" (*etnici heresiarchae*), they constituted a foreign body in the Hungarian nation. As, however, the Hungarian Estates were fundamentally Catholic the members of the council considered it impossible for this community also to have Protestant members. Therefore, in their view the king, on the basis of his Catholic royal power, had the right to restore Church lands and consequently Church buildings also to their former owner, the Catholic Church.[50] The authors also gave historical legitimacy to this proposal by referring to sundry statutes prescribing the persecution of heretics from the Medieval legal history of Hungary.[51]

Rudolf employed the third argument when in January 1604 he decided (as had been done in Austrian towns) to confiscate Lutheran churches and schools in the royal free towns in Upper Hungary and ban their ministers from the towns.[52] He did this, to the advantage of the Catholic Church, on the grounds that the royal free towns were "the property of the king and the Holy Crown".[53] The term "property of the crown" (*peculium coronae*) originally referred to those of the king's estates that he could not grant.[54] In this context, however, Rudolf used this term as an argument to justify his disposing at will of his own property.

At the Diet in Gálszécs on 26 September 1604 this argument of the king's was discussed in detail, as we are informed by an eye-witness.[55] At the Assembly the

---

48 "A magyar királyi tanács katholikus tagjainak véleménye" 521–522.
49 *Ibid.*, see: *Tripartitum*, Part. I, Tit. 11.
50 "A magyar királyi tanács katholikus tagjainak véleménye" 521–522.
51 *Ibid.*, 520.
52 See: Bocatius, *Opera Quae Extant Omnia: Prosaica*, 508–518, ÖStA Wien, HHStA, Ungarn. Hungarica Fasc. 433. Miscellanea Konv. E. Die Angelegenheit der Kasschauer Kirche betr. Akten aus den "Hungarica" Okt. 1603 -Sept. 1604, fol. 1–73.
53 *Corpus Juris Hungarici*, 940–9 57.
54 Eckhart, *A szentkorona-eszme*, 139.
55 "A Gálszécsi gyűlésből Belgiojosohoz küldött biztottsága egyik tagjanak tudosítása e bizottságnak Belgiojosoval folytatott tárgyalások [Report on the negotiations with Belgiojoso of a member of the commission sent from the meeting in Gálszécs to Belgiojoso]," in: MOE X 596. The report is in

Protestant Estates protested at the king's behaviour. On this occasion Count Giacomo Barbiana Belgiojoso, Captain of Upper Hungary, held talks with the dissatisfied Estates: he had been charged with implementing the king's decision. In the king's name he ruled that in the Habsburg Empire the principle of *cujus regio, ejus religio* (the religion is his who holds the region, the right of patronage) held good. This meant that the owner of land decided what religion the serfs living on it should follow. As the royal free towns were in the possession of the king – said Belgiojoso – the king might decide at will about his own property like any other landowner. From this it followed that the king might decide to whom the churches in his towns were to be granted, and which clergy he would employ. In Belgiojoso's view the king had the right to restore the Protestant church in Kassa to the Catholics, and that any that opposed this committed lèse-majesté.

The Protestant Hungarian Estates replied to this threat by stating that they were independent of the king, free Hungarian subjects, and belonged to the community of the Estates. This statement they justified by saying that in their view the organic metaphor of the country had been confused with the device of the towns being property of the crown. In order to gain a full understanding of this line of thought we must analyse the Estates' reasoning step by step. According to the reporter, the Estates replied to the king's agent that there was a basic difference between serfs and royal free towns. Serfs were their owners' property and did not own land. They defined the legal position of the towns and came to the essence of the matter by declaring:

> They are called free towns because their freedom is equal to the lords' and ours [sic], liberty is one, *non sunt peculium regis, sed peculium coronae; coronae regni, membra regni* [They are not property of the king, but property of the crown; the crown of the kingdom, the parts of the kingdom] . . .[56]

The Estates' political message sounded as if the towns were owned not by the king but by the crown, and thus must be comparable to the Estates in terms of freedom of religious practice. In their view, it could be deduced from the situation of the towns that not only were they independent of the king but furthermore the same freedom applied to them as to the "lords", by which the delegates understood the nobility of Hungary and their political and religious rights. This identity they presented by the use of a metaphor taken from building and an organic one: the towns as the pillars of the country (*regnum*) and as parts of the body of the country (*regnum*). Both

---

narrative form, in a mixture of Latin and Hungarian. We give the technical terms in the original language.
56 *Ibid.*, 597.

metaphors served to persuade the listener that as pillars and parts of the body of the country, the towns belonged to the community of the Hungarian Estates, and therefore had equal rights with the Estates.

It therefore seems that in formulating the link between the property of the crown and liberties the Estates were inspired by the familiar fourth paragraph of the first part of Werbőczy's book of laws, on which the nineteenth century Doctrine of the Holy Crown too is based.[57] In this section the sixteenth century lawyer also explains and justifies the Hungarian nobility's thesis concerning "one and the same liberty", that the nobility are all equal in every respect as they all share in the property of the crown in the form of grants of land. Through this, the nobility are "members of the Holy Crown" (*membra sacrae coronae*) and all of them have such political liberties. In respect of the reasoning based on the idea of crown lands, the text formulated in 1604 departs from the book of laws. In Werbőczy, the granting of crown lands to nobles serves as justification for the thesis of the identical political rights of the nobility.

The Protestant Estates rather reasoned further that, as the towns were in the possession of the crown, they enjoyed the same freedom as the nobility. By this they made the concepts receive crown lands and be in the possession of the crown of the country identical in meaning: freedom was the consequence of both, since the nobility gained independence from the king just as the towns did as a result of this status. This appears to be a contradictory explanation, because the crown lands ultimately belonged to the king, as he himself stated in the argument repeated above. This could also be based on the fact that in the Austrian territories the archducal towns belonged to the *Camera* lands (*Kammergut*), which were under the jurisdiction of the emperor and the *Camera*, the financial organs.[58] Eckhart explains this contradiction, saying that it means that "… the Estates went further than the theory formulated in Werbőczy's book of laws …"[59]

However, Werbőczy did not take into account the royal free towns, nor do they feature in his summary of inhabitants of the country that enjoyed political freedom. This is why Eckhart states that the Estates interpreted the Doctrine of the Holy Crown as it applied to the towns, and so were able to make it appear that the towns enjoyed the same political rights as the rest of the Estates.[60] In his opinion, a new approach to the Doctrine of the Holy Crown may be observed in this politically charged seventeenth century document.

The question is whether Eckhart's explanation really equates with the Estates' political views. From the account it is clear that the Estates intended to make the

---

57 *Tripartitum*, Partis I, Tit. 4.
58 Németh, *Várospolitika*, vol. I. 266.
59 Eckhart, *A szentkorona-eszme*, 151.
60 *Ibid.*, 140.

point that the citizens of the towns could not be treated in the same way as serfs, with their restricted freedom, as the citizens enjoyed the same religious freedom as the nobility because the towns were in the possession of the crown. The delegates upheld with detailed reasoning the assertion that the towns enjoyed the same political rights as the nobility:

> His Majesty summons them likewise to the National Assembly *peculiaribus literis*, as he does prelates, other lords and counties etc. They have a free vote, equal in weight with those of other status. *Tempore electionis regis* [At the time of the election of the king] too they are of equal standing with the other Estates.[61]

The Protestants reasoned, by analogy with the possession of political rights, that the towns enjoyed the same religious freedom as the other Hungarian Estates, and that in terms of freedom of religious practice their "being in the possession of the crown" meant the same as "enjoyment of crown lands" did for an individual. According to the Estates, this opinion concerning the concept of being in the possession of the crown justified the townspeople's free practice of religion in opposition to the king. Therefore the Estates once again advanced the organic metaphor when explaining before Belgiojoso why they took the part of the towns and why they objected to the king's decision: "Seeing this affair that has befallen the towns, they are in sympathy with them, deplore their case, saying that they are members of us, we cannot desert them . . ."[62] The delegates made use of the organic metaphor to illustrate that the Protestant towns too were parts of the political body of the country.[63]

This is the first time that the towns of Hungary appear on the scene as parts of the body of the country, because this expression does not occur in the Middle Ages.[64] The protestors fortify this device by the declaration that the other Estates would not tolerate "…that anyone should injure this part of the body, because it would injure them too and cause them too pain." The concept of the crown and the organic image of the Hungarian Estates are kept distinct: the towns are parts of the body of the country, although the Estates do not name them as belonging to the body of the crown.

---

61 MOE, X, 597.
62 *Ibid.*
63 Kálmán Benda, "Az országgyűlések az újkori magyar fejlődésben [The Diets in the Early Modern Hungarian development]," in Kálmán Benda and Katalin Péter, eds., *Az országgyűlések a kora újkori magyar történelemben* [The Diets in the earlymodern Hungarian history] (Budapest: MTA Történettudományi Intézet: Országos Pedagógiai Intézet, 1987) 9.
64 József Gerics, "Az "ország tagja (membrum regni)" és az "ország része (pars regni)" kifejezés középkori magyarországi használatáról [On the Medieval use in Hungary of the expressions "member of the real, (membrum regni)" and "part of the realm (pars regni)"]," in Rozsondai, *Jubileumi*, 88–89.

As Eckhart states in his work, a year later, in the so-called Szerencs Declaration or *Querelae* – the content of which we shall discuss later in this chapter – the royal free towns are for the first time named as belonging to the body of the crown. *Querelae* argues for the rightfulness of the Hungarians' rebellion against Rudolf. The central theme of the document is that the king has infringed the liberties of the Estates. The term part of the body of the crown appears in the section dealing with the infringement of free religious practice. The authors declare that freedom of religious practice is the supreme freedom that any noble or landowner can enjoy on his estates, and that neither the king nor any prelate may appoint any priest contrary to the wishes of the landowner on his land.[65] After that they say: "... The magnates, nobility, lords and royal free towns as members of the crown of Hungary enjoy this right in freedom and peace..."[66] In this passage the authors call both the royal free towns and the (titled and untitled) nobility part of the body of the crown.

This excerpt from *Querelae* does not impart the Doctrine of the Holy Crown either, but rather may be taken as a summary of the development which ensued in 1604 in the Hungarian Estates' thought about the legitimation of the free practice of religion. The aim of *Querelae* is, once again, only the justification of the free practice of religion by the citizens of the towns. The attainment of this aim is served by the following premise: those that are in the possession of the crown enjoy the same rights as those who are in possession of crown lands. This equation is not so much concerned with political rights as rather with the free practice of religion. The legitimating function of the concept towns as parts of the body of the crown extends, therefore, only to the justification of the right of citizens living in the royal free towns to free practice of religion.

According to László Péter, like the organic metaphor and the significance of the crown used by Werbőczy, the allusion to the Estates as part of the body of the crown may be taken as a special argument devised in the interests of a peculiar political goal – the defence of the right of the royal free towns to free practice of religion. This metaphor occurs only once in the hundreds of documents of legal and religious content published in the seventeenth century, and was used only in connection with religious freedom. According to István H. Németh, the towns used this crown lands argument throughout the seventeenth century, primarily in self-defence.[67] In

---

65 "Querelae, excusationes cum protestatione Regni Hungariae praesertim partium superiorum coram Deo et toto orbe Christiano," in MOE, XI, 175.

66 '(...) *in quorum usu pacifice et libere tam magnates, nobiles et domini, civitatesque liberae, tanquam membra Coronae Hungariae extiterant;* (...)'. Ibid.

67 Németh, *Várospolitika*, vol. 1, 496–498. In August 1608 an assembly of the league of towns was convened in connection with the taxation of the towns. The people of Lőcse had informed the senate in Kassa in advance that they intended to raise their taxes in harmony with the other inhabitants of the country rather than in accordance with a special regulation. The town councillors enquired

the last third of the seventeenth century the government turned this round in its endeavours to centralise, and identified the crown with the king; the description of crown lands was again applied to the towns, however, and this was made identical with the Austrian concept of *Kammergut*.[68]

For this reason, duly noting the defined meaning, special connection and limited use of the concept, it cannot be deduced that there is any question of a coherent notion of the crown as a body politic or of the acceptance of this idea. The Hungarian crown received a new legitimating significance only in this special connection. The Hungarian Estates did not "… go beyond Werbőczy's theory…", as Eckhart stated, but made use of a metaphor similar to Werbőczy's to legitimate another political message. This significance had nothing in common with what has later been read into political writings of the Early Modern period. The re-invented concept of the crown and the Doctrine of the Holy Crown, both of which originated in the nineteenth century, therefore, have no seventeenth century roots.

The exchange of views (see below) that took place between Belgiojoso and the Protestant citizens of Kassa on 27 October 1605 – during the Bocskai rebellion – supports this inference. Belgiojoso was fleeing from Bocskai's forces and would have liked to seek refuge inside the walls of the town. According to the chronicles the townspeople would not let him in and shouted from the walls that they would never have him in their midst again as he was "…the sworn enemy of Hungary and common liberty, and undermined the law of the land…".[69] From this it appears that the essence of the political debate was not the significance of the crown but its interpretation in connection with the societal freedom of the Estates.

The song on Bocskai and the crown

After this interlude about a tale organically linked to the crown, we shall return to the activity of Bocskai's court. The earliest known soldiers' song associated with the court to have appeared in print dates from December 1604; in it the new,

---

indignantly what entitled them to this, "because the king alone can impose taxes on the towns, which are the certain property of the crown and not of the inhabitants of the country or the king". *Ibid.*, 154. In October 1636, when the Hungarian *camera* declared the military tax on the towns it emphasised in its proposal to the Diet , that "…the royal free towns are the property of the Holy Crown of the Kingdom of Hungary and members of the Estates". *Ibid.*

68 This is evidenced by the view expressed in 1672 by Kristóf Cseróczy, deputy legal director of the Szepes *camera*, to the effect that "It is quite certain that the royal free towns are the property of the Holy Crown…", and that for this reason the taxation imposed on the towns (and likewise the landowners) were a matter for the *camera* alone to decide. *Ibid.*, 266.

69 Quoted in Nagy, "*Megint fölszánt*," 49.

legitimating significance of the crown occurs and love for the fatherland and the nation supports the justness of the Bocskai rebellion. The words were written by János Debreceni Szappanos (Ioannes Smigdatopoeus Debrezinus, 1589?–1620?) and published in the pamphlet *Militaris congratulatio comitatus Bihariensis* of 1605.[70] Szappanos was active as an archivist to the Nagyvárad chapter and its official poet, and had composed extended poetic works on historical subjects even before the rebellion.[71] In 1607 there was a reference to the *Historia Hungarica* – now lost – on which he was working at the time, and for the printing of which Bocskai left money in his will.[72] As he dedicated *Militaris congratulatio* to Bocskai, and it tells of his activity as a commander, it is also probable that Bocskai commissioned the work and bore the expense of its printing.

The pamphlet containing the soldiers' song was written to glorify Bocskai's prowess as a military leader. The work is full of laudatory expressions and has a long Latin title. This is followed by a dedication in verse form, addressed to Bocskai, also in Latin, after which comes the Hungarian verse. The use of the two languages reflects the purpose for which the sections were written. The title and the dedication are intended for the patron, Bocskai, while the song of praise has the requirements of a different audience in view. The Hungarian poem has the aims of proving to his forces Bocskai's capability as a leader and of bolstering the army's morale. This audience, however, could probably read Hungarian not much better than Latin, and it is likely that after appearing in print the song was circulated by oral tradition.

The legitimating role of the soldiers' song can be recognised in its verse form: it is a song of praise about Bocskai published in the name of the leaders of the troops of the Hajdús. The Hajdú army consisted of lesser nobility and peasantry who had been driven off their land in the sixteenth century by the conquering Ottomans and had therefore enlisted as soldiers.[73] Werbőczy's concept of the *natio Hungarica*

---

70 Joannes S. Debrecenis [János Szappanos Debreceni], *Militaris congratulatio Comitatus Bihariensis: Ad Ilustrissimum Principem et Dominum, Dn. Stephanum Botskai de Kis Maria...* (Debrecini: Paulus Rhaeda Lipsensis, 1605). Little can be known for sure about Szappanos' career. He was presumably the son of a citizen of Debrecen and studied in Wittenberg. He was an official of the Nagyvárad chapter archive. After joining Bocskai he probably became chaplain to one of the Hajdú commanders. Klaniczay, *A Magyar irodalom*, vol. 1., 96–97; Tibor Klaniczay and Béla Stoll, eds., *Régi Magyar Költők Tára XVII. Század*, vol. 1 (Budapest: Akadémiai Kiadó, 1959) 581–584.
71 István Bitskey, "Bethlen Gábor," 3.
72 Gábor Szigethy, ed., *Bocskai István testámentumi rendelése* [The last will of István Bocskai] (Budapest: Magvető, 1986) 21.
73 Kálmán Benda, *A Bocskai-szabadságharc* [The Bocskai war of freedom] (Budapest: Művelt Nép Könyvkiadó, 1955) 7–8. In the early sixteenth century, when southern Hungary was being penetrated by Turkish armies, the *Hajdús* were in the main drawn from the Serbian population. As the Ottomans pushed forward over Hungarian-populated territory the number of Hungarians among the *Hajdús* increased proportionately. See: Nagy, "*Megint fölszánt*," 81–95.

as nobles fighting for the Catholic faith and loyal to the king could certainly not have been applied to these soldiers. The majority of them were Protestants, and – as is evident from a variety of ordinances and legal texts – the king, the nobility and the peasantry alike looked on them as the dregs of Hungary.[74] The Lutheran minister István Magyari complains of the Hajdús in 1602 with the following words:

> Are these the warriors of Christendom? Is this how Christendom must be defended? In this way we ourselves are destroying ourselves. Even the Turk does not treat his subjects so. Oh, how many homesteads have been ruined because of these vagrant warriors. We shall not set Hungary free by means of these.[75]

In the political background of the song was the fact that the rebels and Hajdús did not take Bocskai's prowess as a leader for granted, as he had a very bad reputation in Transylvania.[76] In the years preceding the rebellion he (like Illésházy) had been closely associated with the Habsburg court and took the side of the Habsburg dynasty.[77] Scarcely ten years previously, on the famous Bloody Carnival (1596) he had had numerous Székelys and Transylvanian lords executed for proposing to break from Rudolf and attach the Principality to the Ottoman Empire. After the king had begun to threaten him personally, Bocskai popularised the policy for which he had earlier had others executed for treason.[78] It was therefore important for him to change the negative opinion that had been formed of him. A commission for a laudatory poem fitted this requirement. In the poem Szappanos depicted Bocskai's actions in the first months of the rebellion as divinely legitimated. In 1604 he had succeeded in persuading the elected leaders of the Hajdús to join the rebellion against the king, and thereby achieved an unexpected victory over Rudolf's much superior forces.[79] Szappanos explained this victory by attributing what followed to God's intervention. Bocskai's struggle was therefore not a simple rebellion but a "divine cause" – as the poet relates in the thirteenth stanza.[80]

---

74 See among others *Corpus Juris Hungarici*, 1602:19.tc.
75 Magyari, *Az országokban*, 164.
76 Nagy, *Kard és szerelem*, 77.
77 István Fazekas, "Adalékok az ifjú Bocskai István bécsi udvarban eltöltött éveihez [Additional information on the years spent in Vienna by the young István Bocskai]," *Studia Caroliensia* 1(2006) 73–85.
78 István György Tóth, "Alternatives in Hungarian History in the Seventeenth Century," *Hungarian Studies* 15/2 (2000) 173.
79 László Makkai, "István Bocskai's Insurrectionary Army," in János M. Bak and Béla K. Király, eds., *From Hunyadi to Rákóczi: War and Society in Late Medieval and Early Modern Hungary* (New York: Social Science monographs/Brooklyn College Press, 1982) 281–283.
80 Debreceni János Szappanos, "Militaris congratulatio comitatus Bihariensis," in Klaniczay and Stoll, *Régi Magyar Költők Tára*, vol. 1., 258.

After that, Szappanos guides the minds of the Hungarian Estates to confront the image of the lawless king. He states that Satan had bewitched Rudolf, because God had turned against the Christians and the fatherland, and that was the cause of the suffering of the Hungarians and the Christian world.[81] But help is at hand – says the poet: God has had mercy on the Hungarians through the person of Bocskai and will punish Rudolf. In the first stanza, therefore, the Hajdús sing of Bocskai as the Heaven-sent liberator of the Hungarians, who has descended as the soldier of Christ to look after the Hungarians' liberty and well-being.[82] Szappanos portrays Bocskai as the Christian preserver of the fatherland and the nation. In this, his description brings to mind Berger's above-mentioned work. It was probably not his own ideology that he formulated in his images; the influence of the Bocskai court can be taken almost for granted.

In these strophes, Szappanos transforms the traditionally negative image of the Hajdús by showing them as pious defenders of the fatherland and God's implements in the struggle against Satan. God's work is not only the arrival of Bocskai but also the Hajdús' joining in the rebellion, after which they changed their ways – this from the Hajdús' mouths. In the fourth stanza the Hajdús acknowledge that for a long time they had been living a sinful life.[83] For this reason God had no longer been with them and they had feared him, but since Bocskai has been among them God has once more vouchsafed them his mercy.[84] Thanks to the coming of Bocskai the wicked Hajdús have become the pious and courageous defenders of the fatherland, as it turns out in the fifth stanza. The Hajdús pray and call on the name of Jesus for aid, "Let us live in warlike fashion..." and they will lay the enemies of the fatherland low. The solders' song ends: "It is time for us to lay about us for our poor, lovely fatherland, our Hungarian Crown."[85]

The poet (or whoever it was from whom he took the idea) varies the image of the Hungarian Estates by calling the Hajdús a nation (*nemzet*).[86] This thought was at odds with tradition because until then, first and foremost it had been the Estates (in the sense of *regnum*), and even more so the nobility, that had been so designated.[87] The poet Rimay, mentioned above, also belonged to the nobility, and

---

81 *Ibidem*, 258.
82 *Ibidem*, 257. "Az szep szabadsagra, Magyarsag javara" [For the beautiful freedom, for the good of Hungary].
83 *Ibidem*, 257. "Mert nagy sok volt bününk" [Because we have many and great sins].
84 *Ibidem*, 257.
85 *Ibidem*, 257.
86 *Ibidem*, 259, 260. ('nemzetünk' [Our nation]).
87 Murdock, *Calvinism*, 300; Klaniczay, *Stilus*, 14. Furthermore, in the sixteenth century a sharper distinction was made between certain persons' politico-legal origin designated by the concept *natio*, and their linguistic-ethnic affiliation designated by the concept *gens*. In this connection Tibor Klaniczay points to the example in 1597 of a certain '*Gregorius Schwonaritsch Scharwariens,*

we must examine his use of this term in this particular connection. As Szappanos has a special political aim with this new meaning – to be precise, the vindication of Bocskai's leadership in the eyes of the rebels and his troops – he also changes the notion of the legitimating role of the Estates. Szappanos explains this deliberate change of meaning by declaring that the Hajdús had been given a mission by God. Inherent in this mission is to defend the Church and Christendom by defending the fatherland from the wicked king.[88] Because of this mission the Hajdús, now leading an exemplary life, are under the protection of Heaven and above man-made rank, because they are bound to the world not by the law but by the Church – says the poet.[89] The soldiers are therefore encouraged to patriotism, and urge each other on in the song to struggle "… for the Church, the true knowledge…".[90] The display of the Hajdús as pious warriors, fighting for Church and fatherland is naturally in its entirety a figment of the imagination, as friend and foe alike complained during the rebellion that the Hajdús brought havoc and destruction upon Hungary. The yoking together of the Church and politics in the historical portrayal of the Estates – as Arno Strohmeyer has noted at the same period in the Austrian territories – is actually more a tendency to give history a religious slant (*Konfessionalisierung der Geschichte*).[91]

By creating for the Hajdús the same image of true, Heaven-sent representatives as of the Hungarian Estates, the poet shows Bocskai as the national ruler of the Hungarians who takes up the struggle against the heretical king Rudolf. According to Benda, this line of thought has its roots in Calvinist political thinking and can be compared to tendencies in the Netherlands.[92] Szappanos presents Bocskai as God's elect, comparing him with biblical figures,[93] on one occasion Moses[94] and

---

Pannonia natione, Croata genere' (Hungarian by origin, Croat by nationality). See: Tibor Klaniczay, "Die Benennungen 'Hungaria' und 'Pannonia'als Mittel der Identitätssuche der Ungarn," in Tibor Klaniczay, S. Katalin Németh, and Paul Gerhard Schmidt, eds., *Antike Rezeption und Nationale Identität in der Renaissance insbesondere in Deutschland und in Ungarn* (Budapest: Balassi, 1993) 107.

88 Szappanos, "Militaris," 259.
89 'Az Ecclesiahoz, Nem a külsö jokhoz, Köttetünk ez vilagon.' *Ibidem*, 259. In this context *ecclesia* refers to the community of Protestant believers.
90 *Ibid.*, 258.
91 Arno Strohmeyer, "Konfessionalisierung der Geschichte? Die ständische Historiographie in Innerösterreich an der Wende vom 16. zum 17. Jahrhundert," in Joachim Bahlcke and Arno Strohmeyer, eds., *Konfessionalisierung in Ostmitteleuropa* (Stuttgart: Steiner, 1999) 221–247.
92 Benda, "A kálvini tanok," 322–331.
93 Emil Hargittay, *Gloria, fama, literatura. Az uralkodói eszmény a régi magyarországi fejedelmi tükrökben* [Gloria, fama, literatura. The ideal prince in the old mirror of princes in Hungary] (Budapest: Universitas, 2001) 26.
94 Szappanos, "Militaris," 259.

three times Gideon.⁹⁵ Furthermore, Bocskai, who came from a small Hungarian village in Bihar county, is even linked to Jesus, who came from Nazareth – both of them changed the world.⁹⁶ By the example of these biblical leaders, who knew that the support of God was at their backs in their struggle against lawful authority, the poet justifies Bocskai's taking up arms.

In addition to religious parables Szappanos also uses a worldlier symbol in support of Bocskai: the Hungarian crown. In his poem he introduces the concept of our crown, and links it to the concepts of fatherland and nation. The Hajdús struggle "… for our poor, lovely fatherland and our Hungarian crown…", as we have quoted above from stanza 5.⁹⁷ In stanza 12, however, the poet brings up the image of the insulted crown, when he makes the Hajdús complain that the king's soldiers disrespect the Hungarian crown: "The Hungarian Crown, the desire of the world, they trample underfoot…"⁹⁸ In stanza 15 the Hajdús elevate Bocskai to king by means of our crown, but in the next stanza they say that in fact it is not they but God himself that has made him king of the fatherland. It appears that Szappanos interprets the crown as a symbol of the fatherland and a genuine tangible crown, and combines these two interpretations in the term "our crown".

Here Szappanos is using the Hungarian crown as a means of justifying Bocskai's role as leader of the rebellion. It is a thought worthy of attention, because the crown originally legitimated royal power. Szappanos' concepts of nation and crown, however, are not like the concepts of *natio* and *sacra corona* in Werbőczy. In *Tripartitum* the function of the concepts of *natio* and the crown of Hungary is to prove the right of the Hungarian nobility freely to elect the king. Based on this meaning of the crown are the rights of the Hungarian nation (*natio Hungarica*) to elect the king, and under strictly defined conditions to dethrone him or resist him if he infringes the rights of the nobility or otherwise abuses his power.

Szappanos further develops the concept of *natio* by calling the Hajdús members of the *natio Hungarica*, and identifying them with the Hungarian nation (*magyar nemzet*). This identification he justifies by reference to the grace of God, which is with the Hajdús. He then links Werbőczy's political theory to the notion of nation (*nemzet*). As the traditional significance of the crown justifies the right of the *natio* to elect the king, while Szappanos identifies the Hajdús with the Hungarian Estates, it is logical for the crown to play a part in his poem about the Hajdús and Bocskai. He supports Bocskai's role as leader by means of the concept of the Hajdús as

---

95 Ibidem, 258 and 260. The depiction of Bocskai as Gideon was frequently used during the rebellion. See also: Ambrus Földvár, "Historia de victoria Gedeonis," in Klaniczay and Stoll, *Régi Magyar Költők*, vol. 1, 380–389 and idem, "Alia historia de iisdem disturbis," in *ibid.*, 436.
96 Szappanos, "Militaris," 259.
97 Ibid., 257.
98 Ibid., 258.

the Hungarian nation (*nemzet*) and the image that has been created about the Hungarian crown.

In addition to the notion of *natio*, Szappanos (or the Bocskai court) also further develops the concept of the crown. He uses the term "our Hungarian Crown" instead of the Holy Crown (*sacra corona*), which alludes to a modified meaning. The difference between the meanings derives from the change of views concerning the character of the Hungarian Estates, the legitimation of royal power and the legitimating significance of the crown.

As a result, the concept and image of the Hungarian Crown in this text has a triple role. Firstly, to show the lawful nature of Rudolf's loss of his royal power. This the poet depicts by the image of the trampled crown. Secondly, the crown has the political significance sketched earlier for the Estates, and none the less is bound to the nation (*nemzet*). As, according to the poet, the Protestant Hajdús constitute the true nation, or rather the Hungarian Estates, the crown is their due. In the poem the crown has lost its holy adjective, instead of which it is called "our Hungarian crown". As true members of the nation, the Hajdús fight for the freedom of the Hungarians and together with it for their crown, and in order that the significance of the crown which is revealed to the Estates may assert itself. Thirdly, according to Szappanos the significance of the crown also includes the Hajdús' right to resist the lawfully crowned king and by the grace of God elect their own king and crown him with the crown which is theirs. By this means the crown is connected in this conception with the Habsburg emperor's crisis of legitimacy, and with the political character of the Estates and their liberties.

Szappanos' description of the crown is not based on an actual condition, as the crown had never yet been in Hajdú hands, nor had Bocskai been crowned with it. For the writer, the significance of the crown was the link connecting the modified concept of the Hungarian nation and the image portraying Bocskai as the national king of the Hungarians. Szappanos formulates in poetic fashion, in imagery, a political concept of the Hungarian nation. This concept satisfies the requirement that the followers of Bocskai be enabled to prove the rightfulness of rebellion against the lawful king. Furthermore, the concepts of the Hungarian Estates and the crown which had taken shape were altered by Szappanos' adaptation of Werbőczy's concept to the political circumstances of 1604. By means of the political imagery of the soldiers' song Szappanos simultaneously initiated a cultural change. The crown no longer legitimated exclusively royal power, but the changed image of the Hungarian nation. In this latter meaning, which first found expression in the soldiers' song about Bocskai, the crown is detached from the king but connected to the concepts of the fatherland and the Estates of the Hungarians, and to the image of the national leader of the Hungarians who is to liberate the fatherland. The change in the significance of the crown may also be observed in the vocabulary used. Instead of the Latin term *sacra corona* Szappanos uses the Hungarian "our

Hungarian crown", which alludes to a lasting connection between the crown as a symbol and the Hungarian Estates.

Thus, Bocskai and his followers created the image of the threatened Hungarian Estates by once more projecting the old themes connected with national self-identity and linking them to new political and religious ideas. In their view the godless tyrant Rudolf and his Austrian followers were menacing the freedom and well-being of the Estates and the country. The aim of the rebellion was therefore the establishment of freedom and unity under a national ruler.

The justification of the Bocskai Rebellion in *Querelae*

The notions formed and changed of the Hungarian Estates were first revealed outside Hungary by a partial Diet held in Szerencs from 16 April 1605 onwards. Estates from Upper Hungary and Transylvania took part. Bocskai had convoked the Hungarian Estates with the intention of obtaining from them material support for the continuation of the rebellion.[99] The assembled Estates gave voice to their complaints against the king, formulated the aims of the rebellion and discussed the strategy to be pursued.

The time for the Diet came at a turning-point in the rebellion, as the rebels had already scored their first military victories over Rudolf's forces and won the support of the Ottomans. On the occasion of the Assembly Bocskai's leadership was confirmed by his election as Prince of Hungary. After this election he swore an oath to the effect that "…he recognised those liberties and laws of his Hungarian followers which were accepted by the will and consent of the Estates…".[100] Thus, Bocskai was enabled to appear in Hungary and elsewhere as the Estates' elected national prince in contrast to the crowned Austrian king, who had lost his power over the Hungarians. In this way Bocskai justified the rightfulness of the rebellion, confirmed his own position in power, and united the rebellious regions of Hungary against Rudolf under his leadership as national prince of the Hungarians.

The best-known text that justifies the causes and aims of the rebellion against the king is known in modern times as the Szerencs Declaration and is titled *Querelae, excusationes cum protestatione Regni Hungariae praesertium Partium superiorum*

---

99 Benda, *A Bocskai-szabadságharc*, 33.
100 See the memoranda of the Calvinist preacher Péter Alvinczi: Kálmán Benda, ed., "Alvinczi Péter kassai prédikátor történeti följegyzései 1598–1622 [The historic notes of Péter Alvinczi, the preacher of Kassa 1598–1522]," in *A Ráday Gyűjtemény évkönyve 1955* [The year book of the Ráday collection 1955] (Budapest: Ráday Gyűjtemény, 1956) 14, MOE, XI, 155. Coronation did not follow election, only the dispatch of a Venetian emissary circulated in Prague to that Bocskai had crowned himself with the crown of King St László. *Ibid.,* 129, note 2.

coram Deo et toto orbe Christiano (hereinafter: *Querelae*).[101] We do not know exactly when this document was written or if it ever was made public, since no dated copy is known to us and only a few contemporary copies survive (about this more later). It was presumed till now that it was composed in January 1605 and promulgated at the Diet at Szerencs in April of that year.[102] Sándor Papp has argued convincingly that at least one declaration did already exist before June 1605 in manuscript.[103] Therefore did exist at least four different political texts at the same time with an almost similar content.[104]

The significance of *Querelae* is that it not only justified the rightfulness of the rebellion, was widespread and does exist in many copies, but also served as the basis for numerous political writings in the seventeenth century, as we will see in the next chapters. Many of the subjects that were used in those writings – for example, the image that had been formed of the Hungarian Estates – can be traced to *Querelae*. The function of the image formed of the Estates was to legitimate their rebellion against the lawful king. The *Querelae*, therefore, likewise marks the beginning of a new developmental period, and it is important for us to consider in detail the way in which it came into being, together with the questions of how the text is constructed and what topics arise in it.

Querelae has at least one predecessor, titled *Hungarica gentis Excusatio maxime necessari…*, which explains in a similar way to the German Electors and the Christian peoples the reasons for the Bocskai rebellion.[105] It is preserved in only two

---

101 "Quaerelae, excusationes cum protestatione Regni Hungariae praesertim partium superiorum coram Deo et toto orbe Christiano," in MOE, XI, 169–184. Károly made this edition on the basis of one copy he found in Vienna.

102 László Makkai, "Bocskai és Európai kortársai," 486; László Nagy, "A magyar politikai történetéhez (az 1605-ös kiáltvány Európa népeihez) [On the Hungarian political history (on the declaration for the European people, 1605)]," *Magyar Tudomany* 88 (1981) 358–365; László Nagy, "Ki volt a szerzője a szabadságért fegyvert fogott magyar rendek Európához intézett kiáltványának? [Who was the author of the declaration to Europe written by the Hungarian estates who took up the weapons to defend freedom?]," in Varjas, *Irodalom és ideológia*, 176; Teszelszky and Zászkaliczky, "A Bocskai-felkelés," 49–121.

103 Sándor Papp, *Török szövetség - Habsburg kiegyezés. A Bocskai-felkelés történetéhez* [Turkish alliance – Habsburg conciliation. On the history of the Bocskai Uprising] (Budapest: Károli Gáspár Református Egyetem - L'Harmattan, 2014) 134–173.

104 Teszelszky and Zászkaliczky, "A Bocskai-felkelés," 49–121; Papp, *Török szövetség*, 171.

105 "Ad Sac. Romani Imperij Potentiss, Sereniss et Illustriss Electores, Principes, ac Duces, Urbes Imperiales, Germania Provincias, caeterasq totius Christianitatis Regiones omnes et singulas, Hungarica gentis Excusatio maxime necessari, Curilla contra Caesaris Romani Exercitum arma ceperit. Judas Maccabeus," in *Acta in Ungarn, Böhmen und Schlesien. 1604-1609*, Biblioteka Cyfrowa Uniwersytetu Wrocławskiego, MF 9961, fol. 37r.-41r.

copies.¹⁰⁶ According to Papp the so-called Declaration of Korpona was written on the basis of *Querelae*, and was named after the Diet in Korpona in December 1605.¹⁰⁷ This text was formulated less stronger than *Querelae*, as it was a rewritten version of it with a German audience in mind. It was signed and sealed by members of the Hungarian Estates and sent with Bocatius to the German Estates, where it was presented to the Electors. Still, *Querelae* is considered as the most influential and widely distributed political text related to the Bocskai uprising, although it was never published till the nineteenth century and only exists in manuscript copies from the seventeenth, eighteenth and nineteenth century.¹⁰⁸

We are relatively well informed about the composition of *Querelae* and similar texts by the circle of humanists around Bocskai of this and similar political texts, thanks to the detailed account of the interrogations of Bocatius after he was captured by the Emperor's men in 1606 and from Bocatius' memoirs (1611). According to Bocatius, the main reason for the production of a political text in defence of the Bocskai and the Hungarian Estates was the appearance of a tract printed in Nuremberg in which *gens Hungarica* was reproached for joining the Ottomans "… at the cost of the blood of Christians and Germans…".¹⁰⁹ From this it follows that the writing of *Querelae* coincided with the necessity of justifying the relationship to the Ottomans.

It is impossible to specify the authorship of *Querelae* and similar texts, about which there has long been a debate in Hungary.¹¹⁰ Illésházy, Bocatius and Mihály Káthay, Bocskai's chancellor and most important advisor, have been named as the possible authors.¹¹¹

It is more likely that *Querelae* was composed by a group of authors, as Bocatius wrote in his memoirs. From his description of the creation of another similar political text it is evident that different people came together to compile each such

---

106 "Ad Sac. Romani Imperij Potentissimos, Serenissimos et Illustrissimos Electores, Principes, ac Duces, Urbes Imperiales, Germania Provincias, caeterasque Totius Christjanitatis Regiones omnes et singulas, Hungarica gentis Excusatio maxime necessari, Cur illa contra Caesaris Romani Exercitum arma sumpserit? 3. Juni 1603," HHStA: Böhm 1075. Miscellanea Hungarica. fol. 1–7r.

107 Wolfgangus de Bethlen [Farkas Bethlen], *Historia de rebus Transsylvanicis*, vol. 6 (Cibinii: Martin Hofmeister, 1793) 353–372; István Katona, Historia *Critica Regnum Hungariae stirpis Austriacae*, Tomulus IX, ordine XXVIII (Budae: Typis Regiae Universitatis, 1794) 453–479; Bocatius, *Opera Quae Extant Omnia: Prosaica*, 383–391 ; Papp,

108 Teszelszky and Zászkaliczky, "A Bocskai-felkelés," 49–171.

109 Johannes Bocatius, "Olympias Carceraria," in Bocatius, *Opera Quae Extant Omnia: Prosaica*, 119.

110 In 1883 Károlyi stated that Illésházy could not have been the author as at the time that Querelae was written he was still not in Hungary. MOE, XI, 140, note 2. According to Papp, Querelae was written during the Diet of Korpona where Illésházy was present. Papp, *Török szövetség*, 173.

111 Nagy, "Ki volt a szerzője," 175–185; László Nagy, *Botránykövek régvolt históriánkban* [Stumblingstones in our long past history] (Budapest: Akadémiai Kiadó, 1997) 150–154.

text.[112] He tells us that the German pamphlet greatly annoyed Bocskai. Later, the Estates gathered at the Diet (presumably that at Korpona, according to Papp[113]) commissioned Illésházy, György Hoffmann, Rimay and Bocatius to write a response. This was to set out the reasons for the rebellion and the conditions for peace. The other topic, however, was to be the great danger that menaced Christendom if peace were not made with the Ottomans.[114] Bocatius then states that Illésházy's idea was selected and describes its content, which in broad outline agrees with the text of the *Querelae*.

Considering the importance of a text of key significance from the point of view of the Bocskai rebellion, it is quite strange that we know not much about its origin, nor how else its content was circulated during the rebellion. It cannot have been just a draft, as we know it had been distributed, but it did not have an official status like the Declaration of Korpona. We only know that, according to the inventory of documents found in his luggage, Bocatius took two copies of *Querela* with him on his diplomatic mission to the German Electors.[115] In addition to *Querelae* he also carried *Hungaricae gentis Excusatio maxime necessaria* and the Declaration of Korpona.

Árpád Károlyi based his edition of *Querelae* on a copy preserved in the Haus- Hof- und Staatsarchiv in Vienna, without specifying precisely where it was found.[116] A nineteenth century edition of another copy, published from the collected manuscripts of Bocskai's historian István Szamosközy, has not been used much.[117] Historians still use the Károlyi edition and quote it without having ever compared it with the original text. To this day, no critical edition of the text has been produced, although it is the most widespread and influential political text of the Bocskai Rebellion.

The reason why I will analyse the content of *Querelae* in depth instead of *Hungaricae gentis Excusatio maxime necessaria* or the Declaration of Korpona, is that much more later copies were preserved of *Querelae* and that also it has been used widely in later political texts, as I will show in the next chapters. It is true that only

---

112 "Interrogatoria für Johann Bocatium," in Bocatius, *Opera Quae Extant Omnia: Prosaica*, 224 (ad 20). For the text, see: *idem*, 383–391.
113 Papp, *Török szövetség*, 172.
114 Bocatius, "Olympias Carceraria," in *ibid.*, 119.
115 *Item Quaerelae etc.*, in: "II/B Inventaria 2," in *ibid.*, 472.
116 See: MOE, XI, 184.
117 Sándor Szilágyi, ed., *Szamosközy István történeti maradványai. 1542–1608* [István Számosközy's historic relics] (Monumenta Hungariae Historica. Scriptores XXX) vol. IV. (Budapest: Magyar Tudományos Akadémia Könyvkiadó Hivatala, 1880) 295–308. The manuscript can be found in ELTE Egyetemi Könyvtár, LEO 1358.

a few copies of *Querelae* date from the time of Bocskai.[118] The only manuscript which definitely dates from around 1605, and which was perhaps handed over by Bocatius or sent by the Bocskai court, was found in the collected papers of the Diet of Silesia.[119] There exists a fragment of a copy written by Illésházy, which was preserved in his collected notes but which was never sent.[120] Other copies found their way to Western Europe by the work of information brokers, diplomats or adherents of Bocskai, and can be found in Paris (Bibliotheca Colbertina)[121] and Bern (Bibliotheca Bongarsiana)[122]. It is not certain if Bocskai or the members of his court ever intended them to reach these destinations, or whether they came there by chance. Still, the relatively large number of copies dated after the end of the Bocskai rebellion and preserved in Hungarian and Austrian manuscript collections shows us the importance of this text, its use and its wide distribution in Hungary.[123]

The political aim of the content of *Querelae* was to obtain support in Christian Europe for Bocskai's rebellion against the Habsburg emperor's policies. The appeal to Europe was made in the knowledge that meanwhile Bocskai was, behind the scenes, seeking the support of Christian Europe's greatest enemies, the Ottomans. The content of the text, therefore, was required to justify on the one hand the rightfulness of the rebellion against the Hungarians' lawful king, and on the other hand the Hungarian-Ottoman liaison. According to the authors, the cause of the rebellion was the king's lawless rule, for which reason this was the most important point in the argument. The Hungarians were forced, in consequence of the king's policies which were set to destroy Hungary and its people, to rise against the lawful ruler, and had to seek assistance from the Ottomans. This was based on a detailed

---

118 One copy in HHStA in Vienna can have been found in the luggage of Bocatius, but we have no definite proof of that. See: ÖStA Wien, HHStA Ungarn. Hungarica Fasc. 431C. Konv. A. Nachtrag 1601–1621, fol. 17r.-21v.; *Item Quaerelae etc.*, in "II/B Inventaria 2," in Bocatius, *Opera Quae Extant Omnia: Prosaica*, 472.

119 *Acta in Ungarn, Böhmen und Schlesien. 1604–1609*, Biblioteka Cyfrowa Uniwersytetu Wrocławskiego, MF 9961, fol. 110r.

120 OSZK Quart. Lat. 316, 14r.-19v.

121 Charles de La Roncière, ed., *Catalogue des manuscrits de la collection des cinq cents de Colbert* (Paris: Ernest Leroux, 1908) 61.

122 Herman Haagen, ed., *Catalogus codicum Bernensium (Bibliotheca Bongarsiana)* (Bernae: B. F. Haller, 1875) 140.

123 ÖStA Wien, HHStA Ungarische Akten Comi. Fasc. 394. Konv. A. 1605, fol. 1r.-15v.; ÖNB, Cod. Ms. 8448, fol. 27r.-40r., fol. 41r.-fol. 42v. (second part is a fragment); OSZK Fol. Lat. 520, fol. 30r.-42v.; OSZK Fol. Lat. 3411, fol. 76r.-84r.; OSZK Fol. Lat. 3606, fol. 33r.-41v. (Codex Isthvánffy); MOL I 7, vol. 34, fol. 123r.-127v. See also: *Querelae Excusationes et Protestatio Regni Hungariae 1604*, Cambridge University Library, Add. MS 8686 f. 58, referred to in György Kurucz, *Guide to Documents and Manuscripts in Great Britain Relating to the Kingdom of Hungary from the Earliest Times to 1800* (London-New York: Mansell, 1992) 2, which origins from an eighteenth century Hungarian collection.

account of what had happened over the years to Hungary and its people as a result of Rudolf's policies.

The most powerful image which the argument was called on to support was the depiction of nation and fatherland as the "bastion of Christendom" (*propugnatio christianorum*). In this image the territory of the Kingdom of Hungary (and the Hungarian people) is shown as an imaginary wall protecting Western Europe from the danger of attack from the East by the pagan Ottomans.[124] The depiction was based on the idea that the defence of Christendom in the Christian community of Europe was the sacred mission of the Hungarians. This notion was of Medieval origin and had grown up in the Hungarian royal court. Its original function had been to justify the Hungarian kings' expansionist power politics in Central Europe. As such, it was linked to the portrayal of the Hungarian king as "defender of Christianity" (*defensor christianitatis*),[125] and in consequence of the threat from the Ottoman Empire, as it spread on the southern borders of Hungary, it appears quite frequently in the fifteenth century.

The role of the image changed in the early sixteenth century after the Battle of Mohács in 1526, which brought about the ruin of Medieval Hungary. Now it became necessary to convince the powers of Europe that their strategy with regard to Hungary was of importance for the defence of Europe, and that therefore the maintenance of the country's original frontiers was essential. As recovery of the lost territory of Hungary remained for a long time merely a political desire, the image of the bastion of Christendom was called upon to underline the necessity for Christian Europe to hold what remained.

---

124 Lajos Terbe, "Egy európai szállóige életrajza [The biography of a European winged word]," *Egyetemes Philologiai Közlöny* 60 (1936) 297–350; József Deér, *Pogány magyarság, keresztény magyarság* [Heathen Hungarians, Christian Hungarians] (Budapest: Holnap, 1938, ²1993) 219–262; Kálmán Benda, *A magyar nemzeti hivatástudat története a XV-XVII. században* [The history of the Hungarian idea of a national vocation in the sixteenth and seventeenth century] (Budapest: Bethlen Nyomda, 1937); Ágnes R. Várkonyi, "A török kiűzésének tervei Európában és Magyarországon [The plans of the expulsion of the Turks in Europe and Hungary]," in Ágnes R. Várkonyi, ed., *Magyarország keresztútjain* [Hungary on crossroads] (Budapest: Gondolat, 1978) 177–184; Ágnes R. Várkonyi, "A török kiűzésének eszméje a magyar politikai gondolkodásban a XVII. század közepén [The idea of the expulsion of the Turks in Hungarian political thought around mid-seventeenth century]," in *ibid.*, 393–403; Lajos Hopp, *Az "antemurale" és "conformitas" humanista eszméje a magyar-lengyel hagyományban* [The humanist idea of "antemurale" and "conformitas" in Hungarian-Polish tradition] (Budapest: Balassi Kiadó, 1992); Ágnes R. Várkonyi, "Az egység jelképei a megosztottság másfél évszázadában [Symbols of unity in the divided one and a half century]," *A hadtörténeti múzeum értesítője* (Acta Musei Militaris in Hungaria) 4 (2002) 65; Kees Teszelszky, "In search of Hungary in Europe," in Kees Teszelszky, ed., *A Divided Hungary in Europe: Exchanges, Networks and Representations, 1541–1699* (Vol. 3). (Cambridge: Cambridge Scholars Publishing, 2014) 7–8.

125 Deér, *Pogány magyarság*, 256.

The depiction of Hungary as bastion or bulwark of Christendom arose in numerous forms in the sixteenth and seventeenth centuries, principally in so-called lament literature in the Holy Roman Empire.[126] The genre takes its name from the content and style of the works. The principal theme of these writings was the lamentable condition of Hungary and her people, which was presented to the eyes of the European community in the form of emotionally charged laments. In these the image of the bastion was combined with the theme of the sufferings of the Hungarians, as the authors declared that the situation of country and people was the result of a divine mission. The purpose of these literary works was to obtain economic, military and political support in Europe, and especially in the Holy Roman Empire, for the struggle against the Ottomans that continued on Hungarian soil.

The appearance of *Querelae* marked a development in this genre, as it once again modified the legitimating function of the depiction.[127] The principal aim of it was to obtain support in Europe for the rebellion in Hungary against the king's policies. The role of the image of bastion of Christendom was in this case not a call for financial support for the Holy Roman emperor, but the justification of the political message of Bocskai and the rebels. The legitimating sense was given expression in the text in the following three ways. Firstly, by introducing the Hungarian Estates and Hungary to the intended reading public. Secondly, by presenting the link between the peoples of Europe and the Hungarian Estates. Thirdly, by trying to undermine the legitimacy of the emperor's power in Europe. Bocskai's political message came to readers and hearers through the portrayal of the Hungarian Estates, the connection with Europe, and a negative image of the emperor.

Querelae opens with an account of the Hungarians, the Hungarian Estates and their place in Christian Europe.[128] The most significant characteristic of the Hungarian people is suffering, the consequence of the war against the Ottomans, the burden that the Hungarians and Hungary have undertaken as the bastion of Christendom. In this way the authors introduce the Hungarians to Europe as a united people. Here they refer to a familiar situation, as the theme of the sufferings of the Hungarians was widely known through countless news-sheets and pamphlets on the situation of Hungary that had appeared in Europe. After briefly summing up

---

126 Mihály Imre, *"Magyarország panasza": a Querela Hungariae toposz a XVI-XVII. század irodalmában* ["Complain of Hungary": the Querela Hungaria topos in the sixteenth and seventeenth century literature] (Debrecen: Kossuth Egyetemi Kiadó, 1996) 160; Sándor Őze, *„Bűneiért bünteti Isten a magyar népet". Egy bibliai párhuzam vizsgálata a XVI. századi nyomtatott egyházi irodalom alapján* [God punishes the Hungarian people for their sins" A research on Biblical parallel on the basis of sixteenth century printed religious literature] (Budapest: Magyar Nemzeti Múzeum, 1991).

127 Imre, *"Magyarország panasza,"* 161.

128 MOE XI 168.

the history of the fight against the Ottomans the authors move on to the character of the Hungarian people. According to them, the Hungarian is strong, trustworthy and steadfast, keeping and defending the faith, and preferring death to having to be parted from the Christian peoples. In their opinion this was why Hungary constantly rejected the Ottomans' offers of peace.

Next the story takes an unexpected turn, when the authors declare that the bastion of Christendom, contrary to all expectations, is crumbling. They state that this has not been caused by the enemy's cannon, but that the Hungarians' own elected and duly sworn king has undermined and destroyed these walls. Next the image of the destruction of the wall is explained. They say that at the start of his reign the Hungarians stood by their king heart and soul. They enthusiastically elected Rudolf as king and crowned him after he had promised to recognise their laws and liberties. After that, too, they had uncomplainingly paid him so much in taxation and placed such great forces at his disposal as no king in the course of history had received. Even now that the war against the Ottomans had been going on for fifteen years, the Hungarians bore this burden strongly, bravely, and without complaint.

According to the compilers of *Querelae*, the break then came when the Hungarians became completely exhausted in the defence of Christendom and their own country and hoped for a better future.[129] Then, Rudolf had decided to take advantage of the situation and implement his plan as proposed gratitude to the loyal Hungarians the defenders of Christendom. He was intent on destroying the Hungarians and making Hungary into a possession of the Empire, bringing it under the power and jurisdiction of the House of Austria (the Habsburg dynasty). The authors suggest that the king decided so for the sake of the funds which realisation of this plan would have brought him. He carried it out under the guise of the defence of Christendom, using funds and troops which he had received from the Christian states to defend Christendom.

After that, arguments are adduced to show that Rudolf had indeed implemented such policy. The first argument stated that the Emperor king had wished to acquire omnipotence in his empire and therefore endeavoured to put an end to the special status in it of Hungary.[130] He listened to wicked counsellors and took no account of God, the law, or justice, but made use of his omnipotence (*absoluta potentia*) to become a tyrant – opined the authors.[131] Following Illésházy, they stated that Rudolf had set himself above the law, and, invoking his sovereign state, requited any opposition with the weightiest punishment. In their view only God had infinite

---

129 *Ibid.*, 170.
130 *Ibid.*, 171.
131 *Ibid.*, 171–172.

power, but even He was ruled by law, as the wise state day by day. Rudolf, however, was a mortal man and was bound by the law and by his own oath – the compilers of *Querelae* flung in the king's face.

The second argument referred to the way in which Rudolf had organised preparations for war in Hungary.[132] The authors state that the king had ruined the country with the huge numbers of soldiers that he had quartered there. They declare that the whole Hungarian people were groaning under the reign of terror of this army. Rudolf had decided to withhold the mercenaries' pay on account of complaints against them, but they made good the loss by robbing the local inhabitants even more. Then the king had caused the money, intended for the defence of Hungary, to be put into his own state treasury. Next the authors made a connection between the financial support received from Europe and the affair of the imperial crown which Rudolf had had made in 1602, and stated that this crown had been paid for with money intended for the defence of Christendom.[133] They say that this unnecessary and costly crown reflected the emperor's shameful ambitions to power.

The third argument points to the link between the rights of ownership and political rights in Hungary. According to the authors, Rudolf created the *Cameras* in order to squeeze the maximum amount of money possible out of Hungary by the confiscation of estates, by which he not only violated the right of ownership but also imposed restrictions on political rights.[134] The king granted the confiscated estates to those that promised not to oppose his decisions in the Diet – say the authors. Furthermore, the king had acquired even more power for himself by bringing "German peasants" into the ranks of the senior clergy and the titled nobility. At the same time, he did not keep his promises. The authors sigh: "… if it not possible to live by the law, it is not possible to live at all."[135]

The fourth argument too was connected to the way in which by a change in the balance of nationalities in Hungary the balance of power had shifted in the king's favour. The authors state that officialdom in Hungary has seen the replacement of Hungarians by Austrians.[136] By this they mean the central offices, which have come under Austrian control. The compilers of the *Querelae* once more refer to the image of the bastion of Christendom when they say that the Austrians – bearing in mind the recent losses of the castles of Eger and Kanizsa – are less capable of defending the Christian world. The purpose of the decisions was simply to enable the king to derive even more profit from Hungary through the continuation of the war.

---

132 *Ibid.*, 180.
133 'Hinc regia corona recens fabricata (…) et alia id genus multis centenis millium tallerorum constantia (…).' *Ibidem*, 173.
134 *Ibid.*, 174.
135 *Ibid.*
136 *Ibid.*, 174–175.

The fifth argument claims that Rudolf has restricted his subjects' freedom of religious practice. In this passage the authors make use of the members of the crown image that has already been discussed. They insist that God has given landowners power over the bodies of their serfs, but not over their souls, and that included their religious convictions.

In sixth place the authors cite the weakening and destruction of the aristocracy. Rudolf deliberately, for his own ends, alters the resolutions of the National Assembly, and does not keep his promises. In this way he forces the Hungarians to take Austrians into their ranks while confiscating the estates of Hungarian nobles. The destruction of the aristocracy leads to the weakening of the Estates too. According to *Querelae*, the Hungarians had protested against these enactments, but to no purpose. At this point the authors refer to a letter of 1603, in which, according to them, a majority of the Estates addressed a protest to the king, who allegedly did not receive it. The authors therefore declare that Rudolf is a shadow rather than a king. His sole purpose is to destroy the nobility, weaken the laws, and reduce the once so flourishing Hungary to the status of a colony.

After revealing what Rudolf's policies, in fact, consisted of, the authors turn to his governance between 1603 and 1605. In so doing they discuss in detail the injustices inflicted on certain aristocrats, so justifying the presence among them of several such as, for example, Bálint Homonnai Drugeth, Bocskai's right-hand man, and Illésházy. The authors pay particular attention to the case of Illésházy, as he had joined the Bocskai rebellion not long before the publication of *Querelae*. Then they declare that the Hungarians have the right to armed opposition, though recourse has never been had to it. They state, relying on certain articles in Werbőczy's book of laws, that under Hungarian law the inhabitants of the country may bear arms against the king if he flouts the law.[137] The Hungarians only took up arms, however, after the king had used force against them and had given orders for the devastation of Upper Hungary, the destruction of the aristocracy, the confiscation of their estates and the replacement of Hungarian aristocrats with Austrians as he had done in Transylvania, which had been the immediate reason for the rebellion.

After making known its cause, the authors give an account of Bocskai's leading role in the rebellion in a mythical description of the events. The picture that they draw of Bocskai and the Hajdús as the embodiment of the Hungarian nation agrees with the description to be read in Szappanos' laudatory poem. In this account, the authors present the rebellion as an event in which all Hungarians are united under a leader sent from God to free the fatherland from a king that rules in lawless fashion, and from an alien people. With the help of God, Bocskai had succeeded in escaping when the king's troops arrived to attack his forces. After that, the leader

---

137 *Ibid.*, 180.

had sent the Hajdús a letter requesting help, informing them of the danger facing the Hungarians. They, together with Bocskai's serfs, had defeated the Austrian army. In the end, the people had joined Bocskai because they saw in him the saviour of the fatherland.

The compilers of *Querelae* further developed Szappanos' device of the Estates by including in the plot Bocskai's connection with the Ottomans. They state that Rudolf had thrown against Bocskai forces that had been meant for the defence of Christendom. After that, Bocskai had been forced to seek help from the Ottomans. The authors say that he did this not of his own free will but out of necessity, and that he had only resolved to do it so as to be able to protect the Hungarians. Furthermore, Bocskai had found even the most natural enemies of Christendom more honourable, better disposed and more trustworthy than the Christian emperor. They go on to say that Almighty God was on the side of the rebels, because He comes to the defence of the oppressed and for their sins takes a kingdom from one people and gives it to another. After this there begins the political message of Bocskai and his followers.[138] The authors state once again that the only cause of the rebellion was the necessity to save the Hungarian nation from destruction. Here they refer to natural law (*jus naturae*), according to which even dumb animals have the right to defend themselves from danger. They implore Christendom to stand up for the Hungarians and to oppose the emperor. Then the image changes and the authors again display the nation as Hungary and the "bastion of the whole of Christendom". Once Hungary and the Hungarian nation are free of Rudolf – the authors of the *Querelae* believe – they will once more defend Christendom like a bastion, as in any case they have always done. But now that the Hungarians are allied to the Ottomans, the authors believe, the Austrian territories, Moravia, Poland and the Czech Kingdom are no longer safe, because "… for him [the sultan] that has once conquered Hungary nothing remains impossible."[139]

The compilers of the *Querelae* then turn their attention to Rudolf's personality and attempt to compare his character and policies.[140] In this their purpose is to show that his tyrannical policies are rooted in his personality. They believe that his actions have been detrimental to his empire, his subjects and himself; he has demolished his own defensive wall in destroying Transylvania, which Zsigmond Báthory had voluntarily presented to him. He has bled his subjects white and is intent on annihilating them. The authors fear that that fate awaits the rest of the Habsburg Empire too, since the king's shameful plans spring from his wicked nature. They characterise his politics as tyranny arising from melancholia (*morbus*

---

138 *Ibid.*, 182.
139 *Ibid.*
140 *Ibid.*, 183.

melancoliae), from which there came nothing but profitless plans and evil thoughts. Because he was sick, Rudolf did not heed good advice, shut himself away from the world, was immersed in his sickness and did not behave in a manner appropriate to his royal dignity.[141] The writers go so far as to suggest that the king was not a Christian and therefore set no store by the wisdom and ordinances of God, and maintained a scandalous relationship outside marriage. They also opined that Rudolf's mental condition was the reason why he rejected proposals for peace with the Ottomans, whereas their acceptance – even if to his damaged and sick spirit it was not so – would clearly have been to the advantage of his subjects.[142] They therefore called on the princes of Europe to confront Rudolf's melancholia and sickness and rise to the defence of Christendom.

By this passage the authors meant to express the view that because of his illness Rudolf had fallen into the clutches of the Devil, and meant to drag the whole of Christendom to perdition with him. In contrast to this, Bocskai was depicted as the saviour of the Hungarian nation, sent by God. In the concluding lines they call once more on the princes of Europe to defend Christendom by hastening to the aid of Hungary.[143] In the authors' conception the Bocskai rebellion had become a continuous struggle between a noble Christian knight and a heretical tyrant, the war between good and evil which was fought out on the territory of the Kingdom of Hungary.

The notion of the liberty of the Hungarian nation had become the most important element of the rebels' ideology. In the extensive correspondence that Bocskai conducted with the Hungarian aristocracy and others he emphasised on numerous occasions that the most important purpose of the rebellion that he was leading was the winning of the freedom of the Hungarian nation.[144] To the Estates the concept of freedom originally referred to the free election of the Hungarian king, the single right enjoyed by the Hungarian Estates as such, which was linked to the tradition of the crown and thus gained justification. In the course of the rebellion the development of the idea of nation modified this idea, as is clear from Bocskai's correspondence and the content of *Querelae*. In these sources freedom of the nation means that the Hungarian Estates would freely elect the national king, who would unite the country and the Estates, and defend their laws and privileges and their right to the free exercise of religion.

---

141 Rudolf's illness was an important topos in the propaganda against him. See Evans, *Rudolf II*, 44–48.
142 MOE. XI, 183–184.
143 *Ibid.*, 184.
144 István Bocskai's letter to Miklós Istvánffy, 16 June 1605, published in: Molnár, *Fürst Stefan Bocskay*, 129–130; also: István Bocskai to Miklós Thurzó, Kassa, 17 June 1605. *Ibid.*, 130–131.

To conclude this chapter: the notion of freedom of the Hungarian nation referred to the right of the Estates to elect themselves a king who would implement their political programme. The further course of the rebellion, together with the connected political thinking and action, was thereafter directed to the justification of this ambition.

V. The Ottoman crown of Bocskai

The request for a new crown

In order to attain their political goal, the rebellious Hungarian Estates had to elect themselves a new king. As the Holy Crown of Hungary was in the possession of the Habsburg king, a new crown appeared on the political scene. In 1605 Bocskai asked the Ottoman sultan for a crown, which he received that same year in November.[1]

The purpose of the request for a crown was firstly to make the emperor hold negotiations with the rebels, which previously he had refused to do. Secondly, that Bocskai should realise the threat adumbrated in *Querelae*, which content was analysed in the last chapter, to ally the Hungarians to the Ottomans. Thirdly, that Bocskai should confirm that the crown was significant for Hungarian society, and especially that it was evidence of the freedom and rights of the Hungarian nation and at the same time of their relative independence of the House of Habsburg.[2]

The new crown was an important symbolic piece on the political chessboard of Hungary for all sides. The gift of a crown gave the Ottomans a further opportunity to recover Transylvania, take it under the jurisdiction of the Ottoman Empire and legitimate this action with the consent of the Hungarian Estates, as at the time this part of the country was in Rudolf's hands.[3] As a tangible visualisation of Ottoman authority in Central Europe the gift echoed the legend of the gift of a crown from

---

1 Parts of this chapter are from a revised version of Kees Teszelszky, "The Hungaroteutomachia and the Holy Crown of Hungary," in Gergely Tóth and Kees Teszelszky, eds., *Johannes Bocatius - Hungaroteutomachia vel colloquium de bello nunc inter Caesareos et Hungaros excitato: Magyarnémetharc, avagy beszélgetés a császáriak és a magyarok között most fellángolt háborúról* [Hungarian-German struggle, or a conversation between the adherents of the emperor and the Hungarians on the now flared up war] (Budapest: ELTE BTK Középkori és Kora Újkori Magyar Történeti Tanszéke and the Transylvania Emlékeiért Tudományos Egyesület, 2014) 79–120.
2 These aims emerge from the extensive correspondence between Bocskai and Illésházy. For example, in one letter Illésházy is of the opinion that the king – since the House of Austria would not exist without Hungary – was afraid that Hungary would be parted from the House of Austria. Illésházy's letter to Bocskai, 6 June 1605 published in: Sándor Szilágyi, "Bocskay István és Illésházy István levelezése 1605 és 1606-ban. (I. közlés) [The correspondence between István Bocskay and István Illésházy in 1605 and 1606. First part]," *Történelmi tár* 1 (1878) 8. On 26 August 1605 Illésházy wrote to Bocskai that the king intended to make Hungary a province of Austria. Jankovics, *Literátor-politikusok levelei*, 28.
3 Sándor Papp, *Die Verleihungs-, Bekräftigungs- und Vertragsurkunden der Osmanen für Ungarn und Siebenbürgen: eine quellenkritische Untersuchung* (Wien: Verlag der Österreichischen Akademie der Wissenschaften, 2003) 117.

the Pope in 1000.[4] Before the time came for the presentation of the crown and before agreement had been reached on conditions the Ottoman and Hungarian emissaries held lengthy talks in Constantinople.[5] These ended on 24 April 1605, and the parties set out the conditions and significance of the presentation in an agreement. With regard to its tone the text falls between a preliminary contract and an informal account of the talks, and in it a sort of meaning of the crown also surfaces. The writer begins by stating that those belonging to the Hungarian nation are Bocskai's subjects. If Hungarian territory and nation come under the power of the Ottoman sultan peace will quickly come to the country. For this reason, among others the nation requests the sultan to offer assistance against the Austrians in such a way that the property of the Hungarian crown is spared, and Austrian territories ravaged instead.[6]

An agreement on the nature of the Hungarian Estates and the exercise of power in the country is followed by details of the coming coronation. In the Hungarians' opinion this has to be done with a crown which has exceptional significance from the point of view of the Ottoman Empire. However, the Hungarians' wish to perform the ceremony with so powerful a symbol – as it emerges from the document – caused some anxiety to the Ottomans. The sultans had never before bestowed a crown on a vassal, but had always given them maces or banners in token of subjection to Ottoman power according to the Ottoman tradition.[7] One after another the Ottoman delegates asked advice from the Hungarians on the question of the crown and coronation.[8]

The Vizier proposed that Bocskai be given a crown jewel which they describe as the "Greek emperor's crown", but this was in poor condition. The Ottomans therefore asked the Hungarians whether they should have a new one made or the old one repaired. When the Hungarians proposed that a new crown be made, the Ottomans asked for a pattern. Nor were the arrangements for the coronation ceremony free

---

4 Cf. Cecily J. Hilsdale, "The Social Life of the Byzantine Gift: The Royal Crown of Hungary Re-Invented," *Art History* 31 (2008) 602–631.

5 "Korláth István, Kékedy György és Mehmed kihája 1605. május 24-én kelt követjelentésének [The diplomatic reports of István Korláth, György Kékedy and exchange officer Mehmed, dated 24 May 1605]," in Ferenc Csonka and Ferenc Szakály, eds., *Bocskai kíséretében a Rákosmezőn* [In the escort of Bocskai on the field of Rákos] (Budapest: Európa Könyvkiadó, 1988) 159–169; MOL Eszterházy cs. lt. Rep. 46. fasc. G. and László Nagy, "Okmányok a Bocskai-szabadságharc idejéből [Records from the time of the Bocskai war of freedom]," *Hadtörténelmi közlemények* 3–4 (1956) 323–330.

6 "Korláth István, Kékedy György és Mehmed kihája," 168.

7 Cf. Victor Ostapchuk, "Cossack Ukraine in and out of Ottoman orbit, 1648–1681," in Gábor Kármán and Lovro Kunčević, eds., *The European Tributary States of the Ottoman Empire in the Sixteenth and Seventeenth Centuries* (The Ottoman Empire and its heritage, vol. 53) (Leiden – Boston: Brill, 2013) 150.

8 "Korláth István, Kékedy György és Mehmed kihája," 168–169.

of complication. For example, the Ottoman envoys asked how Bocskai should be addressed after the coronation. The Hungarians said that king would be the most suitable form of address as Bocskai was to be crowned king, since in that way the Hungarian territories would join him most quickly and there would be calm sooner in the Kingdom of Hungary.

After that, the emissaries link the significance of the new crown to the tradition of the Holy Crown with a prayer that may be read at the end of the document. They pray that "… the Lord may give this crown to the glory of God, the spiritual refreshment of the prince, the rebuilding of the poor, ravaged fatherland and the future peace of the Hungarian nation."[9]

Then they write "God grant that the prince be able to recover the Holy Crown of our saintly kings, which is now in Austrian hands, together with the country, which is in a ruinous condition." This prayer is the first indication that the desired presentation of the crown given by the Ottomans was connected to the significance of the Holy Crown.

The presentation of and handing over of the Ottoman crown (1605)

The presentation of the Ottoman crown to the Hungarians and the handing over of the crown to Bocskai finally took place on 11 November 1605 in Ottoman-occupied territory at Rákosmező, outside Pest. Bocskai was presented with a crown, a sabre and a coronation robe by Lalla Mohamed, the Grand Vizier, on behalf of the sultan. Several that were present, such as Bocskai's right-hand man Bálint Homonnai Drugeth, the preacher Péter Alvinczi and Bocatius, wrote descriptions of the ceremony.[10] Of these it is Bocatius' work that is, for several reasons, the most important to us: firstly, because it is most often quoted as giving a reliable and factual account of what took place; secondly, because it had the greatest influence on the analysis of the significance of the coronation, and thirdly, because we may regard this work as the most important informant on the fiction of the refusal of the crown.

As writer, teacher, and politically active citizen of Kassa, Bocatius was one of the most significant figures of late humanist culture in Hungary.[11] He was regarded as the best teacher in Hungary, and his pupils were trained to occupy high public positions. He called himself *Reipublicae Literariae et Politicae Rector*, and could

---

9 *Ibid.*
10 See the summary in Csonka and Szakály, *Bocskai kíséretében a Rákosmezőn*, 97–153.
11 The father of Bocatius (also known as Bock, Bok, Bogas, and Bogáthy, 1569–1621) had been a merchant in Germany. János was educated in Dresden and Wittenberg, where he was top of his year, and then lived in Hungary. Franciscus Csonka, "Vita Ioannis Bocatii," in *ibid.*, 9–29,

claim authorship of some noteworthy Latin verse and prose.[12] At the same time he was also elected magistrate by the citizens of Kassa. In 1598, at the proposal of Archduke Maximilian Habsburg he was appointed court poet and historian, and at the same time was granted Hungarian nobility. He held talks with Belgiojoso over the expropriation of the Lutheran church in Kassa, then joined the rebellion under the influence of events, and worked as historian of Bocskai's court and as a diplomat. In early 1606, after Bocskai's coronation, he travelled to German territory to raise support for the political aims of the rebellion.[13] While doing this he was captured and imprisoned, only regaining his liberty in 1610.[14]

One of the last things that he wrote before being imprisoned was a letter dated 26 November 1605, during the Diet at Korpona, addressed to Bocskai on the subject of the handing over of the crown given by the Turks. This was in Bocatius' luggage when he was captured immediately on leaving Hungary. He was then interrogated in detail and made to account for his activity on behalf of Bocskai. The very first question put in his interrogation was whether he was the author of this letter.[15] We have the interrogators to thank for an independent picture of the political background to this and other of Bocatius's writings during the Bocskai rebellion. Under interrogation Bocatius said that he had been present willy-nilly at Rákosmező, but "as a listener and spectator of stories" (*auditor et spectator fabulae*).[16]

Although it is a fact that the account is written in letter form, we cannot regard it as a faithful description by a single eye-witness despite this admission. First: this supposition is based on the fact that Bocskai had earlier used the format of a letter addressed to a fictitious person to transmit individual definite political messages.[17] The letter was never, to the best of our knowledge, printed during Bocatius' lifetime, but when he was captured there were two contemporary copies of it in his possession, one of which I discovered in the Haus-, Hof- und Staatsarchiv in Vienna.[18] Apart from that, several manuscript copies from the seventeenth century have come down to us.[19]

Secondly, Bocatius himself writes about his role in the dissemination of Bocskai's ideas, of which the said letter also speaks. In one passage, an unnamed Hungarian

---

12 Bocatius is one of the few Neo-Latin writers of Early Modern Hungary whose (almost) complete works are available in a modern critical edition. Iohannes Bocatius, *Opera quae exstant omnia*, vol. I-III, Franciscus Csonka ed. (Budapest: Akadémiai Kiadó, 1990–1994).
13 Teszelszky, "Üzenet az utazótáskában," 127–147.
14 As a result of his stormy career his work falls into two periods: pre-1606 and post-1610.
15 "Interrogatoria für Johann Bocatium," in Bocatius, *Opera Quae Extant Omnia: Prosaica*, 217.
16 "Confessiones [Ultimo mense Augusto 1606]," in *ibid.*, 231.
17 See the above-mentioned *Copey eines Sendtschreibens...*, addressed to a German 'Freyherr'.
18 ÖStA Wien, HHStA Ungarische Akten, 149/C, fol. 3–18.
19 See Kulcsár, *Inventarium*.

points out to the prince that it will be known in Vienna and Prague within five days that he has met the Ottomans.[20] According to the letter, Bocskai considers that "that does not matter", then turns to Bocatius and asks him "… whether he has collected enough material to write a poem about this". Bocatius replies in the affirmative, and adds that "… if he had the time, the space, and the strength he could write a thicker book than Virgil."[21] From this it may be deduced that – according to Bocatius – Bocskai had the intention of informing all Europe of the event. Bocatius was therefore given the task of preparing a brief account of the event in keeping with Bocskai's ideas. This confirms that the role of the description of the coronation in the strategic plan of the rebellion was to impart Bocskai's political message to the Prague court and Christian Europe.

The most important message in *Querelae* and Bocatius' letter is the call to restore the liberties of the nation. This topic is given expression in various ways in the description of the coronation. At the start of the letter the description of the scene and the actions carried out in connection with the presentation, for example, recalls the time when the Hungarian Estates were still free.[22] The place is Rákosmező, where, according to Bocatius, "the Hungarians held Diets in the days when Hungary was still a strong country". He describes how councils had been held there about the country's wars with its enemies, and here the kings had been elected. By this he alludes emphatically to the idealised notion of the nation's ancient liberties, as was also done in works discussed above.

The political ideas emerge principally in the passage in which certain definite persons speak. These texts too have been so constructed as to convince the reader or hearer about Bocskai's ideas. For example, Bocatius describes the content of a speech on the subject of the Ottoman-Hungarian alliance given by the Grand Vizier to a Hungarian audience. The writer states that he only partly understood what the Vizier said.[23] Despite this, the content of the letter agrees precisely with that of *Querelae*. It is therefore highly likely that Bocatius put into the Ottoman's mouth a text that corresponded to Bocskai's ideas.

The substance of the speech is that the Vizier wishes to find a way out of the problems with the Habsburg king that the Hungarians list in *Querelae*. Bocatius refers to the unjust acts perpetrated by the king and justifies the Hungarians attaching themselves to the Ottomans. At the same time, he touches on the question of the

---

20 Iohannes Bocatius, "*Relatio vel epistolica commemoratio conventus inter sereniss[imum] Hungariae Transylvaniaeque principem Bochkay et inter Machumetum Vezerium habiti in campo Rakos ex adverso ripae Danubii et Budensis civitatis die 11. Novembris in festo nimirum D[ivi] Martini anno 1605. Ad amicum ἄδηλου. Authore Bocatio poeta*," in Bocatius, *Opera Quae Extant Omnia: Prosaica*, 87–110.
21 Ibid., 98–99.
22 Ibid., 88–89.
23 Ibid., 101.

self-identity of the Hungarian Estates by sketching the conflict as a struggle by the Austrian nation against the Hungarians, in the course of which the Hungarians seek refuge from Teutonic injustice with the hostile Ottomans. At the start of his speech the Vizier states that in contrast with the devastation presently being wrought by the Germans in Transylvania, the situation of the country when under Turkish rule was like a golden age.[24] He believes that the German people was never the friend of the Hungarians and that the Austrian kings never defended the Hungarians but waged war against them instead. He therefore thanked the Hungarians for finally befriending the Turks, an alliance which would never be to their shame but always to their advantage.

Then the Vizier (or Bocatius) paints a picture of the friendship of the two peoples, once more using for the purpose the concepts of the Hungarian Estates and the Hungarian crown.[25] At the same time, he emphasises the bad characters of the Austrian king and people and states that the Turks will protect the Hungarians as if they were of Turkish stock (*gens*). He further promises that the ancient rights of the Hungarians will be recognised. The Ottoman ruling house had never yet committed the crime of breaking its word or going back on an agreement as long as the other party too kept its word and the agreed conditions. It was, however, the custom with the Germans, Austrians and their kings, the Vizier points out, to make promises in ostentatious fashion and then not to keep them, but to lie and deceive.[26] In contrast, the Turks were well-intentioned, fair and honest: if the Hungarians maintained the new friendship they would soon appreciate the good fortune of the "kingdom and Crown of Hungary" (*regnum et Corona Hungariae*).[27] The proviso was that the Hungarians should continue on the road that they had started on and not allow themselves to be diverted by the Germans even if they promised mountains of gold, because they would be tricked again, said the Ottoman Vizier.

The passage on the crown is of interest because the Holy Crown was at that time in Prague and had not yet come into Bocskai's hands. By the crown Bocatius or the Vizier might also mean the crown presented to Bocskai by the Turks, as it is never called the Crown of Hungary. Furthermore, the concept of the crown returns later in the document. It is more likely that by this observation the significance of the Crown of Hungary is separated from the person of the king, and re-connected to the concept of the Hungarian Estates and their ancient liberties (*libertas antiqua*). The term crown therefore is a substitute for the liberties of the Hungarian Estates in this passage.

---

24 *Ibid.*, 100.
25 *Ibid.*, 101.
26 *Ibid.*
27 *Ibid.*, 101.

After explaining and justifying the link between the Hungarians and the Turks, Bocatius describes the ceremony called upon to set the seal on this. He emphasises that the parties took great pains to explain to one another the significance of the symbols and ceremonies. This is made possible for him by communicating to the reader the political message of the festivity in the light of a variety of elements that form them. According to the document, the coronation began with the bringing in of the crown presented by the Turks, and the other gifts.[28] Bocskai was first girded with a sabre and the Turks explained its significance. The sabre in itself was clearly not sufficiently important from the point of view of the message that Bocatius wishes to impart in his description, because he does not quote in detail the Turks' account of it.[29] We may surmise another possible reason – that the comments on the sabre were contrary to Bocskai's and Bocatius' intentions. Then the Turkish emissaries placed the crown on Bocskai's head and spoke of the significance of that too.[30] The description of the coronation is pivotal for the understanding of the crown presented by the Turks and the Hungarian crown, and is therefore the most important part of the document.

According to Bocatius, the prince accepted the crown with thanks, and said that he "… regarded it as a gift that he had proved worthy of the crown, and had no intention of abusing it … "[31] Then he stated that while the Austrian emperor lived, he was reckoned ruler in accordance with law, privilege and custom as he had been elected king in keeping with the customary ceremonies of the fatherland.[32] The account states that Bocskai emphasised that he "… wished to keep a clear conscience and had no desire to do anything contrary to the law of the fatherland." The letter goes on to say that Bocskai repeated what he had said in Hungarian and swore an oath "… that he would never do anything contrary to the ancient liberties".[33] Bocatius writes that Bocskai "… would not make use of the crown, for fear of infringing the rights of anyone, or violating the liberties of the land …". The prince charged those present not only with remembering his words but also with making them widely known.[34]

---

28 *Ibid.*, 102.
29 *Ibid.*
30 *Ibid.*
31 *Ibid.*
32 *Ibid.*
33 *Ibid.*, 102–103.
34 *Ibidem.* Bocskai also received a crown from the Saxon delegates of Brassó together with the associated regalia, which had previously been in the possession of the kings of Moldavia and Wallachia, to the east of Transylvania. *Ibid.*, 108.

The myth of the refusal of the Ottoman crown

It is obvious that the writer concentrated on what Bocskai said. In the final analysis, it is not so much the presentation of the crown by the Turks or the ceremonial involved that is of decisive importance in changing the meaning of the thinking about the crown, the power of the king and the Hungarian Estates, but rather Bocatius' description of the refusal of the Ottoman crown by Bocskai. Bocskai's words – whether truly reported or not – were considered to be his, because the document achieved wide circulation and had considerable influence. Bocatius' account of the events at Rákosmező is the most important source for modern history writers, and has been accepted as a verbatim record of Bocskai's words.[35]

Even today, what Bocskai said and the description of the events are assessed on the basis of Bocatius' observations. Many Hungarian historians have praised Bocskai's courage in refraining from having himself crowned king with the crown given by the Turks.[36] In their view, acceptance of the crown and the title of king would have brought about a rift between the Habsburg Empire and Hungary, while at the same time an undiplomatic rejection of the crown would have drawn a hostile reaction from the sultan. The conditional rejection of the Hungarian crown is a crucial episode in Hungarian historical literature and an important element in the national identity. Bocskai is shown as the national king of the Hungarian people who, on the occasion of the presentation of a crown by the Turks, succeeded by his well-chosen words in preserving the independence of Hungary between the two aggressive great powers. These modern assessments are indeed based on Bocatius' depiction – as is clear from other contemporary writings and the political associations of the time – but do not correspond with the contemporary significance of the event.

Firstly, Bocatius' text does not correspond to the Ottomans' conception of the coronation. For their authorities, Bocskai's symbolic restraint had no meaning because the crown and coronation – that is, a Christian symbol and ceremony – had no place in Ottoman political thinking. Bocskai had accepted the crown as a

---

35 Heinrich Marczali, *Ungarisches Verfassungsrecht* (Tübingen: J.C.B. Mohr, 1911) 11; Angyal, *Rudolfs II. ungarische Regierung*, 84, Benda, *A Bocskai-szabadságharc*, 40; Molnár, *Fürst Stefan Bocskay*, 85–86; Gábor Barta, "Az Erdélyi Fejedelemség első korszaka (1526–1606) [The first period of the Principality of Transylvania (1526–1606)]," in Béla Köpeczi, ed., *Erdély története* [History of Transylvania], vol. I (Budapest: Akadémiai Kiadó, 1987) 535; Péter F. Sugar, ed., *A History of Hungary* (Bloomington, Indiana: Indiana University Press, 1990) 98; Ferenc Szakály, "Virágkor és hanyatlás 1440–1711 [The Golden Age and its decline, 1440–1711]," in Ferenc Glatz, ed., *Magyarok Európában* [Hungarians in Europe], vol. II (Budapest: Háttér Kft.-Téka, 1990) 177; Tóth, "Alternatives in Hungarian History," 173; Lendvai, *The Hungarians*, 112; Winkelbauer, *Ständefreiheit und Fürstenmacht*, vol. I, 145.

36 Benda and Fügedi, *A magyar korona regénye*, 153–154; Makkai, "A Bocskai-felkelés," 736; Barta, "Az Erdélyi Fejedelemség első korszaka," 535.

gift, and therefore in the eyes of the sultan and the Ottomans had become a vassal.[37] In Ottoman sources he is subsequently referred to as "king of Hungary", even when he had supposedly declined the title.[38] The following quotation from a letter to Bocskai from Ali, pasha of Buda, shows this double status of both vassal and king: "Our mighty Emperor has taken under his wings His Majesty King István Bocskai, the Hungarian lords and Hungary, and made a great vow."[39]

Secondly, the accounts of other eyewitnesses at the ceremony differ from Bocatius'. According to him, Bocskai charged those present with remembering his words, while others write not one word about Bocskai's rejection. His right-hand man and designated successor Bálint Homonnai Drugeth, for instance, described the presentation of the "sultan's gift".[40] Szamosközy, the other court historian, does not devote a single word to the rejection in the poem that he wrote on the gathering at Rákos.[41] Alvinczi states that Bocskai had himself crowned and on the occasion also received a sabre and a banner as gifts; when presenting them the pasha said: "With this crown the invincible Emperor of the Turkish nation presents Your Majesty with Hungary entire and complete, together with its ancestral liberties."[42]

---

37 "Illustrious padishah, since last year there have been sent twice to the slave king Bocskai as a sign of favour sumputous kaftans, jewelled swords and daggers, wonderful horses, and the crown which belongs [only] to kings which they call krona." Cengiz Orhonlu, *Osmanli Tarihine Aid Belgeler. Telhisler (1597–1607)* (İstanbul: İstanbul Üniversitesi Edebiyat Fakültesi, 1970), 114. Thanks to the orientalist Petr Štěpánek for this quote and translation.
38 Papp, *Die Verleihungs-, Bekräftigungs- und Vertragsurkunden*, 126; ÖStA Wien, HHStA, Ungarische Akten, Fasc. 149 Konv. D., fol. 21r.-24v. (Letter of Pasha Suleyman, 1605); *Rex Botischkai*, idem, fol. 50r.; Letter of Ali Pasha of Buda, Buda: *Stephano Rege excellentissimo*.
39 Letter of Ali Pasha of Buda to István Bocskai, Buda, 24 December 1605, published in Gustav Bayerle, ed., *The Hungarian Letters of Ali Pasha of Buda 1604–1616* (Budapest: Akadémiai Kiadó, 1991), 34. On Bocskai's royal appellation see: *ibid.*, XV.
40 "Homonay Bálint irasa az Bocskay Fejedelem dolgairól [Bálint Homonay's writing about the thing of Prince Bocskay]," OSZK Fol. Hung. 1089, mentioned in Csonka and Szakály, *Bocskai kíséretében*, 137; Eszter Venásch, "Drugeth Bálint Homonnai hadinaplójának kiadatlan része [An unpublished part of Bálint Drugeth Homonnai's war diary]," *Lymbus. Magyarságtudományi forrásközlemények* [Lymbus. Hungarologian source editions] (Budapest: Magyar Országos Levéltár; Balassi Bálint Magyar Kulturális Intézet; Nemzetközi Magyarságtudományi Társaság, 2007), 19–46.
41 István Szamosközy, "Budához midőn a költő Bocskay István kíséretében megfordult a török táborban a Rákos mezején, 1605 november havában [To Buda, when the poet turned in companion of István Bocskay in a Turkish camp at the Field of Rákos in the month of November 1605]," in Tibor Klaniczay, ed., *Janus Pannonius – magyarországi humanisták* [Janus Pannonius – Humanists of Hungary] (Budapest: Szépirodalmi könyvkiadó, 1982), 495–496.
42 "Ezzel a koronával a buszurmány nemzet győzhetetlen császára Felségednek ajándékozza az egész és teljes Magyarországot, ősi szabadságával." Kálmán Benda, "Alvinczi Péter kassai prédikátor történeti feljegyzései 1598–1622 [The historical notes of Péter Alvinczi, Preacher in Kaschau 1598–1622]," *Ráday Gyüjtemény Évkönyve* [Yearbook of the Ráday collection], vol. 1 (1955), 16.

Alvinczi adds that "… he has described what he saw …".[43] If Bocskai really had spoken the well-known words, and they had really been so significant to those present and his contemporaries, surely they would appear in the journals of his more important advisors.

Thirdly, Bocskai himself makes no mention of any kind of rejection in his political testament. This, written at the end of 1606, summarises and justifies his actions during the rebellion. Without saying a word about rejection, he gives a detailed account of how he acquired the power of prince and mentions that the Ottoman emperor crowned him while the "other emperor" confirmed his status as prince.[44]

Fourthly, there is no trace of rejection in the correspondence of contemporaries and other sources of the time. In his letter from Léva of 18 November 1605 to Archduke Matthias, Zsigmond Forgách describes the presentation of the crown but says nothing about rejection.[45] In the reports of the peace negotiations between the delegates of the emperor and Bocskai, the ceremony at Rákosmező is called a coronation.[46]

Fifthly, there is not a single reference to rejection in historical works on Bocskai. Not long after Bocskai's funeral Menyhért Bornemisza of Vác, chaplain to Bálint Homonnai, wrote a poem of almost four hundred lines on Bocskai's life.[47] Of these, almost thirty are devoted to the coronation and the presentation of the crown given by the Turks. Six stanzas describe the crown itself and its supposed origin.[48] Although a number of stanzas agree with Bocatius' description, Bornemisza does not so much as mention rejection, but calls Bocskai "king of the Hungarians".[49] In other laudatory poems composed on the prince's death in 1606 no mention is to

---

43 *Ibid.*
44 '(…) melyben annak utána csakhamar a két hatalmas császárok közül az egyik, a török, meg is koronázott (…).' Szigethy, *Bocskai István testámentumi rendelése*, 12.
45 '(…) *ut Vezerius plenam authoritatem tractandi pacem nomine Swltani Bochkaio concedat, ita ut quidquid ipse cum sua Matte' concluerit illud ratum gratum, firmumque in perpertuu' maneat, quibus sic transactis Coronam ei a Swltano dono missam, magna solemnitati Vezerius exhibuit, quam novam, leuiqus ponderis esse asserit; ipse autem Vezerius equos 14 dono eidem obtulit, quos inter duos solum alicuisa momenti, reliquos claudos, vetustos multo pabulo saginatos, fuisse refert.*' ÖStA Wien, HHStA, Ungarische Akten, Fasc. 149 Konv. A., fol. 127.r.-v.
46 '*Quam enim hic contra Regem suum legitime oloctum unctum et coronatum, hostem Christiani Nominio non solum in auxilium vocaverunt.*' MOL I 47 Hoffinanz Ungarn, Bocskayische Friedensakte, Fasc. 15434 (January 1606), fol. 203r.
47 Ményhárt Bornemisza Váczi, "[Históriás ének Bocskay Istvánról] [Historic songs about István Bocskay]," in: Klaniczay and Stoll, *Régi magyar költők tára*, vol.1, 269–298.
48 *Ibid.*, 281–284.
49 *Ibid.*, 284.

be found of rejection,[50] nor is there any in his epitaph, which was composed by Rimay.[51] Finally, even before he was imprisoned Bocatius was commissioned by the prince to write a laudatory poem; this was carved on a marble tablet and on 25 October 1605 placed in the house where Bocskai had been born.[52] The poem recalls the presentation of the crown and the title received from the sultan, but here too there is no mention of rejection.[53]

If the most important source for this event, which originated so soon afterwards, does not even mention it, it is doubtful whether the so-called rejection was in fact voiced, and whether the familiar words were indeed spoken. Essentially, what is important is not what in Bocatius' text is fiction and what fact, but rather what were the political circumstances of the words in his description which may never have passed Bocskai's lips. In order to find the answer to this question we must examine the use made of Bocatius' description in later accounts of the coronation ceremony. We must note here that the description of Bocatius was only published in the eighteenth century: till then, it circulated in manuscript and travelled through reception in other works.[54]

These sources can be divided into two groups: one group makes no use at all of the description of the rejection, while the other does use it. To the first and larger group belongs one of Berger's works, dated 1612, in which the writer, as one of the

---

50 "Az felseges Boczkai Estvannak meg halasrol [On the death of his highness István Bocskai] [cantio optima Boczkaidys]," in Klaniczay and Stoll, *Régi magyar költők tára*, vol. 1, 369–371 and János Filiczki, "Alia cantio," in *id.*, 378.

51 János Rimay, "Bocskai István sírfelirata," in Eckhardt, *Rimay János összes művei* 88–89. This verse was published even in Dutch in 1619, see Hieronymus Oertel, *De Chronycke van Hungari* [The chronicle of Hungary], Peter Neander, tr. (Amsterdam: Jan Evertszoon Cloppenburch, 1619).

52 Iohannes Bocatius: "Prosopodeia diei sui veneris," in Ioannis Bocatius, *Opera Quae Extant Omnia: Poetica*, vol. I (Budapest: Akadémiai Kiadó, 1990) 598–601; ÖStA Wien, HHStA Ungarische Akten, Fasc. 149 Konv. C. 1605 s.d., fol. 43r.-v. Under interrogation Bocatius admitted being the author, and stated that the work had been done on Bocskai's commission. "Interrogatoria für Johann Bocatium," in Bocatius, *Opera Quae Extant Omnia: Prosaica*, 598. This method of deifying Bocskai in the guise of a memorial tablet is one of the earliest known examples of the genre in Hungary.

53 "Hídvégi Mikó Ferenc emlékirata - részlet [Part of the memoirs of Ferenc Hídvégi Mikó]," in László Makkai, ed., *Bethlen Gábor krónikásai* [The chronicles of Gábor Bethlen] (Budapest: Gondolat, 1980), 31.

54 Bocatius' work was first published with the title: Iohannes Bocatius, "Commentatio epistolica de legatione sua ad Stephanum Botskay," in Matthias Bél, ed., *Adparatus ad historiam Hungariae* (Posonii: Royer, 1735) 330–336. Two examples of reception abroad: János Nadányi, *Florus Hungaricus, sive rerum Hungaricarum ab ipso exordio ad Ignatium Leopoldum deductarum compendium* (Amstelodami, Ex officina Joannis à Waesberge: 1663) 345; Louis De May [Du May de Salettes], *A discourse, historical and political, of the War of Hungary, and of the causes of the peace between Leopold the First, Emperor of the Romans, and Mahomet the Fourth, Sultan of Turkey. ... Translated in English.* [by Sir James Turner] (Glasgow: Robert Sanders, 1669) 63.

first, writes of the presentation of the "Greek crown", which is, moreover, in his view "... scandalous with regard to the Hungarian crown ..."[55] In one manuscript of his great work on the history of the Kingdom of Hungary, he wrote a similar text.[56] Ferenc Hídvégi Mikó (1585–1635), court historian to Prince Gábor Bethlen of Transylvania, calls the event simply coronation "with a Greek crown" in his memoir of 1613.[57] Péter Révay too discusses the coronation in a work of the same year, but makes no mention of the rejection.[58] The historian Gergely Petthő (1570–1629) wrote of the event in about 1626, saying that the Vizier "... placed the crown on Bocskai's head in the name of the sultan..."[59] In a work of 1662 János Szalárdi, court secretary to Prince György Rákóczi of Transylvania, only mentions the fact that Bocskai's coronation took place at Rákosmező.[60] From these writings it appears that the writers were unaware of Bocatius' work.

A common feature of the few writers that do mention the rejection is that all of them are strong Habsburg supporters, in close contact with the court – by which means Bocatius' work may have reached them. The most influential taking up of the description, without acknowledging its source, is in the history book of Hungary by Miklós Istvánffy (1538–1616). As palatine of the Hungarian kingdom (*locumtenens palatialis regni Hungariae*) until 1608, he was the principal adviser in Hungary to the Habsburg emperor.[61] Istvánffy was the most important figure in the pro-Habsburg faction in Hungary, strongly anti-Bocskai and at the same time Illésházy's greatest enemy. He was also known as a humanist and a historian: he wrote his book about the history of Hungary between 1608 and 1613. In 1608 he lost the election to Illésházy and in addition suffered a stroke, as the result of which he was unable to complete his history because from then on, he stammered and his right-hand

---

55 Elias Berger, *Trinubium Europaeum* (Francofurti: apud Godefridum Tampachium, 1612) 40; Idem, "Trinubium Europaeum," in Melchior Goldast, ed., *Politica Imperialia, sive discursus politici, Acta Publica, Et Tractatus...* (Francofurti: Ex Off. Typogr. Johannis Bringeri: 1614) 722–742.
56 [Elias Berger], *Historia Hungarica ab a. 1572 usque ad a. 1606*, ÖNB, Cod. 8464, Fol. 252v.-253r.
57 "Hídvégi Mikó Ferenc emlékirata," 31.
58 Petrus de Rewa [Péter Révay], *De sacrae coronae regni Hungariae* (Augustae Vindelicorum: Christopher Mangus, 1613) 54.
59 Gergely Petthő, *Rövid magyar kronika* [Short Hungarian chronicle] (Kassa: Akademia, 1753) 172.
60 Ferenc Szakály, ed., *Szalárdi János siralmas krónikája* [Woeful chronicle of János Szalárdi] (Budapest: Magyar Helikon, 1980) 85–86.
61 Emma Bartoniek, *Fejezetek a XVI-XVII századi magarországi történetírás történetéből* [Chapters from the history of Hungarian historiography in the sixteenth and seventeenth century] (unpublished manuscript, Budapest, 1975) 344; Gábor Nagy, *Vicissitudines (Előkészület Isthvánffy Miklós Historiaeja kritikai kiadásához)* [Vicissitudines. (Preparation of a critical edition of Miklós Isthvánffy's Historiae)] (Doctoral thesis, University of Miskolc, 2005) 23–24.

shook. His work was published only in 1622, after his death.[62] The description of the rejection gained acceptance through this very influential book.[63]

Although Bocatius never published his description of the coronation, the rejection returns in a few lines in a heroic poem by him about Mátyás II in 1614.[64] This – also a strongly pro-Habsburg work – came from the time when Bocatius had been released from prison and was trying to regain the favour of the Habsburg court. Bocatius' description also came, through Istvánffy's book, into the work of Franz Christoph Khevenhüller, historian of the Habsburg court.[65] Bocskai's explanation of the rejection too is to be found in this work, and in which the significance of the Holy Crown is also mentioned: "The frequently mentioned Bocskai said several times of this that he would not accept the crown which the Grand Vizier had given him to the detriment of His Royal Majesty of the Kingdom of Hungary and the ancient crown of that same country."[66]

From the way in which this borrowing is used it is clear that the role of Bocatius' description sends a topical political message to a very special audience – the Habsburg emperor and his close circle of advisers most relied on for Hungarian affairs. This is evident from a letter of 12 December 1605 from Zsigmond Forgách to Archduke Matthias.[67] The message agrees with the ideas contained in *Querelae* which were described in the third chapter. On this occasion, however, these ideas are made known to the intended audience in a form different from the summons issued to Christian Europe. On the one hand, the coronation ceremony took place outside Pest on Bocskai's initiative, which was meant, through all channels – such as emissaries that were present and spies – to shake up and alert the king, the foreign diplomats and the courts of Europe. On the other hand, by means of Bocatius'

---

62 Nicolaus Istvánffy, *Historiarum de rebus Ungaricis Libri XXXIV* (Coloniae Agrippinae: Hieratus, 1622).
63 We do not know how Istvánffy came by this text, but a ms in his library – dated 1614 – is one of the earliest to contain Bocatius' description. OSZK Fol. Lat. 3606 II. 119–130.
64 Iohannes Bocatii c[ivis] Cassov[iensis], "Matthiados carmina heroica," in Bocatius, *Opera Quae Extant Omnia: Poetica*, vol. II, 750–802: '(...) *Regnantis munus Mahometea Othomenide amicum / Impositures erat capiti diadema recusans, / Quod regis tutilo Bochkaius, instar honesti / Accipiens doni tetulit, convivia nobis* (...)'. Ibidem, 775.
65 '(...) alda ihme der Obriste Vezier eine Griechische Cron (die er nicht ahnemmen) auffstritzen unnd verehren woellen (...)'. Franz Christoph Khevenhüller, *Annales Ferdinandei ...*, vol. VI (Regenspurg: Christoff Fischer, 1643) 214.
66 'Ober das so saget mehr gedachter Botschkay, daß er die Cron, so ihme von Vezier Bassa zugeschickt, zu Abbruch der Koenigl. Maijest. deß Koenigreich Hungern und desselben uhralten Cron, nich angenommen.' Article in the peace treaty of 23 June 1606 in *ibid.*, 3057.
67 The archive of the *Camera* of the Viennese court, quoted in Lajos Thallóczy, "Bocskay István koronája [The crown of István Bocskay]," *Archaeologiai értesítő* 16 (1884) 167–168, note 2; Ipolyi, *A magyar szent korona*, 109–110, note 4.

description Bocskai was also disseminating an image and an assessment of the coronation beyond the borders of Hungary.

Bocatius' Hungaroteutomachia

Relatio was not the only text written by Bocatius which influenced the ideas on the Hungarian crown. Another text on the development of the meaning of the crown at the time of the Bocskai Rebellion is titled: *Hungaroteutomachia vel colloquium de bello nunc inter Caesareos et Hungaros excitato*.[68] It is a text in dialogue form in which the political message of Bocskai is communicated with the world outside the Hungarian borders. It was written to spread the newly constructed image of the Hungarian crown and the Hungarians in Europe, but instead of reaching its intended audience, copies of it were deeply buried in Austrian, German and Italian archives, only to be published in the twenty-first century.

As Gergely Tóth has argued convincingly, Bocatius can be considered to be the author of the *Hungaroteutomachia*.[69] This work reveals also most vividly the enigmatic nature of the writer and his controversial views on the politics, religion and history of Hungary — and above all on the crown of Hungary. Although the text of *Hungaroteutomachia* was not published till 2014, it cannot be said that no one has ever found or seen this work, or that it has never been studied by a historian. Hungarian scholars knew for many years of the existence of at least one of the manuscripts in the *Ungarische Akten* of the Hof-, Haus- und Staatsarchiv in Vienna, but no one thought of editing or publishing a comprehensive study of its contents.[70] The first historian to quote and translate parts of the original manuscript in Vienna was Árpád Károlyi, in 1899. He used its content extensively as a source for his analysis of the way in which contemporary works reported the

---

68 Tóth - Teszelszky, *Johannes Bocatius - Hungaroteutomachia vel colloquium de bello nunc inter Caesareos et Hungaros excitato*.

69 On the history of the manuscript, see: Gergely Tóth, "*Hungaroteutomachia*. Authorship, textual tradition and the principles and structure of publication," in Tóth - Teszelszky, *Johannes Bocatius - Hungaroteutomachia vel colloquium de bello nunc inter Caesareos et Hungaros excitato, 33*; Gergely Tóth, "Az erazmista szatirikus és a bebörtönzött mártír. Bocatius két műve, a Hungaroteutomachia és az Olympias carceraria [The Erasmic satiric and the imprisoned martyr. The two works of Bocatius: the Hungaroteutomachia and the Olympias carceraria]," in: Anita Fajt, Emőke Rita Szilágyi and Zsombor Tóth, eds., *Börtön, exilium és szenvedés. Bethlen Miklós élettörténetének kora újkori kontextusai* [Prison, exilium and suffering. The Early Modern contexts of Miklós Bethlen's life story] (Budapest: Reciti, 2017) 61–75.

70 As confirmed orally by István Fazekas, former Hungarian archive delegate at HHStA and Géza Pálffy.

Bocskai Revolt.[71] Interestingly, he quotes the content of the *Hungaroteutomachia* far more often than *Querelae*. Although he apparently found the text interesting, he did not publish it elsewhere. This may have had something to do with his poor opinion of the supposed author, considering the text to have been written by an "ultra-Calvinist and wild Hungarian author" with a "bloody mouth".[72] As Károlyi expresses a positive opinion about Bocatius elsewhere in his volume, it is clear that he did not understand the true nature of this political text as a literary construction in the form of a dialogue representing several conflicting political viewpoints — nor did he consider Bocatius to be its author.

Károlyi's book on the Early Modern Diets of the Hungarian Estates, with editions of related sources, had a tremendous influence on the study of the Early Modern political history of Hungary and the view on the Bocskai Revolt in the twentieth century. However, it did not encourage other scholars to devote attention to the manuscript of the *Hungaroteutomachia*. It is mentioned only by Géza Lencz in his 1917 dissertation on the Bocskai Revolt. He described the content as follows: "Das sehr interessante Schrift - stück übt scharfe Kritik über die damaligen Zustände."[73] More than 50 years were to pass before another reference appeared about the work in the historical literature. László Makkai wrote erroneously in his 1974 analysis of the ideological background to the Bocskai Revolt that the author of the *Hungaroteutomachia* must have been a follower of the emperor.[74] We can only assume that Makkai based his opinion on a loose reading of Károlyi. It is not likely that he had ever seen the original source. As far as we know, no other Hungarian or foreign scholars have studied the manuscript or made a thorough analysis of its contents. The quoted historians were unaware of the real author, the meaning of the work and the background to the manuscript.

Based on the acerbic comments on Hungarian politics that it contains, we can state that the writing and distribution of the *Hungaroteutomachia* must have been closely related to the propaganda campaign carried out by Bocskai's court at the end of 1605, as has been described in the previous chapter. As such, it belongs among a large group of similar and interrelated documents written and distributed by the followers of Bocskai between 1604 and 1606 in order to influence the image of Bocskai and the Hungarian rebels abroad, and especially the opinion of the Protestant Estates in the German lands.[75]

There is no extant source that refers to the gathering of material for the *Hungaroteutomachia* in particular, nor do we know anything about exactly when or

---

71 MOE XI., 221, 226, 283–285, 288, 296, 308–309, 316–317.
72 MOE XI., 288, 296.
73 Lencz, *Der Aufstand Bocskays*, 29.
74 László Makkai, "Bocskai és európai kortársai," *Történelmi Szemle* 17 (1974) 488.
75 Teszelszky and Zászkaliczky, "A Bocskai-felkelés," 68–109.

where the text was written. We have no information about whether Bocskai ever commissioned its writing, or whether it was simply another work in Bocatius' huge oeuvre relating to Bocskai. In contrast, the writing of the declarations referred to above can be followed on the basis of letters, diaries and other sources from the circle surrounding Bocskai, as I have shown in the previous chapter. The later works of Bocatius in particular, including his memoirs, are themselves a valuable source of information about how they came into being. Even the content of the *Relatio*, written in 1605, reveals information about its origins. Bocatius had promised the Hungarian prince to describe the event at which he was present — that is, the ceremony of the handing over of the Turkish crown to Bocskai.[76] He kept his promise, writing the *Relatio* after his return. No such clues are contained in the *Hungaroteutomachia*, as neither Bocatius himself, nor Bocskai, play a role in it. The whole work revolves around fictional characters that represent opinions held by the different sides in the Bocskai Revolt.

Far more important to our understanding of the origins of the *Hungaroteutomachia* is the diplomatic mission undertaken by Bocatius, which began at the end of December 1605 and came to a wretched end at the beginning of February 1606. As almost all our sources on the *Hungaroteutomachia* are related to this mission, we can assume that the composition of the work must also have been closely related to its goal. The earliest reference to the *Hungaroteutomachia* can be found in the list of items confiscated from Bocatius after his arrest in the German town of Nordheim. The detailed list was compiled by Philippus Rust, town clerk and judge of Nordheim on 26 February, 1606, in the presence of a man referred to as "Kayserlicher Haubtman".[77] The date can thus serve as a *terminus ante quem* for the genesis of the manuscript. The clerk unpacked Bocatius' possessions item by item and wrote down in detail what he found, according to his understanding of Latin and German. Bocatius' money, packed in three purses, was first taken from the "verschloßen runden Wadtsack" (closed round backpack), then a diamond ring, a gift from the Elector Palatine, was found, followed by some loose letters and a number of letters bound together.

It is important that the manuscript of *Hungaroteutomachia* was found on top of the luggage (and was only the fifth item on the list).[78] The inscription on the

---

76 Cf. Bocatius, "*Relatio vel epistolica*," 98–99.
77 ÖStA Wien, HHStA, Ungarische Akten. Miscellaneae Fasc. 433. Akten, betreff. den Stadtrichter von Kaschau, Johann Bocatius 1606. fol. 36–37. Published as: "II/B Inventaria 2," in: Bocatius, *Opera Quae Extant Omnia: Prosaica*, 467481.
78 "5. Item, Hungaroteutomachia vel colloquium de bello nunc inter Caesareos et Hungaros excitato. Dialoi tres. Germanus, Hungarus, Italus, Polonus, Transylvanus: collocutores; Turca, per Caelium Palaemonem. Nec Hungaroteutomachinationum, nec Hungaroteutomorum, sed solius veritatis amicum. Ots in quarto undt ungehefftet." *Ibid.*, 468. A contemporary, abridged version of the

title page of the manuscript was copied in detail by the writers of the inventory. Immediately after this the manuscript of *Relatio* was found: one of the handwritten descriptions of the ceremony of the handing over of the Turkish crown.[79] This is perhaps no coincidence, as I will argue below. It is possible that the two manuscripts were at the top of the bag as Bocatius may have intended to hand them over to a printer in the German lands. However, we have no proof that Bocatius indeed planned for them to be published, as there is no extant source material concerning his intentions. There was only one manuscript of the *Hungaroteutomachia* found among Bocatius' belongings, according to the inventory. Including this one, which was preserved in Vienna, there are only three known copies of the manuscript, all written in the same hand, which ended up in very different places in Europe.

As Tóth states in his study, we can assume that one of the two students who travelled with Bocatius and who were also detained with him after his arrest, served as a copyist.[80] This suggestion is confirmed by Bocatius himself in his memoirs, as he refers in several places to his secretary, including his background and activities. If Teuffel indeed produced the written copy of the *Hungaroteutomachia*, then he also could have copied more texts for Bocatius or Bocskai. The two copies of the *Relatio* found in Vienna and Munich, as well as the copy of the *Excusatio* that was possibly left by Bocatius on behalf of the Estates of Silesia, were all written in the same hand as were all the copies of the *Hungaroteutomachia* in Vienna and Munich.[81]

How did these copies from the possession of Bocatius end up in different corners of Europe? As only one copy is mentioned in the inventory, and as the majority of the handwritten items on Bocatius' list turned up in the Habsburg archives in Vienna, we can assume that the copy now in Munich was left in Heidelberg by Bocatius during his meeting before he was detained. The copy, which was originally kept in the Protestant Correspondence Archive of the Elector Palatine in Heidelberg and discovered by Márton Zászkaliczky, was transferred to Munich after the Siege of Heidelberg in 1622. The manuscript now in Vienna must have been confiscated

---

same list, which was written in the same hand and bearing a similar date, was found by Márton Zászkaliczky in the Bavarian Main State Archives (Bayerisches Hauptstaatsarchiv) also features the *Hungaroteutomachia* as the fifth item. Extract aus dem Inventario… Jo. Bocatio… Bayerisches Hauptstaatsarchiv, München, Kasten Schwarz. 16712. fol. 84v.

79 "6. In einem Schnur seindt nachfolgende Stucke zusamen gebunden in quarto. Relatio vel Epistolica commemoratio conventus inter Serenissimum Hungariae, Transylvaniae, Valachiae Transalpinae principem etc. [rec. et] inter Mahumetem Vezerium habiti in Campo Rakos ex adverso ripae Danubii et Budensis civitatis. Die undecima Novem[bris] in festo nimirum D[ivi] Martini an[n]o Do[mi]ni 1605." *Ibid.*

80 Tóth, "*Hungaroteutomachia*. Authorship, textual tradition and the principles and structure of publication," 33.

81 Acta in Ungarn, Böhmen und Schlesien. 1604–1609. Biblioteka Cyfrowa Uniwersytetu Wrocławskiego, MF 9961, fol. 37v.

when Bocatius was detained in Nordheim. After that, it must have been transferred to the imperial administration in Prague and finally ended up in the Ungarische Akten of the Haus-, Hof- und Staatsarchiv. We can therefore assume that the copy in Vienna is identical with the one described on the list. Nevertheless, we have no way of knowing for sure how and when the manuscript now in Munich reached the Elector Palatine. The third copy was found by Tamás Kruppa in the archive of the papal nuncio in Prague, Giovanni Stefano Ferrero, who wrote extensively on Hungary.[82] How Ferrero obtained this copy remains a mystery. All that can be known for sure is that the three manuscripts remained unpublished in the archives for more than 400 years.

The unusually small number of known, preserved manuscripts of such an outspoken and well-written political text raises questions about the nature of the intended readership — questions that also have some bearing on when and why Bocatius wrote the text. As far as we know, the manuscript was never published, nor do we have any proof that it was ever disseminated further in manuscript form outside the three known copies by the same hand. We do not even have proof that it was read by any contemporaries outside the small circle of people concerned with Bocatius and his mission, as there is not a trace of any reception of the text at that time. There is not a single copy, not even a draft, in any of the collections in Hungary related to the administration or members of Bocskai's court, not to mention the complete lack of references to this work from anyone in Bocatius' own intellectual circle.

All this suggests that the creation of *Hungaroteutomachia* followed a very different course from that of other propagandistic writings defending the Bocskai Revolt. There are many extant copies of *Querelae*, for example, and it was widely read and discussed both during and after its creation, although it was not mentioned to be disseminated. Although similar in some respects, the *Hungaroteutomachia* also stands apart from the *Relatio*, of which at least eight known contemporary copies still exist in collections in Hungary, Romania, Austria and Germany.[83] A copy was even preserved in the notebook of Márton Pribizer (Martin Pribizerus), a schoolboy from an unknown Lutheran Latin school in the east of Hungary dating around 1610 to 1612.[84] We also know that the text of *Relatio* was widely read already at the time of the Bocskai Revolt and was extensively used after the revolt in the Habsburg and Hungarian historiography of the seventeenth century, as we have shown in the previous chapter.

---

82 Archivio di Stato di Biella, Famiglia Ferrero della Marmora, Fondo Ferrero, Cassetta XVI, Cartella 18, Fascicolo 287/13.

83 Cf. Bocatius, "*Relatio vel epistolica,*" 87. ÖStA Wien, HHStA, Ungarische Akten, 149/C fol. 3–18; MTAK, Budapest, K 75, fol. 39v–51v.

84 MTAK, Budapest, K 63, fol. 135r–150r.

As the *Hungaroteutomachia* was composed at roughly the same time as other, similar texts legitimating the Bocskai Revolt that were taken abroad, and as there are no other copies known in Hungarian territories, we may suppose that Bocatius did write it not long before or during his travel to the German lands and that he was also planning to have this work published or disseminated abroad. He no doubt hoped for a wide readership among the supporters of the Hungarian cause, both within the Protestant German lands and beyond. However, it cannot simply be assumed that he had such a plan from the outset.

The distribution of a sensitive political or religious text only in manuscript form was not uncommon in those days. One example is the *Repraesentatio pacis generalis* on the Dutch Revolt, written anonymously by the Dutch envoy Pieter Cornelisz. Brederode at roughly the same time as the *Hungaroteutomachia*.[85] This manuscript was indeed found in the luggage of the Hungarian envoy, but many other handwritten copies exist apart from this one and as far as we know, it was only published in 1607 and 1608 in printed form.[86] We must not forget that at this time it was also possible to write for an individual reader or a small audience, producing a work in a single manuscript copy for an important patron or a selected target audience. During his career as a humanist, Bocatius wrote and published many works exclusively for the benefit of a patron or a small circle of readers, among them the recently discovered *Lessometria*.[87]

Bocatius builds up *Hungaroteutomachia* using quotations from the bible and from many classical and Early Modern authors. His political arguments are extracted from contemporary political pamphlets, newspapers and broadsheets published by followers of the emperor or the Hungarians, and from political declarations written by members of Bocskai's court. It also builds on his former work. This, then, is a pattern into which other works of his might plausibly be fitted, including the *Relatio*. The *Hungaroteutomachia* reveals most tellingly the place and function of Bocatius in the circle around Prince Bocskai. Bocatius' job, in the winter of 1605–1606, was to construct a political theory to legitimate Bocskai's rebellion. Although he denied this strongly in his confessions and apology, the content of all his works points in this direction.

The relationships between the *Hungaroteutomachia* and the intellectual currents of the Bocskai Revolt are as involved and complex as everything else about this work and its author. The dialogue form appears particularly apposite for Bocatius' presentation of the major themes of the Bocskai Revolt. The *colloquium* (colloquy)

---

85 Uwe Sibeth, "Gesandter einer aufstandischen Macht. Die ersten Jahre der Mission von Dr. Pieter Cornelisz. Brederode im Reich (1602–1609)," *Zeitschrift für historische Forschung* 30 (2003) 19–51.
86 "II/B Inventaria 2," 471; Cf. Sibeth, "Gesandter"
87 Kees Teszelszky, "Joannes Bocatius egy ismeretlen művéről [About an unknown work of Joannes Bocatius]," *Irodalomtörténeti Közlemények* 112 (2008) 92–93.

format requires opposing participants, with the truth emerging through conflict and the resolution of diverse opinions. The dialogue form was a popular literary style and there are many Renaissance examples, also from Hungary. The form goes back to the Ancient Greek descriptions of the intellectual conversations between Socrates and his students, while Erasmus' *Colloquia Familiaria* is an Early Modern example of the genre.

A well-known dialogue related to Hungary is one of the oldest Hungarian-language broadsheets: the so-called "Image of True Religion", written by Albert Szenci Molnár and published in 1606 which contains a dialogue between a female character personifying Religion, and a symbolic Human, who can be identified as the reader of the text.[88] The broadsheet was disseminated at the same time as an apology defending Bocskai's religious views. The dialogue was published only shortly after the composition of the *Hungaroteutomachia* (1606), but was inspired by a sixteenth-century Dutch model. The dialogue form, just as the *Hungaroteutomachia*, also fits into the pattern of a slowly-developing public sphere in the Hungarian territories in around 1605, in which political matters were discussed in public, in manuscripts and sometimes even in printed form.[89]

We can assume that the dialogue form was equally popular during the Reformation because it provided a symbolic *persona* for the author, whose views might be controversial from a political or religious point of view, or even directed against the authorities. The writer could always state that the unwelcome opinion came from the mouth of one of the participants in the dialogue. It is no surprise that Bocatius used this strategy to defend himself, as the supposed author, after he was detained, as we read in the account of his interrogation. The interrogation took place on 28 August 1606 and was recorded in German and translated into Latin, as were the confessions that followed the interrogation. The interrogators followed the order of the list of items found in Bocatius' possession, as one of the first questions referred to the *Hungaroteutomachia*. Bocatius was asked: "Wer die Hungaroteutomachiam gemacht?" (Who wrote the *Hungaroteutomachia*?)[90], which was translated as: "*Quis author Hungaroteutomachiae?*"[91] Bocatius' reply was recorded as follows: "Saget, es sey nicht seine Invention, je doch er habe etliche Argumenta undt meisten Theils daz iehnig was in Persona Germani geredet wurdt, suppeditirt undt bekent, daz es sein Stilus." [92] (He says that it wasn't his invention, but that he added most of the arguments of the German character, who speaks and confesses in his style.)

---

88 See: Teszelszky, *True Religion*.
89 Cf. Jürgen Habermas, *The Structural Transformation of the Public Sphere: An Inquiry into a Category of Bourgeois Society*, translated by Thomas Burger (Cambridge, MA: MIT Press, 1989).
90 "Interrogatoria für Johann Bocatium," in Bocatius, *Opera Quae Extant Omnia: Prosaica* 217.
91 *Ibid*. 221.
92 "Responsoria," in Bocatius, *Opera Quae Extant Omnia: Prosaica* 223.

This was a very clever answer on the part of Bocatius, as the German character in his work personifies the political views of the Habsburg emperor and his followers, and voices the opinions printed in German broadsheets and newspapers on Bocskai and Hungary. The German character thus sums up arguments expressing the content of the Habsburg propaganda and the German newspapers directed against Bocskai in favour of the Hungarian king. Bocatius' answer can be understood as a way of defending himself against allegations that he was one of the masterminds behind the propaganda for the Bocskai Revolt. But his plan was not successful: later, after being tortured: "Bekent, daz sein styly die Argumenten sein ihm" (He confessed that the style and arguments are his).[93]

The *Hungaroteutomachia* is basically a conversation between six anonymous men from six different nations: a German, a Hungarian, an Italian, a Pole, an Ottoman Turk and a Transylvanian, as Bocatius states on the title page of his work. The title of the work also suggests its main theme: it is the description of three fictional conversations, held on three days, during which the participants speak about a variety of topics related to the Bocskai Revolt in Hungary and Transylvania. Among these topics are politics, religion, the House of Habsburg, and the Holy Crown of Hungary. The discussion is between two groups: those in favour of Bocskai, the Protestant Hungarian Estates and their political and religious demands; and those against, who support the cause of the Habsburg dynasty and the Catholics in Hungary and Europe. The Hungarian, the Transylvanian and the Ottoman comprise the first group. The other group consists of a German, who is supported by an Italian and a Polish person. Apart from the Hungarian and the German, the characters do not necessarily represent their nation or country, but rather stand for a political or a religious point of view, either that of Bocskai or that of the Habsburg ruler.

The Transylvanian is a witness to the sufferings of the inhabitants of Transylvania under Habsburg rule. The Ottoman has a minor role in the whole conversation, but supports the Hungarian cause. He personifies the political support of the Ottoman Empire to the politics of Bocskai and the threat towards the Habsburg Empire and Europe. The Italian represents the viewpoint of the pope and the Catholic Church, while the Pole gives voice to the Catholic Estates of the countries neighbouring Hungary and Transylvania and the people who are threatened by the Ottoman menace. The conversations take place in Latin, although all the participants sometimes speak in their own native tongue (German, Italian, Polish, Hungarian and even Turkish), which makes the work vivid and interesting. The Ottoman speaks the Hungarian language now and then to the Hungarian, but does not take an active part in the discussion as he does not seem to speak or understand Latin or German.

---

93 "Responsoria," in Bocatius, *Opera Quae Extant Omnia: Prosaica* 227.

Bocatius explains the title of the work and the choice of characters by referring to the *Batrachomyomachia* (the Battle of Frogs and Mice), a Homeric parody from the Late Hellenistic period. This was a very popular fable in the Early Modern period and the story was reused as a political text in 1595 by Georg Rollenhagen.[94] The lesson learned from the poem is that, in a war between two sides, a third party will always win in the end. Bocatius is clearly pointing to the conflict between the Germans and the Hungarians, which will be ended by the Ottomans who will defeat both and conquer both lands. He returns to this theme in the third dialogue, in which he declares that the emperor's troops had begun to destroy the Hungarian lands, and that the Hungarians were therefore forced to create an alliance with the Ottomans.[95] This was also the basis of his defence of the Bocskai Revolt: the Germans started it, while the Hungarians were only legitimately defending themselves against the German forces.

Remarkably, Bocatius repeated the same argument in 1611 when describing his conversation with the Dutch envoy Pieter Cornelisz. Brederode during their meeting at the beginning of 1606 according to his memoirs.[96] As the theme played an important role in legitimating the Bocskai Revolt abroad at the time of his mission, the *Hungaroteutomachia* may have been written especially for the occasion of the diplomatic meeting with the German protestant electors. The text on the title page reveals the main message of the work. If the Hungarians had not asked for help from the Ottomans, the conflict between the Hungarians and the Germans would have become like Homer's proverbial frog–mouse war: both the Hungarian and the German lands would have been swallowed up by Ottoman force. Bocatius is suggesting here that the Hungarians saved the Germans and themselves by making an alliance with the Ottomans rather than betraying the Christian world. It is not the Hungarians who are responsible for the crisis in the Kingdom of Hungary and the threat to Christian Europe, but the wicked politics of the emperor and the overwhelming force of the German troops directed against the innocent Hungarians.

The first dialogue starts with a meeting between the main characters on a street in a royal free town in the north of Hungary. As the German figure has to disguise himself in Hungarian clothes in order to conceal his German identity, we can assume that the town was Kassa (today Košice in Slovakia) during the Bocskai Revolt. The choice of the royal free town of Kassa as the setting for the conversations is a significant and very symbolic aspect of the work, not least because it was the home

---

94 Georg Rollenhagen, *Froschmeuseler* (Magdeburgk: Andreas Gehn, 1595). It was used again later in a similar way to describe the conflict between the Spanish and the Dutch. S.N., *Batrachomiomachia* (Leiden: I. Burchoorn, 1636).
95 Bocatius, *Hungaroteutomachia*, III. 45.
96 Bocatius, "Olympia," 120.

town of the author himself. The Medieval city played a crucial role in the tumultuous political events before the outbreak of the rebellion, and was also one of the main stages for the revolt during its development. As described in the former chapter, it was the political and intellectual centre of the Bocskai movement and was the seat of Bocskai's nomadic court between 1604 and 1606.

Bocatius was the town judge and the city's central political and intellectual figure. It is therefore no coincidence that the events in Kassa before and during the Bocskai Revolt play an important role in the discussions. Kassa also served as the meeting point of various envoys from different regions and countries. According to Bocatius' confessions, even people from Scotland and the Netherlands were travelling freely in disguise to Hungary at the time of the uprising, although we do not have any proof of that.[97] The description of the setting for Bocatius' conversation thus presents a vivid picture of the exciting daily life in Kassa at the height of the Bocskai Revolt. The city, as a royal free town and a possession of the crown of Hungary, is also an important subject of the conversation.

The meeting between the two groups cannot be considered as a realistic description of a political discussion, as they symbolise the two opposing ideologies that clashed during the Bocskai Revolt. The Hungarian character voices the essence of Bocskai's propaganda. The main lines of the arguments expressed by the Hungarian, but also the Transylvanian and even sometimes the Ottoman, can be understood as a summary of the political thought of Bocskai and his court. This ideology was put into words in declarations, charters, official or humanist letters and other political texts. However, it was not consistent. Bocskai and his court formulated different political messages for each target group. Existing texts were cut up, slightly adapted and reformulated in order to legitimate the actual political message of the day, which might lead to something that contradicted other texts disseminated at the same time.

By creating conversations between characters, Bocatius was using a similar technique to that used by the writers of Early Modern commonplace books.[98] The way in which he constructed his dialogues is reminiscent of the way in which commonplaces were selected, created and used to write new books during the same period. We can therefore understand this work as the careful composition of eloquently formulated commonplaces derived from existing political texts from the Habsburg

---

97 "Confessiones I [Ultimo mense Augusto 1606]," 236.
98 See for this rhetoric technique: Ann Moss, *Printed commonplace-books and the Structuring of Renaissance thought* (Oxford: Oxford University Press, 1996); François Goyet, *Le Sublime du "Lieu Commun." L'invention rhétorique dans l'Antiquité et à la Renaissance* (Paris: Champion, 1996); Robert Bireley, *The Counter-Reformation Prince. Anti-Machiavellianism or Catholic Statecraft in Early-Modern Europe* (Chapel Hill, N.C.: University of North Carolina Press, 1990) 78; Ann Moss, "The Politica of Justus Lipsius and the Commonplace-Book," *Journal of the History of Ideas* 59 (1998) 421.

and Bocskai courts, broadsheets, newspapers and other information sources, mixed with Classical and Early Modern quotes to enforce their rhetorical value. He introduces the reader to various opinions and arguments concerning the Bocskai Revolt and presents the main allegations against the Hungarians, as well as their defence. Although Bocatius leaves the final verdict regarding the righteousness of the uprising to the judgement of his readers, we can still consider the work as an attempt to unify and summarise the various political texts of the Bocskai court and their varying interpretations. He rewrote the mixed and often confusing political opinions of Bocskai's followers into a single political message.

The nature of the text as a short, clear overview of the various arguments pro and contra Bocskai, and the specific form of the text as a dialogue in a realistic setting, betrays the original target audience. Bocatius was writing for foreign readers with a humanist background, who might have been interested in the conflict between the Hungarians and Germans in the east, but who were not willing to dive into the large amount of dry, ideological texts, declarations and heated correspondence produced by both sides. (Bocatius nevertheless brought these with him in his luggage, should anyone be interested.) His readers were instead invited to read a humorous, intelligent, sharp and well-written discussion, short enough to retain their attention. The various parts of the text in Italian, Hungarian, Polish and even in Turkish would have appealed to the taste of the well-educated humanist reader elsewhere in Europe.

The text was not written in the Socratic dialogue form of questions and answers, which would naturally lead to the truth on which all participants could agree. Instead, it is a heated debate in which neither side wins, but all participants have the opportunity to express their opinions. Bocatius presents himself in the afterword as the spokesman of the truth. One of his arguments is that he does not belong to any of the nations taking part in the discussion. (And therefore reveals his identity as author of the text as well.) Another argument is that he only wrote a summary of the various opinions. This is an indication that Bocatius has indeed read all the propaganda documents from both sides and reworked their content into this dialogue.

The conflict between the Hungarians and Germans can be viewed as a true propaganda war, which Bocatius describes as "war of words". Another argument supporting the supposed neutrality of the author is his opinion that all readers should inform themselves of the various arguments, on the basis of which they must reach a conclusion for themselves. Bocatius will not do this for his readers. The conversation ends with the words of the Italian, who declares that every single rebellious Hungarian noble must be wiped from the Earth. The war of words remains without a true winner, although the Italian's final words can also be understood as a warning to the Protestant nobles of Europe that they will share the fate of the Hungarians if they do not support them in their struggle against the Catholic powers who are devastating the Protestants in Hungary.

One of the most fascinating features of the *Hungaroteutomachia* is the innovative way in which the crown is described in the text. In this way, it is an addition to the already mentioned *Relatio*. Above all, the content of the *Hungaroteutomachia* itself provides unambiguous evidence of Bocatius' real erudition regarding the crown's intellectual history and the political history of Hungary. This is not surprising, as Bocatius was a trained scholar in Hungarian political and legal matters. As the envoy of Kassa, he took part in the legal and political discussions during the Diets of the Hungarian Kingdom, for example in Pozsony in 1601. When he became town judge of Kassa, he gave an oration on 9 January 1604, which was published in the same year with the title "Regentenspiegel".[99] Since he outlined his ideas on the ideal government of a town in this mirror of regents, it is a great pity that this work, crucial to an understanding of his political thought, is lost. Bocatius also went on a mission to the court of the emperor in Prague in 1604 to protest against infringements to the status of Kassa as a royal free town that belonged, in his eyes, to the Holy Crown of Hungary. We also know of many petitions to the king from his hand.[100] The *Hungaroteutomachia* suggests the work of an intelligent layman who has effectively collected the necessary information from his surroundings in order to revive the tradition of the Holy Crown in support of the politics of Bocskai. However, as I will argue later, the image of the crown as Bocatius created it in his work is nothing other than a true revival of the age-old tradition of the Holy Crown.

The first dialogue begins with a chance meeting between a Hungarian, a German, a Pole, a Transylvanian, an Italian and an Ottoman in a street in the town of Kassa. It is clear from the start that the real discussion will be between the Hungarian and the German; the others serve merely to emphasise some of the arguments put forward by these two main figures. Bocatius' choice of form is deliberate: it is not Rudolf and Bocskai who are the main actors in the text, but rather the German and Hungarian peoples. The stereotypical representatives of the five nations play a major role in the work, along with the topoi connected to them. In this way, Bocatius presents an excellent depiction of the Early Modern image of these nations.

The discussion starts with an explanation by the German critic regarding the Hungarians. The German's main argument is that the Hungarians are untrustworthy because of their barbarian, even "Scythian", character.[101] The Hungarian counters this attack by pointing out the untrustworthiness of the Germans, who handed over the fortresses of Győr and Kanizsa to the Ottomans and the emperor, who failed to

---

99 Iohannes Bocatius, *Regentenspiegel. Eine Oration vom Standt der Obrigkeit* (Bartfeldt: Klös, 1604). The only known copy of this book was lost after WWII.
100 ÖStA HHStA, Wien, Ungarische Akten fasc. 433; Cf. Bocatius 1992. 499–520.
101 Bocatius, *Hungaroteutomachia*, I. 7–9.

keep his promises to the Hungarians.[102] The Transylvanian strengthens this argument by pointing out the devastation wrought by Basta in Transylvania in the name of the emperor. Basta, too, failed to keep his promise to the Transylvanians. The Hungarian uses the well-known topos of the Hungarians as born soldiers, created not to sing or to write, but to fight and to defend their country.[103] Bocatius then puts the most important demand of the Hungarians in the mouth of the Hungarian — the same demand that can be found in the Petition of Illésházy discussed in the former chapter: If the crown returns to the country and the Germans no longer disturb the Hungarians, they will lay down their weapons immediately.[104]

The meaning of the crown is placed at the centre of the discussion from this point onwards. In fact, Bocatius describes the tradition of the crown and its contemporary meaning in detail in the conversation that follows. First of all, the Hungarian character states that the crown is being kept illegally outside the country's borders, against the laws of the country and the decision of the Estates, which damages and disgraces the Hungarian nation and their loyalty to the king. These words are an exact copy of the content of point four in the Petition of Illésházy. The Hungarian's statement can also be understood as an addition to the political theory of the Holy Crown, which was presented in the *Relatio*. The *Hungaroteutomachia* is therefore strongly related to the *Relatio*, and it is no surprise that the documents were found together in Bocatius' luggage and in the archive in Munich.

The German replies that the Hungarians wish to hand over the Crown to their unlawfully elected ruler, Bocskai, to which the Hungarian responds that Bocskai has been openly and lawfully elected as ruler, with general approval. The German immediately touches on a sensitive topic, stating that Hungary is no longer a free kingdom but a "colony of Austria". Bocatius is repeating here the ideas of the Habsburg dynasty regarding their omnipotence.[105] As the Habsburg dynasty has the right of inheritance to the Hungarian throne, the Hungarian people are nothing but slaves and the king can do with them whatever he pleases. This is the essence of the German's argument: as the Hungarians did not accept the omnipotence of their king, they are guilty of lèse-majesté. (This part of the conversation resembles the already described discussion between Emperor Rudolf and Illésházy.) The Italian supports the German, stressing the guilt of the Hungarians with respect to the Catholic religion. As the Hungarians have rejected the true religion of Catholicism, the king can do with them whatever he pleases, even eliminating them from their own country.

---

102 *Ibid.*, I. 11–12.
103 *Ibid.*, I. 15–18. Cf. *Tripartitum*, Operis Conclusio. 424.
104 Bocatius, *Hungaroteutomachia*, I. 18. Cf. MOL, E211 XXXII. Lymbus II. series 1605–1606, fol. 6r.
105 Cf. Evans, *Rudolf II*, 78–79.

Bocatius uses this strongly-worded statement by the German to explain the true grounds for the rebellion. He allows the Hungarian to reply that this is exactly why the Hungarians are waging war against their ruler. Hungary is a free country, and it is precisely because of this freedom that the Hungarians have taken up their swords. They want to live according to their own traditions. It is their own business to choose their own king. Circumstances may have forced their forefathers to choose a foreign king, but nothing stands in the way of them now choosing a king from their own nation. Bocatius is pointing indirectly here to the election of the Hungarian Bocskai as ruler of the Hungarians, and to Bocskai's words in the *Relatio*.

Bocatius links the topic of the crown to the sensitive question of the legitimacy of Habsburg rule in Hungary. The German spokesman counters this by pointing to the settlement between King Ulászló II and Emperor Maximillian II in 1491 on authority in the Hungarian kingdom. If Ulászló II did not have a son, the Hungarian crown was to pass to the Habsburgs. When Ulászló II's son Lajos II died at the Battle of Mohács in 1526, the right to the Hungarian throne passed automatically to the Habsburg dynasty. King Ferdinánd I was chosen and crowned by the Hungarians. The Hungarian replies to this by stating that the settlement became void on the death of Lajos II. According to him, the Hungarian Estates vowed at the time of the coronation of Lajos II, during the Diet in Rákos in 1505, that they would never choose a king who was not of Hungarian blood, so as to avoid the troubles they now faced with a foreign king. According to the Hungarian, this vow was recorded in an official patent, held by Bocskai himself. This part of the work suggests that Bocatius must have had access to, or at least knowledge of, historical sources on the subject. In order to deprive the Hungarians of their freedom of election, the crown was taken out of Hungary by members of the Habsburg house, since when there had never been a free election of a king in Hungary. The freedom of the Hungarians was taken away by removing their crown from Hungarian territory.

Bocatius links the issue of the sovereignty of the Hungarians to the function of the Hungarians and Hungary in Europe by using the age-old topos of the Kingdom of Hungary as the bulwark of Christianity which we also encountered in *Querelae*. According to the Hungarian character, the Hungarian people are not the slaves of the Germans, nor is Hungary a colony, because the Hungarians and Hungary have defended the Holy Roman Empire as a shield against the Ottomans for many years in the sole interests of the Germans. The German character states that the Germans have sacrificed themselves on Hungarian soil, and that the German lands have paid the price of their defence in vain. The Hungarian replies that the Germans have made use of the Hungarian territory as a defence line, in order to spare the German lands from war. Besides, the Germans have behaved badly in Hungary, pillaging the country and giving themselves up to all manner of vices such as greed and drunkenness. Bocatius counters this with the German image of the Hungarians as barbarians without morals. He quotes a verse by Paul Melissus, professor at the

University of Heidelberg and librarian of the Prince Elector of the Palatinate, which strongly supports his opinion.[106]

At the end of the first conversation, Bocatius uses an argument that perhaps reveals the original target audience of his writing. He reacts to the German's opinion that the money paid for the defence of Hungary was entirely wasted, as there are no results to be seen of the war against the Ottomans. He states that Emperor Rudolf sent German money intended for Hungary to *Belgia*, to fight the Christians there. A similar argument can be found in contemporary Dutch propaganda, in which the Dutch complain that the Habsburgs have sent more money and troops to fight against the Christians in the Low Countries then they have sent for the defence of Christianity against the Ottomans.[107] According to Bocatius, the money that was meant to defend the German countries against the Ottomans was used to put down the Dutch Revolt in the Low Countries. He also states that the three electors of the Saxon lands, the Palatinate and Brandenburg have made public that they will not send any more money to the emperor because of this misuse, which will cause him great harm. Bocatius refers here to a letter from the electors. The fact that he quotes openly from the letter, and uses an argument that was well-known in the Protestant circles of Western Europe, suggests that the text must have been directed to the protestant electors and their followers, whom he would visit at the beginning of 1606.

The second dialogue deals with the question of the authority of the Habsburg king and the subject of religion in the Kingdom of Hungary at the time of the Bocskai Revolt. The conversation takes place one day after the first. Although this is the shortest part of the work, the theme is discussed in great detail, indicating the author's thorough knowledge and erudition on the subject. The Italian starts the discussion by asking the Hungarian about the origins of the revolt.[108] The Hungarian states that the forced takeover of the Elisabeth Church in Kassa by the Catholics was the beginning of all the troubles. This launches a discussion on the question of who has authority in matters of religion in the Hungarian Kingdom, and who is the owner of church property. The debate is similar to the conflict between Illésházy and King Rudolf I on royal authority and ownership. At the heart of the discussion between the Hungarian and the Italian is the question of the ownership

---

106 Paul Melissus, "Ad Carolum Utenhovium, C.F. Patricium Gandavensem. Anno 1566. ex castris," in *Collegii Posthi Melissaei Votvm, Hoc Est, Ebrietatis Detestatio, Atqve Potationis Saltationisque eiuratio: Amethystvs Princeps Sobrietatis* (Francoforti ad Moenvm: Johannes Lucienbergius, 1573) 15–16.

107 [Hubert Languet], De verantwoordinghe des Princen van Oraengien ... [The apology of the Prince of Orange] (S.L.: S.N., 1568). See also: Martin van Gelderen, *The Political Thought of the Dutch Revolt 1555-1590* (Cambridge: Cambridge University Press, 1992) 151-155.

108 Bocatius, *Hungaroteutomachia*, II. 3.

of the church in Kassa, and of who is able to decide on matters of religion in the kingdom. According to the Italian, the king is all powerful in his realm: he can decide on the religion of his subjects and is the sole owner of all church property. All those who resist him are guilty of lèse-majesté. The Hungarian defends the right to private property and the freedom of religion in the kingdom on the basis of the rights and privileges of the Hungarian Estates, which were confirmed by the king at the time of his coronation.

The discussion depicted by Bocatius follows the lines of the earlier political conflict in Hungary, which was fought between representatives of the king and those of the royal free towns at the Diet of Gálszécs on 26 September 1604.[109] This debate was recorded by one of the Protestant representatives of the royal free towns, probably Bocatius himself.[110] The opinion expressed by the Italian in the *Hungaroteutomachia* greatly resembles the views of Count Giacomo Belgiojoso, representative of the king and the Chief Captain of Upper Hungary.[111] The Hungarian repeats the words of one of the representatives (likely Bocatius himself) at the Diet, who wrote that the royal towns possess equal freedom to that of the nobility, as they have an equal vote in the election of the king and possess equal rights at the Diets.[112] It is highly likely that Bocatius used this text, written after the Diet, to construct the important debate on religion in order to inform his foreign readers about this matter.

In the following lines, the Hungarian tries to convince his interlocutors that the authority of the king has its boundaries, and that the Hungarians acted legally to "defend themselves against force" (*vim vi repellere licet*).[113] The right to noble resistance was established in the Golden Bull of King András II in 1222, on which the king swore his oath at the coronation.[114] As Márton Zászkaliczky argued, the right of resistance was one of the main legal arguments used to legitimate the Bocskai Revolt in the Declaration of Korpona, dated November 1605.[115] Originally,

---

109 See the ms in the handwriting of Bocatius: ÖStA Wien, HHStA, Ungarn. Hungarica Fasc. 433. Miscellanea Konv. E. Die Angelegenheit der Kasschauer Kirche betr. Akten aus den "Hungarica" 1603 Okt. -1604 Sept., fol. 1–73.
110 "A Gálszécsi gyűlésről Belgiojosóhoz küldött bizottság egyik tagjának tudosítása e bizottságnak Belgiojosóval folytatott tárgyalásai", in: MOE X. 596.
111 Bocatius, *Hungaroteutomachia*, II. 33–34.
112 *Ibid.*, II. 33–34. Cf. MOE X. 596.
113 Bocatius, *Hungaroteutomachia*, II. 24.
114 *Tripartitum*, I. 9. 6.
115 Zászkaliczky, "The language of liberty," 288; Teszelszky and Zászkaliczky, "A Bocskai-felkelés," 85–86; Márton Zászkaliczky, "A Bocskai-felkelés politikai nyelvei [The political languages of the Bocskai Revolt]," in Gábor Kármán and Márton Zászkaliczky, eds., *Politikai nyelvek a 17. századi első felének Magyarországán* [Political languages in Hungary in the first half of the seventeenth century] (Budapest: Reciti, 2019) 59–60.

only the noble community of landowners enjoyed this right, as stated in István Werbőczy's law-book.[116] However, Bocatius expands this right to the royal free towns, entitling all Bocskai's followers, both noble and townsmen, to the right of resistance.

The basis of this notion of the freedom of the people, as used by Bocatius, is the Protestant religion. He states that in 1572 the majority of the Hungarians were Protestant.[117] The Hungarian character states that due to their Protestant faith, the Hungarians are a free nation (from the viewpoint of religion), as the king promised to respect this (religious) freedom at his coronation.[118] The Hungarians therefore do not have the same status as Austrian farmers, who have no freedom as subjects of the archduke, but they do have (religious) freedom, based on the coronation oath sworn by the king. The Hungarian argues that the royal free towns have the same kind of freedom as the nobles, thus they likewise possess the same right of resistance against any violent infringement of their rights, privileges and possessions, such as the forced takeover of the church in Kassa. As the king is bound by the law of the kingdom due to his coronation with the crown, but has disregarded the religious rights and privileges of the inhabitants of Hungary, including the royal free towns and even the ordinary people, all Hungarians have the right to defend their religious freedom against their unjust ruler.[119] They Hungarians have not sinned against their religion and the ancient customs, but instead have exercised their legal right of resistance.[120]

The author refers to several documents that prove the truth of the words spoken by the Hungarian. Bocatius states that the Hungarians themselves have warned the emperor and his court in texts and protestations on the "rejection of force" (*de repellenda vi*).[121] The Hungarian also says that he possesses the original correspondence between Archduke Matthias and the emperor, which contains their plans to subdue the Hungarian community.[122] Interestingly enough, Bocatius brought with him copies of almost all of the documents quoted in the dialogue, which were found along with the manuscript of the *Hungaroteutomachia*, *Relatio*, *Querelae* and the Declaration of Korpona.

The third and final dialogue addresses the question of the freedom of the people, the law and royal power in the Kingdom of Hungary, and the Hungarians' peace conditions. It is a continuation of the train of thoughts described by Bocatius in the

---

116 *Ibid.*
117 *Ibid.*, II. 50.
118 *Ibid.*, II. 51–54.
119 *Ibid.*, II. 55.
120 *Ibid.*, II. 63.
121 *Ibid.*
122 *Ibid.*, II. 66.

previous dialogue, although references to the work of Werbőczy are now included. The Hungarian starts the discussion by stating that he knows precisely the content of the notion of the freedom of the people (*gens*) in Hungary. He explains the right of protest and resistance on the part of the Hungarian people in the case of the infringement of godly or natural law. The Italian asks what is meant by "people". The Hungarian refers to Part II, Chapter 4 of Werbőczy's *Tripartitum*, which states that the people comprise the bishops, the barons and other aristocrats and all other nobles, including the royal free towns. Bocatius must have added the mention of the royal free towns himself, as it cannot be read in the original work.

The German then asks about the nature of royal power (*potestas*) in the Hungarian Kingdom.[123] The Hungarian replies by telling him that the king is bound by the law.[124] If he rules according to the law, his subjects are bound to obey him. However, the present king does not attend the Diets of the country. He appoints foreign and unsuitable people to important offices, from which Hungarians are excluded. He overrules the decisions of the Diets, favours the Catholics above the Hungarians, and despoils the Hungarians of their property. No one is allowed to visit him in Prague, which is against the law. No one protects Hungarian soldiers against injustice. In conclusion, the king does not do what he is obliged to do according to the custom of the kingdom, nor does he take care of his subjects. Similar complaints can be read in the various declarations of the Hungarian Estates.

The discussion then continues on the question of the legality of resistance against the king. The Hungarian brings up the example of the Schmalkaldic War (1546–1547) against Emperor Charles V, which is described in a work by the historian Johannes Sleidanus.[125] The rebels defended themselves in a letter to the emperor, in which they stated that they were forced to take up weapons in order to defend themselves against an illegal attack. According to Bocatius, the Hungarian revolt has common ground with this German revolt. The German replies that Rudolf was unaware of the misconduct of his troops in Hungary under the command of Belgiojoso. The Hungarian states that he has proof of this in the form of sealed letters, undersigned by the emperor. He says that letters were sent to the princes of the empire to deny this proof, and that the agent of Rudolf, Rotwitz, tried to influence this opinion. Here again, Bocatius anticipates knowledge on the part of his readers, who must have been part of the circle around the Protestant electors. He quotes a history book that was well known in Germany and compares the Bocskai Revolt with a war in Germany. He reacts to information sent by the emperor to the Protestant princes, and presents a counter opinion, based on the

---

123 Ibid., III. 15.
124 Ibid., III. 15–19.
125 Johannes Sleidanus, *De statu religionis et rei publicae Carolo V. Caesare commentarii* (Argentini: 1555) 530–531.

original letters from the emperor which were also found in Bocatius' luggage.[126] All this points to the fact that the *Hungaroteutomachia* was written specifically for Bocatius' mission and that the German princes and their circles must have been the original target audience.

In what follows, the Hungarian character tries to persuade his interlocutors that the Hungarians were forced to fight against Belgiojoso and to ask for help from the Ottomans, as they were no longer able to defend themselves against the emperor's troops. The Hungarian returns to the topos of the fight between the frogs and the mice to explain the reasons for the truce between the Hungarians and the Ottomans.[127] The question of why the Hungarians allied themselves with the Ottomans returns when the Pole states that his country was never allied with the Ottomans but only signed a truce with them. The Hungarian states that the Hungarians were forced to become the allies of the Ottomans, as they were at war with the Germans. The Poles never had to struggle against two enemies. Bocatius supports his statements with many biblical examples, which prove that the alliance with the Ottomans, as the enemies of the faith, is not as exceptional as the German claims. In the end, he even points to the alliance between King Francis I of France and the Ottomans.

The discussion between the German and the Hungarian continues with a debate about the alliance between Prince János Szapolyai and the Ottomans. The same topic was also discussed by Illésházy in his petition to the emperor.[128] In the continuation of the discussion, we hear in the words of the German, the Italian and the Pole those same attacks on the Hungarians that were printed in broadsheets, newspapers and other documents. Bocatius summarises these sources and presents a short comment on them by means of the answers given by the Hungarian and the Transylvanian.

At the end of the third dialogue, the Hungarian sums up Bocskai's peace proposals and the reactions of the German.[129] Remarkably, Bocatius presents here a detailed description of the various peace proposals that were made successively by Basta, the Hungarians and the envoys of the emperor.[130] He thus gives an overview of how the peace negotiations took place, what exactly was proposed, and the reactions of all parties to the proposals. It is clear that the German does not want to hear these details.[131] The Hungarian replies that in this case the Hungarians will act like the Maccabees, the Jewish rebels who sacrificed themselves. After this, their

---

126 "II/B Inventaria 2," 472.
127 Bocatius, *Hungaroteutomachia*, III. 45.
128 MOL, E211 XXXII. Lymbus II. series 1605–1606, fol. 4r.-v.
129 Bocatius, *Hungaroteutomachia*, III. 159–162.
130 Cf. MOE XI.; and the original documentation of the peace talks in MOL, Archivum Familia Thurzó, 2. Doboz, fasc. 5.
131 Bocatius, *Hungaroteutomachia*, III. 159–162.

revenge will fall on the Germans, according to him. Hungary will lose its traditional function as the shield of the Holy Roman Empire.[132] The same threat can be read in *Querelae* and the Declaration of Korpona. Bocatius' message is directed towards his Protestant readers in order to obtain their support for the peace proposals of the Hungarians.

The final description of the peace proposal exactly replicates the points in the already-mentioned Petition of Illésházy.[133] Firstly, religious freedom must be restored, and the Jesuits must be removed from the country. Second, fewer bishops must be appointed, so that elections at the Diets will not be disrupted. This was an important issue, since each bishop possessed one vote. Hungarians must deal with Hungarian affairs. Only some Germans who had risen to the status of the Hungarian nobles should gain access to Hungarian posts. The crown of the Hungarian Kingdom must be guarded in the country itself by two trusted men, according to the old custom. The chambers must be dissolved, the treasurer restored and the king must once again be present at the Diets. Above all, the old privileges and freedoms of the Hungarians must be restored.

Another important issue was that the emperor must make peace with the Ottomans.[134] The Hungarian character states that Bocskai can act as an intermediary between the emperor and the sultan. In return, Bocskai wants to know what he can expect. The Hungarian warns that this opportunity should not be missed. As the goal of Bocatius' mission was to convince the Protestant electors to press the emperor to make peace with the Ottomans, it is clear why he stresses this point. In return, Bocskai wants a truce according to which his present status will remain untouched, and the future election of the king will be guaranteed.

Something then apparently suddenly occurs to the Hungarian.[135] He requests that those who were judged by the emperor should go unpunished. We can understand that he is thinking here of Illésházy. In addition, no one who took part in the rebellion should be punished, and all of Bocskai's property must be respected. The conversation ends with a fierce call from the Italian for the elimination of the whole Hungarian nation.[136] The interlocutors then bid each other farewell.

The third dialogue is followed by an epilogue in the name of the author, in which he explains his own position on the subject. He argues that he was in search of the truth and presents himself as a citizen of the world, not born in any of the countries participating in the discussion. The reader should accept the text from the point of view of these citizens, but should not forget that they are all subjects of Jesus.

---

132 *Ibid.*, III. 186.
133 *Ibid.*, III. 190–198.
134 *Ibid.*, III. 200–201.
135 *Ibid.*, III. 206–208.
136 *Ibid.*, III. 213–218.

The work is followed by an appendix containing five verses written by Bocatius. The verses are written to the Hungarian crown, to the Hungarian people, on Bocskai, to the Jesuits, and on religion, the last being a repetition of the verse on Bocskai. As Gergely Tóth points out, the composition seems to be unfinished and unedited.[137]

As the verses were only preserved in the Munich manuscript, it is even possible that they were never intended to be part of the work and can be considered as separate works on the crown. It may also be the case that they were written especially for this version of the manuscript, as I will argue below. Their content is strongly related to, and supportive of, the political message conveyed in the dialogues. We can also be sure that they were written by Bocatius, as they contain many references to his earlier poetry.[138] Like the copy of the *Hungaroteutomachia*, we can be certain that Bocatius wrote the verses before his visit to the elector at the beginning of 1606. This all leads to the conclusion that the verses were written before 1608, which has been seen, until now, as the year in which the tradition of the Holy Crown was revived in Hungary and firmly rooted in Hungarian political culture.

The verse on the crown is written from the point of view of a Hungarian talking to the crown: the crown is personified and addressed by Bocatius.[139] The main concept is that the crown jewel plays a role in the history of Hungary through the laws, customs and rules of the kingdom and its people, the Hungarians, and is thus responsible for their freedom, religion and destiny of the people and the kingdom.[140] God guides the Hungarian people and the country through the meaning of the Holy Crown. If this meaning is respected, the kingdom and its inhabitants will flourish. If not, they will perish.

The content of this verse can be related to the Protestant eschatological discourse then dominant in the Protestant territories of Europe. Protestant authors saw the history of Europe and current affairs from the perspective of divine providence, as the visible aspect of the cosmic war between Good and Evil. They divided the peoples and rulers of the world according to their assumed place in the divine plan, which was determined by their supposed attitude towards the Protestant faith. On the one side stood the Protestant people, comprising the chosen nations supported by Providence; on the other side were the Catholic Habsburgs and the pope.

Bocatius also presents the Bocskai Revolt from this providential point of view. Although the Hungarians were the weaker side, they were victorious with the help of God, just like David and Goliath.[141] The Protestant Hungarians are portrayed by

---

137 Tóth, "*Hungaroteutomachia*. Authorship, textual tradition," 28–31, Tóth, "Az erazmista szatirikus és a bebörtönzött mártír," 79–120.
138 *Ibid.*
139 Bocatius, *Hungaroteutomachia*, App. I. 45.
140 *Ibid.*, App. I. 45.
141 *Ibid.*, App. I. 75–90.

Bocatius as the chosen nation, fighting "... as long as the law permits ..." against the (Catholic) Italians, the Germans and the pope, who are on the side of evil. The only Protestant people outside the Hungarians who are mentioned by Bocatius are the Dutch. Bocatius relates the fate of the Hungarian rebels with that of the Dutch rebels, stating that "... *rebellamus cum Belgis* ..." (we are rebelling with the Dutch). Both peoples fought for the same (Protestant) cause and stood on the same side. Bocatius explains in no fewer than six lines how the Dutch are fighting, like the Hungarians, against the evil of the Catholic menace and the pope.[142]

It seems odd that Bocatius should defend the Bocskai Revolt by referring to the Dutch Revolt, which he can hardly be expected to know anything about. Nevertheless, the Hungarians must have known of the Dutch Revolt. The Dutch envoy Pieter Cornelisz. Brederode (Brederodius) mentions his Hungarian contacts in a letter to the Dutch Staten-Generaal in 1605.[143] As mentioned earlier, Bocatius had met Brederode in Heidelberg, a meeting that must have been pre-arranged. There can also have been connections between the court of Bocskai and the Dutch Protestants (perhaps those living in exile in Prague or Heidelberg), as Bocatius wrote in his memoirs about Dutch people who visited Hungary during the revolt. It is also noteworthy that the Protestant humanist Albert Szenci Molnár re-used a very symbolic image from the Dutch Revolt to clarify the religion of Bocskai, thus stressing the common fate of both peoples.[144] The Protestant circles in Germany had much sympathy for the Dutch, and the Protestant princes supported their struggle against the Spanish Habsburgs with considerable sums of money. But it was not only the Hungarians who legitimated their rebellion using the Dutch example: it also worked the other way around. Emanuel van Meteren points out in his patriotic history of the Dutch Revolt (1608) the remarkable similarities between the Dutch and the Hungarian revolts.[145] He wrote about Bocskai and the Ottoman crown and even mentions a Hungarian envoy, who must have been Bocatius. The Bocskai Revolt must have been a strong incentive for relations between the Hungarians and the Dutch.

Bocatius ends his verse with a prayer to "our Holy Crown" to save the power (*potestas*) and religion of the kingdom through the defence of ancient virtues. This is a true revival of the Medieval tradition of the crown of Hungary. The Hungarian crown was originally a Catholic symbol of authority in the kingdom, transferred

---

142 *Ibid.*, App. I. 90–100.
143 Nationaal Archief, Den Haag, Staten-Generaal, nummer toegang 1.01.02, inventarisnummer 6016. (9 April 1605).
144 Teszelszky, *True Religion*, 108–110.
145 Emanuel van Meteren, *Commentarien ofte memorien van-den Nederlandtschen staet* [Commentaries or memoirs of the Dutch state] (Schotlandt buyten Danswijck [Amsterdam?]: Hermes van Loven, 1608) 100r-v, 149r.

through a Catholic ceremony from one king to another. The roots of the tradition of the Holy Crown in Hungary are also Catholic in essence, as the Hungarians traditionally trace them back to St István, the first king of Hungary who converted his people to Catholicism. The Hungarian Catholics at the time of Bocatius defended their position by pointing to the legacy of St István.

Bocatius adapted the tradition of the Holy Crown in order to fit it into the Protestant eschatological framework of the Bocskai Revolt and the Protestant rebel tradition in Europe. The Crown is portrayed as the defender of Protestant values through its political meaning. If the ancient Hungarian customs and privileges, which are symbolised by the Holy Crown, are guaranteed by the ruler through the free election of the king and the keeping of the crown on the territory of Hungary, then the Protestant religion will also be secured.

It may seem strange that Bocatius made use of this state symbol, which is not only Catholic in origin but was also in the hands of the emperor at the time the verse was written. The crown had not been in the country for 33 years, since the coronation in 1572 as described in the former chapter. The author even seems unaware that it is kept in Prague, stating in the *Hungaroteutomachia* and in the verse that the crown was in Linz.[146] In another line, he even asks the crown quite seriously where it can be.

Why did Bocatius devote so much effort to reinventing the tradition of the crown, when he did not even know where the tangible crown jewel was? The clue is concealed in the person of Bocskai, his religion, and his political message regarding the restoration of the free election of the king in Hungary by the Estates. Bocatius translates the Catholic tradition of the Holy Crown into a new political theory, based on the person of Bocskai and his image in Hungary as the Protestant saviour of a nation in crisis. The second verse, addressed to the people of Hungary, starts with a reference to St István, the first apostolic king of Hungary, and to his crown, which belongs to the people. Without coronation with the Holy Crown, no one can be a true king of Hungary, writes Bocatius after Bonfini. The people are seeking a sacred person who can wear this Holy Crown. In the third verse, it becomes clear who this person will be. Through the meaning of the crown, Bocskai is presented as a "second István". Just as the first king converted his people to Christianity, so the religion of the second István will now be victorious and faith will be restored.

Bocatius presented the Hungarian ruler in the same way that other Protestant rulers liked to see themselves: as "living Protestant saints" ruling their chosen people and defending their country against the Catholic Habsburg menace, as John Exalto showed in his studies about Dutch Protestant saints.[147]

---

146 Bocatius, *Hungaroteutomachia*, III. 38, App. I. 43.
147 Cf. John Exalto, *Gereformeerde heiligen* [Reformed saints] (Nijmegen: Vantilt, 2005); John Exalto, "Reformed sanctity: Some observations from Dutch religious history," in Thomas K. Kuhn and

The transformation of the Holy Crown of Hungary from the Catholic state symbol of a saint-king and royal power into a symbol of Protestant resistance against Catholic tyranny is similar to the development of the representation of other state symbols and rulers in Protestant countries in Europe, as in the Low Countries. The way in which Bocatius depicted Prince Bocskai in these poems is very much reminiscent of how the Dutch Stadholders William the Silent and Maurice of Orange were portrayed in contemporary prints and broadsheets. It should be no surprise that several of these Dutch propagandistic broadsheets on Maurice were found in Bocatius' luggage.[148]

The positive image of Bocskai even reached the Dutch Republic: Bocskai was presented in contemporary Dutch historiography as a living Protestant saint, the ideal ruler and defender of the Protestant faith in Hungary, even serving as an example for the Dutch Stadholder Maurice.[149] The appendix to the *Hungaroteutomachia* can therefore be seen as a mirror of princes for Protestant rulers in Europe, in the same way as the later works of Berger and Révay on the Holy Crown, of which we will read in the next chapter.

It is thus possible that Bocatius added these verses to the *Hungaroteutomachia* in order to promote the image of Bocskai in Protestant countries as the ideal Protestant ruler and as a living Protestant saint. If this is the case, it is unclear why the other two copies of the *Hungaroteutomachia* do not have the appendix of verses. It seems that they never had such an appendix, and that Bocatius did not plan to add one. So why did he add the verses only to the copy of the *Hungaroteutomachia* that was left in Heidelberg?

It is possible that the lack of these verses had something to do with the original destination of this manuscript and its target audience. Bocatius' mission was originally planned as an opportunity to meet with the electors of the Palatine, Saxony and Brandenburg in Germany. He brought with him letters and documents for all three of them, as seen from the inventory and as proved by the letters in Vienna addressed to the electors.[150] Bocatius had only one copy of the *Hungaroteutomachia* with him when he was arrested on his way to Brandenburg. We know this from the letter from Brederode that Bocatius carried with him and which he had to hand over to the secretary of the prince of Brandenburg.[151]

As there were originally three copies of the *Hungaroteutomachia*, and as no other copy is known to have been left on the journey or sent elsewhere, it is highly

---

Nicola Stricker, eds., Erinnert, Verdrängt, Verehrt. Was ist Reformierten heilig? (Emder Beiträge zum reformierten Protestantismus, Band 16). (Göttingen: Vandenhoeck & Ruprecht, 2016) 21–38.
148 Teszelszky, "Üzenet az utazótáskában," 127–147.
149 Teszelszky, *True Religion*, 144.
150 "II/B Inventaria 2," 480–481.
151 *Ibid.*

possible that each copy was originally intended to be presented personally to the three electors. The copy now in Vienna could have been destined for the elector of Brandenburg. As the only manuscript containing the verses on the crown can be found in Munich, having been left originally in Heidelberg, this copy could have been made especially for the Elector Palatine of the Rhine, Friedrich IV, and could have been presented to him. This does still not explain the existence of the copy in Italy and the lack of the crown verses in it, of which we do not know the exact provenance. Perhaps this was the one intended for the Elector of Saxony and travelled afterwards to Italy.

The gift for the Elector Palatine of the Rhine with a reference to the Holy Crown is perhaps no coincidence. The verses on the crown and the references to a (Protestant) elective king can be related to a discussion at the court in Heidelberg between the advisors of the Elector Palatine on the future king of Hungary in April 1605.[152] This was a very topical question, as at the time Bocskai was elected prince of Hungary on the occasion of the Diet of Szerencs in the same month. One of the advisors to the elector palatine, Michael Löfenius, stated during a meeting on 20 April 1605 that if Hungary wanted to have another ruler, and did not want to have either a Habsburg or a Saxon, then the elector palatine should not refuse the opportunity, as "… someone from the family had already been king of Hungary …" (he referred to Otto of Bavaria).[153] Löfenius was even ready to make a deal with Brandenburg to exclude Saxony.

We do not know if these plans to occupy the Hungarian throne were ever put into action. We should also remember that precisely on the day of this meeting, Bocskai was elected as king, something that Löfenius was probably not aware of.[154] It is therefore possible that Bocatius wanted to make clear to the elector palatine that Bocskai had already been elected as prince of Hungary. As we know, Bocskai was already ill and quite old at the end of 1605 and the discussion about the succession of Emperor Rudolf II was an ongoing theme in the courts of Europe,[155] thus it is also possible that the *Hungaroteutomachia* and the verses were intended as an incentive to the Protestant Elector Palatine Friedrich IV to think about taking over the Hungarian throne.

One of the riddles remaining after reading the work of Bocatius is his description of the tangible crown of Hungary and his reference to an image. As mentioned earlier, no Hungarian had set eyes on the crown between 1572 and 1608 as far as we

---

152 Ritter, *Die Gründung der Union 1598–1608*, 444. (17 April 1605)
153 *Ibid.*; MOE XI. 221.
154 "Orantiuncula ante sole iuramentum," in *Acta in Ungarn, Böhmen und Schlesien. 1604–1609*. Biblioteka Cyfrowa Uniwersytetu Wrocławskiego, MF 9961, fol. 11r.-13v. Cf. MOE XI. 152–154.
155 Luc Duerloo, *Dynasty and Piety: Archduke Albert (1598–1621) and Habsburg Political Culture in an Age of Religious Wars* (Farnham: Routledge, 2012) 232–266.

know, as it was locked far away in the treasury of the imperial castle in Prague. The only realistic drawing of it, made in the sixteenth century, was kept in Germany, as we have shown in the first chapter (see image 4).[156] It was only in 1608, when members of the public were able to view the crown, that artists had an opportunity to draw it and others wrote descriptions of the crown jewel. The first realistic images of the crown were published after 1608 in the work of Jeszenszky, as we will read later.[157] As far as we know, no Early Modern image of the crown was available in Hungary at the time that Bocatius composed his verses.

Bocatius makes a reference to the lack of an image of the crown, writing at the beginning of his verse that "… although our fathers held you between their two hands, now Hungarians no longer know you …".[158] It is of course also possible that the author is trying to say that Hungarians no longer have any knowledge of the tradition of the Holy Crown. However, in the next lines he refers unambiguously to the external appearance of the crown: "How is it possible that no one knows what you look like?"[159] He goes even further, exclaiming that "… the painter depicts the crown as he thinks best".[160] Apparently, there were no realistic images of the crown in his day, as we have shown in the first chapter. Later on, Bocatius asks his readers to believe that he does know what the crown looks like. According to him,

> … it is almost impossible to imagine what I see on you, baskets of pearls, and you are totally (…) made of gold, or perhaps you are made from what one of the wise men from the East once gave to Jesus, this is a gift of heaven. Is it any wonder that everyone's eyes and hearts are attracted to you?[161]

Bearing in mind what the crown actually looks like, it almost seems that Bocatius really had seen it with his own eyes. When reading these lines, we must not forget that the author had a vivid imagination and could easily delude the reader, just as he did in the *Relatio*. It is of course possible that he did possess one of the images of the crown, made during the time of King Mátyás Corvinus and kept at the court of Bocskai. Indeed, pictures of crowns exist among the manuscripts of Mátyás Corvinus and in the already-mentioned historical work of János Thuróczy

---

156 Cf. Buzási and Pálffy, *Augsburg - Wien - München - Innsbruck. Die frühesten Darstellungen der Stephanskrone und die Entstehung der Exemplare des Ehrenspiegels des Hauses Österreich.*
157 Johann Jessenius, *Regis Ungariae, Matthiae II. coronatio; Johan: Jessenio a Jessen, Regio Medico, Descriptore. Adiecta, regni, regumque Pannoniae, brevis Chronographia.* (Viennae: Ludovicus Bonnoberger, 1609).
158 Bocatius, *Hungaroteutomachia*, App. I. 6–7.
159 *Ibid.*, App. I. 8.
160 *Ibid.*, App. I. 9.
161 *Ibid.*, App. I. 29–34.

(see image 2) and on the map of Wolfgang Lazius (see image 5) that bear a slight resemblance to the Holy Crown, but which are not depictions of the crown in the strict sense.

The crown played an important role in the political thinking behind the Bocskai Revolt. If there really did exist an image of the crown at the time of Bocskai, it is remarkable that it was not used in any pictorial publication or any other visual propaganda from the Bocskai court. There is no Hungarian crown visible on any of the noble patents issued by Bocskai as the king of Hungary, nor was it used in his own armour, his princely or royal seal or any other representations used by him, like portraits, coins or jetons.

In the second verse, to the Hungarian people, Bocatius unambiguously refers to an image of the crown, which was meant to accompany the verses: "And now here is painted, what you can see, people, your crown."[162] If this image of the crown really did exist in the time of Bocatius, and if it really resembled the Hungarian crown, it would be one of the oldest depictions of the crown of Hungary. Was it possible that an image of the Holy Crown existed in the court of Bocskai?

There is one source that indeed suggests that such an image could have been made at the time of the revolt. When Bocskai requested a crown from the sultan, a discussion regarding the style of this crown took place between the envoys of Bocskai and those of the sultan. The evidence can be found in the already-quoted letter above from István Korláth, György Kékedy and Mehmed Kethüda written in Constantinople to Bocskai and dated 24 April 1605.[163] The Hungarians asked for a new crown and the Ottomans wanted to have a design from them, so that they could make a new one. Finally, a new crown was made. This means that the Hungarians presented some kind of image of a crown to the Ottomans. We do not know whether this was merely a schematic image of a European royal crown, or whether they sent a depiction of the crown of Hungary. Given the significance of the Hungarian crown for Bocskai and the Hungarian Estates, it is very likely that they tried to obtain a copy of the Holy Crown from the Ottomans.

The image of the Crown in the *Hungaroteutomachia* and in the verses in the appendix is nothing other than the true revival and renewal of the Holy Crown tradition. It is the first serious political and literary text on the meaning of the Crown since Werbőczy's law-book was finished in 1514. It is important to note that Bocatius states nowhere that the entire Hungarian nobility were members of the crown, or had political power based on their membership of the body of the Holy Crown. Nowhere does Bocatius use an organic metaphor when writing about the crown, nor did any of the Early Modern authors after him until the eighteenth

---

162 *Ibid.*, App. II. 2.
163 "Korláth István, Kékedy György és Mehmed kihája," 159–169.

century. The work on the crown again supports the thesis that the Doctrine of the Holy Crown is a modern invention.

However, Bocatius is the first Early Modern author to outline a political theory on the basis of the personification of the Holy Crown, as described in historical examples. He is also the first person to connect such a theory to an image of the crown and to write about the external appearance of the tangible crown in a political text. Not long afterwards, when he was already languishing in the prison in Prague unable to communicate with his fellow intellectuals in Hungary, many others followed his example, as we will see in the next chapters. These authors and their works went on to become famous, while the work of Bocatius on the crown was entirely forgotten and has been buried in the archives till our time.

The question remains as to who, or what, inspired Bocatius to write this work. As stated above, the birth of the *Hungaroteutomachia* must be viewed in relation to many other political texts defending Bocskai and the rebellious Hungarian Estates. As we have seen in the last chapter, the court of Bocskai consisted of some of the most outstanding humanists, writers and poets of the time, including János Rimay, Illésházy, Mihály Káthay, János Debreceni Szappanos and Simon Péchy, to name just a few. These authors worked together on most of the propagandistic writings, but it was only Bocatius who wrote about the Holy Crown.

Bocatius' verse on the Holy Crown resembles most closely the work of the already-mentioned Elias Berger on another of the symbols of the Hungarian Kingdom: his *Rapsodiae De Cruce Insigniis Regni Hungarici* on the Cross of Hungary (1600), which we discussed in the previous chapter. We know that Bocatius read this work, which was the first national epic of the Hungarians, as he possessed even a special copy of this work with added blank pages between the printed text, on which he added his own handwritten verses and his signature (J.B.).[164] It can't be sure that Bocatius was the person one who interpreted the crown as a national symbol in a politically tinged text for the first time, but it is a fact that there has not been any reception of this work, as no one could have read it in Hungary. Bocatius' idea of the crown must be regarded as a highly interesting, but also dead branch in the development of the tradition of the Holy Crown in Hungary around 1605.

From the perspective of the development of the crown tradition after 1606, the *Hungaroteutomachia* and its appendix is one of the most interesting and best written, yet totally unknown, Early Modern sources on the Holy Crown in Hungary. It reveals a great deal about how, in the short period between the end of 1604 and the end of 1605, the crown tradition was revived and redeveloped in Hungary under the influence of anti-Habsburg Protestant political culture. Bocatius' verses

---

164 Berger, *Rapsodiae de cruce insigniis regni Hungarici*. ÖNB, sign. 39.R.11.

and the content of the *Hungaroteutomachia* show that the use of the crown in the representation of the Hungarian Estates can be traced back to the work of the intellectual circle around Bocskai in 1605.

VI. The return of the Holy Crown to Hungary

The end of the Bocskai rebellion and the testament of Bocskai (1606)

After the handing over of the Ottoman crown to Bocskai, Archduke Matthias began negotiations with Illésházy, who acted on behalf of Bocskai. The aim of Bocskai's political strategy was to bring the Habsburg emperor to the negotiating table and force him to concede his opponent's political demands.[1] The essence of the demand put forward by Illésházy was the restoration of those rights of the Hungarian Estates which, in the opinion of the rebels, had been conferred by the ancient Hungarian crown.

What the crown meant to the Hungarian rebels becomes clear from a misunderstanding on that point that arose in the course of the peace negotiations between Illésházy and the Archduke.[2] Illésházy proposed to the delegates that it should not be permissible to offend against the crown and the authority (*auctoritas*) of the king.[3] By that he was referring to the first decree of Ulászló II, made shortly after his coronation. In this, the king had promised to uphold unharmed the liberties, ancient rights and privileges of Hungary.

According to Illésházy, the authority (*auctoritas*) of the crown incorporated the rights of the Estates to oppose the king. From Archduke Matthias' response it is evident that he had not understood Illésházy correctly, and thought that he was referring to the safekeeping of the crown itself. In point of fact, he stated that insofar as it concerned the authority of the crown and the king, the age of Ulászló II and the present time were different. From this it follows, said the Archduke, that a way of storing the crown must be found that differed from that employed in the time of Ulászló II, as Visegrád was in Ottoman hands, and there was nowhere in the whole of Hungary safer than where the crown was at present kept. Then Tiburtius Himmelreich, secretary to the Hungarian Chancellery, indicated that he had understood what the Hungarian delegate was saying, because he declared that the ancient rights and privileges mentioned in Ulászló II's time were not appropriate to modern circumstances. In the end the parties reached an agreement, and on

---

1 Ágnes R. Várkonyi, *A királyi Magyarország 1541–1686* [Royal Hungary 1541–1686] (Budapest: Vince kiadó, 1999), 66–67.
2 The documents that formed the basis of the quarrel have survived to this day: ÖStA Wien, HHStA, Ungarische Akten, Fasc. 149 Konv. A., fol. 62r.-68v.
3 Eckhart, *A szentkorona*-eszme, 131.

23 June 1606 the Peace Treaty of Vienna was signed, which formally brought an end to the rebellion.[4]

In this document both the Hungarian crown and that presented by the Turks acquired once more a legitimating function with respect to the agreement made between the Habsburg emperor and the Hungarian Estates. The treaty recognised the liberties of the Estates, among them freedom of religious practice and the right to elect the king freely. The guarantee of these rights was the Holy Crown of Hungary, since in Article 4 it was laid down that the Holy Crown must return to Hungarian territory.[5] The crown given by the Turks was dealt with in a separate clause titled "As concerns the person of Bocskai" (*Quod personam Bochkay concernit*). In Article 9 the fiction of the rejection of the crown is repeated: "Since, out of respect for the ancient Holy Crown of the country and the right to elect the king freely, Bocskai accepted from the hands of the Turks the crown that he received as a gift ... "[6]

How is it possible for the rejection of the crown to appear in the official text of the Peace of Vienna but not in historical literature from that time? The reason is once again the role, or rather the intention, of the fiction in the restoration to the Holy Crown of the Kingdom of Hungary its original legitimating significance with regard to the right to elect the king freely. That there is reference to the rejection in the treaty but not in historical literature proves that the rejection played an important part in the political consensus involved in the wording of the treaty. The question of whether the event took place at Rákosmező or not was of no importance to Bocskai's contemporaries, as for all of them it had been of use in only one certain political context. The rejection is no longer mentioned in later historical works because it was of no consequence once peace had been made and the Hungarian crown returned to Hungary. If the rejection is even then mentioned in an essay, it is only that Bocatius' work is being quoted.

This apparently rather tangled interplay of fiction and reality by which the Hungarian Estates pursued their rights can be identified with the function of the topos of the Huns as ancestors of the Hungarians. This myth is mentioned in the legal documents of 1608, but in the final article more foreign persons are accepted as members (*indigenatus*) of the Estates with all the rights thereto appertaining.[7] Although the new members of the Estates were not descendants of the Huns, they still acquired all the privileges which they were later able to claim by virtue of imaginary forbears. The Hun-fiction only came into play for the attainment of individual

---

4 Makkai, "A Bocskay-felkelés," 753–755. The commissioners of the Ottoman and Habsburg Empires signed the Treaty of Zsitvatorok on 11 November 1606.
5 Benda, *A Bocskai-szabadságharc*, 153.
6 'Quod Bochkay coronam a Turcis in praeiudicium sacrae antiquae coronae regni et regis Hungariae ac liberae eius electionis non acceperit, (...).' MOE, XI, 859.
7 "Matthiae II. decr. a. 1608 post. cor. (I) 2, art. 27," in *Corpus Juris Hungarici*, 38–40.

definite political aims and if there was no political need of it, it was ignored, as, for example, was done in the acceptance of new foreign members of the Estates. It is also noteworthy that the authors of these ethnic fictions were non-Hungarian foreigners such as Berger and Bocatius.

The change in the significance of the crown did not end with the Peace of Vienna in 1606. In the second half of 1606 Bocskai and Illésházy debated the political future of the Kingdom in an exchange of letters.[8] The most important point at issue was whether Transylvania should remain an independent principality under its own elected prince, or should rather be united with Hungary under Habsburg rule. The political background to the question was whether the peace treaty made with Rudolf could be a sufficient guarantee of the continuation of the independence of Hungary within the Habsburg Empire and of the preservation of the liberties of the Estates.

Illésházy, and with him most of the aristocrats from the Habsburg territories of Western Hungary, was of the opinion that the latter possibility was the more favourable.[9] As he saw it, an independent principality that elected its own prince was a threat to the unity of Hungary: " ... nothing could be more dangerous to the poor Hungarians after the death of a king than that two free elections should remain in our midst."[10] In his view they should strive for the unification of the two parts of Hungary under Habsburg rule so that the country should be able to offer effective resistance to the Ottomans. Bocskai was less optimistic than Illésházy over the intentions of the Habsburg court.[11] His greatest anxiety was that a Habsburg emperor could not be regarded as a national king, as his throne would be outside Hungary, and in consequence the Estates could scarcely act as a counterweight to his power.[12] He was of the opinion that if the Habsburg dynasty took the whole of Hungary into its power it must soon mean the end of Hungary's

---

8 MOE, XII, 362–363, Benda: *A Bocskai-szabadságharc*, 66–67; Makkai, "A Bocskay-felkelés," 750–753.
9 See *inter alia* the letter of a number of high clergy and aristocrats (including Péter Révay), who, led by Istvánffy, protested against Bocskai's dividing Hungary. Vienna, 26 September 1606. MOE, XII, 704–706.
10 Illésházy to Bocskai, Vienna, 13 June 1606. Szilágyi, "Bocskay István és Illésházy István levelezése 1605 és 1606-ban," 282–283.
11 Illésházy to Bocskai, 7 September 1606, *ibid.*, 324–325.
12 In Árpád Károlyi's words: "So great were the waves made in European public opinion by the latter thought, that in the Calvinist court of Heidelberg serious discussion took place over what would happen if Hungary tired of the Habsburgs and wanted another, different king: at one session of the council the advisors of the Elector of Pfalz declared that in that event "as the common good took precedence over the House of Austria" the lord of Heidelberg ought not to refuse the Hungarian crown, "because a count of Pfalz (i. e. Otto of Bavaria) had once been king of Hungary". MOE, XI, 221.

independence within the Empire and of the liberties of the Estates.[13] In his view an unbreakable bond existed between the Hungarian people and Transylvania. Nevertheless, he believed that a strong, independent Transylvanian principality had to remain an Ottoman protectorate so that opposition could be offered at all times to the Habsburg dynasty if danger from the West threatened the interests of the Hungarian people. The strategic division of the country into two must also preserve the balance between the Habsburg and Ottoman great powers. His final conclusion was, therefore, that national unity could be preserved by political division.

In the debate both writers made use of the Holy Crown in support of their views on the unity of Hungary and the Estates. Illésházy's reply to Bocskai said that Bocskai would do the greatest harm "… to the Hungarian crown and the future …" by the division of the country.[14] In his political testament (1606) Bocskai reacted to this accusation. He spoke of the significance to the Estates of both the Hungarian crown and that presented by the Turks.[15] He had divided this nation (*nemzet*) into two parts, and called the two parts (using the word in a political sense) states (*respublicae*) so as to distinguish the term from the concept of nation.

In his testament Bocskai defended the statement that both crowns were needed for the preservation of the unity of Transylvania and Hungary, two states combined in a single nation.[16] This necessity, in his opinion, was created by the current political situation, in which the power of the king of Hungary was exercised by the "German-Austrian nation". This posed a threat to the freedom and independence of the entire Hungarian nation, since there was no freely elected ruler to lead the whole of the Hungarian Estates. He expressed his conception of the situation of the Estates in allegorical fashion, in which the two crowns represented the power of the king of Hungary and of the prince of Transylvania:

> We can, however, see the way [ahead] in the permanent maintaining of conciliation: let neither principality, change though they may each in accordance with free choice, nor *respublica* either strive one against the other through anyone's provocation or incitement. But as long as the Hungarian crown is in the hands of a nation stronger than us, the German, and the Kingdom of Hungary turns on the Germans, it will be at all times

---

13 Bocskai to Illésházy, 18 September 1606. Szilágyi, "Bocskay István és Illésházy István levelezése 1605 és 1606-ban," 331–333. (answer to the letter of 13 June).
14 Illésházy to Bocskai, Trencsén, 9 December 1606, *ibid.*, 635.
15 Szigethy, *Bocskai István testámentumi rendelése*, 15–16. Bocskai wrote the testament shortly before his death in September 1606. A contemporary copy can be found at: MOL P 287 Forgách család. Series 1. 34. cs. Fasc. T. 34, fol. 24–31.
16 *Ibid.*, 14–15.

necessary and profitable to maintain a Hungarian prince in Transylvania, for that will be to their advantage and protection.[17]

In short: while the "German-Austrians" were the stronger and exercised power of the king in Hungary, it was necessary for this situation to be balanced by the power in Transylvania of a freely elected Hungarian prince. Next, he outlined a political idea whereby he presented the situation in which the crown (meaning royal power) was in the hands of a Hungarian king:

> If, however, God were to grant that the Hungarian crown were to come into Hungarian hands in Hungary under a crowned kingship, then we would beckon to the Transylvanians not to remain aloof or stand apart, but indeed to assist as best they could and place themselves under that crown in the old way, on an equal footing. Which we would very much recommend, if ever there is loyal brotherhood among them.[18]

The essence of Bocskai's political message was that it would be possible to unify the Hungarian Estates in the Kingdom of Hungary only if a Hungarian king did it. In other words: it would only be possible and permissible for Hungary to be made one under a king born of the Hungarian people. This view of Bocskai's is not to be taken as a mere political vision, as has often been thought, but rather as his answer to the political question of the time. The political background to the passage quoted was whether Transylvania would join the part of Hungary that was under Habsburg rule. It was his assumption, on which he based his argument, that under the political conditions of the day an elected home-grown prince – whether Bocskai or some other prince of Transylvania – would serve to offset the preponderance of Austrian royal power in Hungary. From that it followed that unification of all Hungary would only be possible if the Hungarian Estates were stronger than the Austrians, because only then would the Hungarian nation be in a position to elect its own king. The strength of the Estates – Bocskai repeats this again and again in his testament and other writings – would be revealed in their political independence supported by certain liberties. In other words: it would only be possible to unite every part of Hungary under the Hungarian crown if the Estates had once more the right to elect the king and crown him with the crown of Hungary.

The significance for the state (*respublica*) of Transylvania of the crown presented by the Turks was, in Bocskai's opinion, that it guaranteed a principality that was

---

17 *Ibid.*, 15. "Testamentoria", MOL P 287 Forgách family. Series 1. 34. cs. Fasc. T. 34 Fol. 26: "magiari corona".
18 *Ibid.*, 16–17.

independent of the Habsburg Empire and where the ruler was freely elected.[19] The existence of this coronation jewel was at the same time a warning to the Austrian emperor, that if he violated the rights of the Hungarian nation in the one state he could always count on the reaction of Transylvania. It followed from this that the Bocskai crown acted as a defender of the liberties of the Hungarian Estates. This was why Bocskai said "… let the Turkish crown and sabre go from prince to prince …".[20] It is therefore no wonder that later, at his funeral in 1607, the Turkish crown too played a conspicuous part.[21]

The views on the crown and royal power expressed in Bocskai's testament had considerable influence on political thought in the seventeenth century concerning the legitimation of rebellion against the Habsburg emperor. Naturally, the Habsburg court followed this Hungarian change of attitude very closely. No fewer than four German translations of Bocskai's testament are to be found in the Haus-, Hof- und Staatsarchiv.[22]

The thinkers and politicians of the later seventeenth century (and the academics of the following period too, not to mention about modern politicians) interpreted Bocskai's testament as legitimation of the procedure whereby he had striven for a political goal – the unification of Transylvania with Hungary as the Kingdom of Hungary. His words – deliberately or unwittingly – were taken out of context and interpreted as a vision of the political future of the country.[23] In the course of this, stress was placed on certain characteristic elements, such as the Hungarian crown, which should no longer remain in the possession of the Austrian king, and the concept of the national king. From these, subsequently far-reaching (and erroneous) conclusions were drawn, such as that Hungary could be regarded as politically independent only if and when the Holy Crown returned to Hungarian hands and the country acquired a national king. This interpretation of Bocskai's testament may have been recognised, among others, at the time of the assumption of power in 1607–1608 by Archduke Matthias, as we shall see later. The effect of the content of the testament is also apparent in Gábor Bethlen's campaign of 1619, which, for lack of space, we shall not examine here.

---

19 *Ibid.*, 16–17.
20 *Ibid.*, 17.
21 Ildikó Horn, "Ismeretlen temetési rendtartások a 16–17. századból [Unknown funeral ceremonials in the the sixteenth and seventeenth century]," *Irodalomtörténeti Közlemények* 5–6 (1998), 760–772.
22 *TESTAMENTARIA DISPOSITIO / Serenissimi Principis et domini, domini STEPHANI Dei gratia Hungariae Transsylvaniaeque Principis et Siculorum Comitis, Coram R.do D'no Petro Alvinczij, et Gener. Paulo Eoruendij Consiliario et Thesaurario, ac Simone Pechio intimo Secretario facta.* ÖStA Wien, HHStA, Ungarn, Fasc. 151 Konv. A. 1606. X–XII, fol. 45r.-110v.
23 See *inter alia*: Árpád Károlyi, *Bocskay szerepe a történetben* [The role of Bocskai in history] (Budapest: Ny. Hornyánszky Viktor, 1898), 16.

The ideas of Illésházy and Bocskai may be regarded as a summary of the development in Hungary between 1600 and 1607 in the tradition of the crown and its role. After 1600 the crown, which in 1572 had still only had any significance at a coronation, symbolised the political rights, liberties and unity of the Hungarian Estates, together with the maintenance of the autonomy of Hungary. This significance is connected to the image formed of the Estates, or rather constitutes part of their self-identity.

Archduke Matthias Habsburg in Hungary

Archduke Matthias Habsburg (1557–1619) has a bad name among modern historians.[24] Because of the "Brothers' Conflict" which he waged with Rudolf between 1606 and 1612, which was at its height in 1607–1608, in numerous studies emphasis has been placed on his supposed bad nature.[25] Most writers rate him a powerful politician, driven by morbid jealousy of his brother Rudolf.[26] Matthias is portrayed as a weak, indecisive and unreliable personality.[27] Robert Evans puts it as follows:

---

24 Matthias II is the only Habsburg emperor of whom no modern biography has been written. In most foreign studies of the Habsburg Empire or dynasty only a few lines are devoted to him. See: Moriz Ritter, "Matthias, Österreichischer Erzherzog und Deutscher Kaiser," in *Algemeine Deutsche Biographie*, vol. 20 (Leipzig: Historische Commission bei der königlichen Akademie der Wissenschaften, 1884), 629–654; Emile Lousse, "Qui donc était l'empereur Mathias?," in Louis Carlen and Fritz Steinegger, eds., *Festschrift für Nikolaus Grass*, vol. I (Innsbruck: Wagner, 1974–1975), 135–143; Brigitte Hamann, "Kaiser Mathias," in Brigitte Hamann and Georg Hamann, eds., *Die Habsburger: ein biographisches Lexikon* (Wien: Ueberreuter, 1988), 353–356; Volker Press, "Matthias 1612-1619," in Anton Schindling and Walter Ziegler, eds., *Die Kaiser des Neuzeit 1519-1918: Heiliges Römisches Reich, Österreich, Deutschland* (München: C.H. Beck, 1990), 114–123; H.G. Koenigsberger, *Monarchies, States Generals and Parliaments. The Netherlands in the Fifteenth and Sixteenth Centuries* (Cambridge: Cambridge University Press, 2001), 280–288.
25 Bernd Rill, *Kaiser Matthias. Brüderzwist und Glaubenskampf* (Graz, Wien, Köln: Styria, 1999); Hannes Leidinger, Verena Schwartz and Berndt Schlipper, *Schwarzbuch der Habsburger. Die unrühmliche Geschichte des Hauses Habsburg* (Wien: Deuticke Verlag, 2003), 51–59; Václav Bůžek, ed., *Ein Bruderzwist im Hause Habsburg (1608-1611)* (České Budějovice: Jihočeská univerzita v Českých Budějovicích, Historický ústav, 2010) (Opera historica, 14.).
26 Andrew Wheatcroft expresses it thus: ".... Matthias seems to have been no less obsessive, but focused exclusively on hatred of his imperial brother...". Andrew Wheatcroft, *The Habsburgs: Embodying Empire* (London: The Folio Society, 1995), 171.
27 Edward Crankshaw, *The Habsburgs* (London: Corgi books, 1971), 109; Evans: "Of Matthias, one of the poorest of all Habsburg rulers, it may be said that he possessed all of the faults of his brother Rudolf II, but none of his redeeming qualities of kindness and cultural interests." Evans, *Rudolf II*, 60. See also: Robert A. Kann, *A History of the Habsburg Empire, 1526–1918* (Berkely: University of California Press, 1974), 43; Geoff Mortimer, *The Origins of the Thirty Years War and the Revolt in Bohemia, 1618* (London: Palgrave Macmillan, 2015), 222.

"It is most logical to consider Matthias' subsequent actions ... as motivated largely by territorial ambition. This was the longest frustration of his life, unsatisfied either by the Netherlands venture or by any other appeals to Rudolf."[28] To sum up, Matthias has found a place in the history books as an average man of no special abilities, who, furthermore, was not even up to standard in his brief reign.[29] Jean Bérenger says: "After such a furious drive to seize power, Matthias did nothing."[30] The question is, can so harsh a verdict be fair on an emperor who was on the throne during one of the most troubled periods of the Habsburg Empire, and on whom, furthermore, we are none too well informed.

Despite his personal imperfections and political mistakes, several writers do credit Matthias with some achievements during his career. According to György Bónis, his most important feat of arms must be the way that he confirmed the Habsburg dynasty's exercise of power in Central Europe and preserved its continuity in a period when that power was in a grave crisis of legitimacy.[31] This was accompanied by the Bocskai rebellion and war with the Ottomans, which together proved the political undoing of Rudolf.[32] The deeper-rooted cause of Rudolf's unsuccessful policies was that his exceptional imperial ambitions clashed with political reality, which according to Evans brought about "... a Samson-like orgy of self-destruction ...".[33] What was more, this crisis was played out at a time when there was great political and religious tension in the Habsburg Empire between the Catholics and the Protestants, and there was also the general European crisis to be reckoned with, including the failure of the banks in Prague. And the costly campaigns against the Ottomans were inconclusive. All these factors could have brought Habsburg power in Central Europe to an end while Rudolf was still on the throne.[34]

Historians like Emile Lousse and Herbert Koenigsberger are more positive in their views of Matthias, taking this background into account. Archduke Matthias could see more clearly than every member of the Habsburg dynasty that the family's

---

28 Evans, *Rudolf II*, 60.
29 Evans wrote of him: "(...) there has been little more posthumous agreement on the merits of Matthias than on those of Rudolf." and: "(...) he was earlier a more militant and sinister figure". *Ibid*. See also: Robert J.W. Evans, *The Making of the Habsburg Monarchy, 1550–1700: an Interpretation* (Oxford: Clarendon Press, 1979), 52, 59.
30 Jean Bérenger, *A History of the Habsburg Empire 1273–1700* (London - New York: Longman, 1994), 259.
31 György Bónis, *Révay Péter* [Péter Révay] (Budapest: Akadémiai Kiadó, 1981), 22.
32 Hans Sturmberger, *Georg Erasmus Tschernembl: Religion, Libertät und Widerstand. Ein Beitrag zur Geschichte der Gegenreformation und des Landes ob der Enns* (Forschungen zur Geschichte Oberösterreichs, vol. 3.) (Linz – Graz: Böhlau, 1953), 141.
33 Evans, *The Making*, 53.
34 Hugo Hantsch, *Geschichte Österreich*, vol. I (Graz: Styria, 1959), 300; Crankshaw, *The Habsburgers*, 106–197.

claims on power in Europe could be secured by means of political concessions to the Estates.³⁵ According to Koenigsberger, Matthias had used this tactic previously as governor of the Netherlands between 1578 and 1581, and tried to fend off the crisis of legitimacy by gradually ceding the Estates' political demands.³⁶ In this way he won their support for his own ambitions for power. The result of this tactic was the steady and non-violent usurpation of his brother's power, and Matthias' crowning success came in his ceremonious installation as emperor in 1612. We do not know whether Matthias – a member of the Erasmist circles in the Habsburg court – owed this achievement to his moderate political views, or to crafty manoeuvring springing from a personal grudge and designed to bring Rudolf down, and the matter has yet never been fully investigated.³⁷ At all events, the Habsburg position with regard to power in Central Europe was maintained during his reign, though the character of that power was modified.

At the same time, the most important element in Matthias' policies – compliance with the Estates – by which he achieved this result, forms a crucial point of criticism for his contemporaries and for historians dealing with his policies.³⁸ According to bishop Melchior Khlesl, Matthias' most respected councillor, the Prince Electors had formed the following negative opinion of Matthias even before he was elected Holy Roman Emperor: "They wanted to elect a man as King of the Romans who was capable of ruling his subjects, not one ruled by them."³⁹ At this juncture we must not forget, when Rudolf's ambitions for power are mentioned, that it was during his reign that the growing influence of the Estates had begun. Herbert Haupt says of this: "As the emperor lost his authority, so the nobility gained in strength."⁴⁰

---

35 Lousse, "Qui donc," 135–143.
36 Koenigsberger, *Monarchies*, 280–288.
37 Howard Louthan, *The Quest for Compromise: Peacemakers in Counter-Reformation Vienna* (Cambridge: Cambridge University Press, 1997), 160, note 23.
38 Bérenger, *A History*, 254.
39 "Sie wolten ainen herrn zum römischen könig wehlen, der seine untertanen regiren kunte und nicht von seinen untertanen regiret wurde." Quoted from a 1608 report by Peter Visser (Visscher) sent to Archduke Albert in Brussels in Anton Chroust, ed., *Der Ausgang der Regierung Rudolfs II. und die Anfänge des Kaisers Matthias* (Briefen und Acten zur Geschichte des Dreissigjährigen Krieges) vol. VI (München: Rieger, 1906), 151, note 1.
40 Herbert Haupt, "From feuding brothers to a nation in a war with itself," in Eliška Fučíkova, ed., *Rudolf II and Prague: The Court and the City* (London: Thames & Hudson, 1997), 238. The growth of authority is one reason why between 1606 and 1608 Rudolf distributed Hungarian aristocratic titles in comparative abundance (25). The new aristocrats also gained political power because they were accepted into the society of the Hungarian Estates and could vote during the Diets. During his reign Mátyás bestowed only one new title annually. See: Peter Schimert, "The Hungarian Nobility in the Seventeenth and Eighteenth Centuries," in Ivo Banac and Paul Bushkovitch, eds., *The Nobility in Russia and Eastern Europe*, vol. II (New Haven: Yale Concilium on International and Area Studies, 1987), 150–151.

The strategy pursued by Archduke Matthias during the brothers' feud brought the Estates into a position of unprecedented power vis-à-vis the emperor, both in the Empire and especially in Hungary. Or rather, the Estates may be regarded as the true winners in the conflict.[41] Such a situation caused a real landside in political relations and therefore brought about changes in thinking about policy and the manner of legitimating the power of the dynasty.

Another debated point in Archduke Matthias' political conduct is to do with his strategy: he brought into the open his plans to cooperate with the Estates, most of all the Hungarians, and openly called on the emperor to hand over power.[42] It is easier to understand this procedure if we look at this factor in connection with the political culture prevalent in Rudolf's reign. Despite his failed policies, the emperor was well regarded by his subjects. His popularity was due to the effective way in which he tried to verbally and visually commend to their attention his ideas about his rule.[43] Archduke Matthias, therefore, tried to win over public opinion by revealing his plans. He hoped to be able to prevent civil war and to win the Estates over to his side.

The Archduke called into question the legitimacy of Rudolf's reign, employing such thoughts and concepts as they might appeal to the audience at which he aimed, and justified his policies in proclamations and other declarations.[44] Despite the interesting aspects of the Archduke's policies, these are not at issue in this chapter, but the focus is on the method by which he legitimated this strategy. In considering this we shall look at how Matthias and the Hungarian Estates justified their ambitions for power, and at the role and purpose therein of the Hungarian crown and the concept of the Hungarian Estates.

Matthias could not have implemented his political strategy had he not had at his disposal men that knew how to put his message over. Therefore, in the period when he was attempting to wrest power from his brother, he gathered about him

---

41 Haupt, "From feuding brothers," 247; Géza Pálffy, *Szent István birodalma a Habsburgok középeurópai államában. A Magyar Királyság és a Habsburg Monarchia a 16. században* [The Empire of St István and the Central European state of the Habsburgs. The Hungarian Kingdom and the Habsburg Monarchy in the sixteenth century] (Doctoral dissertation, Budapest, 2008), 336–352; Géza Pálffy, The Kingdom of Hungary and the Habsburg Monarchy in the Sixteenth Century. [Translated from the Hungarian by Thomas J. and Helen D. DeKornfeld] (Boulder, Colorado: Social Science Monographs–Wayne, New Jersey: Center for Hungarian Studies and Publications, Inc. – New York: Columbia University Press, 2009). (East European Monographs, DCCXXXV.; CHSP Hungarian Studies Series, 18.), 221–234.
42 Bérenger, *A History*, 253–254.
43 See: DaCosta Kaufmann, *Variations*; and Vocelka, *Die politische Propaganda*.
44 Karl Vocelka, "Matthias contra Rudolf: zur politischen Propaganda in der Zeit des Bruderzwistes," *Zeitschrift für historische Forschung*, 10 (1983), 341–351.

several men in a faction that could support him in his ambition. From this group of confidants there developed, over time, what formally became the royal court at the moment of his coronation as king of Hungary. Over the short period 1605–1608 the growth of his power and the character of his circle of courtiers were transformed.[45]

In the first period of his take-over of power the Archduke's main political goal – as governor of Hungary from 1607–1608 – was on the one hand to gain legitimacy among his Hungarian subjects and on the other hand to inspire confidence in his brother. As a result of this policy his brother succeeded in finding a political solution to the legitimacy crisis in the Empire and especially in Hungary. A large proportion of the tasks that Matthias personally undertook, or which were performed on his behalf, were directed at dealing with the persisting crisis in the Habsburg court or in Hungary. He endeavoured to justify these measures in numerous letters to Rudolf or the German princes. The Hungarian section of the archducal faction united the followers of Bocskai and the circle of adherents to the Habsburg dynasty who opposed Rudolf.[46]

Considering the role that Matthias had played in the anti-Rudolf Bocskai rebellion, it is no surprise that we find the majority of Bocskai's supporters in his faction. Now too István Illésházy was his chief councillor, since as palatine he was the leading figure of the pro-Matthias Hungarian Estates.[47] János Rimay too belonged to the faction, and after Bocatius fled from prison he was employed as a court historian. Berger had in 1603 or 1604 been commissioned by Matthias to write a historical work on Hungary.[48] He acted already since 1605 as agent between the Lutheran Illésházy and Matthias.[49] To the annoyance of the Hungarian *Camera* and against its wishes, on 3 July 1607 Matthias appointed Elias Berger court historian.[50] Péter Révay, who wrote later a book about the crown, was one of the Archduke's chief councillors and political strategists. János Jeszenszky held the post of court doctor and historian.

---

45 Volker Press, "The Imperial Court of the Habsburgs," 305.
46 The formation of the court was not free of problems, as many of those loyal to Rudolf I were members of the civil service. See: Holl, *Ferenczffy*, 29–32.
47 Nagy, *Kard és szerelem*, 120–122.
48 Kulcsár, "Berger Illés történeti művei," 246.
49 In December 1607 Illésházy recommended Berger as secretary to the Hungarian Camera. István Illésházy to Leopold von Stralendorf, ÖStA Wien, HHStA Hungarica AA Fasc. 153. Konv. B. 1607. Nov.-Dez., fol. 131–132. 20 dec. 1607, Trencsén. "*P.S. Commendo Illustrissimae Dominationi Vestrae Eliam Bergerum, meum agentem, virum doctum et de Caesarea Maiestate scriptis bene meritum, dignissimum secretarii in Camera Hungarica officio.*" My thanks to Géza Pálffy for this information.
50 István Monok, ed., *A magyar könyvkultúra múltjából: Iványi Béla cikkei és anyaggyűjtése* [From the past of Hungarian book culture: the articles and source collections of Béla Iványi] (Szeged: JATE, 1983), 158–159.

Elias Berger as historian of the Habsburg family

The role, weight and influence of those members of the faction who strove to put into words their leader's political message must not be underrated. Hungarian historians and literary historians have long decried the work of Berger, whom they have labelled an untalented hireling German pen-pusher in the untalented Early Modern period.[51] Kálmán Benda and Erik Fügedi write of him: " ... whom the emperor appointed historian of the Hungarian royal court, contrary to the recommendation of the Hungarian *Camera*, although he knew not a word of Hungarian and had nothing to do with Hungary."[52]

As I have shown in the third chapter, László Szörényi's research has shown that Berger's Latin literary creations are by no means as worthless as has been thought, and that their content may be regarded as an important source for the style of political thinking of his time.[53] His correspondence and his political and literary activity alike show that Berger played a part in the transmission of ideas between the Catholic and Lutheran élites in Central Europe. From 1605 onward, when Illésházy's illness made him his agent at the Archduke's faction, that was certainly Berger's task.[54] Karol Žierotin, principal man in Moravia, wrote to Illésházy on 28 November 1606 that Berger was keeping him constantly informed about talks on the peace to be made with the Ottomans and the conditions of the treaty.[55] Berger's political role next to him being a writer therefore is worth further study.

A key figure, who opened the door to the Habsburg court for him in 1603, was the Dutch lawyer and diplomat Johann Barvitius (?1555–1620).[56] As Imperial Councillor between 1593 and 1607 and Rudolf's personal secretary he was one of

---

51 György Pray, *Index rariorum librorum bibliothecae Universitatis regiae Budensis* (Budae: Regia Universitas, 1790), 126–128; Podhraczky, "Berger Illés," 351–366; Fraknói, "Berger Illés," 373–390; Evans, *The Making*, 152; Evans, *Rudolf II*, 128; Galavics, *Kössünk*, 63–69; Holl, *Ferencffy Lőrinc*; 158–170, 175, 179; Kulcsár, "Berger Illés történeti művei," 245–259.
52 Benda and Fügedi, *A magyar korona*,164.
53 Szörényi, "Berger Illés eposza," 291–300. In his two letters to Illésházy, Žierotín refers to Berger's work as the equal of Jeszenszky's. Peter von Chlumecky, *Carl von Zierotin und seine Zeit 1564–1615*, vol. II (Brünn: A. Nitsch, 1862), LII–LIII, XXXXVII. Letter of 28 November 1606, LXI–LXII, LVII. letter of 4 September 1608. He also mentions Jeszenszky's work in other letters to Illésházy. *Ibid.*, LXIV, LIX. letter of 6 November 1608, LXVI, LXII. letter of 5 April 1609.
54 ÖStA Wien, HHStA, Ungarische Akten, Fasc. 149 Konv. A., fol. 6r-8v. Illésházy to Matthias, 2 November 1605, fol. 10r.-11v. Berger to Matthias, d.d. 3 November 1605, fol. 22r-24v. Cardinal Dietrichstein to Matthias, 5 November 1605. According to Károlyi Berger, "as Illésházy's agent" passed information between Dietrichstein and Illésházy. MOE XI, 209.
55 Chlumecky, *Carl von Zierotin*, vol. II, letters II, LII–LIII, XXXXVII.
56 Stefan Benz, *Zwischen Tradition und Kritik. Katholische Geschichtsschreibung im barocken Heiligen Römischen Reich* (Husum: Matthiesen, 2003), 308.

the most influential personalities of the Prague court.⁵⁷ It was thanks to him that Berger was appointed royal Poeta Laureatus in 1603, against the recommendation of the Hungarian *Camera*. Berger corresponded with such influential persons as Karol Žierotin⁵⁸, Rimay⁵⁹ and the brothers Péter and Ferenc Révay.⁶⁰ Furthermore, we can see from the dedications in his books that he had a whole network of powerful patrons, among others János Kuthassy, Ferenc Nádasdy, Karol Žierotin,⁶¹ István Illésházy, Péter Révay,⁶² and the Palatine Miklós Esterházy,⁶³ not to mention sundry German Prince Electors and bishops,⁶⁴ and of course Archduke Matthias himself.⁶⁵ Finally, he delivered the eulogy at the funeral in 1609 of Illésházy, Palatine of Hungary, dedicated to Tamás Bosznyák, who was a war hero, adherent to Bocskai and later to Matthias. This work again goes to show that Berger played an important role and was held in high regard in the political and literary circles of the Habsburg Empire.⁶⁶ All this offers reliable evidence that Berger certainly "… had something

---

57 Oswald von Gschließer, *Der Reichshofrat. Bedeutung und Verfassung, Schicksal und Besetzung einer obersten Reichsbehörde von 1559 bis 1806* (Wien: A. Holzhausen, 1942), 153; Evans, *Rudolf II*, 73.

58 Chlumecky, *Carl von Zierotin*, vol. I, 272 (13 July 1606); "Eliae Bergero" [Letter, January 1609], in Chlumecky, *Carl von Zierotin*, vol. II, CLVI-CLVII (letter CXXXI.). This letter is about the work *Connubium Hungariae et Bohemiae*, which Berger was writing on Žierotín's commission, and which was published in 1611 in Prague.

59 Rimay's letter to Berger, 26 May 1609. Arnold Ipolyi, "Hely és nemzéktani adalék – Tudósitás Rimay János munkáiról [Information about geography and nation studies – Report on the works of János Rimay]," *Új magyar muzeum* [New Hungarian Museum] 3/12 (1853), 485–486; edition: Arnold Ipolyi, ed., *Alsó-sztregovai és rimai Rimay János államiratai és levelezése* [The correspondence and state writings of János Rimay of Alsó-sztregova and Rima] (Budapest : M. T. Akad., 1887), 53.

60 SNA – ARR Korešpondencia Peter Révay Krč. 81 fol. 271, Berger to Révay, 25 April 1612, fol. 318, *idem*, 7 July1609, Krč. 82 fol. 40, *idem*, 1612, fol. 78, *idem*, 19 January1612, fol. 133, *idem*, 23 January 1613., fol. 147, *idem*, 13 April 1616, fol. 175, *idem*, 7 May 1617, Krč. 83 fol. 44, *idem*, 11 May 1621, fol. 73, *idem*, 1 June 1621. SNA – ARR Korešpondencia Frantisek III Révay Krč. 76, fol. 203 Berger to Ferenc Révay, 24 March 1620, Krč. 77, fol. 125 *idem*. (undated) My thanks to Maroš Mačuha for the two latter references.

61 In: Elias Berger, *Connubium Hungariae et Bohemiae in Matthia II. rege Hungariae et rege Bohemiae coronato denuo sanctitum* (Pragae: Typis Schumanianis, [1611]).

62 In: Elias Berger, *Caduceus seu proba, et brevis invitatio* (Viennae Austriae: Typis Margarethae Formicae, Viduae, 1607), A1r.

63 In: Elias Perger[!], *Duplex speculum chronologicum* (Viennae Austriae, 1635) (manuscript with only printed title page) EK, Ms. G 69.

64 In: Elias Berger, *Trinubium Europaeum*, … (Francofurti: Godefridus Tampachius, 1612); Second edition: Elias Berger, "Trinubium Europaeum," in Melchior Goldast, ed., *Politica Imperialia, sive discursus politici, Acta Publica, Et Tractatus…* (Francofurti: Typis Ioannis Bringeri, 1614.) 723.

65 In: Elias Berger, *Gratulatio Serenissimo Principe ac Domino D. Matthiae Archiduci Austriae…* (Viennae Austriae: Typis Margarethae Formicae, 1607).

66 [Elias Berger], *Oratio funebris in exequiis illustrissimi comitis, palatini Stephani de Ilieshaza comitis Trenchinien: et Liptovien:…* ([Kassa: S.N.], 1609).

to do with Hungary ..." and was very well integrated in political circles of Habsburg Hungary.

If the power of the Habsburg ruler underwent a crisis of legitimacy – as happened in Hungary between 1600 and 1608 – a court historian like Berger had an important part to play in dispelling it. He had to make known his master's political message so that it should connect closely with the political reality of the time and have immediate effect on his audience. For this reason, his work obviously lacked permanent validity but may rather be taken as a series of quick snapshots of the style of current political thinking. This is why Berger's work makes scarcely any impression on the modern observer, and appears to the reader of today to consist of empty, bombastic phrases.

The special task that bound Berger to Archduke Matthias' court must account for the close collaboration that grew up between him, Illésházy and Révay. Illésházy was the chief strategist and theoretician in Matthias' retinue. It was probably Matthias or one of the other two that gave Berger the task of writing pamphlets and speeches intended to transmit a definite political message at special, formal gatherings of the Hungarian Estates such as important National Assemblies or the coronation itself. It may therefore well be imagined that Berger's writings were produced in a similar way to those of Bocskai's court. It seems likely that Illésházy, Révay or others gave Berger specific thoughts – within a political intellectual circle – which he then worked up into speeches or pamphlets.

Archduke Matthias's political goal was the restoration of the Habsburg dynasty's power base in Central Europe, but his method of attaining it differed from his brother's. Rudolf had increased his personal power at the expense of the rights of the Estates. The essence of Matthias' strategy lay in seeking compromise between the various parties, and he granted far-reaching political rights to the Estates of the Empire so as to gain their political, military and economic support in the struggle against the emperor – which in the end de facto cost his personal power. He applied this strategy for the first time when governor of Hungary between 1607–1608, and used it again later in his efforts to gain power over Bohemia and the Holy Roman Empire. The explanation of this strategy must be that he needed effective armed force in his struggle against Rudolf, and this army was available to him in Hungary.[67] The Ottoman challenge had caused Hungarian society to become highly militarised; the two most typical strata were the Hajdús and the *banderia* maintained by the great landowners. For this reason, there were tens of thousands of men constantly under arms in Hungary who could be mobilised in the event of

---

67 Kálmán Benda, "Habsburg Absolutism and Hungarian Resistance," in R.J.W. Evans and T.V. Thomas, eds., *Crown, Church and Estates* (London: Palgrave Macmillan, 1991), 126–127.

a conflict. The support of the Hajdús and the Hungarian soldiery was therefore of decisive importance to Matthias in the first period of his assumption of power.

He also needed political support. This he obtained by plotting against Rudolf with the Estates of various countries in the Habsburg Empire – Hungary, Bohemia, Moravia and the Austrian territories – from 1607 onwards.[68] The principals in this collaboration were Illésházy, Erasmus Tschernembl and Karol Žierotin – the most powerful aristocrat in Moravia and a close personal friend of Illésházy.[69] According to Karl Nehring, the alliance of the Estates had been Illésházy's idea, but considering the intensive connections between the leading figures it could just as well have been the joint brain-child of them all.[70] After Matthias had reached agreement with the reformist politicians of the counties or the aristocracy and their circles, Illésházy remained his most important councillor on Hungarian affairs. He had been the most respected person representing the rebels in the talks leading to the Peace of Vienna (1606). Matthias convened the Estates to a Diet in Pozsony on 10 January 1608 at which delegates from Hungary, Transylvania and the Austrian territories were present. This Diet marked the beginning of his assumption of power.

The essence of the conflict between Matthias and Rudolf was a profound difference of opinion over the political future of the Habsburg Empire and dynasty. The archdukes and the family had already decided that Rudolf was incapable of ruling – he was disabled by his illness – and made Matthias head of the dynasty. The conflict had broken out in 1606, when Rudolf refused to ratify the Peace of Zsitvatorok (1606) between the Habsburg Empire and Ottoman Empire, and the Treaty of Vienna agreement made with Bocskai; Matthias had brought these about after lengthy negotiations. Instead of a peace treaty with the Ottomans and peace in Hungary – which Matthias advocated – Rudolf was intent on launching a new campaign against the Turks. He therefore planned to seek financial support for this from the territories of the Holy Roman Empire at the next Imperial Assembly, to be held at Regensburg in the spring of 1608. In addition, he had no intention of restoring the Hungarian crown to the Hungarians, though the Treaty of Vienna agreement was specific about this. He complained of Matthias in 1607:

When the Archduke Matthias received power plenipotentiary from His Majesty he made shameful peace treaties with the Hungarians and the Turks in which he conceded everything that they might desire or yearn for to the rebels and the Turks, and which would

---

68 Evans, *Rudolf II*, 144; Bahlcke, *Regionalismus*, 322, 336.
69 See the ample (and conspicuously warm) correspondence between them in Chlumecky, *Karl von Zierotin*, vol. I, 300 and vol. II, XXIX–LXII. Although he was known as a very wealthy but very miserly man, Illésházy also sent Žierotín costly gifts. *Ibid.*, vol. I, 554 note 30.
70 Karl Nehring, "Magyarország és a zsitvatoroki szerződés (1605–1609)," *Századok* 120 (1986), 39; Pálffy, *The Kingdom of Hungary*, 221–233.

have had to return to His Majesty's power and possession. And even that was not enough, but even more knavery took place, in that the Hungarian crown, which had always been the property of His Majesty and his forebears, was desired of His Majesty, and what it would all lead to was easy to foretell.[71]

Because of the events that ensued in Hungarian politics Rudolf's crisis of legitimacy reached a crucial stage in November 1607.[72] The situation was very like what Bocskai had envisaged in his testament in 1606. The Hajdús were threatening to rebel afresh because Rudolf would not comply with the terms of the Peace of Vienna, and they wanted their own king.[73] They made known to the Hungarian emissaries that "… they could not rest until the Hungarians had raised one of their own to be king …", and that if need be they would try their luck again with the Ottomans.[74]

The Hungarian Estates were as anxious at this new disturbance as was Matthias. This situation served him as a reason for urging forward a solution to the crisis.[75] By means of an alliance brokered by Illésházy he obtained the support of the Estates. The agreement was sealed in a letter to Illésházy of 13 November 1607, in which he expressed his intention of forming an alliance. By so doing he became leader of the anti-Habsburg faction in Hungary. In the letter he legitimates his power by declaring

---

71 "Als Ertzhertzog Mathias von ihr may. die pleni potenz außgebracht, hatt er mit Hungern und Turckhen einen schandtlichen frieden geschloßen, den er den rebellen vnd Turcken alles nachgeben was sie wünschen vnd begern mögen vnd was ihr may. autoritet vnd guetten namen zue wider seind könde. Ist dem nicht genueg geweßen, sonnder man hatt noch mehr practickhen, das die Vngerisch cron von ihr may. begert worden, weliche doch ihr may. vnd dero vorfahren statts bey sich gehabt, zue was endt ist leichtlich zue gedenckhen." ÖStA Wien, HHStA, Familien Akten Fasc. 1., quoted in: Vocelka, "Matthias contra Rudolf," 345.
72 Tibor Wittman, "Az osztrák Habsburg-hatalom válságos éveinek történetéhez (1606-1618) [On the crisis years of Austrian Habsburg power]," *Acta universitatis Szegedinensies sectio Historica* V (1959), 3–44.
73 Kálmán Benda, "Der Haiduckenaufstand in Ungarn und das Erstarken der Stände in der Habsburgermonarchie 1607–1608," in Dániel Csatári, ed., *Nouvelles études historiques publiées à l'occasion du XIIe Congrès International des Sciences Historiques par la Commission Nationale des Historiens Hongrois*, vol. I (Budapest: Akadémiai Kiadó, 1965), 299–313.
74 Report of Forgách and Dóczy from Kassá to Matthias, 22 November 1607, in Mihály Hatvani, ed., *Magyar történelmi okmánytár a brüsszeli országos levéltárból* [Hungarian historian charters from the country archive in Brussels] (Magyar történelmi emlékek [Hungarian historical relics], vol. 1, Osztály [Class]: Okmánytárak [Charter registers], vol. 3 (Pest: Eggenberger, 1857), 279.
75 Archduke Matthias had prepared the ground for this by holding talks in 1605 about the succession to Rudolf with his brothers Maximilian III, Ferdinand and Ernst Maximilian. A year earlier he had secretly informed his brothers, on the advice of the pope and the king of Spain, that they would recognise him as head of the House of Habsburg and Rudolf's successor. Victor Lucien Tapié, *The Rise and Fall of the Habsburg Monarchy*, Stephen Hardman trans. (London: Pall Mall Press, 1971), 86.

that he is a member of *"nostra Hungarica natio"* (our Hungarian nation).[76] In his own words: "I promise the same to our whole Hungarian nation, as I spring from that nation as did my ancestors, and I regard this country as my native land which I shall never, never, desert . . ."[77] It was therefore possible to show him later as an ideal Hungarian national king, the logical successor to Rudolf and Bocskai, because by that announcement he had defined himself as a Hungarian. He could appear before the rest of Europe as an acceptable, legitimate ruler, as to the Hungarians he was a Hungarian and to Europe a Habsburg. The Archduke was, therefore, on the one hand deliberately using the concept of *natio* and the fact that he belonged to the Hungarian Estates, and forming an image of himself as national king in order to legitimate his ambition for power in Hungarian eyes. On the other hand, he was showing himself outside Hungary to be a Habsburg and Rudolf's natural successor. In Koenigsberger's opinion he had pursued a similar strategy thirty years previously in the Netherlands.[78]

On 20 January 1608 the assembled Hungarian Estates issued the Declaration of Pozsony, in which they justified their joining their political destiny to that of Archduke Matthias.[79] The author of the Declaration is unknown, but as Illésházy was the leader of the Estates it is likely that he had a hand in compiling the text. The Pozsony Declaration is in tune with *Querelae*, as both are written as laments addressed to Europe. Here too Europe is summoned to the support of the Hungarian Estates, and Rudolf's misguided policies and unjust rule cited in argument. At the same time the image of the bastion of Europe and the presentation of the Hungarian Estates as associated with it also emerges.

The most essential difference between the two texts lies in the image formed of the legitimating role of the Estates. In *Querelae* the Estates demonstrate the rightfulness of rebellion against the emperor, whereas in that of Pozsony they try to legitimate the policies of the uncrowned Habsburg. The Estates and the Archduke employ the same means of depiction to support their common political message. This derives

---

76 "(...) *idemque toti nostrae Hungaricae nationi promitto, de qua ut ab attavis meis originem duco ita etiam patriam meam esse agnosco, cui nullo unquam tempore defuturus sum, immo extrema in conservatione ejus attentare non recusabo, ut fusius de his et aliis ex praesentium exhibitore, eui concredere poteris, intelliges.*" Sándor Szilágyi, ed., "Három uralkodói levélke [Three small letters of rulers]," *Történelmi Tár* 1 (1878), 389–390.
77 Ibid.
78 H.G. Koenigsberger, "Epilogue: Central and Western Europe," in Evans and Thomas, *Crown, Church and Estates*, 308.
79 Literae Regnicolis Hungariae Posonij 21 Januarij Anno Domini 1608 per legatis partium Superiorum exhibita. MOL N 49 Lada Diaeta Antiquae Fasc. B. Fol. 10–12. Nagy, *Magyar história 1526–1608*, 499–502; György Pray, *Epistolae procerum regni Hungariae (Pars III. ab anno 1554 ad 1711)*, (Posonii: Ex Typographeo G. A. Belnay, 1806), 93.

from the premise that Rudolf's policies are faulty, as he means to continue the war against the Turks and is unwilling to ratify the peace treaty. The second difference is the way in which the relationship between the Hungarians and the Austrians is described in the Pozsony Declaration. In this instance the Estates hold a positive opinion of the "Germans", whom they praise for their straightforwardness and honesty, as people that keep their word and fulfil their promises. According to the Pozsony Declaration, the authorised Austrian delegates promised that the treaty would be honoured, and it was only because of the emperor's opposition that it was not.[80] Additionally, in another similar document the Estates praise Archduke Matthias for his affection for the Hungarians.[81]

The Pozsony Declaration is the link between *Querelae* and the next, a document written by Matthias – or someone acting on his behalf – in April 1608.[82] This is nothing other than a reply to Rudolf based on what happened in the Diet at Pozsony, by which Matthias clears himself of his brother's accusations. The Declaration contains very detailed argument and originally had fifteen appendices.

This response came into being as a consequence of the political situation that arose in Hungary after the Pozsony Diet. Rudolf reacted exactly as he had done earlier in the case of Illésházy. He accused Matthias and the Estates present of treason, set in motion the confiscation of their property and armed the towns that were loyal to him.[83] In a letter to the assembled Estates, dated 23 January, he writes that the councils taken at Pozsony "… were directed against Our Majesty and Power …".[84] If the Estates were disobedient and persisted in their intentions and desires, he would institute proceedings against them for lèse-majesté. Then on 1 February 1608 Matthias formed an alliance with the assembled Estates for the

---

80 Nagy, *Magyar história 1526–1608*, 501.
81 "… *pro suo, erga Nationem Hungaricam amore* …" in Replicatio statuum et ordinum Regni Hungariae (Pozsony, 30 January 1608), ÖStA Wien, HHStA, Ungarische Akten Comi. Fasc. 395. Konv. A, fol. 117v.
82 "Kurzer bericht der fürstl. Dhlt. Erzherzogs Matthiassen zu Österreich etc. vber das Vngerische Wesen, cum refutatione objectorum. Also einkhomen jm April 1608.," in Hatvani, *Magyar történelmi okmánytár*, 282–295. Unfortunately, this text is quoted without appendices and background information. In addition, it is not entirely clear when or on what occasion it was written. It certainly pre-dates the Imperial Assembly at Regensburg, because that took place in mid-April, and there a decision was taken on the continuation of the war against the Turks. Another edition is printed as: "Staatsschrift Herzogs Mathias an Kaiser Rudolph.," in Joseph Hammer-Purgstall, *Khlesl's, des Cardinals, Directors des geheimen Cabinets Kaisers Mathias, Leben*, vol. II (Wien: Kaulfuss, 1847)154–163 (with no indication of source).
83 Haupt, "From feuding brothers," 239.
84 "Rudolf leirata 1608. január 23-án a rendekhez [Document of Rudolf, dated 23 January 1608 to the Estates]," in Nagy, *Magyar história 1526–1608*, 503.

preservation of peace with the Ottomans and the Hajdús, and addressed a letter requesting assistance to the Estates of Moravia, Silesia and Bohemia.

The aim of this was to justify his anti-Rudolf policy, but taking into account its content and dissemination, it presented his political plans at the same time. As its content is consonant with *Querelae* and the Declaration of Pozsony it is very likely that a number of people collaborated in its composition. The author(s) was/were fully aware of the style of political thought on the matters in question in Hungary at the time. Illésházy may be regarded as one of the most probable authors, as he acted as Matthias' most important Hungarian political adviser. It is at the same time by no means inconceivable that Révay, Berger or other members of Matthias' court made their contributions, though there is no reference to this in the document.

The importance of this document is that the Hungarian crown features in it as "Cron Hungern", and that a meaning is attributed to this term which implies a change of significance. The German term, or a variant of it, appears regularly in official documents and correspondence of the Habsburg emperors and in their political reports dated between 1600 and 1608. In this declaration the term Cron Hungern has three meanings. It occurs most often in a territorial sense, as the Kingdom of Hungary and its territories.[85] Rudolf uses the term "Krone Ungarn" in this sense in a document of 12 January 1608, in which he points out that "the Turks ... are hanging on to that which remained of the Hungarian crown".[86] The second meaning is that connected to Hungarian royal power.[87] This meaning is often brought under one heading with the first, as no distinction is generally made in the sources between crown designating territory and crown as a synonym for

---

85 "... der erzherzog Matthias, wie ich selbs sainer schreiben eines gelösen, hat selbes an der cron Ungern desperiert und sorgt sich schier noch der anreinenden länder ebenfalls." Prince Maximilian's letter to Prince Elector Ernst of Cologne, 8 March 1605, published in Felix Stieve, ed., *Vom Reichstag 1608 bis zur Gründung der Liga* (Briefen und Acten des Dreissigjährigen Krieges), vol. VI (München: M. Rieger, 1895), 46, see also: to the prince's council, *ibid.*, 179 note 1, and that of the Bavarian secret council to Prince Maximilian, 29 March 1608 *cron Ungarn*, *ibid.*, 290.

86 "... dat die Türken (...) das noch uebrige der Krone Ungarn an sich reissen." "Hauptverhandlungen des Reichstags. 1608 Januar 12. Kaiserliche Proposition: § 1," in Moriz Ritter, ed., *Die Gründung der Union 1598–1608* (Briefen und Acten des Dreissigjährigen Krieges), vol. I (München: M. Rieger, 1870), 628. See also: '(...) was von der cron Hungern hinweggerissen worden, wider erobert (...).' *Ibid.*

87 For example, a copy of a letter from Rudolf to Archduke Matthias dated 18 February 1608: "... *cum contra nostram consientam e tempore acceptionis coronae Ungariae prastium grave juramentum omnia augeri, sit, uti im nostrae, protestatione continetur.*" Stephanus Illésházy, *De Rebus...* (ms) OSZK Fol. Lat. 2336 fol. 38v.

royal power. Thirdly, the word can also designate the tangible coronation jewel.[88] It is not always clear which meaning the writer intends the term to have.[89]

In the Pozsony Declaration the most important subject is the need to end the war against the Ottomans. Its author deals with this topic by outlining in some detail the effect of the war on Hungary and surrounding territories. In so doing he distinguishes between the Kingdom of Hungary and other territories of the Habsburg Empire by defining the former by the term "Cron Hungern" and the remainder by their everyday names. Thus, on behalf of Archduke Matthias, he writes that "… the enemy of Christendom has been oppressing "Cron Hungern" and His Majesty Rudolf's other kingdoms and countries for the past sixteen years."[90]

This term which the author uses for Hungary is a reference to the country's special relationship with the Habsburg Empire and its other European parts and to the outstanding role that it played. He derives the importance of Hungary from *Querelae* or another text based on it. In his opinion, this importance is based on the fact that the Kingdom of Hungary, as Cron Hungern, plays a significant role in the defence of the common native land. He expresses this view by means of the description of the new peril resulting from the Bocskai rebellion and the alliance made between Bocskai and the Ottomans. Thanks to the rebellion, the Ottomans will now be able to penetrate deep into the Austrian lands, so that the capital, Vienna, will be imperilled.[91]

Then the author clearly means to make it plain that this is an acute crisis, for which Rudolf is responsible, and that there is need for immediate action. He begins by calling on Rudolf to accept personal responsibility for the sake of his realm, and states that the Empire is suffering great need. The family had frequently warned His Majesty, and Archduke Matthias had kept him constantly informed of the situation.[92] Meanwhile His Majesty had allowed Esztergom to be ravaged, and the rebellious Hungarians had occupied the fortresses needed for the defence of the fatherland. It seemed that as a result of all this, "Cron Hungern" would fall into the hands of the Turks. The "confoedirten feindten," or hostile alliance, was again plundering the Danube lands, and – as Matthias emphatically pointed out – even

---

88 In this sense, the term ocurs most frequently in documents to do with the handing over of the crown on 27 June 1608 and the coronation in Hungary on 19 November 1608.
89 As early as the nineteenth century the use of the concept *Cron Hungern* was causing confusion among German historians, to whom it was not clear whether to take it as the object itself or as kingship. Stieve, *Vom Reichstag*, 86–87 note 1.
90 "Kurzer bericht," 282. Translator's comment: I have tried to edit the following passage to make it clear that an unknown author is writing on behalf of Matthias. The text vacillates on this point, and it sometimes seems that Matthias is writing personally.
91 *Ibid.*, 283.
92 *Ibid.*, 283–284.

the Holy Roman Empire was at risk. "Cron Hungern" was of decisive importance for Rudolf, since the emperor was in fact responsible for the security of the Christian kingdoms and countries.[93]

Next, he describes how Archduke Matthias, as governor of Hungary, had tried to find a solution to the problem. He had attempted to fend off the Ottoman menace and to separate the allies by carrying on peace negotiations with both sides, for which he had received full authority from the emperor.[94] Then he suggests that Rudolf has precipitated the Hajdús' rebellion by constantly postponing ratification of the peace treaty. This has produced protests from the Hungarians and the Ottomans, leading to a further Hajdú rebellion. The Hajdús have again occupied a large part of Hungary, and have been prepared "... to hand over the Hungarian crown to the Turks ...", and indeed "... to elect their own king from their own nation and religion ...".[95] That this had not occurred was due to Matthias' prompt action. In addition, he also mentions that Matthias had continued negotiating with the Ottomans and had held a Diet at Pozsony to resolve the crisis.

In this passage, the author makes use of Bocskai's views on the national king of Hungary – see above for Bocskai's expression of this in his political testament – and the crown. As the crown itself was, at the time, still in Rudolf's possession "Cron Hungern" in this text must not be interpreted as the tangible crown but as Hungarian royal power. In the following passage the Archduke reaches the crux of his exposition:

> The conclusion that must be drawn from the situation that has thus arisen is that His Majesty is dragging into danger the kingship, the realm, the glorious House of Austria and surely the whole of Christendom, risking their loss and ruin, since the Hungarian crown has always been seen as the bastion and preserver of all Christendom and therewith the German nation of the Holy (Roman) Empire, and every intelligent mind and heart must benevolently take into account and ponder that this Kingdom has hitherto belonged for so long to the glorious House of Austria and been in its possession.[96]

---

93 *Ibid.*, 284.
94 *Ibid.*, 285–286.
95 "... die Cron Hungern dem Türggen zu vbergeben..." and "... ainen Khünig Irer nation vnd Religion zu erwöhlen ..." *Ibid.*, 286.
96 "Was nun hierauss, wann es seinen Vortgang, wie darauff gestandten, erraichet, Irer Mt. dero Khünigreich vnd Länndern, dem löblichen Haus Österreich, ja der ganczen Christenhait für ain gefahr, verlusst vnd höchste ruin entstandten, weilen die Cron Hungern jederzait als ain Vormauer der ganczen Christenhait, jnsonderhait des heiligen Reichs Teutscher nation gehalten, vnd durch sy erhalten worden, vnnd bisshero so lange Zeit bey dem löbl. Hauss Österreich continuiert vnd verbliben, das haben alle vernüfftige gemüetter vnd Herzen wolmainent zubedenckhen vnd zu erwegen."*Ibid.*, 286–287.

Here, the author is conjoining "Cron Hungern" (in the territorial sense) and the image of "Vormauer der ganczen Christenhait" (bastion of the whole of Christendom). The meaning of the bastion image is the same here as in *Querelae*, as the author links together as identical the preservation of Hungary and the legitimacy of the power of the House of Habsburg, the "Löblichen Hauss Österreich". If Hungary, in the sense of "Cron Hungern" and "Vormauer der ganczen Christenhait," is threatened, then – so goes the author's argument – not only the Kingdom but also the other regions of the Holy Roman Empire, all of Christendom and the Habsburg dynasty itself will be placed in jeopardy. From this it follows that the preservation of "Cron Hungern" is of vital significance for the legitimacy of the House of Habsburg.[97]

In the document produced in the name of Archduke Matthias it is evident that now once more the crown legitimated Habsburg power, and furthermore was associated with a national concept. This meaning reminds us of Berger's epic of 1600, in which the cross alludes to the preservation of Christendom as the emperor's sacred duty. Berger too conjoins the legitimate nature of imperial power and the strengthening and defence of the Kingdom of Hungary. It is therefore probable that the source of these concepts, novel in Hungarian circles, is to be found in the Archduke's entourage.

In what follows Matthias' author expands on this idea, analysing more deeply the importance for the legitimation of the Habsburg dynasty's power of the meaning of "Cron Hungern" as "Vormauer der ganczen Christenhait". He states that the Archduke had convoked the Pozsony Diet in order to justify the Habsburg dynasty's claims to power.[98] The Estates had assembled because of the shared danger (*communi periculo*) to the Kingdom of Hungary, the other territories and the House of Austria. The Estates and Matthias personally had tried to protect the power of the king: "... His Majesty's imperial and royal standing must be saved from ultimate destruction in the Kingdom and the territories, and thus once more it will be possible to guide and lead everything to a peaceful condition . . ."[99] The Estates criticised Rudolf's governance, and had reached the conclusion that the Vienna Peace should be ratified without delay. If this were not done at once, the crown of Hungary would fall into Turkish hands and would no longer able to perform the task that fell to it as the bastion of Christendom.

---

97 It is striking that in April 1579 Matthias warned Rudolf by an emissary from the Netherlands of dangers menacing the House of Austria: loss of territory and the threat that another ruler would have to be elected. See: Koenigsberger, *Monarchies*, 288.

98 "Kurzer bericht," 287–288.

99 "... Ihrer Mt. Khays. vnd Khünigl. authoritet, souol auch dero Khünigreich vnd Länder vor entlichen interitu vindicirt, vnd alles widerumben in friedtlichen Standt gerichte vnd gebracht werden möchte ..." Ibid., 288.

And can one truly entrust oneself to the benevolent support of empires and other foreign Christian powers? And even if so, were all assistance to arrive far too late when the fire has immeasurably gained ground, when the Hungarian crown as bastion of all Christendom is torn from the Empire in the present unrest – in which, alas, it is at present more involved that is its due – and Hungary falls into the hands of the ancient enemy of the name Christian – of which the possibility remains – and further external dangers too threaten.[100]

Matthias's amanuensis then paints a dreadful picture of the future – if Rudolf were, nevertheless, to persist in his present policies – and links that too to the crown. He draws attention to the suffering of hundreds of thousands of Christians, the eternal servitude threatening Hungary, the Austrian territories and Styria, and the further horrors which the "ancient enemy of the name of Christ" will inflict on Christians.[101] In his view, the peace treaty was the only means of preventing this. Rudolf, however, is reluctant to ratify it, even though it had been agreed on his authorisation. Peace would be best for the kingdoms and for "… His Majesty, the glorious House of Austria and all the countries of Christendom …" in the interests of calling a halt to the rebellion and "… defending the Hungarian crown from terminal decline and destruction …".[102] In addition, if the peace treaties are obeyed the Hungarians will withdraw from the enforced alliance with the Ottomans.[103]

The author declares it Rudolf's task to avert the danger by ratifying the peace treaty; delay is dangerous "… if he does not wish to lose the Hungarian crown in its entirety…".[104] He states that the Hungarian frontiers are the bastions of the German-Austrian nation and Christendom. If Hungary is lost, Germany will be the next victim. That is why it is so very important for peace to be made with the Hungarians and the Ottomans, and for the defence of the frontiers to be appropriately strengthened.[105] If peace is made with the Ottomans the new blaze of rebellion too will be extinguished. He goes on to connect the ratification with religious freedom as another item giving rise to rebellion. He believes that Rudolf has laid excessive

---

100 "Vnd ob man sich woll auff die Reichs vnd anderer ausslenndischer christlichen potentaten treuherzige bewilligung verlassen mechte, wüerde doch bey so vberhandt genumbenen Feuer alle hilff ganz zu spat sein, wan in diser Eyll, wie sichs bishero im werckh laider mehr dan zuvill erzaigt, die Cron Hungern als ain Vormauer der ganzen Christenhait solle vnder ainsten von derselben abgeschnitten vnd in des Erbfeindts Christlichen namens henden, darauff es berait gestanden, khomen, vnd noch bis dati in eüsserister gefahr stehet." *Ibid.*, 289–290.
101 *Ibid.*, 290.
102 "... vnd die Cron Hungern vor endlichem abfall vnd vndergang noch zu erhalten..." *Ibid.*
103 *Ibid.*, 290–291.
104 "die Cron Hungern ganz vnd gar verlieren wellen" *Ibid.*, 291.
105 *Ibid.*, 292.

emphasis on the first paragraph of the treaty, which deals with religious freedom.[106] Like Bocskai, the Hajdús also have made the rebellion into a war of religion, and have sought assistance from the Protestant Prince Electors and rulers outside Hungary. By so doing they have been able to inflame the situation greatly and spread the rebellion far more widely. Rudolf has been meaning to assist "… the only religion that leads to salvation …" and its clergy, but in the meantime, this has led to the destruction of that faith. This why the Hajdús have so clung to their religion in their demands, and to a king that would follow it.[107] The Hajdús have in fact done nothing to harm the Catholic religion. Bocskai proclaimed freedom of the exercise of religion, and in Matthias' opinion this was completely in agreement with the first paragraph of the Peace of Vienna.[108]

By this interpretation the author shows that the stance taken by Rudolf against freedom of religion has damaged his authority by giving the opposition arguments and offering the opportunity for cross-border alliances to be formed. He closes his exposition with the argument that the purpose of his actions had been the defence of the faith, the emperor, the House of Austria and its possessions, the Holy Roman Empire and the whole of Christendom:

> … the overwhelming majority of Matthias's deeds and actions had no other goal than to guard firstly the glory of the Most High God and to further the Roman Catholic faith, which alone brings salvation, to maintain in their former places its priests, to defend His Imperial Majesty, their Imperial and Royal Highnesses, the glorious House of Austria and the said kingdom and territories, and together with these the well-being and happiness of the Holy Roman Empire and the whole of Christendom.[109]

The theory of Illésházy and Berger concerning the crown

In the period when Archduke Matthias was taking over power in Hungary and forming an alliance with the Lutheran Estate of the Habsburg Empire, Illésházy was his principal Hungarian strategist and most influential disseminator of his political

---

106 *Ibid.*, 293.
107 *Ibid.*
108 *Ibid.*, 294.
109 "… das sy auch in diesen Ihren oberczelten actionibus vnd Handtlungen nichts anders, als zuförderist die Ehr des Allerhöchsten erhalt- vnd vermehrung vnser allainseligmachenden Cath. Röm. Religion, derselben Geistlichen standts permansion, Ihrere Khays. Mt. Kays. vnd Künigliche Hochhaiten, des Löbl. Haus Österreichs vnnd derselben Künigreich vnd Landte conservation, ja des Römischen Reichs vnd der ganczen Christenheit wohlfahrt vnd aufnemben gesucht haben." *Ibid.*, 295.

message.¹¹⁰ This is why in 1611, Bocatius calls Illésházy "*Peitho et Siren Hungaricae gentis*" (the Peitho and Siren of the Hungarian people – Peitho was the Classical goddess of persuasion and the three Sirens mythical seductresses).¹¹¹ In addition, various tales of his political and oratorical prowess and achievements were widely circulated.¹¹² Illésházy was a cultured man with wide European horizons. As we shall see, the development of the significance of the crown and the Estates, together with the formation of images of them, was largely the fruit of his thinking. First of all – turning our attention first to the formation of his ideas about the future of the Hungarian Estates – we shall give an account of how he and his colleagues elaborated the concept of the crown.

According to István Hiller, judging by his political activity Illésházy saw the profitable response to the questions facing Hungary not in opposition but in harmonisation of interests with the Habsburg dynasty.¹¹³ The essence of his political thought was the harmonisation of interests among the various factions on the political scene of the Kingdom of Hungary. In the first place that meant that he sought a balance between the political aims of the Habsburg dynasty and those of the Hungarian Estates. Secondly, he strove for a similar balance between the various religious, social and political groupings in the Kingdom. Thirdly, he tried to steer Transylvania and Hungary together onto a common political course.¹¹⁴ Fourthly, by encouraging a peace treaty between the Habsburg and Ottoman Empires he tried to create a stable situation in the three areas of the divided Kingdom of Hungary.

The keyword to Illésházy's thinking is harmony (*concordia*). He endeavoured to achieve this not by setting the partial interests of one defined group before those of others, but by working for the common good (*publicum bonum*) within the framework of the community (*respublica*), and by securing generally accepted compromises. The sole work in which these ideas of Illésházy (or the views inspired

---

110 Benda, "Habsburg-politika," 416; Éva S. Lauter, "A Palatinus Regni Hungariae," 216–217.
111 Bocatius, "Olympias Carceraria," 116.
112 Among others, one anecdote from the correspondence between Matthias and Illésházy. Matthias: "Make me king, then I will see to making you first man in the country." Illésházy: "No, but first do you make me first man in the country, then I will make you king." Quoted in Hiller, "Illésházy István," 85. A second instance occurred at the Diet in January 1608, at which complaints were being voiced against Rudolf. The Croat delegate Tamás Erdődy wondered whether he had gone too far? Illésházy replied: "I shall put an end to what you are concerned over (imperial power) in three days." Quoted in Benda, "Habsburg-politika és rendi ellenállás," 417, note 33.
113 Hiller, "Illésházy István," 85; István Hiller, "Pázmány Péter és a Habsburg diplomáciája [Péter Pázmány and Habsburg diplomacy]," in Emil Hargittay, ed., *Pázmány Péter es kora* [Péter Pázmány and his time] (Piliscsaba: Pázmány Péter Katolikus Egyetem Bölcsészettudományi Kar, 2001), 142.
114 Nagy, *Botránykövek régvolt historiánkban*, 154–156. Nagy considers that this ambition of Illésházy's led to Káthay's death, as the political aims of Illésházy and Káthay were different.

by him) is set out is Berger's *Caduceus, seu proba et brevis invitatio ad comitia pia concordia fida Hungariae Posinii celebranda*.[115] This pamphlet appeared on the occasion of the Diet in Pozsony in 1607, and its dedication is addressed to Révay, who probably commissioned its writing and paid for it to be printed. It consists of a dedication to the patron, a review of the current political situation in the Kingdom of Hungary, a prayer to Christ for Hungary and a further poem in praise of Révay.

The essence of what Berger says in *Caduceus* (herald) is aimed at the justification of the policies of Archduke Matthias and Illésházy. The most important topic in it is the need for peace in *respublica Hungarica*, which it is possible to attain with the aid of harmony and trust (*fides*). Once again, the author makes known this message by sketching the image of the Hungarian Estates, and thereby summons the reader to the "love of the fatherland" (*amor patriae*).[116] It is striking that, unlike political writers on this subject, he presents this idea in terms which allude unmistakably to the Catholic religion. Thus, among other things, he names Pope Clement as one very desirous of peace in Hungary,[117] refers again to the image of the double cross of St István – which also appears in his first work – as a token of the protection of the Christian faith,[118] and at the end of the work, in a prayer for Hungary, he also writes of the "Catholic Christian Church" (*ecclesia christiana catholica*).[119]

From the generally Catholic content of the work and the prayer at the end, the nineteenth-century historian József Podhraczky deduced that Berger, and even perhaps Révay, were Catholics.[120] No one has written more recently on the question of why Révay, a Lutheran, supported a work so indisputably Catholic. Once more, we can find the answer in the political milieu of the time of publication. The greatest opposition to a compromise led by Illésházy between Matthias and the Estates was shown from the Catholic side. After the religious tensions around 1600, the violent Counter-Reformation of 1604 and the generally anti-Catholic mood of the Hungarian rebels, the Catholic Church had little hope of anything good from such an agreement, as they had been the chief losers from the Peace of Vienna. The reason for their opposition was that they were afraid of the Protestants' freedom of religious practice, through which the dominant position in the Empire of the pro-Habsburg Estates and the Catholic Church could be lost. This fear was well founded, because Illésházy considered it an important political goal to put an end to the

---

115 Elias Berger, *Caduceus, seu proba et brevis invitatio ad comitia pia concordia fida Hungariae Posinii celebranda* (Viennae Austriae: Typis Margarethae Formicae, Viduae, 1607).
116 *Ibid.*, B2 r.
117 *Ibid.*, B4 r.
118 *Ibid.*, C2 r.
119 *Ibid.*, C4 v.
120 Podhraczky, "Berger Illés," 356–357.

interweaving of the Catholic Church and the kingship.¹²¹ Accordingly Archduke Matthias did not afterwards invite the bishops to the Diet, no longer asked for advice from the clergy, and granted Church lands to the nobility. The Diet of 1607–1608 was, therefore, partly a setback for the Catholic Church in Hungarian politics, and partly the recovery of their privileges in Hungary by churchmen.

Because of the growing uncertainty, Illésházy and his adherents concentrated their strategy on winning the confidence of the Catholics. Berger's pamphlet, with its message of loyalty, trust and concord was to convince the Catholic members of the *respublica* of the integrity of Matthias's and Illésházy's intentions. The most logical way for them to be able to put such a political message over to the Catholic audience was to make use of Catholic subjects and symbols. The content of the pamphlet, therefore, is to be regarded not as a source on the persuasion of its writer and his patron, but rather as a means whereby Matthias and Illésházy – through Berger's work – tried to draw the Catholic Estates to their side.

The point of view of the pamphlet is most strongly evident in the concluding prayer. As a literary creation, *Caducei votum ad Christum pro Hungaria* belongs to the genre of political prayers for the fatherland. Among others Illésházy and Révay wrote in this genre, which may be regarded as part of the political representation of the Estates. They were led by the purpose of transmitting the political message to the Estates in the form of a prayer to God, the function of which was to strengthen the feeling of interdependence in them. Expression is given to this in, among other things, one of Illésházy's prayers by the collocation *Deus Hungarorum* ("God of the Hungarians"). The first three Protestant prayers from the period 1605–1612 were widely familiar.[122] The fourth is what was previously known as Berger's Catholic prayer, while the fifth appeared in 1613 in one of Révay's writings on the crown. The aim of Berger's work was that the Catholic half of the *respublica* should feel part of the Estates through the author's sketching, with the aid of universally familiar subjects, an image with which the Estates as a whole could identify.

The transferring of the Crown from Rudolf to Matthias (1608)

The next step in the development of the significance of the crown was the formal handing over of power within the House of Habsburg by the endowing of Archduke Matthias by Rudolf with the crown of Hungary. The occasion for this was provided

---

121 Benda, "Habsburg politika," 426–427.
122 The preacher Péter Alvinczi collected the following prayers: "*Precatio Magnifici Illieshazij in Polonia profugi ad ipsom et ex sacris collecta*", "*Oratio pro Hungaria*," "*Gratiarum accio*". All these are published in Ötvös, *Pálffy Kata*, 170–173. See also: [Stephanus Illésházy], *Oratio pro salute Hungariae* …, in Ms. OSZK Quart. Lat. 316. fol. 10r.-13v.

by the threat of a further Hajdú rebellion and war with the Ottoman Empire, coupled with the efforts of members of the family, court officials and representatives of the Estates of the Habsburg Empire to prevail on him to abdicate.[123] Rudolf had given evidence that he could not and would not resolve the worrying situation. This was the moment for Archduke Matthias to take power by force.[124]

> ... his aim was to save the emperor, the House of Austria, its countries, its empire and Christendom from ruin, very close to which a number of countries – Hungary, the Austrian territories and Moravia – already were, for which reason they had formed an alliance with him . . .[125]

The ceremony of transfer of power was preceded by wide-ranging discussions and political complications, the outcome of which was that Matthias received royal power in Hungary and ruled the Austrian territories and Moravia.[126] The final statement by Matthias and Rudolf – the so-called Stará Libeň Agreement – was signed in two tents at the castle of Stará Libeň on 25 June 1608. Matthias' delegation at the discussions was headed by Karl von Liechtenstein and Karol Žierotin. Among the signatories was György Thurzó, who, like Illésházy, was one of the most powerful pro-Habsburg aristocrats in Hungary.

A variety of sources describe the ceremony of the handing over of the Hungarian Holy Crown. We know that the event was immortalised by a painting, an image and at least one print.[127] The relevant official documents relating to the handing over

---

123 Sturmberger, *Georg Erasmus*; Tibor Wittman, "A magyarországi államelméleti tudományosság XVII. század eleji alapvetésének németalföldi forrásaihoz. J. Lipsius [On the Dutch sources for the Hungarian political thought in the seventeenth century. J. Lipsius]," *Filológiai közlöny* 2 (1957), 53–66; Tibor Wittman, "Az osztrák Habsburg-hatalom válságos éveinek történetéhez (1606-1618) [On the history of the crisis years of the Austrian Habsburg power (1606-1618)," 3–44; Tibor Wittman, "Az erdélyi fejdelmek és a magyarországi uralkodó osztály függetlenségi és rendi küzdelmei (1607-64) [The independence and class struggle of the Transylvanian princes and the Hungarian ruling class (1607-1664)," in Éva H. Balázs and László Makkai, eds., *Magyarország története 1526-1790* [Hungarian history 1526-1790], vol. II (Budapest: Tankönyvkiadó, ²1972), 165–166.
124 Haupt, "From feuding brothers," 240.
125 "Sein Ziel ist den Ks.[Kaiser], das Haus Österreich, dessen Länder, das Reich und die Christenheit vor dem Untergange zu bewahren, dem einige Länder schon nahe waren, wie sich denn eben dehalb Ungarn, Österreich und Mähren mit ihm verbündet haben ..." Letter of Archduke Matthias to Prince Maximilian, 20 May 1608, published in Stieve, *Vom Reichstag*, 383.
126 Sturmberger, *Georg Erasmus*; Vocelka, *Rudolf II.*, 114–115; Bahlcke, *Regionalismus*, 341–342.
127 See, *inter alia*, the very detailed reports of Archduke Albert Habsburg's emissary Peter (de) Visschernek to Jacob Fleckhammer, dated 7, 14, 21 and 28 June 1608, in Hatvani, *Magyar történelmi okmánytár*, 12–32, the letter of Archduke Matthias to Archduke Albert of 29 June 1608, *idem*, 33; Haupt, "From feuding brothers," 241–244 (based on: Descriptio germanica expeditionis arch. Matthiae in Moraviam et Bohemiam a 15. Aprilis usque ad 27. Iunii 1608, ms edition ÖNB Cod.

have also survived.[128] The following paradox arises as one studies the evidence: as is evident from written sources and drawings, the ceremony partly focused on the Crown, which was the centre of attention; partly, however, the object itself was given no particular significance alluding to any development of the crown tradition whatsoever. In the painting the crown gives the impression of being one coronation jewel among many. In the drawings and written accounts alike, it is simply called "Hungerischen Kron", "königliche Kron" or "*corona Regni Hungariae*", without any attention being devoted to the possibly special significance inherent in it. The explanation for this neutral drawing and description is that in the written sources and the pictures all that matters is the depiction of the transfer of power within the House of Habsburg. To most of those present the Hungarian crown meant neither more nor less than the office of king of Hungary which Rudolf was ceding to Matthias.

To the Hungarian participants in the ceremony, however, the handing over of the Crown had a special significance because of its tradition. The bishop of Veszprém and chancellor of Hungary, Bishop Bálint Lépes, greeted Matthias and the crown

---

7647); György Závodszky, "Diarium rerum ...," in Bél, *Adparatus* 353–379; Kaspar Ens von Lorch, *Ad rerum Hungaricarum historiam appendix* (Coloniae: Wilhelmus Lutzenkirchen, 1608); Nicolaus Istvanfi, *Historiarum de rebus Ungaricis libri XXXIV* (Coloniae: Antonius Hierat, 1622), 851; S.n., *Nevves ovt of Germanie or The surprizing of the Citie of Prage by the Arch-duke Leopold, and what there passed in the in the moneths of February and March last. With a briefe of the most remarkable things happened within fixe moneths, as well in France and Germany as in Bohemia, Transiluania and Spaine. Translated out of the French Copie, printed at Paris 1611* (London: Printed [by N. Okes] for Iohn Royston and William Bladon, 1612), A2; Pierre d'Avity, *Archontologia cosmica ... opera et studio Jo. Ludovici Gotofredi* (Francofurti ad Moenum: Jennisius, 1628), 395–396, Original edition, Paris, 1613. English translation: Pierre d'Avity, *The estates, empires, & principallities of the world* (London: Printed by Adam: Islip; for Mathewe: Lownes; and Iohn: Bill, [2]1615, 625–626);" Christian Matthiae, *Theatrum historicum theoretico-practicum ...* (Amstelodami, 1668), 1102.

128 Among other things these documents should be preserved among the collected sources from the Diets of 1607 and 1608 in the Kálmán Benda bequest. (Hungarian Academy of Science, Történettudományi Intézet (Institute for the study of History), no catalogue number). This publication of sources was almost ready for the press as long ago as 1980, but has never been printed, although there are still plans to publish it (2022). The section of the work relating to the handing over of the crown is not to be found in either the collection of the Academy, or the Ráday collection in Budapest. Benda refers to this publication in a variety of articles and books as in preparation. A variety of sources on the handing over may also be found in Illésházy's register, "Reversales super Coronae Regni Hungariae receptione" (25 June 1608), in [Stephanus Illésházy], *De Rebus Hungaricis Prothocolon* (manuscript) OSZK Fol. Lat. 2336 fol. 49r.-v., "Cessio Sacrae Caesareae Regiaque Majttis p(...) Regno" 51r.-52v., "Paria literarum Reversalium sua Maittis (...)" 52r.-v., ÖStA Wien, HHStA, Fasc. 395 Konv. A., MTAK, Ms. 5169/21 (Árpád Károlyi bequest). Benda used many of the documents in the book he wrote with Erik Fügedi on the crown.

in a speech.[129] Matthias himself bestowed on the crown the title *Sacra dicti Regni Hungariae corona*.[130] One Hungarian observer wrote: "By having the crown brought back to Hungary in accordance with the Peace of Vienna Archduke Matthias did the greatest deed for the fatherland that he could possibly have done".[131] The anonymous writer expresses the hope that God will now show mercy to the Hungarians and bring them into a peaceful, calm and blessed condition. The arrival of the Crown was therefore associated with positive political changes and the grace of God. This notion also recurs in later texts on Matthias and the crown.

After being handed over the Crown really became the centre of interest. Matthias gave a celebratory lunch in his tent. On this occasion the Crown was put on show – probably on a salver on the dining table – in the manner usual at a coronation.[132] It was the first opportunity since the coronation of 1572 that those present had had of seeing the Crown up close.[133] This helps to explain why there is so much description of the Hungarian coronation regalia in accounts of the event.[134] It is also highly probable that a number of other writers who dealt with the crown – for example, Péter Révay, János Jeszenszky, and Kristóf Lackner and others – used this

---

129 The text of the speech is recorded in Petrus de Rewa [Péter Révay], *De monarchia et sacra corona regni...* (Frankfurt: Thomas Matthias Götzius, 1659), 122–123.
130 See the already quoted manuscripts: "Reversales super Coronae Regni Hungariae receptione [25 June 1608]", in Stephanus Illésházy, *De Rebus Hungaricis Prothocolon* 49v-r, "Paria literarum Reversalium sua Maittis," *idem*, 52 v-r; ÖStA Wien, HHStA Ungarische Akten, Comitalia, Fasc. 395 Konv. B. Fol. 195–201, *idem*, Hoffinanz-Ungarn r. nr. 95. Konv. B. [June 1608], fol. 169–189. Other collections of sources, "Apparatus historicus Nicolai Istvánffy, propalatini regni Hungariae. Collectio litterarum diplomatum memorabilium, manuscriptorum selectissima.," OSZK Fol. Lat. 3606, II k., fol. 91r.-92v. (Istvánffy-collection) and "Liber in qvo omnia acta tvmvltvs Bockaiani cum [sic!] ipsa tvrcicae pacis tractatione in ordinem redacta continentur," OSZK Fol. Lat. 2204, fol. 66r.-69v. (György Thurzó collection).
131 Quoted without attribution in Benda and Fügedi, *A magyar korona*, 146–157.
132 Visscher's report to Fleckhammer, 28 June 1608 in Hatvani, *Magyar történelmi okmánytár*, 32.
133 Tóth, "A koronázási jelvények," 10–11, 19; Géza Pálffy, "A Szent Korona és a koronaláda balesete 1638-ban [The Holy Crown and the accident with the chest of the crown in 1638]," in József Jankovics, Tünde Császtvay, István Csörsz Rumen, Zoltán G. Szabó, eds., *"Nem sűlyed az emberiség!".... Album amicorum. Szörényi László LX. születésnapjára* [Humanity does not drown! Album amicorum for the 60th birthday of László Szörény] (Budapest: MTA Irodalomtudományi Intézet, 2007), 1431–1444.
134 Tamás Vizkelethy gives a detailed list of the coronation regalia in a letter of 6 July 1608 to Ferenc Beniczk about the handing over of the crown. See: MTAK, Ms. 5169/21 (Árpád Károlyi bequest), fol. 14. (Originally in Magyar Nemzeti Múzeum, Beniczky cs. Lt. Fasc. XII. N. 34.) A report from Archduke Albert's emissary, Peter Visscher, to Jacob Fleckhammer, dated 28 June 1608, in addition to listing the crown jewels contains one of the oldest descriptions of the Hungarian coronation cloak: "Auff der Casul ist mit lateinischen lettern gestanden: Casula haec facta est Ao MXXXI et donata a Rege Stephano et sua Conjuge Gisla Sanctae Mariae sitae in Alba." Hatvani, *Magyar történelmi okmánytár*, 32.

occasion, or the exhibition for a larger public in St Virtus' church, to examine and sketch the crown.

After being handed over, the crown became the focus of a disagreement between Matthias and the Estates. The point at issue was whether the crown was to be kept in Austria or in Hungary, and when it was to return to Hungarian soil. Behind all this was the balance of power between Matthias and the Estates, and the definition of his position as king.[135] Rudolf had handed over the crown on condition that the Estates unanimously elected him king. The Estates wanted to strengthen their position by electing their king freely in accordance with the Peace of Vienna and to keep the crown in Hungary. Matthias tried to show his independence of the Estates by keeping the crown in his possession and requiring the Estates to swear loyalty to him. Nor was he willing for the crown to go to Hungary before the election of the king had taken place.[136] The essence of the dispute is clear from the views expressed by the Saxon delegates at the assembly of Prince Electors at Fulda on 30 July 1608, which may be read in the Mainz Protocol: " ... let the crown be restored to the Hungarian Estates, whose concern it is, as in Hungary the kingship is elective and not hereditary ..." (*regnum electivum et non haereditarium*).[137]

According to Hungarian historians the content of this question was largely theoretical, as in fact there could not be a free election of the king. Archduke Matthias held royal power thanks to his brother. Emma Bartoniek has stated that if the House of Habsburg had really not meant there to be an election of king it would not have happened.[138] Considering the current political situation and the actual balance of power, it is no surprise that both parties fought with the weapons of propaganda.

During the preparations for Matthias' coronation a new image appeared in political literature in Hungary. The nature of the future king was established by picturing him as a second Mátyás Corvinus. This was based on the fallacious parallel drawn between Mátyás II and his famous predecessor because of the return of the crown and the identity of name. Surprisingly enough, the same topos was already used during the entry of Archduke Matthias in Brussels in 1578. His adherents and the writers commissioned by them (Illésházy, Berger, Révay, Jeszenszky) showed Mátyás II as the national king of the Hungarians; he would do deeds as great as those of the first Mátyás, if not even greater. This mode of portrayal was in keeping with the prevailing political situation, as just then there was a renewed threat of

---

135 Fraknói, *A magyar királyválasztások*, 186–187.
136 Mátyás II in fact was having the crown repaired and a cracked saphire removed, as is described by keeper of the crown Péter Révay. De Rewa, *De monarchia*, 143.
137 "... die cron Hungern seie den stenden in Hungern, denen sie geburt, geliefert, dan dis ein *regnum electivum et non haereditarium*." See "Mainzer Protokoll des Churfürstentags zu Fulda," in Stieve, *Vom Reichstag 1608*, 449.
138 Bartoniek, *A magyar királykoronazások*, 98.

rebellion by the Hajdús, who were demanding a national king. Furthermore, the memory of the national ruler Bocskai was still alive.

The function of the comparison of the two Kings Mátyás was the establishment of Mátyás II as king. Through the dissemination of this portrayal the identity of the nobility too was strengthened. Mátyás was able to spread this image of himself because an active, spontaneous Mátyás cultus came into being in Hungary, forged by Protestants and Catholics alike.[139] One – if not the most – important stimulus of this cultus in distinguished circles was the appearance of Bonfini's above-mentioned work on the history of Hungary. After a section of it had been printed in Basel in 1543 and a German translation of this section in 1545, the court historian Zsámboky (Sambucus) published a full Latin edition in Basel in 1568 and in Frankfurt in 1581.[140] After that a section was translated into Hungarian and adapted by the Transylvanian Protestant printer, writer and pastor Gáspár Heltai, and published in 1575 while the Latin version was re-issued in Hanau in 1606.[141] Bonfini's work had a tremendous influence, and formed the basis for the historical studies of almost every young aristocrat in Hungary. The cultus was then further spread by historical works, songs and other literary and cultural creations that can be traced back to Bonfini.[142]

In this cultus two topics from Bonfini were significant to the contemporaries of the second or Other Mátyás: the standing of Mátyás Corvinus as national king of Hungary who had unified the Hungarians, and his successful endeavours to recover the Hungarian crown from Emperor Friedrich. Both had been important in the legitimation of Mátyás Corvinus' royal power, and now the Other Mátyás and his supporters made use of these motifs to establish the political situation in 1608.

István Illésházy's speech of 1608 and the work of Berger (1608)

The two topics can first be found in a speech by Illésházy to the Estates assembled in Kassa in July 1608.[143] The purpose of the Kassa Diet was for the Estates to accept

---

139 See: Ildikó Kríza, *A Mátyás-hagyomány évszázadai* [The tradition of Matthias through centuries] (Budapest: Akadémiai Kiadó, 2007); András Kubinyi, *Matthias Rex* (Budapest: Balassi Kiadó, 2001).
140 Kulcsár, *Inventarium*, 81–82.
141 Gáspár Heltai, *Chronica az Magyaroknac dolgairol* [Chronicle on the deeds of the Hungarians] (Colosvarot: Heltaj Gasparné, 1575); Péter Kulcsár, "A történetíró Heltai [The historian Heltai]," in Varjas, *Irodalom és ideológia*, 113–133.
142 Péter Kulcsár, "Utószó [Afterword]," in Péter Kulcsár, ed., *Humanista történetírók* [Humanist history writers] (Budapest: Szépirodalmi Kiadó, 1977), 1193.
143 "Anno 1608. Peroratio sive preambulum propositionum 29. Julii Cassoviae exhibita regnicolis per C. Stephanum Illésházy," *Történelmi Tár*, 2 (1879), 388–389.

Rudolf's abdication and to swear loyalty to Archduke Matthias as a first step to the election of the king. At the same time, the event served to celebrate the return of the crown.[144] The text of the speech was incorporated that same year into one of Berger's works on the joyous return of the crown to Hungary, the aim and content of which we shall consider in the following chapter.[145]

It is the speaker's intention to convince the Estates in the northern parts of Hungary of the necessity to elect Matthias as king. This he does by showing him as the yearned-for national king, led by the best of intentions when the liberties of the Estates and the "public good" (*publicum bonum*) are concerned. An image is invoked to justify his kingship which presents him as Mátyás Corvinus. This depiction makes its first appearance in this text, and is based on Matthias' deeds in connection with the crown, which the speaker compares with those of Mátyás I. In other words, here the crown tradition serves as a link between Matthias Habsburg and the royal power of Mátyás Corvinus. Illésházy bases the image to be formed of Matthias Habsburg on his depiction as a second Corvinus, and with this in mind takes into account his efforts to secure the return of the crown. When Illésházy was describing all this, the crown was not yet in Hungary. Furthermore, in view of the continuing discussions on the Peace of Vienna and the complications that followed the handing over of the crown, it appeared that Matthias had no intention at all of placing it in the hands of the Estates. The topic of the return of the Hungarian crown must therefore be seen as a fiction clothed with the function of a specific legitimation.

In Illésházy's speech this topic serves as the ultimate justification of Matthias' actions while governor of Hungary, and supports his coming acquisition of royal power. The speaker states that Matthias had done everything for the restoration of the liberties of the Hungarian Estates, and in that connection mentions, inter alia, his securing the Peace of Vienna and his forging of the alliance. The most eloquent testimony of his benevolence, however, is Matthias' desire to restore the crown to the Hungarians. For Illésházy too the return of the crown is the link between the image of the ideal king, Mátyás Corvinus, and the future kingship of the Other Mátyás. Therefore, he states that Matthias – just like his predecessor – has taken

---

144 Elias Berger, "Ad Illustrissimum ac magnificum D.D. Stephanum Ilieshazi comitem Trinchinien, & Liptowien D.& Patronum observandißimum," published in: Elias Berger, *D.O.M. Jubilaeus de origine, errore et restitutione S. Coronae Hungariae Regni fortiss. ac felicissi*. (s.l.: s.n., 1608), F1.
145 "Oratio illustrissimi D.D. Stephani Ilieshazi Comitis Trinchiniensis, ac Liptovviensis, Habita ad proceres, & status Hungariae superioris Cassoviae congregatos," in Berger, *D.O.M. Jubilaeus*, F3. The following page numbers were those of the 1863 edition of the speech: Gábor Kazinczy, ed., *Gr. Illésházy István Nádor följegyzései 1592–1603. és Hídvégi Mikó Ferencz históriája 1594–1613. Bíró Sámuel folytatásával* [Count István Illésházy's historic notes 1592–1603 and the history of Ferencz Hídvégi Mikó 1594–1613] (Pest: F. Eggenberger, 1863).

the crown from Austria and given it back to the Hungarians. Together with this, Illésházy declares that as Mátyás Corvinus recovered the crown, indeed, performed even greater feats, so it would be in the case of Matthias Habsburg too.[146]

A political promise couched in these descriptive terms satisfied the hopes of the Estates for a national king comparable to Mátyás Corvinus. In order to be able to address the whole social order of the Estates (*res publica*), Illésházy painted a very effective picture of the crown without drawing attention to any political or religious differences that might exist. The meaning given to the crown in this speech was that it embodied the Estates' political ambitions. Through the portrayal of Matthias' actions, the crown assumed the role of a symbol uniting the Estates.

The concept of the interdependence of the crown and the Estates becomes clear from the structure of the speech. Illésházy begins by picking up the image taken from *Querelae*, depicting the sufferings of Hungary and the Estates as the consequence of their role as bastion of Christendom against the Ottomans.[147] He too declares that the fatherland is in ruins, and therefore the danger looms of Hungary's being unable to continue to discharge its task as defender of Christianity. This at once suggests that even alone, the Hungarians are capable of bearing this burden, but only if and when a solution arises that will ease their situation. This, Illésházy sees in the election of Archduke Matthias as king. The essence of his message is that Matthias would be the right king to ensure that the Hungarians are able further to carry out their duty and defend Europe from the Turks. He declares that God has sent Matthias to prepare the country for this. As governor, he has demonstrated that he can ensure peace in the fatherland and the surrounding countries. Rudolf would not hear of peace and provoked civil war, whereas Matthias would ensure lasting peace.

In Illésházy's argument, the most important symbol and proof of Matthias's political promises is the return of the crown. He links this to three themes: the Hungarian Estates, their liberty and their patriotism. According to Illésházy, the clearest proof of Matthias's good intentions was that he had brought the crown to Hungary and given it back to the Hungarians, since that had for a very long time been the desire of the Estates.[148] He was therefore to be regarded as the defender of the rights of the Hungarian *res publica*, who embodied true patriotism and was of Hungarian blood.

The meaning which Illésházy thus attributed to the crown may be viewed as the outcome of the *Querelae* and Matthias' declaration. He shows the Hungarian coronation jewel, on the occasion of its return, as a symbol of Matthias' having

---

146 *Ibid.*, 331.
147 *Ibid.*, 327.
148 *Ibid.*

saved Hungary and the Estates, and thereby ultimately the whole of Christendom. In conclusion, the presentation of Matthias as national king is at the same time vindication of Illésházy's policy too. He declares that the liberty of Hungary is guaranteed, as Matthias has restored the crown.[149] He thereby repeats the argument used previously in his debate with Bocskai, that the return of the crown would vouch for the freedom of the Hungarian nation and that there would be no need of an independent Transylvania to protect that freedom. In Illésházy's view, the presence of the crown in Hungary would be sufficient guarantee of the political rights and liberty of the Hungarian Estates.

In a speech, the text of which was printed in Vienna together with Illésházy's in 1608, Berger further refined the meaning of the crown outlined by Illésházy.[150] The work was titled: "To Almighty God, a festive garland on the origin, wanderings and restorations of the Holy Crown of the mighty and blessed Kingdom of Hungary, together with a varied garland for the blessed and worthy coronation of the new king of Hungary". This occasional piece was dedicated to "the king and Estates of Hungary", although Archduke Matthias was at the time still only king in prospect. The speech was written before the Diet held in Pozsony in October and November 1608, at which the delegates elected Matthias king on 16 November and Illésházy palatine on 18 November. The coronation took place on 19 November, using the Hungarian crown which had been returned, after the Lutheran Révay and the Catholic István Pálffy had been elected Guardians of the Crown.[151]

It appears from the language and style employed, and from a letter written by Georgius Rhemus (Rem, 1561/2–1625, a German lawyer, philosopher and historian with an interest in Hungary) that Berger probably delivered his speech to the said Diet.[152] As is the case with Berger's other occasional writings, this too was not widely distributed, and no more is known of this publication. The pamphlet contains a

---

149 *Ibid.*, 330.
150 Berger, *D.O.M. Jubilaeus.*
151 Kálmán Benda, ed., *Magyarország történeti kronológiája* [Historical chronology of Hungary] Vol. 2. (Budapest: Akadémiai Kiadó, 1989), 436.
152 Letter from Georgius Rhem(us) to a certain Rittenhausen, 16 December 1608: *"Circumferuntur Oratio habita in coronatione regis Hungariae Matthiae II. a Bergero dicta."* Details quoted in: Dézsi, *Szenci Molnár Albert*, 266, quotation 1. In the same collection there is another letter from a person unknown to Albert Szenczi Molnár, in which there is another reference to a certain Berger and his work, although it is unclear whether this is to be indentified with Elias Berger. *Ibid.*, 269. In his letter mentioned above Asztalos writes that Berger had dedicated his eulogy on Illésházy to Rem, whereas in his *Rapsodiae* ... Berger had also written with his own hand a dedication to Asztalos. See also Kees Teszelszky, "Elias Berger Historia Ungarica című művének keletkezése és háttere (1603/4–1645) [The origin and background of the work Historia Ungarica by Elias Berger]," in Gergély Tóth, ed., *Clio Inter Arma. Tanulmányok a 16–18. századi magyarországi történetírásról*

title page, a dedication, a compilation on the origin, vicissitudes and return of the crown, a page with an inscription to Matthias on an imaginary triumphal arch, a letter to Illésházy, and finally Illésházy's above-mentioned speech.

Berger's is the first work on the historical significance of the Hungarian crown to be written in the Early Modern period. A number of historians assert that Révay was the first to write on the subject, but it was in fact not Révay but Berger.[153] This is considered a key work on the crown and the representative presentation of the Estates. Hungarian historians have hitherto shown only a passing interest in it.[154]

The work was intended to justify Illésházy's election as palatine. He is not even named as such in the pamphlet, which makes it likely that the little work, devised in the interests of him and Matthias, was published before the elections. Archduke Matthias could take his own election as king for granted, but it was not certain that Illésházy would be elected palatine. In the first part Berger praises to the heavens the new king's virtues and deeds, and in the second part extols Illésházy. Then follows Illésházy's speech, which likewise proclaims the glory of Matthias. Berger's work does not, therefore, only speak of Matthias, as Benda and Fügedi stated, but also deals with Illésházy's political ideas and deeds.[155] Berger's speech, like his earlier writings on the Estates and the crown, may be regarded as a sequel to Illésházy's.

The essence of his line of thought in this work is the personification of the crown which is an unmoving mover changing in its changelessness: the crown is an object which, through a significance given to it by God and Man, and through change in the latter significance, affects the fate of the Estates and the fatherland. The crown and its significance are similar to what is described in the poem by János Pannonius, which we used in the first chapter. In this fiction, contrived by Berger and others, the crown personifies the law, order and essence of Hungarian history – in brief, the Hungarian Estates and the true nature of the fatherland – which have been sanctified by God. The essence of the personality of the crown is the power and sanctity received from God, together with the respect that comes from Man. This quality Berger calls the "divine nature" or "faith of the crown" (*numen* or *religio sacrae coronae*). Since, as a result of this sacred significance, the crown presents the true nature of the Estates and the fatherland, the people pay homage to it. According to Berger, the Estates actually honour themselves through the crown. From this it

---

[Clio inter arma. Studies on history writing in Hungary between the sixteenth and eighteenth century], (Budapest: MTA Bölcsészettudományi Kutatóközpont, 2014), 149–168.

153 Emma, *Fejezetek*, 390; Bónis, *Révay Péter*, 43; Bertényi, *A magyar szent korona*, 117; György Szabados, *A magyar történelem kezdeteiről* [The beginnings of the Hungarian history] (Budapest: Balassi, 2006), 103.

154 Wittman, "Az osztrák Habsburg-hatalom,"; Benda and Fügedi, *A magyar korona*, 164; Bónis, *Révay Péter*, 45; Várkonyi, "... Jó Budavár magas tornyán....," 86.

155 Benda and Fügedi, *A magyar korona regénye*, 164.

follows that we may regard this sacred significance of the crown as one of the most important elements in the Hungarian Estates' self-identity in the Early Modern age.

It was not Werbőczy's book of laws but Berger's pamphlet that brought about change in the thinking about the Estates in the Early Modern period. Because of the way that this meaning of the crown – further developed by Révay, among others – spread among the Estates during the seventeenth century, Berger may be regarded as an important renovator of the tradition of the crown. We may therefore record the court historian of Austrian descent – and perhaps even a Catholic – as one of the most important *topoi* of the self-identity of the seventeenth century Hungarian Estates.

The only question is whether Berger may really be regarded as the prime source of the new meaning of the crown. As we have said, his literary output counted – and counts – for little in historical circles. Even Péter Kulcsár expresses a distinctly negative opinion of the originality of his historical writings as he studies a manuscript (believed lost but preserved) of his main work on Hungarian history.[156] Briefly: in Kulcsár's view, Berger's *modus operandi* indicates that he transcribed the work of others (such as Bonfini and Istvánffy) without himself investigating sources.

Contrary to this, Noémi Viskolcz discovered in Budapest and Vienna three parts of the manuscript of this work in codex form, the content of which supports the writer's originality.[157] According to Viskolcz, these codices in Vienna serve to defend Berger, because it is now certain that he had completed his undertaking and written the history of Hungary before King Ferdinánd II ascended the throne in 1618.[158] A collection of sources on the coronations of Rudolf and Mátyás II which Berger copied is also extant.[159]

---

156 Kulcsár, "Berger Illés," 254–255.
157 The three unknown Berger-codices (which I discovered one month after Viskolcz found them): 1. Historia Ungarica ab A.C. 1458., definit autem in A.C. 1490., in 2°; ÖNB, Cod. 8677, 2. Historia Hungarica ab a. 1572 usque ad a. 1606, in 2°, ÖNB, Cod. 8464.; 3. Historia Ungarica ab A.C. 1607., definit autem in A.C. 1618.; ÖNB, Cod. 8229. The codexes in Budapest: [Elias Berger], *Res sub Ferdinando II. imperatore gestae. Pars secunda, continens annos 1631–1633.* EK, G. 70. (manuscript dealing with the period 1631–1633). [Elias Berger], *Res sub Ferdinando II. imperatore gestae. Pars secunda, continens annos 1631–1633.* ELTE Egyetemi Könyvtár Kézirattár G 70. (Continuation of chronicle from 1632–1633) and: [Elias Berger], *Isagoge seu prolegomena duplicia in chronologiam.* 1635. ELTE Egyetemi Könyvtár Kézirattár G 69. (Manuscript with print proof of title page).
158 Noémi Viskolcz, *A mecenatúra színterei a főúri udvarban. Nádasdy Ferenc könyvtára* [The stages of the patronage in the aristocratic court. The library of Ferenc Nádasdy] (Szeged and Budapest: Szegedi Tudományegyetem Historia Ecclesiastica Hungarica Alapítvány, 2013), 292–294.
159 *Descriptio Coronationis Hungarica Serenissimi Imperatoris Maximiliani. A.C. 1563, d: 8 Sept:* ÖNB, Ms. Codex 8674, 1. k., fol. 1r.-fol.12v., and: *Descriptio Coronationis Serenissimi Principis ac Domini; Dni Rudolphi Archiducis Austria. etc.: in Regem Hungariae inaugurati, Posonij die Vigesima quinta Septembris Anno Dni 1572 d:26. Sept:* In: ibidem, 2.k., fol. 13r.-31v. Also a manuscript of Illésházy's work can be found in this codex: [Elias Berger], *Historia Bellorum in Hungaria gestorum, imperante*

Kulcsár declares of another Berger manuscript: "Perhaps he did not intend to write history as such, but to outline a theory with the help of a collection of examples from the history of Hungary."[160] By this Kulcsár is quite right about Berger's early work. It is highly probable that in 1608 it was precisely his task to create a theory of the Holy Crown, based on historical examples, which with proper justification would serve for the current political situation. For this he drew on the inspiration, examples and perhaps the original ideas of others.[161]

If in fact Berger did not himself invent the ideas that he expounded, there must have been three writers – Illésházy, Révay and Pázmány – from whom he borrowed those which he moulded into a theory in 1608. These were the most important and original political thinkers of the time in Hungary.[162] We know from the abovementioned exchanges of correspondence and pamphlets that Illésházy and Révay worked closely together with the court historian.[163] In a speech given by bishop Bálint Lépes (but written by Pázmány) on the occasion when Matthias appeared at the Diet, the destiny of the fatherland and the arrival of the crown are linked together.[164] At the same time, we also know of a document by Révay titled *Postulata conservatorum sacrae coronae* (Requests of the Guardians of the Holy Crown) which he himself wrote before the Diet of November 1608.[165] In this he expressed ideas on the meaning of the crown, based on Hungarian history and similar to the thoughts to be found in Berger's book.[166]

We may regard this document of Révay's as the first version of his later work on the crown (1613), but the text is also related to Berger's ideas on the crown and the destiny of Hungary. Révay states that the crown had often been in danger and had often suffered the blows of fate.[167] Then he summarises the history of the crown, and ends with the statement that an end has now come to its exile. The crown has come back home without the use of force and thanks to divine grace. Then he

---

     RudolphoII. Caesare Rom: Bonae fide conscripta. ÖNB Codex 8674, 3. k., fol. 1r.-39v. See Viskolcz, *A mecenatúra*, 292–294.

160 Kulcsár, "Berger Illés," 258.

161 For the view of Berger on history, see: Elias Berger, *Duplex speculum chronologicum… Isagoge seu prolegomena duplicia in chronologiam* (manuscript) EK, s. G 69.

162 Illésházy too greatly esteemed Révay's wisdom (*prudentia*). Ötvös, *Pálffy Kata*, 8.

163 In 1615 Berger received money for his book on the crown through the intervention of Révay: ÖStA, Hoffinanz–Ungarn, r. Nr. 106. Konv. 1615.II.9.

164 [Pázmány Péter], "*Ad Regem Mathiam cum in Ungariam coronam reveheret, qua insigniretur*," in Ferenc Hanuy, ed., *Petri Cardinalis Pázmány epistolae collectae I (1610–1628)* (Budapest: Magyar Királyi Tudomány-Egyetem Nyomda, 1910), 29–35.

165 "[1608] *Postulata conservatorum sacrae coronae*," SNA, Decreta et mandata regia, fasc. VII. No. 33, quoted in Bónis, *Révay Péter*, 101–103.

166 *Ibid.*, 47.

167 "[1608] *Postulata conservatorum sacrae coronae*," 101.

declares that in order for Hungary to be happy (*felix*) and fortunate (*faustus*), a number of regulations have to be introduced for its safekeeping; these he then lists point by point.[168]

As Illésházy's speech was certainly composed before Berger's work, while Pázmány and Révay probably wrote either at the same time as he did or shortly afterwards, it may confidently be assumed that Illésházy influenced the ideas of all three. Certain thoughts on the crown feature in the works of Illésházy and Pázmány – such, for example, as the personification of it – which are also present in Révay and Berger.[169] Presumably Révay and Berger continued to exchange ideas, but we do not know who made use of whose idea. It could be that the picture that Berger draws of the crown was the joint work of all three, but it is more probable that it was Berger's alone.

The most serious argument for the originality of Berger's ideas is the more detailed elaboration of the crown-theme in 1608. The essence of this is that through the Hungarian Holy Crown, God influences the history of the fatherland, the Estates and the Habsburg dynasty. Berger had already picked up a similar thought when in 1600 he wrote about what the True Cross meant. Through the symbol of the Cross and the Holy Crown God influenced the history of mankind – and in particular that of Hungary and the other parts of the Habsburg Empire. The shaping of Berger's thought and the political circumstances of the time, together with the special task that the writer was given on this exceptional occasion may serve to explain why his crown-theory took such an original form.

The principal thought in the work is set out in the first sentence, in which Berger links the crown to Providence. He makes Matthias declare that he will restore the Holy Crown to a pacified Hungary, put an end to its vicissitudes, and bring back to Hungary the "defending godhead" or "tutelary spirit" (*tutelare numen*).[170] Berger sees the crown as the ultimate achievement for Matthias in his ambitions for the success and happiness of Hungary. He links Matthias' good qualities to the crown and declares that it was because of these qualities that God had pre-ordained the crown to him as a divine gift. Then he describes in detail the anti-Matthias criticism, but makes it plain that God has guided and defined Matthias' destiny

---

168 Ibid.
169 In a speech which Illésházy gave in November 1608, before Mátyás' coronation there is not a word about the crown. [Illésházy István]: "*Oratio, quae salutatus est Rex Posonij 1608 tempore coronationis*," in Illésházy, *De Rebus Hungaricis Prothocolon* (manuscript) OSZK Fol. Lat. 2336, fol. 28r.-v., and: "*Steph: Ilishaj ad Matthiae oratio*," in [Elias Berger], *Historia Ungarica ab A.C. 1607., definit autem in A.C. 1618.*, ÖNB, Cod. 8229, fol. 5r.-6v. In another speech at the coronation Illésházy does mention the crown: *Ibid.*, fol. 55r.-fol 56r.
170 Berger, *D.O.M. Jubilaeus*, A2r.

in accordance with his deserts.[171] The royal crown which he has won is therefore the ruler's merited reward from God. Berger then expresses his hope that Matthias will kindly take part in the "ceremony of the Holy Crown of Hungary" (*Coronae Hungariae Sanctae solemnitas*), by which he means the coronation.[172]

Berger's book continues with a detailed account of the link between the meaning of the crown and its external appearance. First, he states that the crown is holy (*sancta*) and angelic (*angelica*), as it was sent from heaven when the faith was first adopted, and an angel brought it to earth.[173]

On the basis of this holiness, Berger personifies the crown. Its holy power was what enabled St István to Christianise the Hungarians. He supports this link to the Catholic faith by turning to the exterior of the crown. According to him, other writers have called the crown apostolic because it secretly conceals the symbol of the belief that it was put together by the twelve apostles, but it is unclear to which writers he is referring. With that, he refers to the images on the crown and states that the pictures of the apostles are by heavenly hands. They increase the newly crowned king's love for the teaching of the apostles and the Catholic Church.[174] With that, he uses the exterior of the crown to argue in favour of the Catholic Church. This detail in Berger is – as far as we know – the earliest reference to the portraits of the apostles on the crown. We can also state that he must have seen the crown from nearby.

Next Berger joins the known history of the crown to the destiny of Hungary. He states that the survival of the crown over the centuries, and the fact that it has returned to Hungary a number of times, are signs that Providence protects the country.[175] He then gives a brief account of his own *modus operandi* when he says that he will review what has happened to Hungary through the historical vicissitudes of the crown.[176] After that, he comes to the pivotal thought of the work. "As often as this divine and majestic object has been placed in danger by the ordinances of the fate of men, so often have the wavering fortunes of Hungary too, touched by the twists and turns of fate, suffered grievous blows."[177] The first image called on to illustrate this thought is the way in which the pope sent the crown to István in miraculous fashion. Berger connects baptism and the presentation, and

---

171 *Ibid.*, A2v.
172 *Ibid.*, A3r.
173 *Ibid.*
174 *Ibid.*, A3r.-v.
175 *Ibid.*, A3v.
176 By this means he compares the fate of the crown with the wanderings of Odysseus. *Ibid.*
177 "Quotiens enim fato humano divinum hoc, et Augustale instrumentum in diserimen incidit: toties Hungariae foelicitas variata notabilis accepit plagas." *Ibid.*

states that Hungary came into being thanks to divine support, of which the descent of the crown as a gift from heaven was the sign.[178]

In the following passage Berger gives details of the consequences of disharmony (*discordia*) for the country.[179] This sin leads not only to Hungary's unhappiness but also to the wandering (*error*) of the crown, in the course of which it abandons Hungary and falls into the hands of foreign rulers. This seems to imply a contradiction between the supernatural power of the personified crown over the destiny of the country and the same crown's helplessness with regard to its own destiny. Berger resolves this by stating that ultimately the spiritual power (*numen*) of the crown triumphed nevertheless and was victorious, since on the one hand it had been strongly guarded and on the other hand István's divine spirit had not permitted anything to jeopardise good fortune in the bosom of the fatherland. Berger tries to interpret this apparent contradiction by the exterior of the crown, saying that the apostles and martyrs on the golden head-band themselves went into exile and wandered on foreign soil just like the crown, and therefore are concerned over its fate.[180] The portrayal of St István as a king that reigns over the country after his death through his crown, and the significance of the figures of the apostles to be seen on the crown, are inventions of Berger, in whose work these ideas appear for the first time. The function of these portrayals is on the one hand to account for the power of the tangible crown and on the other hand to emphasise the importance of guarding it. This last point is connected with both the Hungarians' demand that the crown be guarded and watched over by Hungarians, and with the election of Révay and Pálffy as Guardians of the Crown after the coronation.

According to Berger, the cause of tension in Hungary and of the sufferings of the crown had been on the one hand dissension among contenders for the throne, and on the other hand division and faction among the aristocracy. The causes of the first and second wanderings of the crown were to be sought in strife among the Estates, who – being divided in the course of voting – had elected a foreign king.[181] This had occurred during the struggle for the throne that followed the extinction of the House of Árpád, when the Bavarian Prince Otto was carrying the crown with him hidden in a wooden box which fell from the carriage onto the road in the darkness. It lay on the busy road for some time, but in the evening, when they were returning, they found it there in the dust. Berger explains this miraculous event, as we described in the first chapter, by saying that by its divine nature the crown had blinded the passers-by. He confirms this later by declaring that at the end of this adventure the crown liberated itself from the godless and impious and breathed

---

178   *Ibid.*, A4r.
179   *Ibid.*
180   *Ibid.*, A4v.
181   *Ibid.*

free in the hands of loyal and faithful citizens.[182] In Márk Kálti's work the function of this miracle is to give supernatural confirmation to the new king's power after a chaotic change of ruler. Berger, intent on transmitting to his audience his thoughts on concord in Hungary, seizes the occasion once more to convince the reader of the power of the crown.

The third wandering of the crown described by Berger is the consequence of its theft in 1439. He states that the cause of this was the civil strife (*civilis discordia*) raging in Hungary at the time, as a result of which a woman was able to steal the crown.[183] He says that it was violence and the letting of blood among Hungarians that led to the crown's deserting the fatherland, since the country had turned against the worship of the Holy Crown (*religio sacrae coronae*), which is the crown tradition. This sin was the cause of much misfortune in the following years, as in contrast to the worship of the Holy Crown "… which was incumbent upon them…", the Hungarians were up in arms against the king for twenty-four years.[184] In this passage, the writer introduces the idea of the worship of the crown in Hungary, which he derives from its supernatural power. He also explains the defeats which Hungary suffered because of its absence, to which it fell victim because of injury to the crown's holy nature.

The first king to offer renewed worship to this holy object was the Divine Mátyás (Mátyás Corvinus), who, according to Berger, was a heavenly blessing bestowed on Hungary as was the return of the crown.[185] This king, amidst the many wars and misfortunes that Hungary had to survive, regarded giving back the crown to the fatherland as the only really important thing that he had done. Berger explains the significance of the matter by declaring that "… without this crown there is no way that the office of royal majesty may be filled, laws made, sacred ceremonies performed, peace strengthened, war waged or any act private or public be accomplished …".[186] By this episode in the history of the crown Berger underpins its function in law; not a single enactment of the king may be seen as lawful in the country if he is not crowned with the Holy Crown. This section ends with the statement that the crown returned home once more after Mátyás had reached agreement with Friedrich.

Next Berger states that the fourth wandering was even more perilous, as in the course of this the crown went into Ottoman hands. While Ferdinánd and János Szapolyai were contending for Hungary the crown fell into the sultan's possession. Thieves attacked Péter Perényi, Guardian of the Crown, and the crown was later

---

182 *Ibid.*, A4v.-B1r.
183 *Ibid.*, B1r. Berger associates this theft with a very negative view of women.
184 *Ibid.*, B1r.
185 *Ibid.*, B1r.
186 *Ibid.*, B1v.

taken to the sultan. This sorrowful image serves to lead the writer to a detailed exposition of what the crown means to Hungary. First, he ponders what an unhappy sign it was that the "likeness of ancestral glory" lay among stolen booty. He says that the crown is "... Hungary's sole true treasure, pledge of war and peace, the grim wages of justice and happiness".[187]

The sultan later released the crown undamaged, which was, Berger says, as good as a sign from God. The crown's wandering continued, however, because, as Berger puts it, dissension was rife in Hungary. This statement – as there are pictures of this on the Holy Crown – he connects again with the exterior of the crown, when he states that even lawful royal power went astray. By that he refers to the pictures of the kings that are on the crown. In the end this association of images connects with the Habsburg dynasty, because Berger later announces "... let the Holy Crown by its own decision show and reveal who is to be the true and inviolable king of Hungary..." by going to Ferdinánd in Vienna. He declares that in this way the crown won a victory, and found peace in the true capital of the Habsburg Empire.

In the following section, Berger defends the absence of the crown when he writes that when it was away the crown enjoyed the support and protection of the Habsburg dynasty. He declares that nothing had been more glorious for the crown than to have been supported by this nation since the Habsburg dynasty owns the most admired crown jewels in Europe and it is they who provide for the Christian religion. Then Berger turns to the symbols of the Holy Roman Empire, including the widely known holy shields (*ancilia*) which descended from heaven, which had always been kept in Rome. He uses these antique symbols to account for the situation that obtains in his own time. He reaches the conclusion that the reason for the survival of the Hungarian crown and its integrity is that it had been set beside the symbols of the House of Austria. He sees the prevailing conditions in Hungary as the best evidence that internal strife is more destructive than hostile force, for which reason the crown had not been safe in Hungary.

Analysis of the condition of Hungary brings in the consideration of Bocskai's coronation with the crown given by the Ottomans. Berger states that this coronation with a false crown was a greater misfortune for Hungary than the previously outlined strife.[188] In his view the holiness and power of the Holy Crown were broken by this ceremony. The sultan had not assembled a diadem from the relics of St István – a reference to an event in 1440 which Berger mentions earlier – but used a crown obtained from the Greeks as spoils of war in "... the ancient rite, the solemn and sacred ceremony of coronation ...". In this Berger once more sees justification for the Hungarian crown's sojourn in Austria, which he considers a divine blessing.

---

187   *Ibid.*, B2.
188   *Ibid.*, B4r.

This shelter given by the Habsburg dynasty had been, in Berger's opinion, evidence of the coming triumph of the Hungarian Estates (*respublica Hungariae*).[189]

The crown's fifth journey is into the royal domestic chapel of the Habsburg dynasty. Berger takes a positive view of this, though he mentions that the leaders and people (*proceres et populus*) of Hungary had drawn up a decree "concerning the restoration of the crown" (its return home), as they were confident that the heavenly powers could be reconciled by its presence in the country.[190] By this Berger is outlining the familiar dilemma: Archduke Matthias wished to keep the crown on Austrian territory whereas the Hungarians wished to take it to Hungary.

The writer advances arguments for the solution of this question which should make the return of the crown to Hungary acceptable to both the Hungarians and Matthias. He begins with the contradictory statement that the Hungarians want to have the crown back because they intend thereby to obtain grace and glory for Matthias; whereas in fact Matthias was opposed to its return.[191] He then states that the Hungarians have a right to their crown since it is their property and because other kingdoms keep their crown jewels on their own soil. In addition, the crown had come into Hungarian possession from heaven and had always been revered as a sacred object, a symbol of military glory and of civil life (*disciplina togata*), in which the benign influences of fortune and law are united. Such a symbol must not be out of the country. The striking thing in this passage is that, according to Berger, the crown is the concern of the Hungarians, meaning the Hungarian Estates.

In the section which follows Berger uses a fiction which he has invented about the crown, in which its appearance – drawn for the benefit of the public – is connected to the description of the events which finally led to its return in 1608. This is a fictitious description, because its purpose is not to reflect events as they actually happened but for Berger, with the assistance of staircase wit, to inform the Habsburg ruler of the Hungarians' political message. That is, he states that Archduke Matthias took upon himself the task of bringing back the crown, but this does not conform to the facts. As we have said earlier, it was the Hungarians' cherished desire that the crown jewels should return to Hungarian soil, but this was entirely contrary to Matthias' wishes; he was unmistakably opposed to the idea. What is more, the politico-religious significance of the crown is Berger's idea (or his patron's), although he states that this had been so for centuries.

Berger resolves the problem of the sequence of events by saying on the one hand that the Hungarians accept this meaning of the crown "as a sort of prophecy".[192] On the other hand, he declares that God has sent Matthias to be the one to take

---

189 *Ibid.*, B4r.-v.
190 *Ibid.*, B4v.
191 *Ibid.*
192 *Ibid.*, C1r.

upon himself the cares of the crown. In this way he takes as proven that this is precisely why the Hungarians asked Rudolf to allow the crown to return to Hungary, to discharge his responsibility for doing so, and to care for the well-being of their fatherland. In addition, Berger informs us that the Hungarians have drawn the king's attention to wars fought previously because of the crown, and he mentions, for example, the wars of Mátyás Corvinus.

For the benefit of the hearer or reader, at the end of the speech there come little sections when Berger declares that God, in His special plan, intends that men shall recognise the outcome of important and wonderful works lest it appear that anything in the world happens by chance. In the view which he adopts of historical events, Berger explains the interconnection of history and the crown, and declares that in what has gone before, he was describing God's plans for the Hungarian people: "God in His independent wisdom, that is, has so ordained that the outcome of a matter shall be common knowledge beforehand, spoken of by all, that it may be possible to determine it in advance, lest it seem as if it had happened by chance."[193] With this opinion he returns afresh to the theme taken up at the beginning of the speech. Berger ends his tale with an idea about God's plan, according to which He has placed the happy outcome and triumph in the hands of the ruler, Mátyás. This He has brought into correlation with a formal appearance like that used in ancient statues of gods.

The second part of the work Berger opens with the extolling of Mátyás II as king of Hungary. On the first page is an imaginary triumphal arch inscribed with Mátyás' previously described virtues and the crown.[194] Next Berger compares the deeds of the two Mátyáses, with the balance naturally in favour of the Habsburg ruler. He declares that Archduke Matthias Habsburg's military successes make him the equal of the first Mátyás. Furthermore, Mátyás II has united the same countries as his namesake. According to Berger, however, the second is even better than the first, because Matthias Habsburg has brought everything to a peaceful conclusion. In both cases the return of the crown may be regarded as Mátyás' triumph. For Berger, however, the second Mátyás is simply better than the first because the Habsburg has accomplished everything by peaceful means. The crown is a divine symbol of those promises which the latter made at the time of forming the alliance. If the crown is be kept on Hungarian soil it will protect liberty and guarantee peace.

Next, Berger goes on to speak of the crown itself, and returns to its significance, which was summarised in the first section.[195] He declares once again that Providence will take Hungary into its care because the crown itself is in the country,

---

193   *Ibid.*, C1v.
194   *Ibid.*, C2r.
195   *Ibid.*, D2v.

and through its divine power, will shield the fatherland from injustice. While the Hungarian nation (*gens Hungarica*) honours the crown through faith in it (*religio sanctae coronae*) God will be with Hungary.[196] At this point Berger remarks that the respect that the Hungarians show for the crown is known everywhere in Europe, but one cannot tell on what he bases this.[197] Recognition of the holiness of the crown guarantees good relationships between king and people and the good fortune of the country, together with piety, liberty and peace. In Berger's opinion the return of the crown is due not only to Matthias, but also to György Thurzó (1567–1616). With the aid of the crowned king and the crown, Hungary is ready to stand guard over the honour and well-being of the whole of Christendom. He ends with the deduction that on account of recent events in Hungary this year must be regarded as the Jubilee of the Holy Crown (*Iubilaeus Sacrae Coronae*).[198]

After this disquisition there begins a laudatory letter addressed to Illésházy in reply to his speech about the crown delivered in Kassa, the text of which is Berger's next chapter.[199] The substance of this letter is that in Berger's opinion it was actually Illésházy that brought about the return of the crown, because it is he that Hungary has to thank for the peace agreement with the Ottomans. His actions guaranteed domestic peace in Hungary and protected the fatherland from ruin. This laudatory passage connects the introductory part of the book with Illésházy's speech at the end, because the theory of the crown described at the beginning, justifies the political system that Illésházy invented and which became law in 1608. The shaping of the system took place at the time when the Bocskai rebellion was ending, the Peace of Vienna being agreed, and Matthias was assuming power. It was intended that the situation with regard to power would finally be settled with the coronation of Matthias. The theory of the significance of the crown guaranteed that the system would stabilise public life in Hungary. In this, the politico-religious significance of the crown communicated in Berger's work functioned both to justify the political compromise that had been Illésházy's brain-child and to set the seal on the lasting status quo between the Estates and the Habsburg king.

Illésházy had tried to create a firm situation in Hungary by bringing about compromise between various parties and interest-groups with a wide range of political and religious backgrounds.[200] The mainstay of the system was a double

---

196 *Ibid.*, D3r-D3v.
197 *Ibid.*, D4r.
198 *Ibid.*, E2r.-E2v.
199 *Ibid.*, F1r.-F2r.
200 This thought of Illésházy's has never yet been analysed or described in detail – perhaps because the series Magyar Országgyűlési Emlékek (Monuments of the Hungarian National Assembly) was broken off at the year 1607, even though all this had been of decisive significance from the point of view of the formation of political order until 1848. See inter alia the following – unfortunately

political arrangement in which the one side balanced out the other. At the top of the system was the king on the throne, keeping his seat in Vienna. Opposite him was the leading representative of the Estates, their most powerful man and principal Hungarian dignity, the palatine.[201] The country's organ of political representation was the Diet, where the leading Estates, ecclesiastical and lay, had their places, as had the representatives of the common nobility and townsfolk, the delegates of counties and towns. This system protected the rights of the Estates, their liberties and privileges – above all the freedom of exercise of religion and the right to elect the king. By way of balance, Hungary's economy, defence and diplomacy were regulated by the central institutions in Vienna – the *Hofkammer*, the *Hofkriegsrat* and the Privy Council. Likewise in the interests of balance an alliance came into being with, on the one hand, the Estates of Austria, Bohemia and Moravia, and on the other hand with the Transylvanians.

The guarantee and symbol of this system was the Hungarian crown, as it was deposited in Hungary and guarded by a Lutheran (Révay) and a Catholic (Pálffy) as Guardians of the Crown, who enjoyed the confidence of the Habsburg emperor and the Estates alike. The crown could be given such a function because the Estates were always ready to elect another king who really would meet their political demands. Whether the crown was able to sustain this significance and function in the social system depended on relations with the ruler, Hungarian military strength, and the effectiveness of the alliance with other parts of the Habsburg Empire and Transylvania. Furthermore, the most essential factor in the continued existence of the system was the preservation of unity among the Hungarian Estates themselves. The change of significance that the crown underwent in 1608 was determined by the internal agreement of the Estates and the political theory (of the crown) addressed by Bocskai and Illésházy to the king and Hungary.

The coronation of Matthias as King of Hungary (1608) and its description by János Jeszenszky

The development described in the preceding section may be observed in a number of ceremonies that took place in 1608 in connection with the crown. The handing over of the crown in June may be taken as one such, as may the festival of the cultus

---

very brief – analyses: László Makkai, "A Bocskai-felkelés," 769–773; Benda, "Az országgyűlések az újkori magyar fejlődésben," 10–11; Benda, "Habsburg Absolutism," 127; Hiller, "Illésházy István" and István Hiller, "Pázmány Péter és a Habsburg diplomáciája [Péter Pázmány and Habsburg diplomacy]," in Emil Hargittay, ed., *Pázmány Péter és kora* [Péter Pázmány and his time] (Piliscsaba: Pázmány Péter Katolikus Egyetem Bölcsészettudományi Kar, 2001), 142.

201 On the function of the Palatine in Hungary, see: Lauter, "A Palatinus Regni Hungariae," 216.

of the crown in Kassa in July. The third came with the election of the king and the palatine in Pozsony – for which the crown was ceremoniously brought to Hungary – and the continued discussion of the coronation promises to which the king had sworn. The fourth and last was the coronation itself, the election of the Guardians of the Crown and the promulgation of laws, likewise in Pozsony. It is striking that the significance of the crown as concerned the Estates was most emphasised when Matthias had not yet given any guarantee at all to Hungary.

Matthias's coronation was preceded by a ceremonious progress with the crown from Vienna to Pozsony on 18 November.[202] This event again was an allusion to Mátyás Corvinus, as – according to Bonfini – he too had brought the crown to Hungary with much ceremony. The function of the ceremony was to establish Matthias as future king. This was followed by the coronation in Pozsony on 19 November.

The coronation ceremony in 1608 became the prototype of subsequent Hungarian coronations, as the order was followed until the last coronation in 1917.[203] The main innovations were the roles played by the lay Estates and the Protestant aristocrats.[204] Thus it was the first time that a Lutheran palatine, Illésházy, took part in the ceremony. During the latter the crown had no role other than that on previous occasions, but its function changed, because this coronation did not simply mean the transfer of royal power, but on this occasion also gave sacral legitimacy to the political and religious compromise. The importance of this symbol was made even more obvious by its entry in procession and by the election of the Guardians of the Crown after the coronation. The crown remained in Hungary, and after being displayed on the table at the formal coronation lunch went back into its chest, which was then sealed and placed for safe keeping in Pozsony castle. This chest was possibly made specially for the occasion, or afterwards on Péter Révay's orders, and was decorated with two faithfully drawn depictions of the crown.[205]

We know of more accounts, pamphlets and pictures of this coronation than of any previous one.[206] The producers of some of these turned their attention – in

---

202 S.n., *Appendix relationis historicae: darinnen kürtzlich erzehlet wird, mit was Ceremonien und Solenniteten die zu Hungarn und Böhem designirte Königl. Wür. Herr Matthias, Ertzherzog zu Österreich, zum Könige in Hungarn in S. Elisabethae Reginae Hungariae, den 19. Novembrie anno 1608 zu Preßburg gekrönet worden* (Leipzig: Abraham Bamber, 1609), A2.
203 Lauter, "A Palatinus Regni," 216; Pálffy Géza, "Koronázási lakomák," 1035. A copy of the original *ordo* can be found here: "Modus et ordo in coronanda sua Maiestatis observatus." MOL N 114 Kovachich Márton György gyűjteménye. Acta diaetalia. I. fol. 55–56.
204 Lauter, "A Palatinus Regni Hungariae," 216–217.
205 Ipolyi, *A magyar szent korona*, 219.
206 See the relevant summary: Kovachich, *Solennia inauguralia* 9–10; Kulcsár, *Inventarium*, 566, 769–670; Ilona Hubay, *Magyar és magyar vonatkozású röplapok, újságlapok, röpiratok az Országos Széchenyi Könyvtárban. 1480–1718.* [Hungarian and Hungary related broadsheets, newspapers

addition to the person of the new king – to the Estates and the significance of the crown. The latter is described not only as an object the purpose of which was derived from the king's God-given power, but is also clothed with a significance connected to the identity of the Hungarian people. In the pictures and descriptions, the crown is imbued with personality, through which it received a blend of meaning, history and operation. This last was an allusion to the supernatural power which the writers attributed to it. The change had already been perceptible in the works of Berger and Illésházy, but after the coronation appeared even more conspicuously in the illustrations.

The explanation of this change of meaning is that this was the first time in the history of Hungarian coronations that the crown had been portrayed from the life, and these pictures were mass-produced and distributed (see images 9–15). The king could be seen, crowned by the recognisable Hungarian crown, on printed matter and on the small coins scattered among the people on the occasion.[207] In contrast to medallions and printed matter from Rudolf's time, those of Mátyás II showed him crowned and bearing the regalia (see images 10 and 11).[208] Virgin Mary, Patron Saint of the Hungarians, was similarly shown for the first time on the medallions, wearing the Hungarian crown.[209] These medallions were produced immediately after the festivities and similar pictures are among the earliest faithful

---

and pamphlets in the National Library Széchényi] (Budapest: Országos Széchényi Könyvtár, 1948), 94–9 5; Géza Pálffy, "Koronázási lakomák," 1069–1070; Noémi Viskolcz, "II. Mátyás magyar királlyá koronázásának egy metszetes ábrázolása 1608-ból [An etched image of the coronation of Matthias II. as King of Hungary]," in Tamás T. Kiss, ed., *Kultúra – művészet – társadalom a globalizálódó világban* [Culture, art and society in a globalizing world] (Szeged: Szegedi Tudományegyetem Juhász Gyula Pedagógusképző Kar, 2007), 155–158. Berger too describes the coronation in a ms in Vienna: "CORONATIO MATTHIAE Secundum in Regem Hungariae," in [Elias Berger], *Historia Hungarica ab a. 1572 usque ad a. 1606* (Manuscript) ÖNB, Cod. 8464, fol. 39r.-86v.

207 Ignácz Acsády, "Magyarország három részre oszlásának története 1526–1608 [History of the division of Hungary into three parts 1526–1608]," in Sándor Szilágyi, ed., *A magyar nemzet története* [The history of the Hungarian nation], vol. V. (Budapest: Athenaeum Irodalmi és Nyomdai Társulat, 1897), 639. According to the descriptions, gold and silver tokens were scattered among the onlookers. See: "Kaysers Matthias Crőnung zu Khőnig in Ungarn. Ao 1608.," (Manuscript) OSZK Fol. Germ. 1116, fol. 26r; Géza Pálffy, Ferenc Gábor Soltész and Csaba Tóth, *Coronatus in regem Hungariae...: Medaliile de încoronare ale regilor Ungariei / Coronatus in regem Hungariae...: A magyar uralkodókoronázások érmei* [The Hungarian coronation jetons], Krisztina Bertók ed., (Cluj Napoca–Budapest: Muzeul Național de Istorie a Transilvaniei și Muzeul Național Maghiar, 2015), 117–141.

208 Lajos Huszár, Habsburg-házi királyok pénzei: 1526–1657 [The money of the Habsburg-house kings: 1526–1657] (Budapest: Akadémiai Kiadó, 1975), XII.–XVI.; Emil Unger, *Magyar éremhatározó* [Guide to the determination of Hungarian tokens] Vol. 2. (Budapest: Ajtósi Dürer Könyvkiadó, 1980), 57–62.

209 *Ibid.*, 57, 58.

depictions of the crown.[210] The crown is also clearly depicted on them as seen from the front and the rear. As medallion images were made from carvings it is highly likely that even more pictures of Mátyás II and the crown were in circulation.

A development similar to the above can be seen in descriptions of the coronation too, in which the emphasis is on those elements of the ceremony which have to do with the novel political changes in Hungary.[211] One of the most interesting descriptions of Mátyás II's coronation is that by the Lutheran János Jeszenszky (Jessenius a Jessen, 1566–1621). He was one of a number of men of learning at Rudolf's court, had studied at Padua, Wittenberg and Leipzig, and been a professor at Wittenberg and Prague.[212] He was one of the disseminators of Neoplatonism and wrote a widely known work on the subject.[213] He was a friend of the Danish court astronomer Tycho Brahe and the court historian Jacobus Typotius, and from 1608 was certainly in contact with Péter Révay too. In that year he joined the court of Archduke Matthias, was present at the handing over of the crown, and took part in the coronation. His books on the occasion appeared a year later.

The publication of Jeszenszky's book in 1609 formed an important part of King Mátyás's European strategy. Coronation in Hungary was for him the first step towards the final goal – the imperial crown and power over the Holy Roman Empire. Jeszenszky justifies his assumption of power in Hungary by a detailed listing of his virtues. His description of the coronation sends a political message to the inhabitants of the Holy Roman Empire. The purpose of the book explains its circulation in so notably wide a circle. Jeszenszky had the Latin text printed in Hamburg in 1609,

---

210 Tóth, "A koronázási jelvények," 11–12.
211 An earlier draft of this chapter has been published partly as Kees Teszelszky, "The Hungarian Roots of a Bohemian Humanist: Johann Jessenius a Jessen and early-modern National Identity (1609)," in Balázs Trencsényi and Márton Zászkaliczky, eds., *Whose Love of Which Country? Composite States, National Histories and Patriotic Discourses in Early Modern East Central Europe* (Leiden and Boston: Brill, 2010), 315–332.
212 Friedel Pick, *Joh. Jessenius de Magna Jessen: Arzt und Rektor in Wittenberg und Prag hingerichtet am 21. Juni 1621; ein Lebensbild aus der Zeit des Dreissigjährigen Krieges* (Leipzig: Barth, 1926); László Mátrai, ed., *Régi magyar filozófusok, XV-XVII. század* [Ancient Hungarian philosophers, fifteenth till seventeenth century] (Budapest: Gondolat, 1961), 48–49; Mout, *Bohemen en de Nederlanden*, 78; László Ruttkay, *Jeszenszky János (Jessenius) és kora 1566–1621* [János Jeszenszky (Jessenius) and his time 1566–1621] (Budapest: Semmelweis Orvostörténeti Múzeum és Könyvtár, 1971), 18–88; Evans, *Rudolf II*, 136–138. Jeszenszky became one of the leaders of the Bohemian rebellion of 1619–1621 and was executed.
213 Johann Jessenius a Jessen, *Zoroaster nova, brevis veraque de universo Philosophia* (Witebergae: Ex Off. Cratoniana, 1593). See also György E. Szönyi, "Scientific and Magical Humanism at the Court of Rudolf II," in Fučíkova, *Rudolf II and Prague*, 224–225.

after which it appeared in German in the same year.²¹⁴ The work appeared again in the same year, this time in an anthology on Mátyás's coronation.²¹⁵

The other purpose of Jeszenszky's work was to justify in the Kingdom of Hungary the new political constitution sanctioned by Mátyás. It provided a historical basis for the new political Estates in Hungary and showed this in such a light that it seemed to have roots going back a century. After that – by means of his work – he made this historical justification known in Europe. Through an inventive account of the history of Hungary – just like his predecessors – he created a new image of the Hungarian Estates. His ideological endeavours formed part of the Estates' strategy to stabilise the new constitution which sprang from the compromise between the Estates and the king.

Jeszenszky's book consists of three sections: a picture of the crown (only in the Latin edition), an account of the coronation, and a chronological list of the kings of Hungary based on Bonfini. The picture of the crown is a milestone in the shaping of its significance, as this is the first printed faithful depiction of it

---

214 Johann Jessenius a Jessen, *Regis Ungariae, Matthiae II. Coronatio*, (Manuscript) ÖNB Codex 8790; Johann Jessenius, *Regis Ungariae, Matthiae II. coronatio; Johan: Jessenio a Jessen, Regio Medico, Descriptore. Adiecta, regni, regumque Pannoniae, brevis Chronographia.* (Viennae: Ludovicus Bonnoberger, 1609); Second edition: Johann Jessenius, *Regis Ungariae, Matthiae II. coronatio* (Hamburg: Georg Ludwig Frobenianus, 1609). Later edition: *Appendix Partis Quartae Chronologiae Ungaricae ..*, in Hieronymus Ortelius *Chronologia oder historische Beschreibung aller Kriegsempörungen und Schlachter so in ober und under Ungern auch Siebenbürgen mit dem Türken geschehen, 1395-1598* (Nürnberg: Sibmacher, 1613, ²1663). In Dutch translation: Hieronymus Ortelius, *De chronycke van Hungarie*, P. Neander, trans. (Amsterdam: Jan Everts van Cloppenburch, 1619). German translation: Johann Jessenius a Jessen, *Der Königlichen Majestät zu Vngarn, Matthiae des Andern dieses Nahmens, Krönung : Gehalten in Preßburg: am Tage S. Elisabeth: im Jahre ... 1608. Neben einer kurtzen Chronica oder ZeitRegister aller Könige der Cron Vngarn*, M. Wolfart Spangenberg tr. (Straßburg: Zetzner, 1609). Modern edition: Johann Jessenius, "Der Königlichen Majestät zu Ungarn / Matthiae des Andern dieses Nahmens / Krönung: ... ," in András Vizkelety, ed., *Wolfhart Spangenberg Sämtliche Werke*, Vol. IV/2 (Berlin and New York: De Gruyter, 1982), 261-316.

215 S.n., *Orationes Gratvlatoriae In Electione, Coronatione, Nativitate, Nvptiis, triumphis, &c. Pontificvm, Imperatorvm, Regvm, Principvm, &c. Habitae à Legatis Virisve suae aetatis doctissimis; Quarum catalogum sequens pagina indicat* (Hanoviae: Typis Wechelianis apud haeredes J. Aubrii, 1613). We do not know whether the French accounts are really based on Jeszenszky's work, but considering its very wide circulation it is very likely. S.n, *Cérémonies observées au couronnement de Mathias, deuxiesme roy de Hongrie* (Paris, Lyon: S.n, 1609). See: Ildikó Gausz, "Magyar koronázás francia szemmel: Riporterek, celebek II. Mátyás koronázási fesztumán [Hungarian coronation through French eyes: journalists and famous people at the celebration of Matthias' coronation]," *Aetas: történettudományi folyóirat* 23/3 (2014), 179-182. There are several other contemporary descriptions by foreigners, for instance: Pierre d'Avity, *Les Estats, Empires et Principautez du Monde* (Paris: Paul Chevalier, 1615), 740-741; English translation: Pierre d'Avity, *The estates, empires, & principallities of the world* (London: Printed by Adam: Islip; for Mathewe: Lownes; and Iohn: Bill, 1615), 625-627.

(images 10 and 11). In the manuscript of the work, preserved in Vienna, there is also a minutely detailed pen drawing of Mátyás II wearing the crown, and a picture of him as King of Hungary, likewise crowned (images 8 and 9). A composition as similar as can be to the printed version is also to be seen on the small coins which were scattered among the public at the coronation and on the medallions and coins struck after the ceremony (images 6 and 7). It is possible that Jeszenszky himself made these drawings, as he was present when the crown was handed over and at the coronation. At the same time, it is conceivable that drawings, engravings, coins and medallions can derive from an earlier, unknown depiction. As Jeszenszky's work circulated so widely we may form the conclusion that it must have become the standard picture of the crown at the time.

Not only was the depiction of the crown faithful, but also the account of the coronation gives the impression of trueness to life. Thus *inter alia* it mentions the colour of the draping of the seats and the characteristic Hungarian costume of those present. It likewise gives in full the texts that were pronounced and the vows that were taken. It describes the event so vividly – like Bocatius's account of the presentation of the crown given by the Turks – that the reader has the feeling that he is actually there.[216] According to Peter Burke, the way in which Jeszenszky's work approaches its subject is in keeping with other historical and antiquarian works of the time by doctors trained in Padua, as was Jeszenszky.[217] In consequence of their profession these doctors made every effort to inspect phenomena carefully, and describe punctiliously what they observed. In addition, Jeszenszky alludes to Classical authors, biblical texts or other relevant examples – sometimes forcedly – and describes the various elements of the coronation in minute detail; these include the crown, the anointing and the dubbing as a knight. This weaving together of medical knowledge, history and political ideas is also typical of other Early Modern doctors.

When the modern reader examines the book, he gets the feeling that various parts of the ceremony were probably not so unequivocal for Jeszenszky's contemporaries. In 1608, the coronation was a sacral event rooted in the Middle Ages and, as the means of legitimation of power, closely connected to the views and concepts of the Catholic Church. Jeszenszky was a Lutheran, and refers to a number of biblical texts (mainly from Maccabees) and connects many events with ancient sources (among others the works of Pliny, Herodotus and Diodorus Siculus) or with individual examples from everyday life. The anointing of the king is an example of the writer's

---

216 He himself refers to this; see: Jessenius a Jessen, *Regis Ungariae,* A3 and Jessenius, "Der Königlichen Majestät zu Ungarn," 303. I have quoted the modern edition, as these pages were numbered.
217 Peter Burke, "Images as Evidence in Seventeenth-Century Europe," *Journal of the History of Ideas* 64 (2003), 294.

free association.²¹⁸ First he mentions St Cyprian's explanation of this, but then he states that the oil ensures a "free disposition" for the king, just as wrestling goes more easily for wrestlers if they use oil. He also refers to the fact that it is oil that prevents a knife from rusting, then ends with an image of the scented balm which causes every man's spiritual condition to be positive.

It seems that the writer, by this and other similar methods, is discreetly turning the attention of the reader away from the original, sacral Catholic context of the ceremony towards a new and positive image of the upright character of the newly crowned king and the idealised Hungarian Estates by means of knowledge and apposite, sometimes mundane examples.

The explanation of the strange method by which Jeszenszky describes the coronation once again is to be found in the political milieu in which the ceremony took place. As a result of the changes in 1608 in Hungary a new power structure came into being. The essence of the change was the growth of the power of the Protestant Estates and the security of their rights; this is shown in the political structure by the installation of an elected palatine. As a consequence of these developments, the Hungarian coronation ceremony itself changed too. One important change, among others, was the free election of the king, together with the determining role in the ceremony played by the Lutheran palatine.²¹⁹

The essence of Jeszenszky's description is that he devotes the necessary attention to the actions performed during the ceremony, and gives in full the vows and other words spoken. By not simply describing all this but also providing an explanation he also justifies the changes in the ceremony itself. As these resulted from the new political constitution, Jeszenszky at the same time legitimates the political changes that had taken place in the Kingdom of Hungary. The significance of his work, therefore, lies not in his precise account of the events of the ceremony but in the way that, as court historian, he interprets the events and presents his interpretation to the wider world. Jeszenszky's writing of history, therefore (like that of Bocatius, Berger, Révay and others), served the political ideas of his master, as Nicolette Mout has established.²²⁰

Jeszenszky's method of trying to justify the Hungarian constitution found inspiration in the writings on the crown of the authors discussed above. This is clear from, inter alia, his introduction and the final lines of the first section. These passages also show agreement with the *Querelae* and the later political texts based on it. Jeszenszky too describes the burdensome situation of Hungary as bastion of Christendom. In his view the cause of the imminent collapse was not only the

---

218 Jessenius, "Der Königlichen Majestät zu Ungarn," 288.
219 Bartoniek, *A magyar királykoronazások*, 98; Lauter, "A Palatinus Regni Hungariae," 216–217.
220 Mout, *Bohemen en de Nederlanden*, 78.

Ottomans but also the growing internal unrest. He states that over the past years Matthias had endeavoured to avert this unrest. In the final section he returns to this subject, after a lengthy description of the coronation.

The most important details in which he speaks of the political changes are, among others, the information on the proceedings of the Diet, the election of the king and the explanation of the crown. The work opens with a description of the preliminaries for the coronation. Following the example of the propaganda of the time, Jeszenszky states that Rudolf had voluntarily surrendered the crown to his brother because he felt no longer capable of ruling.[221] During the Diet Matthias had paid due attention to the views of the Estates and there was lively discussion between them.[222] Cardinal Ferenc Forgách's speech follows, and by that he justifies Mátyás's royal power, pointing to his military successes in Hungary and his efforts to unify the Hungarian people. Next, the Estates propose a motion in which they express their hope that Mátyás will recognise their rights and liberties. In addition, they emphasise that he is the scion of Hungarian kings and refer to him as "father of the fatherland".[223] Then the parties reach agreement and re-establish the office of palatine, whom they will freely elect even before the coronation begins.

As the free election of the palatine was an important political innovation Jeszenszky devotes particular attention to it. He says that it took place after the delegates of the Austrian and Hungarian nations had reached agreement on the conditions. In the process they decided that these were to be four candidates – two Protestant (Illésházy and György Thurzó) and two Catholic (Tamás Erdődy and Zsigmond Forgách) – and that the election would be by simple majority.[224] Illésházy emerged the winner, and was appointed on taking an oath.[225] In Jeszenszky's account, this oath had the following noteworthy content. As we have said earlier, Illésházy had been a leading figure in the Bocskai rebellion and in Matthias' assumption of power, and the debate about the extent of royal power which he had initiated may be seen as the basic cause of the rebellion. As palatine he swore to "… hate and shun all plans leading to rebellion and alliance and conspiracy …".[226] Likewise "… he must preserve unharmed the royal majesty's king's majesty, dignity and highness". In addition, he undertook to do all in his power for the protection of the rights and liberties of the Estates ecclesiastical and lay, without putting his own interests first.

---

221 Jessenius, "Der Königlichen Majestät zu Ungarn," 266.
222 *Ibid.*, 267.
223 *Ibid.*, 274–275.
224 *Ibid.*, 279.
225 The text of the original oath is preserved as: *Juramentum Comitis Palatini Regni Hungariae* (ms). MOL N 114 Kovachich Márton György gyűjteménye. Acta diaetalia. I. fol. 53.
226 Jessenius, "Der Königlichen Majestät zu Ungarn," 280.

(In this act, Illésházy was promising not to do in future what he had done all his political career hitherto ...).

After the oath the actual coronation with the coronation regalia began. Jeszenszky explains the origin of the ceremony by reference to similar ceremonial among the ancient Egyptians, as described by Herodotus and Pliny.[227] It is noticeable that he makes no reference to the Medieval roots of the ceremony, but quotes the above Classical writers. He does, however, deal with the Medieval origin of the regalia. He clarifies the meaning of the Cross by the familiar Hartvik legend.[228] In Jeszenszky's interpretation the king received the Cross as a gift for disseminating the Christian faith, and together with the other crown jewels it symbolises the defence of the country. In the words of Cardinal Forgách, the sword is a symbol of the protection which the king is duty-bound to offer the Church in Hungary. Shortly afterwards Jeszenszky interprets the sword as a symbol of the defence of all Christendom, in this connection referring to the Bible and in particular to Maccabees, the Jewish rebels, which the court of Bocskai also referred to.[229]

In the following section Jeszenszky analyses the significance of the crown, allotting an important role to Illésházy. It was he who had received the crown from Forgách, raised it on high, and asked the Estates whether they wanted Mátyás II as their king, to which they replied with a unanimous "Yes".[230] The crown thus received a new meaning during the ceremony: it was by means of it that the Estates – through their elected palatine – recognised royal power as rightful. It is therefore no surprise that the depiction of the coronation jewel has so prominent a place in the book. Then Jeszenszky, following Berger, speaks of the crown, "… the precious treasure of the Kingdom of Hungary…", which has itself experienced the vicissitudes of fortune.[231] After that he describes the actual ceremony of coronation. Once more he turns to Pliny and other Classical writers to explain this part of the proceedings. Naturally, he does not accept Diodorus Siculus' interpretation to the effect that the massive crown is nothing more than a means of preventing drunkenness.[232] (Perhaps this is a hidden critic from the doctor on the extensive consumption of

---

227 Ibid., 281.
228 Ibid., 285.
229 Ibid., 289. See "Ad Sac. Romani Imperij Potentiss, Sereniss et Illustriss Electores, Principes, ac Duces, Urbes Imperiales, Germania Provinciis, caeterasq totius Christianitatis Regiones omnes et singulas, Hungarica gentis Excusatio maxime necessari, Curilla contra Caesaris Romani Exercitum arma ceperit. Judas Maccabeus," in *Acta in Ungarn, Böhmen und Schlesien. 1604–1609*, Biblioteka Cyfrowa Uniwersytetu Wrocławskiego, MF 9961, fol. 37r.-41r.
230 Jessenius, "Der Königlichen Majestät zu Ungarn," 290.
231 *Ibid.*
232 *Ibid.*, 291.

alcohol by Matthias, as was noted by Illésházy.²³³) Instead, he says, that because of its weight, the crown is a symbol of the weighty burden of sovereignty that lies on the king, and compares the Hungarian crown to the iron crowns made for the rulers of Italy and the Holy Roman Emperor.

Then Jeszenszky, like Berger, brings together the exterior of the crown and its significance. He also writes about another component, which is overlooked in Berger's work – the chains that hang at both sides. According to him, their function is that of the slaves of the king of Persia, of whom Plutarch writes that day and night they whispered into the king's ear that he should do his duty. Here the exterior and the history of the crown once more are linked to the political developments of the day. It is noteworthy that many images of King Mátyás II with the crown, including the drawing in the manuscript of his work, show him from the side and the chains are clearly visible (see images 6, 7 and 9).

After describing the further procedure and conclusion of the festivities, Jeszenszky moves on to the king's taking of the oath, which took place in the open air, outside the church. Mátyás II – in Jeszenszky's account – swore by the Virgin Mary, Patron Saint of Hungary, promising to protect the liberties, rights and privileges of his subjects.²³⁴ In so doing he alluded to the Golden Bull of King András II, and promised to defend the frontiers of the kingdom and at the same time to increase the territory of the country.

It is noteworthy that Jeszenszky ends his account with a peroration in which he extols the Hungarians and the fatherland rather than the virtues of the king. In this way his work ends with a political message that presumably springs from the Hungarian Estates themselves. This passage too was probably inspired by Berger. Jeszenszky begins by showing Mátyás II as the Hungarians' national king, and says that by his graciousness, valour and virtue he is a worthy successor to his namesake Mátyás I. Then he states that nothing else could have been expected from a king who was the ruler of Hungary, that country which was known for its antiquity, fertility and good fortune, and for which therefore the name "Glueckreich" might be suitable. On the basis of the double entendre (*reich* may mean rich or country) Jeszenszky, as a doctor and court historian, gives his diagnosis that Hungary is sick because of Ottoman attacks, and those that speak ill of it name it *Angaria* (land of distress).²³⁵ This medico-political way of seeing things is in keeping with the views

---

233 See the description of the Siege of Esztergom in 1594 by Illésházy, when Archduke Matthias did not come out of the camp for two weeks because of excessive alcohol consumption. Kazinczy, ed., *Gr. Illésházy István Nádor följegyzései*, 9–10.
234 *Ibid.*, 298.
235 This may be seen as the extension of the ideas of sickness in the 'body politic' expressed in the dissertation *Pro vindiciis contra tyrannos...*, which he wrote in 1591, and which was only published

of other humanist medical men that wrote on politics and history.[236] Jeszenszky's opinions fits in very well with Nancy Siraisi's thoughts about those Early Modern doctors who saw in history a curative effect on public life.

Next, he tries to change the negative image of the Hungarian nation that prevailed at the time. His work serves to counterbalance the pamphlets of negative content about the Hungarians which were put about at the behest of Rudolf's court during and after the Bocskai rebellion. To this end, Jeszenszky draws an idealised picture of the Hungarians.[237] They are, says he, a warlike people, who willingly sacrifice their lives for the sake of the fatherland, are satisfied with little pay, in time of war abhor mutiny and indiscipline, are courageous, moderate, virtuous and brave, do not swear or blaspheme. Then, he says, he too belongs to this people by descent, that Hungary is his native land and true fatherland.

Next, he passes his political message, which again he justifies by the use of the bastion of Christendom image. In his dramatic depiction, Hungary is like an enormous dam, by its present condition and character the only such defensive work protecting the Holy Roman Empire from the Turks. As long as Hungary is capable of this the German-Austrian nation can rest calmly and sleep at night in safety, free from anxiety. (We have been able to read this topos previously in *Querelae* and the work of Berger on the Cross.) When, however, this wall, or rather dam, is breached the Ottomans will inundate "Germany" like a tempestuous sea, and the flood will sweep away all freedom. Like in *Querelae*, Jeszenszky closes the first section with an appeal to the Christian princes to be alert, and to give Hungary (the Hungarian Estates) help and support.

It seems that with Jeszenszky's political message of the description of the coronation, a period of political and cultural changes has come to an end in Hungary. A single depiction is to be found in his manuscript, in which the Hungarian crown is portrayed together with King Mátyás II (images 8 and 9) and these images reflect the situation in which the political desires of the Habsburg ruler and of the Hungarian Estates are fulfilled. Jeszenszky tells the Holy Roman Empire that if it wishes to remain in being, it must exert itself to keep political order in Hungary safe.

One must regard the change in the image of the Hungarian Estates and the function of the Crown at the time of the handing over of power and Mátyás's coronation in 1608 as the logical consequence of the transformation which became perceptible through Bocskai's rebellion between 1604 and 1606. Mátyás II and the Estates made

---

in 1614 with a letter to Gulielmus Traunerus of Nürberg, dated November 1612. Johannes Jessenius, *Pro vindiciis, contra tyrannos, oratio* (Francofurti: Ioannes Bringerius, 1614).
236 Nancy Siraisi, "Anatomizing the Past: Physicians and History in Renaissance Culture," *Renaissance Quarterly* 53 (2003), 1–30.
237 Jessenius, "Der Königlichen Majestät zu Ungarn," 303–304.

use of this image and the meaning of the crown to justify and present a joint anti-Rudolf policy in 1607. The crown was shown as a symbol of the bonds between the Habsburg pretender and the Hungarian Estates. The basis for these bonds was the political compromise between king and Estates, which was justified by the newly formed image of the crown and of the Estates. In this thinking the crown functioned as the divine legitimator of the compromise, but in the meanings detailed in this chapter it also embodied the various political, religious and moral elements of that.

VII. Péter Révay's History of the Holy Crown (1613)

Questions and problems

The year 1613 saw the publication of Péter Révay's book on the crown: *De sacrae coronae regni Hungariae ortu, virtute, fortuna, annos ultra DC clarissimae, brevis commentarius*.[1] Nowadays this book is considered the earliest work on the history of the Hungarian crown, and the most important work in the Early Modern period on its significance. As we have already stated in the first chapter, Révay's book was exceptionally popular in the seventeenth and eighteenth centuries, although at the end of the eighteenth century, with the rise of critical history writing in Hungary, public interest in it declined. After the appearance of the first Hungarian translation in 1979, Révay's biography too was published. Once more his thoughts received attention.[2] Historians in the past have considered that he wrote the history of the crown superficially and uncritically, with, furthermore, a naive, Medieval belief in its holiness.[3]

The question is, is this opinion of Révay reasonable? To this day only a few historians have provided an adequate answer to who he actually was, why he of all people wrote a book about the crown, and what the connection is between him and the writers of the works on the crown mentioned above.[4] At the same time,

---

1 Petrus de Rewa [Péter Révay], *De sacrae coronae regni Hungariae ortu, virtute, victoria, fortuna, annos ultra D C clarissimae, brevis commentarius* (Augustae Vindelicorum: Christoph. Mangus, 1613).
2 Hungarian translation by Péter Kulcsár in Tamás Katona, ed., *A korona kilenc évszázada. Történelmi források a magyar koronáról* [The nine hundred years of the crown. Historic sources about the Hungarian crown] (Budapest: Európa könyvkiadó, 1979) 195–232; György Bónis, *Révay Péter* [Péter Révay] (Budapest: Akadémiai Kiadó, 1981). Márton Tárnóc also wrote in 1983: "Péter Révay's work has never been one of the fashionable topics for academic research." Márton Tárnóc, "Bónis György: *Révay Péter* [György Bónis: Péter Révay]," *Irodalomtörténeti Közlemények* 5 (1983) 570.
3 Mátyás Bél, in Johannes Georgius Schwandtner, ed., Scriptores rerum Hun. Veteres ac genuini Vol. II (Vindobonae, Lipsiae: impensis Ioannis Pauli Kraus, 1746) XXVIII; Bartoniek, *A magyar királykoronázások*, 169; Thomas von Bogyay, "Zum Stand der Sankt-Stephan-Forschung. Bemerkungen zu Györffys "István király és müve," *Südost-Forschungen* 38 (1979) 240; Bónis, *Révay Péter*, 61; Thomas von Bogyay, "Über die Forschungsgeschichte der heiligen Krone," in Zsuzsa Lovag, ed., *Insignia Regni Hungariae I. Studien zur Machtsymbolik des Mittelalterlichen Ungarn* (Studien zur Machtsymbolik des mittelalterlichen Ungarn, Vol. I) (Budapest: Magyar Nemzeti Múzeum, 1983) 66; Benda and Fügedi, *A magyar korona regénye*, 167.
4 Gergely Tóth, "Lutheránus országtörténet újsztoikus keretben. Révay Péter *Monarchiá*ja [Lutheran history of the country from a new stoic point of view. Péter Révay's Monarchia," in Gergely Tóth, ed., *Clio inter arma. Tanulmányok a 16–18. századi történetírásról* [Clio inter arma. Studies on history writing in Hungary in the sixteenth to the eighteenth century] Budapest: MTA Bölcsészettudományi

there is as yet no explanation of why he wrote on the significance of the crown in this curious form, nor has there yet been any investigation of his political ideas and their source. In order for us to understand his thoughts on the crown better, it is extremely important to look beyond the frontiers of Hungary, and to examine the form and content of Révay's work in a European context and from the point of view of the development of humanist political thought.

As Quentin Skinner stated: not only does politics change history, but the past can change political thinking.[5] According to Jacob Soll, from the time in the Renaissance when the work of Tacitus was rediscovered and Niccolo Machiavelli (1469–1527) published *Il Principe* and *Discorsi*, both inspired by Tacitus, people in Europe took a different view of the concept of power and the role of history.[6] The concept of God-given authority gave way to that of national interest (*raison d'état*) based on the legitimation of power. This meant that the ruler was no longer seen as God's *locum tenens* in this world but a person whose task it was to take to heart the interests of the country. In order to perform this task well he had to have an appropriate character (*virtus*) and statesmanly wisdom (*prudentia*); equipped with these virtues, he was capable of justly guiding the state. Attention turned from Cicero, moralising defender of the Republican party, to the ideas of the realist Tacitus.

To legitimate royal power, to define how the ruler must behave in the national interests, from the fifteenth century on, politicians and historians have looked more and more often into the past, seeking justification in history.[7] Quentin Skinner has characterised this change in thinking as "history became political theory".[8] In the sixteenth century writers who adopted Tacitus' attitude, like Jean Bodin and Justus Lipsius, made use of the newly discovered Greek and Latin works to analyse the workings of politics.[9] At the same time, the French kings, in an effort to acquire absolute power, insisted that men of learning gather together as many historical

---

Kutatóközpont, Történettudományi Intézet, 2014.) 117–147; Gergely Tóth, *Szent István, Szent Korona, államalapítás a protestáns történetírásban (16–18. század)* [St. István, the Holy Crown and the foundation of the state in Protestant historiography (sixteenth to eighteenth century)] (Budapest: MTA Bölcsészettudományi Kutatóközpont, Történettudományi Intézet, 2016).

5 Quentin Skinner, *The Foundations of Modern Political Thought*, Vol. I. (Cambridge: Cambridge University Press, 1978) 208.
6 Jacob Soll, *Publishing the Prince. History, Reading, & the Birth of Political Criticism* (Ann Arbor: University of Michigan Press, 2005) 22–23.
7 Anthony Grafton, *What was History? The Art of History in Early Modern Europe* (Cambridge: Cambridge University Press, 2007); Jacob Soll, "Introduction: The Uses of Historical Evidence in early-modern Europe," *Journal of the History of Ideas* 64/2 (2003) 149–150; Ernest Cassirer, *The Myth of the State* (New Haven; London: Yale University Press, 1946) 135–173; Herbert Butterfield, *The Statecraft of Machiavelli* (New York: Collier Books, 1962) 61.
8 Skinner, *The Foundations*, Vol. I., 208.
9 Soll, *Publishing the Prince,* 31–33.

sources as possible on the past of the country. They hoped that, based on the sources, they would delve deep into the workings of politics, give a new legitimacy to their own power, and find material for the construction of a new kind of mythology, one which would be able to justify their desires for absolutism.[10] Representatives of the French Estates likewise carried out research into the constitutional roots of their fatherland. They applied the notion of national interest to defend their own political interests against the ruler's absolutist ambitions. According to Soll, history served at one and the same time as a key to absolute power and a weapon with which to oppose it.[11]

But how could history have been formed into political theory? According to Jacob Soll it was the French thinker Jean Bodin (1530–1596) that worked out a systematic method of transforming historical knowledge into pragmatic political theory.[12] In his masterly *Methodus ad facilem historiarum* (1566) Bodin states that the wisdom of the political statesman (*prudentia*) must be founded on the careful analysis of history.[13] If, for some reason, a historian finds it impossible to write about current events taking place in the country, he must study the historical roots of the constitution of his fatherland. According to Bodin, the nature of the constitution will betray all sorts of things about the character of the people of a country, its geographical situation and climate. Bodin's historical method was unprecedentedly popular in European historical studies in the Early Modern period, thus leading to the revival of interest in national character.[14] From then on, the study of history has been regarded as the ideal form of political and moral education.[15]

How, according to Bodin, is it best to become aware of the history of individual countries? The first step in his method is the analysis of the originality and reliability of sources. The second step is the establishment of truths of general validity based on raw source material. These truths emerge from the recognition of the causal links between irrefutable and tested historical facts.[16] Relying on this knowledge, politicians have the power to exert statesmanly wisdom, and in the possession of it can influence events in the country. The key to influence, however, was whether the

---

10 *Idem*, 26. Soll points to the following study: Filippo de Vivo, "Dall'imposizione del silenzio alla "Guerre delle Scriture": Le publicazione ufficiali durante l'Interdetto del 1606-1607," *Studi Veneziani* 41 (2001) 179–213.
11 Soll, *Publishing the Prince*. 26.
12 *Idem*, 27.
13 Jean Bodin, *Methodus, ad facilem historiarum cognitionem* (Paris: Apud M. Iuuenem, 1566); Soll, *Publishing the Prince*. 27.
14 Grafton, *What was History?*, 166.
15 Julian Franklin, *Jean Bodin and the Sixteenth Century Revolution in the Methodology of Law and History* (New York; London: Columbia University Press, 1963, ²1966) 3.
16 Ann Blair, "Humanist Methods in Natural Philosophy: The Commonplace Book," *Journal of the History of Ideas* 53 (1992) 544.

ruler and the *respublica* could be convinced of the historical truth as conceived by a historian. Bodin based his concept of historical truth on the notion of the French lawyer François Baudouin (1520–1573): Divine Providence was to be recognised not only in nature but also in history.[17] Baudouin – and later Bodin – employed the notion of *similitudo temporum*, that is, the (perceptibly) lasting similarity between historical periods, which occurs in the Greco-Latin historian Polybius (c. 203–c. 120 BC).[18] Baudouin had the notion that God's plan for mankind was knowable through the revelation of analogous historical events. Divine truth could be deduced from the historical links that this uncovered. In Bodin's opinion the same parallels could be found in divine, natural and human history.[19] All knowledge could be interpreted taking God's all-embracing plan for mankind as starting-point. The historically based political proposals, therefore, with which the ruler's God-given power was either justified or rejected, gained religious legitimacy by reference to Providence. By this means, political thought in the Early Modern period too acquired a religious interpretation.[20] We have written about Protestant and Catholic religious history in Hungary in a previous chapter.

How could the writer convince the reader or listener of historical truth? According to Bodin, the correct presentation of historical source material was of decisive importance. In processing information he employed a humanist technique, central to which were illustrative quotations and important details taken from the Classics, together with historical examples.[21] In the course of history others have indeed used this method – among others the Roman biographer Suetonius – but Bodin was the first to make use of it to present source materials logically as general regular features of the past.[22] In practice, Bodin's method meant that a writer had to construct his argument or study on a trinity of quotations from authoritative Classical authors such as Tacitus, and examples, ancient and contemporary, relevant to the given

---

17 Franklin, *Jean Bodin*, 116–118.
18 Polybius, *Histories*, Vol. I, 4.
19 Franklin, *Jean Bodin*, 142.
20 Friedrich Polleroß, "From the *exemplum virtutis* to the Apotheosis," in Allan Ellenius, ed., *Iconography, Propaganda, and Legitimation* (Oxford: Clarendon Press, 2008) 53.
21 See: Ann Moss, *Printed Commonplace-Books and the Structuring of Renaissance Thought* (Oxford: Oxford University Press, 1996); François Goyet, *Le Sublime du "Lieu Commun." L'invention rhétorique dans l'Antiquité et à la Renaissance* (Paris: Champion, 1996); Blair, "Humanist Methods in Natural Philosophy," 541–551; Robert Bireley, *The Counter-Reformation Prince. Anti-Machiavellianism or Catholic Statecraft in Early-Modern Europe* (Chapel Hill, N.C.: University of North Carolina Press, 1990) 78; Ann Moss, "The Politica of Justus Lipsius and the Commonplace-Book," *Journal of the History of Ideas* 59 (1998) 421.
22 Earle Havens, *Commonplace Books. A History of Manuscripts and Printed Books from Antiquity to the Twentieth Century* (Yale: Yale University Press, 2001) 47.

subject.[23] His followers applied the quotations to the best possible effect, detaching them from their original or literary contexts, and if necessary adjusting the (political) idea supported by the original author. The Early Modern author, therefore, did not simply repeat the Classical quotations as the person that originally worded them had imagined them, but looked for an interpretation which could offer a straightforward and convincing answer to the problems of the present day.

The new method was much more a rhetorical strategy than a scientific *modus operandi*, as the writer had no intention of putting forward absolute knowledge but was rather endeavouring to convince his audience.[24] The reader probably had to be persuaded of the correctness of a political theory which had come into being through the selective and often dubious interpretation of historical source material. For several writers, ancient culture or personal past meant a mass of really discrete building elements, and by constantly putting them into shapes and polishing them, a novel memorial with meaning appropriate to the age was formed. By virtue of the style and *modus operandi* employed, books had a Classical breadth of argument and convincing force, though with regard to their substance they were Early Modern creations. As Robert Bireley puts it: "They carried the authority of the ancients, but they represented his thoughts."[25] Nevertheless these efforts signalled a cultural change tending towards the rediscovery and re-creation of the Classical age and the writers' own past. In addition, the change led towards the creation of new myths, which the historical research work carried out by the Bodin method underpinned.

According to Julian Franklin, Bodin's second important innovation was that his historical method offered an opportunity for a new kind of comparison of the different European and non-European political systems.[26] In sixteenth-century Europe there were radical shifts in political relationships as the traditional, God-given power of rulers lost ground to the political influence of the Estates and their constitutional demands. For this reason, it became no longer possible to apply the Classical division of the political systems of Aristoteles and Polybius, as several European states could no longer be described as monarchies, aristocracies or democracies. Bodin was the first, in his mighty work *Six livres de la république* (1579), to make a systematic attempt to rework the ancient classification into a new scheme apposite to the new sovereign nation-states that had arisen in Europe. He tried in this way not only to shed light on the constitutional nature of Europe, but at the same time he created a new scale of values by dividing systems of government into despotic and legitimate categories. He declared that the perfect system of

---

23 For the quoted lines, see: Bireley, *The Counter-Reformation Prince*, 78; Moss, "The Politica," 421.
24 Anthony Grafton, *Bring out your Dead: the Past as Revelation* (Cambridge (Mass.): Harvard University Press, 2001) 241.
25 Bireley, *The Counter-Reformation Prince* 78.
26 Franklin, *Jean Bodin* 116–118.

government was that in which, to the best of their ability, the ruler or those in power served the interests of the Estates, and did their best with the instruments of the law to defend their liberties and property.[27] The constitution therefore became the norm which settled the lawful nature of the governing Estates.

Péter Révay's life and oeuvre

Who in fact was Révay? Why did he write a book about the crown, and how did he recreate the past of Hungary? Also known as Petrus de Rewa or Révai (1568–1622), he was a Lutheran baron from Royal Hungary, the part under Habsburg rule.[28] He was a member of the sort of family that had for more than a century played an important role in political, cultural and religious life in Hungary. He was trained from the age of six to fill the highest positions, the purpose of which was for him to acquire profitable skills, while dealing with routine political agendas, and to have at his disposal statesmanly wisdom with which he could best serve the interests of the Hungarian Estates. The denominational background of an educational institution was of little importance from the point of view of the attainment of the goal.[29] He therefore spent three years (1584–1587) studying rhetoric under the Jesuits at the Catholic University of Vienna, and after a further three (1587–1590) received the degree of magister from the Protestant University of Strasbourg.[30]

---

27 Idem, 76.
28 On Révay's life, see: Rafaël Hrabecius, *D.O.M.A. Oratio Funebris In solennibus exequiis Spect. ac Mag. Dni Petri de Reva, supremi ac perpetui Comitis Comitatus Thurocen... Habita in loco sepulturae Ejusdem & Majorum, in templo Martinopolitano... 17. Julij. Anno 1622... Adjuncta est Valedictio Eiusdem Dni Petri de Reva, ... morituri* (Cassoviae: ex officina typographica Danielis Schultz, 1623); Sándor Szilágyi, *Révay Péter és a Szent Korona (1619–1622)* [Péter Révay and the Holy Crown (1619–1622)] (Budapest, 1875); Bónis, *Révay Péter*. On Péter Révay and his family, see: Maroš Mačuha, *Panstvá rodu Révai v ranom novoveku (ekonomický a sociálny kapitál uhorského aristokratického rodu)* [The dominions of the Révai family in the Early Modern period (the economic and social capital of a Hungarian aristocratic family)] (doctoral dissertation, Bratislava 2007) and Miloš Kovačka, Eva Augustínová and Maroš Mačuha, eds., *Rod Révai v slovenských dejinách. Zborník prác z interdisciplinárnej konferencie 16. - 17. September 2008, Martin* [The Révay family in Slovak history. Proceedings of the Interdisciplinary Conference, 16–17 September 2008, Martin] (Martin: Slovenská národná knižnica, 2010).
29 Péter and his brother Ferenc were entrusted to a minister of religion, who made their father regular reports on their progress and the development of their religious views. Bónis, *Révay Péter* 7–8.
30 Hrabecius, *D.O.M.A. Oratio Funebris*, C4r.-D1v., Sándor Eckhardt, "Magyar szónokképzés a XVI. századi Strasszburgban [Hungarian orational education in sixteenth-century Strasburg]," in György Németh, ed., *Értekezések a nyelv- és a széptudományi osztály köréből*, XXVI./5 (1944) 351–363. Bónis, *Révay Péter* 8–9 ; György Gömöri, "A strassburgi akadémián tanuló XVI. századi magyarok

The question of where Révay learnt to put history to use in day-to-day politics has not yet received due attention.[31] He encountered the rhetorical techniques of the time and the use of philosophical and historical source material for the first time at Strasbourg, where he was a pupil of the celebrated Protestant academic Johannes Sturm.[32] His studies were guided by the rector, Melchior Junius (1545–1604), who used to organise lively debates in which the participants first delivered written speeches in public, of which the best were then printed.[33] These were devised by the students systematically collecting quotations on given topics from Classical or Early Modern authors and then using these to construct their own arguments.[34] The way in which Révay used the new rhetorical technique and Bodin's method can be seen clearly in his published speeches.[35] These performances are not to be regarded as independent philosophical works but as exercises from Révay's student years; they served as a sound basis for his later political writings on Hungary.[36]

---

album-bejegyzései [The album inscriptions of sixteenth-century students studying at the academy of Strasburg]," *Lymbus* 3 (2005) 49–55.

31 Klaniczay, "A magyar későreneszánsz," 319; Wittman, "A magyarországi államelméleti" 53–66; Bartoniek, *Fejezetek a XVI-XVII századi történetírás*, 389–403; Bónis, *Révay Péter*, 72–93.
32 Eckhardt, "Magyar szónokképzés," 345–347.
33 Idem, 349–351. See also: Gömöri, "A strassburgi akadémián," 49–55.
34 One subject for debate was 'The situation of Hungary'. Imre, "Magyarország panasza," 311–312, note 464.
35 The published lectures of Révay: [Péter Révay], "Oratio Ciceronis Pro L. Mureana," in Melchior Junius, ed., *Orationum, qae Argentinensi in Academia exercitii gratia scriptae ...* Vol. III. (Argentorati: Lazarus Zetzner Bibliop., 1606, 1620) 97–9 9, 114, 121–122. (4 December 1589). See: Eckhardt, "Magyar szónokképzés," 353. [Péter Révay], "Actio parricidii ad imitationem orationum Philippi Regis Macedoniae, Ejusdemque filiorum Persei ac Demetrii apud Livium Decad. 4. lib. 10. excercitii gratiae instituta," in *ibid.*, 32–35. Idem, "Orationum, quae Argentinensi in Academia exercitii gratia scriptae ..." in Melchior Junius, ed., *Orationum, qae Argentinensi in Academia exercitii gratia scriptae*, Vol. II. (Argentorati: Lazarus Zetzner Bibliop., 1606, 1620) 1007–1010. [Péter Révay], "Oratio. Generosi D. Petri De Revva, Comitis Thuroczensis, de laudibus M. Tul. Ciceronis, recitata, 6. Idib. Ian. 1591," in Melchior Junius, ed., Orationum quae argentinensi in academia, exercitii gratia scriptae & recitatae II. (Argentorati: Lazarus Zetzner, 1594) 208–228, *idem*, "Praetorus ad Ivdices," in *ibid.*, 248–250; *idem*, "Generosi Dn. Petri de Reuva, Comitis Thuroczensis Praetorus sub persona ad Ivdices," in *ibid.*, 281–282. Later edition: *idem*, in Melchior Junius, ed., *Orationum quae argentinensi in academia, exercitii gratia scriptae & recitatae* Vol. II. (Argentorati: Lazarus Zetzner, 1620) 117–129; [Péter Révay], "De illustrium ac generosorum recreationibus orationes...," in *Orationum, quae Argentinensi in Academia exercitii gratia scriptae ac ...* Vol. II. (Argentorati: Lazarus Zetzner, 1594) 10–14. (6 July 1590) Later edition: idem, *Orationum, quae Argentinensi in Academia exercitii gratia scriptae ...* Vol. III. (Argentorati: Lazarus Zetzner, 1611) 189–192.
36 Révay's dissertation: Petrus de Rewa, *Disputatio de Mutuo, materia non minus difficili qvam utili. In inclyta Argentoratensium Academia, exercitii, causa a' Generoso D. Petro de Rewa, Comite Thuroczensi &c. Ungaro, conscripta, & Praeside Clarissimo Viro, Paulo Grasceccio J. V. D. Mense Martio defensa* (Argentorati: A. Bertram, 1591).

Like other Early Modern writers, Révay also composed his works using his own collection of quotations.[37] The extant collections shed light not only on the breadth of his erudition but also on the method that he learnt in Strasbourg for gathering facts and their use for rhetorical purposes. A large part of the collection is made up of hundreds of sentences full of the Latin terms *bona, concordia, democratia* and *natio*.[38] It is noticeable that Révay quotes not only the Classics, such as Plato, but also Bonfini, Zsámboky (Sambucus) and Bodin.[39] In his later studies of the crown Révay applied the method learnt in his student days of working up quotations and historical examples. His biographer Rafael Hrabecius mentions a compilation of historical quotations and sources titled *Viridarium* (Flower garden) which Révay made after finishing his studies, for use in his later works on the crown and Hungary.[40] This presumably furnished him with more building material for the shaping of his political theory. As far as we know, he did not read the aforementioned *Hungaroteutomachia*.

After finishing his studies, Révay had ample opportunity to put what he had learnt into practice, as he played an important part in Hungarian political life between 1598 and 1622. He took the first step in his career in 1598, when he became perpetual főispán (*supremus comes*) of Turóc county.[41] From 1601 onwards he was appointed *commissarius* (országos biztos) on a number of occasions, and so led his own forces against the Ottomans. He played a key role in the political life of the country when in 1605 he became the most influential adviser to Archduke Matthias (at the time still only governor of Hungary) and took part in the talks leading to the Peace of Vienna and the return of the crown.[42] At the Diet of 1608, he and Pálffy were elected "Guardians of the Crown" (*conservator sacrae coronae*), and in 1610 he was given the office of Lord Steward of the royal household.[43] He

---

37 Such are extant from his time in both Vienna and Strasburg: [Péter Révay], *Joannis Molensis Annotationes in Universam Logicam et Mathesim per Petrus Révay* (Manuscript) Főegyházmegyei könyvtár, Esztergom Ms. 272, *Commentario(!) in octo libros Aristotelis de Physice ausculatione*, idem, Ms. 224, *Commentaria in libros Aristotelis de Coelo et Mundo, de Generatione et Corruptione, Metheorologicorum, de Anima et Metaphysicorum*, ibid., Ms. 273 (Vienna); *Annotationes Morales Historicae*, ibid., Ms. 253 (Strasburg). The latter collection was compiled on the conclusion of his studies, but contains no mention of the crown. Bónis, *Révay Péter* 9–12.

38 [Péter Révay], *Annotationes Morales Historicae*, (manuscript) fol. 63 (*natio*), fol. 215 (*concordia*), fol. 315 (*Bono communitas*). This collection contains only 276 folio, while the older one has 1273.

39 *Bodin de resp 2 lib. Cap 68, lib 4 cap 1. Ibid.*, fol. 16. Bonfini: fol. 28, 33, 44, 70.

40 Hrabecius, *D. O. M. A. Oratio Funebris*, F2r.

41 Fallenbüchl, *Magyarország főispánjai* 5–25. On the offices held by Révay: ibid., 61, 104.

42 Bónis, *Révay Péter*, 14–21, Pálffy, *The Kingdom of Hungary and the Habsburg Monarchy in the Sixteenth Century*, 171, 197, 205.

43 On his activity as Guardian of the Crown see the following unpublished sources: MOL, P 1889 bundle 42, fol 1–11. (annual accounts from 1613–1620 and a number of lists of names of military units), and: "*Juramentum Militum Germanorum, in Arce Regia Posoniens: pro praesidio Sacrae Coronae*

was also Master of Ceremonies on the occasion of the coronation in 1613 of Queen Anna and that of King Ferdinánd III in 1618.[44] By virtue of his role in public life, he was in close contact with the internal political shifts of the Habsburg Empire and with the shaping of the destiny of the Hungarian crown.

Révay began to write historical essays about Hungary when on 2 August 1607 Archduke Matthias commissioned him to scrutinise what had happened in Hungary in past centuries, together with the laws brought in by the men of old, and on that basis to provide him with political advice.[45] This task was similar to that given by the French king to his historians in the sixteenth century.[46] Révay was also tasked with reviewing the workings of Hungarian political life and giving new legitimacy to Habsburg power in Hungary. Thanks to his good education, his thourough knowledge of the Hungarian political system and the important role that he played in the country he was the very person for such a task. This request probably connected with the activity of other writers mentioned above, such as Illésházy, Berger, Jeszenszky and Bocatius.

It was a common feature of the writings of the said authors that their subject was the history of Hungary and the country's connection with the Habsburg dynasty. They all used elements of the crown-tradition and Hungarian history to create a myth about the Hungarian Estates and the crown which gave the impression that the constitution of Hungary – which actually came into being in 1608 – had roots going back centuries. The use for political purposes of history and the crown-tradition was an innovation in Hungary, and gave rise to a large number of written works about the crown, together with depictions of it, in the years following 1608. Révay's book on the crown was therefore innovative in that it was helped by favourable political circumstances.

Regni Hungari, relictorum praesentibus Mag: Dno Petro Rewai, Custode eiusdem Sacrae Coronae, et Generoso Domino, N. Thorn, dictorum Militum Capitaneo, sexta die Januarij Anni Domini 1610, per eosdem Milites sub interiorae porta Arcis praestitum." (The oath [of loyalty] to the crown taken by the Austrian forces in the castle of Pozsony for the protection of the Holy Crown of Hungary), MOL, P 1615 Révay family 1, bundle 41. See also Bónis, *Révay Péter* 30.

44 *Ibid.*, 35.
45 *Ibid.*, 24.
46 J.H.M. Salmon, *Renaissance and Revolt: Essays in the Intellectual and Social History of Early Modern France* (Cambridge and New York: Cambridge University Press, 1987) 119–35; Donald R. Kelley, *The Foundations of Modern Historical Scholarship: Language, Law, and History in the French Renaissance* (New York: Columbia University Press, 1970).

The interpretation of the book on the Holy Crown

Révay's book was published in 1613. Judging from correspondence, the manuscript was finished in 1611 or 1612, and publication was planned for 1612.[47] In this period too political changes were taking place in Hungary, which must have served directly as compelling cause for writing. The most important development was that Archduke Matthias and the Estates had reached a political agreement which was sealed by the return of the crown and the coronation of 1608. Following the coronation, it became obvious that in Hungary the political situation was uncertain, and that there still existed those factors – for example, the lack of a strong government, the yawning gap between the Habsburg ruler and the Hungarian people, and the internal unrest – which had undermined political stability before 1608. In 1609 came the death of Illésházy. In him, Hungary lost both its spiritual leader and the intellectual author of the compromise. He was succeeded as palatine by György Thurzó, who also kept up a personal friendship with Révay, who shared his principles. Mátyás II was not so dependent on the Hungarian Estates after his election as king of Bohemia in 1611 and as Emperor in 1612.[48] In the meanwhile there continued to be tensions between the various religious trends, together with the tension that had arisen between the Hajdús and the Estates, not to mention that between Hungary and Transylvania.

The appearance of Révay's book must not be viewed only in this political context but also as a further step in the post-1608 change in the meaning of the crown. The writing of *Hungaroteutomachia*, Berger's pamphlet of 1608 and Jeszenszky's book of 1609 were followed a few years later by several more works on the crown by Bocatius and Berger. In 1611, Bocatius mentions the crown more than once in a book of verse which draws a parallel between the deeds of Mátyás Corvinus and Mátyás II (although this work cannot be related to *Hungaroteutomachia*).[49] In Berger's eulogy of the late Rudolf (1612) he refers twice to the guarding of the crown.[50] In his work *Trinubium* (mentioned in the former chapter), in which, on the occasion of the coronation of Mátyás II as emperor, he painted a picture of a Europe united through the "joining in marriage" of Hungarians, Czechs and Germans, there is once again a mention of the link between destiny (*fatum*) and

---

47 Bónis, *Révay Péter* 48.
48 Wittman, "A magyarországi államelméleti," 54.
49 *Elegia Serenissimo archiduce Matthia etc. circa Pragam castra metante anno 1608*, and: *Ode gratulatoria de coronae Hungaricae restitutione*. Published in: Johannes Bocatius, "Salomon Hungaricus," in Bocatius, *Opera Quae Extant Omnia: Poetica*, 73–78 and in part in *idem*, II, 827–834.
50 Elias Berger, *Spectator theatri extemporanei belli Hungarici...* (Pragae: Typis Danielis Sedesan, 1612) D1r., D2r.

the Hungarian crown.[51] On 26 November of the same year the Estates too, in a speech to Mátyás II, mentioned the angelic crown (*angelica corona*) as the gift of Pope Benedict VII [sic!].[52] By all these references the Estates' political message was recognised even outside Hungary. Révay's book that was published in 1613 belonged to this line of strategy.[53]

The new ideas about the crown were able to spread so quickly because the said writers were in personal contact, constantly corresponding with one another and supporting one another in the writing and publishing of their books on the subject. Révay, for example, corresponded with Jeszenszky and Berger about the crown.[54] Berger and others helped in the writing of Révay's book. Lutheran minister Mátyás Lochmannus, for example, collected data for it and proofread Révay's manuscript.[55] Illés Lány, the Thurzós' chaplain, and Rafael Hrabecius, the Révay domestic chaplain also played similar roles in the genesis of the manuscript. The book did not, therefore, come into being as the result of the author's pleasant spare time occupation, as Révay wrote to György Thurzó in 1614, but we may regard it as a serious piece of writing containing the clear political message to Europe of the Hungarian political élite.[56]

Révay's clandestine purpose with this book was to bring about a political theory concerning the historical connection between the crown and Hungary. This theory would have been invoked on the one hand to create peace and concord in Hungary, and on the other hand to prove to the world that the country was free and independent. With this in mind Révay wrote the history of Hungary, the Hungarians and the crown, in such a way that in the process he convinced the reader of the correctness of his own views.

The essence of Révay's thinking was that through the Holy Crown, God had exercised constant influence on the destiny of the Hungarian people and Hungary ever since the country had been founded. Consequently – as might be read in the title

---

51 Elias Berger, *Trinubium Europaeum, hoc est...* (Francoforti: Tampachius, 1612) 12, 40, 44. For an analysis of Berger's thought in this work, see: Wittman, "Az osztrák Habsburg-hatalom," 32. See also: Kees Teszelszky, "The Crown of Hungary before and after the Hungarian crowning: The use of the Holy Crown of Hungary in Hungarian revolts and Habsburg representation between 1604 and 1611," *Hungarian Studies*, 30 /2 (2016) 172–173.

52 "Gratulatio legatorum Hungariae, in felicissimum reditum, Sac. Caes. Regi atque Matthis, Viennam, anni 1612 die 26 Novembris, in Palatio, coram Caesarem Matte, et senatu habita.," in MOL I 34 (Collection Kollar) fol. 377.

53 The copy numbered OSZK RMK III.1118 in possession of the Hungarian National Library was presented by Révay to Cardinal Melchior Khlesl, who had been Archduke Matthias' most important advisor after Illésházy, and a promoter of the transfer of power within the House of Habsburg.

54 Bónis, 48; SNA – ARR Korešpondencia Peter Révay Krč. 81 (1612).

55 Bónis, 109–112.

56 *Ibid.*

and introduction – his express intention was to offer a brief account (*commentarius*) on the origin (*ortus*) of the Holy Crown of the Kingdom of Hungary more than six hundred troubled years before, its distinguished and victorious nature (*virtus et victoria*), and its destiny (*fortuna*).

The method chosen for writing the history of the crown and the analysis of its significance served as an example (*exemplum*) and a justification of the author's theory on the political life of Hungary. The constituent elements of the theory on the crown agree in the principal points with the contents of the pact made in 1608, thanks to Illésházy's efforts, between the king and the Estates. As we said in the first chapter, this pact may be taken back to a sharing of power by the Estates and the king in which the crown and the law on the one hand were evidence of the rights and sovereignty of the Estates and the country, and on the other hand the Peace of Vienna and the return of the crown testified to the emperor's ruling power.

The book begins with an introductory section consisting of a title page, an engraved image of the crown (see image 12), a dedication, a letter from the author to the reader and an anonymous epigram in honour of Révay. It is possible that Berger wrote this epigram, as in his previously mentioned *Caduceus* he penned a laudatory verse in honour of Révay. Then follows the main body of the work, seventy sections of text written in the form of an apologia, neither divided into chapters nor numbered. This section is closed by two speeches which really contain the final conclusion of the author's analysis. Révay ends the book with letters of recommendation from Berger and Jeszenszky, who had read and commented on the manuscript.[57]

The basis of Révay's political theory is a desire for harmony (*concordia*). He would like to find means of preventing chaos forming in public life, one which could lay the foundation of a power prepared to guarantee security and stability. The dedication to the king, queen and the Hungarian people (*gens*) at the start of the book, like the prayer for king and country in the text (*oratio pro Corona, Rege et Regno*), explicitly stresses that harmony is necessary and that civil war in Hungary must be forestalled.[58]

---

57 Révay shows the letter as a unified whole, whereas it was certainly compounded from two separate letters from Berger. In his book the dateline Regensburg, 20 August 1613 can be read, but the first half is taken from the opening of a letter from Berger written on 15 April 1612. The original of the first part is preserved in the archive containing Révay's correspondence, and at present is designated as: SNA – ARR Korešpondencia Peter Révay Krč. 81 fol. 271, Palmarum, 15 April 1612. The second half is not to be found there, and was perhaps never sent as a letter. Bearing in mind the connection between the writers, it is likely that this text was written with the intention of assisting the dissemination of Révay's ideas, and so it was included in the book as an imaginary letter. I failed to find the original of Jeszenszky's letter in the archive.

58 De Rewa, *De sacrae coronae regni Hungariae*, 97–9 8.

Révay's political theory is based on the permanent link between Providence (*providentia*) and destiny (*fatum*), to which he gives expression in an account of the significance of the crown. His starting-point is that the destiny of Hungary was subordinate to Providence and that through the medium of the crown God personally intervenes in the destiny of king and country.

He pictures the link between Providence and destiny by personalising the crown. The depiction of the crown as a person is embodied in the description of its excellence (*virtus*). In Révay's work this term designates the supernatural power, influence or moral quality of the crown. He states that the Hungarian crown is something which, in its material reality (as an object) but also from a moral viewpoint (as an allegory, a parable or *exemplum*) will stand immoveable amid the storms of the destiny of Hungary. This alludes on the one hand to the historical fact that the crown has been preserved over the centuries. On the other hand, the meaning of the crown is the mark of moral trustworthiness in Hungarian history, since God – as Providence itself – has foreordained the destiny of the king, the country and the Estates through the working of the Holy Crown. From this it follows that God will punish king and nation if the *virtus* of the crown is harmed. This meaning of the word also embraces the impact of the crown on Hungarian history.

The meaning of the crown also forms the starting point of those thoughts of Révay's which refer to the form of the Hungarian state which benefits by it, and to those virtues which, in his view, the rulers of Hungary and the Hungarian people must possess. It is his opinion that the Kingdom of Hungary is linked to the divine origin (*ortus*) of the crown. This, however, is far from saying that the ruler enjoys absolute power. By virtue of the fact that Providence determines the destiny of the country, the only appropriate form of authority in Hungary, as a kingdom under Habsburg rule, is that in which the ruler – who is under the law – is crowned with the Holy Crown. Only thus can peace (*pax*) and harmony (*concordia*) come about in the country. In Révay's view the ideal kingdom can be maintained if the actions of the king and the Estates are directed towards the common good (*bonum publicum*).

The *virtus* of the crown shapes the direction of political activity, and this Révay explains in detail as he presents in detail the virtues of the good statesman. Numerous instances are listed in the book both of the virtuous behaviour of the king and the Estates, and of their quarreling. In the course of this, concrete examples from the history of the crown are listed, in which is revealed a range of good qualities – godliness (*pietas*), honesty (*probitas*), fairness (*justitia*), mercifulness (*clementia*), faithfulness (*fides*) and moderation (*modestia*). Later the author brings together the display of individual virtues with concrete political goals – as, for example, the liberty of the Estates, the independence of the country and deference to the king – by means of which the subject always has relevance.

The essence of the examples is the repeated appearance in them of the crown as the moral touchstone of the actions of the king and the Estates. Some of the examples that Révay quotes are the Medieval miracles, the theft of the crown and its return in 1608. Should the king and/or the Estates perpetrate any impropriety, in so doing they offend the crown, and it leaves the country; God then punishes king, country and people with misfortune. This persistent interaction between the acts of God performed through the crown and the actions of mankind as it comes into contact with them, Révay describes as good or bad fortune. When the crown and its associated moral quality are respected, the common good is guaranteed and an extraordinarily happy situation prevails, which Révay calls the victory (*victoria*) of the crown.

The method by which Révay shapes his own version of Hungarian history is similar to those of Berger and Jeszenszky. Elements that he employs may be found in the works of both, such as the influence exerted on history by destiny. Furthermore – like Révay – both Berger and Jeszenszky make use of examples taken from Hungarian history to present a definite political message to the reader.

Révay is the first to transform his analysis of Hungarian history into a systematic political theory. As a result of its political theoretical content his work cannot be characterised as simply a mirror for princes of the Hungarian Estates.[59] Like the writings of Bodin, this book too is a practical manual of Hungarian political life, full of concrete examples and of use to king and politician alike. In addition, Révay's book, unlike Berger's and Jeszenszky's, became very widely known and exercised considerable influence on the development of national self-awareness in Hungary.

Révay applies Bodin's pious lie method to pass his own political message to his readers. He selects the historical examples in such a way that their content matched precisely the significance of the crown that he was creating.[60] In this way the selection and sequence of the illustrations fitted the desired course of the argument, faithfully reflecting the author's political interpretation. He had used this method as early as 1607 in his first proposition to Archduke Matthias; in this he stated, on the basis of historical examples, that Bocskai's grants of land were not lawful because the prince had not been legitimately crowned king.[61] In the section of the book on the crown titled "The author to the reader" he gives a detailed account of his method and offers a pre-emptive defence of his thoughts about the crown and history against the historians and lawyers of his time. From this it emerges unambiguously that Révay's *modus operandi* and view of history were innovations

---

59 On mirrors of princes in Hungary see: Emil Hargittay, *Gloria, fama, literatura* (Budapest: Universitas Kiadó, 2001).
60 Révay almost never mentions the source of the examples that he uses. For a survey of likely sources see the works of Bartoniek and Bónis. Bartoniek: *Fejezetek* 390; Bónis, *Révay Peter*, 52–61.
61 Advice of Péter Révay to Archduke Matthias, dated Holics, 10 August 1607. MTAK, Károlyi bequest, Ms 5169/4, fol. 84–87. This statement on Bocskai's grants of land was to be read in a supplement on Bocskai's person in a previously mentioned article about the Peace of Vienna.

in Hungary. He is not defending himself against definite historians or lawyers, as Várkonyi supposes, but rather against the dominant views of history and the law which characterised his own time, when neither historians nor lawyers concern themselves with the "honour of the crown".[62]

It is also possible that Révay is alluding here to Ludovicus Tubero's work which was published in Frankfurt in 1603 and which was very negative on the Hungarian tradition of the Holy Crown.[63] Tubero (1458–1527) was a Croatian abbot of a Benedictine monastery near Dubrovnik.[64] He wrote a historiographical work which is especially informative on the history of Hungary after the death of King Mátyás Corvinus. The author was very critical of the Hungarian people and the crown tradition: in this way it can be read as a reaction to the work of Bonfini as well. Tubero did not intend to print it: it circulated in manuscript among his friends to inform and entertain them. One copy found its way to Frankfurt, where it was edited by the city writer and rector of the Latin school Adelarius Cravelius (Gravelein). According to Bónis and Bartoniek, Révay adopts Tubero's text without using quotation marks.[65]

Following Bodin, Révay explains his method by saying that the starting-point of his research is the discovery of historical truth (*veritas*).[66] He declares that those writers who deal with the publication of "… the laws of nations and the customs of peoples …" or "… memorable deeds and words …" (i. e. lawyers and historians) "… probably do mankind the greatest service if, in their fine words, they not only seek the delight of narratives but also preserve the reality and record of events."[67] In this way Révay – just like Bodin – differentiates between historical studies (*historia*) leading to the discovery of truth and mythology, the historiographic tendency concerned with happenings and legends.

Next Révay gives an account of the writing of his book, employing the same theory on which the rest of his argument is based. He states that he has been involved in affairs of state in peace and war and has always busied himself in the service of the Hungarian fatherland, the kings and the Estates, but that even so, fate and the grace of God have made it possible for him to compile this work. Initially his worship

---

62 Várkonyi, "A korona és a Budai vár," 41. For example, in the earlier mentioned historical work of Istvánffy there is not a single reference to what the crown meant to the Hungarians. Istvánffy does not regard the tradition of the crown as important.
63 Ludovicus Tuberonis Dalmatae Abbatis, *Commentariorum De Rebus…* (Francofurti: Impensis Claudii Marnii, & haeredum Joannis Aubrii, 1603).
64 Vlado Rezar, "Ludovicus Cervarius Tubero," in David Thomas and John A. Chesworth a.o., eds., *Christian-Muslim Relations. A Bibliographical History: Volume 7. Central and Eastern Europe, Asia, Africa and South America (1500–1600)* (Leiden – Boston: Brill) 147–153.
65 Bónis, *Révay Peter,* 52–61; Bartoniek, *Fejezetek,* 389–403.
66 De Rewa, *De sacrae coronae regni Hungariae, autor ad lectorem* (no page number).
67 *Ibid.*

of the Holy Crown (*religio sacrae coronae*) made him reluctant to disclose his thoughts, and it was only the urging of kindred spirits and high-ranking politicians that convinced him of the necessity of publishing the book.[68] From this it follows that God influences the destiny of Hungary through the holiness of the Crown, and has inspired the writer to produce this book about it. Thus, Révay endows the book with divine justification, and looks upon himself as God's instrument as its author.

Then he tells us why study of the crown is important, together with this peculiar method of historical investigation that he has used. He follows Bodin in stating that the knowledge of science and history are so necessary that without that adornment a man or a ruler is but a shadow and ghost of himself.[69] In conclusion, he notes that his family, which has for three hundred years been involved in Hungarian affairs of state, has always regarded science, men of learning and culture as the greatest adornment.[70] In his opinion the crown, politics and science are interlinked, as is evident from the account of his method.

Then, following the title, he repeats the purpose of the book and mentions how it came into being: "It is in fact no more than a brief account of the Holy Crown, which I have so put together in clear and simple style that everything that other writers have been able to say about it in dutiful and suitable fashion should here be found all in one." In this way, Révay acknowledges not only that he has selected material but hints that at the same time selected passages from other authors will speak for themselves. As we shall see later, this authorial plan can also be traced in the drawing up of the historical examples. It seems as if the author is convinced that his ideas are untenable, as in the following section he analyses the condemnation to be expected from the lawyers and writers of his time. Révay, the Guardian of the Crown, says "... I have no doubt that the legal experts of our country ... will surely laugh at me and find fault..." and adds that the "... legal experts of Hungary will simply call the book superfluous, while those who cannot fill the lamp with oil or have no oil in their lamps will not have even a truism to say on the subject."[71]

By way of defence the author reveals the essence of his conception at the outset: he means to prove on a basis of "historical truth" (*veritas historica*) that the crown

---

68 *Ibid.*. This is probably a humanist modesty-topos, as similar phraseology may also be seen in the introduction to Kristóf Lackhner [Lackner]'s 1615 work on the crown which was written for Demeter Naprágyi. Christophor Lackhner [Lackner], *Coronae Hungariae emblematicae descriptio* (Lavingae Suevorum: Typis Palatini, excudebat M. Iacobus Winter, 1615), *Dedicatoria*, 13–14.

69 De Rewa, *De sacrae coronae regni Hungariae, autor ad lectorem*. (no page number).

70 According to the dedication of this book, Révay's grandfather was one of those who supported the publication of Bonfini. Antonio Bonfini, *Rerum Ungaricarum decades* (Basiliae: Robert Winter, 1543) A2r-A3v.

71 De Rewa, *De sacrae coronae regni Hungariae, autor ad lectorem*.

is "holy, angelic and apostolic" (*sacra, angelica et apostolica*).⁷² He underpins this announcement with a humanist topos: "I therefore wish that this shall be the holy sacrifice for our nation, both for the cultivation of the record of events (*res memoria*) and in order that by combining the present and the past we may be able to take care for our future ..." The future destiny of Hungary depends on knowledge of the past. The struggle for the common good (*bonum publicum*) of the state of Hungary (*respublica Hungarica*) can best be waged if the king and the Estates possess the appropriate virtues (*virtus et prudentia*). In Hungary one can acquire these virtues by studying the record of events – meaning what has happened to the crown – and acting in accordance with the excellence (*virtus*) of the crown.

Révay addresses this political message not only to the Hungarians but also to other parts of Europe, since – in his own words – it is his intention to explain why his nation regards the crown as holy and why they believed in its holiness: "... and at the same time that other nations may understand for what reason we Hungarians proclaim and believe in the holiness of our crown." In conclusion, he declares that the majesty or sovereignty (*maiestas*) of the crown, its holiness or worship (*religio*) provide him with sufficient defence against evil tongues. By that he says, in effect, that the knowledge of the crown that he has acquired will speak for itself. In Révay's opinion, the concise form and content must have sufficient power of conviction to impart his political message to the reader.

Révay does not divide his book into chapters or sections but, with occasional departures from chronological sequence, relates the history of the crown in the order of occurrence of events. In terms of content the work may be divided roughly into three parts. In the first, the author deals with the history of the Medieval kingdom up until 1526. The second part covers the period from the Battle of Mohács in 1526 till the coronation of Mátyás II in 1608. In the final section Révay gives an account of the events of his own time and of the external features of the coronation regalia. The main text is preceded by the title page (mentioned above), an illustration (see image 12), the dedication and the letter to the reader; the latter explains the arrangement of the book and draws together the most important elements of Révay's thought. The illustration serves to present the most significant idea in the book: Providence, through the crown, exerts an influence on the shaping of the destiny of the country.⁷³

In the print the meaning of the crown is expressed as follows: the title reads SACRA, ANGELICA ET APOSTOLICA REGNI HUNGARIAE CORONA (holy, angelic and apostolic crown of the Kingdom of Hungary, (see image 12)). The three

---

72 Ibid.
73 The illustration is an engraving made, to Révay's instructions, by the celebrated Augsburg engraver Wolfgang Kilian. This is shown by two signatures below the print: *D. Pet. Rew.C. T.* and on the right: *Wolfg: Kilian: Aug: sculp:*

qualities of the crown are reflected in the arrangement of the picture, which is divided into three interdependent horizontal bands, separated by strips of clouds. At the top is the sacral (divine) band, characterised by a shaft of light emanating from a cloud and bathing the crown in its rays. In the central, heavenly band the crown is floating between frothy clouds, held by two Baroque angelic figures in female dress. They are small compared to the mighty object in their hands. Thanks to the proportions, the details of the crown can be so clearly made out that even the pictures of the saints and the texts in the enamels can be seen. Below the crown, separated by another strip of clouds, a small, oval shield with the arms of Hungary is depicted in a Baroque frame. This designates the earthly band, and the link with the apostolic meaning. The crown is placed between the earthly and the divine realities, and performs a role of liaison between the two. Below the picture Révay illuminates this concept in Latin elegiac verse:

Nobile caeligeno resplendens lumine sydus / Dignius anne polo! Dignius anne solo: / Fulge sic patriae: ne fati sera potestas / Te caeli rursus cogat adire lares.
(Heavenly star that looks down on us with divine light, art thou more worthy of heaven or of earth? Shine upon my fatherland – may the awesome power of Fate not steal thee away among the spirits of heaven!)

The adjective "holy" in the title of the print connects with the "divine light" in the first line: both terms refer to the divine origin of the crown and its holiness. "Divine light" and the term "heavenly star" emphasise the belief that the jewel descended from heaven. In this way the crown acquires supernatural power or virtue, and this is nothing other than the holiness of the crown. The direct influence which God exercises on the destiny of the country through the crown characterises the link between the Almighty and Hungary. In the picture this is referred to by the rays of light, in the verse by divine light and in the title by the adjectives holy, angelic and apostolic.

In the dedication which follows the illustration Révay illuminates the permanent connection between God, the crown and the Hungarian people by means of a simile. The dedication is addressed to the king and queen and the Hungarian nation, but on closer examination it appears that actually it is rather the Holy Crown that is central to the text. The author lists the virtues and deeds of Mátyás II, but later makes it obvious that all these excellent qualities and actions are attributable to the "aid of almighty God" through the medium of the "holy, ancient and most worshipful crown of Hungary".[74] The connection between God, the crown and the king is also indicated by the font used for the explanatory text: the reference to

---

74 De Rewa, *De sacrae coronae regni Hungariae*, 2*

God is at the top, in the largest type, centred; the words "Crown of Hungary" stand out in somewhat smaller capitals, and at the same time the name of Mátyás II is in discreet capitals at the start of a line.[75] It is evident that the supernatural power of God and the crown is of greater significance to the well-being of Hungary than the person of the king.

From what follows it emerges that the crown has a special connection not only with heavenly beings but also with the Hungarian nation. After a summary of the deeds of Mátyás II and accounts of events leading to the handing over of the crown in 1608 and the coronation of Queen Anna in 1613 there follows a further series of honorific titles of the crown. The series ends: "… the crown is the symbol of the eternal glory of the aristocracy and people of the noble, worthy, courageous, battle-hardened Hungarian nation … ." From this it follows that in the author's view not only the privileged nobility but also the common people are parts of the Hungarian nation. As in Révay's account the significance of the crown is linked to properties that characterise the entire nation, it may be regarded as a factor unifying the Hungarian race. With that premise Révay embarks on his own exposition, in his account of the meaning of the crown also sketching out the features of the people.

After the introduction Révay states the subject. First, he defines the most important political factors in Hungarian history. One after another he deals with the Hungarian people, royal power and the coming into being of the country and the crown. He refers to the Hungarians by the names of *natio, gens Hungaris, populus* and *aborigines Hunni*. The appellation *natio* first occurs in the first section after the introduction, and after that only once more, fifty pages further on.[76] The terms "people" (*populus*) and "descendants of the Huns" (*aborigines Hunni*) occur once each in the text. By *populus* Révay probably means the (common) people, but in this context there is no indication of the possible political meaning of the word. The use of the term *gens*, on the other hand, permeates the whole book, appearing in the collocations *gens Hungarica* and *gens Hungarorum* – Hungarian people and people of Hungarians. Révay describes the Hungarian people as warlike, and gives martial spirit as the Hungarians' most important quality (*virtus*). He therefore calls them a people warlike by temperament or battle-hardened (*natio bellica*).[77] The nation (*natio*) had inherited this characteristic from their ancestors the Huns. It

---

75 See for example the similar form of dedication in Berger's work of 1612. Elias Berger: *Trinubium Europaeum*.
76 '*natio nostra*'. *Ibid.*, 49.
77 *Ibid.*, 1. Révay alternates the terms *natio* and *gens* when speaking of the Hungarians. He begins his exposition with *natio bellica* on the first page, but on the title page has *gens Hungarica*, on the second page *gens*, and on the third page appear both *natio Ungarica* and *gens Ungarorum*. The term *gens* occurs more frequently in the book than does *natio*. It appears that he uses these words as synonyms.

had enabled the pagan Hungarians to win many a battle against the Christians in many parts of Europe and to occupy Pannonia. Révay declares that "... after they began to shout the name of Christ their virtue and courage only increased."[78] After that, to the terror of their foes they defended the Christian community (*respublica Christiana*). In this way the Hungarians gained the titles of "shield of the faith" (*fidei clypeus*), "defending wall of religion" (*religionis murus*) and "unconquered bastion of Christendom" (*propugnaculum Christianorum invictum*). This characterisation of the Hungarians agrees with that of the writers discussed above and is similar to the content of the Szerencs Declaration too. The explanation of the honorific titles is the concept that the calling of the Estates – to defend Christendom from the heathen – is founded on the most important feature of the Hungarians, courage. In the same way as in the works mentioned above, here too this declaration constitutes the point of departure of the writer's argument.

In what follows Révay again comments on the aim of his book: "From the six hundred years that the Kingdom of the Hungarians (*Monarchia Hungarorum*) has been flourishing I gather together ... that which relates to the holy symbol of majesty of the battle-hardened Hungarian nation (*sacrum diadema Ungariae gentis bellicosissimae*), its origin, victories and destiny." That sentence forms the theme (*propositio*) and epitome (*summa*) of his argument, as is made clear by its explanation set in small type in the margin. The passage quoted says in essence that his work is not about the shaping of the destiny of the people but rather the lasting connection, through the crown, between God and the Hungarians in the form of the Estates. As he has done in the dedication, in this statement of intent he lays the emphasis on the sacral meaning of the crown, the character of the Hungarian people and the political constitution of the country. This principal thought of the book lays the firm foundation on which he builds the political independence of Hungary.

Révay returns to this connection in greater detail when he describes the link between the origin of the Christian faith of *natio Ungarica* and the arrival of the crown in Hungary.[79] He declares that Providence turned pagan superstition into Christian faith. He describes the Hungarians as a formerly bellicose people, destructive by inclination and merciless to their opponents. When they were Christianised their hatred of Christendom was changed into mutual goodwill, and from then on, their strength and weapons were used on the Christian side against all kinds of enemies. The whole community of Christian peoples was the stronger for this miracle, as faith in Christ is the foundation of every virtue. The Hungarians' miraculous con-

---

78 *Ibid.*, 1–2.
79 *Ibid.*

version, the coming of the Holy Crown and the coming into being of the fatherland – henceforth a kingdom – (*patria nostra regnum*) likewise sprang from divine truth.

The function of this section is to reveal, by describing the good offices of Providence, what the conversion of the Hungarians means in the grand plan of God's dealings with mankind. In addition, through the changes that he outlines, Révay also shows that God created the character of the people. The sacral character received from God is, at the same time, an element of his detailed argument: constitutionality and the sovereignty of the Estates are based on the fact that the world needs the Hungarians for the calling laid upon them in Christian Europe and which forms part of God's plan.

Révay then deals with the genesis of the Kingdom of Hungary and the origin of the crown. In this he makes use of Berger's account of the formation of the Kingdom, supplementing it with his own ideas on the second conversion of the Hungarians. He plays down to some extent the importance of papal influence on events, and at the same time states that voluntary conversion would not have sufficed for the Hungarians to become Christians.[80] The Hungarians had once been converted in the time of Charlemagne, but because of internal unrest the true faith had been lost and they had slipped back into the former darkness. Only in the time of Prince Géza and his son István did the Christian faith gain a firm footing, in particular through the building of churches and the strengthening of Holy Mother Church in Hungary. The radical transformation of the wild and unruly people (*indominata gens*) was brought about not merely by the piety and steadfastness of the two rulers, says Révay, but first and foremost divine power (*divina potentia*) evoked it. The status of the kingship became firm, its territory grew, and Hungary changed from a principality into a kingdom. Furthermore, it was enriched by a royal coronation jewel (*Regium Diadema*) which, Révay concludes the section, was surely of all marks of majesty the most praiseworthy (*praeclarum*) and most holy (*religiosum*).

By that account Révay justified the form adopted by the Hungarian state. Legitimacy was based on the proviso that the Hungarians could only fulfil their God-given mission if a king ruled over the nation. In proof of this, the Hungarians had once slipped back into paganism after voluntary conversion.

Next, Révay describes the coming of the crown as the miraculous gift of the pope.[81] He says that Pope Benedict VII had originally intended the holy jewel for the Polish Prince Mieceslav. He narrates how the Polish prince had been cured in supernatural fashion of the blindness with which he had been born, had Christianised his country, and freed it from the darkness of paganism. Then – at precisely the same time as Prince István – he had asked the pope in Rome to give him and

---

80   *Ibid.*, 4.
81   *Ibid.*, 5.

his posterity a crown and the title of king. In consequence of divine intervention, the pope sent a diadem, together with a double cross, to the Hungarian prince in the year 1000.

Here the function of the account of the miraculous gift is the same as in the Medieval chronicles: the justification of the rule of the king and the dynasty. Révay, on the other hand, alters the significance of one element, and so of the whole story, by taking a different view of the meaning of the gift of the double cross. In Werbőczy, Berger and Jeszenszky the cross had been the symbol of the lasting link between the Christianity of Hungary and the constitution of the kingdom. Révay omits all reference to this politico-religious meaning and explains the meaning of the symbol quite differently. According to him, the double cross and its destiny is a symbol and portent of the grief to come later in the history of Hungary, as in the course of time the cross itself was lost.[82] He links his own interpretation to Jeszenszky's analysis of the situation of Hungary, quoting a passage from his book in which he names Hungary (*Hungaria*) Land of Wretchedness (*Angaria*). Révay states that the crown did not share the fate of the cross because, despite all the wretchedness it itself miraculously remained for the benefit of the Hungarians. Révay thus erases the cross from the coming history of Hungary. The sacral meaning of the cross in the work of Berger is transferred to the object of the Holy Crown.

Révay ends his account of the emergence of the crown with a summary of the political situation in Hungary and Europe around the year 1000.[83] This Bodin-inspired comparison is not found in Berger. Révay is of the opinion that all the events that took place at once everywhere in Europe were just as miraculous as the birth of the crown and are comparable to the events of his own time. A number of peoples, such as the Poles, the Danes, and all of northern Europe converted to Christianity at that time. Furthermore, Christian constitutions came into being at precisely the same time in three city-states (*politiae*) or realms (*regna*). The Holy Roman Empire developed at that time too. Révay considers that Europe was even better able to withstand enemies as a result of the alliance of these states. After that, he draws a parallel between the coming of the Hungarian crown and of the Holy Roman Empire when he states that the Emperors Otto and Henrik created an institution similar to "our crown", because like the Hungarian king, the emperor of the Empire is elected by his subjects, the Prince Electors, and that country too had flourished for 600 years.

---

82 *Ibid.*, 6. An extra passage about the cross was attached to the book in an eighteenth-century edition of Révay. Petrus de Rewa, "*De sacrae coronae...*," in Schwandtner, *Scriptores rerum Hun. Veteres ac genuini*, Vol. II., 451. See also: 475. (See also next chapter for a detailed account of the additions to the eighteenth century editions.).

83 De Rewa, *De sacrae coronae regni Hungariae*, 6–7.

This section of Révay's discourse emphasises the reason behind contemporary Hungary. Central to his argument is that the history of the Holy Roman Empire and Hungary has been parallel at two periods. He believes that the existence of Hungary has been important from the point of view of European history because the Hungarians have defended the Christian world from the pagan Ottoman menace. He also stresses the independence of Hungary from the Empire by discussing the circumstances of their respective geneses and political characters (elective kingship), and states that these two were able to stand together against the common enemy better because of historical similarities.[84] By showing the events of the year 1000 as a miracle, what Révay has to say about the changes of his own day wins divine justification.

It is noteworthy that, like Berger, Révay also jumps ahead in time after describing the reign of István. By so doing, both writers leave out of consideration events that are important in early Hungarian history and which, in other books, are always mentioned in connection with the crown. The first such is the short life and early death of István's son Imre and the canonisation of them both, while the second is the dedication of the crown to the Virgin Mary, who has from then on been regarded as the patron saint of Hungary. The explanation of the omission of the two stories is that these themes, with which the Catholic Church sought to legitimate its power and its position in the country, played an ever more important role from the 1600s on in counter-Reformation literature.[85] Révay and Berger were more intent on justifying the political agreement of 1608, which in fact restricted the role and power of the Catholic Church in Hungary to the advantage of the Protestant Estates.

In his description of the troubled conditions under the kings that succeeded István I, Révay continues his account from the time of King Péter (1038–1041 and 1044–1046). Almost all the rulers in this period are shown in a bad light. These kings had an adverse effect on the fate of the crown by not respecting the laws and customs which it symbolised. The purpose of the historical examples adduced is to paint a general picture of the evil doings of the bad rulers, in which Révay's moral teaching holds that a bad ruler is one that does not respect the crown, and is thus detrimental to the well-being of the nation. Although he takes some of his examples from Berger, Révay discusses them in greater detail and transmits his moral message more emphatically.

---

84 Sándor Bene, "A történeti kommunikációelmélet alkalmazása a magyar politikai eszmetörténetben- A kora újkori modell [The use of the historic communication theory in the Hungarian history of political ideas – The Early Modern model]," *Irodalomtörténeti Közlemények* 105 (2001) 301–302.
85 In connection with the Mária-topos see: Tüskés and Knapp, "Magyarország – Mária országa," 573–602.

He begins the description of this period by speaking of the destiny (*fortuna*) of the crown. In the young kingdom, destiny put the symbol of majesty to the test even in its cradle. This he shows by reference to the events in which the pretender Aba stole the crown and drove Péter, the descendant of István I, from the kingdom. The exiled king turned to the Holy Roman Emperor Henry III to regain the crown. The emperor heard his plea, invaded Hungary with an armed force and took the crown. Instead of keeping it himself, however, he gave it back to Péter and put him on the throne.

In addition to illustrating the sins of the kings, these examples also serve to express the independence of the Kingdom of Hungary from the Austrian emperor. Révay's moral is that a good emperor honours the sovereignty of the kingdom by showing respect for the legitimate king of Hungary. A bad emperor does not do that, and therefore God punishes him. Révay thus suggests that the significance of the Hungarian crown is greater than the power of the Austrian emperor. As, in his fiction about the cross, Berger made the verdict on the Habsburg emperor's actions dependent on his rule in Hungary, so Révay too yokes together the destinies of the Austrian ruler and the crown, or the respect shown for the sovereignty of the Kingdom.

Révay therefore begins the next example with a positive opinion of the Holy Roman Emperor Henry III because of the proper respect that he showed for the crown. The emperor "... deserved unfading memory and praise because he preserved the dignity of the Holy Crown ...".[86] This included, in Révay's view, putting the lawful king back on the throne and leaving the Kingdom unharmed. He takes issue with the writers who state that Hungary became a vassal of the Holy Roman Empire, made to pay tax by the emperor. In his eyes, respect for the heavenly (*caelesteis*) and holy (*sacrosanctus*) nature of the crown dictated Henry's actions; these qualities were not, in his words, to be harmed by deceit or weapons.[87] This explanation acts as an example of the virtues desirable in a ruler, as is evidenced by the tale about King Péter, who lost not only the realm but also his life through the violence of the later András I. The fate of the latter, in Révay's opinion, is a warning to other kings. He therefore closes this section on the virtues of princes with a message: "... it is fitting that all those that sit at the government of countries and affairs of state ... use the power granted them by the Godhead moderately, do nothing arrogantly, nothing unworthily, nothing thoughtlessly, nothing violently, and should fear God, who shows no mercy to the sinful."[88]

---

86 De Rewa, *De sacrae coronae regni Hungariae*, 2.
87 *Ibid.*, 9.
88 *Ibid.*

In the following example Révay admonishes the emperor, alluding to the bad name that he acquired when he again invaded Hungary and tried to drive out András I and to steal the crown. András successfully opposed the imperial forces. In Révay's view "... the king defeated the emperor by nothing more than fear of the innocent and the holiness of the crown ...". This defence of the king and Hungary he calls the victory (*victoria*) of the crown. The crown had defended the king who showed respect for the holy nature of the symbol of majesty, and punished the person who had offended against its holiness.

Révay makes use of the notion of the victory of the crown again to emphasise the independence and integrity of Hungary. Any that offend against the king, the crown or the country are punished by God through the crown. He explains the punishment of the crown with the aid of the following example. In keeping with the ideas expressed in Justus Lipsius's *De Constantia* (On Constancy, 1584), for offence against the holy nature of the crown retribution is exacted with divine approval under the "law of compensation in kind" (*lex talionis divinitus rata*).[89] Révay illustrates this retribution with an anecdote about András. András challenged Béla to choose between a crown symbolising royal power and the sword denoting princely power. Béla chose the sword, but shortly afterwards his father-in-law Boleslaw, king of Poland, stole the crown and took possession of the country. Révay declares that there is something to be learnt from the fates of Kings Péter, András I and Béla: "... it is an irrefutable law that a sin is immediately punished by the same sin ...". Anyone that with the assistance of aliens steals the crown and dethrones the lawful king shall end his life in the same way as a victim. Révay draws from the occurrence the moral lesson that the response to the king's sin is the punishment of the Holy Crown (*vindicta sacrae coronae*).

In Révay's eyes, the thought of retribution (*vindicta*) coming from the crown was a further sign that God directly influences the destiny of king and country. Because of its supernatural character this retribution was above all earthly laws: even if his

---

89 Justus Lipsius, *De constantia libri dvo* (Antverpiae: C. Plantini, 1584) First book, part X. On Lipsius and Révay, see: Anna Vargha, Iustius Lipsius és a magyar szellemi élet [Justus Lipsius and the Hungarian spiritual life] (Budapest: Dunántúl Nyomda, 1942). Martinus Schödel compares the ideas of Lipsius and Révay on this subject: Martinus Schödel, *Cum Deo. Disquisitio Historico-Politica, De Regno Hungariae...* (Argentorati: Johannis Rippl, 1629, 1630) A4v, K1v.-K2r., L4v.-M1r. Schödel's work is the best source for the connection between the ideas of Révay and Lipsius, because he indicates precisely from where Révay took Lipsius' ideas. Kees Teszelszky, "Révay Péter és Justus Lipsius eszméi a történelemről és a nemzeti identitásról [The ideas of Péter Révay and Justus Lipsius on history and national identity]," in István Bitskey and Gábor Fazekas, eds., *Humanizmus, religio, identitástudat (Tanulmányok a kora újkori Magyarország művelődéstörténetéről)* [Humanism, religion and identity consciousness (Studies on the Early Modern cultural history of Hungary] (Studia Litteraria, vol. XLV.) (Debrecen: Debreceni Egyetem / Magyar és Összehasonlító Irodalomtudományi Intézet, 2007) 106–113.

subjects believe a king to be a lawful ruler, God can take the crown from him, or oust him from the throne by means of another pretender. Révay shows the workings of divine vengeance by the description of an eleventhcentury event. After the death of Péter, Salamon was regarded as the lawful king but was punished for his sins by the secret will of God.[90] His sin was in fact that he had attacked his fatherland (*patria*) at the head of a foreign army and taken the crown for himself with the assistance of the Austrian emperor. Révay regards it as a sign of the imminent punishment of the wicked king that after the coronation of the lawfully elected King Salamon, the cathedral of Pécs burned to the ground. He states that this event was without doubt connected to the fact that Salamon had offended against the crown by the shedding of his brother's blood, the civil war and his unbridled lust for power. Not long afterwards Salamon was defeated by his brother Géza, into whose hands the crown passed. The reading public of Révay's time was quick to see the parallel between the above (and following) account of the rule of Salamon and Géza and the dispute between the brothers Rudolf and Matthias. Like Salamon, Rudolf too attacked his native land with foreign troops, civil war broke out, and in the opinion of the Hungarian Estates offence was given to the crown.

After listing the sins of Hungarian kings and Austrian emperors, Révay paints the picture of the good and virtuous king, taking as his example (*exemplum*) the rules of Géza and St László. In the legends of their lives, attention is drawn to their heroic deeds, but Révay focuses rather on how they governed Hungary. As, in his view, the deeds of both of them that were connected to the crown display certain resemblances to those performed by Mátyás II, Révay informs the reader of the actions of the earlier rulers in which the virtues expected of Mátyás II are revealed. This connection comes to the fore most clearly in the third section of his book. The first and second sections, therefore, serve as an introduction to the discussion of the rule of Mátyás II and the exhortations that Révay addresses to him and the Estates.

This part of the book opens with the statement that the arrival of the good king is preceded by a sign from God. Géza "… gained the kingdom not only by this fortunate victory but by a miracle and a heavenly prophecy too …".[91] Heavenly angels appeared in a vision to Géza's brother László and placed the crown on Géza's head. This miraculous event is, to Révay, the most reliable argument for the lasting connection between the kingdoms of heaven and earth, to which expression is given through the crown. In his opinion the event shows that because of the holiness of the crown there is a link between heavenly Providence (*caelestis providentia*), the piety of the king (*pietas regis*), and the happiness of the country (*felicitas regni*).

---

90 De Rewa, *De sacrae coronae regni Hungariae*, 14.
91 *Ibid.*

Révay explains this link to the reader by saying that it shows Géza and László to be exemplary Hungarian kings. They honoured the holiness of the crown and so brought happiness to their country. Thus, Géza was able to pacify the realm, acquiring the style of Great (*magnus*). His successor, László, answered even more fully to the picture of the outstanding king, and therefore receives from Révay the description of "God's favourite". He had every virtue that a king requires. Révay writes that "... so rare were László's piety and peerless modesty, he merits great praise in the eyes of posterity."[92]

Révay illustrates László's piety and "peerless modesty" (*singularis modestia*) in a list of his numerous deeds. His peerless modesty was displayed immediately on his election as king. The election took place by general consensus and a unanimous vote (*communi consensu atque voto res declaratur*), but László "... for a long time steadfastly refused this dignity, and would not tolerate that his head should be adorned with the holy symbol of majesty while Salamon lived."[93] Later, however, since the Hungarian nobility, embittered against Salamon, begged him to rule the country he consented to govern with the title of prince. Révay explains that this modesty meant that László was of the opinion that "the fullness of royal worth lay not in the throne but in excellent and praiseworthy acts."[94] This description may also be relevant to the beginning of the reign of Mátyás II, as he too was first governor and only later was elected king.

Among László's prime virtues Révay lists his humility towards the crown. This king "... cherished and worshipped the crown with full reverence and godliness ..." and "... took the sceptre most responsibly ..."[95] Through his merits László won the support of Providence and brought happiness to Hungary. Révay points to László's virtues by describing his constant hostility to Salamon, the banished king. In this example one can perceive the fraternal strife that broke out between the Habsburgs, which ended only with the death of Rudolf in 1612. In the following section another comparison of László and Mátyás II is made. When László realised that the exiled Salamon was causing disquiet in the country, attacking with foreign troops and taking advantage of his benevolence and moderation, he decided to oppose him. Révay stresses that László was spurred on to this action not by concern for his own well-being but by the responsibility that he felt for the fate of the nation and the fatherland. Finally, László achieved victory over Salamon, ended the civil war with a peace agreement, and gained all of Dalmatia and Croatia "for the crown and the

---

92 *Ibid.*
93 *Ibid.*, 15.
94 *Ibid.* This thought recurs in Révay's will. See: Petrus De Rewa, "Valedictio Morituri," in Hrabecius, D. O. M. A. *Oratio Funebris*, K.
95 De Rewa, *De sacrae coronae regni Hungariae*, 15.

Hungarian realm" without shedding a drop of blood.[96] It is also Révay's intention in displaying the ideal king to justify Archduke Matthias' assumption of power, and later in his exposition he similarly evaluates the peaceful nature of this, together with the deeds that he performed for the good of the Estates and the fatherland.

After this account of the rule of the ideal kings there follows a description of more lawless governance. This provides Révay with the opportunity to express a theory about what happened to the crown and the nation in a time of political unrest. He makes use of the notion of the sufferings of the crown which he takes from Berger, and depicts an undesirable condition in which a lawless king torments the crown. The cause of the sufferings is the neglect of the worship of the crown (*cultus sacrae coronae*), as the wicked kings that succeeded László did not hold in honour the political morals for which the crown stood. Révay states that the greatest crime of these kings was tyranny, accompanied by a variety of deceitful acts. The undermining of public morals (the sufferings of the crown) resulting from the king's wrongdoing damaged the public good (*publicum bonum*), and led to the collapse of the harmony which had prevailed in the country. Révay believes that the fate of the crown in this situation is like that of a ship on a storm-tossed sea.

Up to this point Révay has been describing the crown as an object of supernatural significance. From now on he presents it as an active person as Berger too did in his epic. Révay sets the personified crown before the public as the rescuer of the fatherland. He explains the concept of salvation by the expression of a lasting bond between the nation (*gens*) and the worship (*cultus*) and majesty (*maiestas* – here in the sense of sovereignty) of the crown. He characterises the bad king as a ruler who harms the public good (*bonum publicum*). But "… no one should fear that wicked kings will bring shame on the community because by its majesty the crown will preserve the liberty of the nation [*libertas gentis*] from ruin".[97] This protection means that as long as the nation nurtures the worship of the crown, the majesty of the crown will protect the nation. From this it follows that at all times the majesty of the crown rules over the nation. If the nation willingly submits to the rights and morals for which the crown stands, peace and order will return to Hungary, the country will be free from hostile attack and acquire protection, while its bounds will increase. Furthermore, it means that the crown "… has by its holiness and majesty defeated or restrained hostile nations."[98]

The function of the concept of the majesty of the crown is to justify the idea of the unimpaired liberty of the nation. Révay presents the power exerted by the crown over the Hungarian people by means of the concept of majesty. This concept,

---

96 *Ibid.*, 16.
97 *Ibid.*, 17.
98 *Ibid.*

at the same time, also involves the nation being capable of governing itself, because the majesty of the Crown means that the people is able, through the cultivation of the cultus of the Holy Crown, to defend its own unimpaired liberty against the governance of a bad king. Since the cultus of the crown means that the people and the king alike must obey the laws and regulations which God has given them through the crown, it follows that the Hungarian people is independent of the king within the limits of the political moral system imposed by the crown. From the fact, however, that Révay bases this moral system on historical examples it follows that through the concept of the majesty of the crown he regards the Hungarian nation as to a certain extent independent.

Building on this idea, Révay creates a theory of the sovereignty of the Estates, which he validates through a fiction of the Holy Crown. Since his thoughts are based on certain characteristics of the Hungarian people, he makes use of the identity of the Hungarians to justify his political views. Consequently, he demonstrates the correctness of his Early Modern thinking on the sovereignty of the Estates by bringing in the identity of the Hungarian people. In this way the function of the identity of the nation is used to justify the notion of the sovereignty of the Estates. The meaning of the crown defines the principles which decide whether or not a king is a legitimate ruler. If a lawless king is governing the nation the Estates have, to a certain extent, the right of sovereignty.

By linking the notion of the majesty of the crown to a personified object, Révay gives the crown the leading role in Hungarian history. This is why, in the following section, he pays greater attention to things that happen to the crown, such as the repeated thefts of it. At the same time, he makes a distinction between the *diadema* (the crown as an object), the *insigne regium* (the crown as the symbol of royal power) and the Holy Crown (*sacra corona*, the crown in the sense of a supernatural power, linked to the notion of the sovereignty of the Estates). As Guardian of the Crown, he explains the difference between these terms in a series of accounts of disturbances in the reign of István III (1162–1172).[99] While István was leading an army against Dalmatia his brother László, with the help of a few disgruntled nobles, stole the crown, as he thought that in this way, he would easily win the country and be crowned king. Révay declares that the lawful king must have sober judgement and statesmanly wisdom (*prudentia*).[100]

In this he is unmistakably drawing a parallel between past and present events. István III gave way to his brother's madness and, like an experienced sailor, waited for the storm to subside. God, who raises kings to the throne and preserves the crown, did not allow this crime to go unpunished. The criminal came to a bad end,

---

99 *Ibid.*
100 *Ibid.*, 18.

but the crown once more went into the hands of a wicked king and the misfortunes of the lawful king began again. At this point Révay quotes Seneca, who wrote that God puts good men to the test.[101] Révay explains these problems by saying that "God shows no mercy to kings and to those of the highest dignity lest they attribute too much to their good fortune, wealth and power, and become conceited."[102] In the end good prevailed and István recovered the symbols of royalty (*insignia regia*), which can, however, only have happened with the aid of the Holy Crown, through the supernatural power of which God defends the ruler who is gentle, pious and just, and cares for the well-being of his subjects.

The role of these moral tales is connected to the political theory outlined above concerning the sovereignty of the Estates. Révay next produces a series of examples, the task of which is to render more authentic the political theories mentioned earlier. From these it is clear that the legitimacy of the king's reign is linked to the respect that he evinces for the moral system for which the crown stands. Since rights of liberty are bound to this moral system, once more Révay is legitimating only the political ambitions of the nation and the constitution of 1608.

Next Révay, following Bodin, compares the meaning of the Hungarian coronation jewel with that of the symbols of majesty of other European imperial and royal powers. He brings out the differences between the Hungarian and Imperial crowns by reference to the parts played by the two crowns in struggles for the throne in the realms. The dispute between brothers in Hungary took place in the time of King Imre (1196–1204).[103] Imre's younger brother, Prince András, wanted the throne himself. When the two brothers' armies were standing face to face, the lawful king laid aside his weapons and confronted the enemy in full royal splendour, the Holy Crown on his head and the sceptre in his hand. Révay tells us that so affected were the prince and his men by this sight that they craved forgiveness and laid down their arms.

Révay compares this incident with one that occurred in the Austrian imperial court, when Henry V took power from his father, Henry IV. As the emperor sat on the throne his son's emissaries rushed upon him, suddenly snatched the crown from him and tore the sceptre from his hand, then clothed his son with imperial power. Révay uses this occurrence to compare the majesty of the emperor and the Hungarian king. His view is that the Hungarian András evinced greater respect for royal majesty than did Henry V for that of the emperor.[104] The reason for the difference, in Révay's opinion, is that the Hungarian king is regarded as "sacrosanct and inviolable" (*sacrosanctus ac inviolatus*), since his majesty is derived from "our

---

101 *Ibid.* See: Lucius Annaeus Seneca, *De Providentia*.
102 De Rewa, *De sacrae coronae regni Hungariae*, 18.
103 *Ibid.*, 19.
104 *Ibid.*, 20.

Hungarian crown" (*corona nostra*) and its cultus.¹⁰⁵ He quotes from Bonfini the words of the palatine of Hungary, Mihály Guti Ország: "Even were he a dumb wild animal, the king that has been crowned with the holy symbol of majesty cannot be wronged without the committal of grievous sin."¹⁰⁶

By the two differences in meaning between the crowns outlined here Révay means to support his own political theory. In his view kings of Hungary are not omnipotent, but derive their sovereignty from the holiness of the crown. Whether they can retain their royal power depends on whether they nurture the cultus of the crown. As he has already in a previous section asserted that the sovereignty of the Estates too, is rooted in this cultus, he is at the same time proving the validity of his conception of the political rights of the Estates.

Révay continues an argument similar to that used in the previous examples when discussing the legitimacy of the power of the Holy Roman Emperor. He states that in the Roman Empire the crown had no function, and that the emperor took his power as ruler from the title Augustus. He quotes Flavius Vegetius Renatus, who said that after the emperor assumed that title, he had to be shown obedience as a divine being. This quotation also shows that the Hungarian crown is independent and special. By these tales he embarks on a new topic which resembles the idea that Berger formulated in his work on the cross – discussed above – that the Hungarian crown is the most important token of the divine legitimation assuring Habsburg imperial power.

A brief review of the titles and crowns of the king justifies Révay's earlier-stated thesis of the sovereignty of the Estates. If the meaning of the crown has its greatest significance from the point of view of the divine legitimation assuring the power of the Habsburg emperor, and if therefore the emperor's power depends on the way in which he governs Hungary, that means that through the political significance linked to the cultus of the crown the Estates have a certain degree of sovereignty. Révay defends the rights of the Estates through the image of the crown as Berger did with the fiction of the cross.

Révay reviews the failings of the people and discusses the limitations of the sovereignty of the Estates. He states that the sovereignty of the crown can turn against its own people, since offence against the majesty of the crown can only be purged by the destruction of the entire people. The failings of subjects and ruler combined have caused offence to the majesty of the crown. Ambition, in his view,

---

105 "... à Religione fortisan & veneratione Coronae nostrae, à qua Regem Maiestatem suam accipere ab illa sacro sanctum ac inviolatum habire credimus." *Ibid.*

106 "… coronatum sacro Diademate Regem, vel si bellua foret, nunquam sine magno laedi posse scelere." *Ibid.*, 20–21. Révay incorrectly attributed this to Miklós Garai in Bonfini. See: Bonfini, *Rerum Ungaricarum decades*, decadis IV, liber III, 564.

is what poisons or infects society, because it turns one against the other people who are by nature born to support each other but allow the desire for power to lead them and are careless of the "dignity of the holiness of the crown" (*religio huius Coronae auctoritas*).

In the following section, Révay turns to the sharing of power between crown, king and subjects. The reign of András II (1205–1235), which followed a period of unrest, serves as the starting-point for the enquiry. According to Révay, this king ruled well and justly, and gained a reputation for his constant endeavours in the recovery of the Holy Land and Jerusalem.[107] His virtues were also in evidence in his respect for the crown, and this Révay illustrates with the description of a ceremony. "András II, fully armed and surrounded by sounding trumpets and hosts in battle order begged pardon of the crown for the evil deeds of his predecessors."[108] The account of András' deeds and virtues introduces his important decision as ruler, which, according to Révay, was likewise inspired by his respect for the crown. The king published an edict or constitution (*Axioma Regia*), which the country immediately accepted by acclaim. By means of this András II, as Révay puts it, "… perpetuated the freedom of Hungary and bestowed great privileges on the nobility, which, by the custom of the land, every king of Hungary has sworn to maintain."[109] By "constitution" Révay means the Golden Bull (*Aurea Bulla*) promulgated by King András II in 1222, in which are stipulated the rights and liberties of the Estates, including the right of opposition to a king who rules in lawless fashion.[110] Werbőczy refers in a number of places to this section of the Golden Bull, and we also find it mentioned in other legal texts. In addition, the appendix on the right of opposition to a bad king was one of the arguments with which Bocskai justified the rightfulness of the rebellion.[111]

The swearing to the Golden Bull was part of the coronation ceremony, and stood for the compromise that had been achieved between the political demands of the Estates and those of the king. In the order of the ceremony the content of the oath rendered legitimate the king's power and the rights of the Estates. András II actually issued the Bull on the insistence of the nobility, and in its introductory text the origin of the rights of the nobility is taken back to the reign of the first king of Hungary.[112] Révay does not mention these historical facts at all, and not

---

107 *Ibid*. András II also bore the title of "King of Jerusalem".
108 *Ibid*., 25–26.
109 *Ibid*., 25–26.
110 Hóman and Szekfű, *Magyar történet*, vol. I., 491–497.
111 Benda, "Habsburg-politika és rendi ellenállás" 425; Benda, "Le droit de résistance de la bulle d'or hongroise et le Calvinisme," 155–161; Teszelszky and Zászkaliczky, "A Bocskai-felkelés," 149–121; Zászkaliczky, "The language of liberty," 274–295.
112 Hóman and Szekfű, *Magyar történet*, vol. I, 492. See also the admonitions of St István, IV.

without reason. By showing the issue of the Golden Bull as the product of the king's honouring of the crown Révay makes the event appear to be the confirmation by God himself of the rights of the nobility. He justifies the notion of the freedom of Hungary not through the person of a holy king (St István) – as happened in the Golden Bull – but in accordance with his own notion of the holiness of the crown. In this way the notion of the freedom of Hungary becomes the equivalent of the liberties of the Estates and the meaning of the Holy Crown legitimates the concept.

The purpose of the detailed account is for Révay to create a link between the events of 1222 and 1608. This link is based on the agreement between the Estates and the king which reflects the political compromise, in which the king confirmed the rights of the Estates and the constitution defining his own powers as ruler. Révay portrays the crown as the key binding together events which happened in the past and in his own time, and the vindication of the political compromise struck between the king and the Estates. In his view, respect for the crown prompted the agreements reached in 1222 and 1608 between the king and the Estates, and the heavenly host thereby consecrated them. At the same time, by referring to the Golden Bull, which spelled out the freedoms of the nation (*gens*), he also provides a historical basis for the notion of the sovereignty of the Estates.

In what follows, Révay discusses the significance of these ideas for Europe and Christendom. This he does through an account of the victory of the crown, the basis of which is likewise the depiction of the personified symbol of majesty. As starting point of the topic, he takes the events of 1241–1242, when the Mongols invaded Hungary in the reign of Béla IV (1235–1270).

Révay considers it a miracle that the crown remained unharmed amid the battles, and attributes that to divine protection. He states that the crown may surely be called the apostolic crown (*apostolica corona*) because it alone could withstand the savage pagan Mongols in the manner and following the example of the apostles.[113] The crown won victory, and "… when the Godhead drove off the barbarians, putting them to flight, the triumphant crown acquired a glittering military glory."[114] Révay displays the crown as a symbol of victory over the Mongols – a role similar to that of the cross in Berger's work. The account of the Mongol invasion and the image of the triumphant crown seem the least convincing part of the narrative about the crown. Révay sheds no light on the part played by the crown in these events, which is no surprise, as it is not mentioned in the chronicles of the period.[115] In his account of the struggle against the Mongols he links the Hungarian crown to the notion of the

---

113 De Rewa, *De sacrae coronae regni Hungariae*, 24.
114 *Ibid.*
115 The crown is not mentioned, for example, in Master Rogerius' *Carmen Miserabile super Destructione Regni Hungariae per Tartaros* (Mournful song for the destruction of the Kingdom of Hungary by the Tartars) László Juhász, ed., "Carmen Miserabile super Destructione Regni Hungariae per

apostolic crown and the triumphant crown. He uses the most inflated expressions and bombastic vocabulary possible to conceal that the historical basis for these two lofty titles that glorify the wondrous steadfastness of the crown in the midst of the onslaught of the plundering barbarian hordes is limited in the extreme.

In mentioning the apostolic crown and the triumphant crown, Révay is voicing his views of the struggle against the pagan marauders of his own time, the Turks. By using the terms apostolic and triumphant he shows the crown to his own contemporaries as the sign of the Hungarian people's war against the Turks and the symbol of the divine aid which the nation had received through it (to be precise, the apostolic crown), and in which, with the aid of this supernatural power – i. e. the victorious crown – it would finally win victory over the heathen.

In the section following the Mongol invasion Révay returns to the political meaning of the crown in Hungarian circles. With an account of the influence exerted on the crown by the struggles for the throne between Károly Róbert of the House of Anjou and the Czech Vencel, he once more turns to the analysis of the connection between the notion of Hungarian liberty and the significance of the crown. In his opinion the most important consequence of the war was that "the crown had to suffer again", and – just as may be seen in previous chapters – now too, it was rising disquiet in Hungary t hat caused the suffering.[116] For the description of the events he made use of the work of Berger, who described the wanderings of the crown in an identical manner, and like him saw the principal reason for the absence of the crown in internal tension within the Estates. The parallel is not only taken from Berger's work, as we may regard it as an unmistakable allusion to the fraternal strife between Archduke Matthias and Rudolf and to current political conflicts of the time.

In what follows Révay describes the sufferings of the crown. Boniface VIII recommended Károly Róbert as king to the Hungarians, but they wanted nothing to do with the pretender. Despite the pope's wishes they elected Vencel king. Révay explains this reluctance to obey the pope as the Hungarians right to elect the king freely. He writes that "so unbreakable were the cords that bound Hungarian love of liberty to respect for the Hungarian crown that because of them the kindness of Benedict VII was forgotten."[117] Under the heading of kindness Révay understands the presentation of the crown. He informs us that the first time in history that the crown left Hungary it was as the result of disagreement among the Hungarians. They then received a letter of excommunication from the pope. After the coronation of the elected king, Vencel, his father did not return the crown to the Hungarians

---

Tartaros," in Imre Szentpetery, ed., Scriptores rerum Hungaricarum tempore ducum regumque stirpis Arpadianae gestarum, Vol. II. (Budapest: Academia Litterarum Hungarica, 1938) 511–588.
116 De Rewa, *De sacrae coronae regni Hungariae*, 25–26.
117 *Ibid.*, 26.

but took it away to Bohemia. According to Révay, he did this "… in order to test whether it was true that where the crown was, that was the Kingdom of Hungary."[118] As claimed by Révay, this was the first "journey of the Crown", and thus it fell into the hands of foreigners.

Next, like Berger, Révay recounts the well-known miraculous event, also to be found in the already-mentioned Illustrated Chronicle (*Képes Krónika*), when the crown was lost on the highway.[119] A striking difference is to be noted between the text of the chronicle and Révay's account. When Révay used a Medieval legend or excerpt from a chronicle he generally enhanced the role of the crown in the story in line with his own ideas. In this case, however, following Berger, he takes over certain details from the chronicle while omitting the previously quoted text about the crown, angels and Pannonia. What is more, his explanation of the event differs altogether from that in the chronicle and in Berger. The reason for this is that now miracles have a different role. The author of the fourteenth-century Illustrated Chronicle made use of the meaning of the Holy Crown to undermine Otto's ambitions for power and legitimated Károly Róbert's situation by supernatural means. The account of this event in Révay's book serves as justification of the notion that had been formed of agreement inside Hungary. He states that Providence makes use of "Otto's crime" (the loss of the crown) to create harmony (*concordia*) in the fatherland (*patria*).[120] From this it follows that within Hungary the crown is also the symbol of harmony. This last interpretation does not even appear in Berger's work. The thought of a connection between the crown and domestic harmony appears in detail in the account of the reigns of King Károly Róbert and his son Lajos. These kings protected the crown from indifference and discord. The respect which the king showed to the crown and the harmony that had grown up in Hungary once more resulted in the victory of the crown, as the king succeeded in re-establishing the broken links with the Polish king and the Austrian emperor. Through this victory – according to Révay – he ruled over an extraordinarily large kingdom. Révay lists nine countries that paid taxes to the crown: Dalmatia, Croatia, Rama [Prozor-Rama, part of Bosnia and Herzegovina], Serbia, Holics [Galicia], Lodomeria, Cumania, Bulgaria and Hungary.[121] That is the list of those countries which, according to Révay, comprise the crown in the territorial sense, of which more later. The judicial system of Hungary too was consolidated, another important element of the victory of the crown. He also tells us that it can be attributed to the good fortune of the crown that at this time French court procedure was introduced in Hungary. The victory of the crown continued in the reign of Lajos too. Révay borrows from Berger

---

118 (…) *quodque ubicunq; Coronam, ibi & Regnum Hungariae esse* (…). Ibid., 27.
119 Ibid., 28.
120 Ibid., 29.
121 Ibid., 30.

the image of "… the crown resting awhile and breathing freely …", as if the crown is a living being.[122] He says that with this new interpretation of the victory of the crown, respect for it, harmony in Hungary, territorial integrity and a stable judicial system are mutually connected.

In the next section Révay analyses his concept of the internal unity in Hungary and the whole European Christian community with an account of the wars in Europe between Christians and Turks.[123] In his eyes the Ottomans are the new enemies of Europe. This is an allusion to the struggle against the ancient enemies of the continent; to the wars mentioned at the start of the book, which Europe waged against the pagans, among whom the Hungarians too had once been. He sees that even the Ottomans had their place in God's plan. He explains their success in breaking into Europe and the first loss inflicted by them on the Hungarians by saying that both in Hungary and in the European Christian community there was a lack of harmony. Unrest broke out among the Hungarian aristocracy after the death of Lajos the Great (1342–1382); this led to fighting between sundry pretenders which grew into civil war. This ended when Queen Mária married (1385) and passed her power to her husband, Zsigmond (1387–1437), son of the Holy Roman Emperor Charles IV, who brought the country to order. Révay cannot decide whether it was glory or shame that alighted on the crown during this king's reign. He put an end to the domestic unrest, but twice suffered defeat by the Ottomans in Bulgaria. The cause of this was the quarrelsomeness (*discordia*) and frivolity (*levitas*) of the French. In this fighting against the Ottomans the crown was involved for the first time, while the king, by the grace of God and thanks to the assistance of the Holy Crown, left the field of battle alive. According to Révay, the Hungarians' first war with the Turks resulted in the fall of the Byzantine Empire. This was, however, in part the doing of the Ottomans.

Révay is drawing a parallel with his own time, and sending a current political message in his analysis. This is meant for the Bocskai faction and its followers, allied to the Ottomans. We can take what Révay says as a response to Bocatius's account of the Turkish coronation (and Bocskai's words), the content of which was addressed to the Austrian emperor and his Hungarian followers. As Révay was one of the aristocrats of the king's party, it is highly likely that he was familiar with Bocatius' work *Relatio*, in which the Grand Vizier's speech is cited: he pilloried the unreliable Austrians and their emperor, and promised the Hungarians (*gens Hungarica*) that their ancient liberties (*libertas sua antiqua*) would be restored, and he foretold the improvement of the fate of the Kingdom and crown of Hungary

---

122 *Ibid.*
123 *Ibid.*, 31–32.

(*regnum et corona Hungarorum*), for which the nation would have the renewed bonds between themselves and the Ottomans to thank.[124]

Révay disagrees with Bocatius (and Bocskai) as to the outcome of alliance with the pagan Ottomans, and over bad feeling among the Christians. In the section on the fall of the Byzantine Empire, therefore, topics from the Grand Vizier's speech are raised again: loyalty, freedom and good fortune. Révay takes the fall of the empire back to two causes: quarrelling among the Greeks and their fatal alliance to the Turks.[125] He writes that this Christian people called on the Ottomans for help during the civil war because they thought that "… there is more loyalty in the pagan nation than in the Christian." The outcome of the alliance was complete ruin and the loss of freedom. "Thus even the memory of the once flourishing Empire was all but lost."[126] Révay then turns straight to the Bocskai faithful with the observation that the fall of the Byzantine Empire "… served as a forewarning or rather example to all those who perfidiously seek refuge beneath the alluring protection of the Turk, driving their fatherland into the most abject servitude."[127]

Révay's opinion is that the Ottomans will only be defeated if harmony prevails among the Christian alliance.[128] The Holy Alliance (*unio christiana*) against the Ottomans was devised by Aeneas Sylvius Piccolomini, the later Pope Pius II.[129] On this occasion Révay attaches to the crown the unity of Christendom and the metaphor of Hungary as a bastion of Christendom. In his opinion, unity is the will of God, and victory over the pagans His most important stipulation. He therefore hopes that Mátyás II, as emperor, will, with the aid of Christian Europe, defeat the Ottomans. He expresses this hope in the section on the reign of Zsigmond, in which he adumbrates the political situation of his own time. Révay describes how Zsigmond was the first to bring the imperial crown to Hungary. He joined the prestige (*maiestates*) of imperial dignity to the divine nature of the Holy Crown, which was a sign from God that promised great good fortune. God wished that the Hungarians should oppose the ancient enemy of Christendom and through this sign be able to trust even more surely in the assistance of the Christian princes.[130] Since Mátyás II had himself crowned as emperor in 1612, in this section Révay is expressing the hope that the Hungarians will once more receive support from Christian Europe in their war against the Ottomans.

---

124 Bocatius, "Relatio vel epistolica commemoratio," 100–101.
125 De Rewa, *De sacrae coronae regni Hungariae*, 33.
126 *Ibid.*
127 *Ibid.*, 33–34.
128 *Ibid.*, 34.
129 Imre, "Szenci Molnár Albert "Idea Christianorum"-a," 241.
130 De Rewa, *De sacrae coronae regni Hungariae*, 34.

After the interlude on agreement in the Christian world, Révay returns to the question of unrest in Hungary and the discussion of the part played by the crown. Because of renewed difficulties over the crown Zsigmond's reign was followed by another disturbed period. At the request of the Hungarian aristocracy the Austrian Archduke Albert governed the country. As regent, he was not crowned, because the widowed queen Mária, assisted by a lady of her court, had stolen the crown.[131] Albert died shortly afterwards, and Mária had her four-month-old son crowned with the stolen crown. Then she handed over the crown, together with her child, to Emperor Friedrich – thus it travelled abroad for a second time. The account of this incident in Berger's work has been referred to above.

Révay believes that the cause of the unrest among the Hungarians can be traced to this incident. In his view the theft of the crown – an offence against the divine symbol of royal majesty (*divinum Regiae Maiestatis insigne*) – constitutes sacrilege. He believes that the loss of the symbol of majesty brought about recklessness and negligence in the Hungarians.[132] As the result of the absence of the crown hatred took root in the character of the Hungarian people. This was the source of division (*dissidia*) and discord, and led to civil war.

Révay feels that wretchedness is the distinguishing feature of this period when the crown was kept outside of Hungary.[133] He speaks of King Ulászló, who had himself crowned with an item taken from St István's reliquary as the proper crown was in the emperor's hands. This coronation, he feels, was "… contrary to nature, uncustomary and unfortunate, or rather, such as was the condition of Hungary: unhappy, marred by hatred, factionism, the wrangling of contenders for the throne and accursed campaigning."[134] In his opinion, the country and the king had to be punished for the offence to the crown, and for that reason the king himself fell victim to the absence of the crown at the battle of Varna against the Turks in 1444. Then his successor, László V (the Posthumous), tried but failed to recover the crown from the emperor. Révay writes that the emperor – cost what it might – wanted to keep in his possession "… the determinant of the greatness and destiny of Hungary…".[135] This account bears the marks of another such time – in fact the reign of Rudolf (1572–1608) – when the crown was not in Hungary. This period too was characterised by strife, struggles between the powerful, plundering by the military and the personality of an emperor that would not relinquish the crown. With this Révay once again draws a parallel between the political past and the fraternal dispute of his own time.

---

131 *Ibid.*, 35.
132 *Ibid.*, 36.
133 *Ibid.*, 39.
134 *Ibid.*
135 *Ibid.*, 40–41.

The sufferings of the crown and the wretchedness of the country came to an end when Mátyás Corvinus ascended the throne. The greatest feat which this king – therefore described by Révay as the divine Mátyás – achieved, was to bring back the crown to Hungary.[136] After this, Mátyás won brilliant victories over the western and eastern emperors and even pacified Hungary. Like Berger, Révay sees Mátyás' glorious reign as the best evidence of divine Providence "… lying hidden in the Holy Crown …".[137] In this context he discusses it only briefly, as he means to return to this flourishing period of Hungarian history when he glorifies the "divine Mátyás" of his own time, Mátyás II.

Destiny, Christendom and the Holy Crown

After the death of Mátyás I, there soon came an end to the peace of the crown. The country was divided by the warring parties of various pretenders to the throne. Révay suggests that the cause of the unfortunate situation was obviously the illegitimacy of Mátyás' son János. With this passage he sheds light once more on the sins of the kings, because the holy nature of the crown had been offended by this. After this, however – in contrast to what might have been expected, considering the way in which his mind worked – he sought the reason for the sudden destruction of Hungary not in the workings of the crown but in the fact that, in his view, even the Holy Crown itself could not have averted this change for the worse.[138] From this, for the first time in Révay's exposition, it appears that Fate (*fatum*) is stronger than the crown.

The explanation for such a change in the argument is to be found in the politico-theological debate between Magyari and Pázmány, already discussed in chapter 3. Révay adopts a new stance without mentioning any writer as he does so. It is more than likely that he knew the works in question, as his library contained Pázmány's response to Magyari's work.[139] In addition, Révay analysed the ruin of Hungary in accordance with Magyari's theory about the regular change in countries. Both of

---

136 *Ibid.*, 41–42.
137 *Ibid.*, 42–43. On Révay's ideas about Mátyás Corvinus, see: Gergely Tóth, "Matthias Augusto similis": Mátyás király a kora újkori protestáns múltszemléletbe," in Enikő Békés, Péter Kasza, Gábor Kiss Farkas, István Lázár and Dávid Molnár, eds., *A reformáció és a katolikus megújulás latin nyelvű irodalma* (Convivia Neolatina Hungarica Vol. 3) (Budapest: MTA Bölcsészettudományi Kutatóközpont Irodalomtudományi Intézet, 2019) 52–56.
138 De Rewa, *De sacrae coronae regni Hungariae*, 46.
139 The book was in the library of Ferenc and Péter's family castle at Szklabina, storage number 247. See Dénes Mednyánszky, "Révay Ferencz szklabinai könyvtára 1651-ben [The library of Ferencz Révay in 1651]," *Magyar Könyvszemle*, 6/6 (1881) 344.

them took this theory from another writer, unknown to us. Révay writes that after the death of Mátyás I, a shift took place in the condition of Hungary. In many other countries too, a similar change – frequently observed by scholars – has taken place every five hundred years.[140] He writes about the fate of the Asian realm, which came under Assyrian rule after 520 years, and refers to the Athenian empire, which became a democracy after 490 years.

Révay adopts a position opposing Magyari and Pázmány in offering a reason for Hungary's dramatic situation which is not Christian in nature. If he had accommodated himself to Magyari's way of thinking as a Lutheran preacher, he would have accounted for this twist of Fate by the will of God, the holy nature of the crown or the sins of the Hungarian race. In contrast to Magyari, however, he expresses the view that the shift had been caused by Fate. In his view, ineluctable destruction followed because of the change in the economy of the State which brought about adjustment of the power-balance in society (*respublica*). Change in society has to take place within the framework of that society. In touching on this question, Révay considers the way in which people adopt political roles, and examines the way in which the individual is capable of influencing his destiny.

Révay begins the next section with a lament for the sins that mankind has committed against society (*respublica*). His first sentence is a cry: "Oh times! Oh morals!" (*O tempora! O mores!*)[141] Then he turns again against religious warfare, as it appears from another quotation which he takes from the Italian humanist Iulius Pomponius Laetus (1425–1497): "The evil demons have so enmeshed our brains that we turn from the real enemy and lay armed and bloodied hands on ourselves and our own."[142] While political and religious division prevails in Hungary and Europe, decay will persist. Révay points out that if the Christian princes do not join forces and defeat the enemy, it is to be feared that the Hungarians will be left in shameful slavery. This topos is also to be found in Archduke Matthias' reply to Rudolf in 1608.

An effort to achieve unity must be made in Hungary and Europe, as that is the only way in which the country's decay can be arrested. In an earlier letter to Lipsius, dated 1592, Révay had expressed a similar idea about a united Christendom, focusing, like Magyari and Pázmány, on the Christians' war against the Turks.[143] His endeavours, however, are not directed at uniting the part of humanity that belongs to a definite denomination in the fight against the pagans, as Magyari and Pázmány had done, as explained earlier. Révay spreads the politico-religious concept of an "… agreement achieved for the sake of Christendom …", without specifying Catholic or

---

140 De Rewa, *De sacrae coronae regni Hungariae*, 46.
141 *Ibid.*, 48. He also applies this exclamation in a letter to Lipsius. Bónis, *Révay Péter*, appendix I, 98.
142 De Rewa, *De sacrae coronae regni Hungariae*, 48.
143 Bónis, *Révay Péter*, appendix I, 98.

Protestant. He finds that the thought must take root in people's awareness that all Christians are one in faith in Christ, and through that faith are citizens of one state (*respublica*). Following St Augustine of Hippo he puts it as follows: "All Christians together must fight under the sign of the cross alone, because our faith is one, and our only country the city of God, of which we are citizens."[144]

As Révay saw it, the cross symbolised the concept of Christian unity in the justification of the Hungarians' political programme. His thoughts in connection with the meaning of the cross are similar to Berger's, whose cross-doctrine inspired him to describe the crown as the symbol of the Estates, and by so doing Révay too presents the influence exerted by God on history. In Berger's epic the Hungarian people receives a sacred mission from God through the gift of the symbol of the True Cross, which is the materialisation of the divine.

Révay clothes the Holy Crown of Hungary with this meaning of the True Cross. It is his view that only the crown symbolises that sacred mission given on this earth to the Hungarians and their kings, as the double cross is the symbol of the wretchedness of Hungary. In Révay's book the sacral working on Hungarian history of the symbol of the Cross, familiar from Berger, is transformed into the working of the holy nature of the Crown.[145]

The explanation of the change is – as we have stated in the preceding chapter – to be found in the political and religious upheavals that occurred between 1600 and 1608. In Révay, the symbolic significance of the crown is less religious and Catholic in content than the symbol of the cross in Berger, but contains much more of a political and Hungarian element. We may regard it as Révay's response to the politico-religious unrest of his time that he developed the notion of the

---

144 De Rewa, *De sacrae coronae regni Hungariae*, 48.

145 In Szörényi's opinion Berger's cross fiction lost its influence because of the political changes that took place after 1604 as a result of the Hungarian rebellion. Szörényi, "Berger Illés eposza a Szent Keresztről," 298–299. Despite this Berger later made use of this theme in a number of pamphlets, among others on the occasion of Ferninand II's coronation, and in his unfinished ms Historia Hungaricae divisa in tres reipublica species. See inter alia: "Oratio autoris de triumpho SS. Crucis," in Elias Berger, *Vindiciae Hungariae* (Viennae Austriae: Gregorius Gelbhaar, 1618) (no page numbers, final page). The subject of the double cross returns in pictorial form in one of György Erdődy's works. Georgius Erdeody, *Gloria virtutis Hungaricae* (Duaci: Typis Viduae Petri Telu, 1633). In addition to Révay's work see a single verifiable borrowing of Berger's cross fiction in a church history of Hungary: Melchior Inchofer, *Annales ecclesiastici regni Hungariae* (Romae: L. Grignani, 1644) 385. It is notable that Inchofer links the cross fiction to the foundation in Hungary of the Order of Crusader Knights (*Crucigerorum equitum ordo*) – of which Berger was a member. The cross is also present on Berger's signet ring, as can be seen on the seal of his letters to Révay (SNA). Precisely what connection there was between Berger, his works on the cross, and the Order has not yet been investigated.

holiness of the crown in order to stimulate an effort to attain harmony.[146] The goal of his crown theory is to urge harmony by way of the unification of a politically and religiously divided country and people, on the basis of a new notion of the Estates. The history of the Holy Crown is an allegory with which to understand the present. By disseminating this idea Révay is telling the Estates – Catholics and Protestants alike – that they are each part of a greater whole, and that the importance of the concept of the Holy Crown points beyond the generally held, contradictory, personal religious convictions and political views.

In the section following the explanation of the cross, Révay appeals to this national sentiment, which in his view, is connected to the crown, and finds expression in the almost religious respect for it. "I call as witnesses those, be they Hungarians or foreigners, that have caught sight of this symbol of majesty afar off: let them say sincerely, did not an incomparable respect for it come over them?"[147] According to his idea, this sentiment is aroused in Hungarian circles by the knowledge that the first king of Hungary, St István, received the crown through a heavenly vision and at an angel's command.[148] Through this tradition the crown is to Hungarians not merely the mark of royal power but also "… the everlasting symbol and memorial of Christian truth acknowledged and proclaimed".[149] Révay makes use of the story of the crown of St István at this point because the Protestant historiographers in Hungary – such as Heltai, mentioned above – also refer to it. He believes that in the historical traditional sense generally accepted by the Estates the crown is the symbol of the shared Christian faith of all Hungarians.

After giving his opinion on the cross, Révay analyses the permanent link between the bonding force of the crown-symbol manifest in the Estates and the religious respect accorded the holy object, then returns to the crown. In so doing – as Berger too had done before him – he employs a physical phenomenon, the magnetic property of the crown. Its holy nature attracts the Hungarians to it. He is unsure whether "… a magnet attracts iron more strongly than the crown, with its mysterious force and magnetic property, draws affection and obedience from the Hungarians."[150] Wherever the crown goes, it always remains in contact with its "warlike Pannonians". This contact is the reason why the Hungarians feel that they must do their

---

146 Bartoniek considers that Révay created this religious significance of the crown under the influence of the interdenominational strife of his time. Bartoniek, *A magyar királykoronázások története*, 169.
147 De Rewa, *De sacrae coronae regni Hungariae*, 49–50.
148 *Ibid.*, 50.
149 "… sed magis ut veritatis Christianae agnitae et professae, Hungarorum aeternum sit symbolum atque monumentum." *Ibid.*
150 *Ibid.*, 50.

utmost to remain in favour with the crown, setting danger at nought, and must defend the crown from all indignity.

After that, Révay analyses the political meaning of the idea and reveals the part played by the religious imagery. This we have already seen in Berger. The protection and guarding of the crown are very important to the Estates because "… here in Hungary the coronation of the king is almost of greater importance than his election, and without the Holy Crown it cannot be lawfully performed."[151] By this means, Révay draws together the Hungarians' religious respect for the crown, the steps taken to protect it, the election of the king, his coronation, and the political rights of the Estates. From this it follows that the presence of the Holy Crown is the guarantee of the free election of the king and surety for the rights of the Estates as set out in the constitution. The essence of what Révay says is that the faith that the Hungarian people places in the supernatural power of the crown justifies its political meaning. They possess political rights because they believe in the holy nature of the crown. Thus, the effect of this cultus not only pours down from Heaven upon the Hungarians, but on the contrary: through the medium of the crown the worship that the people offer to God is also manifested. Révay's political thinking is vitalised by this faith, since he legitimates his views by the concept of the Hungarian Estates.

In the next section, Révay compares the Hungarian and Austrian crowns and proceeds with the exposition of his theme.[152] He states that the Hungarian crown is more important to the Hungarians than the imperial crown to the Austrians. This he demonstrates by explaining the difference in meaning between the royal and imperial coronations. The starting point of his analysis is the fact that – in contrast to the Hungarian coronation tradition – as far as the legality of the power of the Holy Roman Emperor is concerned it does not matter whether he has been crowned or not. According to Révay, a number of emperors – Rudolf I, Konrad I and II, Henry, Louis IV, Ferdinand and Maximilian – were acknowledged as true and lawful emperors with full imperial jurisdiction and authority, even without having been crowned, simply on the basis of election. "There have been a good few emperors who were never adorned with the supreme crown of the Empire, that is to say the golden imperial crown with which only the Roman high priest has the right and privilege to crown, in Rome."[153]

Just like Berger, Révay too states that in Hungary royal power depends strictly on coronation with the Holy Crown. It is indispensable for it to be confirmed

---

151 *Ibid.*
152 *Ibid.*, 50–51.
153 *Ibid.*, 51.

(*redimitus*) and consecrated (*consecratus*) by that means.[154] Even if a king has been elected by unanimous assent of the Estates and has ruled the country magnificently for many a year, without coronation he is regarded as a mere governor. For this reason, Révay continues, every licence, grant of land or privilege originating from an uncrowned king is void and valueless. He states that there are countless examples of this, of which he gives two. Lajos II, who was an elected king, fought courageously against the Ottoman emperor and lost his life in battle. As, however, he had not been crowned with the Hungarian crown, after his death not a single privilege that had been granted was considered to be further valid. Mátyás Corvinus re-confirmed his grants after being crowned, and those thus confirmed became genuinely valid. Hungarian kings have requested and received from the crown their honour (*decus*) and dignity: through the crown they have acquired the power to make merciful and profitable laws, and to annul the profitless ones.[155]

To this day, the importance and effectiveness of the political meaning of the crown from the point of view of royal power is a subject of debate, like we have shown in the first two chapters. Contrary to what Révay asserts, in the course of Hungarian history the crown has not always had such legitimating significance for the king as a lawmaker. Its significance was a function of the shifts in dynastic conditions in Hungary and its legitimating role as a token of majesty. At the time when the Holy Crown of Hungary was not yet spoken of at all, and the crown therefore played no special part in the coronation, the symbol of majesty could not have had the significance that Révay attributes to it. As in the events of 1608, in the fourteenth and fifteenth centuries, following the struggles for the throne, the crown had very great significance from the point of view of the legality of the power of the king over the Estates. For this reason, it is not surprising that Révay takes the examples from this period.

In Révay's argument, the role of the examples is not to prove the rightfulness of royal power but to emphasise that the Hungarians have political rights vis-à-vis the power of the Habsburg ruler. By this, he clearly means to say that it is possible for the Austrian emperor to rule omnipotently in his own country, but in Hungary – in the sense of the significance of the crown – it is not so. The king's power as a lawmaker only comes into effect after his election and investiture with the Hungarian crown. According to Révay, therefore, from the point of view of that power a manifest legitimating significance follows from the fact that the crown itself is the "law of laws" (*lex legum*). Like Berger, Révay too points out that the crown is the embodiment of the law of the land, and he adduces a series of examples

---

154 *Ibid.*
155 *Ibid.*, 52.

from which all this is clear.[156] For example, he mentions that it is the custom of the Hungarians to pay fines and ransoms to the crown, and to swear solemn oaths by the crown. The Hungarians make a practice of bequeathing to the crown their inheritance ecclesiastical and lay, or of promising while still living that they will do so. Furthermore, Révay states that everything in Hungary is the property of the crown, since Hungarians' Estates revert to the crown. At the same time, he describes how a number of royal towns and fortresses are called "property of the crown" (*bona sacrae coronae*), and no one may freely turn them to their own profit nor alienate them from the crown. This is an unmistakable reference to the Rudolf-Illésházy case.

In the next section, the concept of property of the crown is connected to the Hungarian crown taken in the territorial sense.[157] Révay bases this meaning on the notion of the territorial inviolability of the crown, which he links to the crown itself in its physical reality. This concept is based on the following: "… the strength of the crown is so great that any that would injure it is not merely guilty of lèse-majesté but also sins against religion and the deity." The inviolability of the symbol of majesty extends to all those territories which were under the jurisdiction of the Hungarian crown in Révay's time or before. He considers that this applies to not only the Kingdom of Hungary but also to those countries which at any previous time had come under the rule of the Hungarian kings.[158] He writes that

> … those ancient and mighty kingdoms, Slavonia, Dalmatia, Croatia, Bosnia, Serbia, Holics [Galicia], Lodomeria, Cumania and Bulgaria, which were at one time embraced by the kings of Hungary and attached to their realms, and which, in the manner of other kingdoms, beyond all doubt possessed their own crowns, evince so great a degree of affection and respect for this angelic crown that, neglecting their own symbols of majesty, they crave for it with open arms, and recognise as their king only him that has been adorned with this crown.

Thus, Révay says that the crown, as it were, fused into itself the meaning of the symbols of majesty of other countries. He depicts this as "… the angelic crown, by its brilliance, puts the gleam of the crowns of many another kingdom in the shade."[159] He then states that it is thanks to the beneficial actions of the Holy Crown that these kingdoms in the Christian sphere still bear the name of "kingdom", and

---

156 *Ibid.*, 52–53.
157 *Ibid.*, 53.
158 On this territorial meaning of the crown see: Eckhart, *Magyar alkotmány- és jogtörténet*, 125–126.
159 De Rewa, *De sacrae coronae regni Hungariae*, 53.

that their names and reputations are still alive despite the enslavement of large parts of their territory by the Ottoman tyrant. By this he suggests that although a significant part of Hungary is indeed in the power of the Turks, the former country exists in the mind, and so therefore does the memory of the mighty empire.

The function of the theory of the inviolability of the territory of the crown is to make the Habsburg king keep his promise, made in the coronation oath, to re-establish the original territory of the kingdom in the Middle Ages.[160] The countries and realms which Révay reckons to the crown in the territorial sense are identical with those which, in the Middle Ages, made up *Archiregnum Hungaricum* or Greater Hungary. The Hungarian armorist Szabolcs Vajay considers that *Archiregnum Hungaricum* describes the now defunct political alliance consisting of Medieval royal Hungary and the vassal states that lay in an arc around it.[161] He believes that expression was given to the bonds of alliance in the titles borne by Hungarian kings and the heraldic devices in common use which designate the political associations of the individual countries.

The image of the *archiregnum* is nothing more than a political fiction, as in this region the balance of power shifted constantly, as did the boundaries of political alliances. The Medieval Hungarian kings used the fiction of the *archiregnum* to strengthen their territorial demands by including these countries among their titles (see image 2). Following the Ottoman invasion of the south-east in the fifteenth century, in the course of which territories belonging to the Hungarian crown also fell into Turkish hands, the concept took on the character of a political programme. The recovery of the lost territories was an important requirement that the Estates made of the ruler. The heir to the throne would promise even before the coronation that he would recover these territories for the crown, and after the coronation

---

160 Péter, "The Holy Crown of Hungary," 445 and 452–453.

161 Szabolcs de Vajay, "Das 'Archiregnum Hungaricum' und seine Wappensymbolik in der Ideenwelt des Mittelalters," in Josef Gerhard Farkas, ed., *Überlieferung und Auftrag. Festschrift für Michael de Fernandy zum sechzigsten Geburtstag* (Wiesbaden: Guido Pressier, 1972) 647–667; *idem*, "Un ambassadeur bien choisi: Bernardius de Frangipanus et sa mission à Naples, en 1476," in Balázs Nagy and Marcell Sebők, eds., *The Man of Many Devices, Who Wandered Fully Many Ways…: Festschrift in Honour of János M. Bak* (Budapest: Central European University Press, 1999) 550, 554; Géza Pálffy, "Magyar címerek, zászlók és felségjelvények a Habsburgok dinasztikus-hatalmi reprezentációjában a 16. században [Hungarian coats of arms, banners and insignia in the representation of the dynasty and power of the Habsburgs in the sixteenth century]," *Történelmi Szemle*, 3–4 (2005) 241–275; Géza Pálffy, "A Magyar Korona országainak koronázási zászlói a 16–17. században [The coronation banners of the countries of the Hungarian crown in the sixteenth and seventeenth century]," in Orsolya Bubryák, ed., *"Ez világ, mint egy kert…" Tanulmányok Galavics Géza tiszteletére* [This world is like a garden. Studies in honor of Géza Galavics] (Budapest: Gondolat/MTA Művészettörténeti Kutatóintézet, 2010) 17–62. The term *archiregnum* does not occur in the work of Révay, but Berger used the expression *sacra archiregni Hungariae monarchia* in one manuscript. Elias Perger [Berger], *Duplex speculum chronologicum…* (Manuscript) EK Ms. G.69.

the country expected him to fulfil his promise.[162] That is why the image of the *archiregnum* appeared on commemorative medals struck for a coronation. During the ceremony the most distinguished aristocrats of Hungary – among them Révay himself – would carry the banners of these parts of the country: Révay carried that of Serbia in 1608. An elaboration of the concept of *archiregnum* is extant in a poem written by an unknown author for the 1608 coronation, and in which the crown also features.[163] After the coronation the territorial demands were expressed in the titles borne by the rulers and by the inclusion on the king's personal seal of the arms of the lost territories.[164] The concept of the *archiregnum* was also otherwise expressed with the crown; see the image in the Thuróczy chronicle (image 3), paintings with the Hungarian crown and the crests of all its countries, and a similar image with the Hungarian crown in Jakob Fugger, Spiegel der Ehren des Höchst-löblichsten Erzhauses Österreich.[165]

Révay also makes use of the *archiregnum* image several times with the intention of bolstering his political concepts by means of it. The reason why he emphatically connects this territorial interpretation with the crown is that in this way he wishes to prove to the king the rightfulness of this political aspiration. In his depiction the crown has become the symbol of those territorial demands of the Estates which the king must realise. Since, according to Révay, the Hungarian crown is the symbol of territorial demands, it may be imagined that other symbols of the power of the ruler used in this context mean a threat with regard to the said aspirations. This is why he says "… there may not remain any other crown within the frontiers of

---

162 Eckhart, *A szentkorona-eszme története*, 137.
163 MOL I 45, documents from the Vienna archives, Böhmisch-Österreichische Hofkanzlei, documents on Hungarian topics, 1608/6. fol. 348r-v. Géza Pálffy and Gergely Tóth, "Az 'országtáblák', egy új koronavers és a pozsonyi Koronatorony különleges vasajtaja: Újdonságok a szent korona 17. századi történetéhez [The "country tables", a new poem about the crown and a special door in the crown tower of Pozsony]," in Gábor Nagy, János Rada and Noémi Viskolcz, eds., *"…nem egyetlen történelem létezik." Ünnepi tanulmányok Péter Katalin 80. születésnapja alkalmából* ["There does not exist one history" Festschrift for Katalin Péter for her eightieth birthday] (Publicationes Universitatis Miskolcinensis – Sectio Philosophica (2)) (Miskolc: Miskolci Egyetem, 2017) 279–301.
164 See e. g. Rudolf's titles on Bocatius letters patent of nobility: Nos Rudolphus Secundus, (…) Hungariae, Bohemiae, Dalmatiae, Croatiae, Sclavoniae, Ramae, Gallitiae, Lodomeriae Bulgariaeque etc. Rex, (…), in Bocatius, *Opera Quae Extant Omnia: Prosaica*, 395. For royal seals and images on them see: Lajos Bernát Kumorovitz, "Die Entwicklung des ungarische Mittel- und Großwappens," in D. Csatári, L. Katus and Á. Rozsnyói, eds., *Nouvelles études historiques*, Vol. I (Budapest: Akadémiai Kiadó, 1965) 322–328.
165 Johann Jakob Fugger, *Spiegel der Ehren des Höchstlöblichsten Kayser- und Königlichen Erzhauses Oesterreich oder Ausführliche Geschicht Schrift von Desselben...* (Nürnberg: Michael und Johann Friderich Endtern, 1668), 477; See also: Buzási and Géza, *Augsburg - Wien - München - Innsbruck. Die frühesten Darstellungen der Stephanskrone und die Entstehung der Exemplare des Ehrenspiegels des Hauses Österreich.*

the kingdom and the annexed parts, as there is no place for another Sun between heaven and earth."[166] By this phrase he alludes to the crown presented to Bocskai by the Turks, of which he writes that Ahmed, the Turkish tyrant, sent it and Ali pasha placed it on Bocskai's head.

When Révay was writing the book this event was still a sensitive issue in Hungary. That much emerges from the text too, as Révay tells us that he does not mean to write a more detailed account of the end that Bocskai came to and what became of Hungary afterwards, "… lest old wounds be reopened …". He does not, however, fail to point out that the "wiser citizens of the fatherland" (*sapientiores patriae Cives*) realised bitterly and indignantly the true meaning of the crown presented by the Turks, as is also obvious from the text of the Peace of Vienna and the constitution of the country (*constitutio regni*).[167] In the Peace of Vienna and in later statutes there is heated discussion of the lasting tension between the meanings of the Hungarian crown and that given by the Turks. This is why, in 1609, the Estates pronounced that the crown given by the Turks in no way meant danger to the old or angelic crown.[168] On 30 June 1610, György Thurzó in fact handed the crown given by the Turks over to the Habsburg emperor.[169]

After the discussion of the territorial meaning of the crown, Révay continues his work with an account of its guarding and safe-keeping in the past. The role of this section is to legalise the situation which in practice obtained in 1608, when the crown was in the hands of the Estates and back on Hungarian soil. Révay pays no little attention to showing that the crown was at all times under the supervision of the Hungarian nobility (*nobilitas Hungarica*).[170]

Among other things, Révay also introduces a new element into Hungarian history-writing: he is the first to include in the text of his book the whole content of three documents, the text of the oath sworn in 1463 by the Guardians of the Crown, and the two that he and Pálffy swore in 1608.[171] He takes this novel manner of presenting sources from Bodin. His intention is to clarify how the crown had been kept in the olden days and to show the good qualities of the present Guardians. The true purpose of showing the documents is, however, to create an appearance of

---

166 De Rewa, *De sacrae coronae regni Hungariae*, 54.
167 *Ibid*. Révay states that many believe that the crown had been the property of a Serbian ruler.
168 *Articuli Diaetalis Posonienses a MDCIX* (s.l., 1609) art. XX A6 9*-10*. See also: Mihály Zsilinszky, *Az 1609-ki Pozsonyi országgyűlés történetéhez* [On the history of the Diet in Poszony in 1609] (Budapest: Magyar Tudományos Akadémia Könyvkiadó, 1882) 6–20.
169 Kálmán Boldizsár, *Bocskay koronája* [The crown of Bocskai] (Debrecen: Városi Nyomda, 1925) 10. The statute was dated 7 November 1609.
170 De Rewa, *De sacrae coronae regni Hungariae*, 55.
171 *Ibid.*, 56–62. For this 'invention' of Révay's, see: Bónis, *Révay Péter*, 64.

historical continuity between the fifteenth and seventeenth centuries by publishing texts from authentic documents.

The account of this part of the history of the crown shows clearly how Révay tries hard to convey his message to the reader. The crown was the symbol of the political compromise that came into being in 1608 between the king and the Estates. The fact that Hungarians "… stood guard on the Holy Crown …" was to the Estates a guarantee on the basis of which it was possible to remind the king of his promises and to preserve the balance of power in Hungary. Despite the fact that the importance of the pledge was obviously symbolic, it was only after long discussions – during the peace negotiations, and following a clash between Archduke Matthias and the Estates – that an agreement was reached that pleased the Hungarians on where and in what circumstances the crown was to be guarded. Révay provides this new situation with justification by means of the description of the late Medieval method of guarding the crown and the texts of the oaths. In this way he wishes to make it clear that at that time the crown was in the possession of the Estates and that the new political compromise had therefore a historical basis.

Next Révay analyses the causes and results of the battle of Mohács in 1526. Following Berger, he regards the events that followed in that period as the consequences of the Hungarians' moral laxity and loss of respect for the crown. He paints in passionate words a picture of the misfortune that overcame Hungary in the course of which Lajos II lost his life, as did the flower of Hungarian chivalry and the greater part of the Hungarian army.[172] Although Süleyman took Buda he did not destroy the city as he did other settlements. Révay interprets that miracle as a sign from God to the Hungarians – and an admonition – to change their ways. "The All Highest saved the city from the enemy in order to urge our nation to a more honourable life."[173]

Despite God's guidance it was not long before degeneration set in again among the Hungarians. Révay writes of the internecine war that sprang up among the aristocracy and the horrors that went with it.[174] He considers that the gravest sin that the nobility committed against the holiness of the crown was to call on their sworn enemies for help. He compares the wrath of God to the action of a strict doctor in treating a serious disease. God, like a conscientious doctor, permitted the Ottomans to take Buda and the greater part of Hungary. The chronicles are silent on the fate of the crown, he says. Nevertheless, he states that no doubt it was God that saved the crown from the Ottoman peril, since "He it was that revealed the crown to us and gave it to us."[175]

---

172 De Rewa, De sacrae coronae regni Hungariae, 63.
173 '(…) ad vitae melioris studium pellicere voluit.' Ibid., 64.
174 Ibid.
175 Ibid., 65.

At this point in the story a prince of Transylvania plays a dual role: János Szapolyai, who was elected king and had himself crowned. Révay states that this hated king had little respect for the majesty of the crown (*Corona Majestatis* – here meaning authority), which led to dreadful wars. Other nobles supported the struggle for the throne of the Habsburg King Ferdinánd. He could only strengthen his position of power by seizing the crown and driving János Szapolyai out of Hungary; the latter was obliged to seek Ottoman support. It is easy to see how closely the post-Mohács events resembled those of Révay's own time. The function of the historical images is once more to point out the sins of ruler and people. Révay says that Szapolyai's downfall was brought about by a desire for power and greed. He quotes Euripides, who wrote of wicked kings: "Break the law for the sake of power, in all else practise piety."[176] According to Révay, the "Turkish tyrant" was delighted at this unexpected support, and hoped that he would gain Hungary too in the same fashion that he had at that time taken Greece, Bulgaria, Holics [Galicia], and Serbia. Süleyman invaded Hungary with a huge army, took Buda, seized the crown and ceremoniously returned it to János Szapolyai. This episode forms the prelude to the description of the greatest miracle connected to the crown: the story of the guarding of the crown – while all the time it was in the sultan's possession. Here Révay makes use of Berger's work in informing his readers of the danger in which the crown had been.

Révay tries to convince the reader that all this was part of God's plan. He states that the crown fell into the hands of barbarians by the ordinance of ineluctable destiny (*fortuna*).[177] The Guardian of the Crown Péter Perényi was trying to escape the Turks, taking the crown with him, but was captured and, together with the crown, taken before the sultan. Nothing other than a miraculous fate (*mirabile fatum*) brought the worship (*religio*), safety (*salus*) and dignity (*decus*) of the crown into the hands of the Turkish tyrant. Révay immediately draws the conclusion that "… the merciless tyrant was rendered blind by the Godhead, for he did not believe in the crown, nor did he respect its blessedness and had no time for its fame."[178] We have already read in Berger that the crown blinded Süleyman, but only in Révay's book is this incident linked to the divine power of the crown, which is indicated by rays of light in the picture of it and which he asserts is an aspect of its meaning.

This account of the miracle, taken from Berger, is Révay's most important argument for the statement that the influence of Providence on the fate of Hungary is exercised through the crown, and this serves as the introduction to the idea of the desirability of unifying Christendom against the Ottomans. He writes: "Who would venture – I ask – to doubt any longer that the Holy Crown is under the protection

---

176 *Ibid.*, 66.
177 *Ibid.*, 67.
178 *Ibid.*, 68.

of Almighty God? Does this example not, then, substantiate our best belief? Can we, then, doubt any longer that no enemy has power over it?" Then on the basis of the lasting link between God and the crown he argues thus: "If [the crown] is inviolate and triumphant, then the fatherland (*patrium regnum*) too will remain intact."[179] By that he means the moral quality borne by the crown, which must be kept in respect, taking into account the following:

> … let us but remain in the ancient apostolic faith [*prisca religio Apostolica*[, tend and advance the common good [*commodum*], pursue the Ottomans with unremitting hatred, and let there be here at home [*domus*, in the sense of the fatherland] piety [*pietas*], faithfulness [*fides*], and harmony [*concordia*], and whatever we may suffer from the enemy we shall not be broken but shall gain strength from hardship.[180]

This sentence we may take as the summary of Révay's political programme.

Révay continues his discourse with an examination of sixteenth century political relationships in Hungary. In this the link between the Habsburg dynasty and the Hungarians is referred to. The dynasty received its power over Hungary from Providence as the Crown, after a certain amount of confusion, came back into King Ferdinánd's possession from Transylvania.[181] Once again Révay is only sketching the image of the connection between the absence of the crown and the unrest rising in Hungary when he writes that after the wanderings and tribulations of the crown the most grievous conditions prevailed in the country, while the aristocracy (primores) harrassed one another "… with Vatinian hatred …".[182] Dissension is the worst thing that can happen to a country, sighs Révay. He quotes Livy, who says that "Discord among citizens has brought greater destruction to many people than have foreign wars, famine or sickness, as the sorest blow to the land that God sends upon us in his wrath."[183]

Révay then considers the question of why the Hungarian aristocrats decided to call on the Ottomans for help. He cannot understand why János [Szapolyai] and his followers found the support and friendship of the barbarians to be advantageous; they were the enemies and devastators of the fatherland (*patria*), and friendship with the Ottomans had always ended in suppression, destruction and enslavement.

---

179 *Ibid.*
180 *Ibid.*
181 *Ibid.*, 69.
182 A reference to Catullus,14, 3, *Vatinianum odium* – the hatred of the politician Publius Vatinius, whose name became a proverb of disrepute.
183 De Rewa, *De sacrae coronae regni Hungariae*, 69–70.

Evidence of this was the fall of the mighty bastion of Sziget and the ruin of Transylvania. He asks again, other than this what fruit had alliance to the Ottomans borne, and the godless, lawless and measureless pursuit of power? In this context he compares again the period of the reign of János Szapolyai and the situation in his own time:

> Alas, if only we did not in our own time experience a similar fate, if only internal disunities and rebellions did not impede the course of the good fortune of our emperor, by Christ, if the sins of the Christians were not to the profit of the Turks, if our dissension were not the greatest nourishment of their ravenings, the source of their power, then we would know that not only mighty Esztergom was ours, which was captured with much bloodshed and weariness, but Buda too, which Archduke Matthias twice besieged with great and powerful forces ...[184]

After that Révay links together his views on human nature (*natura civica*) and the Hungarian people.[185] He states that people learn in two ways: from their own mistakes or from those of others. The Hungarians' mistake is that they nurture mutual hatred. All this leads to the destruction of the fatherland, because instead of defending it the Hungarian people destroys the land from within. He expresses the hope that "... at least our own misfortunes may in the end make us more careful ...", but he fears that the old tale that he has told will fall on deaf ears.

> The spirits of individuals are so filled and aroused by the desire for vengeance for petty concerns that they would rather be destroyed along with those that they hate than defend the fatherland to which we have been born, and prefer to combine obstinacy with danger rather than compliance with security. What could be more like by nature to dragons and vipers than this impiousness?[186]

Hungarian royal power is best in Habsburg hands. Like Berger, Révay defends this opinion by presenting the Habsburg dynasty's assumption of power as if the crown itself and the Hungarian people had selected this ruling house for themselves. The reason for the crown's choice is the human nature outlined above. He recounts how while Ferdinánd Habsburg was still alive the Estates of the country (*Regni Ordines*) elevated his son Maximilian to kingly dignity, and his father gladly and voluntarily surrendered the crown to him. In this way the crown regained its personality in history. Here too, as above in Berger, we read that public life in Hungary was

---

184 *Ibid.*, 70.
185 *Ibid.*, 71.
186 *Ibid.*, 71–72.

insufficiently secure for the crown, and so it entrusted itself to "… the affection and safe-keeping of the Austrians …"[187]

In this connection, Révay raises the point that in his view the Habsburg dynasty are not blood relations of the Hungarians, and so are not to be regarded as part of the Hungarian Estates (*gens Hungarica*). This section is all the more surprising because Archduke Matthias – inter alia, in his above-mentioned letter to Illésházy – actually emphasised his blood relationship to the Hungarians. It is Révay's opinion that the crown selected the Habsburgs for itself, since the sinfully obtained power of "princes of our own people" was insufficiently long-lived, and furthermore the posterity of the (Hungarian) royal house had become extinct. After the Austrian ruling house had taken possession of Hungary and turmoil had subsided there, the crown could once more watch over general well-being and reputation in complete calm.

Révay makes use of Archduke Matthias' accession to discuss the awkward questions of the succession and the election of the king in Hungary. After the House of Habsburg acquired the Hungarian crown the manner of succession to the throne had essentially changed. He argues that, having in view the purpose of maintaining the unity of Hungary, it is better for the question of the succession to be properly settled in the Kingdom. He considers that a hereditary monarchy is more suitable for preserving the unity of Hungary. King Maximilian followed the example of his father and designated his successor, Rudolf, in good time, and so passed to him the crown and the country with the Estates' approval. In this connection Révay observes that "… it is laudable if rulers are so wise that they seek not their own good but that of our fatherland, and when while they still live they think in good time about the kingship, knowing very well that it is in the nature of mortals to crave the realm and wait impatiently for the dignity of the throne."[188] Transient conditions when power changes hands, are favourable to rebellious and ambitious attempts, and as such dangerous for the country. Révay sighs: "How many woes and dangers follow the deaths of kings, if they have not attended in good time to the succession." For lack of a ruler the nobility disintegrate into warring factions. "Then the state, like a ship without a helmsman, is tossed or even sunk on the stormy sea, of which we have examples in Hungary well known to all and painful enough."[189] Almost every restless period of Hungarian history can be traced to struggles involving succession to the throne.

---

187 *Ibid.*
188 *Ibid.,* 73.
189 *Ibid.*

Hereditary monarchy has the consequence for Hungary that the importance of the election of the king is diminished. The fact that there can no longer be a real free election undermines the liberty of the Estates. Révay anticipates criticism: in fact, the election had never been really free. The election of the king in Hungary took place with the agreement of the entire nobility, but in former times it had often been fought out at Rákosmező by armed force. He believes that it had very seldom happened that the election had passed off with complete agreement when there was a heavily armed crowd present. It had frequently happened that "… the king had been elected to suit him who had with him the greatest strength, most men, for which reason a mockery was sometimes made of freedom of election [*libertas electionis*], and the law grievously infringed."[190]

After thus discussing the question of the transfer of royal power, Révay turns to the reign of Rudolf. The account of this period is unpleasant for him, as the disturbances of the Rudolf years contradict his previously expressed view that the rule of the Habsburgs guaranteed stability. He therefore assesses the events from the point of view of the political compromise achieved between Archduke Matthias and the Hungarian Estates. We are reminded that until 1608, the crown was in the possession and power of the emperor, and thus not in Hungary, and Révay again explains this situation as intervention by God. Like Berger, he states that "… anyone can see that, by the far-reaching grace of divine Providence, the Holy Crown was kept for some seventy years on the domestic altar of the majestic kings, resplendent with imperial honour."[191] During this time war was waged against the Turks with mixed fortunes, "… while we tossed about among internal strife and upheavals …". He therefore records that "… immediately after this the crown returned to the fatherland, with honour gleaming in the defence of blessed peace".[192]

The description of the outlook of the crown

Révay also says that the crown returned to Hungary by the influence of God's intervention. During the negotiations over the Peace of Vienna it was resolved, at divine suggestion, that the crown must be taken back to Hungary. From those words it appears that Révay considers that the emperor would not have wished to be parted from the crown on his own initiative.

He emphasises the divine intervention made through the crown and does his best to explain and finally to justify the situation which arose as a result of the

---

190 *Ibid.*, 73–74.
191 *Ibid.*, 74.
192 *Ibid.*

squalid quarrel between the Habsburg brothers. According to Révay's thinking, the actions of Archduke Matthias during the fraternal quarrel likewise offended the holiness of the crown, as he allied himself to the rebellion against the lawful ruler and forced him to surrender the crown. In that way, rather than show the outcome of the brothers' quarrel as a divine intervention, Révay is able to avoid the conflict arising from further analysis of Mátyás II's actions in this connection.

By the description and assessment of the exterior of the crown and other coronation regalia, Révay links them to the events of 1608. This part of the book poses the question of why he, Berger, Jeszenszky and their contemporaries thought that there was a connection between the exterior of the crown, its political-moral meaning, and the events of that year. In anticipation of this there has already been mention of the explanation offered, for example, of the symbolic role that the crown played at the time of the transfer of power, the cultus of Mátyás I, and thoughts on the connection between the crown and the political rights of the Hungarian people.

A further explanation may be the so-called antiquarianism which was very popular in the sixteenth and seventeenth centuries, and which formed part of the Renaissance movement in the broader sense. Peter Burke considers that one should understand by that expression an obvious interest in the material memories of the past on the basis of which historians attempt to reconstruct the past in its entirety.[193] He states that at the start of the seventeenth century attention turned from written to material monuments – and especially to pictorial representations – which were treated as sources of historical information. Burke called this development the "visual turn". The discovery of pictorial representations also led to attention being paid to the "three antiquities" (past ages, Christianity and the barbarian world), and in Burke's opinion this eventually had huge consequences – inter alia, the development of Early Modern national identity.[194] Artefacts were used to prove all manner of new political theories.[195] From this it follows that we may not regard the studies of Bocatius, Révay, Berger, Jeszenszky and others on the external form of the crown as a particularly Hungarian innovation, but must examine them as works in keeping with the growing international interest in the past.

Révay's description of the crown and the picture that appeared in his book have been dealt with in detail in specialist literature since the eighteenth century, but – especially over the past thirty years – interest has grown constantly outside the academic world too.[196] The Hungarian translation of Révay's book on the crown

---

193 Burke, "Images as Evidence in Seventeenth-Century Europe," 273.
194 *Ibid.*, 282–283.
195 *Ibid.*, 275–278.
196 See among others: Ernő Marosi, "A magyar korona a jelenkori kutatásban és a populáris irodalomban [The Hungarian Crown in the modern research and popular literature]," *Művészettörténeti Értesítő* XXXV (1986) 49–55; Enikő Buzási, "III. Ferdinand mint magyar király (Iustus Sustermans

appeared in 1979, in which the description of the crown could at last be read in Hungarian. Attention was directed particularly to the figure of the Virgin Mary, whose portrait, according to Révay, is to be found on the rear of the crown; today it is not there. In the eighties, a group of Hungarian goldsmiths stated, on the basis of Révay's text, that the portrait of the Virgin on the rear of the crown had been altered into one of the Byzantine Emperor Michael VII Ducas (1071–1078).[197] There was some debate over why the crown as seen today differed from that in the seventeenth century description and illustration, and what was the significance of the difference. As no other Early Modern illustration of the portraits on the rear had survived, the thought of the alteration of the crown – even if it were unintentional – seriously concerned the goldsmiths, as did the possible reason for it.

The debate took a new turn when the historian Géza Pálffy discovered a seventeenth century illustration of the rear of the crown in which the portrait of the Virgin Mary was not to be seen and which corresponded to the current exterior.[198] Pálffy produced the print in Jeszenszky's book which in 1609 had been considered an accurate picture of the crown from the front. As we know that Révay received Jeszenszky's book from Thurzó, and it is beyond doubt that he used it in writing his own, he must have been aware of this picture. For that reason, it is impossible

---

ismeretlen műve az egykori Legánes gyűjteményből)[Ferdinand III. as Hungarian king. (An unknown work of Iustus Sustermand from the past Legánes collection)]," A Magyar Nemzeti Galéria Évkönyve [Yearbook of the Hungarian National Gallery] (Budapest, 1991) 149–158; Endre Tóth and Károly Szelényi, *A magyar szent korona - királyok és koronázások* [The Hungarian Holy Crown: kings and coronations] (Budapest, 1996, ²2000) 19, R. Várkonyi, "... Jó Budavár magas tornyán...," 83–9 4; László Holler, "A magyar királyi koronát ábrázoló, 1620–1621. évi festményekről [On the paintings which depict the Hungarian Royal Crown dated 1620–1621]," *Művészettörténeti Értesítő* 49 (2000) 297–310; Iván Bertényi, "Révay Péter Magyarország Szent Koronájáról írt munkájának forrásértéke [The source value of the work of Péter Révay on the Holy Crown of Hungary]," in: Tibor Seifert, ed., *A történelem és a jog határán. Tanulmányok Kállay István születésének 70. évfordulójára* [On the border of history and law. Studies for the seventieth birthday of István Kállay] (Budapest: Eötvös Loránd Tudományegyetem BTK, 2001) 19–29, Endre Tóth, "A koronázási jelvények," 11–21, Kees Teszelszky, "A magyar korona megjelenése a kora újkori képzőművészetben [The appearance of the Hungarian Crown in Early Modern art]," *Művészettörténeti Értesítő*, 60/1 (2011) 1–10; Enikő Buzási, "Portrésorozatok a 17. századi magyar arisztokraták politikai reprezentációjában [Portrait series in the representation of seventeenth century Hungarian aristocrats]," *Művészettörténeti Értesítő*, 60/1 (2011) 11–21; Géza Pálffy "A Szent Korona balesete 1638-ban," 1432; Buzási and Géza, *Augsburg - Wien - München - Innsbruck. Die frühesten Darstellungen der Stephanskrone und die Entstehung der Exemplare des Ehrenspiegels des Hauses Österreich*; Pálffy and Tóth, "*Az országtáblák*".

197 Ernő Marosi, "A magyar korona a jelenkori kutatásban és a popularis irodalomban [The Hungarian crown in modern research and popular literature]," *Művészettörténeti Értesítő*, 35 (1986) 49–55; Zsuzsa Lovag, "A koronakutatás vadhajtásai [The wildings of the crown research]," *Művészettörténi Értesítő* 35 (1986) 35–48.

198 Géza Pálffy, "A Szent Korona és a koronaláda balesete 1638-ban", 1443.

that he saw anything on the crown other than what is there now, as on the basis of his own observation, the depiction in Jeszenszky, and Berger's description, he must have had an accurate picture of it. Furthermore, the illustration of the crown was to be seen on coins, in coronation memorabilia and indeed even on the crown chest – probably made in 1608 to Révay's own orders. Therefore, any depiction of the crown that differed from these must mean something that fitted his argument and followed from the other ideas which he expressed.

Révay's description begins as follows: "Therefore the crown is of pure gold, moulded into a ring by craftsmanship rather heavenly than human."[199] According to him, the following are depicted on the crown:

> On the periphery a circle of triangular floral spikes at equal intervals … on the front part a likeness of Our Redeemer holding an apple, and on the opposite side one of the Holy Virgin Mother, then a holy row of apostles, Christian kings, emperors and martyrs, as it seems, with Greek letters…[200]

Révay says about the chains: "From the place by the ears on both sides costly, white, shining jewels hang to the ears like pendants …"[201] He follows Jeszenszky in interpreting the meaning of the chains:

> … which strike one another in mutual harmony at even the slight movement of the holy head, so that both ears may be alerted to listening to the truth, divine and human, and that by this means to the fact that everything must be done to the glory of the name of God and to good repute and fame.[202]

Next Révay brings together the outer form of the symbol of majesty with the above-mentioned idea of *archiregnum* and possibly with its image. He states that

> … the nine little chains and nine toppings, which gleam with largish pearls at precise intervals on the parts of the crown to front and back, symbolise the power and brilliance of the nine countries and realms incorporated into Hungary, viz. Dalmatia, Croatia, Slavonia, Serbia, Bosnia, Holics [Galics], Lodomeria, Bulgaria and Cumania.

---

199 De Rewa, *De sacrae coronae regni Hungariae*, 75.
200 *Ibid*. Révay was the first to notice the Greek letters on the crown, so he must have had studied it from close by.
201 *Ibid.*, 76. In the print of the crown eighteen rows of pearls can be seen.
202 *Ibid*.

Then he goes on with reflections containing even more numerology: "I think that this has been done not without purpose, and in the numbers of the toppings, precious stones, portraits and gilded pendants the number nine is very precisely and logically to be made out." This section, which is occupied with numbers, serves to provide grounds for Révay's next utterance, according to which the construction of the crown presents unity and harmony.

The detailed exposé of the crown, its depiction and the explanation form part of the writer's rhetorical strategy by means of which he seeks to convince the Hungarian and foreign reader of his political notions. This tactic is not based on a logically-constructed argument, but on the persuasive force of suggestion both visual and verbal. Révay portrays the exterior of the crown in a veiled manner as the perfect foil for his previously outlined ideas. The immediate, material description of the crown and the illustration of it provide convincing arguments for the justification of his views. Since the Hungarians themselves too were only too ready to believe in Révay's concept, as it completely met their political ambitions, they felt no inclination to criticise this image of the crown. The latter remained fixed in the public mind for centuries because of the lasting connection between the illustration and the political consideration, and it was only late in the eighteenth century – again a time of political change – that it began to be questioned. The meaning of these parts may be interpreted on the basis of Révay's theory of political morals, as is confirmed in what follows. In his view, the craftsmanship of the crown is perfection itself since God desires a perfect crown, king and country, and it is He himself that brings this perfection into being.[203] From the perfect construction it follows that, in Révay's view, the crown, as God's creature, shows how the king, the Estates and Hungary ought to be. In this regard the crown – as a creation consisting of highly significant images, precious stones and decorative elements – is the embodiment of political morals. The manner in which Révay describes the imaginary construction of the crown reminds us of St Augustine's concept of the City of God or the Heavenly Jerusalem from the Book of Revelation. In the immediately preceding section Révay compared the ideal Hungarian nation to the City of God, and so in this section too, the construction of the crown reflects that image.

The function of the image becomes clear when he declares:

> I believe, however, that by the decoration of the crown God sought nothing other than that the crowned king himself – and likewise the whole nation under his leadership –

---

203 *Ibid.*, 77.

should strive most steadfastly for the knowledge, nurture, love and armed defence of the blessed apostolic faith which he has accepted.²⁰⁴

By this Révay quite unmistakably implies that the message which God means to impart through the crown is concealed in its exterior. The essence is the unity of the whole people through the faith which they share. Since he has already defined in a previous section what he understands by the meaning of the Hungarian crown, he now underpins that account by the description given of the exterior of the symbol of majesty. For this purpose, he employs familiar images, such as that of the Virgin Mary, the Patron Saint of Hungary.

The topics and images in Révay's description of the crown have to be contrasted with the desirable perfect condition, and cannot be understood outside their-seventeenth century everyday political context. He does not provide a basic art-history account of the crown, but – as did Berger and Jeszenszky – treats it as a vehicle for his own ideas. By means of the symbol of majesty that he imagines, he presents the ideal condition of king, people and country. The actual situation, however, is far from ideal, but perfection is certainly to be striven for. This is why he writes of the Hungary which he holds to be ideal is that in which the *archiregnum* consists of nine countries; of the perfect Estates, united by the apostolic faith; of the Virgin Mary, the Holy Crown and the perfect ruler. By this, Révay presents a political ideal by means of the idealised crown which in reality does not exist, but he holds a mirror in front of his readers and offers the better future.

Révay goes on to review the other coronation regalia. This section we may regard as reflecting royal virtues. He believes that these items are needed not only on the occasion of a coronation, but also for the purpose of reminding the crowned king of his duties in a "secret sign-language".²⁰⁵ This explanation can be traced almost entirely to Jeszenszky, but Révay adopts only the essence of his way of thought without naming him as his source or referring to the Classical authors on whom Jeszenszky relies. After the crown, St István's coronation cloak is the first item that Révay introduces. He takes its origin back to the first king. In his view the holiness of the cloak is indicated by the wonderful embroidery on it. In Révay's description, on the one side God is seen enthroned in heavenly light, surrounded by the apostles, while on the other side is the victory of Christ in the symbol of the cross.²⁰⁶ At this

---

204 *Ibid.*
205 *Ibid.*, 77–78.
206 A copy of the original description of the casula which perhaps was made by Révay is preserved: "Descriptio Habitus Regis Hungaria visi in solemni inauguratione Mathiae II. Archiducis Austria in Regem Hungaria. Anno 1608. Novembris 19. Textura in Casula Regia." MOL N 114 Kovachich Márton György gyűjteménye [Collection of Márton György Kovachich]. Acta diaetalia. I.

point, Révay makes use of the image of the Virgin Mary as Patron Saint of Hungary. He states that the letters R.R.E.T.O.B VMBRA on the cloak stand for "Queen of the Roman Church and of all Olympus, Holy Virgin Mary, Patroness of the Warlike Kingdom". Another interpretation gives: "Queen of Queens, Blessed conqueror of the World, Holy Virgin Mary, Queen of the Angels".[207] Like Jeszenszky, who considers that the cloak alludes to the king's sinlessness, Révay too explains that this garment symbolises the king's upright character. The king is the likeness and shadow of God; of him it is true that "… we are dust and ashes, since the kingdom of this world is but the shadow of the heavenly and spiritual kingdom." In Révay's opinion the meaning of the cloak is precisely that. From the point of view of the king's dignity, therefore, nothing is more important than God, whose portrait he wears on earth. The king has a duty to acknowledge and worship God, defend holiness and truth, and armed with the Christian faith, to prevail over the enemy.

Next, he turns briefly to the meaning of the sceptre, the orb and St István's sword, and also explains the significance of St István's gloves and sandals.[208] This too he takes from Jeszenszky. The sceptre is the rod of truth and law (*veritas et iustitia*). He considers that its form departs from the traditional, since it resembles the maces used in battle by Hungarian chieftains. Like the crown, the sceptre too is decorated with chains which are to remind the king that, when necessary, he has to fight for the law and the flock (*pro lege et pro grege*). The orb means the unpredictability of the king's fortunes. St István left the sword to posterity – says Révay, following Bonfini – to make with it the sword-strokes in the open air which remind the king to defend Hungary.[209] In conclusion he states that the gloves and sandals symbolise the king's sinlessness and purity. By this interpretation he places the significance of all these regalia in a typically Hungarian-style context, and links it to the identity of the Estates.

Révay continues with the place where the crown is kept. He feels that this has to be a fortress on a high place – near to God – far from people and not too close to royal power. By this he means the hilltop castle of Visegrád, where the crown was originally kept. In his view, the fact that the Ottomans took the castle has symbolic meaning for the condition of Hungary. Connected with this is his thought that Mátyás II had not long before retaken Visegrád and restored it "to us", which to him had been the epitome of the changes of 1608 in Hungary.

---

207 De Rewa, *De sacrae coronae regni Hungariae*, 79.
208 *Ibid.*, 80–81.
209 *Ibid.*, 82.

The reign of King Mátyás II

The account of the ideal place of residence for the crown forms the introduction to a further account of the return of the crown and the reign of Mátyás II. Like Berger, Révay too sees it as the most propitious omen and prelude to the future that the fatherland has received the crown back.[210] He cannot put into words what a triumphal progress, what glory it has been for the Hungarian people (*gens Ungarica*), and what an undying name Archduke Matthias acquired when Rudolf returned the crown, and the huge crowd received the returning symbol of majesty with shouts of jubilation. By the account of this, Révay creates the link between the reigns of Mátyás I and II. Like Berger, Révay too makes use of details taken from Bonfini, and presents the return of the crown and the historical parallel as a favourable omen for the coming successful reign of Mátyás II. He then states that he will compare the two Mátyáses on the basis of the manner in which the crown was recovered. The purpose of the comparison is for him to show that he considers the Habsburg king even more virtuous than his predecessor. The most important argument supporting this statement is that Mátyás II had no recourse to arms in his assumption of power, but rather urged agreement. Révay says that Mátyás I spilled much blood and waged a pitiless war over the return of the crown, and despite it all could only receive it back after paying the emperor six thousand gold forints for it. Mátyás II, in contrast, recovered the crown without any loss of life or bloodshed. Révay then gives a detailed account of the return of the crown and the coronation.

After that, he sings the praises of Mátyás II, and in so doing devotes close attention to what this king has done for the fatherland. In Révay's eyes, his most beneficial act has been to expel criminals from the country (*nostra patria*). He mentions that plotting by enemies has come to an end, the rebelliousness of dissidents has ceased, as have deep-seated hatred and envy; bloodthirsty plans have been abandoned, and the bitterness and devastation of previous years are no more.[211] What remains, says Révay, are heavenly peace and tranquillity, in the protection of which the laws have flourished and the rule of law (*iuris dicendi potestas*) has been restored to its rightful place. Révay assures the reader that "… once more we are happy …", and states that "… after bearing so many blows we have once more come to the golden age" (*aurea tempora*). From the depths of his heart, he wishes that this condition be lasting and constant, and that strife and disaster never trouble them anymore.

Révay writes that the blessed condition that has thus arisen is due not to the king alone but also to the angelic crown (*angelica corona*).[212] He appeals to the reader's

---

210 *Ibid.*, 83–84.
211 *Ibid.*, 87–88.
212 *Ibid.*, 89.

imagination when he states that the crown, as it were, formed an indissoluble union with the mighty realm of the Czech crown and imperial majesty as an additional fundament or key-stone, and in this way brought all these realms beneath its own authority, and so gained the patronage and support of the whole Christian world. By this he means that his proposal for the unity of Christianity, and for that of union between Hungary and the whole of Christendom together, came to life thanks to the accession of Archduke Matthias and the return of the crown.

Next, Révay discusses the sealing of the political compromise brought about by the enactment of laws and the setting-up of the dual commission to guard the crown. He claims that it will only be possible to maintain Hungary's fortunate situation if the crown is properly guarded. The sealing came about through the ceremony of the presentation of the crown. After the dual commission had been sworn in, one of them lifted the crown from its chest and displayed it to the assembled nobility, so that all might be convinced that they were dealing with the true crown.[213] By this he once again confirms the link between the crown and the outlined theory. It appears that the displaying of the crown is formal confirmation of the political compromise of 1608. The crown myth had come to life in its full reality.

Révay then endeavours, with the oath of the Guardians of the Crown which follows, to enlighten the reader on the great respect which the king, the nobility and the Guardians had for the crown in 1608. The picture which he paints is somewhat contrary to the numerous difficulties that arose because of outstanding taxes – not detailed here – with which the Guardians had to contend four years later in order to fund the garrison of Pozsony castle that was charged with guarding the crown.[214] In conclusion, Révay pays attention to the coronation of the queen of Hungary. He tries to show that this too had to be performed with the Holy Crown. The coronation of Queen Anna in 1613 forms the basis for the account. The function of this section is to prove the lawful nature of the ceremony of crowning the queen with the Hungarian crown.

In the penultimate section Révay addresses his fellow Hungarians with a speech to the crown, the king and the country, beginning "To you, stout Hungarians, with whom I share a fatherland" (*Ad vos Hungari fortissimi, cum quibus communis mihi est patria*).[215] The essence of this speech is that the Hungarians must seek unity through guarding and preserving the crown in seemly fashion. In elaborate Baroque language he repeats once more his main point. The Hungarians, thanks be to God, have received once more the Holy Crown, which they had lost again through their

---

213 *Ibid.*, 90.
214 Bónis, Révay Péter, 31–32; and: MOL P 1615 Révay család box 1, item 73, Pozsony, 8 August 1619, Request of the guards of the crown Mátyás Belecij and András Vcijntsij to the palatine; MOL P 1615 Révay család box 1, item 73. Pozsony, 2 January 1620, Request of György Rozsos to the palatine.
215 De Rewa, *De sacrae coronae regni Hungariae* 96.

own neglect. He implores them in the name of affection and respect for the Holy Crown to pray to God for its secure safe-keeping. He believes that the crown had come to Hungary six hundred years previously together with the Christian faith. He appeals to the Hungarians: "Consider with a single will and purpose, that this holy star … may, as in our ancestors' time, find a safe and worthy lodging, and for ever shine upon us." The Hungarians must be on their guard against internal strife and external enemies alike. In his modest work they can find an appropriate means of establishing sure, safe and untroubled protection for the crown. By this he was in fact summoning his fellow Hungarians to put into practice the ideas that he had set out.

Révay ends his book with a prayer for the crown, the king and Hungary (*Oratio pro Corona, rege et Regno*) which embraces his entire argument.[216] This is a prayer similar to the ones that could be seen in the work of Illésházy and Berger, as has been explained in chapter 4. In it he beseeches God to watch over Hungary. He implores Him, who gave this nation (*gens nostra*) the Holy Crown and has guarded it to this day – to preserve the crown in safety, unharmed and flourishing. He prays for the emperor and for our king, the father of the fatherland (*pater patriae*), that he may triumph over his enemies. He begs God to give the Estates harmony, the people peace and quiet, to keep dissension and strife far from them, to uproot from among them hatred and jealousy and let them win the "crown of eternal life". And of course, the prayer ends with an Amen.

Révay's book and the shaping of national identity

In the book Révay presents his thoughts on the sovereignty of the Estates, which he justifies by discussion of the ups and downs of the fate of the crown and the Hungarians. In so doing, he simultaneously gives political meaning to the concept of nation. The fact that the image of the nation had changed in comparison with the ideas of previous writers on the same subject indicates that an awareness of self-identity among Hungarians had developed.

The most significant innovation concerning Hungarian society in this book is that Révay, on the basis of the events of 1608, connects the concept of identity with the interpretation of the political ethos of the crown. Relying on this connection, he states that the Estates have an autonomous right of opposition to a king that acts unlawfully. At the same time, he justifies the royal power of the Habsburgs through the medium of the ethos of the crown. The role of the notion of the Estates is to create political stability in Hungary after a period of great political upheaval. The

---

216 *Ibid.*, 98.

most important implement for the maintenance of the favourable situation that has arisen is the political ethos represented by the crown, which serves as a clear lesson for king and Estates alike. Révay hopes that through the creation of a crown-fiction of an ethical nature – embracing such principles as e. g. the punishment and reward of the nation, and even urging confession and penitence – the Hungarians would strive to lead a virtuous life. With the aid of a reasoned framework of historical examples he outlines the image of Hungarian society and formulates a convincing political statement.

In the knowledge of the intellectual environment in which the book was written, it is clear that Révay took most of the historical examples from recent political and historical works; these too carried a certain current political message which their authors based on the concept of the Estates. Révay chiefly made use of the work of Jeszenszky and Berger, but also dipped into Magyari and Pázmány. At the same time, his book finds its own place among writings on the subject of the crown of Hungary. The allegation that Révay wrote the Medieval political notion of the crown from a religious viewpoint is therefore untenable.[217] His book – a significant element in the political debates of the time – has a clear political message for his own time; he justifies his own standpoint, however, by means of the creation of an apparently original historical fiction, which is in fact based on recent publications and contemporary ideas.

We may state the following of the development of identity in Europe in the Early Modern period. The shaping of this particular form of national self-identity – understanding by the concept of self-identity a change in the meaning of the crown – was the consequence of the existence of a local tradition, but may be seen with regard to its content rather as the outcome of an international intellectual dialogue. The collaboration of *respublica litterata*, public interest in learning about the past, and mutual exchanges between individual writers was the most significant stimulus in the shaping of national identity in Early Modern Hungary.

The question remains as to whether national self-identity really did take shape in Early Modern Hungary along the lines of Révay's thinking. In theory, we could only speak of the existence of national identity if we could demonstrate beyond doubt that the significance of the crown elaborated by him became engraved on

---

217 Mátyás Bél, "Praefatio," in Johannes Georgius Schwandtner, ed., *Scriptores Rerum Hungaricarum Veteres ac genuini*, vol. II (Vindobonae : Kraus, 1746) XXVIII.; Bartoniek, *A magyar királykoronázások története*, 169, Benda and Fügedi, *A magyar korona regénye*, 167. Péter Váczy uses the work of Révay as proof of the existence of the medieval Hungarian folk-belief in the divine origin of the crown. Péter Váczy, "Az angyal hozta korona [The crown brought by the angel]," *Életünk*, 19 (1982) 94–102, especially 9; Bónis, *Révay Péter*, 61, Thomas von Bogyay, "Über die Forschungsgeschichte der heiligen Krone," 66.

the hearts and minds of members of the Estates. In practice, we can provide an answer to this question if we examine the way in which the work circulated. It is not possible, however, to analyse this problem to any depth within the scope of the present study; it would require a completely separate essay.[218] The central topic of the next chapter will be how Révay's book was made use of after his death in 1622. We shall now, with a few relevant examples, make a couple of statements on the lasting connection between his thoughts and the identity of the Estates.

It is obvious from the extraordinary popularity of the book in the late eighteenth century that Révay's ideas on the crown and the Hungarian people laid the foundation of the identity of the Early Modern Hungarian Estates. It is quite remarkable that – with the exception of Várkonyi and Tóth – Hungarian historians have to this day scarcely mentioned the connection.

There are two reasons for this. The main one is the view that prevails in Hungary, that Early Modern national identity is based on Werbőczy's theory.[219] In the previous chapter we have shown not only that the Doctrine of the Holy Crown did not exist at that time, but also that not a single author writing on the crown who is

---

218 We have left out of consideration the already mentioned 1615 work on the crown by Christoph Lackner (Lackhner, 1571–1631), as that, like a mirror of burghers, falls outside the scope of this study. Christophor Lackhner, *Coronae Hungariae emblematicae descriptio* (Lavingae Suevorum: Typis Palatini, excudebat M. Iacobus Winter, 1615). Révay was Lackner's patron, and he inspired Lackner's book, as we may learn from Lackner's autobiography: Gergely Tóth, ed. and trans., *Lackner Kristófnak, mindkét jog doktorának rövid önéletrajza* [Short biography of Christoph Lackner, doctor in both laws] (Sopron: Sopron városi levéltár, 2008). Révay and Lackner took part in the imperial Diet of 1614 at Linz and Révay did him great honour at the Hungarian coronation in 1618. *Ibid.*, 28, 127. Lackner wrote letters to Révay, see the Ms.: Epistole ad Patronos et Amicos. Soproni evangélikus egyházközség levéltára [The Lutheran convent archive, Sopron]. 45. VI. B. fol. 234–235, 237, 257. Lackner's autobiography contains a number of otherwise unknown facts about the book on the crown, the crown itself and the 1618 coronation. On the book: *Ibid.*, 116–117, 133. "He was charged with going into the castle together with other magnates to bring out the crown. Here he wore a chain of honour and saw with his own eyes that mighty treasure taken from the chest, held the sceptre in his hands in the room and touched with his hand everything else, viz. the sandal, the cloak, the orb, the sword etc... then together with the said trustees took the crown and other royal insignia back into the tower, their customary place of safe-keeping. There Lackner with his own hand wrapped up the crown, that mighty treasure … Cardinal Khlesl himself unsealed and resealed the iron chest with unbreakable seals impressed, and the cardinal further personally wrote his name on the wall in red chalk as a memento, as did the rest too." *Ibid.*, 134–136. Lackner also describes an emblematic mural of the crown which was painted in 1618, but which is unfortunately lost now. *Ibid.*, 137–139.

219 One example: Ernő Marosi, "A magyar történelem képei. A történetiség szemléltetése a művészetekben [The Hungarian history in images. The view on historicity in the arts]," in: Árpád Mikó and Katalin Sinkó, eds., *Történelem—kép. Szemelvények múlt és művészet kapcsolatából Magyarországon* [History-image. Excerpts of the relation between past and art in Hungary] (Budapest: Magyar Nemzeti Galéria, 2000) 19–21.

quoted here, refers to Werbőczy in his work. It is important to stress again that in Révay's work there is not a single reference to the organic state-theory about the crown (or the Doctrine of the Holy Crown), nor does the term member of the Holy Crown (*membrum sacrae coronae*) occur.[220]

The second reason is that apart from the political, religious and intellectual context of his time Révay's ideas have not been taken seriously, or have not been understood from the political, religious and intellectual context of his time. Nevertheless, his thoughts gained wide circulation.

The currency of Révay's work can be broadly divided into three categories: to the first belong those works which he himself wrote, and those the production of which he personally inspired or supported; in the second may be listed the writings of others who made use of Révay's work, and in the third are documents depicting the crown and descriptions of its exterior, that were prepared on the basis of the 1613 portrayal. Sharp divisions cannot be made between the three, as Berger's later works, for example, fall into all three categories.

We may regard the continuation of the book on the crown as the first work in the first category; written between 1613 and 1622, it was published only posthumously, in 1659.[221] The second is Berger's extensive work, also supported by Révay, which was already mentioned in a previous chapter. Berger was commissioned to write an illustrated history of the Kingdom of Hungary, but it never appeared in print.[222] He refers in several places in his manuscripts to Révay and his work on the crown. From this it is clear that he continues Révay's line of thought on the crown and the history of the Estates.[223] Like Révay, in his account of King Mátyás II, Berger

---

220 Nevertheless, several researchers still believe that Révay used the Doctrine of the Holy Crown. See inter alia: Hargittay, *Gloria, Fama, Literatura*, 83, note 248; György Szabados, *A magyar történelem kezdeteiről* [On the beginnings of the Hungarian history] (Budapest: Balassi, 2006) 95. Bónis found no trace of the Doctrine in Révay. Bónis, 93.

221 Petrus De Rewa, *De Monarchia Et Sacra Corona Regni Hvngariae Centuriae Septem* (Francofurti: sumptibus Thomae Mattiae Götzii, 1659). A critical edition, Hungarian translation and thorough study of this book by Gergely Tóth and his colleagues was published in 2021. See Péter Révay, *De monarchia et Sacra Corona Regni Hungariae centuriae septem. – A magyar királyság birodalmáról és szent koronájáról szóló hét század*. Ed. Gergely Tóth; the Latin text ed. and transl. by Gergely Tóth, Bernadett Benei, Rezső Jarmalov, Sára Sánta. I–II. (Budapest: Bölcsészettudományi Kutatóközpont, 2021). See also: Gergely Tóth, "Lutheránus országtörténet újsztoikus keretben: Révay Péter Monarchiája," in Gergely Tóth, ed., Clio inter arma (Budapest: MTA BTK Történettudományi Intézet, 2014) 117–147.

222 Holl, *Ferenczffy Lőrinc*, 149–170; Kulcsár "Berger Illés történeti művei," 245–259; Viskolcz, *A mecenatúra színterei a főúri udvarban*, 292–293. For printed material and their importance see also: Mikó and Sinkó, *Történelem – kép*, 293–296.

223 On the meaning of the crown in mss in Vienna: [Elias Berger], *Historia Ungarica ab A.C. 1458., definit autem in A.C. 1490*, ÖNB, Cod. 8677, fol. 21r.-v., 33r.-v., 54r., 60r.-v.; [Elias Berger], *Historia Hungarica ab a. 1572 usque ad a. 1606*, ÖNB, Cod. 8464, fol. 183r.-v., 222r, 253r., 252v.-257r. (on

describes the exterior of the crown and mentions the portraits of the Virgin Mary, the twelve apostles and the Greek emperor.[224] As, however, this manuscript never appeared in print, and so was never circulated or read in Hungary, we will not speak of it in detail.[225] It is possible that due to the changing political circumstances in Hungary and the Habsburg Empire after Mátyás II gave up his throne in 1618, the work of Berger and its content went out of fashion. In conclusion, we must mention Révay's farewell speech, in which he once more refers to the familiar meaning of the crown.[226]

The most important works in the second category are those of historians such as Berger.[227] In 1614 and 1621 Bocatius too refers to Révay and the crown.[228] Gergely Petthő of Gerse (1570–1629) wrote a chronicle about the Hungarians and

---

the gift of the Turkish crown); [Elias Berger], *Historia Ungarica ab A.C. 1607., definit autem in A.C. 1618.*, ÖNB, Cod. 8229, fol. 12v. (on Révay's work on the crown); 53r.-56r. (Illésházy's speech at Mátyás II's coronation) 132r.-133r., 172v-174v.

224 (…) *S. Coronae ex formae vetustatis et sanctatis, plenae sacris salvatoris, Divae Virginis duodecim Apostolorum et Graecorum Imperatorum, in quorum tutela esse dicitur, imaginibus, primis statim invita Paloczius agnovit.* [Elias Berger], *Historia Ungarica ab A.C. 1458., definit autem in A.C. 1490*, ÖNB, Cod. 8677, fol. 33r.

225 The only known example of the use of Berger's manuscript is Thomas Johannes Pessina de Czechorod who quoted from it: *Chronologia Regni Hungariae*. Thomas Johannes Pessina de Czechorod, *Mars Moravicus* (Pragae: Typis Joannis Arnolti de Dobroslawina, 1677) 341.

226 De Rewa, "Valedictio Morituri," in Hrabecius, *D. O. M. A. Oratio Funebris*, K r.-v.

227 As early as 1613 reference is made to the Hungarian crown in a book published on the occasion of Mátyás' coronation as emperor. Johan Marco Aldringen Luxemburgio, "Ad insigne regum ungariae, á Sylvestro ipsis transmissum," in Bernard Praetorius, ed., *Corona Imperialis…*(Norimbergae: Typis Et Imp. Georg. Leop. Fuhrmann, 1613) 51–52; Petrus Fradelius Schemnicens "Plausus in Coronam Caesaream," in *idem*, 73–74. In 1618 the Calvinist Albert Szenci Molnár expressed doubt over the crown legend and listed the crown as angelic handiwork as examples of the 'superstitions' and 'idolatries' of Hungary. Albert Szenczi Molnár, *Secularis concio evangelica, azaz Jubilaeus esztendei prédikáció* [Secularis concio evangelica or preaching for a jubilee year] (Oppenheimii: Typis & aere Hieronymi Galleri Basileens, 1618), appendix. In 1621 Tamás Balásfy attacked Molnár's position using the Lutheran Révay's ideas. Tamás Balásfy, *Christiana responsio ad libellum Calvinisticum Alberti Molnar Hungari, pedagogi Oppenhemiensis* (Viennae: Typis Gregorii Gelbhaar, 1621) 14–18, On the debate, see: Holl, *Ferenczffy Lőrinc*, 83; Géza Galavics, *Kössünk*, 73–74, 143 and the following chapter.

228 Johannes Bocatius, *Hexasticha votiva, vel strena poetica, ominis boni gratia. Anno Deo volente erit melius* (Bartphae: excudebat Iacobus Kléz, 1612). Modern edition: Bocatius, *Opera Quae Extant Omnia: Poetica*, vol. II, 688. Johannes Bocatius, *Matthiados carmina heroica libri duo* (Cassoviae: Iohannis Fischer, 1614). Modern edition: Bocatius, *Opera Quae Extant Omnia: Poetica*, vol. II., 751, 774–775, 783, 799–802. Johannes Bocatius, *Historica Parasceve* (Cassoviae, 1621), in Bocatius, *Opera Quae Extant Omnia: Prosaica*, 53, 58–59, 64, 53, 58–59, 64. In the last two works Bocatius also mentions Berger.

the crown that may be regarded as a continuation of Révay's work.[229] In 1629 his theory became the focus of attention of Strasbourg political history-writing when the Lutheran political historian Martin Schödel chose the book on the crown as the starting-point of his doctoral thesis.[230] The dissertation became something of a collection of quotations containing, inter alia, countless quotations from the works of Révay and various writers, Classical, Hungarian and others. Later Schödel wrote a handbook on Hungarian politics following Bodin's method on request of the famous Elsevier publisher in Leiden (see image 13).[231] It was based on the thought of Révay and Justus Lipsius; this was published twice in 1634.[232] This volume is the single most important source on how Révay's work was read and interpreted in the Early Modern period.

Even the lawyers of whom Révay thought so little, made use of the meaning of the crown that sprang from it, as may be seen in the 1619 work on Hungarian criminal law by János Kitonich, which begins with an "Ode to the crown", to the inspiration of Révay.[233] A similar verse may be found in the work of János Nadányi (1641–1707).[234]

---

229 Gergely Petthő, *Rövid magyar kronika* [Short Hungarian chronicle] (Viennae Austriae, 1660), continuation and reprints 1702, 1729, 1734, 1738, 1742, ²1742 and 1753.

230 Martinus Schödel, *Cum Deo. Disquisitio Historico-Politica, De Regno Hungariae...* (Argentorati: Johannis Reppl, 1629, ²1630). Schödel was a student of the well-known professor Martin Bernegger. Later continuations: Johann Ferdinand Behamb, *Notitia Hungariae Antiquo-Moderae Berneggeriana: Perpetuis Observationibus Condecorata Nec non Indice Tum Marginali, Tum Reali illustrata, emendata* (Argentorati: Georgii Andreae Dolhopffii, 1676). See also: Johann Christoph Becmann, *Historia Orbis Terrarum Geographica Et Civilis ...* (Francofurti et Lipsiae: apud Henr. Joh. Meyeri Haered. & Godofr. Zimmermann, 1673) 714. (further editions: 1680, 1685, 1692 and 1698).

231 [Martin Schödel], *Respublica et Status Regni Hungariae* ([Leiden: Elsevier], 1634, ²1634).

232 Kees Teszelszky, "Respublica et Status Regni Hungariae: Magyarország kora újkori reprezentációja Európában és a republikánus politikai gondolkodásban [Respublica et Status Regni Hungariae: the representation of Hungary in the Early Modern period and the republican political thought]," *Századvég*, 16/61 (2010) 3–11; Béla P. Szabó, "Hungarológiai munkácska államtudományi hangsúlyokkal a 17. század első feléből [Hungarological small work with politological accents from the first half of the seventeenth century]," *Gerundium: egyetemtörténeti közlemények*, 8/1 (2017) 163; Gergely Tóth, *Szent István, Szent Korona, államalapítás a protestáns történetírásban (16–18. század)* [St. István, the Holy Crown and the foundation of the state in Protestant historiography (sixteenth to eighteenth century)] (Budapest: MTA Bölcsészettudományi Kutatóközpont, Történettudományi Intézet, 2016) 69–72.

233 János Kitonich, *Directio Methodica Processus* (Tyrnavia: S.N., 1619). (frontispiece, verso).

234 Ad CORONAM HUNGARIAE. / Gentis magnaminae radians per secula sidus, / clarius anne solo, clarus ane salo: / Dum fulges gemmisque viris, te Praeside dudum, / Patria praesentem credidit esse Deum. János Nadányi, *Florus Hungaricus, sive rerum Hungaricarum ab ipso exordio ad Ignatium Leopoldum deductarum compendium* (Amstelodami: Ex officina Joannis 'a Waesberge, 1663) (frontispiece, verso). The verse is missing from the English translation (London, 1664). TO THE CROWN OF HUNGARY: Star of a great people, shining through the ages, / what is brighter

The third and final category comprises art, as the overwhelming majority of Early Modern depictions of the crown may be traced back to the illustration in Révay (see image 12).[235] To the best of our knowledge, however, no one has raised the question of why precisely this depiction has enjoyed such great popularity. It appeared from the preceding chapter that there were in the Early Modern period numerous pictures and descriptions of the crown that differed from Révay's engraving and description. The crown itself is depicted in a way that differs from the print in Révay in (at least) five paintings that the book inspired.[236] The fact that despite this the picture in Révay gained the role of national icon, speaks volumes for the wide circulation and popularity of the thoughts expressed in the book. The image of the Révay-crown became familiar in other European countries thanks to the print in Schödel's work (see image 13).

The finest example of the circulation of the theory and the image is the picture on the title page of Hieronymus Ortelius' work on the Ottoman wars in Hungary (image 17) (enlarged and revised edition, 1665).[237] The picture by an unknown artist may be regarded as a Catholic allegory of the views which Révay professed on the crown, Hungary and Christian Europe. It shows that even forty years after his death his ideas were alive and thriving.

---

than you alone on the sea: / while you have shone and gleamed with precious stones, as long as you have ruled/ the Fatherland has believed that God has been there. For the crown-text as a Roman tabella, see: László Havas, "Anticiceronianizmus és antitacitizmus mint az európai nemzeti eszme egyik formálója [Anti-Ciceroism and anti-Tacitism as one of the formers of the European national idea]," in István Bitskey and Szabolcs Oláh, eds., Religió, retorika, nemzettudat régi irodalmunkban [Religion, rhetorics and national consciousness in our ancient literature] (Debrecen: Kossuth Egyetemi Kiadó, 2004) 545–548.

235 György Rózsa, *Magyar történetábrázolás a 17. században* [Hungarian historical images in the seventeenth century] (Budapest: Akadémiai Kiadó, 1973); Teszelszky, "A magyar korona megjelenése,"; Enikő Buzási, "A portrésorozatok," 11–21; Buzási and Géza, *Augsburg - Wien - München - Innsbruck*; Pálffy and Tóth, "Az "országtáblák".

236 Attila Pandula, "Egy XVII. századi, heraldikai témájú, magyar olajfestmény [A seventeenth-century Hungarian oil painting with a heraldic theme]," *Turul* 70 (1997) 26–28; Szilveszter Sólymos, "Hozzászólás és kiegészítés [Comments and addition]," *Turul* 71(1998) 39–41; Holler, "A magyar királyi koronát," 297–309; Mónika Zsámbéky "Megjegyzés a magyar királyi korona 1621. évi ábrázolásaihoz [Remarks on the paintings of 1621 which depict the Hungarian royal crown]," *Művészettörténeti Értésítő* 50 (2001) 341–342; Mikó and Sinkó, *Történelem—kép*, 115; Géza Pálffy, "A Magyar Korona országainak koronázási," 17–53; Pálffy and Tóth, "Az országtáblák".

237 Hieronymus Oertel [Ortelius] and Martin Meyrn, *Ortelius Redivivus et Continuatus oder Ungarische und Siebenbürgische Kriegs-Händel, so vom Jahr 1395. biß auf 1665. mit dem Türcken vorgelauffe* (Nürnberg: Fürst, 1665), title-page. On this title page see: Kees Teszelszky, *Szenci Molnár Albert elveszettnek hitt Igaz Vallás portréja (1606) - True Religion: a lost portrait by Albert Szenci Molnár (1606)* (Budapest: ELTE BTK Középkori és Kora Újkori Magyar Történeti Tanszéke and a Transylvania Emlékeiért Tudományos Egyesület, 2014) 129–130.

VIII. The effect of Révay's book on the crown

The Sylvester Bull

The Sylvester Bull is one of the most intriguing examples of the reception of Révay's work. The document known in Hungary as Sylvester Bull was considered from 1644 till the beginning of the nineteenth century to be the original charter of Pope Sylvester II (999–1003) addressed to the first king of Hungary.[1] In the Bull, István, as prince of the Hungarians, receives the pope's apostolic blessing for placing Hungary (*regnum*) and the Hungarian nation and people (*gens et natio Ungariae*) under the tutelage of the Holy Roman Church. In addition to tutelage, István had requested a crown (*diadema*) and the title of king, and that the Head of the Church should elevate the church in Esztergom to the rank of cathedral and consecrate the episcopates. The pope entrusted Hungary to István and fulfilled his requests on condition that Hungarian kings, lawfully elected by the great men (*optimates*) of the country, should, in person or through their appointees, renew the oath of loyalty and swear obedience to the Holy See. The Head of the Church further granted István the right to have a cross borne before him in token of his apostolic quality (*apostolatus*), and in his apostolic authority (*apostolica auctoritas*) clothed him with the privilege of ordering Church affairs in Hungary himself. In conclusion he informed him that he was about to send to István a crown which had originally been made for the ruler of Poland.

Since the crown figures prominently in the text, the Bull was considered until the end of the nineteenth century to constitute proof of its papal origin and its connection with St István.[2] For the reader living in 1644, however, the content of the Bull had quite a different meaning: in fact, a meaning connected to the political debate concerning the power of the Habsburg ruler that had started in the early years of that century. The Bull explained to the ruler the apostolic status relating to the domain of the Hungarian crown. From the king's point of view, the term apostolic meant that he, as the bearer of the title apostolic king, might not only claim lay power but also exercised authority in the ecclesiastical sphere in his country.

---

1 Georgius Fejér, *Codex Diplomaticus Hungariae ecclesiasticus ac civilis*, vol. I (Budae: Typis typogr. Regiae Universitatis Ungaricae, 1828) 274–277.

2 Ipolyi Arnold, *A magyar szent korona és a koronázási jelvények története és műleírása* [The history and description of the Hungarian Holy Crown and the crown jewels] (Budapest: Magyar Tudományos Akadémia, 1886) 10.

With regard to the king's presumed apostolic status, a debate took place in the second quarter of the seventeenth century over whether the Habsburg ruler had the right to appoint bishops on Hungarian territory (the royal "right of patronage", *jus patronus regius*).³ The Habsburgs justified their privilege by reference to their descent from St István, the first apostolic king of Hungary, to whom – according to them – Pope Benedict VII (974–983) had granted this right together with the crown. The Head of the Roman Church, however – considering that there was no proof of the permanent nature of the apostolic status – questioned the power of the Habsburg rulers in this respect. The consequence of this was that the pope routinely refused to ratify the appointments of bishops that they made. The publication in 1644 of the Bull was, therefore, like a gift from heaven to the king. The allegedly eleventh-century document provided, with retrospective force, an unambiguous answer to this current political question: if the lawful heir to the throne swore loyalty to the pope, as successor to the apostolic king, had he the right to appoint bishops in Hungary?

The struggle for power was not only between the pope and the king, but was felt throughout the Catholic Church.⁴ Tension was caused both by the centralising ambitions of the pope and the Habsburgs, and by the opposition to this which became evident in Hungary. The Hungarian prelates tried to ensure themselves an autonomous position viv-à-vis pope and king alike. For this reason, when a king such as Rudolf or Mátyás II came to the throne, who might be seen as more sympathetic to the Protestants, they sought support in Rome.⁵ In the event, however, that a pope of pro-French tendencies was at the head of the Church and pursued a policy hostile to the interests of the Habsburg Empire, the Hungarian bishops took the Habsburg side.

---

3 On the debate see: Vilmos Fraknói, *A magyar kegyúri jog Szent Istvántól Mária Teréziáig* [The Hungarian patron law from St István till Maria Theresia] (Budapest: Magyar Tudományos Akadémia, 1883) Ferenc Galla, *Marnavics Tomkó János Boszniai püspök magyar vonatkozásai* (Budapest: Római Magyar Tört. Intézet, 1940) 74–84; Péter Tusor, "A magyar egyház és Róma a 17. században [The Hungarian church and Rome in the seventeenth century]," *Vigilia* 64 (1999) 503–513; Sándor Bene, "A Szilvester-bulla nyomában. Pázmány Péter és a Szent István-hagyomány 17. századi fordulópontja [In the footsteps of the Bull of Sylvester. Péter Pázmány and the turning point of the St István tradition in the seventeenth century]," *A Ráday Gyűjtemény Évkönyvei* (1999). (In what follows we shall refer to the extended version of this publication only available in archived form on the web: https://web.archive.org/web/20070719110755/http://www.rgy.hu/bene.htm, accessed on 15 May 2022); Sándor Bene, "A Szilvester-bulla nyomában. Pázmány Péter és a Szent István-hagyomány 17. századi fordulópontja [In the footsteps of the Bull of Sylvester. Péter Pázmány and the turning point of the St István tradition in the seventeenth century]," in László Veszprémy, ed., *Szent István és az államalapítás* [St István and the foundation of the state] (Budapest: Osiris, 2002) 144–146 (abridged version of the former).

4 Bene, "A Szilvester-bulla nyomában," 1*-2*.

5 Péter Tusor, "Az 1608. évi magyar törvények a római inkvizíció előtt: II. Mátyás kiközösítése [The laws of 1608 before the Roman inquisition: Mátyás II excommunication]," *Aetas* 4 (2000) 89–105.

The conflict between Church and ruler was most strongly felt when vacant sees were being filled in the southern and eastern areas of Hungary which were occupied by the Ottomans. These frequently existed in name alone by that time, or had only a fraction of their original area. The bishops who were placed in charge of these dioceses gained in worldly rather than ecclesiastical standing by their appointments, as they often owed their titles to services that had had little to do with religion.[6] The king simply appointed them and often did not even ask for papal ratification (*confirmatio*) at all.[7] These wielders of authority, nominally ecclesiastics but frequently laymen, chiefly served the interests of the king. The debate over the king's right of patronage broke out again and again, reaching its height during the pontificate of Gregory XV (1621–1623).[8] It was this pope who, in 1622, convened a congregation under the name *De Propaganda Fide*, the task of which was to reestablish the hierarchy of the Church in divided Europe.[9] A second purpose of the congregation was to create a mission in the pagan lands of the New World and in the formerly Christian territories of the Old – among others, in the occupied regions of Hungary.[10] In the same year the pope transferred the centre for missionary work in the Balkans from Vienna to Rome.[11]

By so doing the Head of the Church clashed in the political arena with those – Ferdinánd II (1618–1637) and Archbishop Péter Pázmány (1570–1637), primate of Hungary and head of the ecclesiastical province of Hungary – who had claims to lay and ecclesiastical power in the region. Pázmány defended the interests of the Hungarian Estates against the Habsburg ruler, and the interests of the king and the Estates against the pope, and did not want Rome to meddle in the affairs of state of the territories that were occupied by the Turks. The Catholic Ferdinánd

---

6 Galla mentions the example of a violinist who was appointed bishop because he played splendidly for the emperor during a mass. Galla, *Marnavics Tomkó János*, 70.
7 In the period about 1610–1620 the king appointed several bishops in Bosnia, not one of whom was confirmed in appointment by Rome. Sándor Bene, "Hol vagy István király?" (Pázmány Péter és a Szent István-hagyomány fordulópontja) [Where are you King Stephanus? Péter Pázmány and the turning point in the tradition of the Holy Stephanus]," in Zsolt Unger, ed., *Szent István király képe a magyar irodalomban* [The royal image of St István in Hungarian literature] (Budapest: Petőfi Irodalmi Múzeum, 2001) 2, 8.
8 Tusor, "A magyar egyház," 503–504.
9 Peter Guilday, "The Sacred Congregation de Propaganda Fide (1622–1922)", *The Catholic Historical Review*, 6/4 (1921) 479.
10 Antal Molnár, "Relations between the Holy See and Hungary during the Ottoman Domination of the Country," in István Zombori, ed., *Fight against the Turk in Central-Europe in the First Half of the 16th Century* (Budapest: Historia Ecclesiastica Hungarica Alapítvány and Magyar Egyháztörténeti Enciklopédia Munkaközösség, 2004) 192; Peter Rietbergen, *Power and Religion in Baroque Rome. Barberini Cultural Politics* (Leiden and Boston: Brill, 2006) 395–398.
11 Bene, "A Szilvester-bulla nyomában," 4*.

and the highest clergy of the Hungarian Church looked feverishly for arguments to defend their rights against Rome. Ferdinánd instructed his lawyers to search in the Hungarian Chancellery and the papal archives with this in mind. Pázmány too did his share of the work, as we shall show later.[12]

This increasing activity, which had its roots in Vienna, explains the resurgent interest in the position and work of Elias Berger, court historian to the Habsburgs. Between 1619 and 1622 Berger published nothing. This is partly because he had not received his promised salary from the court between 1619 and 1621, but he continued to write his history of Hungary and presented the results in manuscript to the Hungarian *Camera*.[13] During one of the military campaigns of Prince Gábor Bethlen of Transylvania against Ferdinánd, he received a house in Szakolcza from Bethlen on 25 February 1620.[14] According to his own account, he was living in straitened circumstances. His outstanding salary was paid only in 1622 and he received a house in Szakolcza from Ferdinánd (perhaps the same house as the one he received from Bethlen: this is still unclear).[15] In 1624 he received 300 forints from Ferdinánd for the printing of his book on Hungarian history.[16] In 1625 Ferdinánd again made Berger court history writer, after Pázmány had urged his appointment.[17]

In the on-going struggle between Rome and Vienna, a side-product was the literary output of three churchmen: János Marnavics Tomkó (Johannes Tomcus Marnavitius Bosniensis, Ivan Mrnaviae Tomkó, 1580–1639), the Franciscan Rafael Levakovics (Rafael Levakoviae, Levakovich, ?1590–?1650) and the Jesuit Menyhért Inchofer (Melchior Inchoffer, 1580/1585–1648).[18] In 1622 Levakovics and Tomkó were commissioned to compile a Glagolitic missal and breviary, while between 1622 and 1644 the three collaborated in a book on the king's apostolic nature and the meaning of the crown. It is feasible that it was they who composed the text of

---

12 Galla, *Marnavics Tomkó*, 76.
13 For the three years 1619–1621, Berger received no money at all from the Habsburg court. See Frankl [Fraknói], "Berger Illés," 386. For Berger's pay from the *Camera*: Zoltán Fallenbüchl, "A Magyar Kamara és a könyvek [The Hungarian *Camera* and the books]," *Az Országos Széchényi Könyvtár Évkönyve 1968–1969* (1969) 305–317.
14 See ms ELTE Egyetemi Könyvtár Kézirattár, Kaprinai B 19/25, 103–104.
15 In connection with Berger's salary see the accounts of the Pozsony *Camera*: István Monok, ed., *A magyar könyvkultúra múltjából: Iványi Béla cikkei és anyaggyűjtése* [From the history of the Hungarian book culture: the articles and source collection of Béla Iványi] (Szeged: József Attila Tudományegyetem Bölcsészettudományi Kara, 1983) 188.
16 Frankl, "Berger Illés," 386; Kulcsár, "Berger Illés történeti művei," 247.
17 Ferenc Hanuy, ed., *Petri Cardinalis Pázmány epistolae collectae I (1610–1628)* (Budapest: Királyi Magyar Tudomány-Egyetem, 1910) 462. (Before 14 July 1625). Pázmány had Miklós Istvánffy's work on the history of Hungary also published in 1622.
18 R. Aubert, ed., *Dictionnaire d'histoire et de géographie ecclésiastiques* (Paris: Letouzey et Ané, 1995) 979–9 80.

the aftermath. It is striking that – as we shall show later – all these churchmen in the papal service committed to paper views which strengthened the position of the Habsburg ruler against the pope.

This political struggle explains why a large number of publications – historiographic, religious and political – on the historicity of the Habsburgs' apostolic kingship appeared after 1622, more details of which will be given in what follows. As the political problem of the apostolic royal dignity involved the meaning of St István's power as king, the granting of the crown also featured prominently in these works. The Habsburg ruler once again won legitimacy for his power from the Hungarian crown, whereby the significance of the crown was varied once more.

The debate on the apostolic nature of the crown

The term apostolic and the significance of the granting of the crown had even before then played a part in polemic literature in Hungary. It is conspicuous that Pázmány was always actively involved in the development of all new ideas connected to the above.[19] At the same time, it was he who initiated the change in thinking about the substance of the adjective "*apostolus*" which came after 1625. From the sources mentioned above it can be seen that even before 1625 a certain change had been taking place, but this had not yet affected the legitimation of the Habsburgs' apostolic royal power. In other words, before 1625 the subject of the king's apostolic nature was not linked to the Hungarian crown. It was Pázmány who, in his above-mentioned pamphlet of 1603, first made use of the subject of the granting of the Hungarian crown.[20] The function of this work was to advise the Hungarian Estates of their obligation to obey the pope. It does not, however, detract from St István's apostolic dignity. A year later the Catholic members of the Hungarian Council, referring to *Tripartitum*, described the king of Hungary as "apostolic" (*apostolus*) in order to emphasise the ruler's authority in Church affairs to the detriment of the rights of Protestants.[21] In 1606 the Bishop of Csanád, Faustus Verancsics (?1540–1617), wrote a pamphlet on means of renewal of the faith in Hungary in which he states that, thanks to the apostolic King St István, the king exercises a right of patronage which makes it possible for him to decide on ecclesiastical stipends, and that he has likewise the right to appoint bishops, while the pope confirms these appointments.[22] Verancsics does not link this right to the crown, as he only refers to the crown in the

---

19 Bene, "Hol vagy István király?," 1–14.
20 Pázmány, *Felelet Magyari István*, 19. See also: Bene, "A Szilveszter-bulla nyomában" 2*.
21 MOE X, 519.
22 Faustus Verancsics, "A vallás felújításának módszerei Magyarországon (1606) [The methods of renewal of religion in Hungary (1606)]," in Katalin S. Vargha, ed. and trans., *Verancsics Faustus*

territorial sense. In 1608 Berger calls the crown "apostolic" because of the depictions of the apostles to be seen on it. The title "apostolic king" first occurs only in works published for the coronation of Ferdinánd II in 1618, but it is not connected to the crown. Ferdinánd is so called in the pamphlet *Apparatus regius*, published in the same year, but no connection between the crown and apostolic royal authority is made in the text.[23] Even in 1621, the Jesuit Tamás Balásfy (Balásfi, 1580–1625) makes no reference to the crown having any actual apostolic significance. He only accepts Révay's account of the holy nature of the crown as a defence against an anti-Catholic work of the Calvinist Albert Szenci Molnár, as we have seen in the previous chapter.

In 1625, Pázmány started a debate over the apostolic nature of the king of Hungary. After this appointment as Archbishop of Esztergom in 1616 he had received the primacy of Hungary from the pope and been made ambassador of the See of Rome. At the same time, he was chief adviser to the Habsburg ruler on political and religious affairs in Hungary; he had the privilege of crowning kings of Hungary, and was at all times the king's confessor and court chaplain, and as such played a far from marginal part in politics and in the representation of the Estates.[24] So great was Pázmány's influence that Prince Gábor Bethlen of Transylvania called him "Regent of Hungary".[25] In addition to his well-known writings on religious subjects he left a number of less-familiar political works and several pamphlets in letter-form containing political advice, inter alia on the desirability of the Habsburgs' hereditary monarchy.[26] In 1625 he petitioned the pope on behalf of the Hungarian Estates, requesting him to make the veneration of King St István known world-wide.[27]

Machinae novae és más művei [The Machinae novae of Faustus Verancsics and other works] (Budapest: Magvető Könyvkiadó, 1985) 328–329, 333.

23 S.n., *Apparatus regius. Sereniss. ac potentissimo Ferdinando II. Hungariae ac Bohemiae regi. Symbolis regum Hungariae adornatus.* (Viennae Austrae: Gregorius Gelbhaar, 1618). See on this work: Holl, *Ferenczffy Lőrinc*, 193.

24 Ágnes R. Várkonyi, *Europa varietas – Hungarica varietas*, Éva Pálmai and Kálmán Ruttkay trans. (Budapest: Akadémiai Kiadó, 2000) 55–88.

25 Márton Tarnóc, ed., *Pázmány Péter művei* [Works of Péter Pázmány] (Budapest, 1985) 1172.

26 Péter Pázmány, "Két beszéd. Pázmány beszéde II. Ferdinánd megválasztása érdekében a Pozsonyi megyegyűlésen [Two orations. The speech of Pázmány for the occasion of the election during the Diet of Pozsony]," in Miklós Őry, Ferenc Szabó and Péter Vass, eds., *Pázmány Péter válogatás műveiből* [Selection of works of Péter Pázmány], Vol. II (Budapest: Szent István Társulat, 1983) 339–395 (November 1617); Péter Pázmány, "Petri Pazmani Responsum ad Quaestionem: An Ferdinando III. Successionis vel Electionis Jure Regnum debeatur," in Hanuy, *Petri Cardinalis Pázmány epistolae collectae I (1610–1628)* 470–472.

27 Várkonyi, *Europa varietas*, 78.

Pázmány's thinking on the vexed question of patronage (*ius patronus*) developed as follows: in 1625 he defended the king's right to appoint bishops in two letters to Caraffa, the papal nuncio in Vienna, but without referring to the apostolic right.[28] Caraffa, however, disputed the archbishop's position. Next, Pázmány researched sources and found a legal basis more secure than common law and tradition for the defence of the royal right of patronage (*ius patronatus regalis*). In a letter to Ferdinánd dated 5 August 1627, he provides evidence of a change in thinking.[29] He states that the original Bull of Pope Sylvester II, in which he confirmed the king's right to appoint bishops, had been lost. It was therefore his view that the king alone, relying on common law, might claim this power which was confirmed only by such secondary authorities as *Tripartitum*, the legend of Bishop Hartvik, Bonfini's History of Hungary, and the relevant clause of the Golden Bull of András II. The essence of the question was whether the king had the right to appoint bishops and have authority over church stipends, or whether his right was merely to recommend appointments of bishops to Rome.

Eight years later, Pázmány expressed his ideas on this matter in detail in a memorandum of 10 April 1635 which he drafted for the king's benefit.[30] He comes to the king's defence on a number of points. In his view the strongest argument for the right of patronage is that St István had converted the Hungarians to the Christian faith of his own volition. The sainted king had appointed bishops and also chosen men for this dignity who were then confirmed in office by the pope. All this, says Pázmány, emerges clearly from the hymns sung on the Feast of St István, and from the foundation deeds of the dioceses created during his reign. The archbishop then turns to the problem that the royal archive had fallen into Ottoman hands while Buda was occupied, and the Papal Bulls had been destroyed. Despite the fact that he had no tangible evidence, he continued to adhere to the validity of common law. The reply from Rome to Pázmány's document was: perhaps the right of patronage was still valid on the present territory of Hungary, but the king could not exercise it in the lost territories of the erstwhile Kingdom of Hungary.

Pázmány reacted to this with another memorandum addressed to the king, dated 16 June 1635, in which for the first time the crown was mentioned.[31] In this he states that the king may not surrender to the Holy See any right to the filling or granting of a single such bishopric as had at any time been the rightful possession of the Hungarian crown, since it was the duty of the king, following the example of his forebears, to preserve that which belonged to the Holy Crown. Pázmány thus brought the legal and territorial significance of the crown into play. The king's right

---

28 Bene, "A Szilvester-bulla nyomában," 5*.
29 *Ibid.*
30 *Ibid.*
31 *Ibid.*, 6*.

to appoint bishops is indissolubly bound to the Hungarian crown, since this right applies to those territories which are or have been in the possession of the crown. Under the oath which he made to the Estates, the king promised to defend the property of the crown, and thereby acquired kingly power. Pázmány's reasoning said that if the king gave up this right he would offend against the Hungarian crown, and would consequently lose the legitimacy of his kingly power.

In an unpublished manuscript of Elias Berger's dating from 1635, we can discover the same thoughts which Pázmány discussed in his second memorandum too, i. e. those on the royal right of patronage and the connection with the significance of the crown.[32] In this work Berger writes of the Habsburgs' valid royal power over Hungary as the logical final outcome of history, as desired by God. In his opinion, the king's right to appoint bishops is indissolubly linked to the crown, as it applies to those territories that are or have been in the possession of the crown.[33] The king had sworn to the Estates that he would defend the property of the crown, and that was what gained him royal power.

If we follow the debate carefully, we can draw the conclusion that the Habsburg court failed to find reliable sources for a sound legal proof of the king's apostolic rights. It was therefore constrained to base its legal argument on the Medieval Hartvik legend, Bonfini's History of Hungary, and Werbőczy's questionable codification, which had never been confirmed by ruling kings. The political and legal fictions were not good enough to meet the court's requirements, and it had to adjust them to the requirements of the time. It was, however, less important to dust off and freshen up such ancient images than to find convincing and tangible evidence that these fictions in fact had any force in law. In brief: historical political imagination had to become valid legal reality.

To show how this process worked it is important for us to turn our attention to the changes that took place in Rome between 1625 and 1644. The most significant representative of Habsburg interests was Cardinal Francesco Barberini, a notable patron of the Hungarian churchmen who constituted the Collegium Germanicum-Hungaricum in the Vatican. It had been thanks to his support that Pázmány had received his cardinal's hat, and other Hungarians and Habsburg loyalists – among them Tomkó Marnavics – their episcopal croziers. Pázmány maintained a lively contact from Esztergom with Barberini and the Church writers, Tomkó, Levakovics and Inchofer.

---

32 Elias Perger [Berger], *Duplex speculum chronologicum...* (EK Ms. G.69) (With the subtitle: *Monarchia Hungarorum Regalis*) fol. 97–103.

33 *Ibid.*, 97–98. Berger writes again about the significance of the cross: *Ibid.*, 97. He refers to Bodin, Bonfini and Werbőczy. Although the manuscript was fit for print, only the title page of this work is printed.

The first work in which a crown-fiction was used to justify the apostolic nature of the king of Hungary was *De coronis Ungaricis brevis nota*, written in 1626 by Tomkó Marnavics.[34] This was commissioned by Lorenzo Magalotti (1584–1637), papal secretary of state for foreign affairs.[35] We can explain the publication of this by the fact that Count Michael Adolf Althan (1575–1636) presented the pope with a "Hungarian crown" and an Ottoman sword, allegedly the former property of Bocskai, with the intention that the gift should go to the well-known Italian place of pilgrimage, the Casa Sancta at Loreto.[36] We may reasonably suppose that a connection existed between the Count and Bocskai's crown jewels; he had been a member of Rudolf's war council, together with Miklós Istvánffy he had taken part as an imperial ambassador in negotiations with Bocskai, and had probably been present when Bocskai was crowned with the crown presented by the Turks.[37] Furthermore, he had supported missionary activity in the occupied regions of Hungary.[38]

The manuscript on the presentation of the crown is written in an easy style and elegant hand. It contains drawings of the crown and the sword, together with Magalotti's armorial achievements and his motto – Freedom – and a cardinal's hat. From the workmanship and exterior, it may be taken as a specially-designed occasional item, intended only for the cardinal with no thought of publication in print. This is why it remained for so long hidden from the eyes of Hungarian historians. It was discovered by a Hungarian researcher in 1909 who took it for the draft of a book on the crown and made it known as such.[39] It was rediscovered only in 1984, since when its translation into Hungarian has appeared, as has its interpretation.[40] As the people that discovered and published this manuscript were art historians, their main interest was in the description of the crown and the art history aspects of the text. For this reason, they failed to notice the interesting historical elements of the fiction that it contained, and its particular political significance.

---

34 Johannes Tomci Marnavitii, *De coronis Ungaricis nota brevis* (manuscript), dated 1 January 1627. Bibliotheca Apostolica Vaticana Ms. OTTOB. Lat. 2776.
35 Rietbergen, *Power and Religion*, 149.
36 Imre Takács, "Corona Vladislaviana avagy corona Coronensis. Tomkó János kézirata 1626-ból Bocskai István második, későgótikus koronájáról [The *Corona Vladislaviana* or the *corona Coronensis*. The manuscript of János Tomkó (1626) on the second, late Gothic crown of István Bocskai]," *Művészettörténeti Értesítő*, XLIV(1984) 102.
37 Ibid. Available sources are silent on his presence at the coronation. For these activities of Althan's on behalf of Rudolf, see: Von Chlumecky, *Carl von Zierotin und seine Zeit 1564–1615*, vol. I, 551.
38 István György Tóth, "Between Islam and Catholicism: Bosnian Franciscan Missionaries in Turkish Hungary, 1584–1716," *Catholic Historical Review*, 89 (2003) 420.
39 Imre Zsák, "A római Ottoboni Könyvtár hazai vonatkozásai [The Hungarian items of the Ottonboni Library in Rome]," *Magyar Könyvszemle*, 131 (1909) 341–342.
40 Takács, "Corona Vladislaviana," 106–113.

The aim of the work was to persuade the cardinal of a historical fiction which Tomkó linked to the crown presented by Althan. Tomkó states that this was the crown that Bocskai received from the Turks in 1605, and "... with which he finally refused to be crowned ...". From that it is clear that the author – probably through Istvánffy – was aware of the myth of the refusal of the crown. According to Tomkó, the crown fell into Ottoman hands after the battle of Varna in 1444, in which King Ulászló I lost his life. The real crown of Hungary was not in the king's hands from that historical moment when the Habsburg emperor took possession of it in the battle and after an Austrian lady of the court, as was common knowledge, had stolen it. As the crown was not on Hungarian soil, in Tomkó's opinion, the king of Hungary had taken the votive crown from St István's reliquary and been crowned with that. Therefore, in his view, Bocskai's crown that could then be seen in Loreto, was not simply a Hungarian crown jewel with a stormy past, but a symbol of majesty linked to King St István. Tomkó is therefore suggesting that the famous object holds in itself something of the first king's saintliness.

Just like the earlier-mentioned histories of the crown, Tomkó's miraculous tale is a blend of reality and imagination. The manuscript contains a picture of the crown that was presented by Althan to the statue of the Virgin Mary in Loreto, which the art historian Éva Kovács believes is datable to the mid-fifteenth century because of its distinguishing features.[41] Using this dating, Imre Takács identifies the Loreto crown not with the Turkish crown of Bocskai, but with another Medieval crown which Bocskai received from the citizens of Brassó after the coronation at Rákosmező.[42] His actual Turkish crown had been in Vienna since 1609. It is therefore not possible that the votive crown at Loreto is identical with that which he received from the Ottomans and in no way graced the head of Ulászló I, nor indeed did it come from St István's reliquary.

The question remains of why Tomkó fabricated such a cleverly constructed fiction about this crown. We find the answer in a register of the treasures of Loreto. According to the records, a number of Hungarian aristocrats donated votive crowns to this place of pilgrimage in the seventeenth century, so that Count Althan was not the only person to send such a generous gift. Tomkó related this tale about the Hungarian crown, making it more interesting than was the case, so that the presentation of this crown – and its donor – should thus acquire a significance greater than that of other votive crowns. We do not know, however, why Magalotti commissioned Tomkó to write this work.

---

41 Éva Kovács, "Bocskai István loretói koronája [István Bocskai's crown of Loreto]," *Művészettörténeti Értesítő*, XLIV (1984) 114–115.
42 Takács, "Corona Vladislaviana," 103.

A thorough examination of the text leads one to suppose that in addition to the story of the votive crown, Tomkó had another tale to tell. He begins with an account of the origins of the Hungarians. Then he speaks of their adoption of Christianity and the granting of the Hungarian crown – this time the real one. After that, however, he goes at great length into the connection between Althan's donation and the granting of the real Hungarian crown. Again and again, he brings topics – the significance of Ulászló's reliquary crown, Bocskai's coronation and his own invented family history – into contact with the Hungarian crown. All this hints at Tomkó's wish to make a definite message about the crown known to the cardinal.

Bearing in mind the political environment in which the manuscript was written, it is not surprising that the key-word to the theory is the term apostolic. In his discourse Tomkó makes a connection between the meaning of the term, the Hungarian crowns and the kings and people of Hungary. This connection he describes from an Illyrian viewpoint – this is one of the main characteristics of his life's work.[43] This is why he quotes not only such Hungarian humanist writers as Bonfini and Istvánffy, but also the Greeks.[44]

Tomkó's essay – especially the section on the Hungarians – thus differs from the usual contemporary historiographic works on Hungary, which makes us wonder how he is going to treat the subject. He begins with an intelligent and extensive summing up of the origin of the people of Hungary, the Hungarian nation (*gens Ungarica*), which he believes stems from the Huns and Avars.[45] In so doing he also considers the origin of the Latin name – *Ungarus* – which in his opinion is derivable from the name not of the Huns but of the Ugric people, since that was what the Illyrians called the Hungarians after they had occupied their country.[46] He argues that the Latin name for the Hungarians comes from the Illyrians. In this was he delicately informs the cardinal that the Illyrians occupied the country before the Hungarian nation (*gens*) came into being.

After that, Tomkó tells of the Hungarians' conversion to the Christian faith and the arrival of the crown in Hungary, then deals with the subject of the king's apostolic nature. He repeats the familiar story based on the Hartvik legend, but emphasises the first Hungarian king's apostolic role even more than Hartvik. He makes it

---

43 Bene, "A Szilveszter-bulla nyomában," 7*. Tomkó presents himself as a scion of the Illyrian ruling house.
44 Tomkó quotes *inter alia* the *De administrando imperio* of Emperor Constantinos Porphyrogenitos, which had appeared in 1611 in a bilingual – Greek and Latin – version in Leiden. Tomci Marnavitii, *De coronis Ungaricis nota brevis* 3a. In what follows he also names Pliny, Nicetas, Curopalatos and Theophanes.
45 *Ibid.*, 5a.
46 Tomkó's idea on the derivation of the word *Hungarus* shows a surprising agreement with the modern scientific view. See Szűcs, "Theoretical elements," xlvi.

clear that István had completed the baptism of the people and the appointment of bishops even before receiving the papal blessing and the crown. He writes that István summoned apostolic workers (*apostolici operarii*) from the whole of Christendom, "… to conquer foes seen and unseen …", and with their help was victorious.[47] In order to ensure that his posterity remained in Christian piety, István founded an archbishopric in the nation's capital and appointed bishops for other areas of the country.[48] Only when he had thus founded the Hungarian Church did he send Bishop Asztrik to Rome to ask Pope Benedict VII for "royal symbols of majesty" (*regalia insignia*). Asztrik, however, appeared before the "apostolic senate" (*apostolicus senatus*) and told them what apostolic work István had carried out for the sake of the Catholic faith along the Danube. Learning of the king's activity filled the pope and the apostolic senate with delight. For his service to the Church not only was a royal crown bestowed upon the "most Christian king" (*Christianissimus rex*), but he was also clothed with "apostolic authority in his realm" (*in regno apostolica authoritas*).[49] This authority meant that he and his successors had the right to appoint bishops.

According to Tomkó, this new significance also implies that not only the cross but also the crown is an "apostolic symbol" (*apostolica insignia*) of the obedience shown by the king and his successors to the pope. He then declares that the senate decided to bestow on István a cross that could be borne before him, so as by that means too, to elevate the glory of this true and faithful knight and apostle of God, and the king and his successors might forever enjoy this privilege.[50] Then, Asztrik returned to Hungary and Tomkó relates in detail with what honour István received the apostolic insignia. From that time on the king set an example to all by again and again expressing publicly his obedience to the pope and the apostolic senate.[51]

Next, Tomkó speaks of the meaning of the term apostolic and states that to that day the Hungarians worship the crown that was bestowed by God on the Hungarian kings, describing it as "holy" (*sacra*) and "angelic" (*angelica*) and by other lofty appellations.[52] No king, says he, may be regarded as a rightful ruler except if he be crowned with this crown. He quotes the remark of Mihály Guti Országh, mentioned above, about the ox that must be accepted as rightful king if it has been crowned with this crown.[53] Tomkó therefore declares that beginning with the first apostolic

---

47 Tomci Marnavitii, *De coronis Ungaricis nota brevis*, 6a. This account is like a Roman reaction to early missionary work.
48 *Ibid.*, 6r.-v.
49 *Ibid.*, 7r.
50 *Ibid.*
51 *Ibid.*, 7v.
52 *Ibid.*, 8v.
53 *Ibid.*, 8r. Bonfini, *Rerum Ungaricarum*, decadis IV, liber III, 564.

king, all his successors have gained the homage of the subjects by virtue of the worship of the angelic crown.[54] There is no further reference to the cross in the text, because the author deals only with the "angelic crown" when writing about the apostolic kings' authority.

Tomkó next gives an account of the story, which we have already mentioned, about how the crown in St István's reliquary came onto Ulászló I's head, and how the Ottomans presented it to Bocskai. Here he emphasises repeatedly that "… the king is not the lawful ruler without the angelic crown …"[55] He devotes great attention to the incident in which the Ottoman ambassador crowned Bocskai. He states that "… so great was the reverence that Bocskai felt towards the Holy Crown that he would not permit himself to be crowned with any other, but accepted the Turkish crown as a gift".[56] Tomkó ends his work with the statement that the votive crown found its way to Loreto through the agency of Virgin Mary, Patron Saint of Hungary.[57] It seems that Tomkó has a decided view about the apostolic kingship and the Hungarian crown. As he sees it, the king has the right to appoint bishops, but at the same time owes obedience to the pope. The Holy Crown is a symbol of the apostolic kingship, and without coronation by means of it there exists no kingly power. At the same time, the apostolic significance of the crown legitimates the king's authority in the ecclesiastical sphere. As researchers have not, to this day, turned their attention to the political interpretation of the term apostolic, the source of Tomkó's notions about the crown remains unknown. It appears that he bases his thinking exclusively on the histories of Bonfini and Istvánffy, since – as Imre Takács points out – these are the only authors whom he quotes.[58] Many arguments, however, support the statement that Tomkó must also have used Révay's book on the crown.

The structure of the manuscript, the significance of the crown that it outlines, even certain passages in the text match Révay's book. Both begin with an account of the source of the Hungarians, and of the origin and significance of the Holy Crown. Tomkó ends his work with a description of the fate of the Medieval crown. In all probability, the political significance of the crown in Tomkó is taken from Révay – we can be sure that it does not come from Bonfini or Istvánffy. Although the Italian humanist wrote about the crown, the function of its appearance in his work is merely to add to the dignity and praise of Mátyás Corvinus. In Istvánffy, the crown does not play a considerable part. By contrast, in several sections of Tomkó's work we can see a quotation from Révay in connection with the meaning

---

54 Tomci Marnavitii, *De coronis Ungaricis nota brevis*, 8r.
55 *Ibid.*, 8r., 14r., 15r., 17v.
56 *Ibid.*, 16v.
57 *Ibid.*, 18v.
58 Takács, "Corona Vladislaviana," 104 and note 28.

of coronation with the Holy Crown, without which a king of Hungary cannot be a lawful ruler.⁵⁹ He likewise bases the reference to the titles of the crown on the introduction to Révay's work.⁶⁰

Bearing in mind these correspondences, it is remarkable that Tomkó does not even once mention Révay's name or his book. If the thoughts of an author go over and over a given work to such an extent it would be logical for the quoted writer's name also to appear. The explanation for this omission is that in 1621 the Lutheran Révay was considered a pillar of the Protestant Church in Hungary.⁶¹ A book written at the bidding of a cardinal, and furthermore intended to make smooth the career of the author, was best not seen to be based on the work of a Protestant. Nevertheless, we may regard Tomkó's work as the acceptance and further development of Révay's political theory of the crown. The Illyrian writer underpinned the King of Hungary's ambitions for authority, and established his own Illyrian political image and identity into the bargain.

Four years after the manuscript on the crown, Tomkó wrote another work in which he once again drew together Habsburg and Hungarian political ideas, Illyrian identity, ecclesiastical history and the crown. In this book, *Regiae sanctitatis Illyricanae foecunditas*, which was printed in instalments between 1630 and 1631, he writes the lives of "saints of Illyria".⁶² These, however, are the saints who lived between the Roman period and the Middle Ages within the bounds of the "Illyrian land" (in Tomkó's account Dalmatia, Croatia, Bosnia, Serbia, Thrace and Macedonia) and those who, in some shape or form, can be associated with the area.⁶³ Tomkó thus reckons among the saints of Illyria the Hungarian saints István, László and Imre, as in his eyes, Pannonia is part of Illyria.⁶⁴

The book is in four sections. The first comprises the title page which bears the date 1630. The second is a dedication, which the writer addresses to Ferdinánd III

---

59 This occurs in four places: Tomci Marnavitii, *De coronis Ungaricis*, 8r., 14r., 15r., 17v.
60 (…) *CORONAM SACRAM, ANGELICAM, APOSTOLICAM & similibus nominibus appellamus* (…) De Rewa, *De sacrae* (auctor ad lectorem)(…) *et sacra, et Angelica, et Caelestis aliisque summis nominibus appellata tanti apud Ungaros* (…) Tomci Marnavitii, *De coronis nota brevis*, 6r.
61 Albert Szenci Molnár, *Secularis Concio Euangelica; az az, Jubileus esztendei praedikatzo…* (Oppenheimii: typis et aete Hieronymi Galleri Basileen, 1618) 4.
62 Johannes Tomci Marnavitii, *Regiae sanctitatis Illyricanae foecunditas a Joanne Tomco Marnavitio Bosniensi Edita* (Romae: Vaticannis, 1630, 1630). Concerning this work see: Ferenc Galla, *Marnavics Tomkó János boszniai püspök magyar vonatkozásai* [The Hungarian relations of János Marnavics Tomkó] (Budapest: Római Magyar Történelmi Intézet, 1940) 61–68; Sándor Bene, *Egy kanonok három királysága. Ruttkay György horváth históriája* [One prebendary for three kings. The Croatian history of György Ruttkay] (Budapest: Argumentum, 2000) 20–21, 127.
63 Tomci Marnavitii, *Regiae sanctitatis Illyricanae foecunditas…*, A6r.
64 Bene, *Egy kanonok három királysága*, 127.

(who had been crowned in 1626) and his wife Mária. The third section contains a dedication to Francesco Barberini, nephew of Pope Orban VIII (1623–1644). After that comes the text, the fourth and final section. Both dedications are dated 1631. On the titlepage, we see a picture illustrating the jurisdiction or territorial significance of the crown, which presents the concept – mentioned above – of the *archiregnum Hungaricum*. The picture shows the arms of Hungary together with those of Dalmatia, Croatia, Slavonia, Rama [Prozor-Rama, part of Bosnia and Herzegovina], Serbia, Bulgaria, Lodomeria and Holics [Galicia]. On this page one can also see an engraving of the king – as a young man – and other Hungarian saints.

In the dedication to Ferdinánd, the author once more brings out the subject of the connection with the crown of the apostolic kingship and royal authority. The essence of what he says is that the king reigns over the realm of the holy apostolic crown (*sacrae apostolicae coronae regnum*) – Hungary and Illyria – by virtue of the power of the apostolic crown (*apostolica corona*).[65] In addition, the king is closely linked to the people that still live in the region as he is the successor to Constantine the Great. Tomkó also states that in his youth Ferdinánd followed the examples of St Quirinius, St Imre and other saints, but now as king he must keep before his eyes the examples of his glorious predecessors Constantine the Great and the saintly Hungarian kings István and László. The subject of the dedication to Barberini is the link between the cardinal and Hungary and the Hungarian people. According to Ferenc Galla, the dedication is dated 1631 and the title page of the book 1630, because Tomkó first showed the cardinal the printer's proof of the section about King St István, in which there is mention of the apostolic kingship. It was after that that Barberini undertook the cost of printing the book.[66] According to Tomkó's dedication the cardinal evinces great sympathy for the peoples and countries of the Hungarian crown: he is the patron of every Hungarian that goes to Rome, on the wall of his room he has hung a portrait of Mátyás Corvinus, and it was thanks to his intervention that Pázmány became a cardinal. From the publication of the book and the dedication it may be seen that Cardinal Barberini took an active part in matters concerning the debate over the apostolic kingship. In Peter Rietbergen's opinion the cardinal's alignment on national questions of this sort was in keeping with his power politics.[67]

Tomkó makes use of individual elements of the identity of the Hungarian Estates in his book in order to outline his own thoughts about Illyria. He does this in an effort to emphasise the significance of the region for the other parts of Christian

---

65 Johannes Tomci Marnavitii, *Regiae sanctitatis Illyricanae foecunditas...*, A3r.
66 Galla, *Marnavics Tomkó János*, 63; Bene, *Egy kanonok három királysága*, 190–191.
67 Rietbergen, *Power and Religion*, 399–400.

Europe – especially the Catholic territories. Like Révay, Tomkó uses familiar themes – such as, for example, the crown, Hungary as the bastion of Christendom and the inalienable liberties of the Estates – to associate the destiny of Illyria with the political changes that had taken place in Europe.[68] In his view, the Hungarian crown is the factor that creates this connection. Following Révay, he states that it was the Holy Crown that united the varied peoples of the Hungarian land. Tomkó is the first writer to revive the expression "apostolic crown", coined by Révay – see above in the previous chapter. As in Révay, so too in Tomkó the anti-Ottoman struggle waged by the inhabitants of the region serves as the background to the term. At the time when Tomkó was writing, a significant part of the territory of Illyria was under Turkish occupation, while the rest was part of the Hungarian border-fortress system, constantly on a war footing.

The role of the image formed of the crown and the Illyrian nation was to obtain support for the southern regions of Europe in the war against the Ottomans. Tomkó emphasises repeatedly the continuing link between Europe and Illyria. In his opinion, the Illyrian nation had not only manfully opposed the heathen invader but had never converted to the Protestant religion. By contrast, whole parts of Hungary had become almost wholly Protestant. According to Tomkó, the Croatian city of Zagreb could be seen as the last bastion of Catholic Christianity. The Croats, along with the Hungarians and other peoples, had fought under the banner of the kings of Hungary for the freedom of Western Europe, the Catholic faith and Christian culture.[69]

Tomkó's notion of Illyria departs from the development of the Hungarian Estates and views of the crown hitherto outlined. At the focus of the image that he created is not the Hungarian people, but another nation which in his eyes is very similar to the Hungarians. Thus, he depicts his own people, making use of the familiar distinguishing marks of Hungarian identity. In his work the Illyrians possess every element of the Hungarian identity, indeed, by virtue of their inward and lasting link with the Catholic faith they are superior to the Hungarians. Arguing according to Tomkó's logic, therefore, only the Illyrians can be seen as true Hungarians, since they were the only ones who maintained the worship of the Hungarian saints – István and László, and the Virgin Mary as *Patrona Hungariae* – and of the Hungarian crown. In other words, the Illyrian people were the only true Hungarian Estates, as they had preserved their Catholic political identity.[70] This fiction was in keeping with a debate in lively progress at the time, since at the partial Diet in 1608 the Croats

---

68 Tomci Marnavitii, *Regiae sanctitatis*, 68.
69 *Ibid.*, 68.
70 As modern Croat nationalists have completely appropriated this work of Tomkó's, these elements have become part of the national identity of Croatia. See: Stanko Guldescu, *The Croatian-Slavonian Kingdom 1526–1792* (The Hague and Paris: De Gruyter, 1970) 123. Guldescu uses the term the

had threatened to leave the realm of the Hungarian crown if the Diet permitted the Protestants free practice of religion in Croatia.[71]

Through Tomkó's fiction, Révay's book too enjoyed some unexpected publicity, as its contents thus assisted the creation of the identity of a nation other than the Hungarian. The use of the Hungarian identity and the expropriation of the crown continued after Tomkó was appointed Bishop of Bosnia in 1631. With the support of Cardinal Barberini he obtained a relic of the skull of St István for the cathedral of Zagreb.[72] At the same time the cardinal presented the cathedral with an ornate reliquary in the form of a bust decorated with a copy of the Hungarian crown.[73] On this occasion Tomkó wrote laudatory verses on St István, the cardinal, and the sainted king's reliquary and crown.[74] In these he tells an imaginative tale of how St István protected the cathedral from the Ottomans. He also mentions the apostolic dignity of the crown, using the term *corona apostolica* several times. In this work, therefore, Tomkó identifies the Crown with the apostolic dignity of the king of Hungary.

From a publication by Berger, which appeared on the coronation of Mária Habsburg as Queen in 1638, it is evident that the dispute between Vienna and Rome was going strong.[75] Apart from this, the pamphlet also contains a song in praise of Ferdinánd III (1637–1657), in which the author again uses the theme of apostolic dignity.[76] The connection between the crown, the apostolic kingship (*apostolica monarchia*) and the majesty of the apostolic crown (*maiestas apostolicae coronae*) is

---

'Triple kingdom under the crown of St István', and generally strikes a very anti-Hungarian tone in his book.

71 Winkelbauer, *Ständefreiheit und Fürstenmacht*, vol. II, 89.
72 Galla, *Marnavics Tomkó János Boszniai püspök magyar vonatkozásai*, 190–192.
73 The crown placed on the reliquary is a copy of the Hungarian crown made in the Baroque period: *Ad imitationem Angelicae Apostolicaeque Coronae Ungaricae*. Johannes Tomci Marnavitii, *Pro sacris ecclesiarum ornamentis et donariis, contra eorum detractores* (Romae: Franciscus Caballus, 1635) 75. The exterior of the crown does not match Révay's description, but does bear several of the distinguishing features of the original. See: Veszprémy, *Szent István*, 148 (illustration).
74 Tomci Marnavitii, *Pro Sacris Ecclesiarum Ornamentis et Donariis*; Galla, *Marnavics Tomkó János Boszniai püspök magyar vonatkozásai* 187. Galla deals with this work in an appendix to his study of Tomkó. *Ibid.*, 208–229.
75 The work is Sigismund Ferrarius' book on the Dominicans in Hungary. On the ornate titlepage the term 'the apostolic kings' (*apostolici reges*) is used along with the arms of Hungary, and in the dedication Ferdinánd III is named 'apostolic king'. Sigismund Ferrari, *De rebus Ungaricae provinciae sac. Ordinis praedicatorum* (Viennae, 1637). The appendix contains an imaginary sermon by a twelfth-century Croatian bishop, the content of which is entirely Tomkó's fabrication. Fraknói, *A királyválasztások*, 221.
76 Elias Perger [Berger], *D.O.M.A Symbolum Sacrum et Augustum Decem Reginarum Hungariae. Politicè et Historicè Expositum* (S.l.: s.n., 1637) (in the book the coronation is dated 1638). For this work see: Holl, *Ferenczffy Lőrinc*, 164–167, 178–179, 202–203.

emphasised in a poem. He states that the king acquires apostolic rights (*apostolica iura*) through coronation. He legitimates this apostolic dignity in the familiar way by reference to István, the first apostolic king,[77] and follows this by stating that queens do not enjoy these apostolic rights. The content of Berger's pamphlet shows that even more than ten years after the start of the dispute the subject of the king's apostolic dignity was still being bruited about.

Annales ecclesiastici regni Hungariae (1644)

The publication of the supposed aftermath was the next step in the debate over the apostolic dignity. The text first appeared in 1644 in *Annales ecclesiastici regni Hungariae* by the Jesuit Melchior Inchofer.[78] The first part of the manuscript of the book, dealing with the history of the Catholic Church in Hungary, was written in 1641. The text of the Bull was constructed somewhere in the 1630s, and – after Levakovich had given it to Inchofer – appeared here for the first time in print.[79] With this it seemed that this political question was solved once and for all.

That there is a connection between what the crown and the term apostolic mean in the book is obvious right from the title page (see image 14).[80] This is filled almost completely by an engraving, in the central part of which is the title of the book on a white background surrounded by a disproportionately large reproduction of the image of the Hungarian crown inspired by Révay (see image 12) and the arms of Hungary in a Baroque frame. Two saints are shown as supporters of the shield. The border surrounding the white area containing the title is divided into fields in which, in Baroque frames, is a portrait gallery of the Hungarian saints. Of

---

77 Perger [Berger], *D.O.M.A Symbolum Sacrum*, stanza 5.
78 Melchior Inchofer, *Annales ecclesiastici regni Hungariae*, vol. I (Romae: typis Ludovici Grignani, 1644, Posonii: Typis Simonis Petri Weber, ²1796–1797) 256–257. On Inchofer, see also Gergely Tóth, *Szent István, Szent Korona, államalapítás a protestáns történetírásban (16–18. század)* [St. István, the Holy Crown and the foundation of the state in Protestant historiography (sixteenth to eighteenth century)] (Budapest: MTA Bölcsészettudományi Kutatóközpont, Történettudományi Intézet, 2016) 26–31.
79 "They – I mean the Hungarians – are of the opinion that the Pope has no rights over their Country, as they were guided to the knowledge and worship of God by their own kings. For the purpose that more sober thoughts may be instilled into them I have written a letter in the name of Pope Sylvester, and shall endeavour by some means to make it common knowledge among them. I consider it will be good to cause them to believe that this letter has been found in Rome. Nevertheless, I do not propose to do anything without your knowledge and approval." (Letter from Rafael Levakovics to Cardinal Ippolitus Aldobrandini, dated 1638. Adam Franciscus Kollar, *De Originibus et Usu Perpetuo Potestatis...* (Vindibonae: Joannes Thomas de Trattner, 1764) 160–161.
80 Inchofer, *Annales ecclesiastici* (title page).

these, the most striking is that of St István, holding in his hand as his attribute a large apostolic double cross. In addition, below his portrait is a lengthy caption in which he is named as "István the First, the Apostolic King" (*Stephanus primus Rex Apostolicus*). That is, St István was not only the first king of Hungary but also the first apostolic king.

The political aim of the work was to increase the power of the Catholic Estates in Hungary vis-à-vis the king, and to reduce the influence of Rome on ecclesiastical policy and the politicisation of the Habsburg rulers. The contents, therefore, first and foremost strengthened the position of the Catholic Church in Hungary and its bishops, making it the basis for the political historiography of the Church.[81] The book furnished, *inter alia*, arguments appropriate to the politico-religious debate, but the Catholic schools also took material from it for use in their plays.[82]

Inchofer employs a historical method similar to Révay's for the exposition of his political views. He too makes use of apposite historical examples and texts taken from Medieval sources and refers to writers of repute to persuade the reader of the correctness of his political ideas. The Catholic censorship, however, took exception to this, because he borrowed excessively from the work of Caesar Baronius and Hendricus Spondanus (Henry de Sponde).[83] At the same time, the critics in Rome found that he wrote very positively about the Hungarians and more negatively than need be about the other nations.[84] In this they are right: Inchofer shows the Hungarian Catholic community in an extraordinarily positive light by selectively reading Baronius and other authors, making idiosyncratic use of historical examples, and presenting sources that are in keeping with his preconceived message.[85]

The role of the positive image was to justify the rightfulness of the king's demand for apostolic dignity, which Pázmány too had formulated earlier. The pillar on

---

81 Gyula Szekfű, "Szent István," 35; György Szabados, "Párhuzamos gondolatok Attiláról, Szent Istvánról [Parallel thoughts on Attila and St István]," *Aetas*, 2 (2003) 137. For the contradictory nature of the work as seen by Rome and the reaction of the censorship, see: Dezső Dümmerth, "Inchofer Menyhért küzdelmei és tragédiája Rómában 1641–1648 [The struggles and tragedy of Melchior Inchofer in Rome]," *Filológiai Közlöny* 21 (1976) 195–197. On Inchofer, see: Thomas Cerbu, "Melchior Inchofer, 'Un homme fin & ruse," in José Montesinos - Carlos Solís, eds., *Largo Campo di Filosofare, Eurosymposium Galileo 2001* (La Orotava Fundación Canaria, 2001) 588–611; Charles E. O'Neill - Joaquín María Domínguez, eds., *Diccionario histórico de la Compañía de Jesús: Biográfico-temático*, vol. 2. (Madrid: Institutum Historicum, 2001) 1999.

82 Bene, "Hol vagy István király," 13.

83 *Ibid.*, 195. Baronius tried again and again to create a historical basis for the doctrines of the Catholic Church. See: Hubert Jedin, *Kardinal Caesar Baronius. Der Anfang der katholischen Kirchengeschichtsschreibung im 16. Jahrhundert* (Münster: Aschendorff, 1978) 35–37, 49.

84 Inchofer defends himself against the charge with the familiar argument: 'Without Hungary Europe will fall apart.' *Ibid.*

85 Tóth, *Szent István, Szent Korona*, 27.

which Inchofer's argument rested was the content of the aftermath. He brings the text of the Bull into connection with such other sources – for example, *Tripartitum*, the Hartvik legend and Bonfini's work – as Pázmány too had mentioned in his letter to Ferdinánd. The common law outlined by Pázmány became judge-written law with retrospective force, as the author finally justified the political significance of these works on the basis of the items in the Bull.[86] It is therefore possible that the appearance of the *Annales* simply served this political aim, whereas the reference to Tome I served to misguide: that is, Inchofer had no intention at all of publishing further parts of the work.

Inchofer quotes details from an authoritative work and returns again and again in his book to a given eleventh-century event. He links the story to a section of the aftermath and so is able to explain the meaning of the quoted text. Then, however, he furnishes an even fuller explanation by connecting this meaning to later works such as those of Bonfini or Révay. One such example is the account of the heavenly origin of the presentation of the crown. Inchofer begins by quoting Baronius, but then compares the quotation to the Bull.[87] Next, he explains that the Hungarians really believe in the heavenly origin of the crown, using Révay as an authority.[88] Then he makes known the origin of the crown by once more drawing the reader's attention to what the Bull says. The following part of the account is similar to the earlier accounts of the significance of the crown to be found in Berger, Jeszenszky and Révay. Inchofer writes about István's coronation, the coronation robe, and the "dignity of the crown", and compares all this to what is observed in the cases of the rulers of England, Aragon, France and the Habsburg Empire.[89] From this point of view Inchofer's book has much in common with other works on the meaning of the crown.

In describing the reign of the first king, Inchofer states that not only the cross, but also the crown, symbolise the apostolic dignity of the king of Hungary. Central to this view is that the successor to the throne receives the adjective "apostolic" when crowned with "… the true crown, which the Hungarians call holy and angelic …".[90] This token of majesty is the means by which the ruler acquires apostolic dignity. Next, he links this statement to the political significance of the crown, already outlined by Révay. The king only becomes a rightful ruler when he is crowned with the Holy Crown, but this only occurs once he has sworn to respect the rights and

---

86 It is possible that Inchofer's entire oeuvre was produced with this intention, and the "*Tomi I*" reference is misleading. The second section never appeared. The manuscript with notes that may refer to the possible second section can be found in Venice: Biblioteca Nazionale Marciana, Cod. 22.329.
87 Inchofer, *Annales ecclesiastici,* vol. I, 251–252.
88 *Ibid.*, 252–253.
89 *Ibid.*, 258–259.
90 *Ibid.*, 278–279.

laws of Hungary – says Inchofer.⁹¹ In conclusion, he refers to the worship of the Holy Crown (*religio sacrae coronae*) and the legal meaning of the crown, and gives an account of the irregular coronation with the crown taken from István's reliquary.⁹² With this explanation Inchofer, like Révay, legitimates the political system of the Holy Roman Empire, while by his argument he supports the integrity of the Catholic Estates, the Catholic clergy in Hungary, and the Kingdom of Hungary.

A few pages further on, Inchofer links these political views of the crown with the Catholic faith,⁹³ which is, in his view, the source of the holy nature of the crown. Then he turns to the story of the loss of the apostolic cross. Like Révay, he too considers the disappearance of the cross to be a sign of impending misfortune for Hungary. After this he states that the crown arrived in Hungary like the cross, and finally describes its exterior.⁹⁴ Inchofer clothes the crown with a peculiar significance. In his view the precious stones, the parts of the crown and its ornaments allude to the power which István received from the pope. As in an earlier part of his work, Inchofer linked the king's power to apostolic dignity, and as the cross received from the pope has been lost, he suggests at this point that the Hungarian crown is the tangible token of apostolic authority. The paradox of Inchofer's *modus operandi* is that, like Tomkó, he made use of the Lutheran Révay's ideas to create a Catholic image of the crown and the Hungarian Estates. He does not so much as once refer to Révay, but his work contains numerous passages which appear to be directly copied. The fact that Inchofer does not acknowledge the source of the passages cribbed is to do with Révay's religious views, because of which it would have been indiscreet to mention him as an authority. Nevertheless, Révay's views on the apostolic crown and the worship of the Holy Crown did in fact support Inchofer's theory on the apostolic dignity of the king of Hungary.

A surprising and little-known aspect of the aftermath is the inclusion of the Bull in eighteenth century reprints of Révay's book. The first reference to the Bull came in Martin Schmeizel's work on the crown, published in 1712, in which the author linked together the Bull and Révay's work.⁹⁵ After this the Bull is referred to in

---

91   *Ibid.*, 279. Inchofer repeats this statement on page 304.
92   *Ibid.*, 279.
93   *Ibid.*, 304.
94   *Ibid.*
95   Martinus Schmeizel, *Commentatio Historica de Coronis tam Antiquis, quam Modernis … Speciatim de Origine et Fatis Sacrae, Angelicae et Apostolicae Regni Hungariae Coronae* (Jena: Typis Gollnerianis, 1712) (reprinted in a Schwandtner edition) 6–7. For the background to the work, see: Thomas DaCosta Kaufmann, "Antiquarianism, the History of Objects, and the History of Art before Winckelmann," *Journal of the History of Ideas* 62/3 (2001) 433.

all succeeding eighteenth-century editions of Révay from 1732 onward.[96] In 1746 the book was reissued, edited by Károly András Bél and with an introduction by Mátyás Bél, in a collection of sources on Hungarian history.[97] In the introduction, Mátyás Bél says that the text had been revised in 1732 to take account of manuscript notes which András Czemanka, a nobleman of Turóc county, had, with permission from Révay's heirs, copied from the family archive.[98] (No trace is left of this in the Révay family archive in the Slovak National Archive in our times, as far as I know.) György Bónis considers that after editing and publication "... Péter Révay's life's work is complete."[99]

The statement of Bónis cannot be true for the issue of 1732. As is known, Révay passed away in 1622. The writing of the Papal Bull can be dated to the 1630s, and the text first appeared in print in 1644, more than twenty years after Révay's death. From this fact it may be asserted that those additions to his book in the eighteenth-century variant that contain references to the pseudo-Bull cannot have been made during the author's lifetime, from which the deduction may be made that reference to the pseudo-Bull can in no way have come from Révay's hand.[100] The amendments

---

96 Paulus Okolicsanyi, *Commentarius Petri De Réwa Comitis Comitatus de Turócz, De Sacra Regni Hungariae Corona. Ad nostra usque tempora continuatus* (Tyrnaviae: Typis Academicis per Leopoldum Berger, 1732) 5–6; Martinus Schmeizel: *Commentarius Petri De Rewa Comitis Comitatus de Turócz, De Sacra Regni Hungariae Corona Ad nostra usque tempora continuatus* (Claudiopoli: Typis Academicis per Simonem Thadaeum Weichenberg, 1735); Laurentius Podhorszky, *Commentarius Petri de Réwa Comitis etc. Thesis ex univ. Theologia* (Posonii: Typis Franciscii Antonii Royer, 1749).

97 Petrus de Rewa, *Comitis Comitatus de Thurocz, de S. Coronae Regni Hungariae, ultra 700 annos clarissimae, virtute, victoria, fortuna, commentarius, Post augustanam editionem anni 1613 plurimis locis emendatus, et ad nostra usque tempora perductus Animadversiones atque Emendationes Auctoris ex Msc. addidit Carolus Andreas Bel, Phil. Prof. Publ. Lips. et Collegio Minori Principum Collegiatus* in Johannes Georgius Schwandtner, ed., *Scriptores rerum Hung. veteres ac genuini*, vol. II., ed. Matthias Bél (Viennae- Joannes Thomas de Trattner, 1746, ²1766).

98 *Ibid.*, xx. Czemanka was a collector of mss, whose collection was mostly destroyed in a fire. Szinnyei, *Magyar írók*. One remaining ms: OSZK Fol. Lat. 3415. See also Gergely Tóth, "Bél Mátyás ismeretlen történeti forráskiadvány-tervezete [The unknown plan of Mátyás Bél for a history source edition]," *Magyar könyvszemle*, 2 (2011) 188–189.

99 Bónis, *Révay Péter*, 52.

100 A further variation in the text is a supplement which refers to the origin and fate of the cross as a symbol of the Kingdom of Hungary, and to the Polish chronicles *(Annales Polonici)*. (De Rewa, *De sacrae coronae* 6, Schwandtner, *Scriptores rerum*, vol. II, 439). Likewise added to the original text is a passage about Ferdinand, Visegrád, Buda, and the destruction of Linz. (De Rewa, *De sacrae coronae*, 65; Schwandtner, *Scriptores rerum*, vol. II, 461). The passage about Euripides is missing, but in the second edition a section is added about the crown and Sárospatak. (De Rewa, *De sacrae coronae*, 66; Schwandtner, *Scriptores rerum*, vol. II, 462) The passage about Queen Izabella has been rewritten and a reference to Ferenc Révay added, together with an account of how the crown came to Ferdinánd (Schwandtner, *Scriptores rerum*, vol. II, 463). Further, there is a story in the book about difficulties surrounding Gábor Bethlen and the Hungarian crown that arose in 1621,

to the description of the crown and its history are at best re-workings of Révay's text.[101] Gergely Tóth pointed out that this reworking was not a direct interference with the work of Révay's crown text, but partly additions by the eighteenth-century Jesuit editors which did not always show which parts were from the original author and which were new.[102] The final inference is, however, that thus in the eighteenth century editions of the original work unwittingly a novel significance of the crown was created, based on the content of the aftermath.

The reason for the amendments by the Jesuits is that the later edition adjusted Révay's content to the political situation of the early eighteenth century. The title "apostolic queen" was first used in the coronation as queen of Hungary of Mária Terézia, of the House of Habsburg, in 1741.[103] Nevertheless, it was only in 1753 that Pope Clement XIII gave permission for this title to be borne, simply because of the recapture of Hungary in the period 1683–1699.[104] The eighteenth-century revision of the work of Révay cleared the way for the renewed use of the title by providing it with historical justification through the amendments to the original. The frequent publications that date from this period on the cultus of the crown and the apostolic king St István, and on the aftermath too, emanate from the political changes.[105]

---

which had to do with a strange conversation between the pastor Péter Alvinczi and the prince. See De Rewa, *De sacrae coronae*, (1732) 101–102. Bethlen would have liked to be crowned with the Hungarian crown, but Alvinczi stated that only the archbishop of Esztergom could do this. To that, Bethlen replied that after his coronation he would elevate Alvinczi (a Calvinist!) to the rank of archbishop, thus there was no need of him for the purpose of a coronation. In the end, the ceremony of coronation did not take place. The purpose of this (probably imaginary) conversation was to destroy Bethlen's image. It is not likely that this description comes from Révay, and this passage is not found in his later writings either.

101 The description of the crown taken from *De Monarchia* is supplemented with details, but these have been re-written and another text added to the description. From *De Monarchia* comes the idea that the crown was presumably Constantine's gift, and that the portraits of the twelve apostles can be seen on it, and further, that the pictorial display on the crown can be a link between the Churches of Rome and of Constantinople. See: Schwandtner, *Scriptores rerum*, II, 466–467 and: De Rewa, *De Monarchia* in the work of Schwandtner, *Scriptores rerum*. vol. II, 821–824. I made the comparison on the basis of the Schwandtner edition of *De Monarchia*, and could not check whether the transmission of the text was correct.

102 Tóth, "Bél Mátyás ismeretlen történeti forráskiadvány-tervezete," 188–189.

103 It is noteworthy that even in 1638 Berger denies that the queen of Hungary might acquire those apostolic rights through coronation. Berger, *D.O.M.A Symbolum Sacrum*, 5.

104 Kropf, "Pope Sylvester II and Stephan I of Hungary," 292.

105 Bene, "Hol vagy István király," 3. Queen Mária Terézia had established the St István Order, amongst others. In her official representation, she used an image of the Hungarian crown which was inspired by that of Révay. She was also frequently painted with the Hungarian crown by her side. The text of the Bull was published in Hungarian translation in the chronicle of Gergely Gersei Petthő. See: Gergely Petthő, *Rövid magyar kronika* [Short Hungarian chronicle] (Kassa: S.n., 1702, 1729, 1734, 1738, 1742, ²1742, 1753, 1753, ²1990) 110–113.

As a result of the political changes and the references in Révay's book the theory that had been formed about the crown changed too. A full account and analysis of the change in significance of the crown in the eighteenth century would exceed the scope of this book. The change felt in regard to the content of Révay's book, however, influences the way in which it has been assessed in recent evaluations. Nowadays numerous writers refer in their studies not to the original 1613 page-numbers but to those of the 1766 edition.[106] A possible explanation for this is the misunderstanding that the eighteenth-century edition is generally considered the more correct.[107] It is not, however, possible, to properly analyse Révay's ideas on the political significance of the crown on the basis of the content of the eighteenth-century editions.

The aftermath of Révay's work and national identity

After our diversion to the eighteenth-century editions of Révay, let us return to the years about 1650. At this period further political changes were taking place, of which other studies inform us in detail.[108] One aspect of this period has really remained unexplored until now: the publication of the Sylvester Bull, as the most significant stimulant of the renewal of the image of the Estates. While the text of the Bull was republished in another book only in 1679, it had become known in the preceding period through Inchofer's work.[109] The essence of the cultural change that took place under the influence of the political meaning of the Bull resulted from the link between Révay's actual views and the content of the Bull. The new theory that arose as a result of this served to justify current political ideas.

---

106 Among others: Ipolyi, *A magyar szent korona* 108; Szekfű, "Szent István a magyar történet századaiban," 35 (561); Wittman, "Az osztrák Habsburg-hatalom," 31; Bartoniek, *Fejezetek* 401–403; Bogyay, "Über die Forschungsgeschichte," 67.

107 Another possible explanation is that the first edition (1613) was already rare in its time. As early as 1652 Ferenc Nádasdy complained about this, after which he decided to reprint it. Petrus de Rewa, *De sacrae coronae...* (Viennae Austriae: Cosmerovius, 1652), Nádasdy's foreword.

108 See among others: Katalin Péter, *A magyar romlásnak századában* [The centuries of Hungarian decay] (Budapest: Gondolat Kiadó, 1975); Katalin Péter, *A magyar nyelvű politikai publicisztika kezdetei. A Siralmas Panasz keletkezettörténete* [The beginnings of political writing in the Hungarian language. The history of the origin of the "Sad Complaint"] (Budapest: Akadémiai Kiadó, 1973) 8–68; Géza Perjés, *Zrínyi Miklós és kora* [Miklós Zrínyi and his time] (Budapest: Gondolat Kiadó, 1965, Budapest: Osiris, ²2002); Ágnes R. Várkonyi, "Európai játéktér – magyar politika 1657–1664 [European playground – Hungarian politics 1657–1664]," in Gábor Hausner, ed., *Az értelem bátorsága. Tanulmányok Perjés Géza emlékére* [The courage of the intellect. Studies in remembrance of Géza Perjes] (Budapest: Argumentum Kiadó, 2005) 577–614.

109 István Kereskényi, *Corona Apostolico-Basilica seu Stephani I. Regis Hungariae* (Cassoviae: S.n., 1679). The work came into use after 1679 through the reprint of Petthő's chronicle mentioned above.

One driving force behind the change was Révay's grandson Ferenc Nádasdy (1623–1671), the wealthiest aristocrat in Hungary, a converted Catholic and Lord Chief Justice.[110] He was one of the principal protagonists of the political programme worked out after the signing in 1648 of the Treaty of Westphalia. The most significant distinctive feature of the programme – with a view to the new offensive aimed at finally driving the Ottomans out of Hungary – was the urge for harmony in Hungary as well as in Europe.[111] The success of the plan – as far as Hungary was concerned – depended on political collaboration between the Habsburg Empire, Hungary, Transylvania and Croatia.[112] The most important aristocrats, such as Miklós Zrínyi (1620–1664), Viceroy of Croatia, and Prince György II Rákóczi of Transylvania (1621–1660), were convinced that there was need of collaboration, but that did not prevent political and religious differences.[113] From 1650 on Nádasdy worked as a politician, writer and patron of such works as disseminated these ideas.[114]

The image that had been formed of the crown was an important tool from Nádasdy's political ideological point of view. In 1652 he re-issued Révay's book and provided it with a new foreword, in which he updated Révay's ideas.[115] In doing so, he linked the theory of the crown with his supporters' political programme, and the

---

110 Nádasdy's mother Judit was the only one of Révay's daughters that did not die at an early age.
111 Ágnes R. Várkonyi, "Vienna, Buda, Constantinople," *The New Hungarian Quarterly* XXV (1984) 1–7.
112 On the part played by the pope, see: Antal Molnár, "Relations between the Holy See and Hungary," 208.
113 On this policy, see: Várkonyi, *Europa varietas*, 55–187, Nádasdy himself converted to Catholicism only in 1643, and his 40,000 serfs were forced to return to the bosom of the ancient Church.
114 György Rózsa, "Nádasdy Ferenc és a művészet [Ferenc Nádasdy and art]," *Művészettörténeti Értesítő* XX (1970) 185–202; Galavics, *Kössünk kardot az pogány ellen*, 77–85; Nóra G. Etényi, "A Nürnbergi nyilvánosság és a Nádasdy Mausoleum [The public opinion in Nürnberg and Nádasdy's Mausoleum]," in Pál Fodor, Géza Pálffy and István György Tóth, eds., *Tanulmányok Szakály Ferenc emlékére* [Studies in memory of Ferenc Szakály] (Budapest: MTA TKI Gazdaság- és Társadalomtörténeti Kutatócsoportja, 2002) 121–138; Enikő Buzási, "Gondolatok Nádasdy Ferenc mecenatúrájáról, avagy mikor készült az árpási főoltárkép? [Thoughts on the patronage of Ferenc Nádasdy or when was the altar-piece of Árpás made?]" in Nóra G. Etényi and Ildikó Horn, eds., *Idővel Paloták.... Magyar udvari kultúra a 16–17. században* [Palace with time. Hungarian court culture in the sixteenth and seventeenth century] (Budapest: Balassi Kiadó, 2006) 582–625. In this way, for example, he assisted with money and information the well-known Amsterdam cartographer Johan Blaeu (1630–1673), who in 1664 dedicated to him one of his maps of Hungary. Nádasdy also bought printing equipment in Amsterdam. Rózsa, "Nádasdy Ferenc," 188. In Blaeu's atlas there is a description of the political system in Hungary, which agrees with Nádasdy's ideas. Blaeu *inter alia* writes of the 'elected king' and the 'elected *locum tenens*'. Johannes Blaeu, *Het koningrijck Hvngaryen* [The kingdom of Hungary] (Amsterdami: apud Guiljelmum et Iohannum Blaeu: [1647]) (map) OSZK TM 06656 v.
115 According to an inventory, Nádasdy owned two etching plates with depictions of the Holy Crown. Rózsa, "Nádasdy Ferenc és a művészet," 202, note 106.

Counter-Reformation that had been taking place in Western Hungary. Thanks to Pázmány's exertions, in Western Hungary, numerous aristocratic families together with their serfs, had returned to the Catholic faith, among them the Nádasdy family.[116] Since 1570 the Principality of Transylvania had been a separate state, less tied to other parts of Hungary politically. The link between Croatia and Hungary too had weakened. Religious differences and the changed foreign relationships resulting from the Treaty of Westphalia (1648) had caused these parts of the country to grow apart.

Nádasdy addressed the message in the foreword to the Estates of the whole of Hungary. Like Révay, the essence of his words was a desire for harmony (*concordia*) in the country, but now, in 1652, this desire served the purposes of the political programme of Nádasdy and his contemporaries. Without mentioning religious differences, he called for harmony between the various parts of Hungary and with the peoples of the adjacent countries. Even so, his writing was a powerful advocacy of the Catholic faith as a significant binding force, and he underpinned his discourse on the crown and the Estates by the use of examples taken from Bonfini and Werbőczy.

What is important here is not so much Nádasdy's political discourse as the method by which he justified it all by means of the image – different from earlier ideas – of the crown that had formed. The essence of the change in this image lay in the expression "the angelic crown of our apostolic kingdom" (*Angelica regni nostri apostolici corona*) and in its meaning. According to Nádasdy, God had presented the crown to István through Pope Sylvester II in order that there should be peace and harmony (*pax et concordia*) in Hungary. In consequence of the presentation of the apostolic crown (*apostolica corona*) the nation (*gens*) became identified with the apostolic faith. As Révay still regarded Benedict VII as the presenter of the crown, while Inchofer, on the basis of the Bull, considered that it had been Pope Sylvester, it is highly likely that Nádasdy, in compiling his own text, made use of Inchofer.

In Nádasdy's text, the role of the concept of the apostolic crown (*apostolica corona*) differs from that in Révay's and Inchofer's works, because this thought no longer serves for the legitimation of a certain political compromise, the power of the apostolic king, or the position of the Catholic Church in Hungary. In Nádasdy, the function of this concept is the justification of his own political programme – placing the interests of the Estates to the fore – which is not directed against the king. Bearing in mind that at that period the leading personalities in the Estates were the Catholics, the idea could only work if it were given a Catholic significance. Thus, in 1652, the idea of the apostolic crown was linked to the idea of the Catholic

---

116 Péter, "A haza és a nemzet," 222–228.

community. It may therefore be presumed that Nádasdy's work was actually a response to one of Inchofer's.

The genesis of the link between the Catholic community and the crown was referred to a year later by László Liszti (Listius, 1628–1663) in his book *Magyar Márs* (Hungarian Mars, 1653).[117] This contains an epic poem of Catholic colouring on the wars of the Hungarian Estates, to whom it is dedicated. A picture of the crown is to be seen at once on the titlepage. Then there is mention of the crown in two stanzas, to be exact, those about King St István and the arms of Hungary. In the first stanza the author states that the "nation" (*nemzet*) was given the crown so that it should "... re-establish respect for God ...".[118] In the second stanza, which mentions the armorial bearings, Liszti writes that God sent the "angelic crown" in order that it should "... remain for ever, and that there should be nothing that takes precedence over it ...".[119] In these two lines the Catholic faith and the Hungarian people are once again linked through the crown by the author's declaration: God sent the crown to the Hungarian Estates. By this, the meaning of the crown legitimated the Catholic religious persuasion of the Estates.

In the period when the above-mentioned writings on the new significance of the crown were published, several other sources appeared which also contained depictions of the crown.[120] There is no space for discussion of these in the present study, but for the sake of completeness we shall mention a couple of them. To begin at the beginning: in 1659 there appeared Révay's second, much fuller study of Hungary and the Hungarian crown, in which too there was a newly-made print of the crown.[121] An analysis of this extensive work is too much for the limits of this work, but we can assert that the concept created of the crown conforms to that in the first edition. In this too Nádasdy's brief dedication to László Révay speaks of the "... angelic crown of our apostolic kingdom ...".[122]

The second work of this kind that we shall consider bears the title *Mausoleum Regni Apostolici Regum & Ducum...* (Mauseleum of the Kings and Princes of the Apostolic Kingdom . . .) which was published in 1664 by Ferenc Nádasdy, who also

---

117 László Listius, *Magyar Márs avagy Moháchz mezején történt veszedelemnek emlékezete* [Hungarian Mars or the loss which happened on the field of Mohács] (Viennae: Mathé Cozmerovius, 1653).
118 *Ibid.*, 6.
119 *Ibid.*, 80.
120 For the political background to this change in significance of the crown see: Noémi Viskolcz, "Kié a könyvtár? Lipót kísérlete a Bibliotheca Corviniana maradványainak megszerzésére [Who owns the library? The attempts of Leopold to acquire the remains of the Bibliotheca Corviniana]," *Acta Historiae Litterarum Hungaricarum* 29 (2006) 283–288.
121 Rewa, *De Monarchia*.
122 *Ibid.*, 4.

wrote the foreword.[123] It contains a number of illustrations of rulers and kings of the Hungarians, some of them wearing the Hungarian crown. Latin captions to the illustrations are by the humanist Nicolaus Avacini (1611–1686) and German captions by the Lutheran divine Sigmund von Birken (1626–1681).[124] The illustrations were originally intended for Elias Berger's historical work, and were presumably prepared in the 1630s, at the time of his renewed literary activity.[125] The meaning of the crown in Mausoleum is in step with Nádasdy's political programme and does not differ significantly from that discussed in the earlier works mentioned.[126] In Nádasdy's work there is no reference at all to the organic constitution of the crown (or Doctrine of the Holy Crown), nor does the term "members of the Holy Crown" (*membra sacrae coronae*) occur in it.[127]

The most noteworthy change with regard to the meaning of the crown in this work is to be found – in scarcely perceptible form – on the titlepage (see image 15). On closer examination of the crown in the illustration, it is evident that on the right-hand page, precisely where the picture of Christ was, that of Mary, Patron of Hungary, is to be seen (see image 16). According to Révay's description of 1613, the portrait of Mary was on the rear of the crown. The unknown artist has taken Révay's picture (see image 12) and description of the crown as a basis but has placed the likeness of Mary on the right-hand page. The role of this new depiction of the crown is to confirm the above-mentioned theory about the crown and the apostolic Catholic community. The portrait of Mary on the crown is connected with the changing political situation and underpins the Hungarian Estates' demand for sovereignty. By the modification of Révay's depiction of the crown, the Catholic reworking of the theory developed by him had been achieved.[128] The already-

---

123 S.n., *Mausoleum Regni Apostolici Regum & Ducum* (Norimbergae: Apud Michaëlem & Joannem Fridericum Endteros, 1664, fascimilé-edition Budapest, ²1991). Latin editions appeared in 1667, 1688, 1752, 1758 and 1779, Hungarian editions in 1661, 1697, 1773. Kulcsár, *Inventarium*, 673.

124 György Rózsa, *A Nádasdy Mausoleum* (Separate attachment to the facsimile edition of Nádasdy's Mausoleum) (Budapest: Akadémiai Kiadó, 1991) 7–14.

125 *Ibid.*, 9–14, Galavics, *Kössünk kardot az pogány ellen*, 61–69; Holl, *Ferenczffy Lőrinc*, 149–170.

126 For the background to the genesis of the work see: Nóra G. Etényi, "A nürnbergi nyilvánosság és a Nádasdy *Mausoleum*," in Fodor, Pálffy and Tóth, *Tanulmányok*, 121–138.

127 György Rózsa believes that the Doctrine of the Holy Crown is the basis of this work. Rózsa, *A Nádasdy Mausoleum*, 7–14.

128 Nádasdy's image of the crown was re-used in the following works: Johann Adam Xavier Schad, *Effigies Ducum et Regum Hungariae* …, (S. l., s.n., 1687) and: Carolus Franciscus Palma, *Heraldicae regni Hungariae specimen, regia, provinciarum, nobilimque scuta complectens*… (Vindobonae: Joannis Thomae de Trattnern, 1766) which contains the following text: "De apostolicorum Hungariae regum insignibus". Cf. Buzási and Pálffy, *Augsburg - Wien - München - Innsbruck. Die frühesten Darstellungen der Stephanskrone und die Entstehung der Exemplare des Ehrenspiegels des Hauses Österreich*.

mentioned allegory depicted on the title page of Hieronymus Ortelius' work on the Turkish wars in Hungary (1665, image 17) can be considered as inspired by these views of Nádasdy.[129] The picture by an unknown artist may be regarded as a Catholic allegory of the views which Révay professed on the crown, Hungary and Christian Europe.

In this chapter we have been able to observe how Révay's work gained ever newer meaning as his thoughts on the crown were made use of in other textual settings. By the introduction of a new supposedly Medieval source and by modifying Révay's ideas to the content of this, the portrayal of the Hungarian Estates assumed a Catholic character. From the aftermath of the book, it has also emerged that it not only exerted influence on the Hungarian identity of the Estates, but also had a stimulating effect on the development of self-identity of the Illyrian nation by the Croatian Estates, ultimately leading to the formation of a Croat national identity, separate from the Hungarian one. At the same time, these ideas also legitimated the political programme of a supra-national alliance. The altered political circumstances justified even the modification of Révay's depiction of the crown.

By analysing Révay's work we have been able to draw the conclusion that ideas formed of the crown and the image of the Hungarian Estates in association with it are not to be taken as of permanent validity and constant, but that their interpretation depends on the political situation of the moment. From the analysis it has become clear that what appear to be identical concepts have been used in different ways, sometimes, indeed, for the justification of conflicting political goals, and in the process, it has not been the political or religious convictions of individual writers and earlier interpretations of the subject that have defined the meaning of particular terms.

---

129 Hieronymus Oertel [Ortelius] and Martin Meyrn, *Ortelius Redivivus et Continuatus oder Ungarische und Siebenbürgische Kriegs-Händel, so vom Jahr 1395. biß auf 1665. mit dem Türcken vorgelauffe* (Nürnberg: Fürst, 1665), title-page. On this title page see: Teszelszky, *True Religion* 129–130.

Conclusion

Political traditions can have deep roots and long shadows. This also goes for the tradition of the Holy Crown of Hungary, which started in the Middle Ages and is still alive today. This book treats the development of Early Modern national identity in the Hungarian Kingdom and the changing of the meaning of the Holy Crown of Hungary between 1572 and 1664, with a special focus on the developments in the period 1600–1613. Using a constructivist method of research, I have shown the relation between the change of the legitimising function of the Hungarian crown and the formation of an Early Modern national identity in Hungary. This legitimising function was expressed in the development of the tradition of the Holy Crown by the Hungarian Estates and the rulers, politicians, orators and historiographers of the kingdom.

The Medieval tradition of the Holy Crown is probably older than the tangible crown itself. It was based on the so-called St István's crown or Holy Crown of Hungary, the Medieval crown with which the kings of the Hungarian kingdom were crowned and which was assembled in the thirteenth century. The cultus of the Holy Crown starts with the first king St István, who was crowned king of Hungary with a crown received from the Pope in 1000 or 1001, according to the tradition.

The modern political Doctrine of the Holy Crown in Hungarian political culture is an invention of a Medieval tradition using elements of the ancient cultus. According to the doctrine, the king, church and nobility divided power among themselves in the mystical body of the Holy Crown, of which the tangible Medieval crown is the embodiment of this concept from the foundation of the kingdom. The starting point for my approach was the notion that this doctrine is a modern invention, following the work of László Péter and Ferenc Eckhart. It is based on one sentence from the law book of István Werbőczy published in 1517. This nineteenth-century doctrine makes it impossible to understand the meaning of the crown in Hungarian political culture in the Early Modern period and before. Due to the influence of the modern doctrine, Early Modern sources about the meaning of the crown have not been properly studied till now.

The role of the Hungarian crown in the political culture of Hungary differs from the history of other regalia elsewhere in Europe. The physical crown acquired symbolic significance in the Kingdom of Hungary much later than in other countries of the Christian world: it started after the Árpád dynasty died out in 1301. The importance of the tangible crown to claims of power by the Hungarian kings increased in the course of the Middle Ages and stimulated the formation of a tradition of the Holy Crown. This was mainly due to the violent succession of royalty and the growth of the power of the Estates.

The crown did not have a set meaning in the Medieval period, and there was an intentional development of the tradition of the Holy Crown which achieved its apex during the reign of Mátyás Corvinus. The crown tradition persisted all through the Middle Ages and became even more important since the Medieval Kingdom of Hungary came to an end in 1526, when the country was divided in three parts. The more the kingdom and the Estates became disunited and the relation between ruler and Estates was stressed, the more important the tradition of the Holy Crown and its holiness became. During this development, the cultural community of Hungarians transformed into a political community. The crown began to symbolize the unity of the as-yet divided Hungarian political community and of the kingdom, and its holiness legitimised the political claims of the Estates.

It is therefore not surprising that the most drastic change of the tradition of the crown happened during a string of severe political and religious crises in the Habsburg Empire and the Hungarian kingdom. This change was the result of the events during the Bocskai rebellion (1604–1606), the first anti-Habsburg uprising in Central Europe, the handing over of the Ottoman crown to Prince István Bocskai (1605), and the coronation of King Mátyás II (1608) as king of Hungary. The revival of the tradition of the crown took place in the unpublished work of János Bocatius (1605), which was continued in, but also influenced by the speeches, published and unpublished work of Elias Berger (1600–1608), István Illésházy (1607 and 1608) and János Jeszenszky (1608 and 1609). It is remarkable how important the role of foreign outsiders like Berger and Bocatius was in the construction of the Early Modern national identity in Hungary and the revival and revision of the Medieval tradition of the Holy Crown.

After having been kept outside of Hungary and having been absent in the political culture for a long time, the tangible crown of Hungary and its symbolic meaning returned to the centre of political culture in the Hungarian kingdom in 1608 as the symbol of the political demands of the Estates and the authority of the Habsburg pretender to the Hungarian throne, Archduke Matthias. The political compromise between King Mátyás II and the Hungarian Estates was legitimised, symbolised and personified by a new image and narrative of the returned crown, its holiness and the united Hungarian community under Habsburg rule. The Medieval Catholic tradition of the Holy Crown was thus revived and refreshed. The cumulation and codification of this tradition took place in the work of Péter Révay on the Holy Crown, which saw the light in 1613.

The description of the crown tradition in the work of Révay was very influential and determined the Early Modern Hungarian national identity till the rise of modern nationalism in Hungary at the end of the eighteenth century. One major change of his ideology took place during the Counter-Reformation halfway through the seventeenth century, when the crown history written by the Lutheran Révay was adapted to the Catholic narrative about the crown using the Bull of Sylvester, an eleventh-century fiction of a papal bull made up in the seventeenth century.

If we step aside from the beaten path of the nineteenth-century narrative about the history of the Hungarian nation and the Doctrine of the Holy Crown based on canonical sources, and instead follow the whimsical path of the development of Early Modern national identity in Hungary, we will find a wealth of forgotten writers, unknown images, unstudied archives, lost manuscripts and surprising ideas. The Holy Crown lives on in the history of Hungary, waiting to be discovered.

Epilogue

When I first met the Holy Crown in the Hungarian National Museum around 1994, I knew that there would be a lifelong relationship between us two. I was struck by the complexity that is linked to this object, this idea and the way the past and the present are linked underneath. It was through this that I came closer to my Hungarian identity. It also helped me to discover my Dutchness better, because I needed this source to be able to connect these two distant points in Europe through the traditions of the past. It was through my studies that I got to know the Hungarian language better, and it was through researching and analysing the sources that I truly understood how important a role the Hungarians played in shaping European culture.

Fate has brought me together with great scholars in my research, whom I respect not only as my colleagues, but also as my friends. I would like to highlight two of them, to whom I owe a great debt of gratitude and respect. They were once friends at the university, then one of them emigrated to the West in 1956, the other stayed in Hungary. László Péter (1929–2008) became Professor of Hungarian History at the University of London, the other person, Ágnes R. Várkonyi (1928–2014) Professor of Medieval and Early Modern Hungarian History at ELTE University, in Budapest. Unfortunately, I only met László Péter once in the Netherlands, but I have a few letters from him. Ágnes R. Várkonyi was not only my doctoral supervisor, she and her husband Kálmán Ruttkay were also close and special friends of our family.

When I met my wife Marika for the first time in the spring of 2000 at the University of Amsterdam, I fell in love with her instantly. She was the first person with whom I could spontaneously talk about the Holy Crown, and I felt that this relationship was also a life-long one. During my doctoral research, I became a father twice, crowning our private life with two great children. In 2003, our first son Mátyás at the age of one, first saw the crown in the Parliament with me. Our second child, Péter, as a confident two-year old appeared with his elder brother at the reception after my PhD defence in 2006. When my Hungarian book about the crown was published in 2009, our one-year-old little girl Ágnes, was also present at the first time for such an important occasion. She has really crowned and completed our marriage.

Just like fatherhood, the research connected to the crown is the most important part of my life. I dedicate this book to those who could not have made this project possible without their professional or personal support, to those I could always count on, who constantly inspired me and reassured me that I was on the right path. Köszönöm mindenkinek!

Images

1. The Holy Crown of Hungary on display in 1938. Fortepan / Zsolt Pálinkás

2. The Holy Crown of Hungary in the Chronicle of János Thuróczy (1488). OSZK, Inc. 1143.

3. The Holy Crown of Hungary as an object and as a concept. King II. Ulászló and his children on the patent of nobility of the Gersei Petheő family (1507). HU-MNL-OL-DL 86051.

4. The Crown of Hungary in the Fugger Chronicle (1547–1555). Bayerische Staatsbibliothek, Cgm 895, fol. 308v.

5. The Crown of Hungary on the map of Wolfgang Lazius (1556). OSZK TR 2501.

6. Coronation jeton of King Mátyás II. (1608). Magyar Nemzeti Múzeum Éremtára.

7. Coin from the reign of King Mátyás II. (1612). Magyar Nemzeti Múzeum Éremtára.

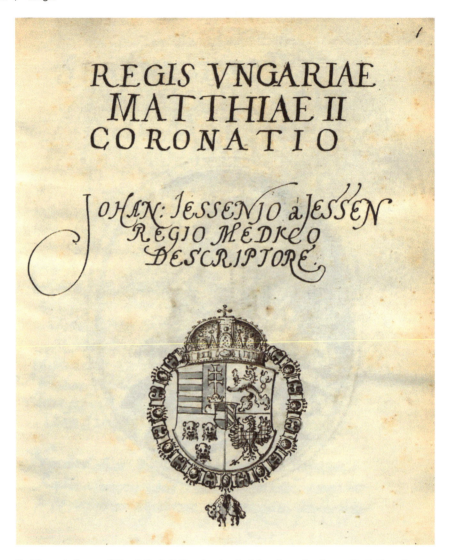

8. The coat of arms of King Mátyás II. Pen drawing in: Johan Jessenio a Jessen, Regis Ungariae, Matthiae II. Coronatio (1608–1609). ÖNB, Codex 8790, fol. 1v.

9. King Mátyás II. Pen drawing in: Johan Jessenio a Jessen, Regis Ungariae, Matthiae II. Coronatio (1608–1609). ÖNB, Codex 8790, fol. 1r.

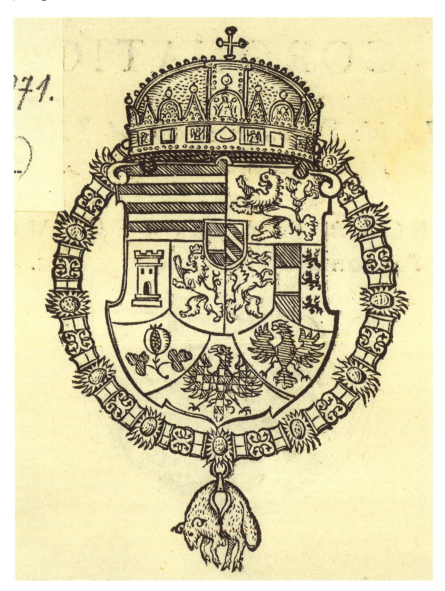

10. The coat of arms of King Mátyás II. Published in: Johan Jessenio a Jessen, Regis Ungariae, Matthiae II. Coronatio (Viennae Austriae: Bonnoberger, 1609). OSZK, RMK III. 1071.

11. Detail of the coat of arms of King Mátyás II. Published in: Johan Jessenio a Jessen, Regis Ungariae, Matthiae II. Coronatio (Viennae Austriae: Bonnoberger, 1609). OSZK, RMK III. 1071.

12. Image of the holy crown of Hungary in: Petrus de Rewa [Péter Révay], De sacrae coronae regni Hungariae ortu, virtute, victoria, fortuna, annos ultra D C clarissimae, brevis commentarius (Augustae Vindelicorum: Christoph. Mangus, 1613). OSZK, RMK III. 1118

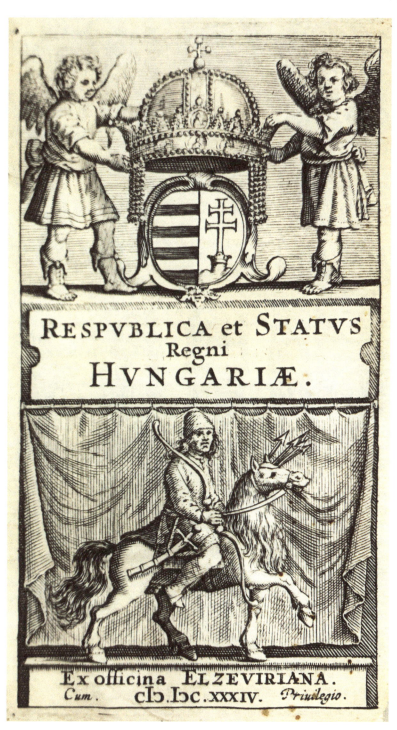

13. Title page of: [Martin Schödel], Respublica et Status Regni Hungariae ([Leiden: Elsevier], 1634, ²1634). Collection Kees Teszelszky.

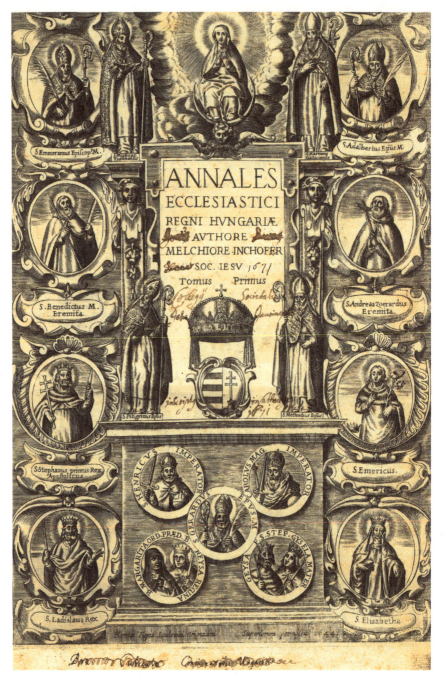

14. Title page of: Melchior Inchofer, Annales ecclesiastici regni Hungariae, vol. I (Romae: typis Ludovici Grignani, 1644. Library of the Benedictines of Győr

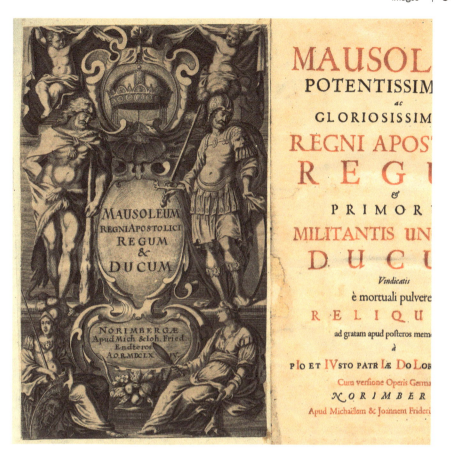

15. Title page of: S.N., Mausoleum Regni Apostolici Regum & Ducum (Norimbergae: Apud Michaëlem & Joannem Fridericum Endteros, 1664). Main Library of the Archabbey of Pannonhalma, 82-A-14.

16. Detail of the Crown in: S.N., Mausoleum Regni Apostolici Regum & Ducum (Norimbergae: Apud Michaëlem & Joannem Fridericum Endteros, 1664). Main Library of the Archabbey of Pannonhalma, 82-A-14.

17. Hieronymus Oertel [Ortelius] and Martin Meyrn, Ortelius Redivivus et Continuatus oder Ungarische und Siebenbürgische Kriegs-Händel, so vom Jahr 1395. biß auf 1665. mit dem Türcken vorgelauffe (Nürnberg: Fürst, 1665). Main Library of the Archabbey of Pannonhalma, 123b-C-2.

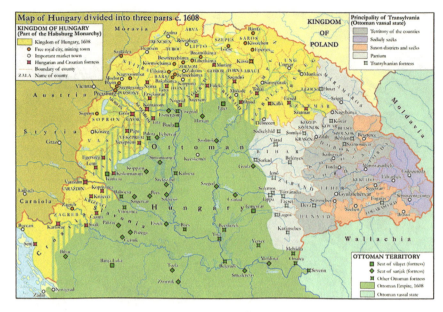

18. Map of Hungary in 1608, made by Béla Nagy (2022).

List of images

1. The Holy Crown of Hungary on display in 1938. Fortepan / Zsolt Pálinkás
2. The Holy Crown of Hungary in the Chronicle of János Thuróczy (1488). OSZK, Inc. 1143.
3. The Holy Crown of Hungary as an object and as a concept. King II. Ulászló and his children on the patent of nobility of the Gersei Petheő family (1507). HU-MNL-OL-DL 86051.
4. The Crown of Hungary in the Fugger Chronicle (1547–1555). Bayerische Staatsbibliothek, Cgm 895, fol. 308v.
5. The Crown of Hungary on the map of Wolfgang Lazius (1556). OSZK TR 2501.
6. Coronation jeton of King Mátyás II. (1608). Magyar Nemzeti Múzeum Éremtára.
7. Coin from the reign of King Mátyás II. (1612). Magyar Nemzeti Múzeum Éremtára.
8. The coat of arms of King Mátyás II. Pen drawing in: Johan Jessenio a Jessen, Regis Ungariae, Matthiae II. Coronatio (1608–1609). ÖNB, Codex 8790, fol. 1v.
9. King Mátyás II. Pen drawing in: Johan Jessenio a Jessen, Regis Ungariae, Matthiae II. Coronatio (1608–1609). ÖNB, Codex 8790, fol. 1r.
10. The coat of arms of King Mátyás II. Published in: Johan Jessenio a Jessen, Regis Ungariae, Matthiae II. Coronatio (Viennae Austriae: Bonnoberger, 1609). OSZK, RMK III. 1071.
11. Detail of the coat of arms of King Mátyás II. Published in: Johan Jessenio a Jessen, Regis Ungariae, Matthiae II. Coronatio (Viennae Austriae: Bonnoberger, 1609). OSZK, RMK III. 1071.
12. Image of the holy crown of Hungary in: Petrus de Rewa [Péter Révay], De sacrae coronae regni Hungariae ortu, virtute, victoria, fortuna, annos ultra D C clarissimae, brevis commentarius (Augustae Vindelicorum: Christoph. Mangus, 1613). OSZK, RMK III. 1118
13. Title page of: [Martin Schödel], Respublica et Status Regni Hungariae ([Leiden: Elsevier], 1634, ²1634). Collection Kees Teszelszky.
14. Title page of: Melchior Inchofer, Annales ecclesiastici regni Hungariae, vol. I (Romae: typis Ludovici Grignani, 1644. Library of the Benedictines of Győr
15. Title page of: S.N., Mausoleum Regni Apostolici Regum & Ducum (Norimbergae: Apud Michaëlem & Joannem Fridericum Endteros, 1664). Main Library of the Archabbey of Pannonhalma, 82-A-14.
16. Detail of the Crown in: S.N., Mausoleum Regni Apostolici Regum & Ducum (Norimbergae: Apud Michaëlem & Joannem Fridericum Endteros, 1664). Main Library of the Archabbey of Pannonhalma, 82-A-14.

17. Hieronymus Oertel [Ortelius] and Martin Meyrn, Ortelius Redivivus et Continuatus oder Ungarische und Siebenbürgische Kriegs-Händel, so vom Jahr 1395. biß auf 1665 mit dem Türcken vorgelauffe (Nürnberg: Fürst, 1665). Main Library of the Archabbey of Pannonhalma, 123b-C-2.
18. Map of Hungary in 1608, made by Béla Nagy (2022).

Bibliography

Primary sources

Manuscripts and archives

[Berger, Elias], Descriptio Coronationis Serenissimi Principis ac Domini; Dni Rudolphi Archiducis Austria. etc.: in Regem Hungariae inaugurati, Posonij die Vigesima quinta Septembris Anno Dni 1572 d: 26. Sept: (…), ÖNB, Cod. 8674, fol. 13r.–31v.

[Berger, Elias], Historia Hungarica ab a. 1572 usque ad a. 1606, ÖNB, Cod. 8464.

[Berger, Elias], Historia Ungarica ab A.C. 1458., definit autem in A.C. 1490, ÖNB, Cod. 8677.

[Berger, Elias], Historia Ungarica ab A.C. 1607., definit autem in A.C. 1618., ÖNB, Cod. 8229.

[Berger, Elias], Isagoge seu prolegomena duplicia in chronologiam. 1635. ELTE Egyetemi Könyvtár Kézirattár G 69.

[Berger, Elias], Res sub Ferdinando II. imperatore gestae. Pars secunda, continens annos 1631–1633. ELTE Egyetemi Könyvtár Kézirattár G 70.

[Bocskai, István], Testamentaria dispositio… MOL P 287 Forgách család. Series 1. 34. cs. Fasc. T. 34.

[Révay, Péter], Annotationes Morales Historicae, Főegyházmegyei könyvtár, Esztergom, Ms. 253.

[Révay, Péter], Commentaria in libros Aristotelis de Coelo et Mundo, de Generatione et Corruptione, Metheorologicorum, de Anima et Metaphysicorum, Főegyházmegyei könyvtár, Esztergom, Ms. 273.

[Révay, Péter], Commentario[!] in octo libros Aristotelis de Physice ausculatione, Főegyházmegyei könyvtár, Esztergom Ms. 224.

[Révay, Péter], Joannis Molensis Annotationes in Universam Logicam et Mathesim per Petrus Révay, Főegyházmegyei könyvtár, Esztergom Ms. 272.

Acta in Ungarn, Böhmen und Schlesien. 1604–1609, Biblioteka Cyfrowa Uniwersytetu Wrocławskiego, MF 9961.

Archivio di Stato di Biella, Famiglia Ferrero della Marmora, Fondo Ferrero, Cassetta XVI, Cartella 18, Fascicolo 287/13.

Bayerische Staatsbibliothek, Cgm 895.

Bayerisches Hauptstaatsarchiv, München, Kasten Schwarz. 16712.

Cambridge University Library, Add. MS 8686.

Commentariolus de coronatione Maximiliani II., OSZK Ms. Lat. 2275, fol. 162–173.

ELTE Egyetemi Könyvtár Kézirattár, Kaprinai B 19/25, 103–104.

ELTE Egyetemi Könyvtár, LEO 1358.

Benda Kálmán hagyatéka, Hungarian Academy of Science, Történettudományi Intézet [Kálmán Benda bequest, Institute for the study of History], (no catalogue number).
Illésházy, Stephanus, De Rebus Hungaricis Prothocolon, OSZK Fol. Lat. 2336.
MOL E 200 Acta diversarum 24. tétel. (Illésházy).
MOL I 47 Hoffinanz Ungarn, Bocskayische Friedensakte, Fasc. 15434.
MOL I 7, vol. 34.
MOL I 45, documents from the Vienna archives, Böhmisch-Österreichische Hofkanzlei, documents on Hungarian topics, 1608/6.
MOL I 34 (Collection Kollar).
MOL N 114 Kovachich Márton György gyűjteménye. Acta diaetalia. I.
MOL N 49 Lada Diaeta Antiquae Fasc. B.
MOL P 1615 Révay család 1 cs., 73. tétel.
MOL P 1341. Raktári szám 2. fasc. 10–12.
MOL, Archivum Familia Thurzó, 2. doboz, fasc. 5.
MOL, E 204 "Perger" Elias 1645.01.25.
MOL E 211 XXXII. Lymbus II. series 1605–1606.
MOL N 114 Kovachich Márton György gyűjteménye. Acta diaetalia. I. fol. 53.
MOL P 1615 Révay family 1, bundle 41.
MOL P 1889 bundle 42.
MOL R 64, 25 April 1603.
MOL Eszterházy cs. lt. Rep. 46. fasc. G.
MOL P 1341. Lad. 1 fasc. 10–12.
MOL P 287 Forgách család. Series 1. 34. cs. Fasc. T. 34.
MTAK, Budapest, K 63, fol. 135r–150r.
MTAK, Budapest, K 75, fol. 39v–51v.
MTAK, Ms. 5169 (Árpád Károlyi bequest).
Nationaal Archief, Den Haag, Staten-Generaal [National Archive of the Netherlands, The Hague, S , nummer toegang 1.01.02, inventarisnummer 6016. (9 April 1605).
ÖNB, Cod. 8790.
ÖNB, Cod. 7647.
ÖNB, Cod. 2920.
ÖNB, Cod. 8229.
ÖNB, Cod. 8464.
ÖNB, Cod. 8677.
ÖNB, Cod. 8448.
ÖNB, Cod. 8674.
ÖStA Wien, HHStA Hoffinanz-Ungarn r. nr. 95. Konv. B. [June 1608].
ÖStA Wien, HHStA Hungarica AA Fasc. 153. Konv. B.
ÖStA Wien, HHStA Ungarische Akten Comi. Fasc. 394. Konv. A. 1605, fol. 1r.–15v.
ÖStA Wien, HHStA Ungarische Akten, Comitalia, Fasc. 395 Konv. B.
ÖStA Wien, HHStA Ungarische Akten, Fasc. 149 C, fol. 49r.

ÖStA Wien, HHStA Ungarische Akten, Fasc. 149 Konv. C.
ÖStA Wien, HHStA Ungarn. Hungarica Fasc. 431C. Konv. A. Nachtrag 1601–1621.
ÖStA Wien, HHStA, Fasc. 395 Konv. A.
ÖStA Wien, HHStA, Ungarische Akten Comi. Fasc. 395. Konv. A.
ÖStA Wien, HHStA, Ungarische Akten, Fasc. 149 Konv. A.
ÖStA Wien, HHStA, Ungarische Akten, Fasc. 149 Konv. D.
ÖStA Wien, HHStA, Ungarische Akten, Fasc. 433.
ÖStA Wien, HHStA, Ungarn, Fasc. 151 Konv. A.
ÖStA Wien, HHStA, Ungarn. Hungarica Fasc. 433. Miscellanea Konv. E. Die Angelegenheit der Kasschauer Kirche betr. Akten aus den "Hungarica" Okt. 1603 -Sept. 1604.
ÖStA Wien, HHStA: Böhm 1075. Miscellanea Hungarica. fol. 1–7r.
ÖStA, Hoffinanz–Ungarn, r. Nr. 106. Konv. 1615.II.9.
OSZK Fol. Germ. 1116.
OSZK Fol. Hung. 1089.
OSZK Fol. Lat. 520.
OSZK Fol. Lat. 2204.
OSZK Fol. Lat. 2336.
OSZK Fol. Lat. 2336.
OSZK Fol. Lat. 3411.
OSZK Fol. Lat. 3415.
OSZK Fol. Lat. 3606.
OSZK Quart. Lat. 316.
Perger [Berger], Elias, Duplex speculum chronologicum…, EK Ms. G.69.
Schödel, Martinus, Cum Deo. Disquisitio Historico-Politica, De Regno Hungariae…(Argentorati: Johannis Rippl, 1629, 1630).
SNA – ARR Korešpondencia Frantisek III Révay Krč. 76–77.
SNA – ARR Korešpondencia Peter Révay Krč. 81.
SNA – ARR Korešpondencia Peter Révay Krč. 82.
SNA – ARR Korešpondencia Peter Révay Krč. 83.
Soproni evangélikus egyházközség levéltára [The Lutheran convent archive, Sopron], 45. VI. B.
Tomci Marnavitii, Johannes, De coronis Ungaricis nota brevis (manuscript), dated 1 January 1627. Bibliotheca Apostolica Vaticana Ms. OTTOB. Lat. 2776.

Printed sources

[Berger, Elias], Oratio funebris in exequiis illustrissimi comitis, palatini Stephani de Ilieshaza comitis Trenchinien: et Liptovien: ([Kassa: S.N.], 1609).
[Bocskai, István], Apologia et protestatio... (Bartphae: Jacobus Klös, 1606, [2]1608).
[Languet, Hubert], De verantwoordinghe des Princen van Oraengien… [The apology of the Prince of Orange] (S.L.: S.N., 1568).

[Schödel, Martin], Respublica et Status Regni Hungariae ([Leiden: Elsevier], 1634, ²1634).
Avity, Pierre d', The estates, empires, & principallities of the world (London: Printed by Adam: Islip; for Mathewe: Lownes; and Iohn: Bill, ²1615).
Avity, Pierre d', Les Estats, Empires et Principautez du Monde (Paris: Paul Chevalier, 1615).
Avity, Pierre d', The estates, empires, & principallities of the world (London: Printed by Adam: Islip; for Mathewe: Lownes; and Iohn: Bill, 1615).
Avity, Pierre d', Archontologia cosmica ... opera et studio Jo. Ludovici Gotofredi (Francofurti ad Moenum: Jennisius, 1628).
Balasfi, Thomas, [Balásfy, Tamás], Christiana responsio ad libellum Calvinisticum Alberti Molnar Hungari, pedagogi Oppenhemiensis (Viennae: Typis Gregorii Gelbhaar, 1621).
Bartoniek, Emma, ed., "Legendae Sancti Stephani regis maior et minor atque legenda ab Hartvico conscripta," in Emericus Szentpétery, ed., Scriptores Rerum Hungaricarum tempore ducum regumque stirpis Arpadianae gestarum, Vol. II (Budapestini: Typ. Reg. Univ. Litter. Hung., 1938), 363–448.
Becmann, Johann Christoph, Historia Orbis Terrarum Geographica Et Civilis ... (Francofurti et Lipsiae: apud Henr. Joh. Meyeri Haered. & Godofr. Zimmermann, 1673, 1680, 1685, 1692, 1698).
Behamb, Johann Ferdinand, Notitia Hungariae Antiquo-Modernae Berneggeriana: Perpetuis Observationibus Condecorata Nec non Indice Tum Marginali, Tum Reali illustrata, emendata (Argentorati: Georgii Andreae Dolhopffii, 1676).
Bél, Matthias, Notitia Hungariae novae historico geographica, vol. II (Viennae Austriae: Paulus Straubius, 1736).
Benda, Kálmán, "Alvinczi Péter kassai prédikátor történeti feljegyzései 1598–1622 [The historical notes of Péter Alvinczi, Preacher in Kaschau 1598–1622]," Ráday Gyüjtemény Évkönyve [Yearbook of the Ráday collection], vol. 1 (1955), 16.
Benessovinus, Johannes, Brevis et succincta descriptio pompae funebris, in honorem sacratissimi ac gloriosissimi monarchae, divi Maximiliami II ... conscripta (Pragae: Melantrichus, 1577).
Berger, Elias, "Trinubium Europaeum," in Melchior Goldast, ed., Politica Imperialia, sive discursus politici, Acta Publica, Et Tractatus... (Francofurti: Ex Off. Typogr. Johannis Bringeri: 1614), 722–742.
Berger, Elias, "Ad Illustrissimum ac magnificum D.D. Stephanum Ilieshazi comitem Trinchinien, & Liptowien D.& Patronum observandißimum," published in: Elias Berger, D.O.M. Jubilaeus de origine, errore et restitutione S. Coronae Hungariae Regni fortiss. ac felicissi (s.l.: s.n., 1608), F1.
Berger, Elias, Caduceus seu proba, et brevis invitatio (Viennae Austriae: Typis Margarethae Formicae, Viduae, 1607).
Berger, Elias, Connubium Hungariae et Bohemiae in Matthia II. rege Hungariae et rege Bohemiae coronato denuo sanctitum (Pragae: Typis Schumanianis, [1611]).
Berger, Elias, Domus augustissimae Austriae. Columnae sidera Caesares monarchae archiduces (Viennae Austriae: Ex Officina Typographica Francisci Kolbij, 1602).

Berger, Elias, Rapsodiae de cruce insigniis regni Hungarici et sanctissimis, et de gestis pro Cruce Christi inclutorum Hungariae Regum Faelicissimis: secundum fidem historicam pro Immortali Gloria Hungariae, pro nomine Christi tot seculis Pugnantis (Olomutii: Typis Georgij Handelij, 1600).

Berger, Elias, Spectator theatri extemporanei belli Hungarici... (Pragae: Typis Danielis Sedesan, 1612).

Berger, Elias, Trinubium Europaeum (Francofurti: apud Godefridum Tampachium, 1612).

Berger, Elias, Vindiciae Hungariae (Viennae Austriae: Gregorius Gelbhaar, 1618).

Bergerus, Elias, Idyllia de virtvte bellica, fortitvdine, is est de militiae christianae origine, progressu u u dignitate utilitate. Additis panegyribus in exemplo dvcis et herois antiqvis et veris comparati avthore Elia Bergero poeta lavreato caeseo (Pragae: Typis Chumanianis, 1603).

Bergher, Elias, Gratulatio Serenissimo Principe ac Domino D. Matthiae Archiduci Austriae... (Viennae Austriae: Typis Margarethae Formicae, 1607).

Bethlen, Wolfgangus de [Farkas Bethlen], Historia de rebus Transsylvanicis, vol. I-VI. (Cibinii: Martin Hochmeister, 1793).

Bijvoet Williamson, H. M., ed., and tr., The Memoirs of Helene Kottanner (1439–1440) (Woodbridge, Suffolk: Boydell & Brewer, 1998).

Blaeu, Johannes, Het koningrijck Hvngaryen [The Kingdom of Hungary] (Amsterdami: apud Guiljelmum et Iohannum Blaeu: [1647]).

Bocatius, Ioannes [János Bocatius], Opera Quae Extant Omnia: Prosaica, ed. Franciscus Csonka (Bibliotheca Scriptorum Medii Recentisque Aevorum, n.s. 12) (Budapest: Akadémiai Kiadó, 1992).

Bocatius, Iohannes, "Commentatio epistolica de legatione sua ad Stephanum Botskay," in Matthias Bél, ed., Adparatus ad historiam Hungariae (Posonii: Royer, 1735), 330–336.

Bocatius, Iohannes, Opera quae exstant omnia: Poetica, vol. I-II, Franciscus Csonka ed. (Budapest: Akadémiai Kiadó, 1990–1994).

Bocatius, János, Öt év börtönben [1606–1610], Ferenc Csonka, ed. and trans. (Budapest: Európa Könyvkiadó, 1985).

Bocatius, Johannes, Hexasticha votiva, vel strena poetica, ominis boni gratia. Anno Deo volente erit melius (Bartphae: excudebat Iacobus Kléz, 1612).

Bocatius, Johannes, Matthiados carmina heroica libri duo (Cassoviae: Iohannis Fischer, 1614).

Bodin, Jean, Methodus, ad facilem historiarum cognitionem (Paris: Apud M. Iuuenem, 1566).

Bonfini, Antonio, Rerum Ungaricarum decades (Basiliae: Robertus Winterus, 1543).

Bonfini, Antonio, Rerum Ungaricarum decades quatuor cum dimidia, Iohannes Sambucus ed., (Francofurti: Andreas Wechelus, 1581).

Boronkai, Iván, ed., Opera quae supersunt / Iohannes Vitéz de Zredna (Budapest: Akadémiai Kiadó, 1980).

Chlumecky, Peter von, Carl von Zierotin und seine Zeit 1564–1615, vol. II (Brünn: A. Nitsch, 1862).

Chroust, Anton, ed., Der Ausgang der Regierung Rudolfs II. und die Anfänge des Kaisers Matthias (Briefen und Acten zur Geschichte des Dreissigjährigen Krieges vol. VI) (München: Rieger, 1906).

Csiky, Kálmán, Sándor Kolozsváry, Gyula Nagy, Kelemen Óváry, Lőrinc Tóth and Márkus Dezső, eds., Corpus juris hungarici: magyar törvenytár, 1000–1895. Vol. 3 1608–1657, évi törvényezikkek [Corpus juris hungarici: Hungarian law collection, 1000–1895. Vol. 3. Law articles from the years 1608–1657] (Budapest: Franklin-Társulat, 1896).

Eckhart, Sándor, ed., Rimay János összes művei [All the works of János Rimay] (Budapest, 1955).

EK, Ms. G 69.

Elias Perger [Berger], D.O.M.A Symbolum Sacrum et Augustum Decem Reginarum Hungariae. Politicè et Historicè Expositum (S.l.: s.n., 1637).

Ens von Lorch, Kaspar, Ad rerum Hungaricarum historiam appendix (Coloniae: Wilhelmus Lutzenkirchen, 1608).

Erdeody, Georgius [György Erdődy], Gloria virtutis Hungaricae (Duaci: Typis Viduae Petri Telu, 1633).

Fejér, Georgius, Codex diplomaticus Hungariae ecclesiasticus ac civilis, vol. I (Budae: Typis typogr. Regiae Universitatis Ungaricae, 1828).

Ferrari, Sigismund, De rebus Ungaricae provinciae sac. Ordinis praedicatorum (Viennae, 1637).

Fugger, Johann Jakob, Spiegel der Ehren des Höchstlöblichsten Kayser- und Königlichen Erzhauses Oesterreich oder Ausführliche Geschicht Schrift von Desselben... (Nürnberg: Michael und Johann Friderich Endter, 1668).

Hammer-Purgstall, Joseph, Khlesl's, des Cardinals, Directors des geheimen Cabinets Kaisers Mathias, Leben, vol. II (Wien: Kaulfuss, 1847).

Hanuy, Ferenc, ed., Petri Cardinalis Pázmány epistolae collectae I (1610–1628) (Budapest: Magyar Királyi Tudomány-Egyetem Nyomda, 1910).

Hatvani, Mihály, ed., Magyar történelmi okmánytár a brüsszeli országos levéltárból [Hungarian historian charters from the country archive in Brussels] (Magyar történelmi emlékek [Hungarian historical relics], vol. 1, Osztály [Class]: Okmánytárak [Charter registers], vol. 3 (Pest: Eggenberger, 1857).

Heltai, Gáspár, Chronica az Magyaroknac dolgairol [Chronicle on the deeds of the Hungarians] (Colosvarot: Heltaj Gasparné, 1575).

Horányi, Alexius, De Sacra Corona Hungariae, ac de Regibus eadem redimitis Commentarius (Pest: Typis Trannerianis, 1790).

Hrabecius, Rafaël, D.O.M.A. Oratio Funebris In solennibus exequiis Spect. ac Mag. Dni Petri de Reva, supremi ac perpetui Comitis Comitatus Thurocen... Habita in loco sepulturae Ejusdem & Majorum, in templo Martinopolitano... 17. Julij. Anno 1622... Adjuncta est

Valedictio Eiusdem Dni Petri de Reva, ... morituri (Cassoviae: : ex officina typographica Danielis Schultz, 1623).

Inchofer, Melchior, Annales ecclesiastici regni Hungariae, vol. I (Romae: typis Ludovici Grignani, 1644, Posonii: Typis Simonis Petri Weber, ^{2}1796–1797).

Ipolyi, Arnold, ed., Alsó-sztregovai és rimai Rimay János államiratai és levelezése [The correspondence and state writings of János Rimay of Alsó-sztregova and Rima] (Budapest: M. T. Akad., 1887).

Istvanfi, Nicolaus, [István Istvánffy], Historiarum de rebus Ungaricis Libri XXXIV (Coloniae Agrippinae: Hieratus, 1622).

Jankovics, József, ed., Literátor–politikusok levelei Jenei Ferenc gyűjtéséből (1566–1623) [Letters of writers and politicians from the collection of Ferenc Jenei (1566–1623)] (Budapest – Szeged: JATE, 1981).

Jessenius a Jessen, Johann, Der Königlichen Majestät zu Vngarn, Matthiae des Andern dieses Nahmens, Krönung : Gehalten in Preßburg: am Tage S. Elisabeth: im Jahre ... 1608. Neben einer kurtzen Chronica oder ZeitRegister aller Könige der Cron Vngarn, M. Wolfart Spangenberg tr. (Straßburg: Zetzner, 1609).

Jessenius a Jessen, Johann, Zoroaster nova, brevis veraque de universo Philosophia (Witebergae: Ex Off. Cratoniana, 1593).

Jessenius, Johann, "Der Königlichen Majestät zu Ungarn / Matthiae des Andern dieses Nahmens / Krönung: ... ," in András Vizkelety, ed., Wolfhart Spangenberg Sämtliche Werke, Vol. IV/2 (Berlin and New York: De Gruyter, 1982) 261–316.

Jessenius, Johann, Regis Ungariae, Matthiae II. coronatio (Hamburg: Georg Ludwig Frobenianus, 1609).

Jessenius, Johann, Regis Ungariae, Matthiae II. coronatio; Johan: Jessenio a Jessen, Regio Medico, Descriptore. Adiecta, regni, regumque Pannoniae, brevis Chronographia (Viennae: Ludovicus Bonnoberger, 1609).

Jessenius, Johannes, Pro vindiciis, contra tyrannos, oratio (Francofurti: Ioannes Bringerius, 1614).

Juhász, László, ed., "Carmen Miserabile super Destructione Regni Hungariae per Tartaros," in Imre Szentpetery, ed., Scriptores rerum Hungaricarum tempore ducum regumque stirpis Arpadianae gestarum, Vol. II. (Budapest: Academia Litterarum Hungarica, 1938), 511–588.

Junius, Melchior, ed., Orationum quae argentinensi in academia, exercitii gratia scriptae & recitatae Vol. II. (Argentorati: Lazarus Zetzner, 1594).

Junius, Melchior, ed., Orationum, quae Argentinensi in Academia exercitii gratia scriptae ... Vol. III. Vol. III. (Argentorati: Lazarus Zetzner, 1611).

Kalt, Marcus de, Chronicon Pictum. Képes Krónika [Illustrated chronicle], László Mezey, ed., and László Geréb, tr., vol. I–II, (Budapest: Magyar Helikon, 1964).

Katona, István, Historia Critica Regnum Hungariae stirpis Austriacae, Tomulus IX, ordine XXVIII (Budae: Typis Regiae Universitatis, 1794)

Debrecenis, Joannes S., [János Szappanos Debreceni], Militaris congratulatio Comitatus

Bihariensis: Ad Ilustrissimum Principem et Dominum, Dn. Stephanum Botskai de Kis Maria... (Debrecini: Paulus Rhaeda Lipsensis, 1605).

Katona, Tamás, ed., A korona kilenc évszázada. Történelmi források a magyar koronáról [The nine hundred years of the Crown. Historic sources about the Hungarian Crown] (Budapest: Európa könyvkiadó, 1979).

Kazinczy, Gábor, ed., Gr. Illésházy István Nádor följegyzései 1592–1603. és Hídvégi Mikó Ferencz históriája 1594–1613. Bíró Sámuel folytatásával [Count István Illésházy's historic notes 1592–1603 and the history of Ferencz Hídvégi Mikó 1594–1613] (Pest: F. Eggenberger, 1863).

Kereskényi, István, Corona Apostolico-Basilica seu Stephani I. Regis Hungariae (Cassoviae: S.n., 1679).

Khevenhüller, Franz Christoph, Annales Ferdinandei ..., vol. VI (Regenspurg: Christoff Fischer, 1643).

Kitonich, János, Directio Methodica Processus (Tyrnavia: S.N., 1619).

Klaniczay, Tibor, and Béla Stoll, eds., Régi Magyar Költők Tára XVII. Század [Collection of old Hungarian poets], vol. 1 (Budapest: Akadémiai Kiadó, 1959).

Klaniczay, Tibor, Reneszánsz és Barokk (tanulmányok a régi magyar irodalomról) [Renaissance and Baroque (Studies on the ancient Hungarian literature)] (Budapest, Szépirodalmi Könyvkiadó, 1961).

Kollar, Adam Franciscus, De Originibus Et Usu Perpetuo Potestatis... (Vindibonae: Joannes Thomas de Trattner, 1764).

Kovachich, Martinus Georgius, Vestigia comitiorum apud Hungaros (Budae: typis Regiae Universitatis, 1790).

Kulcsár, Péter, ed., Humanista történetírók [Humanist history writers] (Budapest: Szépirodalmi Kiadó, 1977).

Lackhner, Christophor [Lackner], Coronae Hungariae emblematica descriptio (Lavingae Suevorum: Typis Palatini, excudebat M. Iacobus Winter, 1615).

Lipsius, Justus, De constantia libri dvo (Antverpiae: C. Plantini, 1584).

Listius, László, Magyar Márs avagy Mohách mezején történt veszedelemnek emlékezete [Hungarian Mars or the loss which happened on the field of Mohács] (Viennae: Mathé Cozmerovius, 1653).

Liszty, János, "II. Miksa beiktatásának rövid leírása," in A korona kilenc évszázada [The 900 years of the Crown], Tamás Katona ed. (Budapest: Helikon, 1979), 176–191.

Magyari, István, Az országokban való sok romlásoknak okairól [On the causes of the many disasters in Hungary], ed. Tamás Katona (Budapest: Magyar Helikon, 1979).

Makkai, László, ed., Bethlen Gábor krónikásai [The chronicles of Gábor Bethlen] (Budapest: Gondolat, 1980).

Matthiae, Christian, Theatrum historicum theoretico-practicum... (Amstelodami, 1668).

May, Louis De [Du May de Salettes], A discourse, historical and political, of the War of Hungary, and of the causes of the peace between Leopold the First, Emperor of the

Romans, and Mahomet the Fourth, Sultan of Turkey. ... Translated in English [by Sir James Turner] (Glasgow: Robert Sanders, 1669).

Melchior, Junius, ed., Orationum, qae Argentinensi in Academia exercitii gratia scriptae, Vol. II. (Argentorati: Lazarus Zetzner Bibliop., 1606, 1620).

Meteren, Emanuel van, Commentarien ofte memorien van-den Nederlandtschen staet [Commentaries or memoirs of the Dutch state] (Schotlandt buyten Danswijck [Amsterdam?]: Hermes van Loven, 1608).

Nadányi, János, Florus Hungaricus, sive rerum Hungaricarum ab ipso exordio ad Ignatium Leopoldum deductarum compendium (Amstelodami, Ex officina Joannis à Waesberge: 1663).

Nagy, László, "Okmányok a Bocskai-szabadságharc idejéből [Records from the time of the Bocskai war of freedom]," Hadtörténelmi közlemények 3–4 (1956), 323–330.

Oertel [Ortelius], Hieronymus, and Martin Meyrn, Ortelius Redivivus et Continuatus oder Ungarische und Siebenbürgische Kriegs-Händel, so vom Jahr 1395. biß auf 1665. mit dem Türcken vorgelauffe (Nürnberg: Fürst, 1665).

Oertel, Hieronymus, De Chronycke van Hungari [The chronicle of Hungary], Peter Neander, tr. (Amsterdam: Jan Evertszoon Cloppenburch, 1619).

Okolicsanyi, Paulus, Commentarius Petri De Réwa Comitis Comitatus de Turócz, De Sacra Regni Hungariae Corona. Ad nostra usque tempora continuatus (Tyrnaviae: Typis Academicis per Leopoldum Berger, 1732).

Ortelius, Hieronymus, Chronologia oder historische Beschreibung aller Kriegsempörungen und Schlachten so in Ober und Under Ungern auch Siebenbürgen mit dem Türken geschehen, 1395–1598 (Nürnberg: Sibmacher, 1613, [2]1663).

Ortelius, Hieronymus, De chronycke van Hungarie, P. Neander, trans. (Amsterdam: Jan Everts van Cloppenburch, 1619).

Őry, Miklós, Ferenc Szabó and Péter Vass, eds., Pázmány Péter válogatás műveiből [Selection of works of Péter Pázmány], Vol. II (Budapest: Szent István Társulat, 1983).

Palma, Carolus Franciscus, Heraldicae regni Hungariae specimen, regia, provinciarum, nobilimque scuta complectens… (Vindobonae: Joannis Thomae de Trattnern, 1766).

Pannonius, Janus, "De corona regni ad Fridericum Caesarem," in Sándor V. Kovács, ed., Jani Pannonii opera omnia (Budapest: Tankönyvkiadó, 1987) 202.

Pázmány, Péter, Felelet az Magiari Istvan sarvari praedicatornak az orzag romlasa okairul irt könivere [Answer to what István Magyari write about the causes of the many disasters in Hungary] (Nagyszombatba: typ. capituli Strigoniensis, 1603).

Pázmány, Péter, Isteni igazságra vezérlő kalauz [Guide to Divine Truth] (Posonban: [S.N.], 1613).

Perger[!], Elias, Duplex speculum chronologicum (Viennae Austriae, 1635).

Pessina de Czechorod, Thomas Johannes, Mars Moravicus (Pragae: Typis Joannis Arnolti de Dobroslawina, 1677).

Petthő, Gergely, Rövid magyar kronika [Short Hungarian chronicle] (Kassa: S.n., 1702, 1729, 1734, 1738, 1742, [2]1742, 1753, 1753, [2]1990).

Podhorszky, Laurentius, Commentarius Petri de Réwa Comitis etc. Thesis ex univ. Theologia (Posonii: Typis Franciscii Antonii Royer, 1749).

Praetorius, Bernard, ed., Corona Imperialis... (Norimbergae: Typis Et Imp. Georg. Leop. Fuhrmann, 1613).

Pray, György, Epistolae procerum regni Hungariae (Pars III. ab anno 1554 ad 1711) (Posonii: Ex Typographeo G. A. Belnay, 1806).

Pray, György, Index rariorum librorum bibliothecae Universitatis regiae Budensis (Budae: Regia Universitas, 1790).

Rady, Martyn, "The Gesta Hungarorum of Anonymus, the Anonymous Notary of King Béla: A Translation," The Slavonic and East European Review, 87/4 (2009), 681–727.

Rewa, Petrus de [Péter Révay], De monarchia et sacra corona regni Hungariae centuriae septem... (Francofurti: Thomae Mattiae Götzii, 1659).

Rewa, Petrus de [Péter Révay], De sacrae coronae regni Hungariae ortu, virtute, victoria, fortuna, annos ultra D C clarissimae, brevis commentarius (Augustae Vindelicorum: Christoph. Mangus, 1613).

Rewa, Petrus de, "Comitis Comitatus de Thurocz, de S. Coronae Regni Hungariae, ultra 700 annos clarissimae, virtute, victoria, fortuna, commentarius, Post augustanam editionem anni 1613 plurimis locis emendatus, et ad nostra usque tempora perductus Animadversiones atque Emendationes Auctoris ex Msc. addidit Carolus Andreas Bel, Phil. Prof. Publ. Lips. et Collegio Minori Principum Collegiatus", in Johannes Georgius Schwandtner, ed., Scriptores rerum Hung. veteres ac genuini, vol. II., ed. Matthias Bél (Viennae- Joannes Thomas de Trattner, 1746, ^{2}1766).

Rewa, Petrus de, De sacrae coronae... (Viennae Austriae: Cosmerovius, 1652).

Rewa, Petrus de, Disputatio de Mutuo, materia non minus difficili qvam utili. In inclyta Argentoratensium Academia, exercitii, causa a' Generoso D. Petro de Rewa, Comite Thuroczensi &c. Ungaro, conscripta, & Praeside Clarissimo Viro, Paulo Graseccio J. V. D. Mense Martio defensa (Argentorati: A. Bertram, 1591).

Rimay, János, Balassi epicedium, ed. Pál Ács (Budapest: Balassi Kiadó, 1994).

Ritter, Moriz, ed., Die Gründung der Union 1598–1608 (Briefen und Acten des Dreissigjährigen Krieges, vol. I) (München: M. Rieger, 1870) 628.

Rollenhagen, Georg, Froschmeuseler (Magdeburgk: Andreas Gehn, 1595).

S. N., "Supplicatio Regni Ungariae," in Gábor Kazinczy, ed., Gr. Illésházy István Nádor följegyzései 1592–1603. és Hidvégi Mikó Ferencz históriája 1594–1613. Bíró Sámuel folytatásával [Notes by Count Palatine István Illésházy 1592–1603 and the history of Mikó Ferencz Hidvégi 1594–1613. With the sequel of Sámuel Bíró] (Pest: F. Eggenberger, 1863), 120–129.

S. N., Apparatus regius. Sereniss. ac potentissimo Ferdinando II. Hungariae ac Bohemiae regi. Symbolis regum Hungariae adornatus (Viennae Austrae: Gregorius Gelbhaar, 1618).

S. N., Appendix relationis historicae: darinnen kürtzlich erzehlet wird, mit was Ceremonien und Solenniteten die zu Hungarn und Böhem designirte Königl. Wür. Herr Matthias, Ertzherzog zu Österreich, zum Könige in Hungarn in S. Elisabethae Reginae Hungariae,

den 19. Novembrie anno 1608 zu Preßburg gekrönet worden (Leipzig: Abraham Bamber, 1609).
S. N., Batrachomiomachia (Leiden: I. Burchoorn, 1636).
S. N., Cérémonies observées au couronnement de Mathias, deuxiesme roy de Hongrie (Paris, Lyon: S.n, 1609).
S. N., Nevves ovt of Germanie or The surprizing of the Citie of Prage by the Arch-duke Leopold, and what there passed in the monehts of February and March last. With a briefe of the most remarkeable things happened within six monehts, as well in France and Germany as in Bohemia, Transiluania and Spaine. Translated out of the French Copie, printed at Paris 1611 (London: Printed [by N. Okes] for Iohn Royston and William Bladon, 1612).
S. N., Orationes Gratvlatoriae In Electione, Coronatione, Nativitate, Nvptiis, triumphis, &c. Pontificvm, Imperatorvm, Regvm, Principvm, &c. Habitae à Legatis Virisve suae aetatis doctissimis; Quarum catalogum sequens pagina indicat (Hanoviae: Typis Wechelianis apud haeredes J. Aubrii, 1613).
S. N., Warhafftige Newe Zeitung/ Wie und was massen sich dess Sigismundi Bathori Mutter Bruder Steffan Botschkai genandt/ gegen unserm Christlichen Keyser/ sampt den Deutschen Kriegsvolck/ Trewlos und Meineydig verhalten/ dem Türcken gehuldet unnd sich ihm untergeben (Prag: Nickel Strau, 1605).
S.N., "Descriptio coronationis in regem Hungariae Posonii," in Márton György Kovachich, Solennia inauguralia serenissimorum... (Pestini: Typis Matthiae Trattner, 1796) 23–28.
S.N., "Anno 1608. Peroratio sive preambulum propositionum 29. Julii Cassoviae exhibita regnicolis per C. Stephanum Illésházy," Történelmi Tár, 2 (1879) 388–389.
S.N., Collegii Posthi Melissaei Votvm, Hoc Est, Ebrietatis Detestatio, Atqve Potationis Saltationisque eiuratio: Amethystvs Princeps Sobrietatis (Francoforti ad Moenvm: Johannes Lucienbergius, 1573).
S.N., Mausoleum Regni Apostolici Regum & Ducum (Norimbergae: Apud Michaëlem & Joannem Fridericum Endteros, 1664, fascimilé-edition Budapest, [2]1991).
Sambucus, Ioannis, De corona serenissimi Rodolphi regis Ungariae, &c. Archiducis Austriae, &c. 25. Septemb. 1572. ad status Regni, & alios Ioan. Samb. oratiuncula (Viennae Austriae: typis Blasii Eberi 1572).
Sambucus, Iohannes, "In moerore funeris Maximiliani II. Laudatiuncula," in Antonio Bonfini, Rerum Ungaricarum decades (Hanovia: Typis Wechelianis, apud Claudium Marnium, & haeredes Ioannis Aubrii, 1606), 816–826.
Schad, Johann Adam Xavier, Effigies Ducum et Regum Hungariae ..., (S. l., s.n., 1687).
Schmeizel, Martinus, Commentarius Petri De Rewa comitis Comitatus de Turócz, De Sacra Regni Hungariae Corona Ad nostra usque tempora continuatus (Claudiopoli: Typis Academicis per Simonem Thadaeum Weichenberg, 1735).
Schmeizel, Martinus, Commentatio Historica de Coronis tam Antiquis, quam Modernis ... Speciatim de Origine et Fatis Sacrae, Angelicae et Apostolicae Regni Hungariae Coronae (Jena: Typis Gollnerianis, 1712).

Schödel, Martinus, Cum Deo. Disquisitio Historico-Politica, De Regno Hungariae… (Argentorati: Johannis Reppl, 1629, ²1630).

Schwandtner, Johannes Georgius, ed., Scriptores rerum Hun. Veteres ac genuini, Vol. II (Vindobonae, Lipsiae: impensis Ioannis Pauli Kraus, 1746).

Schwandtner, Johannes Georgius, ed., Scriptores Rerum Hungaricarum Veteres ac genuini, vol. II (Vindobonae : Kraus, 1746).

Sleidanus, Johannes, De statu religionis et rei publicae Carolo V. Caesare commentarii (Argentini: 1555).

Stieve, Felix, ed., Vom Reichstag 1608 bis zur Gründung der Liga (Briefen und Acten zur Geschichte des Dreissigjährigen Krieges, vol. VI) (München: M. Rieger, 1895).

Szakály, Ferenc, ed., Szalárdi János siralmas krónikája [Woeful chronicle of János Szalárdi] (Budapest: Magyar Helikon, 1980).

Szenczi Molnár, Albert, Secularis concio evangelica, azaz Jubilaeus esztendei prédikáció [Secularis concio evangelica or Preaching for a jubilee year] (Oppenheimii: Typis & aere Hieronymi Galleri Basileens, 1618).

Szentmártoni Szabó, Géza, "Balassi Bálint halála [The death of Bálint Balassi]," in János Rimay, Balassi epicedium, ed. Pál Ács (Budapest: Balassi Kiadó, 1994) 82.

Szigethy, Gábor, ed., Bocskai István testámentumi rendelése [The last will of István Bocskai] (Budapest: Magvető, 1986).

Szilágyi, Sándor, ed., "Három uralkodói levélke [Three small letters of rulers]," Történelmi Tár 1 (1878), 389–390.

Szilágyi, Sándor, ed., Szamosközy István történeti maradványai. 1542–1608 [István Számosközy's historic relics] (Monumenta Hungariae Historica. Scriptores XXX) vol. IV (Budapest: Magyar Tudományos Akadémia Könyvkiadó Hivatala, 1880).

Tarnóc, Márton, ed., Pázmány Péter művei [Works of Péter Pázmány] (Budapest, 1985).

Thurocz, Joannes de, Chronica Hungarorum (Augsburg: Erhard Ratdolt, 1488).

Tomci Marnavitii, Johannes, Pro sacris ecclesiarum ornamentis et donariis, contra eorum detractores (Romae: Franciscus Caballus, 1635).

Tomci Marnavitii, Johannes, Regiae sanctitatis Illyricanae foecunditas a Joanne Tomco Marnavitio Bosniensi Edita (Romae: Vaticannis, 1630).

Tuberonis Dalmatae Abbatis, Ludovicus, Commentariorum De Rebus… (Francofurti: Impensis Claudii Marnii, & haeredum Joannis Aubrii, 1603).

Venásch, Eszter, "Drugeth Bálint Homonnai hadinaplójának kiadatlan része [An unpublished part of Bálint Drugeth Homonnai's war diary]," Lymbus. Magyarságtudományi forrásközlemények [Lymbus. Hungarologian source editions] (Budapest: Magyar Országos Levéltár; Balassi Bálint Magyar Kulturális Intézet; Nemzetközi Magyarságtudományi Társaság, 2007), 19–46.

Verancsics, Faustus, "A vallás felújításának módszerei Magyarországon (1606) [The methods of renewal of religion in Hungary (1606)]," in Katalin S. Vargha, ed. and trans., Verancsics Faustus Machinae novae és más művei [The Machinae novae of Faustus Verancsics and other works] (Budapest: Magvető Könyvkiadó, 1985) 328–329, 333.

Verbőczy[!], István, Werbőczy István Hármaskönyve, Sándor Kolosvári and Kelemen Óvári, eds., and trans. (Budapest: Magyar Tudományos Akadémia, 1894).
Veszprémi, István, Magyar országi öt különös elmélkedések, I: A Magyar Szent Koronáról [Five special reflections, I: on the Hungarian Holy Crown] (Pozsony: Simon Péter Weber, 1795).
Werboecz [Werbőczy], Tripartitum opus iuris consuetudinarij inclyti regni Hungarie... (Viennae Austriae: Joannes Singrenius, 1517).
Wolkan, Rudolf, ed., Der Briefwechsel des Eneas Silvius Piccolomini. I. Abteilung: Briefe aus der Laienzeit. I. Band: Privatbriefe (1431–1445) (Fontes Rerum Austriacarum) (Wien: Hölder, 1909).
Wolkan, Rudolf, ed., Der Briefwechsel des Eneas Silvius Piccolomini. I. Abteilung: Briefe aus der Laienzeit (1431–1445) II. Band: Amtliche Briefe (Fontes Rerum Austriacarum) (Wien: Hölder, 1909).

Research literature

Abaffy, Erzsébet, and Sándor Kozocsa, eds., Magyar nyelvű kortársi feljegyzések Erdély múltjából. Szamosközy István történetíró kézirata [Contemporary historic notes in the Hungarian language from the Transylvanian past. István Szamosközy's historical manuscript] (Budapest: Magyar Nyelvtudományi Társaság, 1991).
Acsády, Ignácz, "Magyarország három részre oszlásának története 1526–1608 [History of the division of Hungary into three parts 1526–1608]," in Sándor Szilágyi, ed., A magyar nemzet története [The history of the Hungarian nation], vol. V. (Budapest: Athenaeum Irodalmi és Nyomdai Társulat, 1897).
Almási, Gábor, The Uses of Humanism: Johannes Sambucus (1531–1584), Andreas Dudith (1533–1589) and the Republic of Letters in East Central Europe (Leiden – Boston: Brill, 2005).
Anderson, Benedict, Imagined Communities (London – New York: Verso, 2006) (revised edition).
Anderson, Jeffrey C., "The Esztergom Staurotheke," in Helen C. Evans and William D. Wixom, eds., The Glory of Byzantium: Art and Culture of the Middle Byzantine Era, A.D. 843–1261 (Exhibition catalogue) (New York: The Metropolitan Museum of Art, 1997) 81.
Angyal, Zoltán, Rudolfs II. ungarische Regierung; Ursachen, Verlauf und Ergebnis des Aufstandes Bocskai (Budapest: Athenaeum, 1916).
Aubert, R., ed., Dictionnaire d'histoire et de géographie ecclésiastiques (Paris: Letouzey et Ané, 1995).
Bahlcke, Joachim, "Modernization and state-building in an east-central European Estates' system: the example of the Confoederatio Bohemica of 1619," Parliaments, Estates and Representation, 17/1(2010) 61–73. DOI: 10.1080/02606755.1997.9627014.

Bahlcke, Joachim, Regionalismus und Staatsintegration im Wiederstreit (München: Oldenbourg, 1994) 310–311.
Bak, János M., "Magyar királyi jelvények a középkorban [The Hungarian crown jewels in the Medieval period]," A Hadtörténeti Múzeum Értesítője 4 (2002) 17–21.
Bak, Janos M., "The Kingship of Matthias Corvinus: a Renaissance state?," in Tibor Klaniczay and József Jankovics, eds., Matthias Corvinus and Humanism in Central Europe (Budapest: Balassi, 1994), 45–46.
Bak, János M., ed., Coronations: Medieval and Early Modern Monarchic Ritual (Berkeley: University of California Press, 1990).
Bak, János M., Königtum und Stände in Ungarn im 14.–16. Jahrhundert (Wiesbaden: Steiner, 1973).
Bak, János M., Péter Banyó and Martyn Rady, eds. and trans., The Laws of the Medieval Kingdom of Hungary, Volume 5, The Customary Law of the Renowned Kingdom of Hungary: A Work in Three Parts Rendered by Stephen Werbőczy (The 'Tripartitum'). The Laws of Hungary (Series I: Volume 5) (Idyllwild, CA and Budapest: Charles Schlacks Jr and Department of Medieval Studies, Central European University, 2005).
Bak, János M. and Géza Pálffy, Crown and Coronation in Hungary 1000–1916 A. D. (Research Centre for the Humanities, Institute of History and the Hungarian National Museum, 2020).
Bárány-Oberschall, Magda von, "Localization of the Enamels of the Upper Hemisphere of the Holy Crown of Hungary," Art Bulletin 31/2 (June 1949), 121.
Bárány-Oberschall, Magda von, Die Sankt Stephanskrone und die Insignien des Königreiches Ungarn (Wien–München: Verlag Herold, 1961).
Barta, Gábor, "Az Erdélyi Fejedelemség első korszaka (1526–1606) [The first period of the Principality of Transylvania (1526–1606)]," in Béla Köpeczi, ed., Erdély története [History of Transylvania], vol. I (Budapest: Akadémiai Kiadó, 1987), 532–535.
Bartoniek, Emma, "A koronázási eskü fejlődése 1526-ig [The development of the coronation oath till 1526]," Századok, 5(1917) 37.
Bartoniek, Emma, "Corona és regnum," Századok, 68 (1934) 321.
Bartoniek, Emma, A magyar királykoronázások története [The history of Hungarian coronations of kings] (Budapest: Magyar Történelmi Társulat, 1938).
Bartoniek, Emma, Fejezetek a XVI-XVII századi magarországi történetírás történetéből [Chapters from the history of Hungarian history writing in the sixteenth and seventeenth century] (unpublished manuscript, Budapest, 1975).
Bayerle, Gustav, ed., The Hungarian Letters of Ali Pasha of Buda 1604–1616 (Budapest: Akadémiai Kiadó, 1991).
Benda, Kálmán and Erik Fügedi, A magyar korona regénye [The Novel of the Hungarian Crown] (Budapest: Zrínyi Nyomda, 1979).
Benda, Kálmán, "A kálvini tanok hatása a magyar rendi ellenállás ideológiájára [The influence of Calvinist ideas on the resistance ideology of the Hungarian Estates]," Helikon 17 (1971), 322–329.

Benda, Kálmán, "Az országgyűlések az újkori magyar fejlődésben [The Diets in the Early Modern Hungarian development]," in Kálmán Benda and Katalin Péter, eds., Az országgyűlések a kora újkori magyar történelemben [The Diets in the Early Modern Hungarian history] (Budapest: MTA Történettudományi Intézet: Országos Pedagógiai Intézet, 1987), 4-5.

Benda, Kálmán, "Bocskai István székhely nélküli fejedelmi udvara [The mobile princely court of Bocskai István]," in Ágnes R. Várkonyi, ed., Magyar reneszánsz udvari kultúra [The Hungarian Renaissance court culture] (Budapest, 1987), 158-165.

Benda, Kálmán, "Habsburg-politika és rendi ellenállás [The Habsburg politics and Estate resistance]," Történelmi Szemle 13/3 (1970), 420-426.

Benda, Kálmán, "Le droit de résistance de la bulle d'or hongroise et le Calvinisme," in Béla Köpeczi and Éva H. Balázs, eds., Noblesse française, noblesse hongroise: XVIe-XIXe siècles (Budapest: Akadémiai Kiadó, Paris: Éditions du CNRS, 1981), 155-161.

Benda, Kálmán, "Der Haiduckenaufstand in Ungarn und das Erstarken der Stände in der Habsburgermonarchie 1607-1608," in Dániel Csatári, ed., Nouvelles études historiques publiées à l'occasion du XIIe Congrès International des Sciences Historiques par la Commission Nationale des Historiens Hongrois, vol. I (Budapest: Akadémiai Kiadó, 1965) 299-313.

Benda, Kálmán, "Habsburg Absolutism and Hungarian Resistance," in R.J.W. Evans and T.V. Thomas, eds., Crown, Church and Estates (London: Palgrave Macmillan, 1991), 126-127.

Benda, Kálmán, A Bocskai-szabadságharc [The Bocskai war of freedom] (Budapest: Művelt Nép Könyvkiadó, 1955).

Benda, Kálmán, A magyar nemzeti hivatástudat története a XV-XVII. században [The history of the Hungarian idea of a national vocation in the sixteenth and seventeenth century] (Budapest: Bethlen Nyomda, 1937).

Benda, Kálmán, and Katalin Péter, eds., Az országgyűlések a kora újkori magyar történelemben [The Diets in the Early Modern Hungarian history] (Budapest: MTA Történettudományi Intézet: Országos Pedagógiai Intézet, 1987).

Benda, Kálmán, Bocskai István [István Bocskai] (Budapest: Művelt Nép, 1955).

Benda, Kálmán, ed., "Alvinczi Péter kassai prédikator történeti följegyzései 1598-1622 [The historic notes of Péter Alvinczi, the preacher of Kassa 1598-1522]," in A Ráday Gyűjtemény évkönyve 1955 [The Yearbook of the Ráday collection 1955] (Budapest: Ráday Gyűjtemény, 1956), 5-26.

Benda, Kálmán, ed., Magyarország történeti kronológiája [Historical chronology of Hungary] I-II (Budapest: Akadémiai Kiadó, 1989).

Bene, Sándor, "'Hol vagy István király?' (Pázmány Péter és a Szent István-hagyomány fordulópontja) [Where are you King István? Péter Pázmány and the turning point in the tradition of St István]," in Zsolt Unger, ed., Szent István király képe a magyar irodalomban [The royal image of St István in Hungarian literature] (Budapest: Petőfi Irodalmi Múzeum, 2001) 2-8.

Bene, Sándor, "A Szilvester-bulla nyomában. Pázmány Péter és a Szent István-hagyomány 17. századi fordulópontja [In the footsteps of the Bull of Sylvester. Péter Pázmány and the turning point of the St István tradition in the seventeenth century]," A Ráday Gyűjtemény Évkönyvei (1999).

Bene, Sándor, "A Szilvester-bulla nyomában. Pázmány Péter és a Szent István-hagyomány 17. századi fordulópontja [In the footsteps of the Bull of Sylvester. Péter Pázmány and the turning point of the St István tradition in the seventeenth century]," in László Veszprémy, ed., Szent István és az államalapítás [St István and the foundation of the state] (Budapest: Osiris, 2002), 144–146.

Bene, Sándor, "A történeti kommunikációelmélet alkalmazása a magyar politikai eszmetörténetben- A kora újkori modell [The use of the historic communication theory in the Hungarian history of political ideas – The Early Modern model]," Irodalomtörténeti Közlemények 105 (2001) 301–302.

Bene, Sándor, Egy kanonok három királysága. Ruttkay György horváth históriája [One prebendary for three kings. The Croatian history of György Ruttkay] (Budapest: Argumentum, 2000).

Benkő, Loránd et al, eds., A magyar nyelv történeti-etimológiai szótára [The Hungarian language historic-etymologic dictionary], vol. II (Budapest: Akadémiai Kiadó, 1970).

Benz, Stefan, Zwischen Tradition und Kritik. Katholische Geschichtsschreibung im barocken Heiligen Römischen Reich (Husum: Matthiesen, 2003).

Bérenger, Jean, A History of the Habsburg Empire 1273–1700 (London - New York: Longman, 1994).

Bernát Kumorovitz, Lajos, "Die Entwicklung des ungarische Mittel- und Großwappens," in D. Csatári, L. Katus and Á. Rozsnyói, eds., Nouvelles études historiques, Vol. I (Budapest: Akadémiai Kiadó, 1965) 322–328.

Bertelli, Sergio, "Rex et sacerdos: The Holiness of the King in European Civilization," in Allan Ellenius, ed., Iconography, Propaganda, and Legitimation (Oxford: Clarendon press, 1998) 123–145.

Bertény, Iván, Szent István és öröksége: Magyarország története az államalapítástól a rendiség kialakulásáig, 1000–1440 [St István and his heritage: the history of Hungary from the beginning of the state till the formation of the Estates, 1000–1440] (Budapest: Kulturtrade, 1997).

Bertényi, Iván, "Révay Péter Magyarország Szent Koronájáról írt munkájának forrásértéke [The source value of the work of Péter Révay on the Holy Crown of Hungary]," in Tibor Seifert, ed., A történelem és a jog határán. Tanulmányok Kállay István születésének 70. évfordulójára [On the border of history and law. Studies for the seventieth birthday of István Kállay] (Budapest: Eötvös Loránd Tudományegyetem BTK, 2001), 19–29.

Bertényi, Iván, A magyar szent korona [The Hungarian Holy Crown] (Budapest: Kossuth Kiadó, 1996); Tóth, Endre and Károly Szelényi, A magyar szent korona. Királyok és koronázások [The Hungarian Holy Crown. Kings and coronations] (Budapest: Kossuth Kiadó, 2000).

Bireley, Robert, The Counter-Reformation Prince. Anti-Machiavellianism or Catholic Statecraft in Early-Modern Europe (Chapel Hill, N.C.: University of North Carolina Press, 1990).
Birnbaum, Marianna D., Humanists in a Shattered World. Croatian and Hungarian Latinity in the Sixteenth Century (Columbus: Slavica Publishers, 1986), 13–20.
Birnbaum, Marianna D., Janus Pannonius - Poet and Politician (Zagreb: Jugoslavenska akademija znanosti i umjetnosti, 1981).
Bitskey, István, "A vitézség eszményének változatai a XVI–XVII. század fordulójának magyar irodalmában [The variants of the ideal of gallantry in the sixteenth and seventeenth century Hungarian literature]," in Tivadar Pétercsák, ed., Hagyomány és korszerűség a XVI–XVII. században (Eger, 1997), 203–212.
Bitskey, István, "Bethlen Gábor és a két Rákoczi György irodalompolitikája [The literature politics of Gábor Bethlen and the two György Rákoczi's]," Magyar Könyvszemle 102 (1980) 3.
Bitskey, István, Hitviták tüzében [In the fire of the religious debates] (Budapest: Gondolat, 1978).
Blair, Ann, "Humanist Methods in Natural Philosophy: The Commonplace Book," Journal of the History of Ideas 53 (1992), 544.
Boeckler, Albert, Die "Stephanskrone", in Percy Ernst Schramm, ed., Herrschaftszeichen und Staatssymbolik: Beiträge zu ihrer Geschichte vom dritten bis zum sechzehnten Jahrhundert (Stuttgart: Hiersemann, 1956).
Bogyay, Thomas von, "Über die Forschungsgeschichte der heiligen Krone," in Zsuzsa Lovag, ed., Insignia Regni Hungariae I. Studien zur Machtsymbolik des Mittelalterlichen Ungarn (Studien zur Machtsymbolik des mittelalterlichen Ungarn, Vol. I) (Budapest: Magyar Nemzeti Múzeum, 1983), 66.
Bogyay, Thomas von, "Zum Stand der Sankt-Stephan-Forschung. Bemerkungen zu Györffys "István király és müve," Südost-Forschungen 38 (1979) 240.
Bogyay, Thomas von, Stephanus rex (Wien–München: Herold, 1976).
Boldizsár, Kálmán, Bocskay koronája [The Crown of Bocskai] (Debrecen: Városi Nyomda, 1925).
Bónis, György, "Ferenc Eckhart," Zeitschrift der Savigny-Stiftung für Rechtsgeschichte: Germanistische Abteilung 75/1 (1958), 596–600.
Bónis, György, Révay Péter [Péter Révay] (Budapest: Akadémiai Kiadó, 1981).
Boronkai, Iván and Ibolya Bellus, eds., Lexicon Latinitatis medii aevi Hungariae, vol. III, (Budapest: Argumentum Kiadó - Akadémiai Kiadó, 1991).
Buckton, David, "The Holy Crown in the history of enamelling," Acta Historiae Artium 43 (2002) 14–22.
Bukovinská, Beket, "Zu den Goldschmiedearbeiten der Prager Hofwerkstätte zur Zeit Rudolfs II," in Leids Kunsthistorisch Jaarboek, 1 (Delft: Primavera Press, 1982) 71–82.
Burke, Peter, "Images as Evidence in Seventeenth-Century Europe," Journal of the History of Ideas 64 (2003), 294.

Burns, James H., ed., The Cambridge History of Medieval Political Thought c. 350–c.1450 (Cambridge: Cambridge University Press, 1988).

Butterfield, Herbert, The Statecraft of Machiavelli (New York: Collier Books, 1962).

Buzási, Enikő, "Gondolatok Nádasdy Ferenc mecenatúrájáról, avagy mikor készült az árpási főoltárkép? [Thoughts on the patronage of Ferenc Nádasdy or when was the altar-piece of Árpás made?]" in Nóra G. Etényi and Ildikó Horn, eds., Idővel Paloták.... Magyar udvari kultúra a 16–17. században [Palace with time. Hungarian court culture in the sixteenth to seventeenth century] (Budapest: Balassi Kiadó, 2006), 582–625.

Buzási, Enikő, "III. Ferdinand mint magyar király (Iustus Sustermans ismeretlen műve az egykori Legánes gyűjteményből)[Ferdinand III. as Hungarian king. (An unknown work of Iustus Sustermand from the past Legánes collection)]," A Magyar Nemzeti Galéria Évkönyve [Yearbook of the Hungarian National Gallery] (Budapest, 1991), 149–158.

Buzási, Enikő, "Portrésorozatok a 17. századi magyar arisztokraták politikai reprezentációjában [Portrait series in the representation of seventeenth century Hungarian aristocrats]," Művészettörténeti Értesítő, 60/1 (2011) 11–21.

Buzási, Enikő, and Géza Pálffy, Augsburg - Wien - München - Innsbruck. Die frühesten Darstellungen der Stephanskrone und die Entstehung der Exemplare des Ehrenspiegels des Hauses Österreich. Gelehrten- und Künstlerbeziehungen in Mitteleuropa in der zweiten Hälfte des 16. Jahrhunderts (Budapest: MTA Történettudományi Intézet, 2015).

Bůžek, Václav, ed., Ein Bruderzwist im Hause Habsburg (1608–1611) (České Budějovice: Jihočeská univerzita v Českých Budějovicích, Historický ústav, 2010) (Opera historica, 14).

Cassirer, Ernest, The Myth of the State (New Haven; London: Yale University Press, 1946).

Cerbu, Thomas, "Melchior Inchofer, 'Un homme fin & ruse,'" in José Montesinos - Carlos Solís, eds., Largo Campo di Filosofare, Eurosymposium Galileo 2001 (La Orotava Fundación Canaria, 2001), 588–611.

Charles Tilly, "Reflections on the History of European State-Making," in Charles Tilly and Gabriel Ardant, eds., The Formation of National States in Western Europe (Princeton, N.J.: Princeton University Press: 1975) 3–83.

Concha, Győző, "Közjog és magyar közjog. Viszontválasz a Nagy Ernő jogtanár úr Közjogáról írt bírálatomra adott válaszra [Public law and Hungarian public law. Response to Ernő Nagy law teacher's answer to my criticism of his Public Law]," Magyar Igazságügy, 35/2 (1891), 46–62.

Couch, Philippa, Esztergom Staurotheke (undergraduate thesis, London, Courtauld Institute of Art, University of London, 2010).

Crankshaw, Edward, The Habsburgs (London: Corgi books, 1971).

Csonka, Ferenc, and Ferenc Szakály, eds., Bocskai kíséretében a Rákosmezőn [In the escort of Bocskai on the field of Rákos] (Budapest: Európa Könyvkiadó, 1988).

DaCosta Kaufmann, Thomas, "Antiquarianism, the History of Objects, and the History of Art before Winckelmann," Journal of the History of Ideas 62/3 (2001), 433.

DaCosta Kaufmann, Thomas, Variations on the Imperial Theme in the Age of Maximilian II and Rudolf II (New York: Garland Publishers, 1978).

DaCosta, Thomas, Kaufmann, "Remarks on the Collections of Rudolf II: the Kunstkammer as a Form of Representatio," Art Journal, 38-1 (1978) 22-28.

Daloul, Zaynab, "Berger Illés és a Domus Augustissimae Austriae columnae sidera c. eposza," in Enikő Békés and Imre Tegyey, eds., Convivium Pajorin Klára 70. születésnapjára [Convivium for the seventieth birthday of Klára Pajorin](Debrecen and Budapest: Institutum Doctrinae Litterarum Academiae Scientiarum Hungariae, 2012) (Classica, Mediaevalia, Neolatina, Vol. 6), 63-73.

Daniel, Ladislav, "The Myth of the Prince between Rome and Prague around 1600," in Lubomír Konečný, Beket Bukovinska, and Ivan Muchka, eds., Rudolf II, Prague and the World: Papers from the International Conference, Prague, 2-4 September, 1997 (Prague: Artefactum, 1968) 50.

Décsy, Sámuel, A magyar szent koronának és az ahoz tartozó tárgyaknak historiája [The History of the Hungarian Holy Crown and the Objects which Belong to it] (Vienna: Alberti Ignátz, 1792).

Deér, Josef, Die heilige Krone Ungarns (Wien: Herman Bohlaus, 1966).

Deér, József, "Eckhart Ferenc: A szentkorona-eszme története," [The history of the Doctrine of the Holy Crown] Századok, 76 (1941), 201-207.

Deér, Jozsef, "A magyar királyság megalakulása [The formation of the Hungarian Kingship]," in A Magyar Történettudományi Intézet Évkönyve [The Yearbook of the Hungarian Institute for the Study of History] (Budapest: Magyar Történettudományi Intézet, 1942, reprint Budapest: Attraktor, 2010), 1-88.

Deér, József, Pogány magyarság, keresztény magyarság [Heathen Hungarians, Christian Hungarians] (Budapest: Holnap, 1938, ²1993).

Deutsch, Karl W., Nationalism and social communication (Cambridge, Mass: M.I.T. Press, 1966).

Duerloo, Luc, Dynasty and Piety: Archduke Albert (1598-1621) and Habsburg Political Culture in an Age of Religious Wars (Farnham: Routledge, 2012).

Dunbabin, Jean, "Government," in James H. Burns, ed., The Cambridge History of Medieval Political Thought c. 350-c. 450 (Cambridge: Cambridge University Press, 1988) 498-501.

Dümmerth, Dezső, "Inchofer Menyhért küzdelmei és tragédiája Rómában 1641-1648 [The struggles and tragedy of Melchior Inchofer in Rome]," Filológiai Közlöny 21 (1976), 195-197.

Eckhardt, Sándor, "Balassi Bálint utóélete [The reception of Bálint Balassi]," Irodalomtörténeti közlemények 72/4(1955) 421-427.

Eckhardt, Sándor, "Magyar szónokképzés a XVI. századi Strasszburgban [Hungarian orational education in sixteenth-century Strassburg]," in György Németh, ed., Értekezések a nyelv- és a széptudományi osztály köréből, XXVI./5 (1944) 351-363.

Eckhart, Ferenc, "Bocskai és hiveinek közjogi felfogása [The concept of public law of Bocskai and his adherents]," in Sándor Domanovszky, ed., Emlékkönyv Károlyi Árpád születése nyolcvanadik fordulójának ünnepére [Book of remembrance to celebrate the eightieth anniversary of the birth of Árpád Károlyi] (Budapest: Sárkány Nyomda, 1933), 133-141.

Eckhart, Ferenc, "Jog és alkotmánytörténet [History of law and constitution]," in Bálint Hóman, ed., A magyar történetírás új útjai [The new roads of Hungarian historiography] (Budapest: Magyar Szemle Társaság, 1931, ^{2}1932), 269-320.

Eckhart, Ferenc, A szentkorona-eszme története [The History of the Doctrine of the Holy Crown] (Budapest: Magyar Tudományos Akadémia, 1941, Máriabesnyő-Gödöllő: Attraktor, ^{2}2003).

Eckhart, Ferenc, Magyar alkotmány- és jogtörténet [Hungarian constitutional and legal history], Barna Mezey, ed. (Budapest: Osiris, 2000).

Eckhart, Ferenc, Magyar alkotmány- és jogtörténet [Hungarian constitutional and legal history], (Budapest: Vörösváry Soksz., 1946, Máriabesnyő-Gödöllő: Attraktor, 2000).

Engel, Pál, Gyula Kristó and András Kubinyi, Magyarország története 1301-1526 [History of Hungary 1301-1526] (Budapest: Osiris, 1998).

Engel, Pál, The Realm of St. Stephen. A History of Medieval Hungary 895-1526, Tamás Pálosfalvi, tr. (London-New York: I. B. Tauris, 2001).

Erdő, Péter, and József Török, eds., Doctor et apostol: Szent István tanulmányok [Doctor et apostol: studies on St István] (Budapest, Márton Áron Kiadó, 1994).

Etényi, Nóra G., "A Bocskai-szabadságharc európai propagandája [The European propaganda of the Bocskai rebellion]," Confessio 3(2006) 24-34.

Etényi, Nóra G., "A Nürnbergi nyilvánosság és a Nádasdy Mausoleum [The public opinion in Nürnberg and Nádasdy's Mausoleum]," in Pál Fodor, Géza Pálffy and István György Tóth, eds., Tanulmányok Szakály Ferenc emlékére [Studies in memory of Ferenc Szakály] (Budapest: MTA TKI Gazdaság- és Társadalomtörténeti Kutatócsoportja, 2002), 121-138.

Evans, Robert J.W., Rudolf II and his World. A Study in Intellectual History 1576-1612 (Oxford: Thames and Hudson, 1973, 1997).

Evans, Robert J.W., The Making of the Habsburg Monarchy, 1550-1700: An Interpretation (Oxford: Clarendon Press, 1979).

Exalto, John, Gereformeerde heiligen [Reformed saints](Nijmegen: Vantilt, 2005).

Exalto, John, "Reformed sanctity: Some observations from Dutch religious history," in Thomas K. Kuhn and Nicola Stricker, eds., Erinnert, Verdrängt, Verehrt. Was ist Reformierten heilig? (Emder Beiträge zum reformierten Protestantismus, Band 16). (Göttingen: Vandenhoeck & Ruprecht, 2016) 21-38.

Fallenbüchl, Zoltán, "A Magyar Kamara és a könyvek [The Hungarian Camera and the books]," Az Országos Széchényi Könyvtár Évkönyve 1968-1969 [The Yearbook of the National Library 1968-1969] (1969), 305-317.

Fazekas, István, "Adalékok az ifjú Bocskai István bécsi udvarban eltöltött éveihez [Additional information on the years spent in Vienna by the young István Bocskai]," Studia Caroliensia 1(2006), 73-85.

Fillitz, Hermann, Die österreichische Kaiserkrone und die Insignien des Kaisertums Österreich (Vienna - München: Herold, 1959).

Fraknói, Vilmos, "Berger Illés magyar királyi historiographus [Elias Berger Hungarian royal historiographer]," Századok 6 (1873), 373–390.
Fraknói, Vilmos, A magyar kegyúri jog Szent Istvántól Mária Teréziáig [The Hungarian patron law from St István till Maria Theresia] (Budapest: Magyar Tudományos Akadémia, 1883).
Fraknói, Vilmos, A magyar királyválasztások története [The history of the elections of Hungarian kings] (Budapest: Athenaeum, 1921, reprint: Máriabesnyő–Gödöllő: Attraktor Kft, 2005).
Fraknói, Vilmos, Werbőczi István életrajza [Biography of István Werbőczi] (Budapest: Magyar Történelmi Társaság, 1899).
Franklin, Julian, Jean Bodin and the Sixteenth-Century Revolution in the Methodology of Law and History (New York; London: Columbia University Press, 1963, ^{2}1966).
Frimmová, Eva, "Humanista Eliáš Berger v službách Habsburgovcov [Humanist Elias Berger in the service of the Habsburgs]," in Miloš Kovačka – Eva Augustínová – Maroš Mačuha, eds., Zemianstvo na Slovensku v novoveku. Časť 2. Duchovná a hmotná kultúra [Developments in Slovakia in the Early Modern period. Part 2. Spiritual and material culture] (Martin: Slovenská narodná knižnica, 2009), 100–115.
Fügedi, Erik, Kings, Bishops, Nobles and Burghers in Medieval Hungary, ed. János M. Bak. (London: Variorum, 1986).
Fügedi, Erik, The Elefánthy: the Hungarian Nobleman and his Kindred, ed. Damir Karbic, with a foreword by János M. Bak (Budapest: Central European University Press: 1998).
Fülep, Ferenc, Éva Kovács, Zsuzsa Lovag, eds., Regni Hungariae I: Studien zur Machtsymbolik des mittelalterlichen Ungarn (Budapest: Népmuvelési Propaganda Iroda, 1983).
Gábor, Gyula, A kormányzói méltóság a magyar alkotmányjogban [The governor's dignity in Hungarian constitutional law] (Budapest: Athenaeum, 1931).
Galavics, Géza, Kössünk kardot az pogány ellen. Török háborúk és képzőművészet [Let us gird on the sword against the heathen. Turkish wars and art] (Budapest: Képzőművészeti Kiadó, 1986).
Galla, Ferenc, Marnavics Tomkó János Boszniai püspök magyar vonatkozásai (Budapest: Római Magyar Tört. Intézet, 1940).
Galla, Ferenc, Marnavics Tomkó János boszniai püspök magyar vonatkozásai [The Hungarian relations of János Marnavics Tomkó] (Budapest: Római Magyar Történelmi Intézet, 1940).
Gausz, Ildikó, "Magyar koronázás francia szemmel: Riporterek, celebek II. Mátyás koronázási fesztumán [Hungarian coronation through French eyes: journalists and famous people at the celebration of Matthias' coronation]," Aetas: történettudományi folyóirat 23/3 (2014), 179–182.
Gelderen, Martin van, The Political Thought of the Dutch Revolt 1555–1590 (Cambridge: Cambridge University Press, 1992).
Gellner, Ernest, Nations and Nationalism (Ithaca: Cornell University Press, 1983).
Gerics, József, "Az 'ország tagja (membrum regni)' és az 'ország része (pars regni)' kifejezés középkori magyarországi használatáról [On the Medieval use in Hungary of the expres-

sions 'member of the real, (membrum regni)' and 'part of the realm (pars regni)']," in Marianne Rozsondai, ed., Jubileumi csokor Csapodi Csaba tiszteletére [Jubilee bouquet in honor of Csaba Csapoi] (Budapest: Argumentum, 2002), 88–89.

Gerics, József, "Szent István királlyá avatásának körülményeiről [About the circumstances of the coronation of St István]," Művészettörténeti Értesítő, 33 (1984) 97–101.

Gieysztor, A. "Gesture in the Coronation Ceremonies of Medieval Poland," in János M. Bak, ed., Coronation, Medieval and Early Modern Monarchic Ritual (Berkeley: University of California Press, 1990), 163.

Gindely, Anton, Rudolf II. und seine Zeit, vol. I–II (Prague: Tempsky, 1863–1865).

Goyet, François, Le Sublime du "Lieu Commun." L'invention rhétorique dans l'Antiquité et à la Renaissance (Paris: Champion, 1996).

Gömöri, György, "A strassburgi akadémián tanuló XVI. századi magyarok album-bejegyzései [The album inscriptions of sixteenth-century students studying at the academy of Strassburg]," Lymbus 3 (2005), 49–55.

Grafton, Anthony, Bring out your Dead: The Past as Revelation (Cambridge (Mass.): Harvard University Press, 2001).

Grafton, Anthony, What was History? The Art of History in Early Modern Europe (Cambridge: Cambridge University Press, 2007).

Gschließer, Oswald von, Der Reichshofrat. Bedeutung und Verfassung, Schicksal und Besetzung einer obersten Reichsbehörde von 1559 bis 1806 (Wien: A. Holzhausen, 1942).

Guilday, Peter, "The Sacred Congregation de Propaganda Fide (1622–1922)", The Catholic Historical Review, 6/4 (1921), 479.

Guldescu, Stanko, The Croatian-Slavonian Kingdom 1526–1792 (The Hague and Paris: De Gruyter, 1970).

Györffy, György, István király és műve [St István and his work] (Budapest: Gondolat, 1977).

György Tarczai, Az Árpád-ház szentjei [The saints of the House of Árpád] (Budapest: Szt. István Társulat, 1930).

Haagen, Herman, ed., Catalogus codicum Bernensium (Bibliotheca Bongarsiana) (Bernae: B. F. Haller, 1875).

Habermas, Jürgen, The Structural Transformation of the Public Sphere: An Inquiry into a Category of Bourgeois Society, tr. by Thomas Burger (Cambridge, MA: MIT Press, 1989).

Hajnik, Imre, Egyetemes európai jogtörténet a középkor kezdetétől a franczia forradalomig [General European history of law from the medieval beginning till the French Revolution] (Budapest: Eggenberger, 1875).

Hamann, Brigitte, "Kaiser Mathias," in Brigitte Hamann and Georg Hamann, eds., Die Habsburger: ein biographisches Lexikon (Wien: Ueberreuter, 1988), 353–356.

Hamza, Gábor, ed., Tanulmányok Werbőczy Istvánról – Studien über István Werbőczy (Budapest: Professzorok Háza, 2001).

Hargittay, Emil, and Ágnes Varga, "A hitvitáktól a gyakorlati politikáig (Pázmány Péter politikai pályájának alakulása) [From the religious discussions to the practical politics (the development of Péter Pázmány's political career]," in Béla Varjas, ed., Irodalom és ideológia a 16–17. században [Literature and ideology in the sixteenth and seventeenth century] (Budapest: Akadémiai Kiadó, 1987), 316.

Hargittay, Emil, Gloria, fama, literatura. Az uralkodói eszmény a régi magyarországi fejedelmi tükrökben [Gloria, fama, literature. The ideal prince in the old mirror of princes in Hungary] (Budapest: Universitas, 2001).

Haupt, Herbert, "From feuding brothers to a nation in a war with itself," in Eliška Fučíkova, ed., Rudolf II and Prague: The Court and the City (London: Thames & Hudson, 1997), 238.

Havas, László, "Anticiceronianizmus és antitacitizmus mint az európai nemzeti eszme egyik formálója [Anti-Ciceroism and anti-Tacitism as one of the formers of the European national idea]," in István Bitskey and Szabolcs Olah, eds., Religió, retorika, nemzettudat régi irodalmunkban [Religion, rhetorics and national consciousness in our ancient literature] (Debrecen: Kossuth Egyetemi Kiadó, 2004), 545–548.

Havens, Earle, Commonplace Books. A History of Manuscripts and Printed Books from Antiquity to the Twentieth Century (Yale: Yale University Press, 2001).

Hetherington, Paul, "Studying the Byzantine Staurothèque at Esztergom," in Christoph Entwistle, ed., Through a Glass Brightly: Studies in Byzantine and Medieval Art and Archaeology Presented to David Buckton (Oxford: Oxbow books, 2003).

Hiller, István, "Pázmány Péter és a Habsburg diplomáciája [Péter Pázmány and Habsburg diplomacy]," in Emil Hargittay, ed., Pázmány Péter és kora [Péter Pázmány and his time] (Piliscsaba: Pázmány Péter Katolikus Egyetem Bölcsészettudományi Kar, 2001), 142.

Hilsdale, Cecily J., "The Social Life of the Byzantine Gift: The Royal Crown of Hungary Re-Invented," Art History 31 (2008), 602–631.

Hilsdale, Cecily J., Byzantine Art and Diplomacy in an Age of Decline (Cambridge: Cambridge University Press, 2014).

Hobsbawm, Eric, Nations and Nationalism since 1780: Programme, Myth, Reality (Cambridge, Cambridge University Press, 1992, 2nd ed.).

Hofer, Tamás, "Construction of the 'Folk Cultural Heritage' in Hungary and Rival Versions of National Identity," in idem, ed., Hungarians between "East" and "West": three Essays on Myths and Symbols (Budapest: Néprajzi Múzeum, 1994), 34–35.

Holl, Béla, Ferenczffy Lőrinc. Egy könyvkiadó a XVII. században [Lőrinc Ferenczffy. A book publisher in the seventeenth century] (Budapest: Magyar Helikon, 1980).

Holler, László, "A magyar királyi koronát ábrázoló, 1620–1621. évi festményekről [On the paintings which depict the Hungarian Royal Crown dated 1620–1621]," Művészettörténeti Értesítő 49 (2000) 297–310.

Holtzmann, Robert, ed., Die Chronik des Bischofs Thietmar von Merseburg und ihre Korveier Überarbeitung: Thietmari Merseburgensis Episcopi Chronicon (Berlin: Weidmann, 1955).

Hóman, Bálint – Gyula Szekfű, Magyar történet [Hungarian history], Vol. I.-II, (Budapest: Egyetemi Nyomda, ^{3}1936).

Hóman, Bálint, ed., A magyar történetírás új útjai [The new roads of Hungarian historiography] (Budapest: Magyar Szemle Társaság, 1931, ²1932).

Hóman, Bálint, Szent István (Budapest: Egyetemi Nyomda, 1938).

Honemann, Volker, "The Marriage of Matthias Corvinus to Beatrice of Aragon (1476) in Urban and Court Historiography," in Martin Gosman, Alisdair MacDonald and Arjo Vanderjagt, eds., Princes and Princely Culture, 1450–1650 (Leiden – Boston: Brill, 2005) 213.

Hopp, Lajos, Az "antemurale" és "conformitas" humanista eszméje a magyar-lengyel hagyományban [The humanist idea of "antemurale" and "conformitas" in Hungarian-Polish tradition] (Budapest: Balassi Kiadó, 1992).

Horn, Ildikó, "Ismeretlen temetési rendtartások a 16–17. századból [Unknown funeral ceremonials in the sixteenth and seventeenth century]," Irodalomtörténeti Közlemények 5–6 (1998), 760–772.

Hubay, Ilona, Magyar és magyar vonatkozású röplapok, újságlapok, röpiratok az Országos Széchenyi Könyvtárban. 1480–1718 [Hungarian and Hungary related broadsheets, newspapers and pamphlets in the National Library Széchényi] (Budapest: Országos Széchényi Könyvtár, 1948).

Huszár, Lajos, Habsburg-házi királyok pénzei: 1526–1657 [The money of the Habsburg-kings: 1526–1657] (Budapest: Akadémiai Kiadó, 1975).

Imre, Mihály, "Magyarország panasza": a Querela Hungariae toposz a XVI–XVII. század irodalmában ["Complaint of Hungary": the Querela Hungaria topos in sixteenth and seventeenth century literature] (Debrecen: Kossuth Egyetemi Kiadó, 1996).

Ipolyi, Arnold, "Hely és nemzéktani adalék – Tudósítás Rimay János munkáiról [Information about geography and nationstudies – Report on the works of János Rimay]," Új magyar muzeum [New Hungarian Museum] 3/12 (1853), 485–486.

Ipolyi, Arnold, A magyar szent korona és a koronázási jelvények története és műleírása [The history and description of the Hungarian Holy Crown and the crown jewels] (Budapest: Magyar Tudományos Akadémia, 1886).

Jászay, Pál, "A' magyar nyelv' történetének vázlata [Sketch of the history of the Hungarian language]," in A' magyar tudós társaság' évkönyvei [The Yearbooks of the Hungarian academic society], vol. VI (Buda: a Magyar királyi egyetem, 1845), 279–280.

Jászay, Pál, A' sz. kir. városok szavazatjoga országgyüléseken [The right to vote of the free royal towns during the Diets] (Pest: Heckenast, 1843).

Jedin, Hubert, Kardinal Caesar Baronius. Der Anfang der katholischen Kirchengeschichtsschreibung im 16. Jahrhundert (Münster: Aschendorff, 1978).

Kann, Robert A., A History of the Habsburg Empire, 1526–1918 (Berkely: University of California Press, 1974).

Kantorowicz, Ernst, The King's Two Bodies: A Study in Medieval Political Theology (Princeton: Princeton University Press, 1957).

Karácsonyi, János, Szent István király oklevelei és a Szilveszter-bulla [The charters of King Sz. István and the Bull of Sylvester] (Budapest: Magyar Tudományos Akadémia, 1891).

Kardos, József, A szentkorona-tan története: 1919–1944 [The history of the Holy Crown doctrine: 1919–1944] (Budapest: Akadémiai Kiadó, 1985).

Károlyi, Árpád, Bocskay szerepe a történetben [The role of Bocskai in history] (Budapest: Ny. Hornyánszky Viktor, 1898).

Károlyi, Árpád, Illésházy István hütlenségi pöre [The infidelity case against István Illésházy] (Budapest: Magyar Tudományos Akadémia, 1883).

Karpat, Josef, "Corona Regni Hungariae im Zeitalter der Arpaden," in Manfred Hellmann ed., Corona Regni. Studien über die Krone als Symbol des Staates im späteren Mittelalter (Darmstadt: Wissenschaftliche Buchgesellschaft, 1961) 298–299.

Kecskeméti, Gábor, Prédikáció, retorika, irodalomtörténet [Sermon, rhetorics, history of literature] (Budapest: Universitas, 1998).

Kelleher, Patrick, The Holy Crown of Hungary (Rome: American Academy in Rome, 1951).

Kelley, Donald R., The Foundations of Modern Historical Scholarship: Language, Law, and History in the French Renaissance (New York: Columbia University Press, 1970).

Klaniczay, Gábor, Holy Rulers and Blessed Princesses. Dynastic Cults in Medieval Central Europe, Éva Pálmai, tr. (Cambridge: Cambridge University Press, 2002).

Klaniczay, Tibor, "Die Benennungen 'Hungaria' und 'Pannonia' als Mittel der Identitätssuche der Ungarn," in Tibor Klaniczay, S. Katalin Németh, and Paul Gerhard Schmidt, eds., Antike Rezeption und Nationale Identität in der Renaissance insbesondere in Deutschland und in Ungarn (Budapest: Balassi, 1993) 107.

Klaniczay, Tibor, ed., A magyar irodalom története [The History of Hungarian literature], vol. I-II (Budapest: Kossuth Könyvkiadó, 1964).

Klaniczay, Tibor, ed., Janus Pannonius – magyarországi humanisták [Janus Pannonius – Humanists of Hungary] (Budapest: Szépirodalmi könyvkiadó, 1982).

Klaniczay, Tibor, Stilus, nemzet és civilizáció [Style, nation and civilisation], Gábor Klaniczay and Péter Kőszeghy, eds., (Budapest: Balassi Kiadó, 2001).

Knapp, Éva and Gábor Tüskés, "Magyarország – Mária országa [Hungary—the country of Mary]," Irodalomtörténeti közlemények, 5–6(2000) 585.

Koenigsberger, H.G., "Epilogue: Central and Western Europe," in R.J.W. Evans and T.V. Thomas, eds., Crown, Church and Estates (London: Palgrave Macmillan, 1991), 308.

Koenigsberger, H.G., Monarchies, States Generals and Parliaments. The Netherlands in the Fifteenth and Sixteenth Centuries (Cambridge: Cambridge University Press, 2001).

Kovačka, Miloš, Eva Augustínová and Maroš Mačuha, eds., Rod Révai v slovenských dejinách. Zborník prác z interdisciplinárnej konferencie 16. - 17. September 2008, Martin [The Révay family in Slovak history. Proceedings of the Interdisciplinary Conference, 16–17 September 2008, Martin] (Martin: Slovenská národná knižnica, 2010).

Kovács, Éva and Zsuzsa Lovag, A magyar koronajelvények [The Hungarian crown jewels] (Budapest: Corvina Kiadó, 1980).

Kovács, Éva, "Bocskai István loretói koronája [István Bocskai's crown of Loreto]," Művészettörténeti Értesítő, XLIV (1984), 114–115.

Kríza, Ildikó, A Mátyás-hagyomány évszázadai [The tradition of Matthias through the centuries] (Budapest: Akadémiai Kiadó, 2007).

Kubinyi, András, Matthias Rex (Budapest: Balassi Kiadó, 2001).

Kulcsár, Péter, "Berger Illés történeti művei [The historical works of Elias Berger]," Magyar Könyvszemle 110 (1994) 245–259.

Kulcsár, Péter, ed., Inventarium de operibus litterariiis ad res Hungaricas pertinentibus ab initiis usque ad annum 1700 – A magyar történeti irodalom lelőhelyjegyzéke a kezdetektől 1700-ig [Inventory of all historic literature on Hungary from the beginnings till 1700] (Budapest: Balassi Kiadó, 2003).

Kurucz, György, Guide to Documents and Manuscripts in Great Britain Relating to the Kingdom of Hungary from the Earliest Times to 1800 (London-New York: Mansell, 1992).

Kurz, Otto, "A gold helmet made in Venice for Sultan Sulayman the Magnificent," Gazette des Beaux Arts, 74 (1969), 249–258.

László Péter, Hungary's Long Nineteenth Century: Constitutional and Democratic Traditions in a European Perspective, Miklós Lojkó, ed. (Central and Eastern Europe: Regional Perspectives in Global Context) (Leiden- Boston: Brill, 2012).

László, Péter, "Ius Resistendi in Hungary," in László Péter and Martyn Rady, eds., Resistance, Rebellion and Revolution in Hungary and Central Europe: Commemorating 1956 (London: Hungarian Cultural Centre, UCL, 2008), 45–65.

Lauter, Éva S., "A Palatinus Regni Hungariae a 17. századi Magyarországon [The Palatinus Regni Hungariae in seventeenth-century Hungary]," in Ildikó Horn, ed., Perlekedő Évszázadok. Tanulmányok Für Lajos történész 60. Születésnapjára [Centuries. Studies offered to Lajos Für for his 60th birthday] (Budapest: Eötvös Loránd Tudományegyetem Budapest Bölcsészettudományi Kar Középkori és Kora–újkori Magyar Történeti Tanszék, 1993), 216–217.

Leidinger, Hannes, Verena Schwartz and Berndt Schlipper, Schwarzbuch der Habsburger. Die unrühmliche Geschichte des Hauses Habsburg (Wien: Deuticke Verlag, 2003).

Lencz, Géza, Der Aufstand Bocskays und der Wiener Friede (Debreczen: Hegedüs und Sándor, 1917).

Lousse, Emile, "Qui donc était l'empereur Mathias?," in Louis Carlen and Fritz Steinegger, eds., Festschrift für Nikolaus Grass, vol. I (Innsbruck: Wagner, 1974–1975), 135–143.

Louthan, Howard, The Quest for Compromise: Peacemakers in Counter-Reformation Vienna (Cambridge: Cambridge University Press, 1997).

Lovag, Zsuzsa, "A koronakutatás vadhajtásai [The offshoots of the crown research]," Művészettörténi Értesítő 35 (1986) 35–48.

Macartney, Carlisle A., Studies on Early Hungarian and Pontic History, László Péter and Lóránt Czigány, eds. (Aldershot: Variorum, 1999).

Macartney, Carlisle A., The Medieval Hungarian Historians. A Critical and Analytical Guide (Cambridge: Cambridge University Press, 1953).

Mačuha, Maroš, Panstvá rodu Révai v ranom novoveku (ekonomický a sociálny kapitál uhorského aristokratického rodu) [The dominions of the Révai family in the Early Modern period (the economic and social capital of a Hungarian aristocratic family)] (doctoral dissertation, Bratislava 2007).

Makkai, László, "A Bocskai-felkelés [The Bocskai rebellion]," in Zsigmond Pál Pach and Ágnes R. Várkonyi, eds., Magyarország története 1526–1686 [History of Hungary 1526–1686], vol. I (Budapest: Akadémiai Kiadó, 1987), 709–775.

Makkai, László, "A Habsburgok és a Magyar rendiség a Bocskai-felkelés előestéjén [The Habsburgs and the Hungarian Estates at the dawn of the rebellion of Bocskai]," Történelmi Szemle, 13 (1974), 162–163.

Makkai, László, "István Bocskai's Insurrectionary Army," in János M. Bak and Béla K. Király, eds., From Hunyadi to Rákóczi: War and Society in Late Medieval and Early Modern Hungary (New York: Social Science monographs/Brooklyn College Press, 1982), 281–283.

Makkai, László, "Magyari és műve [Magyari and his work]," in Magyari István, Az országokban való sok romlásoknak okairól [On the causes of the many corruptions in Hungary], ed. Tamás Katona (Budapest: Magyar Helikon, 1979), 187–206.

Makkai, László, "Mindszenti Gábor emlékirata [The memoir of Gábor Mindszenti]," in László Makkai, ed., Mindszenti Gábor diáriuma öreg János király haláláról [The memoir of Gábor Mindszenti on the death of old King János] (Budapest: Európa Kiadó, 1977), 36–37.

Makkai, László, "The Crown and the Diets of Hungary and Transylvania in the Sixteenth Century," in R. J. W. Evans and T. V. Thomas, eds., Crown, Church and Estates (London: Palgrave Macmillan, a division of Macmillan Publishers Limited, 1991), 81.

Makkai, László, "Bocskai és európai kortársai," Történelmi Szemle 17 (1974), 488.

Mályusz, Elemér, "Az Eckhart-vita," Századok 64 (1931), 416.

Marczali, Heinrich, Ungarisches Verfassungsrecht (Tübingen: J.C.B. Mohr, 1911).

Marosi, Ernő, "A magyar korona a jelenkori kutatásban és a populáris irodalomban [The Hungarian crown in the modern research and popular literature]," Művészettörténeti Értesítő XXXV (1986), 49–55.

Marosi, Ernő, "A magyar történelem képei. A történetiség szemléltetése a művészetekben [The Hungarian history in images. The view on historicity in the arts]," in: Árpád Mikó and Katalin Sinkó, eds., Történelem-kép. Szemelvények múlt és művészet kapcsolatából Magyarországon [History-image. Excerpts of the relation between past and art in Hungary] (Budapest: Magyar Nemzeti Galéria, 2000), 19–21.

Mátrai, László, ed., Régi magyar filozófusok, XV-XVII. század [Ancient Hungarian philosophers, fifteenth till seventeenth century] (Budapest: Gondolat, 1961).

Mednyánszky, Dénes, "Révay Ferencz szklabinai könyvtára 1651-ben [The library of Ferencz Révay in 1651]," Magyar Könyvszemle, 6/6 (1881), 344.

Mezey, Barna, "Utószó [Afterword]," in Ferenc Eckhart, Magyar alkotmány- és jogtörténet [Hungarian constitutional and legal history], Barna Mezey, ed. (Budapest: Osiris, 2000), 423–424.

Mezey, László, ed., Athleta Patriae: tanulmányok Szent László történetéhez [Athleta Patriae: Studies on the history of Saint László] (Budapest: Szent István Társulat, 1980).

Molnár, Andrea, Fürst Stefan Bocskai als Staatsmann und Persönlichkeit im Spiegel seiner Briefe 1598–1606 (München: Trofenik, 1983).

Molnár, Antal, "Relations between the Holy See and Hungary during the Ottoman Domination of the Country," in István Zombori, ed., Fight against the Turk in Central-Europe in the First Half of the 16th Century (Budapest: Historia Ecclesiastica Hungarica Alapítvány and Magyar Egyháztörténeti Enciklopédia Munkaközösség, 2004), 192.

Monok, István, ed., A magyar könyvkultúra múltjából: Iványi Béla cikkei és anyaggyűjtése [From the past of Hungarian book culture: the articles and source collections of Béla Iványi] (Szeged: JATE, 1983).

Mortimer, Geoff, The Origins of the Thirty Years War and the Revolt in Bohemia, 1618 (London: Palgrave Macmillan, 2015).

Moss, Ann, "The Politica of Justus Lipsius and the Commonplace-Book," Journal of the History of Ideas 59 (1998) 421.

Moss, Ann, Printed Commonplace-Books and the Structuring of Renaissance Thought (Oxford: Oxford University Press, 1996).

Mout, Nicolette, Bohemen en de Nederlanden in de zestiende eeuw [Bohemia and The Netherlands in the sixteenth century] (PhD dissertation, Leiden: Universitaire Pers, 1975).

Nagy, Gábor, ed., Magyar história 1526–1608: forrásgyűjtemény [Hungarian history 1526–1608. Collection of sources] (Debrecen: Tóth Könyvkereskedés és Kiadó, 1998).

Nagy, Gábor, Vicissitudines (Előkészület Isthvánffy Miklós Historiaeja kritikai kiadásához) [Vicissitudines. (Preparation of a critical edition of Miklós Isthvánffy's Historiae)] (Doctoral thesis, University of Miskolc, 2005).

Nagy, László, "A magyar politikai történetéhez (az 1605-ös kiáltvány Európa népeihez) [On the Hungarian political history (on the declaration for the European people, 1605)]," Magyar Tudomany 88 (1981) 358–365.

Nagy, László, "Ki volt a szerzője a szabadságért fegyvert fogott magyar rendek Európához intézett kiáltványának? [Who was the author of the declaration to Europe by the Hungarian Estates who took up arms for freedom?]," in Béla Varjas, ed., Irodalom és ideológia a 16–17. században [Literature and ideology in the sixteenth and seventeenth century] (Budapest: Akadémiai Kiadó, 1987), 175–187.

Nagy, László, "Megint fölszánt magyar világ van..." Társadalom és hadsereg a XVII. század első felének Habsburg–ellenes küzdelmeiben ["It is again an uplifted Hungarian world ..." Society and army in the first half of the seventeenth century in the struggle against the Habsburgs] (Budapest: Zrínyi, 1985).

Nagy, László, A Bocskai–szabadságharc katonai története [The military history of the Bocskai rebellion] (Budapest: Akadémiai Kiadó, 1961).

Nagy, László, Botránykövek régvolt históriánkban [Stumbling-stones in our long history] (Budapest: Akadémiai Kiadó, 1997).

Nagy, László, Kard és szerelem: török kori históriák [Sword and love: Stories from the Turkish period] (Budapest: Gondolat, 1985).

Necipoğlu, Gülru, "Süleyman the Magnificent and the representation of power in the context of Ottoman-Habsburg-papal rivalry," Art bulletin, 71(1989), 401–427.

Nehring, Karl, "Magyarország és a zsitvatoroki szerződés (1605–1609)," Századok 120 (1986), 39.

Nelson, Janet L., Politics and Ritual in Early Medieval Europe (London: Hambledon Press, 1986).

Németh, Gyula, "Hunok és Magyarok [Huns and Hungarians]," in Gyula Németh, ed., Attila és Hunjai [Attila and his Huns] (Budapest: Akadémiai Kiadó, 1940), 265–271.

Németh, István H., "A szabad királyi városi rang a kora újkorban [The free royal town rank in the Early Modern period]," Urbs. Magyar Várostörténeti Évkönyv, Vol. I (2006), 109–122.

Németh, István H., Várospolitika és gazdaságpolitika a 16–17. századi Magyarországon [City politics and economical politics in sixteenth and seventeenth century Hungary] vol. I.-II. (Budapest: Gondolat, 2004).

O'Neill, Charles E., - Joaquín María Domínguez, eds., Diccionario histórico de la Compañía de Jesús: Biográfico-temático, vol. 2. (Madrid: Institutum Historicum, 2001).

Orhonlu, Cengiz, Osmanli Tarihine Aid Belgeler. Telhisler (1597–1607) (İstanbul: İstanbul Üniversitesi Edebiyat Fakültesi, 1970).

Ostapchuk, Victor, "Cossack Ukraine in and out of Ottoman orbit, 1648–1681," in Gábor Kármán and Lovro Kunčević, eds., The European Tributary States of the Ottoman Empire in the Sixteenth and Seventeenth Centuries (The Ottoman Empire and its Heritage, vol. 53) (Leiden – Boston: Brill, 2013), 150.

Ott, Joachim, Krone und Krönung: die Verheißung und Verleihung von Kronen in der Kunst von der Spätantike bis um 1200 und die geistige Auslegung der Krone (Mainz am Rhein: Philipp von Zabern, 1998).

Ötvös, Péter, ed., Pálffy Kata leveleskönyve: iratok Illésházy István bujdosásának történetéhez 1602–1606 [Correspondence book of Kata Pálffy: documents on the exile of István Illésházy] (Szeged: Scriptum, 1991).

Őze, Sándor, "Bűneiért bünteti Isten a magyar népet". Egy bibliai párhuzam vizsgálata a XVI. századi nyomtatott egyházi irodalom alapján [God punishes the Hungarian people for their sins". A research on Biblical parallel on the basis of sixteenth century printed religious literature] (Budapest: Magyar Nemzeti Múzeum, 1991).

Őze, Sándor, and Norbert Spannenberger, "Zur Reinterpretation der mittelalterlichen Staatsgründung in der ungarischen Geschichtsschreibung des 19. und 20. Jahrhunderts," Jahrbuch für Geschichte und Kultur Südosteuropa 2 (2000), 62.

Pálffy, Géza, "A bécsi udvar és a magyar rendek a 16. században [The Viennese court and the Hungarian Estates in the sixteenth century]," Történelmi Szemle 3-4 (1999), 331–369.

Pálffy, Géza, "A Magyar Korona országainak koronázási zászlói a 16–17. században [The coronation banners of the countries of the Hungarian crown in the sixteenth and seventeenth century]," in Orsolya Bubryák, ed., "Ez világ, mint egy kert..." Tanulmányok

Galavics Géza tiszteletére [This world is like a garden. Studies in honor of Géza Galavics] (Budapest: Gondolat/MTA Művészettörténeti Kutatóintézet, 2010), 17–62.

Pálffy, Géza, "A magyar nemesség I. Ferdinánd bécsi udvarában [The Hungarian nobility in the Viennese court of Ferdinand I.]," Történelmi Szemle, 45/1–2(2003), 45–59.

Pálffy, Géza, "A Szent Korona balesete 1638-ban [The accident of the Holy Crown in 1638]," in József Jankovics, ed., "Nem sűlyed az emberiség!"... Album amicorum Szörényi László LX. Születésnapjára [Mankind is not lost! Album amicorum for the 60th birthday of László Szörényi] (Budapest: MTA Irodalomtudományi Intézet, 2007, 1431–1444.

Pálffy, Géza, "Der ungarische Adel und der Kaiserhof in der frühen Neuzeit (eine Skizze)," in Václav Bůžek and Pavel Král, eds., Šlechta v habsburské monarchii a císařský dvůr (1526-1740) [Nobility in the Habsburg Monarchy and the Imperial Court (1526-1740)] (České Budějovice: Historický ústav Jihočeské univerzity, 2003), 133–152.

Pálffy, Géza, "Magyar címerek, zászlók és felségjelvények a Habsburgok dinasztikus–hatalmi reprezentációjában a 16. században [Hungarian family crests, flags and crown jewels in the dynastic–power representation of the Habsburgs in the sixteenth century]," Történelmi Szemle 3–4 (2001), 241–277.

Pálffy, Géza, "The Impact of the Ottoman Rule on Hungary," Hungarian Studies Review, XXVIII(2001), 109–111.

Pálffy, Géza, and Gergely Tóth, "Az 'országtáblák', egy új koronavers és a pozsonyi Koronatorony különleges vasajtaja: Újdonságok a szent korona 17. századi történetéhez [The 'country tables', a new poem about the crown and a special door in the crown tower of Pozsony]," in Gábor Nagy, János Rada and Noémi Viskolcz, eds., "...nem egyetlen történelem létezik." Ünnepi tanulmányok Péter Katalin 80. születésnapja alkalmából ["There does not exist one history" Festschrift for Katalin Péter for her eightieth birthday] (Publicationes Universitatis Miskolcinensis – Sectio Philosophica (2)) (Miskolc: Miskolci Egyetem, 2017), 279–301.

Pálffy, Géza, Ferenc Gábor Soltész and Csaba Tóth, Coronatus in regem Hungariae...: Medaliile de încoronare ale regilor Ungariei / Coronatus in regem Hungariae... : A magyar uralkodókoronázások érmei [The Hungarian coronation jetons], Krisztina Bertók ed., (Cluj Napoca–Budapest: Muzeul Național de Istorie a Transilvaniei și Muzeul Național Maghiar, 2015).

Pálffy, Géza, Szent István birodalma a Habsburgok közép-európai államában. A Magyar Királyság és a Habsburg Monarchia a 16. században [The Empire of St István and the Central European state of the Habsburgs. The Hungarian Kingdom and the Habsburg Monarchy in the sixteenth century] (Doctoral dissertation, Budapest, 2008).

Pálffy, Géza, The Kingdom of Hungary and the Habsburg Monarchy in the Sixteenth Century, Thomas J. and Helen D. DeKornfeld, tr., (Boulder, Colorado: Social Science Monographs–Wayne, New Jersey: Center for Hungarian Studies and Publications, Inc. – New York: Distributed by Columbia University Press, 2009. (East European Monographs, DCCXXXV.; CHSP Hungarian Studies Series, 18).

Pandula, Attila, "Egy XVII. századi, heraldikai témájú, magyar olajfestmény [A seventeenth century Hungarian oil painting with a heraldic theme]," Turul 70 (1997) 26–28.

Papp, Sándor, Die Verleihungs-, Bekräftigungs- und Vertragsurkunden der Osmanen für Ungarn und Siebenbürgen: eine quellenkritische Untersuchung (Wien: Verlag der Österreichischen Akademie der Wissenschaften, 2003).

Papp, Sándor, Török szövetség – Habsburg kiegyezés. A Bocskai-felkelés történetéhez [Turkish alliance – Habsburg conciliation. On the history of the Bocskai Uprising] (Budapest: Károli Gáspár Református Egyetem - L'Harmattan, 2014).

Parker, Geoffry, "The political World of Charles V," in Hugo Soly and Willem Pieter Blockmans, eds., Charles V 1500–1558 and his Time (Antwerpen: Mercatorfonds, 1999), 155.

Pauler, Gyula, "Ki volt Hartvich püspök? [Who was Bishop Hartvich]," Századok, 16 (1883) 803–804.

Perjés, Géza, Zrínyi Miklós és kora [Miklós Zrínyi and his time] (Budapest: Gondolat Kiadó, 1965, Budapest: Osiris, ²2002).

Péter, Katalin, A magyar nyelvű politikai publicisztika kezdetei [The start of journalism in the Hungarian language] (Budapest: Akadémiai Kiadó, 1973).

Péter, Katalin, A magyar romlásnak századában [The centuries of Hungarian decay] (Budapest: Gondolat Kiadó, 1975).

Péter, Katalin, Papok és nemesek. Magyar művelődéstörténeti tanulmányok a reformációval kezdődő másfél évszázadból [Priests and nobles: studies on cultural history from hundred fifty years after the beginning of the Reformation] (Budapest: Ráday Gyűjtemény, 1995).

Péter, László, "The Holy Crown of Hungary, Visible and Invisible," The Slavonic and East European Review, 81(2003), 32.

Péter, László, "Die Verfassungsentwicklung in Ungarn," in Adam Wandruszka, Peter Urbanitsch, and Alois Brusatti, eds., Die Habsburgermonarchie, 1848–1918. Verfassung und Parlamentarismus, Bd. 7 (Wien: Verlag der Österreichischen Akademie der Wissenschaften, 2000), 239–261.

Péter, László, Hungary's Long Nineteenth Century: Constitutional and Democratic Traditions in a European Perspective, Miklós Lojkó, ed. (Central and Eastern Europe: Regional Perspectives in Global Context) (Leiden- Boston: Brill, 2012).

Péter, László, The Antecedents of the Nineteenth-century Hungarian State Concept: A Historical Analysis. The Background of the Creation of the Doctrine of the Holy Crown (PhD thesis, Oxford, 1966).

Pick, Friedel, Joh. Jessenius de Magna Jessen: Arzt und Rektor in Wittenberg und Prag hingerichtet am 21. Juni 1621; ein Lebensbild aus der Zeit des Dreissigjährigen Krieges (Leipzig: Barth, 1926).

Podhraczky, József, "Berger Illés magyar történetíró [Elias Berger Hungarian historiographer]," Tudománytár Értekezések XII (1843), 351–366.

Podhraczky, József, "Illésházy István nádor élete [The life of Palatine István Illésházy]," Új magyar múzeum [New Hungarian Museum], I (Pest, 1856) 299–321, 370–390.

Podhraczky, József, "Mikor és miért vitette Rudolf király Prágába a' magyar koronát [When and why did King Rudolf bring the Hungarian crown to Prague]," Tudománytár Értekezések XI (1842) 374.

Polleroß, Friedrich, "From the exemplum virtutis to the Apotheosis," in Allan Ellenius, ed., Iconography, Propaganda, and Legitimation (Oxford: Clarendon Press, 2008), 53.

Press, Volker, "The Imperial Court of the Habsburgs," in Ronald G. Asch, and Adolf M. Birke, eds., Princes, Patronage and the Nobility. The Court at the Beginning of the Modern Age, c.1450–1650 (London: German Historical Institute, 1991), 302–303.

Press, Volker, "Matthias 1612–1619," in Anton Schindling and Walter Ziegler, eds., Die Kaiser des Neuzeit 1519–1918: Heiliges Römisches Reich, Österreich, Deutschland (München: C.H. Beck, 1990) 114–123.

Radnóti, Sándor, "The Glass Cabinet. An Essay about the Place of the Hungarian Crown," Acta Historiae Artium 43 (2002), 83–111.

Rady, Martyn, "Bocskai, Rebellion and Resistance in Early Modern Hungary," in László Péter and Martyn Rady, eds., Resistance, Rebellion and Revolution in Hungary and Central Europe: Commemorating 1956 (London: UCL SSEES, 2008) 57–66.

Rady, Martyn, "Stephen Werbőczy and his Tripartitum," in János M. Bak, Péter Banyó and Martyn Rady, eds. and trans., The Laws of the Medieval Kingdom of Hungary, Volume 5, The Customary Law of the Renowned Kingdom of Hungary: A Work in Three Parts Rendered by Stephen Werbőczy (The 'Tripartitum'). The Laws of Hungary (Series I: Volume 5). (Idyllwild, CA and Budapest: Charles Schlacks Jr and Department of Medieval Studies, Central European University, 2005), xxvii–xliv.

Rady, Martyn, Customary Law in Hungary: Courts, Texts, and the Tripartitum (Oxford: Oxford University Press. 2015).

Rady, Martyn, Nobility, Land and Service in Medieval Hungary (London: Palgrave Macmilan, 2000).

Révay, Péter, De monarchia et Sacra Corona Regni Hungariae centuriae septem. – A magyar királyság birodalmáról és szent koronájáról szóló hét század, ed. Gergely Tóth; the Latin text ed. and transl. by Gergely Tóth, Bernadett Benei, Rezső Jarmalov and Sára Sánta. I–II. (Budapest: Bölcsészettudományi Kutatóközpont, 2021).

Révész, Kálmán, "Bocskai István apológiája [The apology of István Bocskai]," Protestáns Szemle 18 (1906), 285–309.

Rezar, Vlado, "Ludovicus Cervarius Tubero," in David Thomas and John A. Chesworth a.o., eds., Christian-Muslim Relations. A Bibliographical History: Volume 7. Central and Eastern Europe, Asia, Africa and South America (1500–1600) (Leiden – Boston: Brill), 147–153.

Richardson, Brian, Printing, Writing and Readers in Renaissance Italy (Cambridge and New York: Cambridge University Press, 1999).

Rietbergen, Peter, Power and Religion in Baroque Rome. Barberini Cultural Politics (Leiden and Boston: Brill, 2006).

Rill, Bernd, Kaiser Matthias. Brüderzwist und Glaubenskampf (Graz, Wien, Köln: Styria, 1999).
Ritter, Moriz, "Matthias, Österreichischer Erzherzog und Deutscher Kaiser," in Algemeine Deutsche Biographie, vol. 20 (Leipzig: Historische Commission bei der königlichen Akademie der Wissenschaften, 1884), 629–654.
Roncière, Charles de La, ed., Catalogue des manuscrits de la collection des cinq cents de Colbert (Paris: Ernest Leroux, 1908).
Roth, G., ed., Peter Eschenloer, Geschichte der Stadt Breslau (Münster: Waxmann, 2003).
Rózsa, György, "Nádasdy Ferenc és a művészet [Ferenc Nádasdy and art]," Művészettörténeti Értesítő XX (1970), 185–202.
Rózsa, György, A Nádasdy Mausoleum (Separate attachment to the facsimile edition of Nádasdy's Mausoleum) (Budapest: Akadémiai Kiadó, 1991).
Rózsa, György, Magyar történetábrázolás a 17. században [Hungarian historical images in the seventeenth century] (Budapest: Akadémiai Kiadó, 1973).
Ruttkay, László, Jeszenszky János (Jessenius) és kora 1566–1621 [János Jeszenszky (Jessenius) and his time 1566–1621] (Budapest: Semmelweis Orvostörténeti Múzeum és Könyvtár, 1971).
Ruzsa, György, "Quand la staurothèque byzantine d'Esztergom est-elle arrivée en Hongrie?," in Anna Tüskés, ed., Omnis creatura significans: Essays in Honour of Mária Prokopp (Budapest: CentrArt, 2009), 47–48.
Sachs, Oliver, The Man who Mistook his Wife for a Hat and Other Clinical Tales (New York: Summit Books, 1985).
Salmon, J.H.M., Renaissance and Revolt: Essays in the Intellectual and Social History of Early Modern France (Cambridge and New York: Cambridge University Press, 1987).
Schimert, Peter, "The Hungarian Nobility in the Seventeenth and Eighteenth Centuries," in Ivo Banac and Paul Bushkovitch, eds., The Nobility in Russia and Eastern Europe, vol. II (New Haven: Yale Concilium on International and Area Studies, 1987) 150–151.
Schramm, Gottfried, "Armed Conflicts in East–Central Europe 1604–1620," in R.J.W. Evans and T.V. Thomas, eds., Crown, Church and Estates (London: Palgrave Macmillan, 1991), 176–195.
Schulze, Wilfried, "Estates and the Problem of Resistance in Theory and Practice in the Sixteenth and Seventeenth Centuries," in R.J.W. Evans and T.V. Thomas, eds., Crown, Church and Estates (London: Palgrave Macmillan, 1991), 171.
Sibeth, Uwe, "Gesandter einer aufstandischen Macht. Die ersten Jahre der Mission von Dr. Pieter Cornelisz. Brederode im Reich (1602–1609)," Zeitschrift für historische Forschung 30 (2003), 19–51.
Sinkó, Katalin, "Árpád versus Saint István. Competing Heroes and Competing Interests in the Figurative Representation of Hungarian History," in Tamás Hofer, ed., Hungarians between "East" and "West": three Essays on Myths and Symbols (Budapest: Néprajzi Múzeum, 1994), 9–26.

Sinkovics, István, "Szamosközy István [István Szamosközy]," in István Szamosközy, Erdélyi története [1598–1599, 1603] [The History of Transylvania], trans. István Borzsák, ed. István Sinkovics (Budapest: Magyar Helikon, ²1977), 20–23.

Siraisi, Nancy, "Anatomizing the Past: Physicians and History in Renaissance Culture," Renaissance Quarterly 53 (2003), 1–30.

Skinner, Quentin, The Foundations of Modern Political Thought, Vol. I.-II. (Cambridge: Cambridge University Press, 1978).

Skinner, Quentin, Visions of Politics: Volume I: Regarding Method (Cambridge: Cambridge University Press, 2002).

Soll, Jacob, "Introduction: The Uses of Historical Evidence in Early-Modern Europe," Journal of the History of Ideas 64/2 (2003), 149–150.

Soll, Jacob, Publishing the Prince. History, Reading, & the Birth of Political Criticism (Ann Arbor: University of Michigan Press, 2005).

Sólymos, Szilveszter, "Hozzászólás és kiegészítés [Comments and addition]," Turul 71(1998), 39–41.

Sroka, Stanisław, "Methods of Constructing Angevin Rule in Hungary in the Light of Most Recent Research," Quaestiones Medii Aevi Novae, 1 (1996), 77–90.

Strohmeyer, Arno, "Konfessionalisierung der Geschichte? Die ständische Historiographie in Innerösterreich an der Wende vom 16. zum 17. Jahrhundert," in Joachim Bahlcke and Arno Strohmeyer, eds., Konfessionalisierung in Ostmitteleuropa (Stuttgart: Steiner, 1999), 221–247.

Sturmberger, Hans, Georg Erasmus Tschernembl: Religion, Libertät und Widerstand. Ein Beitrag zur Geschichte der Gegenreformation und des Landes ob der Enns (Forschungen zur Geschichte Oberösterreichs, vol. 3.) (Linz – Graz: Böhlau, 1953).

Sugar, Péter F., ed., A History of Hungary (Bloomington, Indiana: Indiana University Press, 1990).

Szabados, György, A magyar történelem kezdeteiről [On the beginnings of the Hungarian History] (Budapest: Balassi, 2006).

Szabó, Béla P., "Hungarológiai munkácska államtudományi hangsúlyokkal a 17. század első feléből [Hungarological small work with politological accents from the first half of the seventeenth century]," Gerundium: egyetemtörténeti közlemények, 8/1 (2017), 163.

Szakály, Ferenc and István Hiller, "Illésházy István (1540–1609)," in Árpád Rácz, ed., Nagy képes millenniumi arcképcsarnok [Great illustrated Millennium portrait hall] (Budapest: Rubicon–Aquila–Könyvek, 1999), 82–83.

Szakály, Ferenc, "The early Ottoman Period, including Royal Hungary, 1526–1606," in Peter F. Sugar, Péter Hanák and Tibor Frank, eds., A History of Hungary (Bloomington: Indiana University Press, 1990), 85.

Szakály, Ferenc, "Virágkor és hanyatlás 1440–1711 [The Golden Age and its decline, 1440–1711]," in Ferenc Glatz, ed., Magyarok Európában [Hungarians in Europe], vol. II (Budapest: Háttér Kft.-Téka, 1990), 177.

Szántó, Iván, "The cross-cultural heritage of a Byzantine reliquary," in Dragana Cicović Sarajlić, Vera Obradović and Petar Đuza, eds., Traditional and Modern in Art and Education (Kosovska Mitrovica: University of Prishtina, 2018) 23–31.

Szekfű, Gyula, "Szent István a magyar történet századaiban [St István in the centuries of Hungarian history]," in Jusztinián Serédi, ed., Emlékkönyv Szent István király halálának kilencszázadik évfordulóján [Book to commemorate the 900th anniversary of the death of King St István], vol. III, (Budapest: Magyar Tudományos Akadémia, 1938, revised ed. 1988) 1–80.

Szilágyi, Sándor, "Bocskay István és Illésházy István levelezése 1605 és 1606-ban. (I. közlés) [The correspondence between István Bocskay and István Illésházy in 1605 and 1606. First part]," Történelmi tár 1 (1878), 8.

Szilágyi, Sándor, "Három uralkodoi levélke [Three small letters of rulers]," Történelmi tár 2 (1879) 389.

Szilágyi, Sándor, Révay Péter és a Szent Korona (1619–1622) [Péter Révay and the Holy Crown (1619–1622)] (Budapest, 1875).

Szörényi, László, "Berger Illés eposza a Szent Keresztről és a magyar történelem [The epic of Elias Berger on the Holy Cross and the Hungarian history]," in Marianne Rozsondai, ed., Jubileumi csokor Csapodi Csaba tiszteletére [Jubilee bouquet in honor of Csaba Csapoi] (Budapest: Argumentum, 2002), 298.

Szörényi, László, Hunok és jezsuiták: fejezetek a magyarországi latin hősepika történetéből [Huns and Jesuits: Chapters from the history of Hungarian Latin heroic epic writings] (Budapest: AmfipressZ, 1993).

Szűcs, Jenő, "Theoretical Elements in Master Simon of Kéza's Gesta Hungarorum (1282-1285)," in László Veszprémy and Frank Schaer, eds. and tr., Simonis de Kéza Gesta Hungarorum (Budapest and New York: Central European University Press, 1999), xli.

Szűcs, Jenő, Nation und Geschichte. Studien, Johanna Kerekes, tr. (Köln–Wien: Böhlau, 1981).

Szvitek, Róbert József and Endre Tóth, eds., A koronázási jelvények okmányai [The charters of the crown jewels] (Bibliotheca Humanitatis Historia, XVIII.) (Budapest: Magyar Nemzeti Múzeum, 2003).

Takács, Imre, "Corona Vladislaviana avagy corona Coronensis. Tomkó János kézirata 1626-ból Bocskai István második, későgótikus koronájáról [The Corona Vladislaviana or the corona Coronensis. The manuscript of János Tomkó (1626) on the second, late Gothic crown of István Bocskai]," Művészettörténeti Értesítő, XLIV(1984), 102.

Tapié, Victor Lucien, The Rise and Fall of the Habsburg Monarchy, Stephen Hardman trans. (London: Pall Mall Press, 1971).

Tárnóc, Márton, "Bónis György: Révay Péter [György Bónis: Péter Révay]," Irodalomtörténeti Közlemények 5 (1983), 570.

Terbe, Lajos, "Egy európai szállóige életrajza [The biography of a European winged word]," Egyetemes Philologiai Közlöny 60 (1936), 297–350.

Teszelszky, Kees and Márton Zászkaliczky, "A Bocskai-felkelés és az európai információhálózatok: Hírek, diplomácia és politikai propaganda, (1604-1606) [The revolt of Bocskai and the European information networks: News, diplomacy and political propaganda, 1604-1606]," Aetas – Történettudományi folyóirat 27/4 (2012), 121-149.

Teszelszky, Kees, "A magyar korona megjelenése a kora újkori képzőművészetben [The appearance of the Hungarian Crown in Early Modern art]," Művészettörténeti Értesítő, 60/1 (2011) 1-10.

Teszelszky, Kees, "Elias Berger Historia Ungarica című művének keletkezése és háttere (1603/4-1645) [The origin and background of the work Historia Ungarica by Elias Berger (1603/4-1645)]," in Gergely Tóth, ed., Clio Inter Arma. Tanulmányok a 16-18. századi magyarországi történetírásról [Clio inter arma. Studies on history writing in Hungary between the sixteenth and eighteenth century] (Budapest: MTA Történettudományi Intézet, 2014), 149-168.

Teszelszky, Kees, "In search of Hungary in Europe," in Kees Teszelszky, ed., A Divided Hungary in Europe: Exchanges, Networks and Representations, 1541-1699, Vol. 3 (Cambridge: Cambridge Scholars Publishing, 2014), 7-8.

Teszelszky, Kees, "Joannes Bocatius egy ismeretlen művéről [About an unknown work of Joannes Bocatius]," Irodalomtörténeti Közlemények 112 (2008), 92-93.

Teszelszky, Kees, "Respublica et Status Regni Hungariae: Magyarország kora újkori reprezentációja Európában és a republikánus politikai gondolkodásban [Respublica et Status Regni Hungariae: the representation of Hungary in the Early Modern period and the republican political thought]," Századvég, 16/61 (2010), 3-11.

Teszelszky, Kees, "Révay Péter és Justus Lipsius eszméi a történelemről és a nemzeti identitásról [The ideas of Péter Révay and Justus Lipsius on history and national identity]," in István Bitskey and Gábor Fazekas, eds., Humanizmus, religio, identitástudat (Tanulmányok a kora újkori Magyarország művelődéstörténetéről) [Humanism, religion and identity consciousness (Studies on the Early Modern cultural history of Hungary] (Studia Litteraria, vol. XLV.) (Debrecen: Debreceni Egyetem / Magyar és Összehasonlító Irodalomtudományi Intézet, 2007), 106-113.

Teszelszky, Kees, "Üzenet az utazótáskában. Diplomáciai kapcsolatok Németalföld és Magyarország között a Bocskai-felkelés alatt [Message in a trunk. Diplomatic relations between The Netherlands and Hungary during the Bocskai Uprising]," in Nóra G. Etényi and Ildikó Horn, eds., Portré és imázs. Politikai propaganda és reprezentáció a kora újkorban [Portrait and image. Political propaganda in the Early Modern period] (Budapest: L'Harmattan, 2008), 127-147.

Teszelszky, Kees, "The Crown of Hungary before and after the Hungarian crowning: The use of the Holy Crown of Hungary in Hungarian revolts and Habsburg representation between 1604 and 1611," Hungarian Studies, 30 /2(2016), 172-173.

Teszelszky, Kees, "The Hungarian Roots of a Bohemian Humanist: Johann Jessenius a Jessen and Early-Modern National Identity (1609)," in Balázs Trencsényi and Márton Zászkaliczky, eds., Whose Love of which Country? Composite States, National Histories and Patriotic Discourses in Early Modern East Central Europe (Leiden and Boston: Brill, 2010), 315–332.

Teszelszky, Kees, Szenci Molnár Albert elveszettnek hitt Igaz Vallás portréja (1606) – True Religion: a lost portrait by Albert Szenci Molnár (1606)(Budapest: ELTE BTK Középkori és Kora Újkori Magyar Történeti Tanszéke and a Transylvania Emlékeiért Tudományos Egyesület, 2014), 1–80.

Teszelszky, Kees, True Religion: a lost portrait by Albert Szenci Molnár (1606) or Dutch–Flemish–Hungarian intellectual relations in the early–modern period (Budapest: ELTE BTK Középkori és Kora Újkori Magyar Történeti Tanszéke and the Transylvania Emlékeiért Tudományos Egyesület, 2014) 81–183.

Thallóczy, Lajos, "Bocskay István koronája [The crown of István Bocskay]," Archaeologiai értesítő 16 (1884), 167–168.

Timon, Ákos, Magyar alkotmány- és jogtörténet különös tekintettel a nyugati államok jogfejlődésére [The Hungarian constitutional and legal history in light of the legal development in western countries] (Budapest: Grill Károly Könyvkiadóvállalata, 1902).

Tóth, Endre, "A Szent Korona apostollemezeinek keltezéséhez [On the origin of the Holy Crown's plates with the apostles]," Communicationes Archaeologicae Hungariae (1996) 181–209.

Tóth, Endre, and Károly Szelényi, A magyar szent korona - királyok és koronázások [The Hungarian Holy Crown: Kings and coronations] (Budapest, 1996, ²2000).

Tóth, Gergely, "Lutheránus országtörténet újsztoikus keretben. Révay Péter Monarchiája [Lutheran history of the country from a new stoic point of view. Péter Révay's Monarchia," in Gergely Tóth, ed., Clio inter arma. Tanulmányok a 16–18. századi történetírásról [Clio inter arma. Studies on history writing in Hungary between the sixteenth and eighteenth century] (Budapest: MTA Bölcsészettudományi Kutatóközpont, Történettudományi Intézet, 2014.), 117–147.

Tóth, Gergely, "Az erazmista szatirikus és a bebörtönzött mártír. Bocatius két műve, a Hungaroteutomachia és az Olympias carceraria [The Erasmic satiric and the imprisoned martyr. The two works of Bocatius: the Hungaroteutomachia and the Olympias carceraria]," in: Anita Fajt, Emőke Rita Szilágyi and Zsombor Tóth, eds., Börtön, exilium és szenvedés. Bethlen Miklós élettörténetének kora újkori kontextusai [Prison, exilium and suffering. The Early Modern contexts of Miklós Bethlen's life story] (Budapest: Reciti, 2017), 61–75.

Tóth, Gergely, "Bél Mátyás ismeretlen történeti forráskiadvány-tervezete [The unknown plan of Mátyás Bél for a history source edition]," Magyar könyvszemle, 2 (2011), 188–189.

Tóth, Gergely, "Matthias Augusto similis": Mátyás király a kora újkori protestáns múltszemléletbe," in Enikő Békés, Péter Kasza, Gábor Kiss Farkas, István Lázár and Dávid Molnár, eds., A reformáció és a katolikus megújulás latin nyelvű irodalma (Convivia Neolatina Hungarica Vol. 3) (Budapest: MTA Bölcsészettudományi Kutatóközpont Irodalomtudományi Intézet, 2019), 52–56.

Tóth, Gergely, and Kees Teszelszky, eds., Johannes Bocatius - Hungaroteutomachia vel colloquium de bello nunc inter Caesareos et Hungaros excitato: Magyarnémetharc, avagy beszélgetés a császáriak és a magyarok között most fellángolt háborúról [Hungarian-German struggle, or a conversation between the adherents of the Emperor and the Hungarians on the new flared-up war] (Budapest: ELTE BTK Középkori és Kora Újkori Magyar Történeti Tanszéke and the Transylvania Emlékeiért Tudományos Egyesület, 2014).

Tóth, Gergely, ed. and trans., Lackner Kristófnak, mindkét jog doktorának rövid önéletrajza [Short biography of Christoph Lackner, doctor in both laws] (Sopron: Sopron városi levéltár, 2008).

Tóth, Gergely, Szent István, Szent Korona, államalapítás a protestáns történetírásban (16–18. század) [St. István, the Holy Crown and the foundation of the state in Protestant historiography (sixteenth till eighteenth century)] (Budapest: MTA Bölcsészettudományi Kutatóközpont, Történettudományi Intézet, 2016).

Tóth, István György, "Alternatives in Hungarian History in the Seventeenth Century," Hungarian Studies 15/2 (2000), 173.

Tóth, István György, "Between Islam and Catholicism: Bosnian Franciscan Missionaries in Turkish Hungary, 1584–1716," Catholic Historical Review, 89 (2003), 420.

Tóth, Zoltán József, Szemelvények a Szent Korona-tan 20. századi történetéből. Az Eckhart-viták története [Excerpts from the twentieth history of the Doctrine of the Holy Crown] (PhD thesis, Miskolc University, 2005).

Tóth, Zoltán, A Hartvik legenda kritikájához (a Szt. Korona eredetkérdése) [On the critics of the Hartvic-legend (the question of the origin of the Holy Crown] (Budapest: Ranschberg, 1942).

Trencsényi, Balázs and Márton Zászkaliczky, "Towards an intellectual history of patriotism in East Central Europe in the Early Modern period," in Balázs Trencsényi and Márton Zászkaliczky, eds., Whose Love of Which Country?: Composite states, national histories and patriotic discourses in Early Modern East Central Europe (Leiden-Boston: Brill, 2010), 1–74.

Trencsényi, Balázs and Márton Zászkaliczky, eds., Whose love of which country?: Composite states, national histories and patriotic discourses in Early Modern East Central Europe (Leiden-Boston: Brill, 2010).

Trevor-Roper, Hugh, Princes and Artists. Patronage and Ideology at Four Habsburg Courts 1517–1633 (London: Thames and Hudson, 1976).

Truhlář, Antonín, and Karel Hrdina, eds., Enchiridion renatae poesis Latinae in Bohemia et Moravia cultae, vol I. (Praha: Academia, 1973).

Tusor, Péter, "A magyar egyház és Róma a 17. században [The Hungarian church and Rome in the seventeenth century]," Vigilia 64 (1999), 503–513.

Tusor, Péter, "Az 1608. évi magyar törvények a római inkvizíció előtt: II. Mátyás kiközösítése [The laws of 1608 before the Roman inquisition: II. Mátyás excommunication]," Aetas 4 (2000), 89–105.

Unger, Emil, Magyar éremhatározó [Guide to the determination of Hungarian tokens] Vol. 2. (Budapest: Ajtósi Dürer Könyvkiadó, 1980).

Váczy, Péter, "Az angyal hozta korona [The crown brought by the angel]," Életünk, 19 (1982) 456–460.

Vajay, Szabolcs de, "Das 'Archiregnum Hungaricum' und seine Wappensymbolik in der Ideenwelt des Mittelalters," in Josef Gerhard Farkas, ed., Überlieferung und Auftrag. Festschrift für Michael de Fernandy zum sechzigsten Geburtstag (Wiesbaden: Guido Pressier, 1972), 647–667.

Vajay, Szabolcs de, "Un ambassadeur bien choisi: Bernardius de Frangipanus et sa mission à Naples, en 1476," in Balázs Nagy and Marcell Sebők, eds., The Man of Many Devices, Who Wandered Full Many Ways: Festschrift in Honour of János M. Bak (Budapest: Central European University Press, 1999), 550, 554.

Varga, Benedek, "Szempontok a Bocskai-felkelés ideológiájának európai kontextusához [View points on the European context of the ideology of the Bocskai Rebellion]," Studia Caroliensa 1 (2006), 29–41.

Vargha, Anna, Iustius Lipsius és a magyar szellemi élet [Justus Lipsius and the Hungarian spiritual life] (Budapest: Dunántúl Nyomda, 1942).

Várkonyi, Ágnes R., "'...Jó Budavár magas tornyán...' A magyar államiság szimbólumairól Mohács után [...'On the high tower of good castle Buda...' On the symbols of the Hungarian statehood after Mohács]," in Hagyomány és történelem [Tradition and history] (Eger, 2000), 77–100.

Várkonyi, Ágnes R., "A Bocskai–szabadságharc nemzetközi háttere (Európai jelenlét és a magyar történelmi távlat) [The international background of the Bocskai freedom war (European presence and the Hungarian historical perspective]," in Klára Papp and Annamária Tóth–Jeney, eds.,"Frigy és békesség legyen..." A Bécsi és a Zsitvatoroki béke ["Let there be joy and peace..." The Peace of Vienna and Zsitvatorok] (Debrecen: Debreceni Egyetemi Történelmi Intézet, 2006), 21.

Várkonyi, Ágnes R., "A korona és a Budai vár [The crown and the Castle of Buda]," in Tanulmányok Budapest múltjából [Studies on the past of Budapest] 29 (2001), 37–47.

Várkonyi, Ágnes R., "A magyar államiság Mohács után [On the Hungarian statehood after Mohács]," in Jenő Gergely and Lajos Izsák, eds., A magyar államiság ezer éve, kultúra és tudomány a magyar államiság ezer évében [Thousand years of Hungarian statehood, culture and science in the thousand years of Hungarian statehood](Budapest: ELTE Eötvös K., 2001), 121–139.

Várkonyi, Ágnes R., "Az egység jelképei a megosztottság másfél évszázadában [The symbols of unity in hundred fifty years of division]," A Hadtörténeti Múzeum értesítője - Acta Musei Militaris in Hungaria [The bulletin of the Military Museum], 4 (2002), 59–69.

Várkonyi, Ágnes R., "Európai játéktér – magyar politika 1657–1664 [European playground – Hungarian politics 1657-1664]," in Gábor Hausner, ed., Az értelem bátorsága. Tanulmányok Perjés Géza emlékére [The courage of the intellect. Studies in remembrance of Géza Perjes] (Budapest: Argumentum Kiadó, 2005), 577–614.

Várkonyi, Ágnes R., "Vienna, Buda, Constantinople," The New Hungarian Quarterly XXV (1984) 1–7.

Várkonyi, Ágnes R., A királyi Magyarország 1541–1686 [Royal Hungary 1541–1686] (Budapest: Vince kiadó, 1999).

Várkonyi, Ágnes R., Europa varietas – Hungarica varietas, Éva Pálmai and Kálmán Ruttkay trans. (Budapest: Akadémiai Kiadó, 2000).

Várkonyi, Ágnes R., Három évszázad Magyarország történetében 1526–1790, Vol. I. A megosztottság évszázada; 1526–1606 [Three centuries in the History of Hungary, 1526–1790. Volume I: the century of division] (Budapest: Korona, 1999).

Várkonyi, Ágnes R., Magyarország keresztútjain. Tanulmányok a XVII. századról [Hungary's crossroads. Studies of the seventeenth century] (Budapest: Gondolat, 1978).

Vásárhelyi, Judit P., ed., Szenczi Molnár Albert válogatott művei [Selected works of Albert Szenczi Molnár] (Budapest: Magvető, 1976).

Vásárhelyi, Judit P., Eszmei áramlatok és politika Szenci Molnár Albert életművében [Lines of thought and politics in the life work of Albert Szenci Molnár] (Budapest: Akadémiai Kiadó, 1985).

Viskolcz, Noémi, "II. Mátyás magyar királlyá koronázásának egy metszetes ábrázolása 1608-ból [An etched image of the coronation of Matthias II. as king of Hungary]," in Tamás T. Kiss, ed., Kultúra – művészet – társadalom a globalizálódó világban [Culture, art and society in a globalizing world] (Szeged: Szegedi Tudományegyetem Juhász Gyula Pedagógusképző Kar, 2007), 155–158.

Viskolcz, Noémi, "Kié a könyvtár? Lipót kísérlete a Bibliotheca Corviniana maradványainak megszerzésére [Who owns the library? The attempts of Leopold to acquire the remains of the Bibliotheca Corviniana]," Acta Historiae Litterarum Hungaricarum 29 (2006) 283–288.

Viskolcz, Noémi, A mecenatúra színterei a főúri udvarban. Nádasdy Ferenc könyvtára [The stages of the patronage in the aristocratic court. The library of Ferenc Nádasdy] (Szeged and Budapest: Szegedi Tudományegyetem Historia Ecclesiastica Hungarica Alapítvány, 2013), 292–294.

Visser, Arnoud, Johannes Sambucus and the Learned Image (Leiden and Boston: Brill, 2005).

Vivo, Filippo de, "Dall'imposizione del silenzio alla "Guerre delle Scriture": Le publicazione ufficiali durante l'Interdetto del 1606–1607," Studi Veneziani 41 (2001), 179–213.

Vocelka, Karl, Die politische Propaganda Kaiser Rudolfs II. (1576–1612) (Wien: Verlag der Österreichischen Akademie der Wissenschaften, 1981).

Vocelka, Karl. "Matthias contra Rudolf: zur politischen Propaganda in der Zeit des Bruderzwistes," Zeitschrift für historische Forschung, 10 (1983), 341–351.

Wheatcroft, Andrew, The Habsburgs: Embodying Empire (London: The Folio Society, 1995) 171.

Winkelbauer, Thomas, ed., Österreichische Geschichte, Ständefreiheit und Fürstenmacht: Länder und Untertanen des Hauses Habsburg, vol. I (Wien: Ueberreuter, 2003).

Wittman, Tibor, "Az erdélyi fejdelmek és a magyarországi uralkodó osztály függetlenségi és rendi küzdelmei (1607–64) [The independence and class struggle of the Transylvanian princes and the Hungarian ruling class (1607–1664)]," in Éva H. Balázs and László Makkai, eds., Magyarország története 1526–1790 [Hungarian history 1526–1790], vol. II (Budapest: Tankönyvkiadó, ²1972), 165–166.

Wittman, Tibor, "Az osztrák Habsburg-hatalom válságos éveinek történetéhez (1606–1618) [On the history of the crisis years of the Austrian-Habsburg power (1606–1618]," Acta Universitatis Szegedinensis. Sectio Historia V (1959), 3–44.

Wittman, Tibor, "A magyarországi államelméleti tudományosság XVII. század eleji alapvetésének németalföldi forrásaihoz. J. Lipsius [On the Dutch sources for the Hungarian political thought in the seventeenth century. J. Lipsius]," Filológiai közlöny 2 (1957) 53–66.

Yates, Frances A., Astrea: The Imperial Theme in the Sixteenth Century (London and Boston: Routledge, 1975).

Yates, Frances A., The Occult Philosophy in the Elizabethan Age (London: Routledge, 1979).

Zászkaliczky, Márton, "The language of liberty in Early Modern Hungarian political debate," in Quentin Skinner and Martin van Gelderen, eds., Freedom and the Construction of Europe, vol. I (Cambridge, Cambridge University Press, 2013) 274–295.

Zászkaliczky, Márton, "A Bocskai-felkelés politikai nyelvei [The political languages of the Bocskai Revolt]," in Gábor Kármán and Márton Zászkaliczky, eds., Politikai nyelvek a 17. századi első felének Magyarországán [Political languages in Hungary in the first half of the seventeenth century] (Budapest: Reciti, 2019) 11–84.

Zemon Davies, Natalie, The Gift in Sixteenth–Century France (Oxford: Oxford University Press, 2000).

Zsák, Imre, "A római Ottoboni Könyvtár hazai vonatkozásai [The Hungarian items of the Ottonboni Library in Rome]," Magyar Könyvszemle, 131 (1909), 341–342.

Zsámbéky, Mónika, "Megjegyzés a magyar királyi korona 1621. évi ábrázolásaihoz [Remarks on the paintings of 1621 which depict the Hungarian royal crown]," Művészettörténeti Értesítő 50 (2001), 341–342.

Zsilinszky, Mihály, Az 1609-ki Pozsonyi országgyűlés történetéhez [On the history of the Diet in Poszony in 1609] (Budapest: Magyar Tudományos Akadémia Könyvkiadó, 1882).

Index

A
Ákos, Timon 31
Almási, Gábor 70
Althan, Michael Adolf 303, 304
Alvinczi, Péter 93, 127, 133, 134
Anderson, Benedict 30
András II (King) 81, 153, 222, 256, 301
Asztalos, András 82
Attila (the Hun) 53, 59, 81
Avacini, Nicolaus 322

B
Bak, János M. 34, 35, 37, 50, 98
Balásfy, Tamás 300
Balassi, Bálint 95
Baronius, Caesar 313
Bartoniek, Emma 197, 239
Barvitius, Johann 178
Baudouin, François 228
Bél, Károly András 316
Bél, Mátyás 316
Benda, Kálmán 64, 94, 109, 178, 202
Benessovinus, Johannes 69
Bérenger, Jean 174
Berger, Elias 32, 77–85, 87, 108, 135, 161, 165, 169, 177–180, 185, 188, 192, 193, 197, 199, 201–212, 215, 219, 221–223, 233–236, 238, 245–248, 252, 255, 257–259, 262, 263, 265, 267, 268, 273, 274, 276, 278, 279, 281, 283, 285, 287, 288, 290, 291, 298, 300, 302, 311, 314, 322, 326
Bethlen, Gábor (Prince) 136, 172, 298, 300
Birken, Sigmund von 322
Bocatius, János 31, 64, 65, 92, 93, 114–116, 127–138, 140–143, 146–162, 164, 165, 168, 177, 191, 218, 219, 233, 234, 260, 261, 291, 326
Bocskai, István (Prince) 13, 31, 32, 67, 77, 82, 86, 90–96, 105–107, 109–112, 114, 116, 118, 121–123, 125–128, 130–135, 137–145, 147, 149, 151, 156–158, 160–162, 164, 166–173, 179, 181, 183, 187, 190, 198, 201, 209, 213, 256, 260, 261, 272, 303, 304, 307, 326
Bodin, Jean 15, 32, 226–229, 231, 232, 238–240, 246, 254, 272, 292
Bonfini, Antonio 48–50, 84, 160, 198, 203, 214, 217, 232, 239, 255, 284, 285, 301, 302, 305, 307, 314, 320
Bongars, Jean 116
Bónis, György 174, 239, 316
Bornemisza, Menyhért 134
Brederode, Pieter Cornelisz. 143, 146, 159, 161
Burke, Peter 218, 279

C
Concha, Győző 19
Czemanka, András 316

D
DaCosta Kaufmann, Thomas 68
Debreceni Szappanos, János 106, 108, 110, 165
Deér, József 26, 28

E
Eckhart, Ferenc 18, 20–31, 94, 98, 99, 102, 104, 105, 325

Engel, Pál   38
Evans, Robert J. W.   67, 173, 174
Exalto, John   160

F

Ferdinánd I (King)   60, 61, 151, 209, 274–276
Ferdinánd II (King)   203
Ferdinánd III (King)   233, 308
Forgách, Ferenc   220, 221
Forgách, Zsigmond   134
Fügedi, Erik   178, 202

G

Galla, Ferenc   309
Géza I (King)   44, 250, 251
Guti Országh, Mihály   50, 255, 306

H

Hajnik, Imre   19, 20
Hartvik (Bishop)   14, 42, 49, 221, 301, 302
Heltai, Gáspár   198, 266
Hídvégi Mikó, Ferenc   136
Hiller, István   191
Hoffmann, György   115
Homonnai Drugeth, Bálint   121, 127, 133
Hrabecius, Rafael   232, 235

I

Illésházy, István   32, 67, 71–76, 86, 87, 89, 93, 95, 114–116, 119, 121, 136, 150, 152, 156, 157, 165, 167, 169, 170, 173, 177–183, 185, 190–194, 197–202, 204, 205, 212–215, 220–222, 233, 234, 236, 269, 277, 287, 326
Imre (Saint-Prince)   41, 247, 308, 309
Inchofer, Menyhért   298, 302, 312–315, 318, 320, 321
Istvánffy, Miklós   89, 136, 137, 203, 303–305, 307

J

János Zsigmond (Prince)   61
Jászay, Pál   73
Jeszenszky, János   32, 163, 177, 196, 197, 216–223, 233–236, 238, 246, 279–281, 283, 284, 288, 314, 326

K

Kálti, Márk   44, 45, 47, 208
Kantorowicz, Ernst   33, 34
Károlyi, Árpád   75, 115, 138, 139
Karpat, Josef   43
Káthay, Mihály   92, 94, 95, 114, 165
Kézai (de Kéza), Simon   52, 53, 57–59
Khlesl, Melchior   175
Kitonich, János   292
Klaniczay, Gábor   41, 42, 44
Klaniczay, Tibor   96
Knapp, Éva   84
Koenigsberger, Herbert   174, 175, 183
Kovács, Éva   304
Kruppa, Tamás   142
Kulcsár, Péter   203
Kuthassy, János   79, 81, 179

L

Lackner, Kristóf   196
Lajos II (King)   151, 268
Lajos the Great (King)   56, 259, 260
Lány, Illés   235
László (Saint-King)   41, 44, 45, 250–252, 308–310
László V (King)   46, 262
Lencz, Géza   139
Lépes, Bálint   195, 204
Levakovics, Rafael   298, 302, 312
Lipsius, Justus   15, 226, 249, 264, 292
Liszti, László   321
Lochmannus, Mátyás   235
Luxemburg, Erzsébet of (Queen)   46

M

Magyari, István   83, 107, 264, 288
Makkai, László   139
Mária (Queen)   262
Marnavics Tomkó, János   298, 302–311, 315
Master P. (Anonymous)   51
Matthias (Archduke)   13, 32, 76, 78, 89, 99, 134, 137, 154, 167, 172–177, 179–184, 186–190, 193–197, 199–202, 204, 205, 210–212, 214, 217, 220, 223, 232, 233, 238, 250, 252, 258, 264, 273, 276–279, 285, 286, 326
Mátyás Corvinus/Mátyás I (King)   31, 37, 45, 47–50, 54, 62, 81, 84, 163, 197–200, 208, 211, 214, 222, 234, 239, 263, 264, 268, 279, 285, 307, 309, 326
Mátyás II (King)   13, 32, 37, 76, 82, 137, 197, 198, 203, 211, 214–217, 220, 222, 223, 234, 235, 241–243, 250, 251, 261, 263, 279, 284, 285, 290, 291, 296, 326
Merseburg, Thietmar von   39
Mout, Nicolette   219

N

Nadányi, János   292
Nádasdy, Ferenc II   83, 85, 179
Nádasdy, Ferenc III   30, 319–323
Naprágyi, Demeter   86, 87, 89
Nehring, Karl   181
Németh, István H.   104

O

Ortelius, Hieronymus   293

P

Pálffy, Géza   63, 64, 280
Pannonius, Janus   47
Papp, Sándor   113–115
Pázmány, Péter   83–85, 87, 204, 205, 263, 264, 288, 297–302, 309, 313, 314, 320
Péchy, Simon   93, 165
Perényi, Péter   208, 274
Péter, Katalin   70
Péter, László   18, 20, 25–29, 31, 34, 40, 42, 62, 98, 325
Petthő, Gergely   136, 291
Podhraczky, József   192
Polybius   228

R

R. Várkonyi, Ágnes   60, 70, 72, 73, 75, 289
Rem/Rhemus, Georgius   201
Révay, Ferenc   179
Révay, László   321
Révay, Péter   13, 14, 32, 86, 95, 136, 161, 177, 179, 180, 185, 192, 193, 196, 197, 201–205, 207, 213, 214, 216, 219, 225, 230, 232, 234–236, 238, 239, 241, 243, 244, 249, 251, 253, 287, 288, 290, 300, 307, 308, 310–316, 318–323, 326
Rietbergen, Peter   309
Rimay, János   92, 93, 95, 96, 108, 115, 135, 165, 177, 179
Rudolf (King)   13, 30–32, 67–74, 76, 81, 86, 89–91, 95, 97, 100, 104, 107, 108, 111, 112, 117, 119–123, 125, 149, 150, 152, 155, 162, 169, 173–178, 180–190, 193–195, 197, 199, 200, 203, 211, 215, 216, 220, 223, 224, 234, 250, 251, 258, 262, 264, 269, 277, 278, 285, 296, 303

S

Schmeizel, Martin   315
Schödel, Márton   292
Siraisi, Nancy   223
Skinner, Quentin   17, 226
Smith, Anthony   18
Soll, Jacob   226, 227
Spondanus, Hendricus   313
St István (Saint-King)   13, 14, 17, 34, 36, 38–42, 44–46, 48, 50, 84, 160, 206, 207,

209, 247, 257, 266, 283, 284, 295, 299, 301, 304, 307–311, 313, 317, 320
Süleyman the Great (Sultan)   60, 61, 209, 273, 274
Sylvester II (Pope)   32, 42, 295, 301, 318, 320, 327
Szalárdi, János   136
Szamosközy, István   86, 115, 133
Szapolyai, János (Prince)   60, 61, 156, 208, 274–276
Szenci Molnár, Albert   82, 144, 159, 300
Szörényi, László   81, 178
Szűcs, Jenő   51–54

T

Takács, Imre   304, 307
Thuróczy, János   49, 163
Thurzó, György   194, 212, 220, 234, 235, 280
Timon, Ákos   20, 21
Tóth, Endre   37
Tóth, Gergely   15, 138, 141, 158, 317
Tschernembl, Erasmus   181
Tubero, Ludovicus   239
Tüskés, Gábor   84

U

Ulászló I (King)   46, 49, 262, 304, 305, 307
Ulászló II (King)   54, 55, 151, 167

V

Vajk (Prince)   14
Virgin Mary (Patroness of Hungary)   14, 42, 84, 215, 247, 280, 281, 283, 284, 291, 304, 307, 310, 322
Viskolcz, Noémi   203
Vitéz, János   47

W

Werbőczy, István   13, 19, 20, 24, 27–29, 31, 32, 54–59, 65, 81, 94, 96–98, 100, 102, 104–106, 110, 111, 121, 154, 155, 164, 203, 246, 256, 289, 290, 302, 320, 325

Z

Zászkaliczky, Márton   141, 153
Žierotin, Karol   178, 179, 181, 194
Zsámboky/Sambucus, János   69, 70, 198, 232
Zsigmond (King)   23